THE OXFORD COMPANION TO THE
WINES OF NORTH AMERICA

THE OXFORD
COMPANION TO THE
WINES
OF NORTH
AMERICA

EDITED BY
BRUCE CASS

CONSULTANT EDITOR: JANCIS ROBINSON

OXFORD
UNIVERSITY PRESS

OXFORD
UNIVERSITY PRESS

Great Clarendon Street, Oxford OX2 6DP

Oxford University Press is a department of the University of Oxford.
It furthers the University's objective of excellence in research, scholarship,
and education by publishing worldwide in

Oxford New York

Athens Auckland Bangkok Bogotá Buenos Aires Calcutta
Cape Town Chennai Dar es Salaam Delhi Florence Hong Kong Istanbul
Karachi Kuala Lumpur Madrid Melbourne Mexico City Mumbai
Nairobi Paris São Paulo Shanghai Singapore Taipei Tokyo Toronto Warsaw
and associated companies in Berlin Ibadan

Oxford is a registered trade mark of Oxford University Press
in the UK and in certain other countries

Published in the United States
by Oxford University Press Inc., New York

British Library Cataloguing in Publication Data

Data available

Library of Congress Cataloging in Publication Data

Data available

ISBN 0-19-860114-X

1 3 5 7 9 10 8 6 4 2

Typeset in Fairfield
by Alliance Phototypesetters, Pondicherry, India
Printed in the United States of America

Contents

Contributors

INTRODUCTORY ESSAYS:

Dan Berger, long-time business and wine writer, including ten years on staff at the *Los Angeles Times*.

Merry Edwards, winemaker and enological consultant based in Sonoma, CA. Resume includes extraordinary success at wineries ranging from Mt Eden to Matanzas Creek.

Jon Fredrikson, wine industry analyst whose consulting business, Gomberg, Fredrikson & Associates, publishes North America's most respected wine market report.

Philip Freese, international viticultural consultant. Currently splits time between CA and a vineyard in South Africa owned with wife Zelma Long.

Lucie T. Morton, author and viticultural consultant long recognized for seminal work in the American east.

Peter Granoff, MS, one of the founding partners of Internet wine retailer Virtual Vyds, now called Wine.com. Formerly sommelier at Campton Place and Square One in San Francisco.

Fritz Hatton, auctioneer and former Director of Christie's Wine Department in the US.

Jim Lapsley, proprietor of organic winery Orleans Hill in Woodland, CA, and administrator of the UC Davis Extension programs in wine.

Carole Meredith, PhD, Enology and Viticulture professor at University of California, Davis.

Jancis Robinson, MW, Consultant Editor.

Larry Stone, MS, sommelier at Rubicon restaurant in San Francisco. Formerly sommelier at Charlie Trotter's Restaurant in Chicago.

Ron Subden, PhD, Microbiology professor at University of Guelph in Ontario, Canada.

Jean-Michel Valette, MW, currently President of Franciscan Estates. Previously wine industry analyst for investment bankers Hambrecht & Quist. In addition to being one of the few American Masters of Wine, credentials include a Harvard MBA.

A–Z TEXT:

BCC **Bruce Cass**, General Editor.

RTS **Bob Slaktowicz**, former wine newsletter writer, wine broker, and partner in a Colorado winery. Currently employed by a Denver fine wine store, and a writer of mystery novels.

LFB **Linda Bramble, PhD**, psychologist turned wine writer. Resident of St Catharines in the Niagara Peninsula, wine columnist for the local newspaper, part-time employee at the top retail wine store in Buffalo, NY.

LAO **Louise Owens**, wine columnist for the *Dallas Morning News*. Formerly employed by importer/distributors in New York then Dallas.

PWF **Patrick Fegan**, proprietor of the Chicago Wine School, author (*Wineries of America: A Traveler's Guide* and *The Vineyard Handbook: Appellations, Maps and Statistics*), and wine columnist for the Chicago *Tribune*.

RF **Richard Figiel**, proprietor of Silver Thread Vyd in New York's Finger Lakes AVA. Former Editor of the *International Wine Review* published in Ithaca, NY.

RAI **Ronald Irvine**, co-author and publisher of *The Wine Project: Washington State's Winemaking History* (Sketch Publications). Former proprietor of Pike & Western, a fine wine retail store in Seattle's famous Pike Place Market. Currently director of the Washington Wine Archives.

RGL **Richard Leahy**, Editor at *Vineyard & Winery Management* and organizer of the Wineries Unlimited trade show, and coordinator of the International Eastern Wine Competition. Formerly a longtime resident of Charlottesville, VA.

RS **Ron Subden**, see above.

Preface

THIS book is particularly important and timely because North America is both a huge, relatively untapped potential market for wine and a producer with explosive, yet still embryonic, vineyard development in hundreds of regions all within the last fifteen years.

Wine is made in almost all of the US states (ND being the lone absolute exception), four Canadian provinces, and six Mexican states. In most of these places it has a two-phase history—having risen to prominence with immigrant groups, then dying out in the first half of the 20th century primarily due to Prohibition, then seeing a revival in the last decades of the millennium, often due to new viticultural advancements. North America's spasmodic bouts with temperance attitudes have created a patchwork mosaic of wine communities and bewildering regulations. This degree of complexity doing business is matched, and compensated, only by the size of the potential dollar market.

Capturing the diversity of regulation, controversy, history, culture, topography, and climate was a task worthy of an Oxford Companion. Moreover, North America is the ancestral home of many more grape species than anywhere else on earth. The role of vines other than European vinifera makes much of this tale completely unique.

Two callings compete when one tries to organize a book such as this one. At heart it is a reference work. In service to that end, one attempts to separate discrete bits of information and place them where they may be most easily located. Hence the section of alphabetical headwords, such as 'active dry yeast' and 'Aguascalientes' through 'ZAP' and 'Donald Ziraldo,' common to all Oxford Companions. But wine so readily lends itself to stories. And effectively telling stories requires assembling related bits of information. One of the marvelous things about wine is the way compelling points about it draw background bits from fields as diverse as science, economics, psychology, history, and politics. In service to that end, we have chosen in this book to depart somewhat from other Oxford Companions by including a group of fifteen essays at the beginning which explore some of the pressing contemporary issues of the North American wine scene.

All the essays and most of the headword entries are identified by their contributors' names or initials. Gathering information on a geographic area as large, complex and diversified as North America is understandably difficult. Few centralized agencies exist which have much of this information readily at hand. Moreover our regional contributors have generally made names for themselves as wine writers in their local areas by virtue of their expertise on the international scene; research on their local wines was a labor of love. They all deserve a tremendous amount of credit for the effort they have expended on behalf of this book. The explosion of North American vineyard plantings in the last few decades, and the advancement of viticultural understanding during that period, make this book quite a bit more challenging to edit, at least in the sense of being topically accurate, than authoritative Oxford Companions devoted to subjects which saw the greatest flowering of their activity in the historical past.

Wine being a subjective artform, we have encouraged contributors to state opinions. Sometimes reasonable people may disagree. Such is the nature of art. In the end, however, the final choice of words has been mine. The contributors deserve credit for the well turned phrases; I am responsible for the excesses.

In working on this book, Jancis and I referred to it as 'the daughterbook.' The motherbook, *The Oxford Companion to Wine*, contains material on wine in general, both technically and internationally. The daughterbook contains information specific to North America: technical innovations and peculiarities, regions and dominant wineries. When a technical explanation common to all wines is needed, we cross-reference the appropriate entry in the motherbook. In several instances there are entries in both books on a similar topic. They are not duplicative. In these instances, OCW is meant to be the overview; OCWNA is meant to provide supplemental depth.

Special thanks to Edwin Pritchard, Pam Coote, and Alison Jones for their measured yet thorough and articulate work improving the language and clarity of this book.

BRUCE CASS

San Francisco
April 2000

Abbreviations and Conversions

ABC	Alcoholic Beverage Control (VA)	mi	miles
ADY	active dry yeast	MLF	malolactic fermentation
AVA	American Viticultural Area	mph	miles per hour
B	Brix	MS	Master Sommelier
btl	bottle	Mt	Mount
BWE	Beringer Wine Estates	Mtn	Mountain
C	Celsius	MW	Master of Wine
CC	country club	Natl	National
CEO	chief executive officer	OAS	Organization of American States
Ch	Chateau	OGWA	Organic Grapes into Wine Alliance
Co	County	PNW	Pacific Northwest
COD	cash on delivery	ppm	parts per million
Dept	Department	Rd	Road
DNA	deoxyribonucleic acid	RS	residual sugar
Dom	Domaine	SAQ	Société des Alcools du Québec
F	Fahrenheit	SF	San Francisco
FDA	Food & Drug Administration (US)	SLO	San Luis Obispo
ft	feet	SO_2	sulfur dioxide
gal	gallons	sq ft	square feet
g/l	grams per liter	sq mi	square miles
HPLC	high performance liquid chromatography	TA	total acidity
Hwy	Highway	t/a	tons per acre
IAREC	Irrigated Agricultural Research Extension Center	TDA	Texas Department of Agriculture
		TWGGA	Texas Wine & Grape Growers' Association
in	inches	UC	University of California
INRA	Institut de la Recherche Agronomique	UCLA	University of California at Los Angeles
Intl	International	Univ	University
LCBO	Liquor Control Board of Ontario	V.	*Vitis*
LDB	Liquor Distribution Board (Canada)	VP	Vice President
MBA	Master of Business Administration	Vyd	Vineyard
mgmt	management	WCTU	Women's Christian Temperance Union

CANADIAN ABBREVIATIONS

AB	Alberta	NF	Newfoundland	PE	Prince Edwards Is.
BC	British Columbia	NS	Nova Scotia	QC	Quebec
MB	Manitoba	NT	Northwest Territories	SK	Saskatchewan
NB	New Brunswick	ON	Ontario	YT	Yukon Territory

US STATE ABBREVIATIONS

AK	Alaska	ID	Idaho	NC	North Carolina	SC	South Carolina
AL	Alabama	IL	Illinois	ND	North Dakota	SD	South Dakota
AR	Arkansas	IN	Indiana	NE	Nebraska	TN	Tennessee
AZ	Arizona	KS	Kansas	NH	New Hampshire	TX	Texas
CA	California	KY	Kentucky	NJ	New Jersey	UT	Utah
CO	Colorado	LA	Louisiana	NM	New Mexico	VA	Virginia
CT	Connecticut	MA	Massachusetts	NV	Nevada	VT	Vermont
DC	District of	MD	Maryland	NY	New York	WA	Washington
	Columbia	ME	Maine	OH	Ohio	WI	Wisconsin
DE	Delaware	MI	Michigan	OK	Oklahoma	WV	West Virginia
FL	Florida	MN	Minnesota	OR	Oregon	WY	Wyoming
GA	Georgia	MO	Missouri	PA	Pennsylvania		
HI	Hawaii	MS	Mississippi	PR	Puerto Rico		
IA	Iowa	MT	Montana	RI	Rhode Island		

CONVERSIONS

Length

metric		*imperial*
1 millimeter [mm]		0.0394 in
1 centimeter [cm]	10 mm	0.3937 in
1 meter [m]	100 cm	1.0936 yd
1 kilometer [km]	1,000 m	0.6214 mi

imperial		*metric*
1 inch [in]		2.54 cm
1 foot [ft]	12 in	0.3048 m
1 yard [yd]	3 ft	0.9144 m
1 mile [mi]	1,760 yd	1.6093 km

Volume/capacity

metric		*imperial* (British)
1 liter [l]		1.76 pt
1 hectoliter [hl]	100 l	21.997 gal

imperial (British)		*metric*
1 pint [pt] (20 fl oz)		0.5683 l
1 gallon [gal]	8 pt	4.5461 l

imperial (USA)		*metric*
1 pint (16 fl oz)	0.8327 UK pt	0.4731 l
1 gallon	0.8327 UK gal	3.7854 l

Area

metric		*imperial*
1 sq m [m²]	10,000 cm²	1.1960 yd²
1 hectare [ha]	10,000 m²	2.4711 acres
1 sq km [km²]	100 ha	0.3861 mi²

imperial		*metric*
1 sq foot [ft²]	144 in²	0.0929 m²
1 sq yard [yd²]	9 ft²	0.8361 m²
1 acre	4840 yd²	4046.9 m²
1 sq mile [mi²]	640 acres	2.59 km²

Mass

metric		*imperial*
1 gram [g]		0.0353 oz
1 kilogram [kg]	1,000 g	2.2046 lb
1 tonne [t]	1,000 kg	0.9842 ton

imperial		*metric*
1 ounce [oz]		28.35 g
1 pound [lb]	16 oz	0.4536 kg
1 stone	14 lb	6.3503 kg
1 hundredweight [cwt]	112 lb	50.802 kg
1 ton	20 cwt	1.016 t

Temperature

Fahrenheit

Under standard conditions, water boils at 212° and freezes at 32°.
To convert Celsius into Fahrenheit, multiply by 9, divide by 5, and add 32.

Celsius (or Centigrade)

Under standard conditions, water boils at 100° and freezes at 0°.
To convert Fahrenheit to Celsius, subtract 32, multiply by 5, and divide by 9.

Note to the Reader

SEVERAL conventions have been employed in this book to reduce redundancy, hopefully thereby improving readability. This book is intended as a reference work for both consumers and for the trade; for technical people within the trade and for marketing people; for Europeans who have been drinking wine all their lives but have never visited North America, and for North Americans who know the places and the local cultures, but not very much about the product.

A good place for everybody to start is the page of Abbreviations and Conversions (pg ix). Since so much of the book is about the United States we have chosen to employ feet, pounds, acres, and Fahrenheit degrees rather than metres, grams, hectares, and Celsius degrees. We have assumed US dollars unless Canadian dollars are indicated.

Sometimes confusion can persist when two words are similar for measurements which are not exactly equal. For instance, an American ton is 2,000 lbs; while a metric tonne of 1,000 kilograms, or 2,200 lbs, is also spelled ton by many English speakers, notably Australians. We use American tons throughout this book. We have generally chosen US spellings (eg color rather than colour), but editing was a US/British collaboration, so occasional crossovers do occur. Never is one quite so aware of the truth imbedded in the joke that the British and Americans are one race separated by a common language than when editing a book together. We have given each other many prolonged chuckles while clearing up these discrepancies of perception. My favorite, although it has been deleted from the text, was Jancis's reaction when I described the passenger on a motorcycle as 'riding sissy.' I simply could not convince her that phrase was a technical term referring to the seat's backrest.

This book is richly cross-referenced. That is an effort to gain the smooth readability that comes with mutually understood jargon, yet always provide readers a pathway to find full explanation of shortcut phrases. Explanations of relevant/useful topics are included alphabetically under the appropriate headword.

Note there are two different types of cross-reference. SMALL CAPITAL TYPE indicates a cross-reference to a topic explained within this book. An asterisk preceding a word (*) indicates a cross-reference to *The Oxford Companion to Wine*, second edition. While there may be some legitimate complaints about using cross-references to a separate book, these pale compared to the enormous advantage of being able to cite technical terms such as MLF (malo-lactic fermentation) without repeating such a lengthy explanation in this work. It is our impression that few people will read this book from beginning to end. Most users will look up discrete topics at various times as their interest is piqued. The cross-referencing technique is a means to allow each reader to tailor their experience with the book to their level of interest at the time, as well as to their overall existing level of expertise.

There are close to 2,000 wineries in North America. This book is not intended to be an exhaustive listing of license holders, nor a catalogue of contact names and numbers. Those functions require almost daily adjustment and are better performed by annual directories such as *Wines & Vines* or *Vineyard & Winery Management*. Our goal is to present the big picture of what is happening around North America. Thus wineries found with their own alphabetical headword entry are those chosen to provide some insight on personalities, history, business practices, production technique, or regional peculiarities. Wineries included as subheads within a geographic headword are the best of the rest, selected to provide a good sampling of that particular region.

The Index is the best place to start when looking for information on a specific winery, perhaps a name vaguely remembered from a bottle label. Hundreds of North American wineries are listed alphabetically in the Index with their city and state plus a reference to the relevant geographic entry in the text.

Similarly, very few people have individual headword entries in the text, yet this book is loaded with revealing portraits of wine industry personalities. The Index is the best place to begin if one wishes to locate people quickly by name. Our goal in the text has been to use descriptions of people to add a human face to the context of points about technical, economic, or political advancements throughout history in various regions. We do not mean to imply the individuals named are the only ones with significant accomplishments. We merely chose representative examples. Such is the burden of an editor. Many more people and wineries are worthy of mention than space and perceived readers' attention span will allow. I made these decisions, and I did so alone. So very alone. Occasionally they were somewhat arbitrary. Readers though can rest assured that whenever a choice of this type was required, the general point has been made. The editing slight will be felt only by the person or winery not selected, and sharply only by their PR employees.

Because of this effort to make big-picture points about the comprehensive range of producing areas throughout North America, it is unfair to draw conclusions about quality based on relative lines of allocated space. There are 240 wineries in Napa Valley, and two in all of Nebraska. Not providing elaborative text on a winery in Napa does not mean we think the discussed winery in Nebraska makes better wine than the ignored winery in Napa. It merely means we were able to make our points about what is going on in Napa by choosing from a surfeit of examples. The points were set; the examples could be chosen based on interest and story value. In Nebraska the examples were set, and editing judgement had to be applied to choose between what points would be most germane.

Much the same explanation applies to geographic regional names. Attention has been paid to governmentally approved appellations (AVAs in the US), and they can all be found in the Index, because these are the names which will be found on labels. Nevertheless, not all AVAs have their own alphabetical headword entry because it is often easier to compare their characteristics within the context of a larger geographical unit, such as a county. A minor district AVA located in Maryland may have its own headword, while a much more productive and prestigious AVA located in California may not, simply because the Maryland AVA is the only example of vine growing in that part of the country while the California AVA is more clearly depicted by a compare-and-contrast technique within some larger California viticultural context. An example would be Sonoma Mtn AVA which is covered under the encompassing Sonoma Valley AVA.

Likewise there are many wine-growing districts that must be discussed for a comprehensive understanding of North American viticulture which do not have governmental approval for specific names. The Index is the best place to find these references too, because some will have their own headword entry

1920 until 1933, the sale of alcoholic beverages was illegal in the US, although production of wine for a family's own use was permitted. This loophole created a huge increase in grape production for homemade and illegal wine. 'Homemade' wine consumption reached some 140 million gal in 1930. This represented the equivalent of 1.2 gal per capita as compared with 2.0 gal consumed today. Wine consumption fell sharply in 1934 when spirits and beer again became legally available for sale.

The legacy of Prohibition and the temperance movement still remains a powerful force in both the US and Canada. The states' rights option following Repeal produced a legal quagmire of obstacles to mass wine distribution in the US. Lack of access to supermarket shelves in about one-half the states is probably the most burdensome marketing obstacle. PA still maintains a monopoly on distribution through state owned warehouses and retail stores. NY does not permit the sale of food and wine in the same retail premises. In Canada each individual province controls the importation and distribution of alcoholic beverages through liquor control boards. Only one province, Alberta, is now entirely private. A major objective of the liquor boards is to generate tax revenue for the provincial governments, as well as making a significant contribution to the federal government. As a result wine retail prices are very high, especially when compared to the US, reducing consumer demand. To avoid paying high taxes and prices at government stores, many Canadians in Ontario and British Columbia make their own wines at FERMENT ON PREMISE facilities. This homemade wine production is estimated to be roughly equivalent to all Canadian domestic wine sales through government outlets.

From the end of Prohibition in 1934 until the late 1950s, wine consumption in North America consisted primarily of high alcohol 'dessert' wines, often imbibed by blue collar workers as an inexpensive substitute for distilled spirits, which were taxed much higher. A CA port, a NY sherry, or an indiscriminate Muscatel provided an inexpensive form of alcohol for 99 cents a quart or less. Although sherries and ports were still popular, the volume of dessert wines declined sharply in the mid-1950s as disposable income rose, enabling more Americans to purchase distilled spirits. Dessert wines continued to be significant until their total unit sales finally were surpassed by table wine sales in 1967. Today, roughly two-fifths of American adult consumers do not consume any beverage alcohol because of religious, health, or other reasons. Among those adults who do drink beverage alcohol, beer has traditionally been the dominant beverage of choice. Since the repeal of Prohibition, beer consumption has far outpaced consumption of both wine and distilled spirits in the US. At 5.9 billion gal (1998), beer is still eleven times larger than wine by volume of consumption.

Distilled spirits have remained the second most popular alcoholic beverage type in America over the past six decades. It was not until 1980 that wine consumption surpassed consumption of distilled spirits by total volume for the first time. When compared by volume of actual liquid consumed, however, the gallonage of total spirit drinks still exceeds wine consumption since spirits usually are diluted with ice and water or mixers when consumed. In addition, when converted to pure alcohol (converted at averages of 80 proof for spirits, 11% alcohol by volume for table wine, and 4.5% alcohol by volume for beer) the consumption of distilled spirits alcohol exceeds all wine alcohol consumption, but is below that for beer.

Of those adults who do consume alcohol, a relatively small percentage consumes a high percentage of the total in each beverage category. About one-eighth of all adult drinkers consume approximately seven-eighths of the total table wine sold in the US. While both beer and spirits are believed to have broader consumer bases, heavy levels of consumption still are concentrated in a relatively small portion of the adult population.

TABLE WINES BECOME POPULAR

Table wine consumption was minimal in the early days following Repeal. At the time table wine consumers consisted primarily of foreign-born immigrants from wine drinking nations who generally drank inexpensive table wines. Unfortunately this base of regular table wine consumers gradually declined as these immigrants died and their progeny adopted American drinking habits along with other typical American lifestyles.

Beginning in the late 1950s and early 1960s, a new generation of wine consumers began to emerge. These early table wine drinkers were generally sophisticated younger people (25 to 45 years of age) with above-average income, education, and cultural development. Growing national affluence, European travel, and strong publicity for wine brought about an awakening of consumer interest in traditional table wines. The number of new wine consumers swelled greatly when the post-war baby boomers reached drinking age in the mid-1960s.

As American consumers began to learn about wine, they favored simple, domestically produced, rather sweet, entry-level wine beverages such as generic blends and 'pop wines' (specialty fruit wines), as well as imported Spanish Sangrias, German Liebfraumilches, and Portuguese Rosés. In the 1970s Lambruscos became the principal entry-level product, only to be replaced in the 1980s by CA White Zinfandel. White Zin and other *blush wines grew substantially in volume, and today make up well over one-third of all wines sold below $5 per 750 ml bottle. These wines are purchased by millions of consumers who prefer the sweet, fruity character of White Zin to the perceived 'sour' taste of dry table wines.

The popularity of *jug wines (inexpensive wines using generic names such as Chablis and Burgundy, and sold in 3-, 4- or 5-liter container sizes) grew rapidly in the 1970s in part because of the enormous popularity of the 'white wine cocktail.' Some consumers shifted away from distilled spirits, and especially whiskeys, to white wines. Preferences went from beef and bourbon to fruit and white wine. Table wine consumption grew during this period at the remarkably high rate of almost 10% per year, and table wine shipments nearly tripled from 1970 to 1980. The strong market attracted new consumer-oriented marketers, including Coca-Cola of Atlanta, Nestlé, and Pillsbury to the business. The industry ramped up production capacity enormously, planting thousands of acres of vineyards and constructing huge new wineries. Wine advertising and promotion reached all-time highs in 1982. There were predictions that American wine consumption would grow rapidly in the ensuing decades. Unfortunately, this rosy picture failed to materialize.

Contrary to the wine industry's expectations, North American table wine consumption declined in the 1980s. In fact sales of all alcoholic beverages fell as popular attitudes towards alcohol consumption changed. At the time, beverage alcohol was considered incompatible with growing concerns about health and fitness. More stringent Driving While Intoxicated (DWI) laws were passed (see BAC). In the US the minimum drinking age was raised to 21 years in all states. The federal government mandated warning labels and sulfite labels on wine containers. These labels told women, 'do not drink wine if you are pregnant.' This warning inhibits consumption, even among those who are not pregnant. The government and many large corporations sponsored advertising campaigns against drunk driving and excess alcohol consumption. 'Just say no to alcohol (including wine) and drugs,' said the federal government using Nancy Reagan as their spokesperson. There was considerable negative publicity about the adverse health aspects of alcohol and drugs.

Nonetheless major new wine industry developments began during the 1980s, the most important being the establishment of premium wine industries in CA, WA, OR, NY, and in other states and Canadian provinces. At the same time, common jug wine consumption, which dominated North American markets up to the mid-1980s, deteriorated significantly. There was huge overcapacity and production in CA. Prices and profitability plummeted. Eventually all the major corporations, including Coca-Cola, Seagram, RJR Nabisco, and National Distillers, exited the volume end of the industry. Without the profitability and the big marketers, consumer advertising for wine dropped to about 10% of its peak level in real dollars. For about a decade, from the mid-1980s to the mid-1990s, there was relatively little consumer advertising for wine. This circumstance certainly limited creation of new American consumers.

WINE RENAISSANCE OF THE 1990s

In the early 1990s several important developments created renewed consumer interest and demand for wine. The most important factor was promulgation of medical evidence suggesting moderate consumption of table wine is healthful. In Nov 1991 CBS television broadcast a *60 Minutes* segment describing the *French paradox. This single program enlightened millions of consumers about the possible health benefits of moderate wine consumption. The show reported that the French, who are heavy wine consumers, have lower rates of heart disease than consumers in other countries even though they often consume rich foods high in fat content. Since the original French paradox segment was broadcast, scores of other medical research studies have been released describing healthful benefits from moderate wine consumption.

In Jan 1996 the US Food and Drug Administration released new Dietary Guidelines that greatly enhanced wine's status compared with the previous guidelines, which had proclaimed that alcohol had 'no net health benefit.' The revised guidelines are more supportive of wine with meals, proclaiming 'drinking can be beneficial' and 'alcoholic beverages have been used to enhance the enjoyment of meals throughout human history.'

An aging North American population has been particularly receptive to these reports on wine's possible health benefits. After years of languishing with relatively little trade advertising and being hindered by anti-alcohol sentiment, wine received much favorable attention in the national media. This exposure stimulated a renewal of interest in table wine, and particularly high quality varietal wines. With wine presented in a favorable light, cultural attitudes about drinking wine became more positive. In addition, lifestyle preferences changed in a way that made wine a part of better living.

A rising consumer appreciation for quality wines and other premium products, including coffees, juices, craft beers, and gourmet foods emerged in the 1990s. A growing economy and higher disposable income helped consumers realize these preferences. In the US total table wine consumption expanded at an annual growth rate of over 5% from 1991 to 1998. Importantly, consumer demand for higher quality, premium varietals grew at about twice this rate in units and at more than three times this rate in terms of dollar expenditures.

Red wines were the primary beneficiaries of the favorable health news stories, even though much of the medical research covered broader beverage alcohol issues. In the early 1970s red wines were the most popular wine type, but white wines surpassed them in popularity after that. From 1991 to 1998 renewed interest in red wines raised their consumption in the US by about 170%, while white and rosé wines grew by just 14%. Growers throughout the world planted thousands of acres of red grapes, especially Merlot, Cabernet Sauvignon, and Syrah in response to this preference trend.

Consumer demographics

In the US and Canada about 70% of adults do not drink table wine. In Mexico only a tiny percentage of the adult population drinks it. Of the relatively small proportion of American adults who do enjoy wine, how can we identify 'typical' wine consumers?

Regular wine consumers are mostly affluent people who have good jobs and have attended college. Nearly three-fourths of all table wine is imbibed by consumers with household incomes over $35,000. Furthermore the incidence of consumption increases considerably as household income rises. Blue collar and lower income workers consume relatively little wine. In the US females drink more wine than males, consuming around 54% of all table wine. Wine is the least male dominated alcoholic beverage.

The vast majority of table wines are consumed by Caucasians. The incidence of consumption for Asian and Hispanic consumers is low. This does not bode well for American wine consumption growth because the new waves of immigrants from Hispanic and Asian nations are unlikely to expand the wine consumption base as their counterparts from traditional wine consuming nations did a century ago. As consumers age there is a greater propensity to drink wine. Young adults often begin consuming beverage alcohol employing beer or malt coolers and gradually drink more wine as they age. Thus adults of 35 years or more consume about three-quarters of all table wine. Table wine draws the oldest profile of any beverage category. Moreover the mid-life period generally favors activities centered on home and family; these are preferred times for wine consumption. Over four-fifths of table wine is consumed at home and three-fifths is consumed with dinner.

One last factor remains, that of residence. Adults who live in cities consume almost twice as much wine as consumers in suburban areas.

Thus a 'typical' picture emerges of a fairly affluent, well-educated, middle-aged, family oriented Caucasian consumer who enjoys wine with family and friends, generally at home with the evening meal.

Why Americans do not drink wine

Millions of consumers who fit the general demographic profile for wine drinkers still are not regular wine consumers for a variety of reasons.

About two-fifths of American adults abstain from alcoholic beverages entirely. Strong anti-alcohol religious beliefs are a powerful force influencing both public policy and private attitudes. The legacy of Prohibition, restricting the distribution of wine in many states and creating an anti-alcohol culture, also maintains a strong influence on wine consumption.

Research has shown that most Americans regard wine as a formal, 'special occasion beverage.' Many believe that wine is just for congratulatory, festive, or romantic meal events. Wine is often seen as not appropriate for the quick, casual dinners experienced as the norm today by many families, and especially those with two working spouses. This appears to be a major barrier blocking increased wine consumption.

Other Americans rarely drink wine because they do not want to open an entire bottle of wine at once. Many consumers do not understand wine can stay fresh for several days in an open container. This suggests that smaller containers, such as the 187 ml bottle, could have considerable sales potential. Possible customers are often discouraged by their lack of wine knowledge. These consumers believe they cannot tell the difference among wines and are confused by the many wine types and complicated foreign names. Wine is a mystery to them. Consumers often do not know which wines to serve with which foods.

They are intimidated by wine terminology and do not want to make the wrong choice or appear foolish when purchasing wine. This is especially true in restaurants where the traditional wine steward can make the uninformed wine buyer feel quite uncomfortable. The ease and simplicity of wine-by-the-glass service in restaurants has contributed to its considerable growth over the past decade because people can make a simple choice without the traditional wine service ritual.

Current consumption trends

North American wine consumers are continuing to shift upscale in their quality preferences. For two decades they have been moving up to the leading premium varietals from inexpensive generic blends and jug varietals such as French Colombard. In recent years the fastest growing wines have been 'high premium' wines priced at roughly $7 and above per bottle at retail, a big step up in quality from the relatively inexpensive, mediocre quality Chardonnays and Cabernet Sauvignons that sparked the growth in premium varietals in the 1980s. Among CA table wines, for example, high premium table wines climbed by nearly 14% per year over the decade through 1998, while 'everyday wines' priced below $7 expanded by just 1%. The highest quality table wines are growing at the fastest rates. CA table wines priced above $25 per bottle at retail jumped by an average of 23% a year over the same ten years. At the end of the millennium many of America's finest wines remain in short supply and are on allocation to the trade and consumers.

Once established wine drinkers have enjoyed better quality wines, it may be difficult for them to consume lower quality products. As their palates mature, their quality threshold rises, and they crave better quality wines. Producers around the world currently are expanding production to satisfy this growing demand for improved quality.

Chardonnay is the largest selling single varietal in North America, accounting for 15% of the volume and a quarter of the dollars. Among white varietals Sauvignon Blanc is a distant second. There is evidence of growing consumer interest in high quality Sauvignon Blanc, but quantities are small compared with the demand for high-end Chardonnay.

Among red varietals Cabernet Sauvignon remains the most popular wine, but Merlot is rapidly closing in on its lead, and soon after the turn of the century may become the largest selling red wine on the continent. A greater proportion of Merlot sales are in the lower price ranges, however, and Merlot is believed to be an entry-level red wine. Cabernet Sauvignon is considered the finest, and is the most expensive red wine, although many Cabernets contain some Merlot in their blends.

These top four varietals—Chardonnay, Sauvignon Blanc, Cabernet Sauvignon, and Merlot—constitute more than three-quarters of all red and white varietal wines sold in North America. Although much smaller in production, there is growing consumer interest in Zinfandel (made almost exclusively in CA), Pinot Noir, Syrah, and Sangiovese. Among white varieties Pinot Gris and Viognier are growing in popularity, but remain tiny in sales.

Conclusion: outlook is for quality wine growth

North America has undergone a long but constrained relationship with wine since it was introduced to the continent centuries ago. Continuing social, religious, economic, and legal barriers to wine consumption growth are formidable. In the foreseeable future, wine is not likely to be adopted as a regular mealtime beverage by more than just a small percentage of the continent's population. Nonetheless there is a sizeable and growing market for wine in North America. An aging population of baby boomers, receptive to favorable health news and with disposable income to spend, will form the primary market during the first decade of the 21st century. Expanded industry advertising and promotion will attract new wine drinkers and will increase the consumption rates of infrequent consumers. An enlarged supply of high quality wines from around the world may reduce retail prices, creating greater value for consumers and thus encouraging greater consumption. Continued relatively strong economic conditions will lift demand, especially for high-end wines.

Quality wines will enjoy the strongest growth prospects in future years as American consumers grow in both absolute numbers and discernment. Commodity jug wines, in contrast, are likely to weaken in sales as consumers move upscale.

Although North America lacks the deep-rooted wine traditions of many European nations, a relatively small segment of the continent's population are regular wine consumers who enjoy wine frequently. This group will gradually expand over the next decade, especially as greater quantities of fine wines from around the world become available in North American markets at reasonable prices.

2

How Good are North American Wines?

Jancis Robinson, MW

THERE is now no shadow of a doubt that the very best North American wines reach as high a level of quality as the best Europe can produce. They are often different, typically being much more open, approachable, and much easier to drink at 2 or 3 years old than their European counterparts. But this is by no means a bad thing, especially since the world's consumers seem ever more impatient to pull corks and are unwilling or unable to maintain their own cellars. Longevity is not such a highly rated virtue in a wine as it once was.

It is only to be expected that the US produces some very fine wine for it produces such a lot of it. Only France, Italy, and Spain produce more wine and have more vineyards dedicated to wine (and only Turkey produces more raisins than CA). Add to this the combination of a series of bursts of economic growth together with wine's newfound respectability as a recreational pursuit, and you have a market for top quality wine at decidedly elastic prices. Since the production levels of such wines cannot hope to keep pace with the amount of disposable income available to buy them, it is hardly surprising that the gap between the most and least expensive wines in North America has been widening.

Were this essay about many other parts of the world—France or Australia, for example—this would be a cue to remark on the irony of the fact that just as the difference in price between best and worst wines is greater than it has ever been, the difference in quality is narrower than ever before. But I am not sure this is true of North America. While other countries benefit from improved technology and large numbers of discerning but value-conscious wine drinkers who concentrate wine trade and media attention onto maintaining a decent standard at the bottom end of the market, the focus of attention in the US seems to be much more on the top end, those elusive 95-point bottles, for example. Jon Fredrikson's essay in this book (Wine and the American Consumer, p 1) spells out just how few Americans are responsible for the great majority of wine consumption.

Although in the early 1970s Gallo's jug wines were arguably the most technically proficient in the world, CA has not maintained its competitive edge. It is my contention that while a small quantity of truly great wine is made in North America (not all of it expensive—see below), the quality of mass market wines would be very much higher if the market were more demanding, and more numerous. There is a sense in which wine producers feel they hardly need to try with the big volume labels because (a) they are so rarely evaluated in public and (b) the American wine drinker is relatively unsophisticated anyway.

There seems to me no reason why the vast CENTRAL VALLEY of CA could not be producing seriously well-made, reliable, extremely inexpensive everyday wine—in just the same way as Australia's irrigated inland regions currently are. The quality of CA's jug wine and fighting varietals may have been creeping up, but it has not been improving fast enough to keep pace with what is available from Chile, Australia, the Languedoc, even South Africa in some cases. There are of course structural problems. There has so far been a shortage of processing plant close to the bulk of Central Valley vineyards. Large producers, influenced by what might be called the Coca-Cola effect, may also overestimate the amount of sweetness required in a mass market wine.

If the basic wine produced in the US is not as good as it could be, its Canadian counterpart is quite literally shocking. Under the auspices of provincial monopolies such as the LCBO, Canadian wine drinkers are routinely sold blends labeled Product of Canada which are wines imported in bulk from whichever country can offer the best deal. And one of the more telling stipulations of superior Vintners Quality Alliance, or VQA, wines has been that they may not contain added water. It is high time that wine labeling was reformed in Canada.

Yet, at the top end again, Canada produces some extremely fine wine indeed. Just as the vineyards of upstate New York just over the border from Ontario are capable of providing real vinous treats, however much they may be reviled by supposed sophisticates in Manhattan. At least Canadians, unlike New Yorkers and the English, are actively proud of their own wines . . .

As for Mexican wine, I am unable to comment on the quality of wine commonly available in Mexico, but perhaps the fact that annual per capita consumption of wine there is less than a third of a bottle (as compared with about ten bottles in both Canada and the US) is testament enough. I have certainly encountered some extremely interesting Mexican wines exported from Mexico to both Britain and the US.

In between the best and worst of wines is a host of overpriced, often dull offerings interspersed with efforts which, even if they clearly come from vineyards or cellars which are some distance from the peak of their powers, prove that there is great wine potential in even the most unlikely corners of North America. Many of these producers have been working in relative isolation. When one considers the extraordinary progress made by the tight-knit clan of CA wine producers over recent years, it is clear that the future may be very bright indeed.

United States

CALIFORNIA

Blessed with a wide range of climates extremely well suited to vine growing, CA not surprisingly produces some of the finest wines in the world (see above). The Wine State's most obvious strength so far has been in its full-bodied, tenderly made, flatteringly ripe, finest Cabernet Sauvignons, the best of which have sufficient but well-hidden tannins to continue to develop in bottle for a decade or two. Like all CA wines, they are less obviously dry (in the sense of not sweet) than their Bordeaux prototypes—and it is too early to say whether Meritage reds will last as long as a first growth Médoc from a great vintage. Straight Cabernets have a long enough history to suggest that they lack the long-term aging potential of a fine red Bordeaux, but the style of those CA Cabs from the 1960s and 1970s was more full blown than their more recent incarnations. The various subdivisions of the NAPA VALLEY and warmer parts of SONOMA are the most rewarding areas for Cabernet lovers, although the likes of RIDGE Montebello in the SANTA CRUZ MTNS show that the overpublicized counties by no means have the monopoly on great CA Cabernet.

Just as red winemaking wobbled a little in the early to mid-1980s, so too did white winemaking. Great CA Chardonnay is a relatively recent phenomenon, with an even shorter track record. Indeed, the number of such wines which give more pleasure at even 5 years old than at 2 or 3 years old can be counted on the fingers of one hand. But the pleasures of a Chardonnay as fine as MARCASSIN or KISTLER are so hedonistic and so immediately obvious that it seems almost churlish to enquire about their old or even middle age. While equivalent white burgundy crouches sullenly in the glass if poured before its fourth birthday, most of these wines are drunk long before they reach this stage. The Sonoma coast and SANTA BARBARA are obviously areas with enormous potential here.

Where there is great Chardonnay, there should be great Pinot Noir . . . which there is, to a very much more limited extent, in CA. Yet the likes of WILLIAMS SELYEM, Saintsbury, AU BON CLIMAT, ROCHIOLI, and Gary FARRELL have proved the worth of RUSSIAN RIVER, SANTA MARIA, and CARNEROS as Pinot Noir sources of *potentially* world class. I have yet to find a bottle of CA Pinot as truly thrilling, complex, and deep flavoured as the best bottles of red burgundy, but these miracles represent approximately 1% of Burgundy's production. Only OR and parts of New Zealand can so far match CA's potential as a Pinot Noir producer. Far too much Pinot Noir however, just like common or garden CA Chardonnay (and Merlot, which has rarely been taken seriously by CA producers), is sweet, simple, and thoroughly unchallenging.

From the great race to plant Italian and Rhône grape varieties some extremely attractive wines have emerged, even if their added ripeness almost invariably makes them extremely dissimilar to (though not always inferior to) the European archetypes. But this obsession with the modish seems bizarre to an outsider smitten by the inherent quality of CA's very own grape Zinfandel, which itself combines much of the attractions of Italian and Rhône reds. All over the world we have seen and benefited from a re-evaluation of grape varieties that have over decades adapted themselves to a particular part of the world (Shiraz in Australia, Pinotage in South Africa, Malbec in Argentina, for example). Many Californians are still guilty of undervaluing the grape they have been dealt by history, albeit still hazy history (see Genetics essay, p 57). Zinfandel is a unique wine and the epithet 'red' should be redundant.

Given the state's climatic range, it is perhaps surprising that it is not matched by the range of wines produced. With very few exceptions, CA Sauvignon Blanc is almost unrecognizable to the outside world, being much fatter and oilier and, yet again, sweeter. Only North American palates reject any hint of leafiness/herbaceousness/grassiness, call it what you will, in a wine's aroma, whether red or white. (On that basis, young Château Cheval Blanc and many a Graves could well be overlooked.) There are very, very few sparkling wines that match even the mid-range currently being produced in France's Champagne region (where, ironically, standards have recently been much improved in answer to perceived competition from the New World)—and this is true not just in CA but throughout North America.

Although it had a history of making some fine (Johannisberg) Riesling, especially late harvest versions, CA seems to have abandoned aromatic wine styles altogether—while its cuisine screams with increasing urgency for such wines in place of heavy, unappetizing commercial Chardonnays. And, perhaps the most curious thing in a land of virtually unlimited sunshine and dessert fanatics, where cheese is rarely offered at the end of a meal, hardly any CA wine producer takes sweet wine even halfway seriously.

PACIFIC NORTHWEST

WA's glossy, wonderfully bright reds occupy a special place in the world of wine—a sort of cross between the open opulence of CA and the crispness of Bordeaux. Merlot and both Cabernets are clearly perfectly at home here (even if Merlot can find winters as cold as 1996 tough going). L'Ecole 41's Semillon suggests this variety could have a future here, in a style that reflects the reds' position in the world. Syrah is getting there.

OR's strong suit has been obvious for years, and is likely to become considerably stronger in every sense as Burgundian clones of Pinot Noir become more widespread. The best wines, and in particular the best vintages, can give considerable pleasure—and rarely suffer CA's besetting sin of excessive sweetness—but in my experience are yet to rise above the level of a premier cru Côte de Beaune.

MIDWEST

This region with its long history of growing hybrids (MO having been the country's prime wine producer for years) can do a fine job with them. The dark-skinned NORTON grape is a particular success here and can produce wines with genuine distinction, a counterpart to no other wine in the world—as (Marechal) FOCH can be in the hands of a producer such as WOLLERSHEIM of WI. Producers in both WI and OH have shown themselves capable of making fine, ageworthy Rieslings, even if the former may, like so many American producers, vinify grapes trucked in from another state. MI's strength, as one might expect, seems to be in creating ICEWINES to rival those of Ontario across the lake.

NORTHEAST

You have to have been raised on Concord grape jelly to truly appreciate the special flavors of wines made here and in the Midwest from grapes with LABRUSCA in their genetic make-up (see Vine Family essay, p 54), but NY state has many other pleasures to offer discerning, unprejudiced wine drinkers. Long Island may have the monopoly on respectable copies of red bordeaux and white burgundy, but the Finger Lakes can produce Rieslings that withstand international comparison, as well as some extremely conscientiously made sparkling wine. (MA has its own, rather tarter answer to Konstantin FRANK's efforts, from Westport.)

MID-ATLANTIC AND THE SOUTH

As Thomas Jefferson suspected, VA clearly has great potential as a wine producing state, even if for the moment the wines are slightly vapid imitations of French classics, albeit with no shortage of ripeness. Chardonnay and Cabernet Franc seem particularly promising at this stage.

SOUTHWEST

The TX vignoble is, as one would expect, big, and some fine Cabernet and Cabernet/Merlot blends have already emerged to take a vivacious bow. One of North America's best-kept wine secrets, however, is GRUET's NM sparkling wine—not fine and creamy, but certainly appetizing. Even AZ can offer a decent Pinot Gris.

Canada

The quality of Canada's best wines will surprise many—except for Canadians, of course. The warmest summers can ripen even Cabernet Sauvignon quite respectably in Ontario's best vineyards such as those of the BEAMSVILLE BENCH. Rieslings both sweet and dry are obviously well adapted here, withstanding comparison with fine Mosel, but Ontario is, not surprisingly, the proud producer of the world's greatest quantity of Icewine, tingling sweet liquids pressed out of frozen grapes. Vidal and to a lesser extent

Riesling are the grapes for these truly world-class wines. British Columbia's wines have less distinction—so far.

Mexico

Baja California's robust reds, typically based on Italian grapes or Petite Sirah, have no need to make any apology. They are robust, confident, slightly rustic, and represent a wine style that is, alas, fading fast from the world wine map as winemakers increasingly worship at the altar of sophistication.

3

Commentators and the Wine Media

Jancis Robinson, MW

THE North American wine market is distinguished by, although not unique in, its reliance on a small number of commentators. It is perhaps not surprising that a single commentator can wield great power in the US, where one publication may have more than 80 million readers. But since wine drinking is not a majority occupation, such publications are not the ones with a regular wine column and it is not in the American mass market that the oracular power of the wine guru rests. Such is the stranglehold of regulation on the interstate commerce in alcoholic drink for most of North America (see Distribution essay, p 21) that it is extremely difficult for wine columnists even in newspapers such as the *New York Times* to give much useful information on how to obtain bottles glowingly reviewed. Instead it is an elite world of wines, selling for substantial two- and sometimes even three-digit figures, that has been transformed by the pronouncements of just two or three wine reviewers. That these wines are available in strictly limited quantities means the most garlanded can command prices which would have been unthinkable a decade ago.

The chief agent of recent change has been the Score, the points out of 100 allocated to each wine reviewed. This much copied system of objectivizing wine quality was introduced in the late 1970s when young Baltimore lawyer Robert M. Parker Jr decided to launch a newsletter, the *Wine Advocate*. In the consumerist climate of the time, when Ralph Nader was at his most voluble, Parker was fueled by what he saw as a wine press too craven or too obligated to provide genuine criticism of wines that failed to live up to their reputation. He provided, and continues to provide, fulsome notes to back up these scores out of 100 but could not possibly have foreseen how often readers would skip the words to concentrate on the numbers alone, numbers which have had an extraordinary impact on the world of wine. This has not just been an inflation of fine wine prices, but because they can be readily understood even by those who do not speak English, the Scores have helped considerably to spread the gospel of wine enthusiasm to non-Anglophone parts of the world such as Asia and Latin America.

In the beginning a typical issue of the *Wine Advocate* would include scores anywhere between the high 60s (for seriously disappointing bottles) and high 90s. Today, it concentrates on wines between the low 80s and (an increasing number) the high 90s plus an increasing roster of super-glorious 100-pointers. Consumers loved this shorthand. It enabled those with a subscription to the *Wine Advocate*, with its insider quality, to feel good about ordering expensive wines, because they were sanctioned by a confident, hard-working, obviously independent taster.

Producers loved points, at least when they garnered lots of them. They could charge virtually whatever they wanted for a wine in the high 90s. Those producers tarnished with the ignominy of steady 70s would either call in help or call it a day. This effect has been a laudable result of the Score; its chief disadvantage the fact it overlooks variability of different bottles and the subjectivity involved in wine assessment. Retailers used points shamelessly to sell their wares, but rued the Score, bemoaning the fact that 'over 90, you can't buy the wine; under 85, you can't sell it.' As time went on, points became more and more powerful. Producers would wait for the Score on a pre-release wine before deciding on a price. Inevitably the 100-point system has been adopted more widely, by rival newsletters such as Stephen Tanzer's *International Wine Cellar*, and by North American wine magazines and on-line services, most notably what was then AOL's Drinks guide and the *Wine Spectator*, whose readership is measured in six figures rather than the five-figure numbers who read the *Wine Advocate*, *Wine & Spirits* magazine, or the *Wine Enthusiast*. It has not necessarily spread to other newsletters and on-line services, which number subscribers in four figures, such as *International Wine Cellar*, *Connoisseurs' Guide*, the *Underground Wine Journal*, and the *California Grapevine*.

Wine Spectator, a glossy newsstand magazine, has done much to glamorize wine, wine producers, and, most vitally, wine consumers. When *Cigar Aficionado* was launched from the same New York stable in the early 1990s, it rapidly overtook its vinous older brother as a publishing success. *Wine Spectator* may not represent quite such a honeypot to advertisers of luxury goods, but it remains the world's biggest selling wine magazine and wine retailers have been happy to use its tasting panel's scores whenever they happen to suit their purposes better than Parker's.

As a result of all the retail hype, often extended into widely published ads, vastly many more people are aware of Parker and his influence than have ever seen his newsletter. Nowadays retailers or producers deliberately choose to quote a flattering score from Parker, *Wine Spectator*, Tanzer, or another halfway credible-sounding publication, or they may cite an award from a show or competition. Those with more weight than most in North America include: the CA State Fair, which administers a taste examination to judges but only accepts CA wines; INTERVIN, which has an international following and is particularly strong on Canadian wines; the *Dallas Morning News* Competition; the ORANGE CO FAIR, which is run by a consumer club; and the EASTERN WINE COMPETITION, which gets wide participation from states other than CA.

The French and, particularly, Australians use medals even more vigorously than Americans as an aid to wine selection and promotion. The state wine shows of Australia and their highly reputable judges are just as trusted a guide to the best wines as the agricultural shows run alongside them to the 'best of breed' and a very significant proportion of all Australian wine is entered into at least one show. In the US, on the other hand, a bronze medal is regarded as almost a negative attribute. Which is one reason the shows are shunned by the great majority of established artistic producers who feel they have more to lose than to gain by having their wines judged in formats which often yield highly capricious results, and against fields largely composed of newcomers and commercial factories. Within France the Paris and Mâcon Fairs are probably the most prestigious sources of medals but here, as in most European wine producing countries, personal connections with vintner friends, family, and a particular wine region provide the strongest motivating force for wine buyers. For the great majority they may be much less reliable than following a Parker or *Wine Spectator* selection, but they are probably more personally satisfying.

Highly developed wine markets such as Great Britain, Germany, and the Netherlands tend to rely on a matrix of different commentators, whose palates and preferences may or may not correspond with those of individual consumers. Trial and error allows them to weigh a wide range of recommendations, much more often at the bottom end of the price range than the top. In these markets wine is so well embedded in society that television and radio programs on the subject, while not exactly proliferating, certainly exist to a much greater extent than they do in North America, where any substance containing alcohol, no matter how closely associated with religion and culture, no matter how much enjoyed in private, is officially regarded with suspicion and even horror (see The Prohibition Paradox, p 17). The Canadian wine market is subject to a quite different set of constraints in the form of its provincial monopolies on liquor distibution. To fill their columns, Canadian wine writers merely need a close acquaintance with the local liquor board's range.

All North American wine commentators, including the one or two based in Mexico, live a long way from the cradle of wine production. That inconvenience has tended to make them curious about European wine and some of them are easy fodder for public relations exercises on behalf of it. A free trip to France, Spain, or Italy is not to be sniffed at when the distance covered is measured in thousands rather than hundreds of miles—no matter that the host may expect a favorable review in return. Only publications as well heeled as the *New York Times* and *Los Angeles Times* can afford scruples in this respect; both publications make much of their no-freebie policies, but then there are remarkably few full-time wine writing posts in North America. It is in this climate that such independent commentators as the powerful bestowers of points have emerged, and it is no accident it was an American, Mr Parker, who first styled himself a wine *critic*.

Now, thanks to the World Wide Web, consumers have their own voice and their own way of comparing notes, quite literally. On hundreds of wine-dedicated Web sites and chat lines in cyberspace, wine drinkers can publish their impressions and ratings not only of individual wines, but of individual wine commentators, and books like this, too. It seems likely that in this respect at least the wine consumer will, happily, continue to exert ever more power.

4

The Prohibition Paradox

Dan Berger

ANTI-ALCOHOL movements have bubbled up in the US three times since the founding of the nation more than 200 years ago. Most of North America seems to swing wildly between acceptance of alcohol as a beverage that can be used with moderation and condemnation as a demon that ruins. Most other nations seem to understand the virtues of moderate use of all alcoholic beverages, and in some countries even the use of other stimulants and depressants. However, Calvinist reform movements develop regularly in the US. Dr David Musto, a sociologist at Yale University who has studied anti-alcohol movements in American history, says they typically occur in roughly 70-year cycles, and last long enough for the progenitors of the prior movement to have died off so the drawbacks of actual *Prohibition have been forgotten.

The first major 'temperance movement' in the US (really an anti-alcohol movement, as moderate use was not a consideration for the activists) arrived in the first third of the 19th century and focused on the consumption of distilled spirits, which had been a major public activity since the American Revolution, when public drunkenness was rampant. By the 1840s, the topic was on the lips of politicians in every state. That prompted many reasonable minds to address the question of forced abstinence as compared with moderate use.

Abraham Lincoln, in speeches to the Illinois House of Representatives in 1840 and then later to the Washingtonian Society in 1842, is quoted as saying, 'Prohibition will work great injury to the cause of temperance. It is a species of intemperance within itself, for it goes beyond the bounds of reason in that it attempts to control a man's appetite by legislation, and makes a crime out of things that are not crimes. A Prohibition law strikes a blow at the very principles upon which our government was founded.' Lincoln feared a prohibition in which the government creates a culture where flouting the law to obtain it encourages other forms of law-breaking too, with good reason, as it turned out.

The temperance movement of the 18th century reached its peak in the mid-1850s when all of New England, and about a third of all Americans lived under state-imposed prohibition. During the period, there was a decline in consumption of spirits (the major target of the reformers), but there was a significant move toward greater beer consumption. Wine consumption in the US, from Revolutionary times through the middle of the 20th century, was largely confined to fortified products, such as port, sherry, and Madeira, most of it sweeter versions. By the 1870s, moderate consumption of alcoholic beverages was once again accepted as a sane diversion.

The second major wave of anti-alcohol sentiment began slowly with the founding in 1874 of the

Woman's Christian Temperance Union (WCTU), and was pushed along 21 years later by the founding of the Anti-Saloon League. It was the saloon, where men gathered and (so said the women) left their families alone at nights, that was the main target of the reformists. The WCTU and Anti-Saloon League revived the outcry against drunkenness, focusing their attacks on the product itself, not on its abuse, and using the saloon as its symbol. In an ironic twist, many of the reformers were in fact closet abusers themselves. Often, the strongest opponents of alcoholic beverage consumption were upper-class women who volunteered with local organizations to close down saloons. After a long, hard day of fighting the good fight against alcohol, many would return to their comfortable homes and before beginning dinner, would have a shot of a 'women's tonic,' whose main active ingredient was alcohol. The anti-alcohol campaigns of the first decade and a half of the 20th century was driven by political campaigns as fierce as any involving abortion today. As women were gaining the vote, they used it to vote only for candidates who believed in Prohibition. Such power was persuasive to politicians.

By 1917, the anti-alcohol movement had gained such strength that Congress finally passed the 18th amendment to the Constitution mandating a ban on the commercial production and sale of all wine, beer, and spirits. The Volstead Act spelled out how the Prohibition would be conducted, and the amendment was finally ratified in January 1920. The result was called the Noble Experiment. Although the word 'prohibition' has a generic meaning, referring to the passage of laws that make certain acts illegal, by capitalizing 'Prohibition,' the tenor of the times gained a formal name. And yet, breaking the law and getting a tipple was almost as American as voting—more so in many cases.

The reformers believed they had saved America. Under the real belief that they were doing good for society, reformers took pride in Prohibition, assuming it would end alcoholism, save marriages from break-ups caused by drunkenness, and generally save all of America from ruin. What it did in practical terms, however, was to take a product that was legal, popular—and taxable—and, in effect, hand it to organized crime, which could charge what it wanted for it while paying the government nothing. As for America's consumption of alcohol, it never really slackened. Alcohol consumption did initially drop when Prohibition started, but later drinking increased dramatically.

The reformers were convinced of their moral stance. It coincided with quests to purify America with a fervor akin to religious evangelism. These staunch fighters against all forms of evil (the evils they perceived) wanted to establish laws that outlawed certain books, art, music, public dancing, and basically to control human expression. During this period, some laws and codes were enacted that dealt with society's desire to control how people lived, to the degree that many victimless crimes were created. Moreover, the motion picture industry was saddled with a censorship system that limited freedom of speech and stifled creativity in the name of 'decency.'

Throughout the debates leading up to the passage of the 18th amendment, a few lawmakers realized that such a pervasive habit as drinking a few beers or a highball at a dinner party could not be completely eradicated with a few signatures. So they left the door ajar for some citizens to procure alcohol during Prohibition (1920 to 1933) quite legally. For example, medicinal wine could be prescribed by physicians for patients who needed a 'pick-me-up.' Who had such physicians? Wealthy citizens, of course. Sacramental wine was permitted for use in religious ceremonies, such as the Catholic Mass and in Jewish celebrations such as Passover. Prohibition created more sick people and religious converts than at any time in the nation's history.

Moreover, homeowners were permitted to make 200 gal of wine at home for personal use, and by making sacramental and kosher wines, medicinal wines, and by selling grapes and similar products, many

California wineries remained in business during the period. (One such product, a 'brick' of pressed, dried wine grapes, carried a warning label: 'do not add water, sugar and yeast or it will ferment'!) It also permitted the development of some shady businesses, such as the off-site winery. For a fee, an entrepreneur would make your 200 gal of wine for you. Moonshine was crafted in stills, many of them hidden in remote hills; bootleggers carried the hooch surreptitiously to the cities. During Prohibition, there developed a number of ways for Americans to get wine illegally, or marginally legally. Cruise ships that left US waters could serve alcohol. And private clubs called 'speakeasies' grew in every major city.

The anti-alcohol forces were never as active as during the Prohibition period, enlisting many evangelical organizations to join their crusade against consumption. The First World War also helped them make their arguments that grains, such as wheat and barley, should be used for wartime efforts, for food, rather than be fermented into whiskey.

Such political and social movements have major fallacies embedded within them. You lose the concept of a safe threshold of use. Anything you drink is bad. Alcohol itself becomes the bad thing, and if you take a little bit of it, you still have a little badness. By making the product act as the demon, personal responsibility no longer becomes an issue. The Prohibition era was rife with crime and bootlegging. Police forces not only turned a blind eye toward rum-running, but often participated in its delivery. As crime increased, the court and prison systems were overwhelmed, unable to handle the case load. Meanwhile, the hoped-for gains in workplace productivity or reduced absenteeism never materialized. Huge tax revenues were lost while government spending was rising to fight illegal booze sales. Moreover, the difficulty of getting alcohol prompted many drinkers to switch to opium, marijuana, patent medicines, and cocaine—substances that might never have become popular had alcohol been available as an outlet.

Prohibition was clearly an utter failure. By 1933 Prohibition was formally ended with passage of the 21st Amendment to the Constitution that gave control over the distribution and sale of alcoholic beverages to the individual states. However, many areas of the country, fearful of rampant drunkenness once Prohibition had ended, passed strict regulations against consumption in delimited regions. Entire cities and counties were DRY, the term used to describe areas in which no alcohol could be sold. And so-called BLUE LAWS were enacted that prohibited sale of alcoholic beverages on Sundays, or during certain hours. Many of these laws are still in effect today.

For the next 40 or so years after Prohibition ended, the lessons of that period were a major deterrent to a new temperance movement developing. However, deaths as a result of drunken driving instigated a new wave of anti-alcohol sentiment in the late 1970s.

The most recent national (and worldwide) wave of anti-alcohol sentiment started in the early 1980s. Despite growing scientific evidence of *health benefits from moderate, regular consumption of wine, reform groups, using as their major symbol the drunken driver, lobbied Congress to control the sale of alcoholic beverages more rigorously. Finally Congress mandated a warning label on all alcoholic beverages. From Nov 1, 1989 all alcoholic beverages sold in the US have had to carry a Warning Statement.

The reformers pushing for tougher laws against drunken driving focused not on the drivers, but on the product. They used as one of their targets a subtle and insidious form of transparent prohibition. Zero Tolerance is the push in many quarters for lower and lower levels of blood alcohol content (BAC) to determine what constitutes a legal presumption of intoxication. The blood alcohol limit for drunkenness while driving in many states had been 0.10%. However, in the early 1990s, campaigns by Mothers Against Drunk Driving (MADD) and other lobbying groups, coupled with pressure from Reagan administration officials who threatened to withhold highway construction funding from any state refusing to comply, persuaded many states to lower this figure to 0.08%. Opponents of the lowered limit point out that almost all serious accidents involving drinking drivers involved those with blood alcohol levels well above 0.15, and that by lowering the figure to 0.08, all the authorities were doing was creating a new class of official drunks, most of whom were not impaired drivers. Additionally a change in the way authorities calculate what defines an 'alcohol related incident' in the 1980s has actually driven up the statistics. Today, if any individual involved in an auto accident has a blood alcohol content above the legal limit, the accident is considered alcohol related. This includes instances where the driver is sober, with a blood alcohol content of zero, and a passenger is above the legal limit. So much for designated drivers!

Using an argument from the 1900–19 campaigns, the reformers of the 1980s and 1990s said that any use of alcohol was irresponsible, and impairing. Then they pushed for the 0.08% limit to be lowered still, to 0.05 for adults and zero for anyone under 21. Moreover, the federal government in the early 1980s wielded enormous power to force all states to raise their legal drinking age to 21—from as low as age 17 in some states, age 18 in many others, and age 19 in most. The government said any state not in compliance with a 'suggested' minimum drinking age of 21 would receive no federal transportation dollars. Every state eventually complied.

Dr Musto believes the passion and intensity of the typical prohibition movement in the US lasts between 30 and 40 years before subsiding. He suspects the current wave of anti-alcohol sentiment will not abate until about 2020. What may truncate the latest anti-alcohol movement is the rash of evidence emanating from the nation's and the world's finest health institutions, from Boston, Harvard, and Tufts universities, UCLA Medical Center, and even including the federal government's own research. These studies increasingly show evidence that moderate consumption of alcoholic beverages, notably wine, helps decrease the risk of heart disease, and that moderate wine drinkers live longer, healthier lives than abstainers.

Moreover, in 1999, the agency that controls alcoholic beverages in the US, the BATF, approved for use on wine two informational labels that encourage the consumer to obtain a copy of the federal government's nutrition guidelines that refer to the possible health benefits, and another that says the wine producer encourages consumers to discuss consumption with their doctors, a tacit implication that doctors would recognize the health benefits of moderate use.

Despite all this, wine is still equated by many lobbying groups as just another drug to be controlled as strictly as it was during Prohibition. The Noble Experiment failed, but the current wave of reformers did not learn much from their ancestors. Their fight persists.

5

The US Wine Distribution System

Jean-Michel Valette, MW

WHILE not quite as impenetrable as Winston Churchill's 'enigma wrapped in a mystery,' the United States' wine distribution system can be baffling even to the initiated observer. Unlike most other commercial goods, wine in the US does not enjoy treatment under the free trade provisions of the US Constitution but is instead governed by the 21st Amendment. This Act, which repealed *Prohibition (the 18th Amendment), gave the individual states jurisdiction to regulate the commerce of alcoholic beverages. As a result, the US has effectively 50 distribution systems, each with its attendant rules and laws.

One feature common to most state regulations, however, is the imposition of a THREE-TIER DISTRIBUTION system of producers, wholesalers, and retailers on the distribution of alcoholic beverages. Each tier generally has separate licensing requirements, and common ownership of enterprises between tiers is either strongly discouraged or specifically prohibited. The outcome is a firmly entrenched wholesale tier, different in every state, which buys from producers or their agents and sells to retail and restaurant outlets. Direct shipments from producer to retailer, or directly to the end consumer, are not in all cases prohibited but are much less common than in other parts of the world.

The balance of power between producer and wholesaler can vary based on many usual economic and commercial factors such as relative size of company, strength of brand, and information flow to name a few. Individual state regulations also play a significant role, most importantly in regulating a producer's ability to change wholesalers. Such laws, generally called franchise laws, differ greatly from state to state. In certain states, it is very difficult to change wholesalers. Navigating this patchwork distribution system on a national basis can be a daunting task for even the largest producers. Many winemakers, especially smaller ones or foreign entities who cannot afford or do not want a company-owned national sales force, rely on additional tiers such as national marketing agents, importers, or brokers. The exact designation and role of these additional middlemen can depend on whether or not they take title to goods and what types of duties (e.g. marketing as well as sales) they perform. In any case, for almost all wines consumed there is often a long line of intermediaries and MARK-UPS, or commissions, between the producer and the consumer. Often, half or more of the price of a bottle of wine to the consumer is made up of distribution related costs and profits.

Advances in logistics and technology coupled with a major consolidation of spirits suppliers over the last 20 years have had a dramatic impact on the wholesale business. The most visible change is in the number of wholesale operations. Whereas there used to be dozens of small and medium sized distributors in any given market, today there are often only two or three large ones. Yet the number of wine labels and companies has dramatically increased over the same 20 years. As a result, the number of wineries per wholesaler has grown exponentially. With much larger books of suppliers, wholesalers cannot focus as closely on each supplier's business as they once could—nor can suppliers expect them to. Gaining a wholesaler's attention, therefore, has become a more critical and difficult task for any winery owner or marketer. Rising above the clutter often requires the clout of scale, a high degree of product differentiation, strong consumer demand, and/or an effective sales organization. The advantages to a winery of breaking through the attention barrier, however, can be substantial. While the modern-day distributor may be less of an individual brand-marketer than in the past, it is also a much more efficient and effective provider of logistics, data, market reach, and financial stability.

The impact of individual state laws does not stop at the wholesale distribution level. When and where a consumer can buy wine also varies by state and sometimes even by municipality. Unlike their counterparts in the United Kingdom, France, or Australia, many American consumers cannot buy wine in their local supermarkets or food stores. In some markets, wine is not available on Sundays or, in the extreme case of certain DRY counties, ever at all. Over the years, however, as wine has become more a part of American culture, the availability of wine to the consumer has increased. In many states wine is now available in all traditional food and beverage outlets including supermarkets. In others, including major metropolitan areas such as New York, wine is limited to specialized wine and spirits stores. In a few states, called *control* or MONOPOLY STATES, wine sales are only permitted in state-run outlets.

Despite the fact that they cannot sell wine in all states, supermarkets and chain grocery outlets such as club stores account for approximately 20–30% of retail wine sales in the US. Moreover, this percentage is increasing as wine sales in grocery stores are growing faster than the overall market. Not only do consumers appear to be attracted to the convenience and pricing of these stores, but grocery retailers are paying more attention to wine, devoting more shelf-space, promotional displays, and local advertising to the category. Some grocery stores even have dedicated wine consultants to assist consumers in their choices. Grocery share of wine sold is higher for lower priced, high turnover wines than for high priced specialty products.

With supermarket sales legally constrained in many areas, specialty wine and spirits stores remain an important factor in US wine retailing—perhaps more so than in many other wine consuming countries. Again, often because of specific state laws either prohibiting or discouraging chains, these specialty stores are often independent or parts of small chains with much less buying power or clout than supermarkets or the big specialist wine chains in the United Kingdom or France. Often these stores supplement in-store sales with an important volume of direct mail and/or catalog sales. These stores provide an important educational function for the consumer and often provide a better selection of harder-to-find or less well-known wines than mass outlets.

Over the last few decades wine sales have expanded beyond the traditional white tablecloth restaurants. Today, wine has become an important source of profits and new business for hotel chains, lower priced restaurants, and resorts. For example, Disney—which once shunned alcohol—now has a very active and successful wine program at its resort hotels, restaurants, and on its cruise ships, including a staff of wine educators and a CA wine exhibit opening soon at Disneyland.

Except for the mail-order activities of individual retailers mentioned above, there are relatively few direct retailers of any scale in the US. This stands in contrast to a fairly well-developed mail-order channel in many European countries. Again, the difficulty of navigating a complex set of legal restrictions is most likely the main hindrance as direct marketing is a significant channel for other goods in the US. The advent of the Internet has spurred the creation of a new set of well-capitalized 'store-less' retailers (such as wine.com, evineyard.com, and wineshopper.com) which have developed significant consumer and winery interest, but at the turn of the century sales were still small compared with traditional channels.

For years, many wineries have shipped small quantities of wine as a service to winery visitors and other interested consumers. Today, especially for a growing number of smaller wineries, direct shipping to consumers has evolved into their dominant source of revenue. With the advent of low cost computing to track individual mailing lists and the emerging availability of low cost courier and shipping sources, direct shipping has for some become more practical and economic than navigating the three-tier system. This evolution is not without controversy. Whereas shipping companies, state regulators, and anti-alcohol lobbyists often turned a blind eye to potential violations of state laws in the past, this is no longer the case. The growth in direct shipping of wine has kindled concerns ranging from the potential loss of state tax revenues to the potential for uncontrolled access to alcohol by minors. In general, too, wholesalers and their industry associations have opposed direct shipping by wineries. The controversy varies significantly by state and is at its most intense in those states where direct shipping of alcohol is a felony punishable by, among other things, loss of one's license to sell alcohol through traditional channels. The issue is much less controversial in those states, called Reciprocal states, which allow the DIRECT SHIPMENT of wine. The table lists Reciprocal states as well as a delineation of states with felony statutes against direct shipping (as of late 1999). For the most current and detailed description of each state's laws on the subject see www.wineinstitute.org, button for winelaw.org, button for direct shipping.

Reciprocal states	States where shipments expressly prohibited	Felony states
CA, CO, ID, IL, IA MN, MO, NM, OR, WA, WV, WI	AZ, AR, DE, KS, ME, MS MT, NY, OK, SD, TX, UT, VA	FL, GA, IN, KY, MD, NC, TN

The reader who has gotten this far surely will have noted the US distribution system for wine is unique and complex. To a large degree, it remains shaped by a state-by-state legal system with its roots planted firmly in the Prohibition era. Over the long run, however, economics often win out over politics. Despite some fairly rigid laws, some signs of fundamental change were already evident by 1999. For example, distributor consolidation is crossing state lines as several large multi-state wholesaler groups expand their reach. At the same time, direct shipping is becoming more of a force and is, in a small way, eroding the exclusive hold of the three-tier system. If and as wine becomes a stronger part of America's backbone, the wine distribution system should continue to evolve in ways which merit attention from consumers and producers alike.

See MEXICO and CANADA for more details of distribution in these countries.

6

Cybersales and the Future

Peter Granoff, MS

THE future of the American wine industry is particularly interesting in the light of the technology revolution and a rapidly changing consumer marketplace, which finds itself increasingly at odds with fragmented and ossified regulatory constraints. One issue is the product itself: does wine have more in common with books, or with heroin? Another issue is philosophical: can any society effectively legislate behavior? Then there is the role of entrenched special interests: should they retain residual benefits when technology passes them by? Finally: are democratic institutions, at least as practiced in the US, capable of resolving these conflicts?

In the summer of 1999, the most heated issue facing the US wine industry was DIRECT SHIPMENT to consumers. Why is the issue heated? In a word, money. When a winery ships directly to a consumer at present, the licensed wholesale and retail tiers of the US THREE-TIER system are bypassed. Naturally the two tiers cut out of the sale are unhappy at what they perceive as a loss of potential business. State regulators, additionally, are upset at the loss of EXCISE TAXES on alcohol, which often represent significant revenue streams for their jurisdictions, and at the loss of control over transactions involving alcohol. These regulators also absorb the irate phone calls from in-state licensees who have been circumvented, and from whom they collect substantial license renewal fees annually.

This emotional debate frequently overlooks the fact that much direct shipping actually originates from retailers across the US who are prospecting for customers further and further from their own physical premises, rather than from a winery. Most wines sold this way have been purchased by the retailer from a local wholesaler. While SALES TAXES in both the originating state and the destination state have likely been lost, all excise taxes in the originating state have been paid. The wholesale tier, which has been most vociferous in its organized opposition to direct shipping, thus ironically benefits handsomely from much of it already. It is also difficult to tell who is winning in this battle as it plays out in our state capitols and courts, as well as in Washington, DC, the federal courts, and in the media.

These details obscure a more fundamental shift taking place in the American wine market. Thomas Kuhn's book *The Structure of Scientific Revolutions* offers an elegant explanation of this, which he calls Paradigm Collapse. First a postulated theory is tested, and eventually becomes a broadly accepted paradigm. Over time the paradigm becomes so entrenched that the set of assumptions on which it rests are obscured or forgotten entirely. When the underlying assumptions cease to be valid, the paradigm is vulnerable to collapse. In the wake of the collapse a new theory is postulated and the process begins anew.

Many of the changes creeping up on the American wine market have long since taken place, or are proceeding at a blistering pace, with the onrush of technology in other industries. These changes are presently held at arm's length by the regulatory structure of the wine industry.

Geographic exclusivity

The current paradigm assumes discrete and meaningful physical boundaries to distribution arrangements. Wineries contract with wholesalers to represent their products in the state where the wholesaler is licensed. In the current regulatory climate, wineries must do this on a state-by-state basis. The assumption is that the wholesaler serves a territory in that state and that state only. Often the wholesaler is selling wine to retailers, who in turn are shipping the wines to other parts of the country, rendering the notion of discrete physical territories meaningless. In other cases the wine is being sold to a chain account as the result of a decision that took place thousands of miles away. A local licensee is hardly needed in this case, as any decent freight handling firm could deliver the goods from a centralized distribution point. E-commerce, and the ability of the Internet to reach a global audience, have rendered geographic exclusivity a relic of history.

Excise or sales tax collection

The current paradigm assumes in-state licensed wholesalers and retailers are the only audit-worthy collection point for state excise taxes and sales taxes (respectively) on wine. This assumption has evolved elaborate, paper-based bureaucracies to manage the process. Meanwhile the entire global banking system functions on electronic movement of funds with audit trails that satisfy the world's finest accounting firms. Every winery tasting room, retailer, and e-commerce firm has credit card processing systems that could just as easily be depositing excise and sales taxes instantaneously at the point of transaction. States already collect sales taxes from hundreds of thousands of merchants with relatively little fraud, and the US government's own Internal Revenue Service proudly heralds the rapid increase in the number of US taxpayers filing their federal tax returns electronically.

Wholesaler consolidation

Sweeping mergers throughout the US wine and spirits wholesale industry in the last quarter-century have created a choke point in the three-tier system. This trend continues unabated. At the same time there has been an explosion in the number of small specialty producers worldwide. Even large producers are increasingly differentiating their portfolios by price, quality, and production level. These two trends run directly counter to each other, and they aggravate tension over direct shipping and over the effectiveness of distribution in general. Larger wholesalers, their protests to the contrary notwithstanding, are poorly prepared to represent small brands, limited production wines, or specialty wines which require extensive explanation, all competing for attention in their 'books' which have grown increasingly bloated by consolidaton. Adaptation to address these marketplace realities must occur at some point.

Well-traveled consumers

The wild card in this game is an individual who visits wine regions around the world adding his or her name to a winery mailing list. When he or she is told that wine cannot be shipped to his or her home state, the response is often bewilderment, outrage, hilarity, or some combination of the three. Consumers are increasingly mobile, affluent, well educated, and comfortable with technology. The wild card orders books from Seattle, CDs from PA, coffee from Central America, clothing from WI, Cuban cigars from Canada or England, and wine from all over the country. The wild card drives from Philadelphia to NJ, or from OH to MO, or travels from England to France through the Chunnel to buy wine. Why? Because prices are lower and selection superior. The wild card sees restrictions on his or her behavior and movements as pointless and mildly oppressive. Those with a vested interest in maintaining the current paradigm for wine distribution in the US are entertaining a fantasy that they can control the wild card.

There are many industries that operate in a regulated climate. The North American wine industry will always be regulated because wine is a socially sensitive product. No responsible citizen would argue otherwise. At issue is the purpose and extent of the regulation, and where the regulatory power actually resides. It is rare that governmental processes modify regulatory restrictions to facilitate change. More often regulations are changed to adapt to a shift in the market that has already taken place. That may be an accurate description of what the wine industry's next quarter-century in North America will look like as states, and maybe even Canadian provinces, come to recognize e-commerce and other forms of direct shipping as revenue opportunities.

How would the industry operate in a climate that recognized the above changes?

The most obvious advantages for the consumer would be a free flow of information and goods. Wineries would be free to market their production via the Internet (or not) wherever they liked and with as much product information as appropriate, provided the excise taxes were paid in the destination state. One or more of the larger shipping companies would facilitate the payment of taxes through a centralized database and ensure that deliveries did not fall into the hands of minors, thus mitigating state concerns about both issues. Wine of all kinds would be staged in a variety of technology-enabled warehouses in key distribution centers around the US. Consumers, restaurants, and retailers alike could order via the Web for delivery to their chosen location. Wholesalers that survived would thrive based on service, selection, and expertise, not on artificial barriers to entry. Real-time inventories would be the standard rather than the exception. When a sales rep made a call, it would be with a laptop, wireless modem, and small printer in tow. Orders, product inquiries, allocations, account status, inventories—all would be immediately accessible. Distribution and logistics would be viewed as cost functions, much as they are in other industries. The most successful players would be those that add genuine value and are the most efficient. Would wine consumption go up as retail price points found new levels? Would the base of wine consumers expand as information became more easily accessible? At the producer level technology would be utilized to manage allocations, inventories, and sophisticated depletion reports, thus at least theoretically liberating wineries to make superior wines and better marketing decisions. Federal labeling requirements and the approval process would be streamlined. Individual state label approvals and their utterly pointless bureaucracies would vanish, thus reducing time to market and eliminating regulatory costs.

Wine is rather unlike most spirits and beers in that wine is different from year to year, even bottle to bottle as it matures in one's cellar. Information is an important component in the enjoyment of a bottle of wine. Electronic delivery has tremendous potential to enhance the amount of information consumers can receive. By contrast, moving information through the three-tiered distribution system is like trying to pump Karo syrup through a brick wall. Perhaps the role of retailers in the future will be to act as a knowledgeable terminal for consumers who do not want to sort through a mass of electronic wine information themselves. Top retailers would perform a valuable role by editing and summarizing information for their customers. By investing in hardware (such as an expensive high bandwidth cable line), software, and expertise that individual, casual wine consumers would not want for themselves, retailers can carve for themselves a service and entertainment function which is particularly important relative to wine. Imagine a retail store environment where pictures comparing vineyards, explanations of winemaking techniques, video presentations of objective wine critiques by colorful personalities, even surveys of consumer opinion can be rapidly marshalled to enhance any consumer's appreciation of a wine he or she is taking home to drink that night.

7

Wine Service in the US

Larry Stone, MS

Over the last 30 years DINING HABITS in North America have evolved out of a condition that might best be compared to a pre-industrialized third world country, into those of a major superpower in the world of wine knowledge and appreciation. The habits of Americans have changed from drinking Blue Nun or Mateus Rosé with their Lobster Newberg at a 'Continental' restaurant, or having a Coca-Cola with their Swanson's TV dinner at home, to ordering a Swanson Sangiovese with a Roasted Quail Salad or an Austrian Smaragd Riesling with Tuna Tartare. In the 1950s and 1960s people ate canned tuna and canned ravioli, frozen TV dinners, and big hunks of beef, and were proud of it. Even fine dining establishments in most parts of the country had limited menus and wine lists, prominently featuring such items as sweetened Portuguese Rosé, Liebfraumilch, Chianti in fiasco, and one or two Extra Dry Champagnes. Mid-level and chain restaurants may have had the three colors of jug wine and a sweetened Oloroso.

There are regional differences in service that are reflected in the development of wine consciousness in America. Of course, the megalopolis spanning WASHINGTON, DC to BOSTON has the longest wine drinking tradition and the highest density of fine dining establishments. Due to its long gastronomic history, there has been an equally prolonged focus on imported wines and cuisines, pre-dating the rebirth of the American wine industry. Not so long ago, on the eastern seaboard, which is still the nucleus of imported wine sales, connoisseurs scarcely condescended to taste CA Cabernet alongside classified bordeaux. Along with this lengthy tradition went a true sophistication about the importance of wine at the table. There were many fine French restaurants that cultivated the cellaring and service of bordeaux and burgundy, such as Lutèce with legendary chef André Soultner. The 21 Club also had a famous cellar with a secret entrance, dating back to before Prohibition, and it maintained special wine storage for its favored customers, such as Richard Nixon or William Paley of CBS. Typical of this earlier era, throughout the US, but especially in the larger cities of the East Coast, was the cool, almost implacable image of the sommelier. It was perhaps due to the timidity of the public itself, or perhaps because of the relative ignorance of many sommeliers at the time, that this pose was common. Unfortunately, this image has persisted in the popular imagination even though the profession has long since discarded it.

One of the first restaurants to make a fresh start and a nationwide impression in terms of wine and food pairings, as well as featuring a superlative cellar, was the Four Seasons restaurant in the Seagram's Building in Manhattan. This restaurant was founded by Joe Baum and Albert Stöckli, and directed briefly but importantly by Georg Lang. But it was brought to enological prominence (since 1973) by the talented

Transylvanian Hungarians Paul Kovi and Tom Margittai, with the help of Alex von Bidder and Julian Niccolini, who were able to create a truly international following for the restaurant with the talented chef Seppi Renggli. This restaurant was the home of the first winemaker dinners in the form of the visionary CA Barrel Tasting Dinners starting in 1976, which were truly groundbreaking for gastronomy as well as for the confidence of CA winegrowers. CA winemakers were invited to discourse on unfinished wines over an elaborate meal in the most respected East Coast restaurant. 'It was the first time we were taken seriously outside of CA,' said Warren Winiarski of STAGS LEAP. These dinners were so successful that they had to be discontinued by 1986, because demand exceeded 2,000 requests for only 230 seats. The restaurant replaced them with an annual Grand Cru Bordeaux dinner. The Four Seasons also promoted the serving of top-end wines for wine-by-the-glass service and often had special tasting menus that paired specific dishes with selected wines. Passing today by the beautifully modern restaurant and building, designed by Mies van der Rohe and Philip Johnson, it is hard to imagine that it began 40 years ago.

In the 1970s the creation of the World Trade Center in New York was crowned by the establishment of Windows on the World with its Cellar in the Sky. Restaurateur Joe Baum was again the driving force. This unique restaurant, whose wine program was exciting and innovative, was the first place where the wine list was more of a feature than the cuisine or ambience. The ambience was indeed dictated by the presence of the well-chosen wine list accompanied by its ambitious wine education program under the direction of Kevin Zraly. He became the most famous sommelier in the Americas and for the last 25 years has continued to direct the Windows on the World Wine School.

NEW YORK CITY has also been home to sommelier groups and consumer classes, which have raised the standard for the last 30 years. That one person can make an important change in a culture is attested to by Master Sommelier Roger Dagorn's decades-long contribution to the teaching of wine service to professionals in New York City through the New York Sommelier Society. Other famous New York sommeliers who have contributed to a true understanding of wines from around the world are Steve Olson, Daniel Johnnes, David Gordon, Karen King, Fred Price, Scott Carney, Michael Bonadies, and the highly honored Andrea Immer. The program of the Institute of Masters of Wine began its outreach into the US here and has the use of the International Wine Center in Manhattan, a for-profit enterprise owned by Mary Mulligan, to help with continuing education and preparation for the Master of Wine examinations.

The other major force in restaurant wine service in the US is on the West Coast. CA especially had a stake in promoting local wineries out of a sense of local pride. In LOS ANGELES, Nathan Chroman, director of the influential Los Angeles Co Fair, also consulted to restaurants, most notably Scandia, which collected an enormous cellar of the finest wines produced in the 1960s and 1970s. In SAN FRANCISCO, the Carnelian Room atop the Bank of America Building and the French Room in the Clift Hotel were also influential in promoting CA wines and directing their clientele on a path of discovery. Indicative of the long way that wine service has come in the west is the story of Chez Panisse. Founded in 1972 and already then representing some of the finest impulses to discover and reinvent anew traditional ideas that has marked CA's contribution to American cuisine, Chez Panisse began with what must now be considered enormous naivety. There were few wines on the list, with the only standard being that Sauternes must be served with dessert, since Sauternes was founder Alice Waters' favorite wine. Gradually Kermit Lynch's and Joseph Phelps' wines made it on, and when Jeremiah Tower became the chef de cuisine he took an interest and began to develop the cellar.

One of the greatest influences on the improvement of wine knowledge and service in the restaurant industry came out of the desire of two Californians to be accredited by the English Court of Master

Sommeliers in the early 1980s. Fred Dame of the Sardine Factory and David O'Connor who worked at the St Francis in San Francisco, went to London to pass the Master Sommelier examination and then actively persuaded the English organization to hold classes and tests in the US. The Court of Master Sommeliers, which began testing in Monterey, CA, in 1986 with the financial help of the National Restaurant Association, has had an especially profound effect on the level of wine service and education in the US through its extremely active testing program. In an average year its volunteers teach and test nearly 360–400 American candidates. Most of these are candidates for the entry-level certificate courses, now held around the entire country, even at Disneyworld in Orlando, FL, and Chicago, New York, Seattle, and other locations. The Advanced course is taken by about 75 people a year, and nearly 40 people apply to sit for the Master examination annually. In 1988 there were ten Master Sommeliers in the US; in 1999 there were 40. The program is a modern one that emphasizes knowledge and accessibility over the more formal school of restaurant service. The main thrust of the program is to produce sommeliers who give appropriate service, but are also skilled in passing along reliable information to customers in a friendly, inviting manner.

The Southeast, especially LA, FL, and GA, was at first connected to the established East Coast European mold, but very quickly have become converts to the modern, CA-oriented wine trade, with its more experimental and inquisitive approach. In ATLANTA, there has developed a strong sommelier community that has been tutored by Yves Durand, who has become the only American director of the International Sommelier Association (ASI). Master Sommelier Michael McNeil, winner of Best Sommelier in the US 1993, and America's first *Master of Wine Tim Hanni have come from there.

Mr Hanni now lives in Napa Valley and has become known for his unique approach to pairing food and wine. He advocates the radical idea of guests altering the balance of salt, acid, and UMAMI in their individual dishes to suit their own individual taste sensitivity to these components, and to create a balance they find most pleasant with the wine being served. Though fascinating and highly instructive, his method is sometimes met with skepticism during food and wine pairings at restaurants by chefs and sommeliers.

The Midwest, outside of CHICAGO, also has an abiding keen interest in French wines, but remains a relative stronghold for German wine sales too. In Chicago in the early 1990s, Charlie Trotter's took American wine service to a higher level with the introduction of Riedel Sommelier glasses, the presence of two full-time on-duty sommeliers, elaborate multi-course wine dinners, and a focus on experimental wine pairings with a non-traditional, eclectic (or personal) cuisine. Charlie Trotter's subsequent wine books were the first specifically written with wine pairing as an essential, even organizational element. His first two sommeliers, Joseph Spellman and this writer, are the only American holders of the Grand Prix de Sopexa, the top international French sommelier award.

The Southwest, which scarcely had any interest in anything but beer and hard spirits 30 years ago, has grown and developed into a gastronomic outpost with PHOENIX, Scottsdale, Santa Fe, Dallas, and Houston developing thriving restaurant communities and a distinctive regional cuisine. SEATTLE had the first Cruvinet wine-saver device on the West Coast in 1981 (at the Red Cabbage, a small restaurant with a large wine list).

One of the most exciting developments over the last 30 years, especially over the last ten years, is that regardless of the region or city, having wine with a meal, especially at restaurants, has become more important to a broad range of people from various professional and cultural backgrounds. The enjoyment of wine is no longer restricted to an elite, ageing, and wealthy upper class. Although at the beginning of the 1990s it seemed that youth, the Gen-Xer's, had rejected wine as a beverage in favor of micro-brews, by the mid-1990s, hop growers and brewpubs were foundering due to the changes in favor of wine-drinking.

Wine and food matching has also had to become contemporary, with experimentation made necessary by having to match wine to cuisines that historically were not consumed with wine, such as South American, Mexican, and southwest US cuisine, or such as the various regional Chinese, East Indian, and Southeast Asian cuisines. It is nearly impossible today to recommend a particular wine or even a class of wines to have with a single dish without first tasting the dish, since such a wide range of seasoning and ingredients is regularly used by the most prominent chefs such as Norman van Aken, Gray Kunz, Charlie Trotter, Jean-Georges Vongerichten, Jean-Louis Palladin, Emerile Lagasse, Susan Feniger and Mary Sue Milliken, Raji Jallepalli, or Elka Gilmore. There are many less well-known chefs who are blending Japanese, Indian, or Vietnamese elements with French or Italian cooking.

It is this newly invigorated era of experimentation, curiosity, and excitement about both food and wine, and how they go together, that will ensure that the next 30 years will be just as vibrant as the last. In Napa, the opening of the American Center for Wine, Food, and the Arts in 2001 will help to facilitate the dialog between wine and food for the next century. So will the fact one of America's top cooking schools, the Culinary Institute of America from Hyde Park in NY's HUDSON VALLEY, has come to compete directly with San Francisco's own CA Culinary Academy by opening a branch in Napa Valley at the former Christian Brothers' landmark Greystone winery building north of ST HELENA. Nor does the US have any sort of monopoly on investigations into local foodstuffs matched to local wines: three residency cooking school programs opened at wineries in Canada's NIAGARA PENINSULA during the late 1990s; and La Embotella-dora Vieja, the superb restaurant run by SANTO TOMÁS winery in Ensenada, Mexico, provides an un-paralleled opportunity to try all the best wines of Baja, even older vintages, with some of the most innovatively prepared, freshest seafood on earth.

See DINING HABITS, UMAMI, NEW ORLEANS.

8

American Wine Auctions

Fritz Hatton

In light of the long history of commercial wine auctions in Europe, auctions of wine in North America are a surprisingly recent phenomenon. Puritans and Prohibitionists can take a certain amount of credit for this, although the American consumer's traditional preference for the grain over the grape played a major role in limiting demand for wine. It was not until the 1960s that fine wine appreciation and collecting by Americans began to spread beyond a tiny European-oriented elite. The primary causes were the promotional efforts of a small band of American wine writers and importers including Alexis *Lichine and Frank *Schoonmaker, the renaissance of American wine production after decades of neglect, and the introduction of public commercial wine auctions in London in 1966.

The most important figure in the development of modern wine auctions, both in Europe and in America, is J. Michael *Broadbent, a member of the British wine trade who established a wine department for the London-based auctioneers Christie's. Although Christie's had sold wines and spirits since they were founded in 1766, the auctions organized by Broadbent from the fall of 1966 constituted the first international public specialty wine auction program. Pioneer American wine collectors such as Drs Bernard Rhodes, Marvin Overton, and Benjamin Ichinose competed with European collectors for the rarest wines, but the wine trade (primarily British) dominated the bidding.

In the late 1960s the American wine and spirits importer Heublein decided to stage promotional wine auctions in the US, thereby introducing the American public to this method of buying fine wine. They invited Broadbent to advise and to conduct its annual auctions from 1969 until 1981. These sales introduced the American public to wine auctions. Heublein's size and extensive national distribution network allowed it to permeate the tangled web of state licensing regulations which otherwise presented an insurmountable barrier to the conduct of public wine auctions in the US. Inasmuch as the primary purpose of these sales was to promote wines owned or represented by Heublein, particularly BEAULIEU VYDS and INGLENOOK, American wines figured prominently in the auctions.

The Heublein auctions received extensive publicity by featuring pre-sale tastings in several cities prior to each sale, and by generating record prices for the rarest wines from European and American collections. The first sale in 1969 comprised 335 lots and achieved a total of a mere (by modern standards) $48,800, with Ch Mouton-Rothschild 1945 selling for $520 per case, one-hundredth of its value in 1999. The auction in 1971 saw a record price of $5,000 for a bottle of Ch Lafite 1846, and included 19th-century bottles of Inglenook Cabernet from the collection of John Daniel, descendant of Inglenook's founder. By

1980 the total sold at the Heublein approached the half-million dollar mark and the record price per bottle had risen to $31,000 for Ch Lafite 1822.

In the late 1970s bidding by American collectors in London auctions and the growth of American wine collections led Christie's to seek to expand its wine department to New York. Negotiations with the NY State Liquor Authority over the course of a year led to an agreement in 1980 to issue a license permitting an auction, but several local retailers and wholesalers (led ironically by Sherry-Lehmann and Peter Morrell, who later began holding their own auctions in New York) obtained a court injunction blocking the sale. Rather than engage in a lengthy legal battle, Christie's elected to move its wine operations to Chicago, where it held wine auctions from 1981 until 1993. Chicago Wine Company began holding wine auctions in Chicago shortly thereafter, and Butterfield & Butterfield obtained a license to hold wine auctions in California in 1985.

In 1993 NY retailers convinced the state legislature to grant wine auction licenses on a limited basis to existing retail wine and liquor licensees, several of whom created joint ventures with the auction houses. The commencement of wine auctions in NY in 1994 was a major contributor to the fine wine boom of the mid-1990s, and the amount typically sold in a day-long wine auction increased from $500,000 to $1–2 million. (American auctions tend to have more lots than their British counterparts.) In 1999 there were five wine auction firms operating in NY (Zachys/Christie's, Sherry Lehmann with Sotheby's, Peter Morrell, Acker Merrill Condit, and Phillips with Park Avenue Liquors); three in Chicago (Chicago Wine Company, Sotheby's, and the internet auctioneer WineBid.com); and three in CA (Zachys/Christie's, Sotheby's, and Butterfield & Butterfield). Zachys/Christie's was the market leader, accounting for just over a third of the US market, which was estimated at $55 million in 1997.

The Napa Valley Vintners' Association, guided by Robert Mondavi and inspired by the Hospices de Beaune auction in Burgundy, decided in 1979 to launch annual auctions to promote Napa Valley wines, with proceeds donated to local hospitals. Michael Broadbent served once again as adviser and auctioneer, and conducted the sales from the beginning in 1981 until 1986. The Napa auction grew from $325,000 in 1981 to $5.5 million in 1999, and is both the model for and largest of all American charity wine auctions. In the 1980s and 1990s charity wine auctions became much more numerous and widespread than commercial auctions. This was a result of their enormous popularity as a fund-raising mechanism as well as their relative freedom from state regulatory restrictions which effectively limit commercial auctions to NY, IL, and CA.

Commercial auctions provide an orderly secondary market for wine and make investing in wine more convenient to collectors outside the trade. Investment in wine is traditionally limited to the finest bordeaux (grands crus and wines of similar quality) which are the only wines to combine the properties of long aging potential, substantial quantities, and a long track record of excellence. Some American collectors follow the British practice of purchasing excess stocks of new vintages from retailers either as futures or upon release, and later reselling a portion of the wine at auction to finance purchases of subsequent vintages. Traditional wisdom held that the price of grand cru bordeaux from the best ('investment grade') vintages would double within five years of release, which was believed to be the optimum time to sell a portion of stock for reinvestment. In the strong wine market of 1999, top bordeaux from the 1995 vintage were selling at auction for approximately double the original US futures price; the price of the same wines from the 1990 vintage had tripled; and the 1982 vintage was thirteen times as expensive. Such returns were obtained only by investors who were careful or fortunate enough to have selected the best wines and the right vintages for *investment.

Prices for the finest and rarest wines of Burgundy, the Rhône, Italy, and CA have also soared in the 1990s. The greatest increases have come from a handful of *CA cult wines. The term CULT WINE has been applied to wines of the highest quality (determined in large measure by the influential wine critic Robert Parker—see Commentators and Wine Media essay, p 14), produced in tiny quantities (200 to 2,000 cases annually), and usually sold directly to consumers via mailing list. Most cult wines are Cabernet Sauvignon based. Because there are long waiting lists for all cult wines they are usually available to new collectors only upon resale. Release prices for these wines average well over $100 per bottle, and auction prices for the same wines range from $200 to as much as $1,000 per bottle, making them more expensive than first growth bordeaux, which are produced in much bigger quantities. As in Bordeaux some wineries have commenced offering these wines to customers as futures well before release, but the tiny quantities involved and restricted allocations limit possible returns to investors.

The most significant factor affecting the auction scene over the next few years is the prospect of an Internet interface with live auctions, as well as the growth of non-time-dependent Internet auctions (see Cybersales essay, p 24).

9

Recent Advances in North American Winemaking

MERRY EDWARDS

AFTER 24 years as a winemaker, I find the challenge renews itself each year: how to make ever better wine. Just as in the fashion world, we are constantly experiencing reruns: winemakers have the opportunity to learn from, and improve on, previous experiences. I am usually startled when asked to name the best wine I have ever made, for it almost certainly has not been made yet.

The most exciting recent advances in winemaking start where every great wine is born: in the vineyard. It is important to understand how vital these improvements have been and will be, to the future of American winemaking. (See North American Viticulture essay, p 44.) Closer *vine spacing has resulted in fewer and smaller grape bunches per vine, along with smaller berries, which in turn has dramatically improved flavor and texture in the resulting wines. Intervine competition also causes reduction of vegetative character in wine that comes from uncontrolled vigor. One key to improving quality is leaf removal in the fruit zone to expose grape clusters to more sunlight and air. This technique improves flavor and aromatics in general, as well as color and tannin content which are so important to red wine quality. That the technique also reduces potential for mildew or rot infestations is a bonus. Once we realize the foundation of wine quality lies in the vineyard, then we recognize a new relationship developing more frequently between grower and winemaker: partnership. Today we see many long-term grape contracts, even in the range of ten years. More and more of them are based on total acreage, with grapes sold by the acre, rather than by the ton. This type of contract can be structured so as to reward low yields, helpful for varieties such as Pinot Noir which tend to be quickly diluted by high tonnage. We see bonuses paid for especially high quality grapes, or a price per ton related to eventual bottle price.

In the arena of active winemaking, the first area of steady improvement has been in equipment versatility and gentleness in fruit handling. Crushers are available which allow the winemaker to choose to crush only a percentage of grape berries, leaving all or a portion to pass through whole and unscathed. This technique is especially beneficial to Pinot Noir, Merlot, Zinfandel, at times Syrah and even softer styles of Cabernet, bringing out full fruit flavors without excessive tannins. Plastic, rubber, and even vibrating belt designs allow whole clusters of Chardonnay to be conveyed directly to a press, without breakage. In general, this type of system is beginning to replace older screw type conveyors, feeding both crusher and press. This innovation prevents maceration of the grape berry or stems with the result that the juices before fermentation are lower in solids and the finished wines contain lower proportions of bitter compounds. High solids can be reduced in whites by juice settling, but with red *must the same opportunity does not exist. Hence the importance of gentle handling.

A major emphasis in equipment design and winemaking technique has been to target maximum extraction of aroma and flavor of red grapes while moderating any potentially rough tannins. A special type of fermenting tank called a Rototank has been adopted from Australia and is being built and installed more frequently in America. This tank is unique in that it looks like a cylinder laid on its side. Inside a very large screw runs parallel to this horizontal axis with a large exit door at one end. After the tank is loaded, it is rotated under the direction of a computer-generated program, turning and mixing the red grape must without any involvement of human labor. The tank may be cooled and heated as it rotates throughout the day and night, in order to speed or slow the fermentation as desired. The frequent mixing obviates the usual need for *pumping over. The Rototank's function is to maximize extraction and efficiency; four to five days in this tank can achieve similar results to standard ten- to fourteen-day fermentations or even extended macerations of up to a month or more. At the end of the desired extraction time, the tank is drained and the screw conveys the spent pomace to a waiting tank, without anyone's having to physically clean out the tank. Wines made in this manner show high color, high fruit intensity, and full texture with generally smooth tannins.

A less sophisticated, but effective mechanism for handling the necessary task of maintaining contact between red juice and skins, where all the important extractives lie, is the pneumatic, semi-automated punch-down system. This is man's attempt to mechanize the ancient, though still practiced, technique of punching down by bare foot. In this case, an air-activated ram forces a perforated disc down through the cap, positioned by manual operation. In order for this system to work well, special tanks with open or removable tops must be used to allow full access to the entire cap being submerged.

Another method for maximizing extraction of red must is a further Australian innovation. The Rack & Return technique is, in a sense, a massive pump over. Almost all the juice is run out from a tank of red grapes. The cap is held at the bottom of the original tank exuding, thanks to the pressure of its own weight, a concentrated liquor. Sometimes this juice is even drained off as a special reserve wine. After a period of time, the juice that was run off is forcefully pumped in on top of the cap, thoroughly saturating it by submersion. This procedure may occur many times during the fermentation. The resulting wines show better color, fuller texture, and smoother tannins. Rack & Return also allows for the removal of some portion of seeds from the fermenter. Seeds contain bitter tannins which can be released during the fermentation. The current focus on seeds and their impact on wine flavor and texture has been extended to using seed maturity as a factor to be considered in harvest timing, along with the usual parameters of Brix, pH, and total acidity. Brown seeds indicate a grape berry that has completed full maturity, while a green seed is a sign that more ripening time is required. Rack & Return is also an opportunity for maximum aeration of the fermenting juice. More phenolic polymerization occurs, stabilizing color, while enhancing tannin development and integration. Aeration is frequently practiced during a standard pump over, where wine splashes through a screen into a sump before being returned on top of the cap. Aeration in many cases is practiced through the first *racking to continue this process.

The use of air has also made the rounds in white winemaking. Forced oxygenation of white juices was practiced in the late 1980s and early 1990s as a backlash against the deeply *reductive winemaking practices that were followed during the previous 15–20 years. Now things seem to have come more into balance with controlled micro-oxygenation as a wider trend. Batonnage or *lees stirring of Chardonnay is commonly practiced. Degrees, length, and frequency of stirring, along with the specific tool, all affect the wine's final flavor, aroma, and texture.

The use of *enzymes is not new to winemaking but the proliferation and specialized nature of available enzymes is. These formulations have come into popular use, especially to increase color and mouthfeel in red wines. Enzymes can also correct problems, by making juices easier to settle, wines easier to filter, and by removing excessive molds and rot from difficult harvests.

In parts of Europe such as Burgundy, where harvests are cool by California standards, winemakers historically allowed their fermentations to begin without cultured yeasts. Under these conditions, the fermentation would not start for many days. At 50–55°F, the red grapes would soak in their own juices, with no alcohol involved. A natural type of extraction occurred which increased the color and textural qualities of the resulting wine over that of a standard fermentation. This same procedure has been adopted by many winemakers in North America, with a slight twist. In CA, WA, TX, Mexico, and the DESERT SOUTHWEST cellars are comparatively warm during harvest, so the tanks must be refrigerated. Perhaps the grapes are crushed and then pumped through a must chiller on their way to the tank. Often dry ice is used to create an inert headspace in the tank to help prevent the fermentation from starting until the desired amount of time has passed. After three to ten days, the tank may be heated using a heat exchanger or by simply running hot water over the tank. Then the tank may be inoculated with yeast or may be allowed to start yeast proliferation on its own.

If this essay seems overly concerned with improvements in red winemaking technology it is because most of the refinements in techniques for cold fermentation of white juices occurred in the 1950s to 1960s, with a concentration on barrel fermentation beginning in the late 1960s. *Sur lie aging of Chardonnay became a widespread fashion starting sometime in the 1970s. The most important advance related to barrel fermented Chardonnay production was probably dependable *malolactic fermentations which began in the mid-1980s with the development of strong, reliable malolactic cultures. More recently, freeze dried cultures have been cultivated which directly inoculate the juice, bypassing the elaborate preparation and yeast multiplication period previously required.

The explosion of barrel fermented Chardonnay has ricocheted around the world, with many markets demanding barrel fermentation of not only this variety but even of more delicate whites such as Sauvignon Blanc, Viognier, and Pinot Gris. As we move into the next century a type of international style seems to be developing, which to some degree is obscuring regional diversity. For example, the winemakers of the delicate Chardonnays of Friuli, Italy, are feeling the pressure to join the world market and so are beginning to use barrels rather than tanks for fermentation. The upshot of the substantial increase in demand for barrels for both reds and whites is that France can no longer supply the majority of North America's, nor the world's, wine barrel needs. This has opened the door for major improvements in the quality of oak barrels coming not only from eastern Europe but also America's heartland, MO, VA, MN, PA, and from OR. Producers in these areas are achieving better wood selection and drying, crafting barrels using more classic European methods and toasting the finished barrel longer and slower. As little as ten years ago the barrels from these areas were non-competitive. Now the gap is narrowing, with these newer coopers providing not only a lower cost alternative to French oak, but different flavor elements to increase wine complexity.

Another area of progress has been in the isolation of more diverse and more reliable yeast strains (see Microbiology essay, p 39). The diversity has been a boon to winemakers, providing yeasts which can create subtle yet important enhancements in wine aroma, flavor, and texture. For example, Chardonnay fermented using Prise de Mousse results in a wine with forward, estery fruit and firm acidity, while Montrachet rounds up the body, and adds both richness and complexity to the aroma. Stylistic opportunities can be found employing Assmanhausen in Pinot Noir versus D254; the former emphasizes berry and spice aromas while the latter increases mouthfeel by promoting the formation of polysaccharide-tannin complexes. Winemakers can choose yeasts to complement a variety or specific terroir.

One mysterious trend has been the production of wines with higher and higher alcohols. Has this been due to the creation of more efficient yeasts? No one really knows. Some 20 years ago, every weight per cent of sugar fermented in a white wine produced about 0.58% alcohol; now that conversion rate has been increased to about 0.62%. This means that harvesting grapes at 23°B used to produce 13.3% alcohol in the finished wine; the same sugar level today results in a wine at 14.3% alcohol. Looking at this another way, harvesting at 24.1°B in 1979 has the same result as harvesting at 22.8°B in 1999. It is a given that in many grape varieties, higher Brix levels generally give more intense, rich wines. How can we now achieve this without producing a wine with too much alcohol?

The answer can be to use reverse osmosis or a spinning cone to remove alcohol from the finished wine. Equipment is available to separate out the alcohol fraction of the wine from a captured aromatic portion. The wine can then be rebuilt using the desired alcohol, adding back the aromatics, and in essence concentrating the remaining components. Aside from simply reducing alcohol, this technique can actually improve the wine's textural feel. Some wineries using this technique intentionally harvest late at high sugars to achieve this effect. In the case of underripe grapes, water can be removed in order to condense flavors. The reverse osmosis procedure can also be used to remove undesirable levels of volatile acidity and in essence rescue a wine which might be unmarketable due to spoilage. The term Miracle Cure is totally appropriate here!

Increasingly sophisticated methods of *analysis in no way substitute for the craft of winemaking, but can give real support in making good decisions. We can look at the initial nutrient status of grape juices and feed them to support a healthy fermentation. In the presence of high levels of spoilage organisms, it can be risky not to filter. In making that judgement we can now monitor growth of the spoilage organism *Brettanomyces, using analysis of the end metabolic product, 4-ethylphenol. We can create an HPLC phenolic profile of a beloved red wine and attempt to duplicate it. Or look at new enological techniques, analyzing each for its effect on color and spectrum of tannins. Our increased understanding of traditional fining agents and the availability of some new ones allows us to treat wines more appropriately and at lower, less invasive levels. At bottling, the pick-up of oxygen can be determined to prevent spoilage. In addition, the level of carbon dioxide can be targeted, along with pH and acid, to create a harmonious mouthfeel.

With all of these improvements on hand, and the future full of exciting, as yet undiscovered improvements, we as winemakers will continue to shoot for the stars. The biggest challenge ahead may be to maintain regional diversity in a time when worldwide forces move us toward an international homogeneity and a rapidly shrinking planet.

10

Microbiology in North American Wine

RON SUBDEN, PhD

s rapidly as research on clones, rootstocks, and trellis systems is progressing in the vineyards of North America, so too is research on the smallest organisms which operate to convert grapes into wine. Micro-organisms and our understanding of them has greatly improved overall wine quality in the last quarter-century.

Pure strain cultures of yeast and lactic bacteria

A particularly important technological advancement beginning in the 1960s that contributed greatly to the proliferation of new wine styles and to consistent quality in wines was development of ACTIVE DRY YEAST (ADY), the preparation of dried selected strains of wine yeast used to start fermentations. The advantage of ADY for winemakers is that they can initiate a fermentation that is more predictable and reliable than fermentations by WILD YEASTS. For the winemaker, the most important quality in a yeast is that it should ferment to dryness. Fermentations that stop before dryness ('stuck' fermentations) are difficult to get started again and often there is a concomitant drop in wine quality. Often fermentations will get stuck because the yeasts become ethanol sensitive due to a depletion of certain sterols in their membranes. The yeast can only synthesize these critical sterols in the presence of oxygen, and oxygen is depleted within the first few hours of any wine fermentation. Using a culture system known as a 'fed batch' process, the ADY producers can ensure a completely respiring culture and make sure that each yeast cell has a sufficient supply of the critical sterol to pass on to its progeny throughout every generation of the fermentation.

It was the choice of wine yeast strain offered by the different ADY manufacturers that prompted the search for specialty wine yeast strains. Each time a new character was identified in wine yeast it added another control for winemakers. The first generation of ADY strains were simply reliable fermenters. They would start the fermentation with a minimum delay after being added to *must, ferment all the fermentable sugars in the must, and be tolerant to all the ethanol they produced. The early start was necessary if the selected yeast were to dominate the wild yeasts during the fermentation.

The second generation of ADY strains which were selected not only extended fermentation efficacy, they also helped winemakers produce different styles of wines. Strains were selected to have good flocculation activity. When the yeast has finished fermenting, winemakers want yeast cells to flocculate, or clump together, and precipitate to the bottom of the tank. Flocculation reduces the need for clarifying additives and greatly facilitates filtration, allowing winemakers to leave the wine alone to mature naturally without manipulation. As cold fermentations retaining the fruity or floral bouquet of some white wines became popular, so many of the yeast strains were also selected to be tolerant of cold fermentation conditions. Most ADY strains are selected for low foaming characteristics because foam forms a ring around the tank at the end of the fermentation which dries out, putrefies, and falls back into the wine causing taints and off-flavors.

To prevent some forms of stuck fermentation, most wine yeast strains were selected or genetically manipulated to be immune to common KILLER YEAST activity. Some winemakers use *sulfur dioxide to incapacitate wild yeasts that are present on grape skins, so selected yeast strains must be resistant to sulfur dioxide. The quest for the perfect yeast strain also includes a search for a wine yeast that does not produce undesirable metabolites such as *hydrogen sulfide, *acetic acid, *acetaldehyde, or ethyl carbamate (a suspected carcinogen), but which will produce metabolites that are organoleptically pleasing.

In addition to the foregoing list of demands for wine yeast fermentation performance, winemakers may have demands that are specific to a particular grape variety, region, or wine style. For instance, in the cool climate grape growing regions of the world one wants a selected wine yeast that will degrade some or all of the malic acid present. But in the hot regions one wants to preserve or even produce the organic acids found in grape musts. Many Gamay wines are constructed to be consumed young. In order to enhance the *aroma of young wines, yeast strains have been selected that produce an estery fruity nose in Gamay and other early maturing wines which would be detrimental to the aroma of a fine Gewürztraminer or a delicate Pinot Blanc. Efforts are made to select wine yeast strains that enhance the varietal character of wines such as Muscat and Sauvignon Blanc. These yeasts produce a special enzyme that can release bound *terpenes. Terpenes are volatile compounds that play a major role in the aromas of fruity or floral wines such as Riesling and Muscat.

Early in the 1980s genetic engineers, encouraged by the search for special wine yeast strains, set out to use the burgeoning recombinant DNA technology to construct strains with properties not found in naturally occurring wine yeasts. This third generation of ADY strains is discussed below.

In addition to ADY there are commercially available preparations of freeze dried bacteria for starting *MLF in wines. The producers are often firms producing lactic acid bacteria for cheese fermentations. The bacteria are more fastidious than the yeast, and often the culture medium is quite complicated. Apple juice is quite often one of the basic ingredients of the lactic acid culture medium. The criteria for selecting lactic acid bacteria for wine production is based on the conditions in which various strains work most efficiently and on their resistance to BACTERIOPHAGE. Manufacturers of active dry lactic acid bacteria select bacteriophage resistant strains and often will use a mixture of up to four different strains gambling that at least one will be resistant to any bacteriophage that may be present in the juice.

Brettanomyces (Dekkera)

One of the microbiological debates which most effectively separates wine judges into Old World and *New World camps is the degree to which some level of infection by the surface yeast BRETTANOMYCES in a wine may be acceptable, or even a desirable contributor to bouquet.

'Brett''s characteristic barnyard odor is a result of a 1 : 10 blend of two compounds formed by the yeast (4-ethyl guaiacol and 4-ethylphenol) formed from compounds present in the wine (trans p-coumaric acid). The average person can detect the blend at a concentration of 435 parts per billion so it does not take much to affect the sensory properties of the wine. The Brettanomyces pathway for the production of the barnyard odor involves two enzymes (cinnamate decarboxylase and vinylphenol reductase) which must be pretty rugged because other wine micro-organisms living in wine (*L. plantarum*) can perform the same reactions but their enzymes are inhibited by the catecheic tannins found in grape musts. There is a consensus among winemakers deliberately using Brettanomyces (see below) that the barnyard character develops in the very late phase of the Brettanomyces growth curve suggesting that 4-ethylphenol may in fact be released from dying yeast cells. When purchasing wines in bulk many buyers will test for Brettanomyces activity by using a gas liquid chromatograph to detect the presence of 4-ethylphenol.

Brettanomyces and the lactic acid bacterium *Lactobacillus hilgardii* are both capable of producing the mousy taint found in some spoiled wines. Mousiness is detected neither in the bouquet nor in the first taste of the wine. It usually presents itself in the aftertaste and its objectionable taste may linger for some time. The taste is due to the closely related compounds (2-acetyl-1,1,4,5,6-tetrahydropyridine and 2-acetyl-1,3,4,5,6-tetrahydropyridine) which are thought to be produced from the amino acid lysine and ethanol. Brettanomyces strains nearly always produce the 4-ethylphenol barnyard character but produce the mousy taint only if there is adequate lysine present in the wine.

It is rather curious that in the last few years there has been renewed interest in Brettanomyces by some North American winemakers interested in adding complexity to their wines. These individuals feel Brettanomyces is part of the natural microflora of any winery using long-term barrel aging, and that some very fine wines throughout history have had a complexity derived from Brettanomyces. Several winemakers have tried to recreate these conditions, but there are a number of problems besetting its use. Brettanomyces is a highly variable species and is not available commercially so winemakers often rely on natural inoculations from barrels that have previously given rise to Brettanomyces cultures. If the winemaker is lucky enough to have the right strain and the wine has the right composition, the faint barnyard character is organoleptically pleasing, the aging process is accelerated, vinegar odor is minimal, and the wine becomes more complex. If the wrong strain is present, the wine has the mousy taint and the wine has a bouquet reminiscent of manure and vinegar.

Historically Brettanomyces has played many roles in winemaking. The first was as a natural resident of beer and wine containers, then a dreaded scourge which was demoted to a minor pest (when it was discovered that it was very sensitive to sulfur dioxide), and currently a biological challenge to harness the metabolic potential of a wild yeast.

Genetically engineered yeasts

Deoxyribonucleic acid (DNA) is the genetic material in the cells of most living creatures including microbes like yeasts, molds, bacteria, and viruses found in must and wine. It is constructed as a chain of four different molecules called nucleotides. The genetic information to produce an enzyme, cell wall, or any other protein in the cell is contained in the nucleotide sequence. Wine yeasts are what they are because they contain a specific sequence of about 12 million nucleotides arranged into 6,000 genes that dictate their structure and metabolism. By contrast, the lactic acid bacteria that perform MLF in wine have less than half the number of genes yeast does. It is the sequence of nucleotides that is the fundamental difference between yeasts, bacteria, and for that matter humans. Changes in the nucleotide sequence or 'mutations' cause changes in metabolism or cell structure. Most mutations to wine yeast strains result in inferior weak strains, but a few may give the yeast desirable attributes such as flocculation, or low foaming. If a researcher wanted to find a special strain for flocculation or other desirable yeast attribute, the process would involve having to monitor hundreds of thousands of fermentations to find a spontaneous mutant with superior flocculation ability. The number of mutations could be increased if the yeasts were mutated (usually by irradiation), but regardless of the process one could only select mutations to the existing yeast functions. This process is also limited by an inability to recombine desirable attributes. If one strain is a good flocculating strain and another strain is non-foaming, it was difficult to make a sexual crossing to combine the two attributes as one would do in corn or cattle breeding. Alternative methods such as cell fusion have experienced only limited success.

Recombinant DNA technology, or genetic engineering, changed all this. Recombinant DNA technology is based on the discovery of enzymes that would recognize and cut DNA at specific nucleotide sequences, other enzymes that could reconnect DNA fragments, and small pieces of circular DNA called plasmids that can replicate themselves in bacterial or yeast strains. Recombinant DNA technology made it possible to cut a gene out of one organism and place it in another totally unrelated species. Recombinant DNA technology made it possible to introduce entirely new genes from bacteria, mammals, molds, or other yeasts into existing selected wine yeast strains. The introduction of new genes was usually an attempt to reduce the need for chemical additives in a wine or to increase the winemakers' control over the fermentation.

A number of examples of genetically engineered wine yeast strains have been constructed, and could possibly come onto the market in the next five to ten years. Researchers working for a large ADY producer have constructed a recombinant strain that has two different types of activity to ensure its dominance in the fermentation population. After water and alcohol, acids are the most prevalent molecules found in wine. In the hot grape growing regions of the world, acid concentrations are often too low and in the cool climate viticultural regions the *acidity is often too high. Acid adjustment in the winery implies that optimal conditions did not exist in the vineyard. Some critics argue wine quality is thus diminished. In order to find a biological method for adjusting wine acidity, several yeast strains were genetically engineered. One strain had a gene for the enzyme (lactic acid dehydrogenase) that would produce lactic acid. Lactic acid is normally produced by MLF bacteria, and can then only be produced by destroying the malic acid present in the wine. The genetically engineered yeast strain can produce lactic acid from grape sugars that are usually abundant in any must from hot viticultural regions.

Two related yeast strains have been produced for winemakers in cool climate regions which tend to produce musts with high levels of malic acid. Traditionally, wineries from these regions have chosen to either produce sweet wines (using sugar to mask the sour acidity), or to lower the acidity by using chalk (calcium carbonate) to precipitate the acids, or to allow lactic bacteria to perform an MLF. Each of the foregoing solutions presents limitations for a winemaker. The market for sweet wines is limited, chalk precipitates more than just malic acid, and the bacteria conducting MLFs are known to degrade floral (terpene) and fruity (ester) notes in the aroma. Genetic engineers are constructing yeast strains that would metabolize the malic acid from high acid musts. Wine yeasts do not have a gene for a protein that will carry malic acid from the must to the inside of the cell where it can be metabolized. Another yeast (*Schizosaccharomyces pombe*), isolated from apple juice, not only has the gene for transporting the malic acid into the cell, it also has another gene that will channel the malic acid into ethanol performing a 'malo-ethanolic' fermentation. Both genes have been cloned and put into wine yeasts where they have fermented all the sugar and malic acid present in the must to produce a wine that was organoleptically sound. This yeast strain is of particular interest to winemakers producing wines with delicate flavors and floral aromas such as Rieslings, Gewürztraminers, and even some Sauvignon Blancs. This yeast is also of interest to brandy producers because they can increase alcohol production.

Another genetically engineered yeast strain that could be introduced in the first decade of the new millennium carries a fungal 'pectinase' gene which breaks down the cell walls of grape particles found in must. As the particles break down they release more juice, more color, and the particles precipitate more rapidly aiding clarification. There are also recombinant yeast strains that enhance glycerol production leading to increased extract and *mouthfeel, enhance flocculation activity (reducing the need for fining agents), and enhance the floral and fruity nature of wines. This latter strain operates by producing an enzyme (β-D-glucosidase) that is capable of keeping free molecules associated with floral notes (monoterpenes) from being bound to complex sugars (glycones).

The introduction of genetically engineered wine yeast is problematic. Technically, most strains simply do not work well enough at present to offer a compelling advantage over existing pure strain cultures. These obstacles, however, will likely be solved in the near future. Non-technical issues may present more obstacles, however. There is strong public reluctance to accept food products that have been processed using anything that has been genetically modified, particularly in Europe where 70% of the world's wine is produced. Some justification derives from a pride in traditional methods and apprehension about new organisms disturbing the biological balance in vineyard and winery. Ever since the introduction of the 'American scourges' in the 19th century (*phylloxera and the *mildews) European governments have been very protective about their vineyard ecology. There are fears that a pectolytic yeast strain, such as the one described above, could escape from a winery and use its pectolytic properties to evolve into a vine pathogen, or that malolactic and malo-ethanolic strains could become uncontrollable in the winery resulting in low acid, flabby wines of distressingly poor quality. Researchers and food and wine producers in the New World point out that in the entire history of genetic engineering no organisms have escaped to become a scourge. The debate continues.

Chatonnet et al. 'The influence of Brettanomyces/Dekkera sp. Yeasts and lactic acid bacteria on the ethylphenol content of red wines,' *American Journal of Enology and Viticulture*, 46 (1995), 463–8.

Degré R., and Shimizu, K., *Wine Microbiology and Biotechnology* (Chur, 1993).

11

North American Viticulture

Philip Freese

ACCORDING to at least two Norse sagas, vines were so common on the east coast of North America at the end of the first millennium that the Scandinavians who colonized the region then called it Wine Land, or *Vínland. The continent they had stumbled upon was in fact a great natural vineyard, where farther south and from coast to coast American native vines rioted in profusion and variety. Cultivation of European vinifera vines began on the East Coast in 1619 when the Virginia Company required 'every householder to yearly plant and maintain ten vines until they have attained to the art and experience of dressing a vineyard either by their own industry or by the instruction of some vigneron.' Meanwhile more successful results with vinifera were well underway at Spanish missions in the hot, dry (less than 40% relative humidity), and principally disease free *mediterranean climate of the DESERT SOUTHWEST and what is now MEXICO, although the mechanical obstacles to providing irrigation had to be overcome. The Huguenots, fleeing late 17th-century persecution in their native France, settled in NY's HUDSON VALLEY and grew native American vines, thus establishing the first successful grape growing area in the US. A vast industry producing not just wine, but jellies and juice, eventually grew up based on the native American Concord grape, still cultivated widely in the NORTHEAST and MIDWEST. And native varieties such as Norton have shown themselves well able to produce wine without off-puttingly 'foxy' flavors in places such as MO and AR. The progression thus begun, is far from finished. Canada and the east continue to increase their plantings of vinifera as well as seeking grape varieties which will combine the native American traits of cold hardiness and disease resistance with the ability to produce pleasant-tasting wine. CA and the Southwest, while combating the odd pest and disease, continue looking for the best fit between vinifera varieties and available *terroir.

Regional differentiation

The territory east of the Rocky Mtns distinguishes itself as the largest area in the world growing such a disparate population of wine grapes. There are more than 75,000 acres of grapes and nearly 600 wineries (35% of America's total), but only 7% of American wine production. Climatic problems come in three forms: severely low winter temperatures; large, rapid temperature fluctuations; and the diseases that accompany hot, humid summers.

Severe winter temperatures that lead to vine trunk freezing and physical damage are often associated with *crown gall. The bacterium causes fleshy galls to appear at the site of vine injury and portions of the vine above the galls may die. Nursery operations during vine grafting or cutting off unwanted shoots or roots can also result in crown gall. Galled vines often produce poor shoot growth. Rapid temperature swings from moderate to severely cold in the late fall and early spring are common causes of splitting in woody tissue and susceptibility to infection. Inland portions of the Pacific Northwest have experienced this problem, as well as vineyards in the East.

In the East, and occasionally in the West too, climatic factors may limit a vineyard's production in one year, which in turn may lead to high production the following year, setting up a progression of alternate bearing cycles which plays havoc with winery economics. Modern developments in agricultural chemicals permit better management of fungal diseases such as *powdery mildew, downy mildew, black rot, and *botrytis. The *phylloxera pest originated in the East on native RIPARIA vines and co-evolved with them, which is why so many phylloxera resistant rootstocks have some *riparia* parentage. VINIFERA vines have therefore to be grafted on to such *rootstocks for survival in the East and in a substantial and increasing proportion of vineyards in CA. (The sandy soils of parts of Long Island provide some protection against phylloxera but vines there are still grafted on to rootstocks for resistance to nematodes in the soil.) Those who grow vines on their OWN ROOTS are less affected by the WINTER KILL problem, however, whereby a scion variety may be killed back to the graft union. This is partially obviated by being able to retrain a surviving shoot from below ground the following year. Pacific Northwest viticulturists are also aware of this advantage and many have been prepared to take the risk of planting ungrafted vines despite the presence of phylloxera in some areas. It also costs less.

In the more mild, albeit arid climatic conditions of the West, different challenges present themselves to vineyardists. A persistent threat has been the bacterial vine disease called *Pierce's which is spread from other host plants into the grapevine by a leafhopping insect called a sharpshooter. In the Northeast the cold winters are sufficient to ward off Pierce's but it is a serious problem in Florida and east Texas, and in the Southeast, where Pierce's has prevented all but the native *Muscadine vines from growing.

Texas root rot, or more properly COTTON ROOT ROT, is a fungus that can kill vines. It is most serious in TX, NM, and AZ on lower elevation, high pH, heavy soils that do not drain well. This disease effectively limits production of grapevines in some regions, although rootstocks based on *Vitis champini, candicans,* and *berlandieri* may be more tolerant to the fungus.

The Pacific Northwest regions east of the CASCADE RANGE enjoy a blend of the climatic advantages cited above: they have winters cold enough to suppress soil-borne fungi, phylloxera, and insect vectors such as sharpshooters; they also have arid summers which eliminate the canopy fungal problems encountered in the humid East and South. West of the Cascades, however, conditions are quite different. Rain and cloud cover is frequent. At these northern latitudes, long days might compensate some for the summer cloud cover. A key factor in the success of Pinot Noir in the WILLAMETTE VALLEY may well be the moderate, but relatively humid ripening weather immediately prior to harvest. Wet, cool harvest conditions can result in failure to fully ripen the fruit, but it is often in precisely these same marginal areas that the very best wines are produced during years of warm, dry harvest conditions (just like *Burgundy).

Phylloxera drives new technology into CA vineyards

Grapevines are a perennial crop with a commercial life expectancy upwards of 30 years. One expects changes in a vine growing region to proceed slowly. No greater exception to this observation exists than phylloxera's second wave of vine devastation on the North Coast regions of CA beginning in 1982. Otherwise unexplained vine decline in Napa Valley vineyards planted on AXRI rootstock led to the discovery of what seemed to be a new biotype of phylloxera. All the intrigue, denial, and finger-pointing one might expect to accompany a financial disaster approximating to one billion dollars in Napa and Sonoma counties alone, did in fact attend the inquiry of how significant parts of the CA wine industry had come to be established on a phylloxera-sensitive rootstock. Nevertheless the industry thrives today, particularly in those same counties. The silver lining was the introduction of many new technical developments in response to the need to replant. A major change occurred in the objectives of grape growing for wine. The past objective of large vines with large crops at an acceptable sugar content is being displaced by balancing vine performance with wine performance.

In the decade from 1987, when the first of the replanting was seriously underway, until 1997, over 85% of Napa's 22,000 acres of AxRI rootstock and 55% of Sonoma's were replanted to phylloxera-resistant rootstocks that were previously virtually unknown in the region. Rootstocks such as 101–14, 140R, 3309, and Riparia Gloire led growers to rethink their methods for growing vines. Whereas AxR rootstock had been tolerant to many virus diseases such as *corky bark and *leafroll carried systemically in grafted scions, the newly adopted rootstocks often succumbed outright or declined after planting.

As replanting progressed, the issue of vine spacing was addressed. Few vineyards were replanted at the wider 8 ft in-row by 12 ft between-row spacing of the previous decade. Densities of 8 ft wide rows became common as growers adopted *vertical trellis and revised canopy orientation. In-row spacing for vines remains a question of matching the potential vegetative capacity of the new vine to the soil. Standard spacing in 8 ft wide rows became 4 to 6 ft for in-row spacing. The objective is to avoid crowding more than five shoots into each foot of space between vines down the length of the trellis system. The research work of investigators such as Smart (1991) and Shaulis (1966) was rigorously applied, albeit in occasionally creative ways.

Canopy and trellis systems

Excess vegetative growth is a common issue in the fertile, deep, clay-loam soils and warm climate of CA, and in summer rain-fed vines in parts of the East. Canopy management techniques developed in the East such as *leaf removal, HEDGING, and removing excess shoots are all aimed at attaining better light penetration into the fruiting zone. This principle also applied to new trellis installations. Attempts at using *Geneva Double Curtain (GDC) and Modified Open *Lyre trellises allowed growers to display better the large canopies of vigorous vines in sites with rich soil. Unfortunately a mistaken idea developed that just adding more crop load to the vines would serve to control vegetative growth. Many winemakers rejected the potential of new trellis types because of these overly productive vines.

Vine density

One of the most hotly debated topics in American viticulture today is the optimum *vine density for balancing wine quality with financial return. The distinct advantage of high vine density, particularly useful in North Coastal CA, is a rapid recovery of yield after replanting. The additional cost associated with higher vine density comes primarily from the added number of rows on any area; not the number of vines within a row. Added benefits to quality are still being investigated.

Clones and grape varieties

Clones of a single variety demonstrate differing growth, fruit, and wine characteristics, albeit much more for some varieties such as Pinot Noir than others. These differences may be subtle, or dramatic, and they will be expressed differently on different sites in different mesoclimates. The relatively short history of vinifera cultivation in North America means we do not have a particularly diverse population of vines from which to select clones. Less than 500 years is not long enough for vines to have naturally *drifted* in their genetic composition (see Genetics essay, p 57). Moreover UC Davis in CA long held that differences between plants were more likely due to differences in virus and viroid content than to genetic composition. CA activity therefore centered on virus elimination rather than on *clonal selection, the painstaking operations whereby specific clones are identified and selected for particular qualities.

The richest source for clonal selections remains Europe with its older vinifera vineyards. In 1988 the French government/nurseryman's association signed agreements with a small number of CA nurserymen to allow them to import their latest selections through the US quarantine system and into American nurseries.

Varieties that have had a large number of separate importations can also be valuable for examination. CA Zinfandel is an excellent example as it seems to have arrived from many different sources. An ongoing project by UC Davis in collaboration with growers and trade groups such as ZAP is an attempt to identify old clones of Zinfandel which are lower yielding, smaller berried, and more characterful than many current clones which were virus treated by Davis. Researchers visit old vineyards looking for vine differences and placing the most interesting specimens in a special heritage collection in Napa Valley's Oakville Research Station. (See Vine Family essay, p 54.)

Vine nutrition

American viticulturists look to plant tissue analysis to determine nutritional balance in their vineyards, while Europeans tend to be more interested in soil composition. Today American winegrowers strive to keep canopies smaller and limit yields as a way to optimize quality of the fruit. American growers, for example, seek sufficient, but not excessive growth, while still providing an adequate *nitrogen supply in the *must to allow the yeast to ferment efficiently. Analysis of American soils prior to vineyard planting reveals considerable regional differences in vineyard nutrition needs. Some coastal CA soils have excess magnesium, for instance, while neighboring sites show deficiencies. Soil samples are taken from pits dug on a grid pattern and the lab analyses then computer modeled on a map to show how gradients of supplements need to be applied. New (to CA) phylloxera resistant rootstocks have differing capacities to take up minerals from the soil, so new nutritional models are being developed. Unlike parts of Europe, much of the American viticultural landscape does not contain high levels of lime or calcium. Many American sites are also low in pH values, some being very acidic (even lower than 5.5 pH). Such conditions can effect the mobility of nutrients into the vines. Low pH value sites need to be prepared for planting by working large amounts of limestone into the soils to facilitate root penetration.

Irrigation

Irrigation may be banned in much of Europe, but then summer rainfall is common and (mostly) adequate there. While Burgundy receives approximately 60% of its annual rainfall during the vines' growing season,

Napa Valley receives less than 15%. In much of America therefore, particularly CA and eastern WA, irrigation is almost an essential part of vine growing, and irrigation management is a key tool in optimizing wine quality. If a vine is given unlimited access to water, it produces a heavy canopy which grows to intercept more sunlight. Regulated 'deficit irrigation' provides the vine with adequate water to grow only enough leaves and shoots to ripen a crop. The idea is to allow the vine to suffer a slight amount of stress, but not enough to stop the functioning of the leaves in ripening the fruit. A grapevine experiencing mild water stress will slow down, and then stop vegetative growth before it stops *photosynthesis and the manufacture of products needed to ripen the berry and preserve the vine. Excessive water stress is negative for both fruit and wine character. Drip is the irrigation method of choice. The amount of water used is dramatically lower than with furrow flooding. Specific placement of the water directly above the root zone maximizes efficiency. When fruit is ripening and soft at the end of the season it is very sensitive to fungal diseases. Drip irrigation allows for watering the vine without wetting the fruit.

Mechanization

Only selected areas of North America have initiated mechanical replacement for activities such as picking and leaf removal, and chiefly those where labor costs are relatively high. Mechanization was pioneered at Cornell, NY, for picking Concord grapes for juice. Using mechanical harvesters on the north coast of CA is still considered by many winemakers a serious quality threat because machines pick too much MOG (matter other than grape). Widespread use of vertical shoot positioned trellis systems means, however, the vineyards are set to readily use mechanical assistance. Non-harvest-related activities such as mechanical lifting and positioning of wires to manage canopies is easily adapted to several manufacturers' machines. Growers all over the US are beginning to use mechanical pre-pruning aids. These machines cut above the fruiting zone, and canes are shredded to a fine mulch.

Baxevanis, J. J., 'The Wine Regions of America, Geographical Reflections and Appraisals,' *The Vinifera Wine Growers Journal* (Stroudburg, PA, 1992).

Gladstones, J., *Viticulture and Environment* (Adelaide, 1992).

Pearson, R. C., and Goheen, A. C., *Compendium of Grape Diseases* (St Paul, MN, 1988).

Shaulis, N., Amberg, H., and Crowe, D., 'Response of Concord grapes to light, exposure and Geneva double curtain training,' *Am. Soc. Hort. Sci* 89 (1966), 268–80.

Smart, R., and Robinson, M., *Sunlight into Wine* (Adelaide, 1991).

facing: Grapes for **Icewine** in Canada are often picked in January. Searching through the snow more than justifies the wines' high prices.
overleaf: One of CA's greatest viticultural assets is its corps of skilled, very hard working, Mexican field hands.

12

Labor in the North American Vineyard

BRUCE CASS

PICKING grapes is hard work. Conditions range from stifling heat and steep hillsides to icy rain and deep mud. Bees and yellowjacket wasps often join the proceedings in great numbers (although they are rendered entirely passive due to a form of apian intoxication caused by such a surfeit of sweet juice).

Pay in North America is not bad by worldwide income standards, but the ratio of effort to dollars is paltry compared to just about any other US job: entry level, menial, manual, whatever. On average US pickers get approximately $100 per ton. The range can go as high as $175 per ton for very selective picking. An extremely fit, experienced, and motivated picker can harvest as much as two tons in a very long day. Your average college kid generally brings in about a third of a ton in eight hours, which makes their take-home pay slightly below US minimum wage.

US citizens sent into the vineyards by their local Unemployment Office usually last until about noon on the first day, then fail to return from lunch. This well-recognized phenomenon, and the wide range of similar agricultural labor required throughout CA, has historically led to demand for hundreds of thousands of migrant, undocumented foreign workers each year. The majority come from rural areas of Mexico, where a four-month season of $100-income days can handsomely support a family all year long. Despite periodic spasms of anti-immigrant xenophobia, and mildly hysterical political rhetoric, the role of the US–Mexico border in this matter seems to be that of a screen to ensure only the most highly motivated workers show up in CA fields. Few reasonable observers would dispute a claim that this clandestine, 600,000-member Mexican labor force constitutes CA's greatest asset in the competitive arena of international fine wine production.

They work very hard. Even teenagers routinely pick more than a ton per day. More importantly, their expertise sets an extremely high world standard. Vine grafting is but one example. Specialized Mexican grafting crews had started to be imported all around the world by the end of the 1990s, where their work in transforming a vineyard from one grape variety to another compared quite favorably to that of local crews. Most vineyard owners report the Mexicans are generally three times faster, and able to achieve a 95% success rate on their grafts compared to a range of 60–80% for local crews. This speed and diligence more than justifies the higher pay demanded by the Mexican crews and the airfare to deliver them to the job. This expertise had been well recognized in CA as early as 1980. Several comparative vignettes exist, but a favorite is the Santa Barbara County plastic surgeon who owned a vineyard he wanted to convert from Riesling to Merlot. Success in grafting is a function of carefully lining up the cambium layers of the

previous page: **Biltmore Estate**, NC.
facing: High elevation vineyards, such as this one in CO, are typical of the dry, cold **Rocky Mtn** and **Desert Southwest** regions.

budwood and the receiving incision, then bandaging the wound until it forms a scar. Not only were all the Mexican field workers quicker than the physician/owner at performing this operation, they achieved their standard 95% take rate, while his best effort was an 85% take.

Comparison of CA's vineyard labor situation to other wine producing regions around the world is instructive. CA's migrant pickers bring in nearly four times as much tonnage per day per individual as their counterparts in South Africa, a racially subdivided population more or less resident on the wine farms of the Cape. South Africa's agricultural labor pool receives year-round housing, some attention to their health care, and patronizing forms of free transportation and education. Nevertheless the cash they receive is little more than a token salary, at least an order of magnitude less than that paid to migrant farm laborers in the US. 'Colored' South African agricultural workers have no incentive to participate more than half-heartedly in wine quality improvement techniques such as selective harvesting. Australia has a very limited labor pool. No matter how well paid (read motivated) Australian pickers may be, there simply are not enough of them. Hence a large percentage of Australian grapes are mechanically harvested, and remote areas such as Coonawarra even rely to a great extent on mechanical pruning.

Theoretically the excellent Mexican labor force at work in CA would represent the same advantage to Mexican wine production if a market could be created for expensive, artisanal Mexican wines. That outcome is speculative, however, at the end of the 1990s because heretofore the Mexican wine industry has been devoted almost exclusively to production of value-priced wines in which the labor force is merely expected to cost less than machines; not to perform tasks unavailable through mechanization.

Canada's border with the US is no less porous than the US–Mexico border, but very few Mexican workers migrate to Canadian wine regions for harvest work. One reason is lower pay. Canadian growers pay approximately C$100 per ton, but that represents one-third less value at 1999 exchange rates than $100 per ton in CA. The other reason is less work. The Canadian agricultural industry is simply much smaller than the traditional migrant labor routes through AZ, CA, OR, WA, or TX and FL. In the OKANAGAN VALLEY of British Columbia the labor pool consists of Asians who come from Vancouver, students who come with something of a holiday attitude from Quebec, and local Native American tribes who have high unemployment rates but may actually own the land on which the vineyards are planted, having leased the property to viticultural companies. Rapid expansion of the Okanagan vineyards during the 1990s has prompted many growers there to move into mechanical harvesting.

In the NIAGARA PENINSULA of Canada and in US growing regions other than the West Coast and Southwest, the harvest for fine wine involves much smaller quantites, a greater number of individual ownership entities, and areas with high population densities. Therefore a much larger percentage of the picking work can be accomplished by 'casual' workers who do it as a respite from other, full-time occupations: housewives, students, friends and supporters of the winery owner, etc. While 'casual' workers may involve a wide range of efficiency levels, pay scales, expertise, and motivation, there can be little debate over the one characteristic they all have in common: the need to schedule their time well in advance. Often they can work only on weekends. Sometimes the work schedule meshes perfectly with ripening of the grapes; sometimes it does not. This disparity between theory and actuality is the great untold story of winemaking. Ask any owner, or most winemakers, how a wine was made, and they will reply with a recitation of how they *planned* to make the wine. But the physical effort to bring tens of tons of grapes out of a vineyard and into the winery is a much less precise process. It cannot be accomplished at the drop of a hat, and getting it done within a few days (plus or minus) of the point the winemaker might consider ideal is actually a very admirable outcome.

Mechanization

One of the advantages of mechanical harvesting is the ability to pick quickly. Rates differ, depending on terrain and the size of the harvester, but in general most mechanical harvesters in use today can do up to a couple of acres an hour. Moreover, they can work at night using headlights, which brings the fruit into the winery at lower temperatures, a definite advantage in hot climates. Because they can run 24 hours a day, machines do help large vineyard owners get their crop into the winery as near to the desired date as possible.

Mechanical harvesting is not a huge financial advantage in CA (and not a financial advantage at all in South America or South Africa). Most of the machines cost something in the order of $200,000, so their use must be amortized over many years to significantly reduce the average picking costs applicable at the end of the 1990s. Machines do not work well on steeply inclined vineyards, nor at all on terraced vineyards. They do not perform much of a selection process when picking, although they will leave behind seriously unripe fruit. Machines tend to split open a proportion of berries, exposing the juice to at least some degree of initial *oxidation. For that reason, even wineries firmly committed to mechanical harvesting will make the marketing point that their most expensive, small lot wines are hand harvested.

Machines work most efficiently on long vineyard rows. However, long vine rows which run over undulating hills may experience uneven ripening from the tops of the hills to the bottoms. It is impractical to pick anything other than an entire row at a time. Similarly, row orientation for mechanical harvesting purposes may at times run counter to desirable row orientation for even ripening. The Okanagan Valley, for instance, sits between 48° and 50° north latitude. Since the angle of the autumn sun is low to the southern horizon at that latitude, a north–south row orientation would be desirable to promote even ripening on both sides of the vine. But mechanical harvesters cannot operate well, nor safely, tilting to the side on an incline. Therefore big growers tend to run their vine rows straight up the hills, even if that means an east–west orientation. Unfortunately, in that circumstance, the clusters on the north side of the row may not ripen as fast as the clusters on the south side of the row, but the machine must pick them both at the same time.

New trellising systems being adopted around the globe have an effect on both mechanization and on hand labor. These new systems differ from traditional methods such as *head trained vines, or the 'CA sprawl,' or the 18-in high South African 'bush vine,' or the French 'goblet' in the sense that the new systems create a specific fruiting zone, usually about waist high, where the clusters form. The specificity of this zone is a requirement for mechanical harvesters, and also a tremendous aid to hand pickers, who otherwise have to search through the vines, often on their knees, to locate the grapes. New trellises which position shoots vertically in a single plane accomplish the above goal for either machines or for hand pickers. New trellises which split the canopy into two parallel portions, in order to let more sunlight penetrate the middle, however, do not lend themselves to mechanical harvest and must be picked by hand.

Quality improvement

The motivation, availability, and cost of vineyard/winery labor are of paramount importance when determining which techniques may be applied in pursuit of enhanced wine quality. Herbicides, for instance, are a labor reducing technique; not any particular financial advantage. Pruning decisions based on the vigor of individual vines, shoot thinning shortly after budbreak, cluster thinning based on overall crop load, leaf pulling, and 'green harvest' to drop excess crop after *veraison are all techniques available to vineyardists with a sufficient pool of suitably experienced and motivated workers, but not available (at least not in equal measure) to vineyardists in regions lacking such a labor resource.

At harvest the most valuable manifestation of a quality labor force is *triage, the selection of top fruit. This technique is particularly important in regions or vintages with marginal weather during harvest. Many authorities comment that the difference between the best producers and the also-rans in a place such as Burgundy is the large percentage of crop top producers leave on the ground during harvest as they systematically reject less-than-perfect, fully ripe clusters or portions of clusters. Applying this concept to more benign climates such as CA means the ability to harvest a block of a grape variety such as Zinfandel, which ripens unevenly, at two or three separate times. In northerly latitudes it might mean picking the south sides of the rows two weeks before the north sides. In the winery, this approach may mean sorting tables or conveyor belts which allow trained workers to remove underripe, raisined, or rotten clusters. The difference in the eventual wine is analogous to the difference between fresh squeezed orange juice and juice reconstituted from canned concentrate.

US immigration

The advantage CA enjoys in the global fine wine economy due to its specialized Mexican labor force is a benefit unevenly recognized either by state policy or by US federal law. Ever since the *gold rush there have been waves of poor immigrants washing into CA prepared to do back breaking labor in exchange for money which would represent high income in their native lands. The fact these people have come of their own volition, even eagerly sought the opportunity, does not erase the discriminatory hardships historically visited upon them by their new neighbors given the standards of these newly adopted neighborhoods. After building the western portion of the transcontinental railroad through the Sierra Nevada, Chinese coolies were treated to a national Exclusion Act which cut off further immigration and barred the resident Chinese from voting and other benefits of citizenship. During the Depression, when Caucasian 'Okies' fled the Dust Bowl of the PLAINS region to work in the wonderland of CA's CENTRAL VALLEY as the massive irrigation projects of that era created overnight agricultural fortunes, the federal government passed the National Labor Relations Act to benefit trade unions, but specifically excluded farm workers.

From the Second World War until 1964 the US ran an official program in cooperation with the Mexican government bringing temporary workers called *braceros* from Mexico to the US for seasonal employment. Today, aged Mexican workers from that era are agitating in Mexico to find out what happened to the 10% of their paychecks that was withheld as a pension fund. Reportedly $150 million was deposited in a Mexican bank, but none of the money has yet arrived in the hands of the *braceros*, who are now in their twilight years. It took ten years of strikes and boycotts by the United Farm Workers' Union in California, and an uncommonly sympathetic Governor, before the CA Farm Labor Act was finally passed in 1975 requiring basic amenities such as toilets in the fields and outlawing brutal management techniques such as the short handled hoe.

At the end of the 1990s several immigration related political issues have once again stirred the pot in which CA's highly skilled Mexican labor force uncomfortably finds itself. CA state initiatives succeeded at the ballot box which would bar undocumented aliens from receiving benefits such as various forms of short-term health care and children's services. Bilingual education was under attack in the schools. Most directly, employers are currently under pressure from tax authorities (as opposed to just the immigration department) to report Social Security numbers for every employee. This last technique is the first time employers have really faced serious penalties for hiring undocumented workers. Under this national program, about 15,000 alien farm workers are supposed to be allowed into the US. Since 600,000 is the approximate number which have been needed to harvest CA's crops in each of the last several years, a great deal of concern is being voiced on all sides of the issue.

13

The Vine Family in North America

Lucie T. Morton

As the earliest visitors to the American continent found (see *Vínland), North America is distinguished by its rich variety of native vine species, which still grow wild in its woodlands and hedgerows. In Europe on the other hand there is just one native species, *Vitis vinifera* or 'the wine-bearing vine,' that is parent to thousands of wine and table grape varieties. The likes of Cabernet Sauvignon and Chardonnay are now known and grown around the world, often in fact on the roots of their North American cousins within the *Vitis family.

While the fruit of European vinifera is prized, its leaves and roots are highly vulnerable to the pests and diseases that afflict vineyards worldwide. Just the contrary is true of the North American vine species which have fruit of restricted commercial appeal, yet which show impressive resistance to the insects and micro-organisms that would harm them. Beyond a vinicultural role in their own backyards, these North American species have been crossed or hybridized with European varieties by breeders on both sides of the Atlantic striving for rustic and hardy vines that produce acceptable quality wine. So popular were they in early 20th-century France that there were nearly 1 million acres of French-American hybrids planted there by the mid-1940s.

The primary American vine species which play a continuing role in wine production are *Vitis labrusca*, *Vitis aestivalis*, *Vitis riparia*, and *Muscadinia rotundifolia*.

The flavor of *Vitis labrusca* is synonymous with 'grape' to Americans weaned on Concord grape juice and the jelly that is well paired with peanut butter. The early US grape industry was based largely on such labrusca dominated wine varieties as Catawba, Diamond, Delaware, Dutchess, Isabella, Ives, and Niagara. The wines produced were often sweet, including the first American kosher wines. Labrusca's marked flavor, described as wild strawberry perfume by devotees and often dismissed as unacceptably *foxy by those raised exclusively on vinifera wines (beauty is in the eye), is attenuated during the aging of fortified wines and also when the fruit is picked relatively green for sparkling wines. In any case, the strong flavors and low sugar of the fruit render it unsuitable for dry table wines.

By contrast, the high sugars, relatively high acids, and deep, if somewhat unstable, color of *Vitis aestivalis* make it the best suited of the native species to dry table wine. Had the Revolution not intervened, the Virginia home vineyard of our first president, enophile George Washington, would have consisted of 2,000 wild *aestivalis* vines. He had assembled the cuttings, but his eight-year absence led to their demise. Cynthiana and Norton are *aestivalis*-type varieties that produced some of the best pre-Prohibition American reds and today are profiting from barrel ageing and modern winemaking in several states east of the Rockies where the summers are long enough to ripen the fruit, notably Missouri and Virginia.

Had George Washington or his fellow enophile Thomas Jefferson lived in Minnesota, he would have vinified *Vitis riparia*, the undisputed champion *Vitis* species for very cold climates. The fruit has a dark color, high acid, good sugars, and a herbaceous flavor that diminishes with ageing. Baco Noir, (Marechal) Foch, and (Leon) Millot are classic riparia-type varieties.

Due to the endemic and deadly *Pierce's disease, Scarlett O'Hara and other denizens of southeastern US would have no grapes at all were it not for the highly distinctive American grape genus Muscadinia (see *botanical classification). The vines have small, round leaves, single or unforked tendrils, and have a more tree-like bark among other characteristics that set them apart from other *Vitis* species. The fruit consists of small clusters of unevenly ripening, marble-sized berries with tough skins and a powerful musky aroma reminiscent of overripe melon. Scuppernong, Magnolia, and Noble are some of the standard Muscadine varieties which produce wines as foreign to Chardonnay as root beer is to lager. Modern breeding programs are producing new Muscadine varieties that have more neutral flavors yet retain their bullet-proof armor against nematodes, fungal diseases, and Pierce's, which one day may be of great use to farm wineries in the South Atlantic and Gulf states.

Their bountiful history notwithstanding, the fruits of and wines made from North American species pale in significance to their roots. In the early 19th century, when the vine destroying phylloxera louse was accidentally transported from eastern North America to the rest of the world on botanical specimens, native American grapevines became the lifeline without which the international vinifera based wine industry faced certain annihilation. The very existence of great wines today is made possible by rootstocks based on the American vine species *Vitis riparia*, *Vitis rupestris*, and *Vitis berlandieri* such as Riparia Gloire, Rupestris du Lot/St George, 3309 C, 101–14 Mgt, 161–49 C, and many more.

Grafting noble vinifera varieties to phylloxera resistant American rootstocks has become accepted practice and is not considered detrimental to wine quality. Growing Euro-American hybrid varieties, however, has caused much angst and controversy both in the New World, where they are legal, and the Old World where they are banned.

But in North America, the use of native American varieties and such vinifera-American crosses as Seyval Blanc, Vidal Blanc, Cayuga Blanc, Chardonel, Chambourcin, Foch, St Croix, Blanc du Bois, et al. is simply a matter of market forces. Here the use of French hybrids, American hybrids, and traditional American grapes is essential to maintaining the locally grown integrity of farm wineries. Most winegrowers today plant vinifera varieties such as Chardonnay and Cabernet Sauvignon provided they will produce reliable crops, without being killed by low winter temperatures or Pierce's, for example. However, on those sites where greater hardiness is required, hybrids may well be used and are vinified in ways designed to bring out their best qualities such as Seyval *sur lie or Vidal ICEWINE. When well made, these wines are often bargains compared to wines made from the more universally famous vinifera varieties.

One need not go beyond the bounds of the classic European winegrape varieties to get caught up in a genetically based trend now occurring throughout North America. Currently, to say one is growing Pinot Noir is not enough. It begs the question of which clone? Pommard, Wadenswil, #115, #777, #927? In addition, where once a handful of Bordeaux varieties were standard fare, nurseries are now busy growing blocks of the latest clonal selections of such fashionable varieties as Mourvèdre, Nebbiolo, Sangiovese, Syrah, Roussanne, and Viognier.

Clonal selection is of critical importance to growers in all parts of the US. Anyone who has studied grape clones from VA to BC knows that—Gertrude Stein notwithstanding—a Cabernet Sauvignon is not a Cabernet Sauvignon is not a Cabernet Sauvignon. There is a Gewürztraminer clone rampant in New England that should be shot—eliminated from the gene pool. Why? It has relentlessly low yields and makes mediocre wine, an extermination combination in any winegrape.

In the areas producing vast quantities of affordable, everyday table wine, clonal choices should be those that are productive, eg have two or three large clusters—many berried, large berried, robust shouldered, and winged—per shoot. Fine winegrowers, whose grapes go into high-dollar bottles and who anticipate high dollars per ton, should be planting clones with fewer, smaller clusters that have fewer, smaller berries.

Chardonnay is a variety where growers have a good range of clonal choices. For example, CA FPMS Chardonnay Clones 4 and 5 have large clusters and produce large crops of very acceptable, very standard fruit. French clones such as ENTAV or Dijon #95 and #96 have relatively lower yields, but their smaller clusters and berries give more flavor at lower sugar contents, a valued trait in cooler regions. There are clones well suited to sparkling wines (INRA-CP #118) and even those (ENTAV #809) which produce Chardonnays with an atypical Muscat character that add to the blender's palette.

As if this topic were not complicated enough, some Chardonnay 'clones' should more properly be called FIELD SELECTIONS because they originated from many vines in a particular vineyard such as WENTE or Spring Mountain. Additionally, there are selections based on imperfectly formed clusters with multi-size berries with names like 'hens & chickens' or 'Mendoza' which may or not be clones in the strictest sense of the word.

Moreover, such vital inputs to wine quality as good sites and good management strongly affect the efficacy of clonal selection. For example, Clone 4 on a low-vigor site with moderate crops may well make better wine than Clone #95 or #96 on a lush site with poor *canopy management. On one thing everyone agrees: that with clones, more is more, meaning that every wine should enjoy the complexity of a multi-clonal composition.

Nurseries have been reaping the benefits of a planting boom in recent years, yet their job is becoming ever more complex as growers are concerned about planting the perfect clone on the perfect rootstock. The health of plant material is also an increasingly complicated issue and the trend is to treat even *certified* cuttings (see PRE-CERTIFICATION CLONES) and rootings to a hot water bath to reduce the chances of infection from tiny organisms from phytoplamsa and bacteria to fungi.

New methods of DNA testing are shedding much-needed light on wine varieties of uncertain origin and unravelling the confusion that comes from locally named varieties entering the international marketplace (see Genetics essay, p 57). Isozyme analysis now provides growers, untrained in ampelography, with an affordable means of verifying trueness to type, even of rootstocks with no leaves. One day these technologies might be used to better characterize the genetic heritage of some of the early American varieties long believed to be crosses that occurred in the privacy of a forest setting.

Just as the earliest visitors to the American continent were struck by the rich variety of indigenous grape flora, foreign visitors to tasting rooms of North American wineries will be struck by the rich variety of flavors provided by local vineyards.

14

North American Geneticists Untangle the Vine Variety Web

CAROLE MEREDITH

THERE are thousands of grape varieties and even more names for them, since many varieties go by different names in different places. Varieties have traditionally been identified by their appearance, a method called ampelography. Cabernet Sauvignon, for example, is quite easy to recognize by its distinctive leaves. However, some varieties look so much alike that even experts find it difficult to tell them apart. Furthermore, even the best ampelographer cannot recognize every variety—there are simply too many of them. To make matters worse, the relatively stable distinguishing characteristics upon which ampelographers rely are not invariable. The same variety grown in two different places may look quite different and important features can also come and go during the growing season.

The application of DNA profiling to grapevines has brought new clarity to issues of grapevine varietal identity. The same methods that can convincingly link a human suspect to a crime can be used to determine the identity of a grapevine by matching its DNA profile to that of a candidate variety. The DNA profile does not change during the growing season or when vines are grown in different places or when they are diseased. It is a stable and objective manifestation of the fundamental genetic identity of a variety.

DNA analysis can also shed considerable light on the origins of old winegrapes. Just as DNA profiling can prove paternity in humans, so can it establish the original parents of a grape variety. From that knowledge the place, and often the time, at which the variety arose may be inferred. Because grapevines are propagated by cuttings or buds and not by seeds, every vine of a variety, even if the variety has existed for centuries, is essentially genetically identical to every other one (with the exception of clonal variants) and all share the same DNA profile. All the individual vines within a variety are derived from a single original vine that grew from a seed. That seed was the result of a pollen grain landing on a grape flower and fertilizing an egg within. If the pollen parent and the egg parent were cultivated varieties (as opposed to wild vines) and if those varieties still exist, DNA analysis can reveal them.

DNA is found in every living cell of a grapevine. It can be isolated from the other cellular components by taking a sample of vine tissue (young leaves are best) through a series of chemical treatments. A very specific and tiny region of the long DNA molecule, called a marker, is then targeted for analysis. This single marker exists in alternative forms in different varieties and these forms can be made visible as dark bands on a clear rectangular gel, each form distinguishable from the others. As more markers are analyzed, the mathematical possibilities for combinations of forms of the different markers quickly become very large. The DNA profile is the aggregate of the results obtained with several markers. Only six to eight markers are needed to produce a unique DNA profile for every grape variety.

Among the findings that have emerged from DNA profiling are the following:

- Petite Sirah, a deeply colored grape that has long been grown in California, was clearly not Syrah, but what was it? DNA profiling has shown that almost all Petite Sirah vines in California are the French grape Durif, although a few are the almost identical Peloursin, an older French variety.
- Zinfandel has been confirmed as the same variety as Primitivo, a grape grown in southern Italy. It has furthermore been shown that Zinfandel is not the same variety as Plavac Mali, the noble Dalmatian grape that had long been a suspect.
- Many old Pinot Blanc vineyards in California are actually the very similar variety Melon de Bourgogne, the grape responsible for the French wine Muscadet.
- Mission, the grape introduced to California by the Catholic missionaries, is the same variety as Pais in Chile but is the same as only one of the several types of Criolla in Argentina.
- Reports that some Merlot in Chile was actually Carmenère have been substantiated.
- Several California synonyms for European grapes have been verified, including Mataro for Mourvèdre, Valdepeñas for Tempranillo, and Black Malvoisie for Cinsaut.

In the relatively short time that DNA profiling has been applied to grape varieties, it has produced some surprising revelations about their origins.

- Not only was Petite Sirah found to be almost entirely Durif, but the ambiguous origin of Durif was also cleared up. Although it had already been reported that Durif was somehow derived from Peloursin, it is now known that Durif originated as a seedling from a cross between Peloursin and Syrah, so the name Petite Sirah is not so far off the mark after all.
- Syrah did not come to France from across the sea as proposed by some. It appears to be French-born, the chance offspring of two grapes from southeastern France, Dureza and a form of Mondeuse.
- Cabernet Sauvignon is the offspring of Sauvignon Blanc and Cabernet Franc. It apparently arose as a seedling from a chance cross-pollination in a vineyard in western France several hundred years ago.
- Almost all the varieties associated with northeastern France, including Chardonnay, were born there and are the offspring of a single pair of parents—Pinot and Gouais Blanc. The contribution of the noble and ancient Pinot was predictable, but that of Gouais Blanc was a surprise. Once widespread in the region, this variety of eastern European origin was considered mediocre at best and was banned several times. Other progeny of Pinot and Gouais Blanc include Gamay Noir, Aligoté, Auxerrois, Melon, and at least ten others.

Further relationships are being investigated in several countries. These studies can be expected to converge eventually to produce a family tree of sorts that will include most of the major varieties. We can look forward to an increasingly clear picture of the ancient migrations and couplings that gave us the classic grapes that we so appreciate today.

15

Organic Wine in North America

JIM LAPSLEY

ALTHOUGH we all know roughly what it means, we will not see the term 'organic wine' on US labels and in advertising until BATF draws up some precise regulations. BATF does recognize that standards exist for the organic production of grapes and thus allows wineries to claim that a given wine is produced from organically grown grapes if supporting documents are submitted at the time of label approval. Similarly, a winery that chooses not to add chemicals such as *sulfites to a wine may place the phrase 'no sulfites added' on a wine label. Should the total sulfites be less than 10 ppm in the wine, the 'contains sulfites' warning may be omitted from the label, although BATF requires that a chemical analysis from a certified laboratory accompany the label approval. For the last half of the 1990s, the US Dept of Agriculture has been attempting to establish national standards for organic foods, which will include wine.

Despite the lack of legal definition, consumers, wineries, and the trade do refer to 'organic wine' and all agree it must start with organically grown grapes. Until the USDA provides a national standard, state law defines what is or is not organic production. In CA organic production generally means no synthetic chemicals have been used in the vineyard for at least three years. Most organic producers maintain vineyard fertility through use of *cover crops or the addition of composted manure. Insect pests are controlled by natural predators and the occasional use of biodegradable soaps or oils. Sulfur, a naturally occurring mineral, is applied as a dust to control *powdery mildew. Organic growers in the eastern US, where *downy mildew is a problem due to higher humidity and summer rains, employ a lime/sulfur/oil mixture. In CA, growers who sell wine grapes as organically grown must register with and be reviewed by their local County Agricultural Commissioner for compliance with the CA Organic Food Act of 1990. In addition, private third party groups such as California Certified Organic Farmers (CCOF), Demeter, and Oregon Tilth, will review and certify organic production of member growers, although such third party certification is not legally required. Although organic grape production is more management intensive than conventional viticulture, it is attracting increasing interest. Several major wineries have converted their vineyards to organic where possible simply because it is an economic way of producing high quality grapes.

The issue of which wines should be considered 'organic' raises serious questions, most revolving around whether synthetically compounded chemicals or processing additives may be used. For many consumers, the term 'organic' implies not just that the raw materials have been organically grown, but that no synthetic compounds have been added to stabilize the food. In the case of wine, since at least the time of *Pasteur, sulfur dioxide has been added as an antimicrobial agent and as an antioxidant, reducing the chance of spoilage or oxidation. Some proponents of organic wine argue that a small percentage of the population is allergic to sulfites and that synthetic materials such as sulfites should not be allowed in 'organic' wine. Other producers point out that yeast themselves generally produce small levels (5–15 ppm) of sulfites during fermentation and that the production of high quality, non-oxidized wine is enhanced by the judicious use of sulfites. The Organic Grapes into Wine Alliance (OGWA), an association of US wineries producing wine from organically grown grapes, allows the addition of sulfur dioxide, but with a free sulfur dioxide of less than 30 ppm and a total of less than 80 ppm and with the sulfur dioxide derived from bubbling gas through water to create a saturated solution, rather than from the addition of sulfite-bearing salts such as potassium metabisulfite. These sulfite levels are within the same range as European standards. USDA is currently reviewing standards for processed organic foods, which includes wine, and its National Organic Standards Board has recommended that sulfites be allowed in 'organic' wine. It thus seems likely that early in this century 'organic wine' will be defined in the US.

At present, wines made from organically grown grapes, with or without sulfite additions, represent about 0.1% of the 200 million-case US market. FETZER, a large winery with national distribution, has launched a line of organically grown wine with sulfites, probably accounting for 50,000 cases, which has been well received by the trade. The handful of wineries comprising OGWA are quite small and in aggregate produce perhaps 100,000 cases of wine from organically grown grapes. The volume of organically grown wine with no added sulfites is probably less than half that amount. US imports of European organic wine are estimated to be below 100,000 cases, so total sales are probably at most 250,000 cases. Although organically based foods are expanding in the general marketplace, it is doubtful that 'organic wine' will move beyond a niche market until the definition of 'organic wine' is resolved and the term can be used freely in marketing.

A

Active dry yeast, a preparation of dried selected strains of wine yeast used to start fermentations. Starter cultures for beer were first used in Denmark in 1886 and first used for wine in Germany in 1891. In contrast to the brewers who universally adopted and still use (except for lambic beers) starter yeast, European winemakers quickly adopted the practice but then rejected it. Winemakers felt that there was more complexity to be gained from using the natural microflora on grapes and the use of starter cultures in wine declined dramatically. The extensive use of wild or indigenous yeasts in winemaking continued on until the 1930s when liquid cultures of selected wine yeasts were commercially available. ADY was introduced in CA in the 1960s and the search for special yeasts for winemaking began in earnest. If one assumes a world production of just under 30 billion liters (8 billion gal) of wine per year, the potential market for ADY (given a dosage rate of 10–20 g/hl) is about 5,000 tons annually. At the dawn of the new millennium the world production of ADY for wine was less than 1,000 tons, so fermentations by indigenous yeasts still dominate world wine production. Most ADY producers are in the business of making bread yeast, which accounts for 95% of their business. ADY for winemaking is a sideline for these industries and wine yeasts are usually produced when equipment is not being used for bread yeast production. Sometime prior to the grape harvest, yeast producers will culture selected wine yeast strains in huge aerated tanks using molasses as a carbon source and ammonium hydroxide as a nitrogen source. Most manufacturers also use a vitamin B supplement. When the yeast population reaches maximum density, the yeasts are harvested, washed, dried, and vacuum packed in metal containers. Shelf life is important because the wine starter yeast will be made all year but used only during the harvest. Shelf life depends on storage conditions. A typical ADY yeast will lose 5% viability per annum if stored at 41°F and 20% per annum if stored at 73°F. When the vintner wants to inoculate a new batch of *must, the yeast is rehydrated in warm water (98 to 108°F) for about five minutes then added to the must to give the desired inoculation density (usually 2×10^6 cells/ml). At this concentration the starter yeast dominates the fermentation and the contribution of the ambient *yeasts is minimized.

See Microbiology essay p 39. R.S.

Aguascalientes, region in the highlands of MEXICO 200 mi north of Mexico City near the town of Zacatecas. Historically a prolific grape growing district, but presently reduced to the production of brandy, primarily through the Domecq brand.

Alabama, state in the SOUTH region whose upper PIEDMONT, with its cooler climate and limestone soils, has potential for quality viticulture. AL currently has six wineries: Braswell's in Dora (Jefferson Co); Bryant Vyd in Talledga (Calidiga Co); Morrione Vyds in Wetumpka (Elmor Co); Perdido Vyds on the Gulf Coast; Pinecroft in Calhoun Co; and White Wind Farms in Shelby Co. All but the last two are in the upper Piedmont north or northeast of Montgomery.

Alabama's growing season ranges from 180 to 300 days, and rainfall is 50–65 in annually. FRENCH HYBRIDS can be grown in the upper Piedmont, and MUSCADINE varieties in the COASTAL PLAIN. Wine consumption is far below the national average. Roughly one-third (23 of 67) of the state's counties are dry. The Alabama Native Farm Winery Act stipulates that 75% of the winery's wine must be grown and produced 'in the vicinity' of the winery, on land owned or leased by the winery. The wines must not exceed 14% alcohol, and the winery may not have an annual production exceeding 100,000 gal. Wineries may not be located in a dry jurisdiction. Wineries may sell wholesale to state-owned stores, or private distributors, or OFF-PREMISE retail to winery visitors. They may offer on-site tastings. Total state wine production is 50,000 gal. Muscadine grape varieties dominate current production. R.G.L

Alban Vyds, premier CA winery in the coastal region of San Luis Obispo Co. In the late 1980s, at a time when *Condrieu had less than 100 acres of Viognier planted, John Alban was considered rather wild-eyed as he began planting 32 acres of the variety in the southern end of EDNA VALLEY. Since then Viognier has been planted all over CA and the *Languedoc, making Alban appear more clairvoyant than crazed.

Alban owns 254 acres, of which perhaps 100 are plantable. Owner of the first winery in North America committed exclusively to *Rhône varieties, he makes an excellent Syrah and is one of the leaders in CA's rediscovery of Grenache as an artisan wine, but his role in defining the characteristics of CA Viognier has been seminal.

An instructive comparison can be made between the Viognier Alban makes from his estate grapes, and a second one he makes (labeled Central Coast appellation) from grapes grown on the warmer, inland side of the coastal range in the PASO ROBLES AVA. His own grapes usually come in at 3.25 pH; the inland grapes come in at 3.45 pH and he *acidifies that must. The estate rarely produces more than 1 t/a; the inland vineyard gets 2 t/a and could get 5. Alban likes to say the inland Viognier is more forward and pleasant, where the estate wine has a more exotic perfume. B.C.C

Alexander, red grape mentioned throughout the literature of the early eastern American experience. Once called the Cape grape and thought to be a pure VINIFERA variety from South Africa, which was the major reason it was accepted by early European-oriented planters. It was subsequently discovered to be an AMERICAN HYBRID, and thought to be a chance crossing. Jean Jacques DUFOUR and others celebrated its wines, although probably because it was one of the few grapes to survive conditions in the NORTHEAST and lower MIDWEST.

Many of the grapes that are now considered to be native American are actually chance hybrids of the indigenous American grapes with vinifera varieties. These latter were planted by early settlers but ultimately failed largely because of the harsh climate. However, in the brief time they flourished, wind and insects spread their pollen to local grapes' flowers and created new varieties. Alexander almost certainly had vinifera genes added to its native labrusca heritage. Although there is some disagreement on this issue, it is generally agreed that many of the popular native American grapes are similarly species crossed.   P.W.F.

Alexander Valley AVA, northernmost AVA in CA's SONOMA CO with some 7,000 acres of vines. Previously seen as distant, it is gradually being pulled into the metropolitan orbit of the greater San Francisco Bay Area by expanding population and more convenient transportation. The AVA comprises both the hills and floodplain of the Russian River which runs south out of Mendocino Co through a steep, rock-strewn gorge then flattens out as it enters the Alexander Valley at Cloverdale. It then flows southeast past Asti, then past Geyserville, which marks the approximate midpoint of the valley. At the southern end of Alexander Valley the river makes an abrupt U-turn to flow northwest again and exit the valley through a narrow gorge between two 1,000 ft peaks in the residential suburbs which form the eastern boundary of Healdsburg. Geologically, Alexander Valley is not just any floodplain. At its southern end it almost captures the river. Soils in the valley floor are the very definition of *alluvial. **Knights Valley** is a much less significant AVA which lies between Alexander Valley and Napa Valley to the southeast. DRY CREEK AVA is west of, contiguous, and parallel to Alexander Valley, separated only by a single ridge of 600 ft high hills.

Historically Alexander Valley was on the frontier of what passed for civilization in Sonoma Co. The Russian fur post at Ft Ross was on the coast at least a day's ride west. The northernmost Spanish mission was at the southern end of Sonoma Valley on San Pablo Bay, a very long day's ride south. Alexander Valley was turned to agriculture by American wheat farmers who traveled overland and displaced the Pomo Indians. Later, at the end of the 19th century, Asti was settled as a philanthropic communal venture initiated by a San Francisco grocer hoping to provide jobs and homes for poor immigrant farmers. He called it Italian-Swiss Colony. The ethnic norms and viticultural traditions of that era dominated the district well into the 1980s and persist visibly today.

Driving north along Hwy 101, the low hills at Healdsburg which separate Alexander Valley from the Santa Rosa Plain to the southwest seem topographically inconsequential. But anyone who has made that passage in a non-air-conditioned vehicle at 5 or 6 pm in Aug can testify to the climatic differential these hills create. At that time of day in late summer a difference of 20°F is possible between the towns of Healdsburg and Geyserville, which are about 5 mi apart. These warm summer temperatures in Alexander Valley produce opulent, forward wines. Cabernets are typified by soft tannins and chocolate notes, which most consumers find quite appealing in wines destined for early drinking.

The Alexander Valley AVA was granted by BATF in 1984. It primarily encompassed the valley floor where almost all of the grapes were planted. In a maneuver which may make sense to marketers, but certainly surprises viticulturalists, the AVA was expanded in 1990 at the behest of Ed Gauer, who wanted his mountainside vineyards east of the valley included. Those vineyards run to as high as 2,400 ft of elevation and are now owned by Jess Jackson's ARTISAN & ESTATES stable.

NOTABLE PROPERTIES

Alexander's Crown, conspicuous Cabernet vineyard with an enviable track record. The wines are made under the Rodney Strong label at WINDSOR VYDS.

Alexander Valley Vyds, site of the property and several historic buildings belonging to Cyrus Alexander, for whom the valley is named. The vineyards are owned and operated by the Wetzel family, pioneers in America's aeronautics industry, and run from the river up into the eastern foothills.

Ch Souverain, winery located right up against the boundary with Dry Creek Valley, tucked into a picturesque foothill nook. The name Souverain was first used by Lee Stewart, who made some of California's most illustrative artisan wines in the 1950s and 1960s at a Napa Valley site which is currently Burgess Cellars. The name was then purchased by Pillsbury during their ill-fated foray into the wine business in 1973. They built a Napa facility (now Rutherford Hill) and the current facility overlooking Alexander Valley. When Pillsbury gave up, the Alexander Valley facility was purchased by a growers' organization and run as a co-op with storage for 3 million gal. They never made money though, and in 1986 Nestlé's Wine World Estates bought the facility, which was subsequently acquired by BERINGER Wine Estates (which include MERIDIAN, Ch St Jean, Napa Ridge, and others). Today Ch Souverain features a top flight restaurant and produces 200,000 cases a year of consistently good value wine under the overall management of Tom Peterson and the winemaking of Ed Killian.

Clos du Bois, winery brand and vineyards begun in 1974 by Frank Woods (English for *Bois*) and some friends from Cornell. Although the line was broad, the quality image eventually came from wholly owned vineyards in Alexander and Dry Creek Valley which were designated on the labels: Calcaire and Flintwood Chardonnays, Briarcrest Cabernet, and the quality flagship Marlstone Merlot/Cabernet blend. When the brand and vineyards were sold in 1988 to Hiram Walker's Wine Alliance (now ALLIED DOMECQ), the purchase price of $40 million was deemed to be 50% for the nearly 500 acres of vineyards and assorted other hard assets, and 50% goodwill for the value of the brand franchise.

Hafner, DIRECT SHIPMENT winery specializing in Cabernet and impressive Chardonnay.

Murphy Goode. Dennis Murphy's family has been farming grapes in Alexander Valley since 1970. Dennis is married to Katie (Wetzel) Murphy, the marketing force behind her family's Alexander Valley Vyds. Together they comprise *the* power couple in Alexander Valley.

Robert Young, vineyard set against the eastern foothills which helped establish Alexander Valley's reputation in the early 1980s when Dick Arrowood, then at Sonoma Valley's Ch St Jean, produced a string of voluptuous vineyard designated Chardonnays from these grapes.

Sausal, converted prune operation planted in 1955, with some Zinfandel vines dating to 1925. Prior to the 1990s most of the wine was sold in bulk, but recently their own label has achieved some prominence, and they now produce some 20,000 cases from 65 acres. Zinfandel is reliably dense and fleshy in a rustic style drawn from the district's traditional roots.

Scherrer, vineyard on an eastside alluvial bench featuring 80-year-old Zinfandel vines. Most of the grapes are sold on a long-term contract to GALLO-SONOMA, but 1,000 tightly allocated cases are made each year by Fred Scherrer for his own label as a sideline to his day job as winemaker for Dehlinger.

Simi, winery on the outer edge of Healdsburg with a long history in the region and a remarkable record of female management, although it was purchased in 1999 by CANANDAIGUA and is now part of their Franciscan Estates fine wine portfolio. The winery began in 1876 when two brothers from *Montepulciano in Tuscany began making wine in San Francisco's North Beach Italian enclave to supplement their produce business. Eventually they bought land in the Alexander Valley to grow grapes, and built a winery there in 1890. At age 14 Isabelle Simi took over when her father and uncle both died in 1904. She continued to run the operation, outlasting both her husband and her daughter, until she sold it in 1970, then she worked in the tasting room for another eight years. Oil man Russ Green was the purchaser in 1970, and his arrival heralded the renaissance of grape growing in Alexander Valley, but his best hire was Mary Ann Graf as winemaker. She had been the first female recipient of an enology degree from UC *Davis (1965). Zelma Long took over as winemaker in 1978, and was elevated to president eventually after the winery was purchased in the early 1980s by *Möet-Hennessy. Today Simi own 275 acres of vineyard: 100 in the Russian River AVA; and 175 in the Alexander Valley. They make 165,000 cases, of which Chardonnay is the biggest proportion, followed by Sauvignon Blanc and Cabernet Sauvignon. Stylistically the wines are noteworthy for the manner in which they integrate their aromatic fruit, wood, and emergent bouquet. This style seems so effortless, it is easy to overlook.

Trentadue, winery making 30,000 cases a year of thick red wine with modest aspirations, but also owners of 190 acres of old, head-pruned vines in the rolling western foothills which have supplied many premium producers including RIDGE.

See also ARTISANS & ESTATES, GALLO-SONOMA, GEYSER PEAK, JORDAN.　　B.C.C.

Allied Domecq, powerful international wine and spirits conglomerate formed in the early 1990s by the merger of Hiram Walker's Wine Alliance, which included CALLAWAY VYDS, and the Spanish company *Domecq. It also owns William Hill Vyds in CA and markets ATLAS PEAK.

Alto Pass, winery located in midwestern ILLINOIS, although it has more to do with, and has had to come to terms with, the deep South. This is southern IL: topographically hilly, which is a break from the notion of flat grain-land, and politically hazardous, at least initially. The glaciers that carved the GREAT LAKES, and flattened almost everything else, did not get this far. Rolling hills are everywhere. Politically the owners, Guy Renzaglia with his son and daughter-in-law, Paul and Marilyn, had to contend with strict religious attitudes about alcohol. They had established a vineyard in 1986 and were successfully selling their grapes to wineries. But their area, Union Co, was a DRY one. Ultimately they won the right to open a winery and to sell their wines from it. Today the Renzaglias turn out a varied list including dessert and fruit wines, but their strength continues

to be in their wines from French hybrids, most notably the Vidal Blanc and the Chambourcin.　　P.W.F.

Altus AVA, one of three ARKANSAS AVAs, all of which are in the northwest of the state. Altus takes its name from the town in which three of the state's four wineries are located. With mountains to the north and south, situated on Lake Dardanelle on the Arkansas River, Altus enjoys a moderate climate for the region. The town of Altus is also the site of Arkansas' largest wine festival in August, named after the town.　　R.G.L.

Amador Co, a cowboy county in CA's SIERRA FOOTHILLS AVA situated immediately north of Calveras Co and immediately south of EL DORADO CO. Amador is distinguished from its neighbors by having its grape growing districts at somewhat lower elevation, which translates into more heat, and thus riper, chewier wines. The little town of Plymouth serves as gateway to both of Amador's approved AVAs: Shenandoah Valley and Fiddletown. Almost all of the wineries are in Shenandoah Valley. The phrase 'valley' is a misnomer when applied to Shenandoah. Actually it sits on a kind of flat, elevated mesa between deeply eroded riverbeds. The vineyards are mainly 1,200 to 1,600 ft of elevation. Fiddletown is a contiguous district running from around 1,600 ft to 2,400 ft. Fiddletown is the cooler of the two, but only boasts 20% of the vines. Soils are locally called decomposed granite. They have very little organic matter to provide fertility, but they are well drained and fairly deep. The color of the soil is a distinctive brick red due to the oxidation of its high iron content (rust). There is also a relatively elevated manganese content. It is not uncommon for overnight temperatures to drop 50°F below the midday high in summer. Most vineyards are planted on gently rolling hillsides and DRY FARMED. Cattle, weekend vacationers from Stockton and Sacramento, and even some large gold mining operations, are important contributors to the county economy.

At least ten separate Zinfandel vineyards in Amador Co date back more than 70 years. Vineyard names such as Grandpere, Eschen, Esola, Deaver, Baldinelli, and Ferrero are particularly choice. About 75% of the 1,700 acres planted in Amador Co are Zinfandel, and it is that variety which has historically given Amador its reputation. Amador Zins are distinctive. They have strong briary or heather smells, high alcohol, and lifted, jammy fruit. In the mouth they leave an impression that can only be approximated by calling to mind whatever *metallic* and *salty* have in common. This flavor is an

acquired taste considered rather attractive, as a structural component, by devotees of the region.

Amador, like most of CA's *gold rush counties, declined dramatically as a wine region following Prohibition. Lying four hours by car from the San Francisco Bay Area, Amador slumbered without a producing winery until the late 1960s, subsisting by selling grapes to knowledgeable winemakers in other regions. In 1968 prominent Sacramento retailer Darrell Corti cajoled Napa Valley's Sutter Home winery (see ST HELENA AVA) to produce a vineyard designated Zinfandel from Deaver Vyd. Two years later Cary Gott began Amador's resurgence as a producing county when he opened Montev1ña (now owned by Sutter Home). Today Amador enjoys a somewhat more defined image in the marketplace than its Sierra Foothills neighbors, and therefore tends to promote itself individually rather than in concert with their efforts.

Syrah is a second variety which does quite well in Amador Co, although plantings did not begin until the mid-1980s. Even more recent, but also showing promise, is Sangiovese. Sauvignon Blanc from Amador is not widely distributed, but it does have a particular claim to notoriety. The same *goût de terroir* which gives Amador Zinfandels their distinctive flavor can be found in Amador Sauvignon Blanc. That slightly brackish note in the finish makes Amador Sauvignon Blanc a specifically good match with artichokes, or with Belon oysters.

NOTABLE PROPERTIES

Amador Foothill. Owner Ben Zeitman's e-mail handle is 'winenerd.' It fits. Zeitman had a noteworthy career as a research chemist for the US National Aeronautics and Space Administration before following his friend Leon Sobon of Shenandoah Vyds to Amador in 1985. Zeitman's wife, Katie Quinn, came to the project with a masters degree in enology from UC *Davis and three years experience at Gundlach-Bundschu in Sonoma. One of the fascinating digressions during a visit to Amador Foothill Winery is how efficient, inexpensive, and clever the passive heating and cooling systems are in their home and in their 10,000 cases per year winery building.

Zinfandels from elderly vineyards were the mainstay at Amador Foothill for years, but the future will likely be carried by barrel fermented, *sur lie* aged Semillon and by Sangiovese. Sangiovese was grafted onto Cabernet Sauvignon vines in the estate vineyard in 1991. Three clones were used: one from Biondi-Santi via Robert Pepi Vyd; another one from *Montalcino; and one from *Chianti Classico.

Karly. Buck Cobb was a fighter pilot, then a nuclear engineer, before starting a winery named for his wife in 1976. He has 20 acres in the Shenandoah Valley planted to eight different varieties, and produces about 10,000 cases a year. Since 1993 Cobb has grown Marsanne and Roussanne. He also has 3 acres of a 'Noir' clone of Grenache which gives him intense color and flavor when cropped under 4 t/a.

The very best item historically in the Karly range, however, has been a Zinfandel from 70-year-old vines planted by Sadie Upton and now farmed by her sons. Cobb buys all the Upton fruit. Some years he blends it into his regular Amador appellation Zinfandel. When he bottles it separately, as in 1986, 1989, 1991, and 1992, it is a wonderfully distinctive drop with plenty of berry and spice to balance the mineral flintiness, high alcohol, and strong extract. As an example of the difficulties involved, all the Upton Zinfandel grapes were eaten by deer in 1994, and the vines barely produced a crop in 1995.

Monteviña, purchased by Napa Valley's Sutter Home Winery in 1988, this important name in Amador wine has moved aggressively into Italian varieties including Sangiovese Grosso, Nebbiolo, and Aleatico. In 1996 a new brand, Terra d'Oro, was introduced to serve as an upmarket label for Zinfandel, Sangiovese, and Barbera.

Noceto, a 3,000-case operation specializing in Sangiovese grown on the property. Owned and run by computer banking consultant Jim Gullett.

Sobon Estate and *Shenandoah Vyds*. Leon Sobon and his wife Shirley moved to the old Steiner Ranch with their six children in 1977, converting the stone garage into a winery they called Shenandoah Vineyards. In 1989 the Sobons took action to preserve the only winery in the district which had survived Prohibition; Adam Uhlinger had built it in 1856. It had been operated since 1911 by the D'Agostini family making wine for sale in cheap jugs to skiers. The hand-hewn beams and rock quarried on the property of the Historic Landmark building now serve as a museum and storage facility for Sobon Estate. Few wine labels in the world can claim to be more attention-grabbing than Shenandoah's phantasmagorical, hypercolored art prints on their fortified Orange Muscat and Black Muscat of Hamburg.

Young's, new estate with excellent Barbera, lovely grounds on which to picnic, and eye-catching original label art painted by owner's married daughter.

See also TERRE ROUGE.   B.C.C.

American Canyon, new CA district without an AVA in the southeast extremity of NAPA VALLEY between the towns of Vallejo and Napa proper. Previously thought too cold, but aggressively planted since 1995.

American hybrids, grape varieties occasionally called native hybrids, spontaneous hybrids, chance seedlings, or indigenous hybrids. In some cases they were discovered and isolated in the wild. Others were the product of research by plant breeders. They may be pure examples of a species native to the North American continent such as *V. labrusca*, *V. riparia*, or *V. aestivalis* (see Vine Family essay, p 54), or they may be some cross with various components of each. Our rule of thumb, however, is that they are *not* the product of research by plant breeders to cross European vinifera vines with one or more of the native American species. Those we call *French hybrids. American hybrids are usually long on cold hardiness and disease resistance, but also tend toward the cosmetic, acetone-like flavors generically called *foxiness. This *lift in the aroma can give the wines an attractive intensity in terms of fruit smells, but they typically lack *extract as well as the weighty flavor concentration to follow through on the *palate.

American oak. In the 1970s, when a North American winemaker said he used French oak barrels, he was implying not only that the wood came from one of the forests in France, but that the staves had been split instead of sawn, air dried for several years instead of kiln dried, and then assembled using the heat of a low fire to gradually bend the staves into the barrel shape while simultaneously *toasting their inside surface. If this same winemaker said he used American oak barrels, he was generally referring to much less expensive barrels which came from coopers in MO, AR, and KY whose primary business was supplying whiskey distillers in their home states. Those assembly line coopers not only used the tighter grained oak from America, but they sawed and kiln dried the staves, bent them with steam, then quickly blew a jet of gas inside to mildly char them. An assembly line cooper might make 2,000 barrels in a day, whereas a French artisan might turn out 25. In 1980 an American oak barrel cost about a quarter what a French oak barrel cost.

Today the issue of wine barrels is more sophisticated in North America (as elsewhere), and much more complicated. There are barrel makers in several locations, although primarily in CA, who use oak from forests in MO, MN, OR, etc, but air dry the staves for several years, then use the slow fire coopering technique to form the barrels. They usually saw the staves, rather than split them, because sawing is a much more efficient use of the log, and tight grained American oak is less likely than French oak to leak. Whether the source of the oak is more important to flavor in a wine than the manner in which the barrel is made is a subject of much conjecture, but most critics would agree the harsh flavors attributed to American oak during the 1970s era probably owed much to kiln drying and lack of toast rather than provenance.

More adroitly made American oak barrels contribute smell and flavor characteristics which are less identifiable as being similar to those found in bourbon, and more fairly compared with the soft, sweet smell of coconut. For that reason it is sometimes preferred by makers of densely ripe and fruity wines such as Syrah and Zinfandel.

See also INNER STAVES.   B.C.C.

Anderson Valley AVA, isolated and somewhat eccentric district in CA's MENDOCINO CO. Anderson Valley is slightly west of the 3,000 ft ridgecrest of the coastal mountains. It opens to the Pacific Ocean along the Navarro River. This *aspect makes it much cooler than the districts on the inland side of the mountains near the city of Ukiah, or near towns such as Willits or Hopland. Until recently, there were 20 times as many grapes grown on the inland side of the mountains as there were in Anderson Valley, so it was rare to find this appellation on a label. In 1983 France's *Roederer champagne house began planting hundreds of acres of grapes which effectively doubled Anderson Valley output.

The towns of Philo and Boonville mark the center of Anderson Valley as it runs northwest along Hwy 128. The southeastern end of the valley floor is 1,300 ft above sea level, while the northwestern extreme is about 800 ft. Fog comes up the Navarro River from the coast, moving in a southeasterly direction and creating a gradient for sunshine ripening hours as it moves into the valley several days each week during the summer. This fog cover slows ripening and benefits grapes such as Pinot Noir and Gewürztraminer. White Riesling and Chardonnay grown anywhere in the valley have much more delicate aromas and much higher acid levels than their inland counterparts; however, they do best when sited at the higher elevation, southeastern end of the valley where they can get enough sun to ripen fully. Thus it is fair to call this upland half of the valley a climatic zone distinct from the lower half, although it is difficult to define where a line separating the two zones should be drawn.

Cabernet and Zinfandel are grown successfully on hillsides above the valley where they will not be affected by the fog. These sites comprise a third climatic zone within the Anderson Valley AVA. Even so, cool breezes from the ocean also slow the ripening process in Cab and Zin to produce much more austere wines than those commonly found in CA. At times these breezes become strong *winds which can virtually cause the ripening process to cease.

The **Mendocino Ridges AVA** covers a large geographic area, but the approved appellation is only for those portions within the defined district which have elevations above 1,200 ft. The overall district pretty much covers the territory south of Hwy 128, from about the eastern edge of Anderson Valley almost all the way to the coast and about as far south as Gualala.

Annual rainfall is high on this side of the coastal ridge in Mendocino Co, averaging well over 40 in annually, more in the higher elevations—one reason Mendocino Co is a favorite destination of mushroom foragers from Oct through Dec each year. The growing season for grapes is extremely long throughout the Anderson Valley AVA. It is not uncommon for Chardonnay to push buds in Feb, but not be picked for table wine until late Sept and even early Oct. Cabernet Sauvignon is routinely picked as late as Nov. Spring *frost is always a problem on the valley floor and some form of protection is mandatory. *Botrytis at the end of the season occurs frequently. A great many apples are also grown in the valley.

Anderson Valley is separated from the warmer eastern half of Mendocino Co by the coastal ridge, and from the main north–south traffic artery (Hwy 101) and its population centers as well. As a result it has a distinct culture in addition to its distinct climate. There is even an enigmatic local patois called *boontling*. Long time residents call wine lovers *seep horners* and describe top quality wines as truly *bahl*. The frontier ethic is everywhere apparent, but modulated today with certain touches of sophistication and irony. Perhaps the best example occurred a few years ago when the publisher of the local newspaper got into a fistfight with a member of the school board. Bruce Anderson, the publisher, had educated his own son at home. Anderson was put in jail, but had no trouble getting the newspaper out. He simply brought his son home from Harvard, where he had gone to university, to run the newspaper for a couple of months.

NOTABLE PROPERTIES

Navarro. Bushy-bearded Ted Bennett was an entrepreneur in the 1960s and early 1970s with a prominent chain of retail stereo stores. When he sold his stake and moved to a 900-acre grazing ranch in the middle of Anderson Valley in 1974, it would have been very difficult to imagine the place as a destination for wine lovers from around the world. It would have also been difficult to find a more beautiful spot. With wife Deborah Cahn, an advertising agency copywriter, Bennett planted 50 acres and built a cozy tasting room. Right from the beginning they concentrated on selling their 15,000 cases to the vacationers speeding along Hwy 128 toward the Mendocino coast every weekend. Today, they share with WINDSOR VYDS in Sonoma and V. Sattui (see ST HELENA AVA) in Napa the distinction of being America's most accomplished DIRECT SHIPMENT wine producers. Their quarterly newsletter is a masterpiece of chatty prose, adroit offering strategy, two-color design, and engaging photography. 'New releases will sell out in few weeks,' Deborah writes under a picture of a kitten gingerly picking its way through the bottles. 'Don't pussyfoot around.'

Navarro scored early critical success with the ethereal aromas of their estate grown Gewürztraminer. They make it dry, which is unusual in CA, and also take advantage of the wet harvests to produce a Cluster Select late picked Gewurz which can be extraordinarily lychee-like early on. Occasionally exceeding 20% RS, these wines have unctuous body and a *volatile lift not unlike many *Sauternes. Although they are not long ageing candidates, as an immediate pleasure they are impossible to pass by. Navarro also makes a fine range of Rieslings which fall into these same categories.

Underappreciated by the American wine press because of their direct shipment focus, Navarro has produced excellent Pinot Noirs since the mid-1980s. These wines show characteristics typical of Anderson Valley: they are light bodied, with cheerful strawberry notes throughout and refreshing acid, but they are not simple wines. The one Navarro calls Méthode à l'Ancienne shows nuances of cinnamon in the nose, mushroomy flavors in the finish, and a leather *bouquet when aged a few years. Most of all, the fruit flavors of these Pinot Noirs linger for a long time.

Pacific Echo. John Scharffenberger moved to Philo in 1981. He deserves the credit for pioneering the Anderson Valley's entry into premium sparkling wines. His impact on the marketplace, however, was not enough to establish the region, and his first winemaking efforts, involving grapes from both sides of the mountains, were merely adequate. Then ROEDERER arrived in 1983 and consumers' concept of Anderson Valley sparkling wines was considerably upgraded. By 1985 Scharffenberger was selling 20,000 cases a year. In 1989 the French champagne house Pommery made Scharffenberger 'an offer he couldn't refuse.' They renamed the winery in 1997, and Scharffenberger left to become a chocolatier.

French capital enabled the brand to acquire a 680-acre ranch on which 180 acres of vineyard are being developed, planted about evenly to Pinot Noir and Chardonnay with a few acres of Pinot Meunier. The impetus to make sparkling wine from Anderson Valley fruit grew out of an impression that hotter climate areas of CA, like Napa Valley, gave too much intensity and a *phenolic character which masked the flavors from yeast *autolysis in a noisy, warm finish. In the beginning, Scharffenberger's sparklers had the basic lemon-flavored, crisp structure common to Anderson Valley, but they lacked texture. Over time, and with better equipment, they have improved steadily. A new facility gives Pacific Echo the capacity to grow to 50,000 cases annually.

Other wineries

Edmeades. The vineyard was first planted in the 1960s by a local physician, whose son established the winery in 1972. The property had been moribund for many years until purchased by Jess Jackson and reopened in 1992 for his ARTISANS & ESTATES stable. Anderson Crest is the name Jackson has given to the estate vineyard on the property, which has been entirely replanted and now consists of 39 acres of Chardonnay plus 25 acres of Pinot Noir. Edmeades releases interesting old vine Zinfandels with single vineyard designations: Ciapusci is tight, with a complicated nose; Zeni has lots of blueberry fruit; DuPratt is the most rustic.

Lazy Creek. Pinot Noir, Chardonnay, and Gewürztraminer are made by former restaurateur Hans Kobler. The 20-acre family vineyard is run by his Swiss-trained son, Norman.

Pepperwood Springs, an 8-acre estate vineyard at 1,000 ft elevation on a south-facing hillside several miles west of Philo. Produces about 800 cases a year of Pinot Noir and Chardonnay. Originally planted in the mid-1970s, then sold in 1980 to Larry Parsons, a blind winemaker who soon began getting publicity as much for the quality of his Pinot Noir as for the curiosity of the braille indicia on the labels he used to tell different vintages apart. After Parsons was unfortunately killed in 1986 in an automobile accident, with his 14-year-old daughter driving, the property was purchased by Phyllis and Gary Kaliher, who in turn have had several impressive releases.

See also GREENWOOD RIDGE, HANDLEY CELLARS, ROEDERER. B.C.C.

Andrés, first established in 1961 in British Columbia by Hungarian émigré and entrepreneur Andras (Andrew) Peller, is CANADA's second largest wine company with a market share of 12% and subsidiaries in BC, Alberta, Quebec, Nova Scotia, and Ontario. In 1971 the company identified correctly consumer demand when it introduced Baby Duck, a low alcohol, sweet sparkling wine, which became the single most popular brand in Canada. In 1994 the company amalgamated with HILLEBRAND, one of Ontario's largest producers of premium VQA wines.

Other Andrés brands sold throughout Canada include Peller Estates, Hoctatler, Dom D'Or, Auberge, Gold Coast, Franciscan, Trius, and various wine kit brands sold to FERMENT-ON-PREMISE operators. As a *négociant, Andrés also imports wines from Chile, Australia, CA, and Italy for bottling in Canada. In Ontario and BC they purchase grapes from local growers to make wines primarily for each respective provincial market. They purchased 210 acres of prime grape growing land in NIAGARA-ON-THE-LAKE, Ontario, on which to plant red vinifera varieties such as Merlot, Cabernet Sauvignon, and Cabernet Franc. Plans are to construct a new winery facility on the site which they will call Peller Estates. Andrés is one of a handful of wine companies who have licenses to sell their wines through retail outlets throughout Ontario province; retail outlets which currently number just over 100. L.F.B.

Andrew Murray, young winemaker bankrolled by a father who loves to cook and entertain, and who also owned a very successful chain of all-you-can-eat Mexican restaurants called El Torito. The winery is on top of a mesa in CA's SANTA YNEZ AVA. There are 35 acres of vines planted along the eroded sides of crevasses in the mesa. For comparison, note that Zaca Mesa winery owns the vines on top of the mesa. Zaca Mesa gets 4–5 t/a; Andrew Murray gets less than 2. But Andrew Murray's vines are sheltered from the prevailing winds blowing up the Santa Ynez Valley from the Santa Barbara coast. Andrew Murray gets riper grapes with more concentrated flavor. He also commands $25 and $30 a bottle. Zaca Mesa and

nearby Firestone make much larger volumes of good value wine priced in the $10 per bottle range. Murray's Syrah is artistically notable; his Roussanne is CA's best.

B.C.C.

Appalachian Mtns, ancient range which separates the East Coast of the US from the interior of the continent by running northeast from northern GA to ME. The Appalachians (in some parts referred to as the Allegheny Mtns) can have elevations over 6,000 ft, with an average elevation between 3,000 ft and 4,000 ft. There are three physiogeologic provinces of the Appalachian region; the Blue Ridge Province of the upper Piedmont to the western slope of the Blue Ridge Mtns (MD, VA, WV, NC, SC, GA); the Ridges and Valleys Province of the entire Appalachian range; and the Appalachian Plateau, in the western parts of PA, MD, WV, and southwestern VA. For viticulture, the most promising of these three provinces is the Blue Ridge. Moderately high elevations, breezes, and cool night temperatures, and the complex, well-drained soils have produced many of the best wines in the MID-ATLANTIC region. The cool climate and well-drained sedimentary soils of the Ridge and Valley Province provides some promising opportunities for viticulture in the Valley of VA and in WV, but further south the region is prone to wide temperature swings in winter which can result in *frost damage to premature buds. Elevations over 2,000 ft can also result in *winter freeze from excessively low temperatures. Accordingly, growers must choose their sites, aspects, and vine varieties carefully in this region. The Appalachian Plateau requires very cold-hardy grape varieties, such as American hybrids, as it has the coldest winters in the Mid-Atlantic region. R.G.L.

Arizona, rapidly growing state in the DESERT SOUTHWEST region, with a large retirement population. Elevation ranges from 70 ft above sea level, along the Colorado River, to 12,633 ft in the mountains north of Flagstaff. An area known as the Mexican Highland in the southeast part of the state harbors most of the quality wine production.

AZ viticulture, much like NM, the neighboring state to the east, was heavily influenced by missionaries. In 1691 at Tumacacori, near the Sulphur Springs plantings of today, *Mission grapes were first planted by a Swiss–Italian Jesuit. The wine industry expanded and flourished well into the 1880s. At that time, AZ wineries exported wine to Los Angeles. But the advent of state Prohibition in 1915 dried out the wine industry. Renewal began between 1969

and 1973 when Gordon Dutt, a soil scientist at the University of Arizona, did extensive test plantings. As a result, serious replanting of vines occurred in 1980. Presently AZ is the second largest producer of *raisin grapes in the US with 4,000 acres, albeit with only about 2% of CA's total. *Pierce's disease can be a major threat, but most AZ vineyardists have learned the disease can be harbored in *cover crops, so they employ clean cultivation.

In 1997 there were 850 acres of wine grapes in the state in three main grape growing regions. Ten wineries produce about 35,000 cases. Two, SONOITA AVA and SULPHUR SPRINGS VALLEY, are in the high desert of the southeast. The area around PHOENIX, called Valley of the Sun, is warmer than the other two. South of Phoenix, *table grapes are grown in an area called the Salt River Valley.

The AZ wine industry has several challenges, water rights prominent among them. Another problem is finding a willing market for AZ wines. While NM seems able to find thirsty consumers for its wines both within and without the state, AZ consumers have been less than wholly supportive of their local wine industry.

NOTABLE PROPERTIES

Callaghan Vyds, located in SONOITA, in southwestern AZ, 50 mi southeast of Tucson. They produce fine Cabernet and Cabernet blends. The 1997 Buena Suerte Cuvée (54% Merlot, rest Cabernet Sauvignon) had intense jammy berriness with really good balance and structure. The 1997 Dry Riesling was wonderfully aromatic with the taste of ripe peaches. The winemaker is Kent Callaghan, who also makes the wines for DOS CABEZAS. R.T.S.

Arkansas, state politically considered a member of the SOUTH region, although AR's winegrowing districts belong more appropriately to the MIDWEST region. These districts are represented by the state's three AVAS; Altus, Arkansas Mtn, and Ozark Mtn (the latter AVA shared with MISSOURI). Muscadine grapes are cultivated in the Mississippi River valley in the east, while French hybrids, Cynthiana, and vinifera are cultivated in the favorable sites in the cooler mountain regions. The growing season ranges from 180 days in the cool Boston Mtns to 240 days in the southeast. Precipitation ranges from 43 to 51 in annually. Challenges to AR viticulture include the grape root borer, spring frost, hail, fungal diseases, and drought.

AR's wine production of 225,000 gal is dominated by its two largest wineries, both located in the town of Altus in northwestern AR. Over half (43 of 75) of AR's counties are dry. Wineries may sell retail ON-PREMISE or OFF-SALE. Private clubs (found in dry jurisdictions) have licenses which allow alcohol sales seven days a week, while public restaurants and retail stores may sell wine, but not on Sunday, as with other alcoholic beverages. As elsewhere in the South and Midwest, the local palate is inclined to sweet wines.

NOTABLE PROPERTIES

Post Familie, winery established in 1880, and still owned/operated by the Post family. Wines are made from Vidal, Seyval, Chardonnay, Muscadines, Cabernet Sauvignon, Cynthiana, and Ives grapes. Production is about 35,000 cases.

Wiederkehr, the largest Arkansas producer making 50,000 cases annually, although they have a capacity of 1,500,000 gal. Products include Chardonnay, Riesling, Cynthiana, and a variety of proprietary blends.   R.G.L.

Arkansas Mtn, one of that state's three AVAS in the mountains south of the Arkansas River Valley near Altus. Cowie and Wiederkehr wineries use this AVA on some of their wines.

Arroyo Grande AVA, region in the southwestern, maritime portion of CA's SAN LUIS OBISPO CO. Unlike EDNA VALLEY AVA, its contiguous, much more homogeneous neighbor to the north, the larger Arroyo Grande region encompasses several different mesoclimates as it runs west southwest from Lopez Lake high in the mountains directly along the shortest path to the sea. Close to the coast, where most of its 450 acres of grapes are grown, Arroyo Grande is quite cold and often fog shrouded. Further up the mountain canyons which surround the lake, above the fog and baked by the sun, Arroyo Grande is fairly hot. This temperature discrepancy generates powerful wind along the arroyo (Spanish for small stream or deep gully). Lopez Lake is one of the premier windsurfing sites in CA.

NOTABLE PROPERTIES

Saucelito Canyon, tiny brand (less than 1,000 cases of single vineyard Zinfandel) exemplifying the amateur enthusiast who matures into a reliable craftsman. The vineyard is the easternmost, warmest extreme of Arroyo Grande AVA. Bill Greenough is descended from a long line of Boston aristocrats. After college in the 1960s Greenough gravitated to an artistic community in the hills behind Santa Barbara. Making wine was a utilitarian function needed to lubricate the endless stream of festivals they

celebrated. Every year they drove to Casteel Vyd near PASO ROBLES, ate poached (not a cooking technique) venison, danced around a fire, and discussed whether Italians deserved civil rights. The next day they would pick several tons of grapes and repair to their homes on Mountain Drive for the selection of the Stomp Queen—never an easy decision since the Queen was supposed to be a virgin, thus limiting the field to fairly young girls. Once a choice was made, everyone would get naked, the grapes would be stomped in large open bins, and a feast would commence. The Mtn Drive Grape Stomp died out in the mid-1970s as the community was disbursed by county building inspectors, but amongst oldtime wine aficionados it carries much the same mythological status as Woodstock does for musicians from the 1960s.

In 1974 Greenough purchased a derelict ranch behind Lopez Lake in the mountains above Arroyo Grande. It had been homesteaded 100 years earlier by an Englishman, Henry Ditmas, who first planted grapes there. It had an underground cellar and an overgrown vineyard, but no electricity. Greenough lived there for ten years and restored the vineyard, bonding his winery in 1982. The vineyard came full circle by winning a Gold Medal at the CA State Fair for its 1986 Zinfandel. It had also taken First Place at the CA State Fair for its 1896 Zinfandel under the St Remy brand.

Soil at the vineyard is deep sandy loam, black in color, but held in place by hillsides full of fossil shells. The soil retains water well. Greenough DRY FARMS the vineyard, but did not lose a single vine during the drought years of 1987–94. The best vintages are the cool ones. In those years harvest occurs in early Oct. Greenough picks in three separate stages in order to blend high pitched, fresh fruit notes with the jammy luxuriousness from extended *hang time. Saucelito Canyon Zinfandels are heavy bodied and traditional in style, but rarely coarse or bitter. They have a cigar smoke complexity to the bouquet more than varietal, berry noses.

Talley Vyds. Brian Talley's grandfather bought 2,000 acres about 8 mi from the coast in 1948. He wanted the flat, loam, and clay land to grow peppers. The hillsides came as part of the deal. Brian's dad graduated from UC Berkeley in 1962 and came back to work on the farm. Today Talley Farms is the fourth largest producer of peppers in CA. Brian's mother does all the telephone sales work with produce brokers herself. Wine and grapes only make up about 5% of Talley Farms' business. Talley is

located at the approximate midpoint of the AVA.

After extensive viticultural analysis Brian's father Don decided in 1982 to try some grapes on the steep hillsides above Talley's vegetable farmland. They have since expanded to 102 planted acres of vines. They sell the majority of the grapes at present and only produce 6,000 cases for their own label. The winery facility, however, has larger capacity and is used for custom crushing services. The largest portion of the estate vines is Chardonnay, followed by Pinot Noir. The Pinot Noir vines include clones taken from La *Tâche in Burgundy and from ROCHIOLI Vyd in the Russian River district of northern Sonoma Co.

Eighty per cent of Talley's vines are on a slope with a south-facing aspect they call Rincon Vyd. The loam and clay topsoil is shallow on this hillside, and it is underlain by limestone. Chardonnay and Pinot Noir yields in Rincon are less than 3 t/a. Talley claims budbreak here is two weeks earlier than it is in nearby Edna Valley. There is also more wind and less *botrytis. The Rincon name is borrowed from a two-story adobe house on the property built in 1863 by the son of the original landgrant holder.

Talley's top-of-the-line vineyard plot for Pinot Noir, called Rosemary's Vyd for Brian's mother, is located 2 mi closer to the coast. This 7-acre vineyard is quite steep and is characterized by white, rocky, limestone soil. The Pinot Noirs from this plot seem to have more weight in their flavor profile and more of a blackberry-like fruit concentration than do those from Rincon.

Laetitia, winery and 187-acre vineyard on an 800-acre property in the westernmost, coastside, coolest portion of the AVA, originally opened as Maison Deutz in 1983. Most of the French champagne houses which came to CA moved to Napa Valley for marketing reasons. William Deutz of Ay arrived in partnership with a division of Nestlé that already had Beringer in Napa and Ch Souverain in Sonoma to attract tourists. Deutz was able to pick his location based on climate for production of sparkling wines. The result was one of CA's best examples of *terroir-influenced wines. Maison Deutz made the easiest sparklers in CA to identify. They had enough acid to give one's dental enamel a case of the shakes. They expressed a clear sense of place, and that expression was, 'Pucker up, Baby!'

When Nestlé sold their CA holdings in 1995, the San Luis Obispo property was sold to a Frenchman who renamed it after his daughter and shifted the emphasis to still wines, particularly a very good Pinot Noir, and a Pinot Blanc which may be one of the few authentic plantings of that variety in CA (most are actually thought to be Melon, the Muscadet grape). In 1999 the property was acquired by the Barnwood Vyd corporation, growers from the tiny northeastern corner of Santa Barbara Co in Cuyama Valley, with investors from Los Angeles. They now make 15,000 cases under the Laetitia label, and another 10,000 under the Barnwood label. The ability to blend their grapes from both vineyards, softening the Arroyo Grande fruit and stiffening the Cuyama fruit, is a win/win situation. The tasting room on Hwy 101, CA's major north–south coastside route, is also important. Cuyama is magnificent in many ways, such as wild flowers in the spring, Indian hieroglyphs, condors, and visible EARTHQUAKE rifts, but it can go weeks without seeing a passing automobile.

BCC

Arroyo Seco AVA, district in CA's MONTEREY CO on the Salinas Valley floor west of Greenfield about two-thirds of the way south from the coast. It is the mouth of a now dry river flowing east out of the Tularcitos Mtns to join the Salinas River. Arroyo Seco is largely defined by its sandy, riverbed soils shot through with rounded stones the size of new potatoes. Equally important, it forms a notch in the western escarpment of the big valley which gives half of the Arroyo Seco AVA protection from the perpetual afternoon winds. *Botrytis is consistent in the irrigated vineyards of this sheltered section within Arroyo Seco. Luscious Gewürztraminers and White Rieslings have been produced from vines in this district regularly for the better part of two decades.

NOTABLE PROPERTIES

Jekel Vyd, started by a Hollywood film producer and considered quite reliable for Rieslings under the winemaking of Dan Morgan and Rick Boyer in the 1980s. Presently owned by Brown-Forman.

B.C.C.

Artisans & Estates, umbrella organizational title for the portfolio of properties assembled by Jess Jackson of CA's KENDALLJACKSON since the late 1980s. KendallJackson's success and phenomenal growth during the 1980s was based on blending wines from several regions to gain complexity. 'Going beyond terroir,' was how winemaker Jed Steele described the process. Artisans & Estates is something of a departure from this blending concept, although one might view it as the corporate complement. The properties which make up the A&E portfolio each have their own winemaker, and specialize in varieties particularly well suited to their region. Hence, for example, Hartford Court is a luxurious facility in the cool Green Valley AVA of western Sonoma Co. Hartford Court specializes in Pinot Noir, Chardonnay, and old vine Zinfandel. Hartford Court has the capacity to produce 40,000 cases, but only 3,000 cases are sold each year under the Hartford Court label, and that total output is divided among ten vineyard designated wines. The wine made at Hartford Court which is not released under the Hartford Court label goes to A&E's La Crema winery in the larger Russian River AVA for inclusion in varietal blends which carry a Sonoma Co appellation. Other A&E properties include: Lakewood in Lake Co, Stonestreet in Alexander Valley, Edmeades in Mendocino's Anderson Valley, Robert Pepi and Lokoya in Napa Valley, Kristone for sparkling wine in Monterey Co, and Cambria in Santa Barbara's Santa Maria Valley. Acquisition of these properties has been so rapid since 1988 that one must assume it will grow further before this book is published.

B.C.C.

ATF, see BATF.

Atlanta, the largest metropolis in the SOUTH excepting FL, and a conventional meeting place, first as a hub for rail lines, today as a hub for airlines. Surprisingly high PIEDMONT elevation (over 1,000 ft in spots) draws occasional snow in winter and qualifies as the second highest elevation major city in the US (after Denver). It is among the top 25 markets for wine consumption in the US, and retail establishments such as wine bars, gourmet grocers, and restaurants have moved quickly to take advantage of this trend. The Atlanta Summit is an annual wine competition each year.

GA is a FRANCHISE STATE with a solid THREE-TIER DISTRIBUTION system and felony penalties for DIRECT SHIPMENT. Even native wineries cannot ship directly to customers. Restaurateurs are given preference by wholesalers over retailers for highly allocated, limited quantity wines. To compete, retailer stores increasingly offer wine classes and events.

R.G.L.

Atlantic Ocean, bordering the East Coast of North America, and comprising 2,069 mi of US shoreline from ME to FL, including an impressive 28,673 sq mi of fecund tidal shoreline. The Atlantic is less saline than the Pacific, and is more turbulent, with strong currents and surging surf which are challenging to both mariners and recreational users. A unique feature of the Atlantic is the Gulf Stream, a current of warm water from the Caribbean which flows northeast all the way to the British Isles, bringing warm, humid air with it and allowing Britain to play host to the planet's northernmost vineyards. Northwest of the Gulf Stream, off New England and Canada's eastern shore, lie the cold, productive fishing grounds of the Grand Banks, and inshore the source of America's lobster bounty.

The Atlantic's major recreational beaches stretch from Virginia Beach through the Carolinas to Florida, in many cases along a low lying strip of barrier islands separated from the mainland by a protected inland waterway. Atlantic City in NJ has been a haven for NY gamblers and beachgoers for decades. Cape Hatteras at the eastern extreme of NC's Outer Banks marks the confluence of two major Atlantic currents, attracting both sport fishermen and an unusual number of historic shipwrecks.

Atlas Peak AVA, CA district in the southern portion of the Vaca mountain range east of NAPA VALLEY. Elevations of 1,200 to 2,600 ft and regular exposure to summer wind pulled from San Pablo Bay toward the hot Central Valley around Sacramento make Atlas Peak a notably cool growing area. At 3.30 pm during July and Aug it is generally 12–14°F cooler than the town of Yountville 10 miles away and directly west on the valley floor. Budbreak, and the entire growing season, are 2–3 weeks later than the Napa valley floor. Soils are primarily volcanic in origin, derived from basalt outflows lifted and fractured by tectonic action. The soil profiles are thin and so well drained that aridity virtually precluded viticulture here historically, even though rainfall is nearly 40 in per year. Irrigation using impounded runoff has helped solve that problem. The AVA encircles much of Foss Valley, a watershed which flows south through Milliken Canyon, and eventually (outside the AVA) through Silverado Country Club, to join the Napa River just north of the town of Napa. The AVA is not contiguous with Stags Leap AVA to the west, which ends at the 400 ft contour line while Atlas Peak has a MEETS AND BOUNDS western border much higher up the ridgeline. Nor does Atlas Peak include more recently planted, although definitely prestigious, vineyards slightly to the south such as Jarvis.

NOTABLE PROPERTIES

Atlas Peak Vyds, a $20 million investment at the end of the 1980s by a venture group composed of *Antinori, *Bollinger, and Whitbread succeeded, with Dick Peterson's help, in carving 450 acres out of the foothills of

Foss Valley, complete with underground mine shaft cellars. In the early 1990s Antinori bought out Bollinger's interest and Whitbread's was acquired by ALLIED DOMECQ. The deal was restructured to make Antinori the landlord and give Allied Domecq the marketing rights. With 120 acres of Sangiovese, Atlas Peak Vyds is on the front of the California wave of interest in Italian varietals.

Pahlmeyer, a CULT WINE made in borrowed facilities for almost a decade, beginning with wines made by Randy Dunn and currently featuring small production wines made by Helen Turley. Pahlmeyer has nearly 200 newly planted acres on both sides of a ridge well up Monticello Rd above Foss Valley.

B.C.C.

Au Bon Climat, premier CA winery, intimately associated with the rise to prominence of SANTA BARBARA CO, and representing a second generation of the pioneering craftsman-sized wineries which began in the 1950s and 1960s. The first wave (see HANZELL, MAYACAMAS, STONY HILL, MT EDEN, RIDGE, CHALONE) began with the European notion that they were places. They were started by middle-aged people with some money and a desire to move into a beautiful, semi-rural setting. Au Bon Climat typifies an outgrowth from that movement. Au Bon Climat shares with those early craftsmen a sense of learning from practical experience rather than from formal academic training, but it departs from the concept of wanting to acquire a specific piece of property. Au Bon Climat was about young, energetic, self-confident people who wanted to make wine, but did not have the money required to purchase land. It is an appealing story for Americans, embodying the bootstrap approach and an eventual triumph of artistry in the marketplace.

Au Bon Climat began in 1982 as a working partnership between Jim Clendenen and Adam Tolmach. In the beginning they picked the grapes themselves, did all the winery chores, and had a two-man bottling line. Clendenen was the salesman; Tolmach was the bookkeeper. Clendenen-Tolmach Vintners opened in a 1,000 sq ft dairy shed at Los Alamos Vyds. The dairy herd had been decimated by some bovine disease, and the landowners had used the insurance money to plant 350 acres of grapes. They let Clendenen and Tolmach use the old shed and some of the stainless steel tanks in exchange for viticultural advice and keeping an eye on the place.

The first vintages of Au Bon Climat Chardonnay and Pinot Noir came from Los Alamos Vyd grapes that Clendenen and Tolmach got to select, and could pick whenever they wanted. They would perform the task in stages over a three-week period giving them a range of ripeness from 20.5°B to 23.5°B. They did not have a crusher, so the Chardonnay was pressed as whole clusters and the Pinot Noir was trod. They did have a gal of French oak capacity for every gal of wine they made. Clendenen stated the departure from the property ownership concept quite clearly at the time, 'In today's market great wine is 90% winemaking knowledge and effort, and 10% being smart enough to select, and connected enough to buy, the right grapes.'

By the latter half of the 1980s Au Bon Climat had become a darling of the trendy American wine scene. Their wines were even being exported to Burgundy. More importantly, Clendenen and Tolmach had moved in a couple of directions which were unconventional for the American marketplace. They adjusted their retail price points up or down depending on their assessment of the vintage quality. They also made some Reserve Chardonnays by picking grapes at 20.5°B, while the skins were still opaque and green, then 'working the wine up in the winery' by forcing it through *MLF and leaving it on the gross *lees in new barrels. Those wines were then bottle aged a few extra years before release.

But circumstances change and the attachments forged in hard physical labor tend to be a province for young men. Tolmach married his childhood sweetheart. Clendenen married a potter whose family owned thousands of acres of ranchland in CA. Los Alamos Vyd was sold to a large Central Valley marketing company. Au Bon Climat operated out of a couple of different industrial sites around Buellton, and sourced grapes from several growers, but gradually the objectives of the partners in Clendenen-Tolmach Vintners diverged. Tolmach sold his rights in the brand to Clendenen and moved to some family property along the Ventura River to pursue his own Ojai label. Clendenen moved into a facility on the Bien Nacido Vyd. He continues the success of Au Bon Climat, but also satisfies his inquisitive entrepreneurial urges in separate cooperative ventures with other winemaking partners including: Vita Nova, a Bordeaux variety label in conjunction with Bob Lindquist of QUPÉ; Il Podere del Los Olivos, an Italian varietal venture; Ici la Bas, Pinot Noirs sourced in OR; and Cold Heaven, a primarily Viognier venture launched with his second wife, Morgan, who is also a winemaker.

B.C.C.

auctions, see also *auctions, come in two flavors: charity and commercial. Commercial (see Wine Auctions essay, p 32) do approximately twice as much dollar volume as charity auctions in the US. Charity auctions have an interestingly gray financial component to them which completely removes the prices paid from any connection to marketplace reality. Wine donors are allowed to write off from their income tax a figure equal to the 'fair market price' of the wine. Since that figure is very difficult to document on rare and obscure bottles, the write-off may be worth considerably more than one's cash investment in many instances, especially to individuals in high tax brackets. Similarly, the prices paid for wines in charity auctions represent a tax deduction to the purchaser of all the money over whatever the donor is taking as a fair market price write-off. When one factors in the publicity value of a very high bid, and the networking value of social interactions at an event such as the Napa Valley Wine Auction, it is not hard to understand why that charity auction was able to raise $5.5 million in 1999 from 2,000 bidders, including Michael Jordan and Robin Williams (a Napa Valley resident). As an example of the fare, $162,000 was spent on a barrel of Cabernet; $95,000 bought a 6 l bottle of red wine, and dinner prepared by Isabel Allende at FRANCISCAN VYDS.

Commercial wine auctions have very different parameters. Here a bloodlessly true marketplace does exist and prices are exactly what the market that day will bear. Individuals hoping for an investment coup acting as wine arbitrageurs should, however, be aware of certain factors. The seller pays a fee (usually in the order of 10–15%) to the auction house, and may be charged for insurance coverage of the wine as well. The buyer also pays a premium to the auction house (typically 10–15%) plus sales tax and any shipping charges. Thus the difference between what the buyer pays, and what the seller receives, is not unlike the MARK-UP between wholesale price and retail price found in most wine stores. Buying wines at retail, then reselling them at wholesale, is a hard way to earn a living.

Harlan Estate, Araujo Eisele, Colgin, Grace Family, Moraga, Screaming Eagle, Dalla Valle Maya, and Bryant Family lead the list of fashionable North American auction wines in 1999. While Caymus Special Selection, Stags Leap Cask 23, Ridge Montebello, and Dunn Howell Mtn represent more venerable examples, the first three are produced in volumes larger than the CULT WINE size. Marcassin in Chardonnay and Turley in Zinfandel would be non-Cabernet examples in the fashionable category. Leonetti would be a non-CA Cab example. Nevertheless new candidates dot the horizon, and therein lies some of the gamesmanship. Whether or not auction demand increases, and whether or not appointment to the exalted ranks by Mr Parker is an actual requirement, remain to be seen. Examples of new candidates in the Cabernet field include names such as Vyd 29, Corison, Seavey, Paradigm, and Abreu.

Butterfield & Butterfield, because of their headquarters in San Francisco (www.butterfields.com) tend to have the broadest offering of CA cult wines in any given year. Christie's (www.christies.com) and Sotheby (www.sothebys.com) do large-volume auctions in several locations each year. Morrell & Co (www.winesbymorrell.com) and Acker-Merrill-Condit do regular wine auctions in NY. A prominent Internet auction site is winebid.com.   B.C.C.

Augusta, first approved AVA in the US (1980). It is a small one, with under 500 acres of vines, located entirely within St Charles Co, MISSOURI just west of St Louis. Bounded on the south by the Missouri River and on the north by a ridge of low hills, it is a strip of land whose south-facing slopes provide excellent drainage for the vines while also offering protection from the cold northern winds. The river to the south radiates its warmth onto the slopes, making them appreciably warmer in the winter. Just over 70% of the AVA is planted to French hybrids—Vidal, Seyval Blanc, and Chardonel predominantly—while 20% is planted to *Norton. As for vinifera, there are also a few acres of Chardonnay and the Bordeaux grapes found at MOUNT PLEASANT VYD.
                                                      P.W.F.

Aurore, or Seibel 5279, French hybrid whose early ripening makes it useful for blending in northeastern states.

AVA, common acronym for **American Viticultural Area**, a specific grape growing area delineated by the US's embryonic attempt to codify the use of geographic names on wine labels. The scheme is administered by BATF, a division of the US Treasury Dept. It is probably a mistake for anyone to draw comparisons too closely between this US system and *appellation contrôlée or any other European system.

Since 1978 BATF has allowed either approved AVAs or three descendingly sized geopolitical units (the whole country, a state, a county) to be shown as appellations of origin on US wine labels. No other general place names are permitted. The only

other place names that are allowed at all are specific vineyard names. The phrase 'American' on a label implies the grapes came from more than one state. The name of a state (eg California) would imply the grapes came from more than one county within that state. As an example, there are 59 counties in CA and 48 of them grow grapes. Counties are the smallest geopolitical unit which can be used as an appellation. Cities (i.e. municipalities) cannot be used as place names on wine labels. Grapes grown within a city's boundaries should use the county name instead.

ATF had approved 107 AVAs throughout the US in the first seven years of the program, as of the end of 1989, but only received petitions and approved 30 more in the next ten years (of which six were sub-appellations dividing up Napa Valley, and three more were in TX).

Anyone may petition for establishment of an AVA. Their application must include, among other things: (1) evidence the proposed name is recognized as referring to the area specified; (2) evidence relating to climate, soil, elevation, and physical characteristics which distinguish the viticultural features of the proposed AVA from surrounding areas; and (3) specific boundaries based on features which can be found on US Geological Survey maps. ATF appends the following caveat to all approved AVA applications: 'ATF does not wish to give the impression by approving a viticultural area that it is approving or endorsing the quality of the wine from this area.'

In all likelihood appellation of origin labeling regulations will eventually have a beneficial effect in the US because place names on wine labels are beginning to educate the American public about such salient issues as the justifiably greater cost of grapes from particular districts and the predictability of stylistic differences between wines from certain districts. The current AVA system, however, is being constructed piecemeal without any comprehensive overview nor long-term plan. That is one of the primary reasons Australian James Halliday cites the system's 'sheer irrationalities' in his *Wine Atlas of California* and American Bob Thompson calls the system 'mildly comic' in his.

There are five general drawbacks to the AVA system:

1. Inconsequential AVAs. Examples in CA include Willow Creek AVA in Trinity Co, Cole Ranch and Benmore Valley AVAs in Mendocino Co, Hames Valley in Monterey Co, and Lime Kiln Valley AVA in San Benito Co. These places contain no wineries and very few grapes. Such vines as do exist there are owned by one grower and sold to

one winery which does not use the AVA name on its label.

2. Official boundary descriptions. Sometimes AVA boundaries make viticultural sense, as when topographic features such as mountain tops, rivers, and elevation contour lines are used. Understandably, and useful from a consumer education standpoint, sometimes boundaries are drawn using easy to identify cultural features like roads. The problem occurs when an AVA boundary is officially described, as they frequently are, using arcane surveyors' references to a grid of rectangles artificially laid out on paper. This problem is so pernicious that few attempts have been made in the literature, even on CA wine, to actually draw maps of the existing AVAs. And all of those attempts have come up with slightly different results. Official BATF descriptions are published in the *US Congressional Record* as written narratives using a technique called MEETS AND BOUNDS. Apparently few of these descriptions have ever been reality checked. One actually reads, '. . . thence north in a southwesterly direction . . .'

3. Meaningless marketing umbrellas. Many AVAs are bigger than they should be for viticultural coherence simply because once the hearing procedure begins, all neighbors immediately outside the proposed borders petition for inclusion. BATF then makes compromises based on political expediency. Sometimes this problem is severe enough to twist the English language, as in the case of Napa Valley AVA. Most English speakers would assume the phrase Napa Valley, at its most expansive, refers to the Napa River watershed. BATF, nonetheless, approved an AVA named Napa Valley which is so large it might as well be Napa Co because it includes all the extremely hot valleys east of Napa which have historically shipped their grapes to Napa wineries. (See ALEXANDER VALLEY for another example where viticultural logic was suspended in favor of bureaucratic ease.)

4. Omission of some useful descriptive names. Because BATF does not initiate any AVA applications, many geographical references which are commonly used by people in the wine industry are not permitted on labels. HECKER PASS in Santa Clara Co, Ukiah Valley in Mendocino Co, and DIAMOND MOUNTAIN in Napa Co are a few CA examples. Perhaps the most illustrative one from CA is CENTRAL VALLEY. Although that is where most of the grapes have been grown historically, no one wants to petition for the right to use it on a label because it has come to signify *jug wine status. Other useful geographic information not approved for

label use would be *greater* specificity than that of existing AVAs. For instance, the western portion of SANTA YNEZ VALLEY AVA versus the eastern portion.

5. Overlapping AVAs. One of the most confusing aspects of the US appellation system is BATF's passive failure to do anything about incongruities along the borders of overlapping, contiguous, or neighboring AVAs. Within Napa Valley the vintners themselves are attempting a cohesive, unusually logical program to divide the valley into sub-AVAs. In San Benito Co, by contrast, the MT HARLAN AVA overlaps the Lime Kiln AVA on one side, but is separated from the San Benito AVA on another side by 200 ft of elevation contour. These discrepancies might be understandable if the region had a thousand years of viticultural history enflaming local growers' prejudices. Mt Harlan, however, only has one winery-grower, and he has been there less than 30 years.

The area around the town of Healdsburg in northern SONOMA CO is worse. Alexander Valley AVA, Russian River AVA, and Chalk Hill AVA all overlap in one particular spot of about 200 acres. It so happens this spot is also included in the Sonoma Coast AVA, which SONOMA-CUTRER winery pushed through the bureaucracy, and in the Northern Sonoma AVA which GALLO pushed through because label regulations require a winery and a vineyard to be in the same AVA for the winery to put Estate Bottled (see US LABEL REGULATIONS) on the label. Add the umbrella North Coast AVA, plus the Sonoma Co and CA state geopolitical appellations which need no AVA approval, and you have eight different appellations under which these few hundred acres of grapes may go to market. As James Halliday put it, 'The intellectual nonsense this makes of the system really needs no elaboration.'

B.C.C.

AxR1, rootstock promoted widely in CA from the 1960s to the mid-1980s, primarily for its productivity. Its parentage is a cross between a vinifera variety called Aramon and a rupestris variety called Ganzin. UC *Davis is often accused of insisting throughout the era of this rootstock's popularity that AxR1 was resistant to *phylloxera, although UC professor A. J. *Winkler's classic textbook *General Viticulture* published in 1962 states of AxR1, 'That its resistance to phylloxera is not high has been demonstrated in other countries.' At its zenith, a majority of CA vines were planted on AxR1 rootstock. In the early 1980s, however, phylloxera infestations were discovered in Napa Valley vineyards planted on AxR1 roots. UC Davis called these phylloxera a 'newly expressed biotype B.' Many fingers were pointed. In Napa Valley alone the financial impact was estimated to be in excess of half a billion dollars.

B.C.C.

Babcock Vyd, SANTA BARBARA CO winery located on a bench 50 ft above the valley floor only 2 mi from the town of Lompoc, a premier example of the cool climate conditions in this westernmost section of the SANTA YNEZ AVA, and quite atypical for CA. The soil of the vineyard is light colored, shallow, and sandy, with very little organic matter. It drains well and may be potassium deficient because the pH of grapes grown here is astonishingly low. Nothing impedes the maritime influence. Fog and wind are common, but frost is not. Positioning on the bench is important. Vines grown in the deeper soils of the valley below produce big crops, but cannot ripen them in such a cold climate. Other benchland growers nearby include Rancho Dos Mundos Vyd half a mile to the south and west, and Rancho San Antonio Vyd which lies between Babcock and Vandenberg Air Force Base, the rocket launching facility on the coast which puts many of the US satellites into orbit.

Brian Babcock had recently graduated from high school and was considering business school in 1982 when AU BON CLIMAT winery purchased some of Babcock's Chardonnay grapes. Flabbergasted by the ripe fruit and low pH, Clendenen and Tolmach designated the wine as their Reserve bottling. They sold it all in a matter of weeks for $20 a bottle. Babcock decided then and there to study enology at UC *Davis instead.

In 1984 the Babcocks built a barn on their property with a bedroom and a kitchen. The winery was subsequently annexed to that structure, a freestanding warehouse was added in 1988, and more space was added in 1997. They produced 15,000 cases in 1998, and hope gradually to grow to 30,000 cases. The biggest part of their volume is Chardonnay, with the top of that range being called Grand Cuvée. It is heavily oaked to complement the wine's hard acid and powerful flavor. Grapes come in anywhere from 21.5°B to 23.0°B, but always at 3.05 pH. The components need bottle age to harmonize.

Babcock's Gewürztraminers and Rieslings have improved steadily over the years. Both get a little time in older barrels and are then blended with unfermented juice to help balance their searing acidity. The top wine of the range though, is a unique Sauvignon Blanc bottled under a separate name, Eleven Oaks. In this case the site's extraordinary flavor intensity seems less abrasive and more primal—think tom toms as opposed to snare drums. The acid is still very strong, but it is more naturally subsumed into the earthy, capsicum, and gunsmoke varietal flavors. At the same time, the extensive oak treatment adds a dimension which pulls the flatter Sauvignon Blanc flavors into a cohesive focus, rather than competing with the already pointed flavors found in underripe Chardonnay. **B.C.C.**

BAC stands for blood alcohol content, expressed as a percentage by volume. It is the figure used to determine the presumption of intoxication in drunk driving cases. Throughout the US motorists stopped by a police officer and suspected of drunk driving have a choice whether or not to submit to a BAC test. If they refuse, their driving privileges may be automatically suspended. If they choose to comply, a breath, blood, or urine analysis may be conducted. Individual states may set their own limits for the presumption of intoxication. In most states that limit used to be some exact point between 0.10 to 0.15%, but since the mid-1980s a great many states have acquiesced to the federal demand for a 0.08% standard. Since 1997 there has been political agitation by groups such as Mothers Against Drunk Driving (MADD) to reduce the standard further to 0.05%. **B.C.C.**

bacteriophage, viruses that attack bacteria. They are important in wine production because certain bacteriophage can attack strains of lactic acid bacteria that perform *MLF. When this happens, the bacteria are killed off by the bacteriophage and the MLF is incomplete. Bacteriophage are very strain specific. They can attack some strains of *Oenococcus* (formerly known as *Leuconostoc*) but not others. Wines that undergo partial MLF due to bacteriophage activity often contain other lactic acid bacteria that are resistant to the bacteriophage and may continue the fermentation at a later date. If the later date is after bottling, MLF occurs in the bottle and the quality of the wine is diminished. See Microbiology essay, p 39.

R.S.

bag-in-a-box, packaging technology called *cask* in Australia, where almost half the wine sold employs it. Not as popular in America, where it was historically easier for the industry to employ large format, 3 or 4 l glass bottles, but still responsible for about 20% of the wine sold. Three companies dominate the field: Franzia is the brand leader at about 45 million gal; followed by GALLO and CANANDAIGUA. The technology is used virtually exclusively for the least expensive *jug wines from CA's CENTRAL VALLEY. The wine is held in a collapsible, somewhat elastic, food-grade polymer container inside a rigid cardboard box. Standard size is 5 l, although bigger sizes are frequently made available to restaurants and some 3 l versions are produced for states such as FL which do not allow bigger sizes. An on-off valve in the form of a spout protrudes through the side of the cardboard box providing service of any amount at a time, eg a single glass. The box is frequently placed in one's refrigerator, allowing gradual consumption over a period of weeks. As wine is removed through the spout, the polymer bag shrinks. Thus air, which would spoil the wine through *oxidation over time, is not allowed to enter the compartment containing the wine. Despite its image of mediocre quality, the technology is quite sound and resourceful. It has made Chillable Red a big category for Franzia. If applied to top quality wine, it would reduce retail cost attributable to individual 750 ml packaging, which is considerable. But there are severe doubts about both medium- and long-term durability. In Britain bag-in-boxes are date stamped, and several studies have shown that once the tap is breached, the wine inside starts slowly deteriorating. **B.C.C.**

Bailly, winery which has been producing wines from grapes grown in MINNESOTA since 1977 when lawyer, David Bailly, decided to apply the knowledge he compiled touring the vineyards of Europe and set up shop just outside the Twin Cities. Currently his daughter, Nan, runs the winery. She farms 12 acres of grapes, mainly Foch, Millot, and Frontenac, as well as buying from other MN growers. Her fruity, Beaujolais-style Marechal Foch is immediately drinkable, while the more structured, Rhône-like Léon Millot needs a bit of bottle age.

P.W.F.

Barboursville Vyds. With 126 acres of *vinifera, Barboursville is one of VIRGINIA's largest wineries at 14,500 cases produced annually. It is owned by Zonin, a large wine producer from *Gambellara in northeastern Italy. Barboursville is in the MONTICELLO AVA, located just east of the intersection of Routes 20 and 33, on the property of the ruins of Governor James Barbour's early 19th-century mansion. Barboursville was one of the first VA wineries to plant an appreciable quantity of vinifera grapes in 1976. Gabriele Rausse, Barboursville's first winemaker, grafted and sold many vinifera vines to new VA vineyards. Under the winemaking skill of Italian native Luca Paschina, Barboursville has won the VA Governor's Cup (for their 1988 Cabernet Sauvignon), expanded their product line to 21 items, and initiated plantings of Italian grape varieties in VA with Barbera, Sangiovese, Pinot Grigio, and Malvaxia (sic).

Barboursville has gained a reputation for clean, aromatic, fresh white wines, particularly Riesling, Pinot Grigio, Traminer Aromatico, Sauvignon Blanc, and Phileo, a proprietary blend of highly scented white vinifera grapes. Cabernet Franc (in a fresher style than the oaked Cabernet Sauvignon) and a sparkling wine are consistently good. In recent years, their regular and reserve Chardonnay and Cabernet Sauvignon have won awards in VA and elsewhere. The winery is particularly proud of its spacious 'Tuscan hall' tasting room, a draw for tourists.

R.G.L.

BATF, US Bureau of Alcohol, Tobacco and Firearms, often merely called **ATF**. This curious agglomeration of portfolios is a department of the US Treasury, but its mandate goes far beyond collection of taxes. Since it was charged with enforcement of Prohibition during the years between 1918 and 1933, many Americans associate the agency with Elliot Ness, its head during that period, who was subsequently lionized by the popular TV series *The Untouchables*. The image of incorruptible warriors against organized crime was, however, peculiar to the Prohibition era. Today that role would be played by the US Justice Dept: 'G-men' as opposed to 'Revenooers.' Nevertheless

ATF's role in the regulation of firearms (and explosives) sometimes puts its employees into controversial situations, and occasional firefights, such as the infamous seige of the Branch Davidian compound at Waco, TX, in 1993.

Reconciling those activities with ATF's role in the licensing of wineries, the approval of AVAs, and decisions about what may or may not appear on US wine labels is grist for a great deal of sarcastic humor within the wine industry. It should be noted, however, that wine label regulation was a portfolio eagerly sought for many years by various Directors of the US Food & Drug Administration, a division of the US Health Dept. For whatever reason that shift in responsibility was vigorously opposed by the major wine industry trade organizations. One must suppose that opposition derived from a fear by CA's largest wineries (the dominant decision-making force on trade organization boards) of the ingredient labeling proposals put forth by ambitious FDA administrators. It is also clear that wine and spirits executives would rather deal with a cumbersome and occasionally tyrannical bureaucracy they know, than with a bureaucracy they see as being sympathetic to NEO-PROHIBITION activists in the US.   B.C.C.

Baxter's Vyd was started by Emile Baxter, an Icarian whose group moved to Nauvoo, ILLINOIS, in 1849. The Icarians were a group of semi-Utopian followers of the philosopher Étienne Cabet, a Burgundian lawyer, teacher, and writer. Evidently they were too much for the French. The sect left, settled first in TX, and then, after the Mormons departed from the colony they had begun at Nauvoo, the Icarians came to take their place. In 1857 Baxter planted his first vineyard. He and his family made wines there from grapes growing along the Mississippi River in far western IL. His sons extended the operations until Prohibition forced them into a grape selling business only. At Repeal, the winery was bonded making it the state's first. Today, it is run by Callan (Kelly) Logan, Baxter's great-great grandson, and his wife Brenda.

P.W.F.

Bay Area, San Francisco, CALIFORNIA region composed of the counties contiguous to San Francisco Bay, i.e. in clockwise order from the north end of the Golden Gate Bridge which spans the mouth of the Bay: Marin, Sonoma, Napa, Solano, Contra Costa, Alameda, Santa Clara, Santa Cruz, San Mateo, and San Francisco (which is both a county and a municipality). The phrase Bay Area is generally employed to

denote the greater metropolitan market, which numbers about 7 million people. San Francisco itself has a resident population of only about 700,000. San Jose, at the south end of the Bay, is presently the largest municipality.

The opening of San Francisco Bay onto the Pacific Ocean is quite small compared to the size of the bay behind it. Given the dense fog frequently found in that spot, it is not at all difficult to visualize how European ships could sail up and down the Pacific coast, hugging the shoreline, starving, and desperate for a safe landfall which would allow them to reprovision, for almost 250 years without sighting one of the planet's finest natural harbors. The Bay was not discovered by European settlers until early Nov 1769 and then, by Gaspar de Portolá, on an overland expedition from San Diego.

Technically a large estuary, the topographical feature which makes San Francisco Bay special is the fertile, protected manner in which so many different ecosystems mesh together within a short, convenient distance. In 1770 it was supporting the densest concentration of Amerindians in the hemisphere, all living peacefully as hunter-gatherers without the need for either settled agriculture or warfare, although both were clearly known to them through contact with outside trading partners. By the end of the 1970s agriculture had come and gone in the region, pushed by urbanization outside the immediate confines of the Bay to a greenbelt of exterior valleys and coastal flatlands on the margins of the greater Bay Area.

The region is stereotypically known for a broadminded tolerance which dates to the *gold rush era. Detractors joke, 'If you could tilt the US by lifting Long Island, everything loose would roll into San Francisco.' Similar to Paris, the Bay Area has long been a magnet for bohemian, creative individuals such as Mark Twain, Ambrose Bierce (*Devil's Dictionary*), Robert Louis Stevenson, America's best early photographers, Jack London, Upton Sinclair, Dashiell Hammett (*Maltese Falcon*), the Beatnik poets, Ken Kesey (*One Flew over the Cuckoo's Nest*), and 1960s rock musicians such as the Grateful Dead and Janis Joplin. In the 1970s it was Gay Liberation, and today it is the multimedia explosion of electronic publishing and the Internet.

The Bay Area's reputation as a restaurant mecca dates to the gold rush as well. The extraordinary mix of people who arrived in a very short time had only one thing in common: they were overwhelmingly male. There was a huge demand for prepared food. There was also a large market for drugs, sex, alcohol, and laundry services. Even 35 years later in the 1880s there were 1,400 entries under the heading 'Liquor Stores' in a San Francisco business directory, and 600 entries under the heading 'Restaurants.' The population at that time was barely over 200,000. (See DINING HABITS.)

Another feature which distinguishes this region from others in CA is the presence of two universities perennially ranked in the top five among all US institutions of higher learning. Stanford and UC Berkeley are not just badges of Bay Area honor. More importantly, their research facilities and inventive capacities are the engines which drive cutting edge, high technology industries in the local area, and thus attract entrepreneurial venture capitalists. It is no coincidence that CA's wine industry is scientifically dynamic and extremely well financed by worldwide standards. Profits and experience from the electronics, computer, bio-tech, medical, and defense engineering industries have all flowed at one time or another into northern CA's winelands.

The WAREHOUSE WINERY phenomenon is strong in the Bay Area. There are many warehouse districts naturally air-conditioned by marine air flow from the Bay. There is also a long tradition of home winemaking dating back to the waves of Italian immigrants who settled as fishermen in San Francisco while sending their cousins to plant vines in the fertile savannas surrounding the Bay. Return-to-the-land counterculture movements repopularized the concept. Three home wine and beer making supply stores existed in Berkeley for 25 years from the mid-1960s. Appropriately enough, the most influential of the bunch was called Wine & The People. Proprietor Peter Brehm initiated many winemakers (some of whom eventually turned pro) all over North America with his annual program shipping them frozen CA grapes.

One of the newest AVAs in the US is the **San Francisco Bay AVA**, approved in 1999, largely at the behest of WENTE Winery located in LIVERMORE VALLEY. The AVA boundaries generally coincide with the Bay Area counties south of the Golden Gate and Carquinas Straits bridges. Although there is some expediency in the AVA for wine writers, and an argument can be made for some degree of marine air influence throughout the AVA, the primary motivation for Wente was to be able to legally link their name with that of San Francisco, rather than less prestigious Livermore, when selling to the 105 international markets they have penetrated in the last decade.

MARIN CO

Visually captivating, Marin straddles the headlands which separate the Pacific Ocean from San Francisco Bay north of the Golden Gate Bridge. It is one of the wealthiest counties in America yet almost militantly New Age oriented. Rich hippies, however oxymoronic that may sound, is an apt description. There is some dairy farming, but calling this area rural is a stretch of the language; almost everyone supports their life-style with outside income.

Historically, Marin Co has always been considered too cold for grapes, and there are no approved AVAs there. This conventional wisdom is being challenged though, and it is not surprising that experimental vineyards are beginning to pop up in Marin. The vast majority of tourists intent on visiting Napa or Sonoma drive through Marin at the beginning and end of their journey. The resident population of Marin has precisely the demographics which typify high-end American wine drinkers (see Wine and the American Consumer essay, p 1): young, white, well educated, wealthy, and employed in an urban area. It is easy to see why Marin Co residents are stereotyped as the 'brie and white wine set' by political pundits seeking a contrast to beer drinking groups in the South or whiskey and cigar crowds in the northern Midwest.

The oldest current vineyard in Marin Co is Pacheco Ranch. Situated in the lee of 2,000 ft Mt Tamalpais, Pacheco Ranch is also the second oldest Spanish land grant in CA continuously occupied by the recipient's family. Juan Pacheco came to CA with De Anza through what is now NM. Juan's son Ignacio was a soldier at the Presidio in San Francisco. They owned the nearby Bull Tail Ranch as well, which was sold in the mid-1980s to film maker George Lucas (*Star Wars*) for his production studio.

As in neighboring SONOMA CO to the north, the sheep and dairy ranchers of western Marin today find themselves at a turning point. Their land is worth a lot of money, although not for the production of wool, milk, or cheese. They are constantly buffeted between environmentalists and developers. Winegrapes provide a very attractive new direction in this milieu. Several small vineyards have been planted in the hills southeast of Tomales Bay since 1995.

NOTABLE PROPERTIES

Kalin, warehouse winery owned and operated by Dr Terrence Leighton and his wife Françoise. Dr Leighton is a microbiology professor at UC Berkeley. Kalin has long specialized in sourcing grapes from old vine-

yards, then conducting lengthy fermentations using strains of yeast specially bred to proceed slowly. The results are always deeply flavorful wines with extraordinary ageing properties. Among their best are dry Semillons made from the El Mocho Vyd in Livermore first planted in the 1870s using cuttings from Ch d'*Yquem.

Thackrey, Sean, winery located north of Bolinas on the Marin coast. Thackrey does not own any vines, but he certainly is not in an industrial park either. He might be this book's lone entry under 'outdoor wineries.' Raised in Hollywood, Thackrey makes wines of epic proportion. Based on grape varieties, he qualifies as a *Rhône Ranger, but that is something of a technicality. It does not matter much which grape varieties Thackrey uses, or really even where he gets them, the operative point is he wrings every ounce of flavor and extract from them, then overlays the whole seething brew with his distinctive barrel treatment. Thackrey wines are in the wood for anywhere from eighteen months to four years. Like body piercing, this style has its fans, and they are committed.

Thackrey produces about 2,000 cases annually. His Syrah, called Orion, is usually the pick of the litter because it retains a substantial whack of fruit to help balance the weight of the wine. His Mourvèdre, called Taurus (Thackrey, like many of his neighbors in Bolinas, is an astrologer), is not as polished in the tannin department as the Syrah. A Petite Sirah, called Sirius, is coarser still. The lightest-bodied item in Thackrey's range, and the most affordable, is a blend of bits and pieces called Pleiades, which often contains some Grenache.

See SONOMA CO, NAPA VALLEY, DELTA (for Solano Co), and LIVERMORE (for Contra Costa Co).

ALAMEDA CO

The urban East Bay including Oakland and Berkeley. Or Berserkly as it has been affectionately called since the Free Speech Movement of the 1960s, is a world marching to its own drummer. There are 40,000 students at any given time in the university. Their influence, and the ethic of unfettered ideas, permeates the community. It is known as the Bay Area's gourmet ghetto because so many marvelously creative culinary professionals started there in bargain priced establishments before moving on to high-end acclaim in white tablecloth districts of San Francisco. Kermit Lynch, the man who pioneered US import of second tier French regional wines such as the *Loire and *Provence, is headquartered there.

NOTABLE PROPERTIES

Edmunds St John. Steve Edmunds was a wine salesman who started a warehouse winery in Berkeley, but he also specialized in painstaking investigation to turn up valuable vineyard sources. Like the others of his ilk, he is often frustrated to see his best vineyard sources snatched away by big business competitors jealous of his success, and alerted to the vineyards' value by tasting an Edmunds St John wine. He makes about 5,000 cases a year in partnership with his wife Cornelia. Most items are 300- to 500-case lots. Edmunds St John is known as a quality producer of *Rhône grape varieties, particularly the Syrah he sources from Durell Vyd in southern SONOMA VALLEY. His Zinfandels are fine as well, and he is presently developing property of his own in AMADOR CO. Les Côtes Sauvages is the proprietary name for Edmund St John's southern Rhône-style blend. It is usually about equal parts Grenache and Mourvèdre with 25% Syrah. It combines fruitiness with a gamey note.

See ROSENBLUM.

See also SANTA CLARA CO, the DELTA (for Contra Costa Co), and SANTA CRUZ MTNS AVA (for Santa Cruz Co and San Mateo Co).

B.C.C.

Beamsville Bench. The NIAGARA ESCARPMENT in ONTARIO, which is the same precipice over which Niagara Falls tumbles on the Canadian border with upstate NY, was once the shoreline of an immense lake out of which the five Great Lakes eventually formed. Its abrupt cliff is about 250 ft in height, composed of several layers laid down over a period of 20–5 million years. In the central part of the NIAGARA PENINSULA, the Escarpment forms two broad terraces called the Beamsville Bench that slope gently towards Lake Ontario. Its location between the lake and the escarpment, its elevation, and its sandy-loam soils together form a particularly successful mesoclimate for wine-growing.

L.F.B.

Beaulieu Vyds, winery started in NAPA VALLEY at the turn of the century by Georges de Latour who had moved there to pursue the cream of tartar business. By 1918 his 300,000 gal capacity and his 240 acres of vineyards made Beaulieu the largest premium producer in Napa. Moreover Latour had parlayed his relationship with the Archdiocese of San Francisco into a national distribution system for sacramental wine which would successfully carry his winery through the dark ages of Prohibition. Quality control and stability problems on his national shipments of these sweet wines were the moti-

vation for Latour to hire André *Tchelistcheff in 1938, two years before Latour himself died. Under Tchelistcheff's guidance Beaulieu's product mix changed and their Georges de Latour Cabernet, universally called BV Private Reserve, emerged to become CA's most famous wine.

Beaulieu was sold in 1969 to the consumer marketing company Heublein, now called United Vintners & Distillers (UDV) and a division of Diageo of which Guinness, Burger King, and Pillsbury are some other divisions. Beaulieu had grown to 1 million cases as of 1998 including several lower priced lines such as Beautour.

In the 1980s BV was making 20,000 cases of Private Reserve Cabernet. Prior to the *phylloxera scare in Napa, and primarily because their image was so tied to Cabernet Sauvignon, they decided to launch an experiment with *clonal selections of Cabernet. They grafted fourteen clones into one of the Rutherford Bench vineyards and fermented those batches separately for seven years before narrowing the study to three or four clones they liked best: a low yielder named Jackson (UCD 6) after an abandoned 1880 agricultural station in the Sierras where it had been found; a better yielder named Mendoza (UCD 4) for its source in Argentina; and the clone(s) planted in 80% of CA vineyards variously called Mirassou, Wente, or Concannon (UCD 7 or 8). Starting in the early 1990s these clones were used to gradually replant the BV PR vineyards. In 1998 only 12,000 cases of BV PR were made, and it will take another eight years before they can get back to their 20,000-case goal. In 1990 and 1991 5% of Merlot was tried in the blend, but that experiment was ended as the increased complexity of the Clones #6 and #4 began to play a larger part in the wine. André Tchelistcheff came back to work at Beaulieu, as a 90-year-old consultant, from 1991 through 1994. On the master's recommendation, winemaker Joel Aiken departed from the BV PR tradition of using exclusively AMERICAN OAK barrels. Today the mix is about half French oak, half American oak. Depending on the characteristics of the vintage, from 70 to 100% new oak is employed. BV PR is quintessentially old-style CA Cabernet, which is to say ripe with plum and unlit pipe tobacco smells, with great impact rather than equivocating complexity, and a background rigidity which gives the wine length in the mouth and the integrity for long bottle maturation. Its track record as an ageing candidate is unassailable, going back to 1936. Even today many connoisseurs consider the 1958 vintage to be the very best in vertical comparisons.

B.C.C.

Bedell Cellars, is located at the center of Long Island's NORTH FORK wine district, in NEW YORK state; a small producer with one of the area's biggest reputations. Perhaps more than any other winery, Bedell raised Merlot to the forefront of Long Island viniculture during the 1980s, which in turn lifted the fledgling district into the world wine arena. Bedell Merlot remains a benchmark wine for the area in both its regular and reserve bottlings, which together account for more than a third of the winery's 8,500-case output. Both wines age in AMERICAN OAK, all new for the Reserve, which comes from a 2-acre block producing exceptionally rich fruit. The use of American rather than French barrels underscores Bedell's reliance on the vineyard and intense fruit character rather than an expensive cellar. Owner-winemaker Kip Bedell has no formal training, an anomaly among first-tier Long Island winemakers.

Chardonnay is Bedell's second wine, showing a much more dramatic difference between a stainless steel fermented regular bottling and a French oak fermented reserve. The 30-acre vineyard surrounding the winery includes smaller acreage of Cabernet Sauvignon and Cabernet Franc (blended into a *Meritage wine), Riesling, and Gewürztraminer. About 40% of production is sold CELLAR DOOR, the rest through a distributor in NY and NJ.

R.F.

Benmarl Vyds, a pioneer in the renaissance of the small NEW YORK farm based wineries, occupies a terraced hillside on the Hudson River 50 mi north of NEW YORK CITY. Grapevines have grown here continuously for two centuries but did not sprout a winery until illustrative artist Mark Miller (now at CHADDSFORD) established a Burgundian-inspired estate in 1971. In his own words it started as 'a whimsical thing' and has retained a certain capricious style. Early struggles with indifferent wholesalers and state regulators led Benmarl to set up a club of 'wine subscribers,' a prototype for the US wine industry. One member was the governor of New York, who endorsed Miller's lobbying efforts for a Farm Winery Law (1976) that opened the regulatory doors for the state's small winemakers.

From a highwater mark of 185 acres, Benmarl's vineyard has ebbed well under 30 acres as the winery takes on an air of nostalgia. An early proponent of the French hybrid varieties, Benmarl has kept the faith, focusing on dry Seyval Blanc and Baco Noir. Wines are sold retail only at the winery, primarily to club members.

R.F.

Benziger, winery in Sonoma Mtn AVA above SONOMA VALLEY largely responsible for launching the *fighting varietal concept in America with their GLEN ELLEN brand in 1980. That brand was sold to United Vintners and Distillers for a reported $40 million in the early 1993 to pay federal estate taxes after Bruno Benzinger died in 1989. Today the Benziger family runs a relatively smaller and more prestige-oriented winery under their own name. They made 180,000 cases in 1998 on a beautifully manicured 65-acre estate next to Jack London State Park. They give well-regarded tours and have produced a number of noteworthy wines in their creatively labeled Imagery series, which accounts for 6,000–7,000 cases annually.

B.C.C.

Beringer, one of the oldest, biggest, and best wineries in NAPA VALLEY, or in North America for that matter. Beringer was started in 1876 by two German brothers from Mainz. The ornate Rhine House they had built on Hwy 29 just north of St Helena has been a landmark for over a century. Fine quality wine at Beringer is, however, a recent development attributable to the Swiss corporation Nestlé which purchased the winery in 1971. They hired veteran winemaker Myron Nightingale, who gradually improved the overall standards while introducing a couple of superlative items, including the Private Reserve Cabernet and Chardonnay, and *botrytized wines made either from Riesling or from Semillon and/or Sauvignon Blanc in the manner of *Sauternes.

The botrytis project was seminal work in CA for which Nightingale and his wife Alice deserve complete credit. They had first experimented with Sauternes-style wine at Cresta Blanca winery in Livermore in 1959 by inducing the botrytis fungus to grow on the grape clusters in the laboratory. The botrytized Semillons at Beringer have about 14% alcohol and taste much more honeyed, from the influence of the fungus, than they do of grapes. The botrytized Rieslings, however, have 7–8% alcohol and intense apricot aromas which blend with the honeyed note very successfully.

Nightingale also trained Beringer's present winemaker, Ed Sbragia, who took the reins in 1985 and proved his mettle by raising the quality of the top-end Cabernets and Chardonnays at least another notch or two in very short order. His 1986 Private Reserve Cabernet was *Wine Spectator*'s Best Wine of the Year in 1991, and his 1994 Private Reserve Chardonnay won the same honor in 1996.

In 1995 Beringer owned 2,000 acres of vineyard in Napa and just over the county line to the north in Sonoma's Knight's Valley AVA. They were making over 2 million cases a year, 40% of which was White Zinfandel. That was when Nestlé sold the company to a group of investors calling themselves Beringer Wine Estates (BWE). That group also owns MERIDIAN in San Luis Obispo Co, Ch Souverain and Ch St Jean in Sonoma Co, the Napa Ridge brand (which actually uses grapes from all over CA), and the Stags Leap Winery in Napa. In aggregate the group has over 16 million gal of production capacity, putting them well up into America's top ten wine producers for volume. Beringer itself increased 25% in both acreage and volume between 1995 and 1999.

B.C.C.

Bernardus, winery tucked deep into the wild recesses of CA's CARMEL VALLEY some 30 mi from the coast. They produce 50,000 cases a year. The winery site was originally planted to Chardonnay by local clothier Robert Talbott, but it is mostly mudstone and not a particularly successful location. Bernardus owns 50 acres on a south-facing hillside ampitheater much closer to the coast (and civilization) in a subdistrict of the Carmel Valley called Cachagua Valley. They planted, mostly Cabernet Sauvignon and Merlot, in 1990 using a fairly dense spacing: 1,660 vines per acre. Interestingly they chose to plant the vines on their own roots. Calling the wine from this vineyard Marinus, they have produced elegant, light-bodied wines to date with very mild tannins and subdued cherry/plum aromas. Very pleasant drinking and smoothly textured, even if hard to notice next to the breathless, expensively produced literature the winery employs for promotion.

Bernardus is owned by Ben Pon, whose father made a lot of money exporting the first Volkswagon Beetles to the US. Ben Pon grew up in Amersfoort, Holland. He drove Porsches six times in the Le Mans road race and competed for the Dutch in skeet shooting during the 1992 Olympics. His company owns the oldest *wijnkoper* distribution house in the Netherlands. In 1999 Pon and his wife Ingrid opened their 57-suite Bernardus Lodge and Marinus Restaurant on Carmel Valley Rd 9 mi inland from the coast in the town of Carmel Valley.

B.C.C.

Biltmore Estate, located in scenic Asheville in the BLUE RIDGE MTNS of NORTH CAROLINA, Biltmore Estate is the fully restored and operational summer retreat of the Vanderbilts, built in the late 1880s. It is one of the most regal estate wineries in the US. It is also one of the largest wineries in the SOUTH at 75,000 cases produced annually. Biltmore claims it is the most visited winery in the US, with 800,000 estate guests annually (although the Robert MONDAVI winery would presumably dispute this). The estate is situated on 8,000 acres which include formal and informal gardens, a 250-room 'French Renaissance château,' and a 90,000 sq ft modern winery built in 1985. Biltmore wines feature three label lines: the George Washington Vanderbilt premium vintage wines, Ch Biltmore vinifera varietals, and Biltmore Estate. Wines produced at Biltmore include varietal Merlot, Cabernet Sauvignon, Chardonnay, Fume Blanc, Riesling, Chenin Blanc, and MÉTHODE CHAMPENOISE sparkling wine.

Viticulture at Biltmore Estate began in 1971 under the direction of William A. V. Cecil, owner of the estate and grandson of the estate's founder, George Washington Vanderbilt. Originally planted with French hybrid grapes, the estate was gradually turned over to vinifera varieties by Cecil under the guidance of French winemaker and teacher of viticulture and enology, Philippe Jourdain. On his retirement in 1995, Jourdain was succeeded by the current winemaker Bernard Delille.

Biltmore Estate aptly demonstrates the dangers of vinifera cultivation in mountain elevations of the South. Night *frost is common as late as May 15, and vinifera vines are vulnerable to premature budding during unseasonally warm periods in Mar and Apr followed by a return to winter temperatures. As a result Biltmore has had to purchase out-of-state grapes to meet its large production. In an effort to thwart this recurrent problem, the estate has constructed a 35-acre lake near the vineyards (see *lake effect), as well as an overhead *sprinkler system.

While a winery in an estate such as Biltmore is worthy of special attention, recent samples of the Biltmore Estate wines revealed nothing of distinction. Of two méthode champenoise sparkling wines, the one with better chemistry and balance was made from 95% CA grapes (1993 vintage). The Vanderbilt Claret 1996, a meritage-style blend of Cabernet Sauvignon, Cabernet Franc, and Merlot, was made of 65% CA grapes and was unimpressive. A Cabernet Franc 1995, of 84% NC grapes was better, but undistinguished. However, the 1995 Biltmore Estate Sauvignon Blanc has performed well in competitions.

R.G.L.

blue laws, a form of local option regulations found in the US which are analogous to 'sin taxes.' In the case of alcohol these regulations usually take the form of restricted hours of sale.

Blue Ridge Mtns (see also APPALACHIAN MTNS). The upper Piedmont on the east slope of the Blue Ridge Mtns is an important region for quality viticulture in MD, VA, and NC (in central MD the range is known as the Catoctin Mtns). Good *air drainage, moderate elevation, moderately late budbreak, and complex soils combine to make this area one of the best in MID-ATLANTIC viticulture.   R.G.L.

Bonny Doon, appropriately sited in CA, but easily the most innovative winery on this or any other planet. It was perched for nearly two decades amongst the redwood trees on the ocean side of the SANTA CRUZ MTNS AVA close to the beautiful campus of UC Santa Cruz, which overlooks Monterey Bay from the north and claims the banana slug for its school mascot. Bonny Doon struggled to sell 10,000 cases a year to a largely cult following for nearly a decade before being discovered by the US wine press at the end of the 1980s. In the following decade, Randall Grahm's incendiary personality, along with his mischievous marketing gimmickry and the extraordinarily competent administrative hand of Gen Mgr Patrice Boyle, engineered meteoric growth. By the mid-1990s Bonny Doon was selling 85,000 cases. They did 150,000 cases in 1998 and expect to top 200,000 cases soon after they complete a planned move into much larger facilities in downtown Santa Cruz.

The signature of Randall Grahm's entrepreneurship has always been unfettered creativity. His headlong rush into new ideas leaves customers and audiences both dazzled and breathless. Hence it is impossible to delineate Bonny Doon's business progression in the space here available. Any summary though, should begin with Rhône varieties because, to quote Grahm, 'It's Rhônely at the top.' Bonny Doon helped pioneer this field in CA when they released Le Cigare Volant from the 1984 vintage. Grahm gets credit for identifying the old vineyards called *Mataro (a Spanish name) in CA as being the Mourvèdre variety from France. He started with a Châteauneuf-like wine which was 85% Grenache and 15% Mourvèdre. Over the years he has moved gradually to reduce the Grenache component (now around 40%), added 20–25% Syrah, and introduced 5–10% Cinsault. Cigare Volant has steadily improved under this program. Grahm found that Grenache was an alternate bearer, setting different sized crops in alternating years. So, the low production crops go into Cigare; the bigger production

crops into a line of *blush wines which Grahm once labeled with all the printing on the back of the label so that it had to be read through the pink liquid. He sold 20,000 cases of that wine.

Among the many other curiosity items Bonny Doon has produced at one time or another, two categories demand special mention. One is the dessert wine produced by *cryoextraction which Grahm calls Vin de Glacière. This is usually Muscat Canelli, but occasionally Malvasia Bianca. It is always rich with blossomy flavor and balanced with a plenitude of acid to take the edge off 10–15% *residual sugar. The other items are not wines at all. They are infusions made by extracting essence of fresh fruits in a grape distillate. Framboise is the most reliable and readily available. It is luscious, almost too concentrated, and half-empty bottles can sit corked for months without losing their intensity. A Cassis version is so concentrated it stains the glass.   B.C.C.

Boordy Vyds, established in 1945 by Philip and Joyce *Wagner, was the first post-Prohibition winery in MARYLAND. Mr Wagner made a significant contribution to eastern US viticulture by cultivating and making wine from French hybrid varieties. Others in NY, the Midwest, and elsewhere in the Mid-Atlantic followed suit, introducing the East to home-grown table wines which had more in common with the character of vinifera wines than with the *foxy American hybrids such as Concord.

Since 1980, Rob and Julia Deford have been carrying on the legacy that their friends began. Today Boordy Vyds is MD's second largest winery and is located in the Long Green Valley in northeastern Baltimore Co. Rob Deford is an enology graduate of *Davis, and although Boordy still produces French hybrids, exemplary Cabernet Sauvignon and Chardonnay also carry the Boordy label. The Chardonnay is a skillfully crafted wine with a well-balanced integration of fruit and oak and fresh acidity. Boordy's most noteworthy wine currently is their Grand Reserve Cabernet Sauvignon. The 1993 vintage, aged in American and French oak for 22 months, unfiltered and aged 13 months in the bottle, demonstrated fully mature fruit, supple tannins, smooth and delicate texture. Eighty per cent of the fruit came from the now-defunct Byrd Vyds near Frederick in the Catoctin hills, whose vineyard Rob Deford declares was the best Cabernet vineyard in the state (it was razed for subdivision development). Unlike many large industry producers who use the phrase indiscriminately, Boordy has only released

two 'grand reserve' Cabernet wines in eighteen years; the second was a 1997 vintage. A Boordy original is their barrel fermented Seyval from 30-year-old vines, which Rob Deford likes to claim was the first commercially produced French hybrid aged *sur lie.

Boordy continues to lead the MD industry, and in 1998 doubled its capacity by acquiring the fruit from 16 acres of vineyard belonging to Catoctin Winery (on South Mtn north of Frederick). The mature vinifera vines planted in 1974 will increase Boordy's production by half, to 15,000 cases, when the vineyard is operating at full capacity in the new century, and will contribute especially to Boordy's impressive Chardonnay and Cabernet wines. Boordy also sources grapes from elsewhere in the Catoctin Mtns and from the Eastern Shore. Thomas Burns is Boordy's winemaker.
                                    R.G.L.

Boskydel Vyd, first bonded winery in MI's LEELANAU PENINSULA AVA. Bernard (Barnie) Rink and his wife Suzanne established Boskydel in 1965 and began experimenting with French hybrid varieties from the start. Today his Soleil Blanc, a Seibel derivative, and his DeChaunac wines, especially the rosé, are palate pleasers.   P.W.F.

Boston, capital of MA and largest city in New England (greater metropolitan population of 3.5 million). Boston's retail wine market is dominated by large chain stores offering a very diverse selection from the world's vinicultural regions. It may be this breadth of inventory is enhanced by a relatively unique legal circumstance, which allows wholesale licenses and retail licenses to be owned by the same business entity, a situation prohibited by TIED HOUSE LAWS in all other American states save CA. European producers have traditionally dominated the Boston market, but somewhat less so in recent years. In keeping with its identity as the de facto capital of New England, Boston has been receptive to the appearance of regional southern New England wines. The annual Boston Wine Festival early each Feb is one of the US's major trade events.   R.F.

boutique wineries, phrase used in the 1970s in reference to small wineries, generally not widely distributed through retail stores, often selling at high prices with demand in excess of supply. The phrase was never much enjoyed by winemaker/owners who performed all the manual labor themselves because they felt it implied a sort of retirement hobby where financial outcome was unimportant. The phrase is losing currency today.

Brettanomyces, also called **Dekkera**, is a spoilage yeast that had been identified in must as far back as 1933 but did not come to the attention of North American winemakers until the mid-1970s in CA. Wine spoiled by Brettanomyces may have a vinegary 'horse,' 'barnyard,' or even 'manure' smell and about 20% has an aftertaste described as 'mousy.' The yeast has two properties that hampered the original discovery of the organism. The first is the organism is slow growing. Microbiological quality control in wineries usually involves spreading a sample of the wine on a petri plate containing the appropriate growth medium to culture the microorganisms present in the wine. These plates are usually examined after four or five days' incubation when most wine yeast colonies are visible. Brettanomyces is unusual because it grows so slowly that the small whitish colonies are not visible until the seventh or eighth day of incubation. Until the discovery of Brettanomyces, plates were usually discarded after five days, so the yeast avoided detection by many wine quality control labs.

The second unusual feature of Brettanomyces was its ability to grow using very low concentrations of nutrients. When the average red wine is *dry after finishing the primary fermentation, it contains about 4.5 g/l of the six carbon fermentable sugars glucose, fructose, and galactose plus the disaccharide trehalose which comes from yeasts which have undergone *autolysis (disintegration after death). This is not enough nutrient to sustain most wild yeast strains that grow in wine. There are several five carbon sugars left but the yeasts cannot ferment these. If an MLF occurs, the lactic acid bacteria ferment the five carbon sugars and the wine, if left in anaerobic conditions, is microbiologically stable and can be aged in a barrel. Brettanomyces, however, can grow on as little as 3 g/l fermentable sugar. If barrels are not cleaned routinely, the long barrel ageing prescribed for some red wines provides an ideal environment for the proliferation of Brettanomyces. Brettanomyces is not commonly found in the grape bloom microflora but is probably ubiquitous in winery equipment. Ironically, it is quite fastidious in its nutritional requirements.

The recognition of Brettanomyces in a wine, and an individual's preference or distaste for it, are controversial issues which can sharply divide judging panels.

See Microbiology essay, p 39.

R.S. & B.C.C.

British Columbia, the most westerly province in CANADA, is much better known for products of the forest than it is for produce of the vine, although grape growing and wine are not new to the area. For many years BC wines enjoyed considerable tax advantages over imports. Sweet local wines made with French and American hybrids were much less expensive than wines from CA or Europe. In 1987 NAFTA ended that protection, shaking up the industry in its wake. While there had been a mild interest in vinifera wines prior to NAFTA, the need to improve quality following NAFTA has induced the BC grape growing and wine industry to blossom since then. Using government assistance, old vineyards have been replaced with newer plantings (cf ONTARIO). As of 1999, BC had 43 wineries crushing grapes grown by over 130 growers on about 4,000 acres of vines.

BC has four designated Viticultural Areas (VA). The most westerly is VANCOUVER ISLAND. The most accessible to an urban population is the broad, glacially carved FRASER VALLEY which opens to the ocean at the city of VANCOUVER. East of the coastal mountains in the center of the province, OKANAGAN VALLEY is home to 95% of BC's grapes. SIMILKAMEEN VALLEY is more or less an offshoot of the Okanagan Valley to its west, surrounded by the abrupt mountains of the CASCADE RANGE. There is an air of excitement spawned by a wine culture emerging out of Vancouver and the neighboring province of Alberta, where cities like Calgary and Edmonton have well-heeled populations and a cosmopolitan world-view. Wine and food appreciation have taken a major leap forward in the last decade, and western Canadians are taking a proprietary interest in locally produced wines.

Grape growing here is not for the feeble though, nor for those light in the wallet. Okanagan land is seven times more expensive than land in eastern Washington over the US border, and plantable vineyards are scarce due to the limited benchland surrounding Okanagan Lake and competition from vacation properties. Large recent plantings have occurred on native Indian lands, or on lands previously under cultivation as orchards.

Much of today's industry was influenced by a group of grape variety studies: two from prior to 1987; one completed in 1992. Helmut *Becker, the renowned German viticulturalist, worked with the BC wine industry from 1977 to 1985 evaluating German varieties and viticultural techniques for BC conditions. Meanwhile John Vielvoye, horticulturist for the BC Dept of Agriculture,

completed and published his grape variety research. The 1992 study looked at Hungarian, French, and German varieties. The ultimate recommendation list was heavy on northern European varieties, but it also indicated certain warm sites might be able to ripen Merlot, Cabernet Franc, and Cabernet Sauvignon. This came as welcome news given the current market's fixation on those red varieties.

All Okanagan vineyards are irrigated. Approximately three-quarters of the vines are on grafted rootstock to protect from phylloxera and/or to encourage earlier ripening. Wines have occasionally to be *deacidified, because of either high acid vintages or vineyards.

Generally, BC wines tend to delicacy and possess a verve of flavor that is subtle and penetrating. These are wines that truly complement food, their naturally higher acidities framing flavors, although they are easily swamped by new oak. Some of the Germanic wines such as Ehrenfelser, Schönburger, or Kerner can make delicious light, intensely fruity aperitif wines. BC also produces remarkably concentrated ICEWINES and other LATE HARVEST styled wines from Riesling, Ehrenfelser, and Vidal.

The BC wine industry is governed by two different branches of government. The Ministry of Small Businesses, Tourism and Culture operates the Liquor Distribution Branch, which controls distribution in the provincial liquor stores that carry wine. The Ministry of the Attorney General oversees licensing and control through its Liquor Control and Licensing Branch. The Canadian Fruit and Inspection Agency plays a role in labeling regulations. The BC Wine Act of 1990 created a BC Wine Institute which oversees and promotes the wine industry, funded through the BC Dept of Agriculture. Matters of quality and appellation origin are handled by VQA, which has had some management problems in BC, entirely separate from its counterpart in Ontario. A federal umbrella entity called VQA Canada was formed in the late 1990s. R.A.I.

Brotherhood, winery 40 mi north of NEW YORK CITY in the HUDSON RIVER Valley. Brotherhood usually inserts 'America's Oldest' into the middle of its name, trumpeting its continuous operation since 1839. A cluster of stone and brick buildings underscored with a warren of vaulted cellars recall the winery's glory days for 100,000 visitors each year. They can sample from a large list of wines including a number of sweet, grapey, old-time *labrusca favorites, some flavored with fresh herbs and spices according to early 19th-century formulas. But new owners have begun shifting Brotherhood's production since the late 1980s toward dry table wines made from vinifera grapes.

Brotherhood's longevity is a testament to adaptability and an ear-to-the-ground attitude over the years, beginning with the first vintage when overplanting in the valley glutted the local table grape market. The winery made sacramental wines during Prohibition, fortified wines in the alcohol-thirsty days after Repeal, and lighter French hybrid table wines during the wine boom of the 1970s. All can still be found on the list. In the 1990s vineyards were established on Long Island with Bordeaux-blend varieties. Cabernet Sauvignon and Merlot are the standouts on Brotherhood's list, particularly for their good value.

Production under the Brotherhood label totaled about 50,000 cases in 1998, distributed in fourteen states and exported to Asia. The winery also sells substantial quantities of wine and hard cider in bulk and bottled to other wineries and private labelers, including a KOSHER line. R.F.

Bruce, David, man and CA winery. Inheritor of all that is eccentric and wild about the SANTA CRUZ MTNS, dermatologist David Bruce wore the mantle well for 30 years. He represents a lineage essential to wine in North America; that of the colorful personality popularizing a beverage which had not theretofore been part of the cultural fabric. Dr Bruce was able to accomplish this role because he is the antidote to wine's image as elitist, tradition bound, and proper. David Bruce was an apprentice of Martin Ray at MT EDEN. The current torch-bearer for this conceptual progression in the Santa Cruz Mtns, a group that has inspired generations of BAY AREA residents, would be Randall Grahm at BONNY DOON. To recognize the relationship between these people and the Santa Cruz Mtns is to begin to feel the 'sense of place' considered fundamental to wine appreciation by most Europeans, but conspicuously lacking in most American wine districts. In the Santa Cruz Mtns it is not a component of the soil; it is an attitude. With Dr Bruce in the 1970s that meant foraging wild mushrooms, an eye for younger women, and swinging from chandeliers during marketing trips to the east coast.

David Bruce built his winery in 1961 on the summit of the mountains which separate the city of San Jose from the city of Santa Cruz. His 15 acres of Pinot Noir and Chardonnay are at 2,200 ft of elevation and almost always above the fog line. David Bruce wines today are much more restrained than they were in the beginning when he did all the work himself. The only thing certain about a David Bruce wine from his first two decades was that it would have the highest standard deviation among scores at any blind tasting.

Chardonnay illustrates the winemaking style which created Dr Bruce's early reputation. True to his mentor, Bruce followed traditional Burgundian practices including lengthy SKIN SOAK, WILD YEAST fermentations in barrel, prolonged *sur lie ageing, and no *filtration. His ripe CA grapes always went through a spontaneous *MLF. The result was intensely yellow-gold wine, that smelled like butter oozing out of freshly baked caramel breakfast rolls, and body so thick the flavor would stick to the roof of your mouth. Reasonable people can argue about the virtues of such wine. In the America of Dr Bruce's youth, if these wines were women, they would have been called 'fast.' There is little doubt, however, that these Chardonnays moved the overall standard in a much more complex and entertaining direction. Dr Bruce also raised the standard for high-end price points several notches.

Less appreciated is Dr Bruce's legacy of tireless vineyard research. He began in the late 1950s poring over historical documents seeking to identify abandoned sites which had been artistically successful vineyards in the previous century. He resurrected Pinot Noir in the district and launched several oceanside experimental plots that blossomed into wineries owned by other people. He made LATE HARVEST Zinfandels from 80-year-old LODI vineyards that bowled consumers over with the trumpet-note force of their sheer 'berriness.' He even made a *White Zinfandel in the 1960s. *And* had the eminent good taste to drop that idea fifteen years before it became America's top selling varietal wine. B.C.C.

Bucks Co, a wealthy rural residential district in southeast PENNSYLVANIA. It contains many of the region's wineries and is situated north of PHILADELPHIA up to the traditional steel town Bethlehem. 'Our vines bud and grapes ripen one to three weeks earlier than higher elevation areas to the north and west,' says Jerry Forest of the county's Buckingham Valley Vyds, attributing this to the moderating influence of the nearby DELAWARE RIVER. R.G.L.

Buena Vista, winery in the Sonoma half of the CARNEROS AVA with 1,360 acres of vineyard producing 500,000 cases a year, including the Robert Stemmler and Haywood brands. In 1999 only 70,000 cases came from Carneros fruit, but 600 acres had been pulled out of Chardonnay and was in the process of being replanted to Cabernet and Merlot. Buena Vista is noteworthy because it helped pioneer the Carneros still wine industry, and is unique in its passion to prove the district's suitability for Cabernet Sauvignon and Merlot.

The winery name dates to 1857 when it was begun in the town of Sonoma by the very flash Agoston *Haraszthy. But after his brief, bright turn on the stage, fortunes declined steadily. Both winery and 400 acres of contiguous vineyards were moribund by the First World War. Purchased and resurrected in the 1940s by the Chairman of United Press Intl, the winery did quite well with its conveniently located cave tasting room during the early years of CA's wine revival. In 1979 a German company, A. Racke, bought the brand and the tasting room (but not the historic vineyards) and sent their youngish male scion and his new bride to manage the property. Marcus Moller-Racke moved production to Carneros, while Anne Moller-Racke began acquiring and planting vineyards. For nearly two decades reliable Chardonnay at modest prices has been the winery's reputation. The Merlot, however, is unique for CA and well worth examination. Ripening slowly in Carneros, it features many of the herbaceous notes one would expect from *right bank Bordeaux rather than CA and in warm vintages can have admirably mulberry-like characteristics. B.C.C.

Bully Hill Vyds, mid-sized winery in NY's FINGER LAKES district, which played a key role in rekindling the area's wine industry during the early 1970s. The winery sits high above Keuka Lake at the original homestead of the Taylor Wine Company, one of the area's early wine dynasties. Walter S. TAYLOR, grandson of that company's founder, opened his new winery here in 1970, surrounded by old family vineyards replanted to French hybrid varieties. Bully Hill has been the major proponent of hybrid varieties in the Finger Lakes and beyond, exploring the possibilities in blends and varietals and popularizing names like Seyval Blanc and Baco Noir. At the same time, the winery honors Finger Lakes tradition with a number of native grape wines, and more recently added Chardonnay and Riesling. A list of nearly four dozen wines leans toward residual sweetness; Bully Hill's mission is to make wine fun and accessible. Their colorful labels feature the often eccentric artwork of the owner. They also list the names of Bully Hill's Finger Lakes grape growers and vigorously promote the provenance '100 percent New York State,' an effort not necessarily applauded by area winemakers who see Bully Hill representing NY's past more than its future. Perhaps the greatest boost Bully Hill has given to NY wine is its role as a training ground for winemakers who have moved on to many other Finger Lakes wineries.

At over 200,000 cases annually, Bully Hill is the state's third largest winemaker; a distant third. The winery complex, with its restaurant and museum of 19th-century wine artifacts, is the Finger Lakes' busiest. Bully Hill wines are distributed in nineteen states.   R.F.

C

Cakebread, winery in the OAKVILLE section of California's NAPA VALLEY on the valley floor adjacent to Hwy 29. Begun in 1973 by Jack Cakebread, who was better known at the time for his photography of the Oakland Raiders football team, and whose financial ability to acquire a Napa retreat was abetted by the family auto body business. Nevertheless Cakebread winery was soon accorded artisan status rarely associated with football or with fender replacement. Son Bruce graduated from UC *Davis in 1978 to become the winemaker. Dense, buttery Chardonnays and rigid, long-lived Cabernets are the most sought after items. Neither are inexpensive and the venture is quite successful, selling nearly 50,000 cases a year nationwide. Replanting after *phylloxera has allowed the winery to introduce a number of new clones and rootstocks.

B.C.C

Calaveras Co, picturesque and remote, southernmost of the three important wine producing counties in California's SIERRA FOOTHILLS AVA. Mariposa Co is further south, second in line after Tuolomne Co, and it does have one winery and a few acres of vines, but it is not a significant player. Calaveras Co wine production is concentrated near the point where Hwy 4 intersects Hwy 49, adjacent to the villages of Angels Camp and Murphys. Sonora, in Tuolomne Co, is the closest town of any size. No AVA application has been made yet for this specific subdistrict. Although off the beaten path, Calaveras Co has seen a large amount of development during the 1990s. The lake at Twain Harte is named for writers Mark Twain (stories such as *Jumping Frog of Calaveras County*, as well as literary classics such as *Huckleberry Finn*) and Bret Harte (*Outcasts of Poker Flat*). Bear Valley ski resort sits at the end of Hwy 4, the Stanislaus River is well regarded in whitewater kayaking circles, Emigrant Wilderness is a popular backpacking destination, and the whole region serves as northern entrance for tourists visiting Yosemite National Park.

Calaveras Co vineyards are primarily planted at elevations from 1,500 ft to 2,400 ft. That makes these vineyards cooler than most in their immediate neighbor to the north, Amador Co, but not as cold as many in El Dorado Co, the third of the major Sierra Foothills producers. Calveras Co soils are interesting because on top they have the normally acidic, weathered volcanics common to the Sierra Foothills, but below they have a more alkaline subsoil with high carbonate content. At lower elevations where eroded soils can collect, this situation leads to somewhat greater vine vigor in Calveras Co than in either Amador or El Dorado.

NOTABLE PROPERTIES

Black Sheep, winery on the edge of Murphys making very respectable Zinfandel.
Stevenot, oldest operating winery in the district, making 40,000 cases. Barden Stevenot was raised in the region and became successful in real estate there. His vineyard is at 1,800 ft of elevation nestled in an extremely beautiful canyon. Despite a thoroughly professional winemaker and a significant investment in Dargaud & Jaegle barrels, the quality of the wines has never reached the level necessary to attract critical attention.

See also KAUTZ-IRONSTONE.   B.C.C.

Calera, California winery and vineyards which are the sole viticultural practitioners in the Mt Harlan AVA of San Benito Co. Mt Harlan is 2,400 ft high, and sits inland from the coast about 20 mi, but nevertheless overlooks Monterey Bay and the mouth of the Salinas Valley in next-door MONTEREY CO. Owner Josh Jensen's *raison d'être* is growing vines on *limestone as a means of following the Burgundian model. Whether or not this theory makes any sense in a sunny climate, on a site which receives very little rain, and none at all during the summer, is the subject of much conjecture. Few quibble, however, with the assertion that Calera is among the better makers of Pinot Noir in California.

Jensen grew up in an affluent suburb of Berkeley, CA, took an undergraduate degree in History from Yale, then a Masters in Anthropology from Oxford, where he rowed on the crew. He worked the 1970 crush at *Domaine de la Romanée-Conti and the 1971 crush at Domaine Dujac in Burgundy while traveling through France learning to speak the language. Jensen, incidentally, is one of only six American members of the French dominated Académie Internationale du Vin, having been elected in 1994 (his neighbor Richard Graff of CHALONE was another one). Jensen started Calera in 1975 after returning from Burgundy and spending two years searching for a site with the limestone soil he wanted. Calera means limekiln in Spanish, and an illustration of an old one found on the property appears on the label.

From the beginning Calera was an artistic struggle. Finding and storing enough water to keep the vines alive is difficult, especially in drought conditions such as they experienced in 1987–91. Even today the estate vineyards produce less than 2 t/a. The winery is a fascinating piece of architecture built on six levels down the side of a mountain for gravity flow purposes. The four Pinot Noir vineyards on the estate are vinified and bottled separately. They all have different *aspects in this hilly terrain. The 14-acre Jensen Vyd, 5-acre Selleck Vyd, and 5-acre Reed Vyd were all planted in 1975. The 11-acre Mills Vyd was planted to Pinot Noir in 1984 along with the estate's 6-acre Chardonnay vineyard. Viognier was planted experimentally in 1985, and extended to 7 acres in 1989, making Calera one of California's first entrants into a varietal category which has been rapidly expanding ever since.

The style of Calera estate Pinot Noirs is rustic. They are *whole bunch fermented in open topped fermenters using WILD YEAST. These days a roof-mounted hydraulic plunger is used for *pigeage. Gravity flow and egg white fining are the standard procedures.

Although Calera makes 30,000 cases, only 5,000 come from the estate. The other 25,000 cases each year of Chardonnay and Pinot Noir are produced from grapes purchased elsewhere in the CENTRAL COAST. Both of these wines are competitively priced for the mid-range market. This technique has turned Calera into a viable business and allowed Jensen to pursue his artistic quest on Mt Harlan.   B.C.C.

California, state with 12% of the US population and 96% of all the North American vinifera vineyards. There are more than 800,000 acres of vines in CA, which would rank the state fifth among countries worldwide. Nearly 425,000 of those acres are producing wine: 410 million gal in 1997, worth $11.4 billion at retail. CA shipments account for 71% of the total US wine consumption. But wine only accounts for 8% of CA's farm output. Agriculture is the largest segment of the CA economy. Computers, the entertainment industry, oil, and defense all play significant roles as well. Although barely half as populous as France or England, CA's overall economy is larger than either and would rank seventh among nations worldwide.

HISTORY

Westernmost of the contiguous United States, *California is separated from cultures to the east by a ring of high mountains. Originally settled by some of the first human inhabitants of the Americas, as attested by hearth remnants found on Santa Rosa Island, native Indian civilizations found CA so abundant they never had reason to forgo hunter-gatherer technologies in favor of settled agriculture, even though they exchanged trade goods with the agrarian Indian populations to the south and east for nearly 2,000 years.

The white men first on this scene were Hispanic. Seventy years before the British landed at Jamestown, VA, to begin what is traditionally thought of as the colonization which begat the US, Francisco Vásquez de Coronado explored the DESERT SOUTHWEST and claimed for the Spanish crown a territory which is larger than Europe is from the Elbe to the Atlantic. The sheer size of this territory made it virtually impossible to administrate effectively from far off Mexico City. It took nearly 200 years for the Spanish to stumble upon the fertile heart of CA. When they did so, they rapidly set about establishing their *mission economy, which relied on conscript Native American labor. European diseases took a heavy toll. CA's Native American population dropped from approximately 310,000 in 1769, the year Portola discovered the San Francisco BAY AREA, to 30,000 by the denouement of the *gold rush in 1860.

When MEXICO achieved independence from Spain in 1821, CA was still an afterthought. By the middle of the 1830s, there were more than 30,000 US settlers living in what is today called TEXAS, but was then still part of Mexico. Those settlers brought black slaves with them, which directly contravened Mexican law. In 1835 the Mexicans responded militarily and, despite a well-remembered victory at the Alamo (near San Antonio, TX), they were conclusively defeated at San Jacinto in 1836. The relatively sleepy coup which flared up on the plaza in SONOMA, CA, twelve years later was little more than a sidelight to US President James Polk's continuing war with Mexico, which was primarily fought along the RIO GRANDE and in the coastal mountains from Veracruz to Mexico City. That extremely bloody and destructive invasion was ended by the 1848 Treaty of Guadaloupe Hidalgo in which the US paid $15 million for more than half the territory of Mexico, including Alta California.

To put these ethnic antecedents in perspective, in 1990 there were 21 million people of Mexican parentage living in the US. Two-thirds of them were born in the US. Half the remainder were legal immigrants who had become naturalized citizens. In the Los Angeles Co public school system 64% of the children spoke Spanish at home. 'We lost Alta California on the battlefield, but we'll win it back in the bedroom,' has been a popular Chicano witticism throughout the Golden State for a century and a half.

The gold rush stocked northern CA with Anglo citizens overnight, but southern CA's arid landscape remained thinly populated until the arrival of the Southern Pacific railroad in the mid-1870s. Jean Louis Vignes had begun growing grapes along the Los Angeles River in 1820, but when he sold the vineyard in 1855 it still had not amounted to much. The great irrigators of the American West were actually the Mormons. They settled in the UTAH desert to escape religious persecution from Easterners who took a dim view of polygamy. The Mormons survived near Salt Lake City by digging canals to bring water from the Wasatch Mtns to their crops. They pioneered the wagon route around the southern end of the Sierra Nevadas and through the Mojave Desert into the LOS ANGELES Basin because they wanted a sea port for the state they were creating (which they called Deseret) so that newly converted Saints from Europe could arrive without having to traverse land controlled by Gentiles. They also wanted to grow olives, grapes, sugar cane, and cotton. One hundred and fifty Mormon families came to San Bernardino, 40 mi southeast of Los Angeles, in 1851. They purchased 35,000 acres and set up their second biggest community.

Anaheim was another cooperative halfway between Los Angeles and San Bernardino. It was the 1857 brainchild of 50 German immigrants who moved from San Francisco seeking a warmer, drier climate. Each man subscribed $750 and they bought 1,065 acres of sandy loam on the Santa Ana River, marrying the river's name to their word for home. They specialized in grapes and rapidly became the best wine producing area in CA. By 1883 fifty wineries in these two districts, which comprise the foothills leading up to the present-day ski area on Mt Baldy, were producing more than a million gal annually from 10,000 acres of vines. That is half again the size of the present-day wine industry in OR.

Southern CA viticulture, however, met a series of disasters. As with the rest of CA, vineyard acreage had boomed in the wake of the *phylloxera epidemic's virtual annihilation of European vineyards between 1860 and 1880. As European production began to rise again, CA was faced with a massive oversupply. Then *Pierce's disease, a systemic bacterial infection spread by an insect vector and originally called Anaheim disease, dealt a *coup de grâce* to the southern CA wine industry. By 1886 it was little more than a shadow of its former size. Several wine marketing companies held on, consolidating the remains, but real estate booms of the 20th century catalyzed by the glamour of Hollywood pretty much ended agriculture as a force in the Los Angeles Basin.

Prior to the gold rush, the CENTRAL COAST and South Coast were CA's primary wine producing areas because the Franciscan padres got vines into the ground almost as soon as they completed living quarters at the missions. There were more than 20 missions along the route from San Diego to San Francisco, each a communications nexus out of which would branch independent ranchos, often on land granted by the Spanish crown as compensation for military service. Cattle and the sale of hides to ships sailing around the Horn (cf *Two Years before the Mast* by Richard Henry Dana written in 1820) were mainstays of the CA economy from 1770 until 1848. For three-quarters of that period winemaking, and the role wine played in the local communities, was largely initiated by the friars. Secularization of the missions following Mexican independence, and the concomitant loss of Native American labor, put the dampers on most of those vineyards. The SIERRA FOOTHILLS enjoyed a surge during the gold rush, but their distance to markets meant that those vineyards withered once the miners left and boom towns shriveled. From 1885 until national Prohibition began in 1920, the San Francisco Bay Area was the dominant factor in California viticulture, and the foothills surrounding SANTA CLARA VALLEY were the quality centerpiece. Demand for grapes was high during Prohibition because heads of households could legally make 200 gal of wine a year. That demand, and the beginning of irrigation projects, spurred the CENTRAL VALLEY boom which catapulted CA into North American viticultural dominance in the middle of the 20th century (supplanting MISSOURI in that role). As US wine consumption began to rise following the Second World War, the Central Valley was the volume engine and the Santa Clara Valley was the quality sector, featuring producers such as Paul Masson, Almaden, and Mirassou. (See DINING HABITS.)

It was not until well into the 1960s that public perception acknowledged NAPA VALLEY as Santa Clara's quality superior. Right about that same time urbanization and the emergence of the computer industry functionally ended Santa Clara Valley's agricultural ambitions. The late 1960s and early 1970s were the launching pad for California's fine wine resurgence. The baby boomers started to come of drinking age and the concept of artisan, BOUTIQUE wineries caught fire following the model of California pioneers such as CHALONE, HANZELL, MAYACAMAS, STONY HILL, MT EDEN, and RIDGE.

The convenience of Napa Valley as a destination one hour's drive away for day trippers from the metropolitan Bay Area exerted inexorable pressure on land prices in Napa. As these rose, growers and younger, more entrepreneurial winemakers began to cast their nets more widely. By the mid-1980s SONOMA CO had achieved a place in public perception as a worthy rival to Napa. This perception was important. Prior to 1985 Sonoma was merely seen as the more rustic, less society-oriented of the two growing regions. After 1985 consumers and winemakers alike began altering their preconceptions about the suitability of cooler climate, coastal influenced vineyard sites. That opening of minds, that broadening of attitudes set the stage for a period of experimentation and quality improvement which continues in California today. By the mid-1990s the Central Coast had been rediscovered through this process and had risen dramatically in terms of public image. It remains to be seen whether the Sierra Foothills, especially in higher elevation, cooler climate zones, will receive the next wave of public acclaim from this process, but already growers and young winemakers are launching exploratory ventures there, drawn by land prices one-tenth of those Napa Valley commands.

GEOLOGY

Serpentine is the CA State Rock. It is a component of the ophiolitic series found in places such as Oman, Tierra del Fuego, Pakistan, New Guinea, Newfoundland, and Cyprus which in the 1960s helped prove the theory of Plate Tectonics. Some 20 plates cover the earth's surface, virtually floating on the molten basalt of the earth's core and moving against each other. In this manner the materials of the earth's crust may be transported long distances over hundreds of millions of years.

The Pacific plate is moving north and subducting, or disappearing beneath, the North American plate in a line along the California coast. This subduction scrapes some material off the Pacific plate and emplaces it on the North American plate. It also creates tremendous heat, which melts rock below the surface, giving rise to volcanic activity. Additionally, the movement of the plates (which we recognize as EARTHQUAKES) creates enormous pressure, raising mountains and ripping open valleys.

Three hundred million years ago the continent of North America met the ocean somewhere between Nevada and Utah. Three major emplacements have occurred, delivering and deforming what is now the land mass of California. An emplacement is when an island arc (such as Japan, Newfoundland, Madagascar, Sumatra, and New Zealand) arrives on a spreading seafloor plate at the edge of a continental plate.

Molten rock, formed by the subduction, rises as a series of plumes. This activity has formed the Sierra batholith, a 25,000 sq mi hunk of granite. Current conjecture says the bottom is about 6 mi deep. The Sierra batholith is gradually being raised and tilted by the pressure between the two tectonic plates. Geologists describe it as a trapdoor, hinged on the western side of the mountains, being pushed up to form a sudden escarpment on the eastern side of the mountains. Wagon trains arriving with emigrants from the East Coast in the latter half of the 19th century had to find a way to climb a grade which rises some 8,000 ft (to a pass through the 15,000 ft ridge tops) in a horizontal distance of about 10 mi. In winter these mountains get twice as much precipitation as the city of SEATTLE does, and commonly have 40 ft of snow, occasionally forming drifts 100 ft deep. These are young mountains, sharply crested with dramatic vertical drops, not the rounded, eroded mountains to which these settlers were accustomed in the East.

The total distance across California is not far, 40 mi in the coastal mountains, 50 mi in the Central Valley, and 90 mi in the Sierras. It is comparable to a trip through the Apennines, the Po Valley, and the Alps, on the way from Genoa to Zurich. One big difference is the Central Valley. There are few comparisons on the planet. It is as flat as a pancake, 50 mi wide and 400 mi long. It was not carved by the action of water running out of the mountains; 3 million years ago the Coast Range and the Sierras rose up around it. The Sierras came up fast because of the structural integrity of the granite batholith. Technically the Central Valley is a structural basin filled with sediments. For the most part though, these sediments arrived long before the surrounding mountains arose. Many of the sediments are marine shales from the Eocene Age formed when the continental shelf was located in Idaho and Nevada, and when California's prolific winegrowing districts were nothing but deep blue sea.

The Coast Ranges rose more slowly than the Sierras. They are composed of fragmentary marine scrappings bulldozed by the North American plate as it rides on top of the spreading seafloor. These Coast Range soils are so confused, so tortured, of such widely varied origins, they are called the Franciscan mélange. They formed initially as islands when sediments of the coastal plain were pushed and folded up from a horizontal position to a near vertical one. Up through this mess rose volcanoes spewing liquid lava and airborne ash. Such complicated origins create many soil-type opportunities for winegrowers in these regions today, but they simultaneously deny easy geological analysis to neophyte viticultural investors looking for blanket solutions, as well as to conscientious wine writers seeking *gout de terroir* explanations which can be broadly applied. In the last 25 million years several terranes, or island arcs in addition to the original three, have been emplaced to form the winegrowing regions of California's Central Coast AVA. The beautiful serpentine rocks found at Land's End in San Francisco overlooking the Golden Gate Bridge are ophiolites delivered to California from a *spreading center* by the Pacific seafloor.

Ripping off corners of huge tectonic plates can also relieve pressure in one part of the globe and rotate a plate slightly. The Pacific plate is currently the earth's largest. It covers two-thirds of the Pacific Ocean. Some three and a half million years ago it shifted direction by 11° to the northwest. This swing is documented most clearly by looking at the Hawaiian Islands *hot spot*. Volcanic magma from the earth's molten core rises to the surface at a fixed location there, building a series of islands as the Pacific plate moves over that hot spot. In the Pliocene Epoch, while Oahu was on top of the hot spot, the Pacific plate shifted direction, putting an 11° bend in the line of the Hawaiian Islands. This event was important for today's California wine industry because it also shifted the direction of the pressures exerted by the Pacific plate on the North American plate.

A rough line between the two plates is generically called the San Andreas Fault, but it is actually a bundle of interwoven fractures that may be some 50 mi wide and 10–15 mi deep. As the sides of these faults move, particularly in mountains of soft composition, they can pull away from each other as one section of the fault line moves quickly and another one remains relatively hung up. The result is called a *pull-apart basin*. Unlike high elevation, water sculpted, erosional valleys, pull-apart basins are remarkably deep and often have sharply defined, eye-catchingly tall mountains surrounding them. Tahoe in the Sierras is a pull-apart basin. In California's North Coast AVA pull-apart basins have formed NAPA VALLEY, SONOMA VALLEY, Ukiah Valley, Clear Lake, and Lake Berryessa. Worldwide, two quite prominent pull-apart basins would be the Red Sea and the Gulf of California between Mexico and Baja California.

TOPOGRAPHY AND CLIMATE

California has a *mediterranean climate. Except in abnormal circumstances, rain is delivered to California by the Jet Stream. Throughout summer and early autumn the Eastern Pacific High Pressure Ridge forces the Jet Stream north into British Columbia, Washington, and Oregon. As days become rapidly shorter after the Fall Equinox (21 Sept), and temperatures drop in the more northerly latitudes, this high pressure ridge breaks down, allowing storms to move into California as they rotate counterclockwise around low pressure areas off the northern California coast. More rain falls north of San Francisco than in the Central Coast because the storms start earlier and are more frequent. However, elevation is equally important in determining overall annual rates of precipitation for any given site. That is why the city of San Francisco gets less rain than either the Santa Cruz Mtns to the south or Mt Tamalpais in Marin Co to the north.

As the earth spins, the surface at the equator moves with greater velocity than the surface nearer the poles. This differential, along with more constant sun exposure, produces a consistent trend of rising air over the tropics. Rising air cools, and drops its moisture in the tropical rainforests. Then, the now-dry air tumbles from high in the atmosphere out into the Horse Latitudes (20°–35° north and south) where deserts girdle the globe. As this air comes down it is compressed into warm, dry, high pressure systems. California's winegrowing regions are right on the margin of these arid Horse Latitudes, ie between 33° and 40°N. Humidity, and the *fungal diseases that accompany it, are much less of an issue in California than in practically any other fine wine region of the world. *Organic viticulture has great potential in the Golden State.

Being 10° further south than France, California enjoys growing conditions that are not determined by the angle of the sun as much as they are by the relationship of any particular site to the Pacific Ocean. Hence differences show up much better in a cross-section of the state from west to east, than they would in a comparison from north to south, which might be more applicable in Europe or the East Coast of North America.

On the westerly edge, coastal valleys are formed where rivers and seasonal creeks run directly to the ocean. FOG is the predominant climatic characteristic. To the north, where rain falls heavily, the nutrient value of the soils is meagre. Dense fog in the north favors conifer forests, which turn the topsoil acidic with their duff. To the south carbonate-rich marine sediments result in higher pH, more alkaline soils. Temperatures are mild and DIURNAL TEMPERATURE FLUCTUATION is minimized along the coast. It never freezes (witness citrus and avocados grown commercially north of San Luis Obispo) and midday summer temperatures rarely exceed 80°F.

The growing season in California's coastal valleys is prolonged by the cool temperatures and by the number of hours each day during which fog may effectively mask sunlight. Late ripening grape varieties rarely do their best in these conditions. Early ripening varieties, however, benefit from lengthened *hang time and often deliver a unique combination of intense, clear varietal aroma with delicate nuances. Sites with a high degree of fog cover frequently produce elevated malic acid levels.

Most coastal valleys, such as SANTA YNEZ and ANDERSON, run east–west. Wind, elevation, and depth of topsoil are more important considerations than whether a vineyard is sited on the north-facing or the south-facing side of the valley or canyon. A wind-protected site is essential. Elevation must be high enough (generally over 800 ft) to get above at least some of the late summer fog. More than a foot or two of topsoil is difficult to find once one climbs higher than the 200–300 ft high coastal plain.

Above 1,500 ft one enters a second viticultural zone, the coastal ridges, such as MT EDEN and RIDGE VYDS in the SANTA CRUZ MTNS AVA. These areas may get 4–8 hours more sunlight than the coastal valleys by the simple expedient of rising above the fog line. Moreover, high plateaus and sliding, friable soils, once derived from marine sediments, can occasionally produce vineyard sites with 3–15 ft of top soil. They can ripen Cabernet Sauvignon, but they are marginal zones for it which do best in the warmest vintages. Coastal ridge Cabs are good candidates for long periods of bottle age. The biggest problem on the coastal ridge tops is wind. Hence the best vineyard sites are usually on the lee (eastern) side of the ridge and often two or three sets of ridges away from the coast. Most of the ridge lines run north–south, or parallel to the coast.

In the lower, more eroded, piedmonts and fans of *alluvium typical of the inland side of CA's Coast Range (particularly south of San Francisco) oak-studded grasslands dominate the landscape. This third topographic zone is CA's best quality soil profile for growing grapes. The rain arrives from the west and falls in the coastal mountains. Sites in this third zone are often in the RAIN SHADOW of mountains, which lessens the impact of storms arriving to mark the transition from dry summer to wet winter. On the steep sides of the ridges, topsoil is thin because rain has washed it away. Water carries this material toward the inland river valley. The creeks and streams run swiftly at the high elevations, then more slowly when they start to flatten out closer to the valley. The biggest soil particles fall out of the water first. These are the pebbles and *gravel which make up the foothills along the margins of valleys. The topsoils in these piedmonts are quite porous because water subsequently flows through these large particles easily without adhering to their (relatively) minimal surface area. Closer to the valley center, the water slows even more and drops the next smaller sized particles, *sand. Sandy soils have a low water retention capacity, but are still better than gravel soils. The smallest sized particles pool in the center of the valley floodplain where they settle as the water from spring floods evaporates. Small particles, *silt, retain water well thanks to their considerable surface area. The smallest particles form *clay.

Topsoils of CA's piedmont areas, such as the bench in Napa Valley's OAKVILLE and RUTHERFORD AVAs, are also quite deep, usually 30–80 ft, and not as likely as river bottomland to be rich in nutritive organics. Vineyards grown on piedmont soil profiles often have huge root systems. Nevertheless they must, if not heavily irrigated and fertilized, struggle to produce minimal vegetative growth each year. These conditions naturally result in small, intensively flavored crops.

The fourth topographic zone is thus inland river valley floodplains, such as the low lying areas in DRY CREEK VALLEY AVA and in the middle of Napa Valley's Oakville and YOUNTVILLE districts. In these areas soils are also quite deep, but they are composed of sandy clays with much more organic matter in them. These *loams spell greater vine vigor and more production. The flow of a valley's river cuts a trough. When the outside of a bend in the moving water sheers off soil in a piedmont area, leaving land at a higher elevation with a sharp vertical drop to the present floodplain, CA farmers call that a *bench*. These are much prized for grape growing. Typically, however, generations of farmers have channeled rivers into the center of the valley to prevent flooding and have smoothly graded the land toward the hillsides to make cultivation easier. This obscures the exact location of the bench and makes for vitriolic debate whenever a political process attempts to demarcate different areas for labeling purposes, such as defining AVA boundaries.

Inland valleys, often pull-apart basins, in the Coast Range are steep sided and narrow, usually running north–south. Although few distinctions are made on labels as to grapes grown on one side of these valleys versus the other, there is a difference. The eastern sides of the valleys receive less rain, and have rockier, less eroded soil profiles. More significantly, they receive direct sunshine later in the day, when ambient air temperatures are high, as the sun sets behind the western mountains. Vineyard sites in the western foothills get their share of direct sunlight earlier in the day as the sun rises behind the eastern mountains, while ambient air temperatures are low; then are shaded by the western mountains in the late afternoon. Both zones three and four have relatively large diurnal temperature fluctuations, but the timing of the variation is different depending on site.

The fifth topographic zone on an eastward cross-section of CA is the Central Valley. Temperatures are high. There is no summer fog. Rich soils go down thousands of feet and crop loads are always quite high, frequently over 10 t/a. In addition to irrigation canals moving water hundreds of miles, there is a huge underground aquifer. Vines tend to be spaced widely so work can be easily done with machines. Land is relatively inexpensive because agricultural uses do not compete with residential uses. Grape prices are approximately one-third those in premium Coast Range districts.

CA's sixth topographic zone is the piedmont of the Sierra Nevada to an elevation of around 1,500 ft. This band along the front of the mountain range has a unique soil composition because of its high proportion of weathered *granite. Visually the soil is distinctly red in many places because its high iron content oxidizes to form rust. In other places the soil is light colored, quartz-rich, sand to pebble sized deposits spread out in alluvial fans. These are placer mine tailings washed out of the mountains between 1850 and 1870. This sixth topographic zone terminates somewhere between 1,200 and 2,000 ft of elevation, primarily because of temperature. The lower elevations have much warmer weather, particularly at night. They also have much deeper soils.

The higher elevations of the Sierra Nevada are a seventh zone. These sites tend to be relatively new properties, and CA winegrowers are just beginning to learn how big *diurnal temperature variations at altitudes over 2,000 ft create entirely different characteristics than those found in neighboring vineyards 1,000 ft lower. It is a mistake to lump all producers from these mountains together. In zone six alcohol levels are always high, but the wines have a full-bodied suppleness. The reds feature soft tannins and jammy fruit. In zone seven the wines are much lighter bodied, with thinner flavor profiles, and much higher natural acid levels. These wines can have quite intense aromas, but they tend to be higher toned, more perfumed, more *lifted. Unless winemakers pay close attention to *phenolic management, the natural acidity in zone seven red wines can push the tannins forward and make them seem harsh, astringent, and bitter. These vineyards get at least a couple of days of snow every winter and a lot of rain. It is difficult to find sites with much topsoil at all, but it is easy to find sites with *schist. Vine yields in zone seven are low, and access to water must be considered. Planting is much more expensive than in flat country. Deer and bird depredation is high because no other crops are likely to be grown nearby. Zone seven has a more *continental climate than any other zone in CA, but it is still only in the third category out of five on the Smart/Day scale, thus very moderate relative to the rest of North America. The Smart/Day scale is sometimes called mean average range (MAR), and is calculated (in the northern hemisphere) by subtracting the mean temperature for Jan from the mean temperature for July. Low results indicate a maritime climate; high results a continental climate. WINTER KILL is never a problem in any CA vineyards.

VINTAGES

CA does have climatic variations from year to year. These may be too subtle for immigrants from Chicago to recognize, but most grapevines are more sensitive than people raised in Chicago.

CA's side of the coin which causes winter kill in the Midwest is an occasional winter so mild there are no freezes at all. That circumstance allows grape pests to overwinter in sufficient numbers to cause significant crop damage during the subsequent spring and summer. More commonly, severe rain storms during a winter season can cause *flooding in sections of vineyard, even submerging the vines for some number of hours. Despite hysterical media coverage, this type of event is of little consequence to CA vineyards. Flood waters recede quickly, and permanent damage only occurs if vines or trellises are ripped out of the ground by the force of the flood current. More commonly, earth subsidence (ie mudslides) eradicate small numbers of vines on terraced, hillside vineyards. Long-term, gradual erosion is a much more sinister issue.

The amount of rainfall during Jan and Feb (when CA gets 80% of its precipitation) is not as important as the amount during Mar and Apr when vines are beginning to grow. *Drought during winter, as happened in 1976 and 1977, then again in 1987 and 1988, can have serious repercussions. It reduces the amount of water available for spring irrigation and frost protection, as well as the amount of water retained in the ground. Normal rainfall ranges annually from 20 in to 40 in for North Coast districts; 15 in to 25 in for the Central Coast. Those figures are, however, averages based on periods of more than 100 years. In actuality, the common experience is several years at 10 in followed by several years at 40 in. None of the recent fluctuations between drought and flood are out of the ordinary. Analysis of tree growth rings clearly documents periods in the last millennium when severe drought lasted 15–20 years in CA, and periods when rainfall was triple the wettest years of the 20th century. In severe drought conditions vine metabolism is restricted. High alcohol, low flavor is the norm in those circumstances. The first year of a drought often produces some concentrated, impressive, long-lived wines, but subsequent years more often produce awkward, rough, charmless wines.

*Frost danger usually passes in CA by mid-Apr. Although in 1980 there was a frost in Napa Valley on May 10, and in 1970 there were 20 nights of frost in Apr there. Frost is a matter of considerable concern in CA because so many vineyards are planted on valley floors. Overhead sprinklers are usually the first line of defense. They are expensive though, because most of the water needed to run them must be stored in some sort of impoundment reservoir. *Wind machines are also seen commonly where topography is suitable. Diesel *smudge pots are no longer used. LONG PRUNING is rare, but some small vineyardists swear by it.

Rain during flowering (average occurrence around the first week of June) is extremely rare in CA, although 1995 saw some in the southern districts and 1994 even included a freak hailstorm the last week of May in Napa. More germane is the possibility of poor pollination due to sluggish performance by bees in overcast, cool, or foggy weather. Equally deleterious can be berry shatter from spikes of really hot weather during flowering.

Overall temperatures during the July and Aug ripening period in CA definitely play a role in determining wine quality. By the end of Aug/early Sept, wineries are usually starting to harvest grapes in CA's North Coast. The Central Valley usually starts three weeks earlier; the Central Coast three weeks later. Weather during the Sept harvest period is a crucial quality indicator in CA because of the generally warm temperatures. Rain during harvest is commonplace in most northern European winegrowing districts, but cold temperatures by that time slow the growth of *rot there, and rapidly shortening days have already stopped vine growth and lignified stems. Significant rain during Sept in CA can destroy the quality of the crop with rot in the space of a week. Winemakers who produce very limited quantities can hand-sort clusters on a *triage board before they go into the crusher. Large wineries must usually forgo this pleasure. Either way, vines will have absorbed a lot of water which dilutes flavors, acid, and sugar in the berries. Brief showers do not cause problems. Actually the most typical weather pattern for CA's North Coast winegrowing districts is a couple of days of cloud and drizzle in late Sept (not enough to affect the grapes), followed by two to three weeks of sunny weather called Indian Summer. Spectators at Stanford football games in Oct go shirtless to improve their tans; while their friends at Notre Dame wear suits, parkas, and ear cozies.

One weather pattern is unusual because of its effect on Sept rains in CA. *El Niño causes a warming of the surface waters in the Pacific Ocean driving everything further north than usual. Warm water fish like marlin come into Monterey Bay, bonita are caught off the Sonoma coast. Sept is HURRICANE season in the northern hemisphere. In the eastern Pacific these storms normally get no further north than Mexico, although they always cause big surf in Baja. In El Niño conditions (1982 and 1983 are the classic example) rain not only arrives in CA in Sept, it arrives from the south (rather than the northwest), and it is tropically warm (not Alaska cold). El Niño conditions are abnormal, but they do seem to return on a 10–15 year cycle.

The flip side of the weather issue occurs when CA's harvest is attended by heatwaves. In extremely hot weather, grapes ripen so quickly that large wineries cannot pick them or process them through their equipment fast enough. Inevitably some grapes will be left on the vine until they are overripe. Small wineries are less likely to have this problem because the volume of grapes they process allows more flexibility.

This table is a forced ranking by decade; not a set of absolute scores. That means every digit must be used once in each decade: one year must be assigned the 1; and only one year can receive the 10.

VINTAGE CHART
Inland Valley Cabernet/Zinfandel

1970	9	1980	8–	1990	9
1971	2	1981	5	1991	3
1972	1	1982	3	1992	1
1973	10	1983	1	1993	6
1974	7+	1984	6	1994	7+
1975	6	1985	10	1995	10
1976	4	1986	7	1996	4
1977	3	1987	9–	1997	5
1978	8–	1988	4–	1998	2
1979	5	1989	2	1999	8

1958 ***, extremely heavy winter rains and flooding all over CA, then spring frost. Cool growing season, then a warm, dry, late harvest. Spectacular wines everywhere. Virtually impossible to find today. André Tchelistcheff thought 1958 Beaulieu Private Reserve Cabernet was the best wine he ever made. It sold for $500 a bottle in 1992 and was magnificent. In the late 1980s I tasted both a Pinot Noir and a Chardonnay from Hanzell Vineyard's 1958 vintage. Hanzell's 1958 Chardonnay was the first time French oak barriques were used in CA. That wine was spectacular in the late 1970s, without a hint of quit.

1964 *, severe spring frosts, mild growing season, warm and dry autumn. Excellent reds.

1965 & 1967, large crops, light-bodied reds. Not distinguished.

1966 **, drought conditions in spring cut size of crop and concentrated flavors. Warm, dry weather at harvest allowed vintners to get the grapes very ripe. Reds had richness to go with the extractive structure all wineries sought.

1968 ***, great reds; poor whites. Very warm growing season, which continued well into autumn, delivering every bit of ripeness desired by the standards of the day. That reputation made this vintage the most collectible of its time, and many reds survive to appear at auction. Now past their peak, the Cabernets are still capable of generating a tarry, leather bouquet with hours of staying power.

1969 **, a cool growing season produced really exceptional whites and lighter-bodied, fruity reds which matured quite elegantly but were not highly thought of at the time. Reds from mountain vineyards can be bargains even today. High initial SO_2 levels kept Chardonnays going for a long time.

1970 ***, a mild winter with lots of rain produced early budbreak. Then severe spring frosts reduced the crop to half its average size. A warm, dry autumn ripened everything fully. Flavor saturation of these wines was remarkable, although the heavy-bodied, extractive winemaking style of the period was always a bit ponderous. Cabernets from great sites are still vibrant, full of chewy flavors and redolent of cigar box bouquet.

1971 & 1972, not very good vintages because of problems ripening the crops. 1971 was a cool growing season that started late due to spring rain, then finished later still due to a big crop after the tiny one in 1970. As a result many 1971 Cabernets were thin and vegetative. 1972 had the triple trouble of spring frost, severe heat in July and massive rain in Sept. Mold went crazy and nothing of interest remains today.

1973 ***, a wet, very cold winter, but warm spring with early budbreak. Then a long, moderate summer, resulting in a late harvest under dry, cool conditions. The crop was large. Whites were good. Reds seemed awkwardly tannic in youth, especially when compared to the softer, higher pH reds of 1974. However, the secret of the 1973 reds was natural acidity pushing the tannins forward; not overextraction. Undervalued and *closed* until well into the 1980s, these reds blossomed after 12–15 years in the bottle.

1974 ******, spring weather was cool and summer was not unusually hot, but harvest occurred in extreme heat. Crop was large, but nevertheless became extremely ripe. Whites were not impressive at all; nor were Pinot Noirs. Cabernet and Zinfandel produced luscious, smooth wines which took the rapidly expanding market by storm. OPEC had changed forever the notion of inventory storage when they quadrupled oil prices in 1973, driving interest rates through the roof. The 1974 CA Cabernets could not have been styled better to take advantage of that situation: they were ripe; they were ready; and they were priced right because there was too much of them. Today their texture is still enjoyable, but hints of raisin character detract from the bouquet.

1975 *****, cold spring with frost and rain followed by a downright cold growing season. Harvest was late, and both Cabernet and Zinfandel got rained on. Chardonnays were spectacular, best of the decade and capable of very long life. Pinot Noirs were equally wonderful. Cabernets were thin bodied and as acidic as CA has ever produced. At the time, such structure was considered substandard, and the 1975 Cabernets were much maligned, especially arriving on the heels of the much ballyhooed 1974s. When the 1975 Cabs started coming onto the auction block in 1985, they were deeply discounted. Today all that has changed. The 1975 Cabs are seen as light bodied, but capable of exquisite bouquet development (ie 1975 is CA's most Bordeaux-like vintage, just as 1982 might be considered a very CA-like vintage for Bordeaux). Deleterious effect of the rain makes the vintage variable from property to property though.

1976 **& 1977**, two drought years at a time when CA wineries were ill-prepared to mitigate the effects in the vineyard or in the winery. 1976 was a hot year with dehydrated berries and low acid. Junk for whites. Some reds were nicely concentrated, but overall too alcoholic. 1977 was more of the same, but with rain at the end of the season. Wineries were better prepared to avoid high tannin and alcohol, but that knowledge could not compensate for the lack of flavor development.

1978 ******, lots of winter rain (twice the average for a normal year) broke the drought and helped produce a very big crop. Harvest was long and dry, but too hot in Sept. Chardonnays and Pinot Noirs were excessively alcoholic. Zinfandels were only above average, but Cabernets were very good. Excellent examples of what CA Cabernet can do

with 20 years in the bottle. More time would be pushing one's luck.

1979, heat waves in late Aug–early Sept were followed by extensive rains. Some wineries were able to pick before the downpour, and some excellent Chardonnays were made. Cabernet Sauvignon was highly variable. Cabernets picked before the rain were not physiologically ripe; those picked during the rain were dilute. Zinfandels were not at all impressive.

1980 ******, there is no better vintage to illustrate the chasm between mainstream, production-oriented wineries in CA and their tiny, craftsman-sized competitors. A difficult vintage for volume producers, and therefore widely panned, but an excellent example of a cool growing season. It was one of the longest growing seasons, and latest harvests, in CA history. It was also a large crop. In general 1980 wines have very high acid levels and low pH. The irony about 1980 was the summer's most pronounced hot spell occurred during the last week of Sept/first week of Oct. Temperatures went to 110°F. Grapes, which had been maturing slowly, all finished ripening at once. Harried pickers passed out in the vineyards. Big wineries could not process the grapes fast enough. They had to leave some of their grapes on the vine too long, resulting in raisined smells for varieties like Zinfandel and Cabernet Sauvignon. Micro-wineries did not have these difficulties scheduling their harvest, and were thus able to produce balanced red wines which aged well beyond normal expectations. Big wineries generally produced anomalies of big body, ripe smells, and high acid.

1981 *** & 1984 ***, both these years were hot growing seasons with early vintages and little or no rain during harvest. 1981 saw most of the heat in June and July reducing the crop by 20% and starting the harvest three weeks before normal. There was a smattering of rain at the end of Sept in 1981, but very few grapes were left to get caught. 1984 was warm throughout, a normal sized crop, and no rain until late Oct. Both vintages produced fleshy, fragrant wines which dazzled consumers and show judges with their opulence and maturity when first released. After five years they began to show the diminishing effects of such an ebullient youth. Cabernets from these years make a fascinating study. Those from Napa Valley are starting to tire. Those from cooler areas like the Santa Rosa plain in Sonoma Co and the Santa Ynez Valley in Santa Barbara Co are among the best vintages those locations have produced. Merlot from Santa Ynez in

1981 and 1984 was particularly prized. Although too elderly now, 1981 really put Monterey on the map for Chardonnay in CA, while it produced middle-of-the-road whites in CA's inland valleys.

1982 & 1983, these two vintages shared the characteristic of rain during harvest. 1982 was a huge crop and a cool growing season. 1983 was a warm growing season and an average sized crop. Nevertheless, in both instances El Niño delivered a great deal of Sept rain which arrived from the south, thus catching the Central Coast first. Pinot Noirs from the North Coast in 1982 were excellent wines, but Pinot Noir was about the only variety picked before the rain. There were also a number of interesting botrytized aromatic whites, but they have now lived beyond their realistic life expectancy. Most Cabernets from 1982 are thin bodied and mildly grassy. Hillside vineyards on the eastern side of inland valleys in the North Coast fared best. 1983 Cabernets are generally dull and nondescript. Freaks like 'Botrytis Chardonnay' surfaced in 1983, but they they made no winemaker proud.

1985 ***** & 1986 ***, both were long, cool growing seasons with good weather during harvest. 1985 was, however, much superior. 1985 featured 70–75°F weather from April Fool's Day until Thanksgiving. The size of the crop was slightly above average. 1986 started earlier and finished slightly early. There was a lot of rain during the winter, and the 1986 crop was 15% bigger than average. The autumn was mild, with only a light two-day wet spell beginning Sept 7. After that brief drizzle, which only fell in the northern half of the state, no rain fell until mid-Nov. 1986 Chardonnays from the Central Coast were not as fragrant as normal early on, but they developed beautifully in the bottle. 1985 Cabernets from classic, warm districts like the Rutherford Bench are magnificent. The characteristics that make those Oakville and Rutherford Cabernets so special have been apparent from the minute they emerged from the fermenters: deep, concentrated fruit with bright high tones, supple tannins, and a clear focus held *en pointe* by excellent natural acidity. The 1986s Cabs hinted at those characteristics; the 1985s layered them on with a trowel.

1987 **** & 1988**, although the quality of these vintages is quite different, they can be fairly considered as a pair because they were both drought years. Being the first year of the drought, 1987 got the benefits from vine struggle which showed up as concentration in the red wines. By 1988 dry-farmed vines had simply shut down and produced flavorless reds. The winter of 1986–7 was cold and dry. Snow fell on the mountains between Napa and Sonoma in mid-November, and then again at the end of March. There was virtually no precipitation in between. An extremely warm end of April catapulted the 1987 growing season ahead and flowering began the first week of May. Heat during flowering caused a significant amount of 'shatter,' reducing the size of the crop by 15%. Harvest began in mid-Aug. Hundreds of forest fires throughout CA blanketed the state with smoke for two weeks in early Sept. This event had little effect on the vines other than to reduce sunlight and slow the rate of maturation. Winemakers, who had rushed to prepare for an early harvest, found themselves sitting on their hands. Sales of tartaric acid were brisk in 1987.

Winter 1987–8 was again cold and dry. Acacia trees did not bloom until mid-Feb, two weeks late, but spring passed without any rain. Some vineyards reported flowering before the end of Apr. The last week of May was extremely hot. Then a very strange thing happened—several inches of rain fell throughout the state during the first week of June. In some varieties shot-berries outnumbered normal ones three to one. Crop size was off 40%. Harvest began in early Aug. Prices, which had been creeping up for a year, went through the roof.

1987 Cabernets are instantly recognizable in vertical tastings because of their power and their saturated color. A lot of their impact comes from brutish tannins and alcoholic lift, but they also show depth and complexity in the flavor profile long after other wines have packed their bags. Call them cowboys, call them New York taxi drivers, but definitely call on these wines to do the heavy lifting at any barbecue you host.

1989, there was not enough snow in the Sierras during the winter of 1988–9 to officially end the drought, but there was enough rain at lower elevations to rejuvenate parched grapevines. Vineyards throughout CA rejoiced by setting one of the bigger crops in the state's history. The growing season was mild. Then heavy rains began falling on the North Coast in mid-Sept. It is a vintage most winemakers remember because they needed all their skills to make good wine in difficult conditions. The marketplace sneered at that opinion. Botrytis ran amok in 1989. The fruit intensity of the off-dry Rieslings and Gewürztraminers made them quite desirable. 1989 was also the last good year for botrytis in CA through 1995.

1990 ***, the autumn rains of 1989 stopped in Dec, and 1990's winter was the fourth in a row with below average precipitation. Spring weather was warm, bringing an early budbreak. Heat at the end of May, and a freak thunderstorm in the North Coast, dropped the crop size 30% below average. Growing season temperatures were quite mild, as were temperatures during harvest. There were no fall rains. Cabernets and Zinfandels were fabulous in 1990, especially from inland areas of the North Coast and from the Sierra Foothills. Using suppleness, balance, and fruit weight as the criteria, 1990 is easily the best vintage between 1985 and 1994 for these wines.

1991, average winter precipitation and mild spring weather helped set a huge crop. The growing season was mild, with cold nighttime temperatures. Harvest was one of the latest on record, but dry and very hot. After the marketing disaster of the 1989 vintage and the short supply of the 1990 vintage, it became quite common in CA for winery owners to enthusiastically tout 1991 as the greatest thing since sliced bread, but side by side in a direct vertical comparison the 1990s are always darker and more concentrated. The heat at the end of the season left many of the 1991 reds with a bit of alcoholic roughness, which is all the more apparent given their relative lack of fruit weight.

1992, mild winter weather got budbreak off to an early start, then very hot temperatures throughout the growing season produced one of the earlier harvests on record. There were rainstorms in Oct, but no grapes left out in the vineyard at that point. Years like 1992 tend to favor cooler districts where hang-time can still be achieved. Chardonnays were definitely better quality in the Central Coast than in Napa, and red Meritage blends from the Santa Ynez Valley in Santa Barbara Co represent good value in an otherwise middle-of-the-road vintage for red wines throughout CA. Lots of reliable, forward wines in a year similar to the 1981 and 1984 vintages.

1993 *, huge winter rainfall replenished the water table and filled reservoirs throughout the state. Cool spring weather delayed budbreak, but helped to set a very large crop. Mild temperatures through the growing season made harvest fairly late. There was a hot spell in early Sept which whipped everyone into a lather, then three weeks of overcast weather that put everybody back on the shelf. Rain fell in the North Coast during the overcast period, but only inconsequential drizzle. Chardonnays, aromatic whites, and Pinot Noirs from 1993 are very good quality with strong fruit intensity and full-bodied structure. North Coast Cabernet

and Zinfandel suffered from the three-week hiatus in the middle of harvest, but Zinfandels and Syrahs from the Sierra Foothills are magnificent.

1994 ***, not much winter rain or cold weather. Then a cold, dry spring got budbreak off to a late start, but reduced frost danger to little more than a mild flirtation. A weird storm hit the North Coast in late May, including an afternoon of hail in Napa Valley, but flowering had not occurred yet so damage was minimal. The growing season was long and mild. Harvest was very late, but also completely dry and without any spikes of heat. 1994 Pinot Noirs were luscious with deep color and layers of fruit. Rhonish reds had exceptional focus and made workmanlike examples from the 1992 vintage look substandard in comparison. Zinfandels were excellent, although not as ebullient as the 1995s. North Coast Cabernets in 1994 were the absolute top of the heap. The cool season gave them length and suppleness superior even to the 1995s. Merlot from 1994 was ideal, but the marketplace completely flipped out. By Christmas 1995, when the 1994 Merlots began appearing in stores, not a single drop existed on the bulk market and prices rose an average 25% in three months at the wholesale level.

1995 ***, massive spring rains and flooding. Not much effect in vineyard except late budbreak and delayed harvest. Only moderate temperatures all summer, and no rain at all until December so late harvest was not a problem. Somewhat bigger crop than average in the north, and a significantly smaller than average one in the south where rain interfered with flowering. Exceptionally good quality overall. Cabernets are harder than 1994 and opening very slowly. Good candidates for long bottle age. Zinfandels are better than 1994 with dense berry aromas and superb balance.

1996 *, wet spring causing significant shatter and a slightly smaller crop than normal which ripened very early. Some wineries in Alexander Valley were done with crush by the first week of September. Ripe, adequate wines but not particularly flavorful in the Zinfandels and Cabernets. Nor did the inland valley reds seem to have the type of balance to predict improvement in the bottle over a long period. Chardonnays from Central Coast had impressive fruitiness, as did Pinot Noirs from all coastal districts.

1997 *, dry spring with early budburst. Early flowering brought on by warm May temperatures. Freak early June rain from the south had little or no effect. Harvest began early, then was interrupted by several periods of overcast weather. Not much rain, but ripening proceeded in spasmodic, unpredictable manner. 50% higher production than in 1996!

1998, cold, wet winter and spring ascribed to *La Niña*, a cooling of the equatorial waters in the Pacific Ocean and the flip side of El Niño. The western mountains in Napa Valley received 86 in of rain, more than double their average. More problematic was the duration of the rainy season, which lasted until mid-June delaying budbreak by as much as six weeks. There were 135 days with measurable rain from late Oct to early June. That is two out every three days, a modern record. Summer temperatures were modest. Harvest was fragmented and late with some rain. Crop size was average overall, due to increased acreage coming into production, but smaller than average in most individual North Coast vineyards. Overall quality was mediocre.

1999, very cold winter with rain and cold weather well into May as La Niña conditions continued. Budbreak delayed as much as four weeks. Scattered showers and even some hail in North Coast over Memorial Day Weekend. June coldest ever recorded in Monterey. Half-hearted pollination performance by bees. Lowest accumulated temperature growing season in a quarter century. Normal onset of the rainy season in early October would have been a disaster, but Nature relented, with three weeks of sunny Indian Summer. Long, dry Fall, season. Yields down by as much as 10–50%, albeit much more in Central Coast than North Coast. Color and fruit concentration in the hearty red varieties extraordinary, and natural acid levels well above normal.

VITICULTURE AND WINEMAKING
The period from the late-1960s until the mid-1980s can be instructively viewed as California's adolescence in terms of fine wine development. There were excesses. In the 1960s most of the wines were being made by large wineries using traditional methods applied to grapes grown on the floor of inland valleys. In the 1970s tiny wineries with aggressively experimental owner/winemakers proliferated in cooler growing areas and more marginal soil profiles in the mountains. During the 1980s, the trial and error lessons divined by these risk-taking, radical, fringe winemakers began to be more widely adapted by larger, mainstream wineries. This dynamic culture is not unique to California, but it is more widespread in California than it is in other parts of the world, where winemaking traditions may be more

entrenched or the homogenizing effect of a university winemaking credential may be more frequently demanded. California not only has a large pool of *nouveau riche* capital, often derived from high technology, eager to play in the wine game, but a considerable number of California's most prominent winemaker/owners did not sit for formal winemaking degrees at educational institutions. They came from liberal arts backgrounds, and learned winemaking skills by apprenticing themselves at wineries, often thousands of miles from California.

In the 1970s the dominant criterion for noteworthy California wines was intensity. Chardonnay supplied so many prime examples that Frank Prial, writing in the *New York Times*, opined that California Chardonnay was too strong to be matched to food. Today delicacy, balance, and good natural acidity are just as likely to be articulated goals, with plenty of room in between for producers and connoisseurs to argue. Prior to Dr Olmo's work at UC *Davis in the 1960s, Chardonnay rarely produced more than 2 t/a in California. *Clonal selection has now raised the state average to between 4 and 5 t/a. The phrase 'small-berried old clone' commonly heard at artisan wineries is both a backlash to the perceived productivity orientation of UC Davis, and a reference to a general set of clones which may be obtained with increasing ease either from new budwood imports or from old vineyards which pre-date Olmo's work. The phrase WENTE clone is often used in California to refer to pre-Olmo Chardonnay budwood. As in many other ways, Napa Valley vineyards which required replanting in the 1990s due to phylloxera afforded growers there an opportunity to experiment with a much wider range of clones than they had previously used, and to keep better track of them.

Two examples will suffice. *Millerandage, the presence in the same cluster of normal sized berries and tiny seedless berries (sometimes called 'hen and chicken'), is not common in California because inclement weather from late May into early June (when flowering occurs) is infrequent. To the degree small berries improve wine quality though, certain California growers are interested. UC Davis has developed a Chardonnay clone they call both 1A and Mendoza, which is subject to millerandage in cool flowering conditions. Doug Meador's special Sauvignon Blanc clone at VENTANA VYDS is a less academic example. In the late 1980s Meador noticed that a couple of individual Sauvignon Blanc vines in his vineyard produced fruit with an exotic guava-like aroma. He cultivated cuttings and now sells this

Musqué clonal selection to growers in cool regions seeking the tropical notes which have made Sauvignon Blancs, such as *Cloudy Bay, from *New Zealand's Marlborough district so justifiably famous.

A more controversial vineyard matter illustrating California's dynamic fine wine culture would be the systemic virus called *leaf roll or red leaf. All that beautiful red color in older California vineyards in the autumn is a result of the disease. The virus reduces the vines' vigor and their production of fruit. It also retards ripening, since the color change begins in the leaves when the grapes reach 16° to 19° Brix. Grapes need green leaves with chlorophyll to produce sugar. The virus slows down and eventually stops that part of the ripening process. Researchers at UC Davis set out to eliminate this disease from California vineyards in the early 1960s. Their goal was virus free vines bearing the maximum tonnage of high sugar grapes. UC Davis distributed certified, heat-treated cuttings to nurseries and growers. Today, 95% of the state's vineyards are planted to these virus free vines, which can be readily recognized in the vineyard each autumn because the leaves simply brown starting closest to the trunk, then fall off as opposed to turning red or yellow. UC Davis spokesmen say heat-treated vines give 'more production with no loss in quality.' That is precisely where this California-style argument begins. There is a group of radical fringe winemakers in California who maintain quite vocally that the two most common problems with grapes grown on irrigated, fertile, floodplain soils in warm inland valleys are overproduction and high alcohol levels. Their position is: virus infected vines producing fewer, less ripe grapes should logically result in *better* wine quality, given the way California's conditions differ from marginal ripening areas like northern Europe. 'After all,' virus defenders maintain, 'the aim of grape growing is not healthy vines, but fine wine. Virus naturally polices the more venal motivations of your average grower.' UC Davis feels there are better ways to solve the quality problem than using sick vines. Virus advocates say certified vines grown on deep, fertile, irrigated soils cannot be restrained even by severe pruning, excess shoot removal, and cluster thinning. They call the heat-treated plants 'bull vines' and the grapes 'basketball berries.' Enemies of the virus (that would include *all* UC Davis trained viticulturalists) typically respond by asking, 'tuberculosis might make you thin and attractive, but would it be worth it?' Vigorous debate can be one of the California wine industry's greatest strengths.

Another controversy, intensified by the opportunity/requirement to replant in Napa following phylloxera, concerns trellis systems and vine spacing (see Viticulture essay, p 44). Conventional wisdom had moved from *head trained vines to *cordon training by the mid-1980s, but the 'California sprawl' of leaves was still standard in vineyards. That technique produced large vines, especially in productive sites, with a cylinder of vegetation several yards in diameter running along the cordon, and shoot tips that were still green and growing when the grapes were picked. Proponents of the new theories hold that vines should be spaced and trellises constructed to match the vigor of each site as defined by available water, depth of top soil, and availability of nutrients. That means more vines per acre and smaller trellises on hillsides with thin top soil. Such protagonists prefer narrow vertical canopies with each leaf in the sunlight. They want shoots which grow only to about 3 feet in length with a diameter about that of one's little finger. They want the shoots to stop growing by the end of the season and the stems to lignify. They say grapes are physiologically mature only when the pips turn brown, irrespective of sugar levels the grapes may achieve before then. Most controversially, these radicals claim *higher* crop levels are possible with *better* wine quality when spacing and trellis systems are balanced to any particular site in this manner. Before-and-after wine comparisons always involve vintage differences, so they are far from conclusive, but these theories are attracting new adherents every year in California. Increased *vine density has become a credential frequently cited by growers.

New plantings have always had a faddish currency about them in California. Cabernet Sauvignon and Chardonnay have dominated the marketplace since 1970, so it is not surprising they are among the leaders in new plantings. Chardonnay doubled its acreage between 1990 and 1998 and will soon account for almost half the nearly 200,000 acres of white grapes in the state. Cabernet Sauvignon has also doubled its acreage in that same period, but accounts for only slightly more than 20% of the more than 225,000 acres of red grapes planted. Merlot (see Wine and the American Consumer essay, p 1) accounts for the biggest percentage increase, with acreage growing by a factor of six since 1990 to almost rival Cabernet. Zinfandel, much of it destined for the *White Zinfandel market, has also rebounded to almost double its acreage since 1990. In regaining the 50,000+ total acres it once held, Zinfandel in 1997 pushed slightly

ahead of Cabernet to retake the position of CA's most widely planted red grape. New plantings at the end of the millennium will likely return that crown to Cabernet Sauvignon however.

In the exciting newcomers category Cabernet Franc together with Rhône, and Italian varietals deserve special attention. Cab Franc has more than doubled its acreage since 1990 to well over 2,000 acres while notably retaining its status as California's most expensive grape averaging close to $1,500 per ton throughout the decade. Syrah exploded in 1991–2, from a small base, to expand its acreage by a factor of 35—to more than double the total acreage for Cab Franc. But Syrah was unable to maintain its price point, falling to $850 per ton on average in 1998. In 1993–4 Viognier went through a similar planting cycle, expanding from just a few acres to well over 1,100. Viognier did maintain its price attractiveness, however, averaging about $1,350 per ton throughout the period to take the laurel for most expensive white grape. In 1995–6 the big demand was for Pinot Gris vines. Sangiovese acreage in California also increased exponentially during the 1990s to reach 2,500 acres in 1997.

As new varieties appear in the marketplace, they go through a process educating both consumers and winemakers. Viognier is a recent illustration. The timeframe for defining what a benchmark CA Viognier should taste like, and cost, parallels the development of red Meritage wines in the 1980s. CA Viogniers began appearing from more than a handful of producers in 1992, generally priced between $20 and $30. The only competition at the time came from Condrieu priced over $30. Most of these original CA Viognier vineyards were barely producing 1 t/a. Other than alcohol levels over 13.5%, these first wines shared very few characteristics: some were voluptuously floral, others very tightly restrained; some were cloyingly phenolic, others thin bodied and acidic; a few showed barrel treatment and MLF. Three years later the field had both focused and expanded. French Viogniers from Languedoc and the Ardéche were arriving at $10. HORTON Winery in VA was producing Viognier at 4.5 t/a and selling it for $12 a bottle. The price for most CA producers had settled between $10 and $20, and everyone with more than two years of experience had begun to rein in the alcohols, the phenolic excesses, and the more cosmetic aromatic properties.

This type of maturation in winemaking style can be traced through every aspect of the CA industry since 1970. As cited above, Chardonnay reveals this attitude evolution

clearly because it is so much a product of the winemaker's efforts. In the mid-1980s there were several CA Chardonnays intentionally produced from marginally underripe grapes, then worked up in the winery with vigorous new strains of MLF bacteria, to achieve wines worthy of long bottle age. Another Chardonnay style frequently encountered in CA since 1985 is made by leaving 0.5% RS to create a new balance point in high acid, *fruit-driven Chardonnays. Such a small amount of sugar is not immediately identifiable to the average consumer. It softens one's perception of the individual elements in the wine similar to the way bottle maturation would. It improves mouthfeel. At Show judgings these wines are controversial. They can be adroitly made and worthy of artistic consideration if they come from cool districts, are picked early enough to retain high natural acidity, and have pointed flavor profiles due to concentrating the fruit in lower yields. The best ones have an intense green apple nose and refreshing structural balance that lets you enjoy tense fruit aromas without paying a painful price from thin, searingly acidic, aftertaste. DE LOACH Winery in Sonoma does very well with this technique.

Other evolutions within CA wineries include: (1) greatly reduced levels of *sulfur dioxide (often under 30 ppm total), and frequently none at all at the crusher; (2) much broader interest in use of WILD YEAST for fermentations; (3) much more attention to tannin management techniques seeking full-bodied texture without bitterness or astringency (see Winemaking essay, p 35); (4) *barrel making (see AMERICAN OAK); and (5) *corks, as winemakers seek better ways to sample batches and avoid randomly tainted bottles, or avoid the risk entirely by using plastic closures.

See also *rootstocks, BRETTANOMYCES, Microbiology essay, p 39, and Genetics essay, p 57.

MARKETPLACE

Per capita wine consumption in the US is paltry, about one-eighth that of France or Italy. But it is over three times higher in CA than in the rest of the US or Canada, ie 6 gal per capita in California, about the same as in Germany. San Francisco is the number one market in America for wine, and dead last in sales of soda pop. Moreover, restaurant dining is more prevalent in CA: San Francisco has over 60 restaurants per 10,000 households, that is 20% higher than even New York; and San Franciscans spend an average of nearly $200 per month eating out, 20% more than the national average. Safeway, a national grocery chain, reports CA is among the top three markets nationwide for sales of fresh herbs, bottled water, salad materials, charcoal, and fresh eggs; while ranking among the bottom five markets for sales of baking goods, tobacco, canned vegetables, sugar, desserts, and boxed breakfast foods.

Ethnic diversity has made CA cuisine a crossroads, significantly altered from the northern European models traditionally applied to fine wine. Dinners in CA are as likely to have a fragrant course and a spicy course, as they are to have the meat and dairy courses one might commonly expect. No specific wine/food pairs have yet emerged as classics in CA, but there is definitely a trend toward a regional palate. It is almost a cliche that at some point European wine trade visitors to CA remark that some wine they are tasting is 'too fruity.' That assessment is as incomprehensible to CA wine drinkers as describing some starlet as 'too pretty.' This gradual disconnection between the northern European palate and the CA palate has something to do with the styles of wines indigenous to each place, but it also owes a great deal to foodstuffs frequently encountered. Salsa is the condiment of choice in CA. Cellaring wines for long periods of time is not a common practice. Californians move on average every four years. Solidity may be less highly regarded in a land beset by thousands of small earthquakes every year.

Wine packaging is another form of departure. CA wine labels are designed to make consumers turn their head and look while walking down a store aisle. Visually startling colors and unusual graphics are the coin of this realm. Well-established brands may aim for more understated elegance, but the difference between a group of Old World bottles and a group of CA bottles is usually unmistakable even 30 ft away.

Perhaps cut from the same cloth is the air of celebrity which surrounds certain winemakers in CA. Europeans believe a wine should reflect the place where it is grown. Therefore the winemaker's responsibility is largely to stay out of the way. Californians think of winemakers as artists who play an active role in producing something better than the sum of its parts. CA winemakers can achieve a public following similar to great chefs. It never hurts to promote one's case either. Winemakers in CA are generally expected to perform a public appearance role, at least to some degree. A colorful demeanor will never fully compensate for shoddy winemaking skills, but there are many wonderful winemakers who are somewhat underappreciated in the state largely due to shy and retiring personalities.

Winery architecture plays a similar role. When Australian winemakers see Napa Valley for the first time they are inevitably astonished by the amount of money that has gone into buildings. They think the value of a wine resides entirely inside the bottle. They have not stopped to consider that the population of CA is almost twice that of all Australia, and half again more people come to visit CA each year. Seventy per cent of Americans do not normally drink wine. The value of a wine in CA often draws to a considerable degree on the personal experience a consumer had at the winery. Architecture is part of that experience.

Wine education takes many forms in CA, although the distinction between promotion and objective education is not well recognized by the general public. Winemaker dinners are a frequent form of entertainment at restaurants in large cities whereby the chef presents a menu to pair with a group of wines about which the winemaker will speak. Schools often offer courses in wine appreciation, as do other socially oriented businesses such as health clubs and country clubs. Tasting organizations such as WINE BRATS or the Chaine des Rôtisseurs have numerous chapters throughout the state. Bookstores in CA commonly have a wine section.

Retail wine stores have changed dramatically in CA since 1970. The predatory nature of discount stores has eliminated specialty wine retailers in all but a few sophisticated markets. Discount stores generally price wines at 16–20% over their cost. They move large volumes and minimize their expenditure on amenities and/or customer service. In a state where 850 wineries can sell directly to any store's customers, and ship conveniently for less than $15 a case, retail outlets definitely need some edge. The answer is generally one of the following three: (1) lower prices on well-recognized brands; (2) specialized inventory and very knowledgeable staff; or (3) the convenience of grocery shopping in the same location. In large sections of CA, with populations in the millions, 90% of wine is sold in supermarket grocery store chains.

Zinfandel provides a clear illustration of the forces at work on the CA marketplace. In the 1970s Zinfandel was a red wine, modestly priced, widely planted, and generally associated with reliable value. There was a cult following for intensely ripe, wildly extracted Zinfandels, mostly amongst fringe groups given to tattoos years before Generation X was even born. But red Zinfandel died in the popular marketplace of the 1980s because its image lacked refinement. Vine-

yards were ripped out, and many venerable properties only survived because of the emergence of that curiosity item, White Zinfandel, which appealed to people who had little prior wine experience, ie most Americans. Then red Zinfandel was resurrected by a corps of dedicated winemakers (RIDGE, RAVENSWOOD, ROSENBLUM) and a lighter-bodied, more elegant style pioneered by Dr Jerry Seps at STORYBOOK MTN winery. Most importantly, they moved Zinfandel into the double digits price category. Not only did more exclusive prices improve the image of the wine, but they greatly facilitated winemakers' ability to produce a truly artistic product. Inevitably the pendulum has continued to swing, and in 1999 some Zinfandel prices had begun to edge into the ludicrous range, but this evolution of CA's own grape variety has at least removed it from the endangered list.

One of the lessons of the Zinfandel story above is particularly germane in America. There *is* a point of intersection between the fine wine industry and the community of US health fascists: per capita consumption *can* go down while industry revenues rise. We are even seeing this phenomenon in Italy and in France. The French today only drink 60% as much wine per capita as they did in 1980. *But* they spend more money to do so. The same is true in CA. For 20 years we have been moving towards drinking more moderate amounts of better wine on a more regular basis.

Only 4% of the wine made in CA is priced over $14 per bottle, yet those 5.5 million cases account for 16% of all the dollars spent on wine. Twenty wine companies in CA produce 90% of the wine volume, but they only receive about half of the revenue. For many years tuxedo marketing was the technique by which small, but ambitious wineries distinguished themselves from the bulk producers. They assiduously cultivated an image of exclusivity. And it worked, at least for the quarter-century beginning in 1975.

Speculations about the future are less confident. Many CA wine marketers figure every bottle that could be sold using an elitist image has already been sold. Expanding the market may require a friendlier, more inclusive approach. Jim McCullough, former marketing manager for Gundlach-Bundschu Winery in Sonoma Valley, was a premier example. In 1990 he began printing Chinese fortunes (humorous one-line predictions) on the corks in Gundlach-Bundschu bottles. When his customers in North Carolina hesitated over pronunciation of the winery's name, McCullough started calling it Gunny Bunny. Then in 1993 he and a couple of friends boarded the Napa Valley Wine Train from horseback, wearing bandanas to disguise their faces. They proceeded to force the train's patrons, at gunpoint, to drink Sonoma Valley wine. Many people in the CA wine business agree the industry would be better off with more mounted masked men and fewer tuxedos.

REGULATION

Predictably California has a much less restrictive environment for wine sales than most states. There are no DRY counties. Delivery is legal throughout the state. Excise taxes are low, and licenses to sell only wine or beer are very modestly priced, although the bureaucratic paperwork to acquire one must deter all but the most hardy individuals. California has flirted with TIED HOUSE LAWS, but unlike most states still allows single business entities to vertically integrate if they wish. Hence, one person or company can simultaneously own an import, wholesale, and retail license. Retail wine stores can get tasting licenses, and restaurants can get licenses for off-premise sales. Grocery stores sell wine, and liquor stores may sell food. DRAM SHOP INSURANCE is expensive, but available. Penalties for drunk driving can be $1,000 or more for a first offense, drivers' license suspension, and jail for subsequent offenses.

EXPORT

California, and the US, were never very active in wine exports prior to 1985. Then a period of export marketing subsidies became available to US wineries from the federal government wherein they could recoup expenses for advertising and trade shows overseas, although not for travel or personnel. Most of these subsidies ended in the early 1990s, but California by then was well launched on an export track. In 1997 8% of California's wine production was exported overseas. In 1998 US wine exports were 72 million gal (ten times what they had been in 1986), valued at $537 million, 90% of which came from California. The UK is by far the world's thirstiest consumer of US export wine at nearly 17 million gal, but Japan and Canada make it a race at 14 and 12 million gal respectively. GALLO is by far North America's biggest volume exporter.   B.C.C.

Fletcher, D., *Balanced Vines* (privately published, 1999).

McPhee, J. A., *Assembling California* (New York, 1993).

Nies, J. E., *Native American History* (New York, 1996).

Stone, I., *Men to Match My Mountains* (Garden City, NY, 1956).

Wine Institute Statistics, www.wineinstitute.org

Calistoga, subdistrict which is not an approved AVA, in the northernmost section of CA's NAPA VALLEY. Name refers to the town, founded in 1859 by non-observant Mormon adventurer Sam Brannan, whose activities in San Francisco had earlier helped contribute the word *vigilante* to the English language. The name is a contraction of California and Saratoga, an upstate NY resort also famous for its mineral baths. Brannan failed as a vineyardist, but his town prospered as a vacation destination because of the geothermal springs which dot the landscape. Personalities as famous as Robert Louis Stevenson came to Calistoga before the turn of the century to live and to enjoy local wines made by Jacob Schram, Alfred Tubbs, and the Grimm brothers (now Schramsberg, CH MONTELENA, and STORYBOOK MTN wineries respectively). Today tourists still enjoy sulfur mudbaths and massage every bit as much as the haute cuisine served in top restaurants such as Jan Birnbaum's Catahoula. The Calistoga brand of mineral water has been purchased by Perrier, but some of it is still bottled locally.

The town of Calistoga is 40 mi from San Pablo Bay at the mouth of Napa Valley. Moreover, the valley narrows dramatically at this northern extremity and takes a dogleg west between St Helena and Calistoga. The result is a much warmer climate. From a glider airport located in Calistoga motorless aircraft can ride the rising currents of warm air. Mt St Helena terminates Napa Valley just north of Calistoga, and the soils of the area are volcanic in origin, even though Mt St Helena has never erupted as a volcano. The volcanic soils in Calistoga district vineyards are igneous rock which has come to the surface due to folding and pulling apart at the edge of the tectonic plate (see CALIFORNIA, geology), then eroded in place to form a light, permeable topsoil local growers call TUFA.

It takes twice as long to get to Calistoga from San Francisco as it does to reach the town of Napa, which is one reason Calistoga retained its rural ambiance longer than Yountville and St Helena. Well into the 1970s Calistoga was most prominent as a source of dark, viscous Petite Sirah, pronounced *Petty Sara* by the Italian growers of that era. Today the small footprint of the valley floor is known for strong, earthy Cabernet Sauvignon, and many of the newer growers are looking seriously at steep canyon walls for high quality vineyard sites.

The southern extent of Calistoga as a district is functionally defined by the northern boundary of the ST HELENA AVA. That is the crossroad called Bale Lane, which may or may not concur with the postmaster and with the telephone directory.

NOTABLE PROPERTIES

Araujo, beautiful 35-acre vineyard located in a canyon northeast of the Silverado Trail. First planted by Milt Eisele and vineyard designated on a special Cabernet Sauvignon from Phelps (see NAPA VALLEY) during the period 1971 through 1991. Purchased by Bart and Daphne Araujo in 1990 for $3 million, the winery is firmly in the ranks of the CULT Cabernets. Although its DNA has not been analyzed, many commentators believe there is a unique Eisele clone of Cabernet because the vineyard's track record has always combined deep color and mineral flavors with a beguiling, *lifted perfume.

Clos Pegase, one of several recent, controversial Napa Valley architectural edifices. Jan Shrem is a self-made publishing magnate with a Japanese wife. In 1983 he sponsored a contest through the San Francisco Museum of Modern Art to have a winery and home designed in which he could display his extensive art collection. The competition was won by Michael Graves from Princeton. His winery features huge columns which imply Greece, but 'classical' is not a description easily employed. Intriguing modern sculptures adorn the grounds.

See STERLING, CH MONTELENA, STORYBOOK MTN, DIAMOND MTN.   B.C.C.

Cal-Italia Consorzio, trade group organized in 1997 to promote wines made from Italian grape varieties grown in CALIFORNIA and also bring attention to the considerable contribution Italian immigrants have made to American wine. There are 110 wineries producing wines from Italian grape varieties in CA. Sangiovese is the most faddishly popular variety, offered by 85 wineries in 1999 (including Seghesio winery, owner of 88-year-old vines) even though there were only 2,500 acres of Sangiovese planted in CA at that time, and a third of those were not yet bearing fruit. Barbera was more venerable with 11,000 planted acres. Malvasia Bianca is the stealth variety with 2,400 planted acres but only a handful of producers. Pinot Grigio is a brewing controversy with no apparent correspondence between wine style and any particular winery's choice of the Italianate name versus the Alsace name of the same grape, Pinot Gris. While obscure Italian varieties such as Teroldego and Aleatico are being auditioned in CA, no one seems to be very happy yet with attempts to produce a serious version of the Piedmontese specialty Nebbiolo. Italian regional standards such as Cortese and Arneis are also making appearances in CA, but one must be dubious American consumers will respond well to wines which their producers describe as emphasizing 'the typically soapy varietal character.' The Consorzio's annual festival with wine tasting and a broad selection of Italian foodstuffs is held near to Columbus Day in Oct each year at Ft Mason in San Francisco. www.cal-italia.org

B.C.C.

Callaway Vyds, large CA winery near San Diego, owned by ALLIED DOMECQ. Eli Callaway was the president of Burlington Industries (textile mills and clothes) before he came to TEMECULA in 1969 to start this winery and to precipitate the local land rush. Callaway left the wine business in 1981 (for golf club manufacture) when he sold to distillers Hiram Walker.

Callaway Vyds was selling 80,000 cases in 1981, so one can assume they knew a few things, but Terry Clancy, the manager Hiram Walker hired, nevertheless made a radical decision to completely eschew red wines. They expanded to over 200,000 cases exploiting that market niche, in particular an entirely stainless steel fermented and aged Chardonnay they called CallaLees. In 1989, after Clancy's regime, they returned to red wine production in order to fulfill the demands of the America's Cup yacht race which was held in San Diego. In 1998 they sold 250,000 cases. Of the 700+ acres Callaway owns in Temecula, 560 are Chardonnay. They produce limited quantities of Viognier, as well as several Italian varietals including Dolcetto.

B.C.C.

Canada, country with the largest land area in North America, but only a third as many people as Mexico and only 12% as many people as the US. Canada ranks eighth in the world in Gross National Product. Total acreage of land under wine producing vine (as opposed to vines grown for grape juice) is 14,000 acres. With C$700 million in sales, wine production represents a very small percentage of the total economy. Total of all wine, including imports, sold in Canada in 1999 was approximately 9.3 million cases.

The rationale behind the existing Canadian tax structure on wine was premised on the Prohibition notion that if alcohol was going to be sold in Canada there had to be accompanying social programs to address problems associated with alcohol abuse. To a large extent, the same justification exists today, albeit the pot is now shared between many sectors such as education, transportation, health, and welfare. On average, taxes represent 56% of the total price of a bottle of wine sold through provincial retail stores. In

1999 that represented C$400 million in wine taxes contributed to government coffers.

HISTORY

The first Europeans to explore Canada extensively were French. Hegemony passed to the British in 1763 after a battle on the Plains of Abraham in Quebec, and the subsequent Treaty of Paris. In 1774 the British conceded religious and linguistic guarantees to their Francophone populations along the St Lawrence River in the Quebec Act of 1774. Several battles between the US and the British were fought around Lake Erie during the War of 1812, and the border was eventually settled with the Webster-Ashburton Treaty in 1842. Repatriation of the Constitution from Britain to Canada, including the Charter of Rights, occurred in 1982 under Prime Minister Pierre Trudeau.

Canada and the US have always been strong trading partners. Over the years, Canada has specialized its industries in order to find a niche living next to the much larger and more efficient economy of the US. This specialization enabled the US to export products not made in Canada to Canada. Each country has become the other's largest market. Tensions in trade negotiations have usually stemmed from the imbalance between the two economies, and from Canadians' sense of disadvantage at having to compete with a neighboring market ten times its size, especially on products they both produce. The wine industry has been no exception. With the advent of NAFTA the Canadian wine industry experienced a decline in volume sales from 50% of market share in Canada prior to the agreement, to 38% in 1999. However, it also experienced a rise in dollar sales, driven by Canadian-grown VQA wines. Non-VQA wines may be legally labeled Produce of Canada even if they contain 75% juice or grapes imported from other countries, but the VQA indicium is only allowed on labels for wines which are entirely made from Canadian fruit. In many ways the VQA movement was catalyzed by the challenge presented when Canadian wines had to compete at parity with US imports.

Alcoholic beverages from indigenous grapes have been made for centuries in ONTARIO. Even before French Jesuit missionaries to the Algonquin Indians gathered wild grapes from along the sandy shores of Georgian Bay to make sacramental wines, Indian folklore records Iroquois-speaking tribes offering fermented grape juice to the water god who dwelled below Niagara Falls. Wild riparia grapes still grow in many areas of Ontario winding around roadside fences.

There is ample evidence grapes were being cultivated on the NIAGARA PENINSULA as early as 1840. Porter Adams is recognized as the first man to systematically plant and cultivate vines on a commercial scale, but he was not the first commercial winemaker. In 1811 Johann Schiller, a German mercenary corporal with previous winemaking experience in the Rhine, settled on the slopes of the Credit River in Cooksville, 20 mi east of York (today's TORONTO). He found labrusca grape varieties growing wild and was soon making wine. Schiller is recognized as the father of Canadian winemaking.

Although *home winemaking was common, Schiller had little commercial competition because the area was so sparsely populated by white settlers. Not until an immigrant wave arrived during the 1850–70s did farmers begin to make wine from cultivated vineyards rather than by simply gathering the wild vine. In 1860, a Niagara resident from Port Dalhousie wrote in the *Canadian Agriculturist* that many German farmers in his neighborhood were making large quantities of wine, some of which 'resembled a good Madeira.' Grape grower James C. Kilborne, in the same year, writing from nearby Beamsville, reported 'three years ago four or five barrels of wine were grown from a single vine in one season' and 'the wine very much resembles port.'

Count Justin M. de Courtenay was a grower and neighbor of Schiller who purchased the Schiller property in 1864. He organized local farmers into the Vine Growers' Association which was granted a charter by the Canadian Parliament which included relief from customs duties for twelve years. De Courtenay renamed Schiller's business Clair House Vyds and exhibited his wines abroad. In 1866 another commercial enterprise was launched under the Vin Villa label on PELEE ISLAND, just across Lake Erie from Sandusky, Ohio. 'A company of gentlemen from Kentucky' purchased a farm and planted 50 acres. The southerners were soon joined by two English brothers who planted a 15-acre rival nearby. By 1875 they were harvesting 5 t/a of American hybrid grapes. By 1890, 35 commercial wineries were established in Ontario.

American hybrids comprised the bulk of Canada's early wine industry (and in fact continued to do so until 1980). The often foul flavor of these wines could be camouflaged when fortified with grape distillate or whiskey, the preferred drink of the times, to produce a palatable 'sherry' or 'port' with 20% alcohol. Establishing a life in this spare new land was harsh at best. A glass of sherry or port could alleviate the trauma. That factor, and the potency of this accessible beverage, soon led to a rise in the number of Temperance groups.

Prohibition

By 1900, the booming commercial wine industry of southwestern Ontario had been reduced to nine producing wineries by the successful influence of temperance sentiment on legislation. Vineyards were torn out in favor of tobacco, a dubious conversion in retrospect, but a more profitable venture than vines at the time. Winemaking in Niagara continued as a small industry, with ever smaller profit margins, until the outbreak of the First World War. When the interests of the Temperance lobby coincided with the interests of the federal government, which needed alcohol to make explosives, even that tiny remnant succumbed. On September 15, 1916, four years before similar legislation was passed nationally in the US, Ontario passed a Temperance Act prohibiting sale of any intoxicating liquor, unless authorized to do so for the war effort. No one could 'have, keep, give, or consume liquor except in a private dwelling house.' By 1919 all other provinces followed suit.

It is interesting to note that the WCTU of Ontario was not exerting its influence in a vacuum. The grape growers' lobby pressured a conservative government to exempt native wines from the Temperance Act. The amended legislation permitted wines made from Ontario-grown grapes to be produced by manufacturers who could secure a permit from the Licensing Board. To curb consumption and placate temperance leaders, the Act conceded that every winery could have only one retail outlet, that it must be on their premises, and that customers would be required to go there to buy wine. In a twist of logic, the law also insisted customers *had* to purchase 2 cases or 5 gal at a time.

Distilled spirits were illegal to sell, but it was not against the law to manufacture them. Alcohol was readily available for 'sacramental, industrial, artistic, mechanical, scientific and medicinal purposes.' The only alcoholic beverage that could be sold without prescription or sanction was wine. The consequence of this was a proliferation of overnight wineries set up in barns and basements. During the eleven years of Prohibition, 57 new licenses were issued, resulting in a total of 67 Ontario wineries by 1925. Consumption of Canadian wine quadrupled because of demand from domestic customers and from bootleggers who smuggled considerable quantities across the nearby Canada–US border. It was a Klondike in the east.

Highly sweet and alcoholic ports and sherries dominated the market following Canadian repeal of Prohibition in 1927. Fortification of wines with spirit made from native grapes was allowed from 1931. This legislation pleased the grower who could sell his less-than-inspiring labruscas and the winemaker who could better mask their *foxy flavor. It also satisfied the consumer who found solace in wines with high alcohol content throughout the embittering experience of the Depression.

Upgrading table wines

Experimental vineyards did exist on the Niagara Peninsula during this period. They focused on three basic thrusts of inquiry. The first explored growing *vinifera using alternative vineyard management techniques to protect vines during winter, eg MOUNDING, and to offer better ripening prospects in summer, eg trellising experiments. The second thrust explored the development of winter-hardy vinifera/labrusca American hybrids. The third introduced French hybrids that had been bred in Europe as a means of addressing the phylloxera epidemic.

Viscount Aldemar de Chaunac, a scientist working at Brights Winery in Niagara Falls led the way in the private sector. The Horticultural Research Institute of Ontario in Vineland led the way in the public sector. The Horticultural Station from 1913 to 1937, for instance, experimented with over 57,000 seedlings in a grape breeding program. Fewer than six were felt to have sufficient promise for further experimentation. The outbreak of the Second World War cut off all experimentation that involved European sources of supply. Ontario wineries meanwhile had all they could do just to stay in business. In 1946, just after the war ended, de Chaunac returned from a trip to France with 40 vine varieties including French hybrids and pure vinifera varieties such as Chardonnay and Pinot Noir.

In 1955 Brights Wines produced a small batch of 100% Ontario-grown Chardonnay. Among ten other varieties de Chaunac brought back that adapted well was the French hybrid Seibel 9549. By 1972 it had become the leading red in Ontario, and was soon renamed De Chaunac to honor his contribution. Marechal Foch, another French hybrid in whose lineage were Pinot Noir and Gamay Noir, also did very well. During the 1950s, de Chaunac developed a 7% alcohol sparkling wine called Brights Winette, using labrusca grapes, soon followed by Du Barry's Sparkling Vin Rosé. It was Joseph Peller from Andrés Wines, however, who created a North American wine revolution with his

rendition called Baby Duck. This early wine *cooler fortuitously coincided with the coming of age of the first wave of Baby Boomers, and provided them with an easy transition from Coca-Cola to table wine.

Between 1933 and 1975 no new licenses of note were granted by Ontario to make and sell wine. Larger wineries were encouraged by the province to buy up the licenses that had once proliferated during Prohibition in order to reduce the number of operating wineries. In 1974 only six wineries remained from the all-time high of 67 in the late 1920s. Glimmers of the potential for growing better varietals started to emerge in the early 1950s when the first 100% Ontario-grown Riesling and Chardonnay emerged. But it would be 25 years before anyone took that potential seriously. The first factor was demand, or lack of same. There was not a wine culture in Canada at the time. Anyone drinking wine other than Baby Duck drank Mateus or Castle Mendes, neutral commercial table wines. Toronto in the 1950s had very few restaurants, and those were usually checked-tablecloth, Italian-style serving uninspiring wines in raffia-covered bottles—and never on Sundays. No alcohol could be served in public places in Ontario on Sundays until 1967, and then only from noon to 3pm and 5–9 pm. (It was not until 1997 that beverage alcohol could be sold in liquor stores across the province on Sundays.) The second factor was grower resistance. French hybrids started to get attention, but grower attitudes ranged from indifference to intransigence. Brights adopted a leadership role by assuring their growers a steady market for varieties such as Marechal Foch and Vidal. At Ch Gai, enologist Paul Bosc planted a few rows of Foch, then took that wine to a 1973 tasting in NEW YORK CITY where participants were pleasantly surprised. Local nurseries were cautioned, however, to stick with hybrids and not venture into vinifera for fear it would not survive Ontario's winters. One senior enologist in the area addressed a conference of growers and winemakers saying, 'Growing vinifera in the Northeast is just like having two mistresses. You enjoy them both, but you marry neither.' Fortunately, a few rebel growers saw the potential and planted vinifera vineyards in spite of such warnings.

Sales at LCBO by the early 1970s were starting to confirm a change in consumer tastes. They met this shift by increasing imports of better quality table wines from California and overseas. Producers saw this increase as a competitive threat. This trend started a chain of events which would change forever the nature of the Canadian wine industry.

NAFTA *and the Canadian wine revolution*

Ontario wine producers were feeling undermined. To compete, they began building modern facilities in provinces that had fewer restrictions than Ontario. Supplies of less desirable grapes started mounting in Ontario, while the market for them steadily declined. A low point came in the mid-1980s with a movement in the LCBO away from accepting labrusca-based wines. Growers and industry observers alike forecast that the portending free trade agreement with the US would break the industry completely. Many felt the Ontario industry could not compete without a protective tariff on imports. A small group of progressives, however, regarded free trade as an opportunity to transform the industry from within. Which is what happened.

In 1988 legislation was passed prohibiting any labrusca-based wine to be sold through the LCBO. To compensate growers who felt their industry was being sacrificed to free trade, the Canadian government paid growers to remove their labrusca vines, from 1989 until 1994. Some growers switched to different crops altogether. Some sold their land and left farming. Others began rebuilding and planted their vineyards with vinifera. The paradox though was that visionaries who had devoted themselves to growing vinifera long before the government's initiative did not qualify for these grants. Their only satisfaction today is that they own the oldest vinifera vines in Ontario. It was no coincidence that VQA was finalized in 1988. The movement had started in 1982, when Donald ZIRALDO and Karl Kaiser attempted to export some of their Inniskillin Foch to Europe. They were refused entry. Thus were planted the seeds of reform. In 1986 there were a total of 14,205,074 grape vines in Ontario, most of which were labrusca based varieties. By 1996 the total figure had dwindled to 10,944,455. The figures for 1998 showed an increase to 12,216,451 vines with vinifera varieties topping all other vines planted.

Despite stigmas of the past, Canadian wineries are demonstrating that wines grown in cool climates can possess complex flavors, delicate yet persistent aromas, tightly focused structures, and much longer ageing potential than wines produced in warmer regions of the world. Sales of Ontario wines account for 46% of the total wine market in Ontario, with demand far outstripping supply. Forecasts suggest the industry can expect to grow by 3% every year for the next ten years. That demand would necessitate doubling present vineyard acreage and result in a 12% increase in market share. There is sufficient arable land in which to plant as long as regional planning boards maintain their commitment to agricultural zoning laws. In 1999 there were 60 wineries in Ontario with 17 licenses pending. Nevertheless operations have not proliferated there as much as they have in other jurisdictions because of an LCBO policy restricting new on-site winery retail stores to premises with at least 5 acres of vineyard and a guarantee that the fruit on the property will be used in the wine.

Another trend is the rise of agri-tourism. Redevelopment of Ontario's vineyards, an increase in small to medium-sized operations, and revenue derived from direct winery retail sales have all resulted in a boom for wineries as visitor destinations. Many producers have invested millions of dollars in developing attractive tasting rooms, tour programs, retail stores, educational opportunities, and vineyard events. There is the usual Canadian weather lull in Jan, but from Feb to Dec wine country vibrates with activity—from special new release evenings and winter weekends skiing and mulling wines by the fire, to gala fundraisers, vineyard jazz and theatre in the fields, bicycle tours, barbecues, balloon rides, and a ten day harvest festival which has been acclaimed one of the top four attractions in Canada. Wineries have opened fine restaurants that specialize in locally grown products and tour operators flourish on the burgeoning appeal of other Niagara Peninsula attractions such as gambling in Niagara Falls and the internationally renowned George Bernard Shaw Festival Theatre. Bed & breakfast inns have multiplied to meet the growing demand. Employment related to winery tourism tripled from 1995 to 1997, a welcome respite from economic recession in the early 1990s when the region's manufacturing base collapsed. Estimates set winery visitations at 450,000 annually in the Niagara Peninsula. This success has launched several plans for special galleries and even cooking schools with residential programs.

For many of Canada's smaller wineries, sales are not an issue. Larger operations are concentrating on export markets. They are also looking to markets which should be considered domestic, but which are virtually untapped, in Quebec and Nova Scotia, as well as in the US.

Until new acreage begins producing, however, larger wineries are free to blend their lower-priced wines with imported wines, a practice legal in Ontario even for wines labelled as Canadian under the Wine Content Act. The Act is scheduled to end Jan 1, 2000 but it is expected to be extended for a couple of years. Other people in the industry want to acknowledge that while Canada may be a gifted wine producing country, it should not try to compete with volume producers. The future, these folks contend, is to move up. Many producers have demonstrated they can make wines of uncommon excellence from varieties such as Riesling, Chardonnay, Cabernet Franc, Gamay Noir, Pinot Noir, and of course, late harvest wines and ICEWINES. New entrants in the industry also have the will and the financial wherewithal to aim for the great wine lists, merchants, and cellars of the world.

MARKETPLACE

The population of Canada in the late 1990s was nearly 31 million. Forecasts predict it will reach 40 million by the year 2016. As in the US, the population is getting older because of the long-term slowdown of the birth rate and the increase in life expectancy. The baby boom generation created a huge bulge in the age structure now accounting for almost one-third of Canada's population. Different from US Boomers, the Canadian bulge started later (1947 vs 1946), lasted longer (1966 vs 1964), and resulted in more children per capita being born. They now make up over 40% of the workforce and earn over half of all personal income. Overall, the population is becoming better educated with 40% white collar and 25% classified as holding professional, managerial, and administrative positions. One-third of the workforce hold blue collar occupations. A growing consumer segment of the population is the ethnic market. Minority combined purchasing power is expected soon to exceed C$300 billion annually. The Italian, German, and Chinese communities each have populations over 400,000 people.

Per capita consumption of beer, spirits, and wine is changing. In 1993 Canadians of legal drinking age were consuming 94 l (25 gal) of beer a year. In 1997 that had decreased to 89 l. In the same period, the consumption of spirits also declined from 6 l per capita annually to 5.6 l. Wine is moving, albeit nominally in the opposite direction. In 1993 Canadians were drinking 10.9 l of wine per capita a year. By 1997 wine consumption had grown to 11.25 l. Average Canadian households purchase wine once a month, although in the Maritimes, Manitoba, Saskatchewan, and Alberta they shop every month and a half. Twenty per cent of wine buyers have income over C$70,000 annually. They are purchasing three-quarters of the total wine volume sold and are shopping more frequently.

REGULATORY ENVIRONMENT

Several federal departments regulate the manufacture and sale of wine in Canada. The Dept of Industry regulates packaging, labeling, and trademarks; Revenue Canada regulates excise taxes. The Food and Drug Act (FDA) from Health Canada regulates all beverages which contain more than 2% alcohol by volume and are the product of fermentation normally performed by yeast. This Act lists the types and concentrations of all permissible ingredients and additives.

The federal government levies both an excise duty and sales tax on all alcoholic beverages sold in Canada. The Consumer Packaging and Labeling Act regulates the size and construction of the bottle or box and outlines all label requirements. The Broadcast Act regulates who can be targeted and specifies what can and cannot be said on Canadian radio, television, and telecommunications. Specific advertisements (newspapers, magazines, television, radio, billboard, posters, etc) must be approved by the respective province(s) in which they appear.

When Prohibition was repealed in Canada in 1927, provincial governments were given power to regulate production, purchase, importation, sale, and distribution of alcoholic beverages. Although each province has overlapping regulations with the federal government, provincial legislation is more stringent. In 1994 Alberta privatized liquor sales throughout the province, although all importation, warehousing, distribution, and tax collection remained the responsibility of the province. Only sales were privatized. Ontario is typical of the other provincial systems that are still responsible for all beverage alcohol activities, including retail sales and wholesale distribution (see LCBO).

Although Canadian beer and spirits consumption is down somewhat during the 1990s, that drop is not reflected in loss of revenue for the provincial liquor commissions. Ontario, for instance, did a record-breaking C$2 billion in net sales in 1997, enabling it to hand over to the province a dividend from collected taxes and earnings of C$745 million. For every C$10 bottle of wine sold, C$3.42 goes to taxes and another C$2.25 for provincial profit margin. Canadian consumers pay 56.7% of the retail price of each bottle of wine to the province whenever wines are sold through an official provincial store. When that same bottle is sold through a winery based retail store, the winery saves the LCBO mark-up, but the consumer still pays the same price for the bottle of wine.

There are three types of wine distribution and retailing in Canada: (1) privatized—Alberta; (2) partially privatized—Quebec, British Columbia, New Brunswick; and (3) government managed by Liquor Control Boards—Ontario, Manitoba, Saskatchewan, Nova Scotia, Prince Edward Island, and Newfoundland.

Privatized systems

In Alberta's privatized system all liquor stores are owned by private retailers; however, the Provincial government retains the responsibility for all wholesaling of distilled spirits and regulates the administration, sales, and warehousing of all beverage alcohol. Delivery is in the hands of the private sector. Since privatization in September of 1993 to January 1998, the number of stores rose from 202 to 701, thereby increasing consumer accessibility. Product selection quadrupled and taxes collected by the province rose due to increased sales.

Partially privatized systems

Two major features differentiate partially privatized systems in Canada from other models: who is allowed to purchase and control stocking procedures; and the type of retail licenses permitted. In British Columbia, for instance, the Liquor Distribution Board (LDB) is part of the ministry of Small Business, Tourism and Culture. It does not purchase wine directly, but rather does so through an agent. Agents provide warehousing for their own products. Prior to procuring a product, however, the agent must have approval from the LDB to list that product. In addition to government-operated, full-service retail outlets (221), British Columbia also grants licenses to sell wine at retail to consumers.

Government managed systems

In all other provinces, the provincial government regulates the manufacture, distribution, quality standards, and sales of all beverage alcohol. Wineries can choose to list with the respective Liquor Boards, but their products must first be approved for listing. The advantage of listing is access to a broad distribution network throughout the province; however, store placement is at the discretion of the Liquor Board. In Ontario all wines must first pass a lab test that analyzes maximum concentrations of various chemical compounds. Wines exceeding the LCBO established limits are not accepted. The testing program is considered one of the most stringent in the world. Quality, in this case, is correlated to the health of the wine as well as its effect on the consumer. If approved, the supplier must satisfy the Liquor Control Board of Ontario (LCBO) that there are sufficient numbers of cases to distribute. The application must also be accompanied by a marketing plan to support sales. All advertising and labels must receive prior approval. So must all labels.

The disadvantage of listing with the LCBO is considerably less revenue for the wine producer. In addition to federal and provincial taxes, the LCBO charges amounts variously called merchandising fee, bottle levies, environmental tax, and mark-up. In the end a supplier makes only 35% of the retail sale. When sold CELLAR DOOR, the winery makes 80% of the retail sales price. In April 1999, for the first time in the history of the LCBO, the province passed legislation to allow wine producers to sell directly to restaurant licensees, thus increasing margins for producers and motivating wineries to work more closely with restaurateurs. Direct sales to restaurants had been permitted in BC and Nova Scotia for years.

The Canadian Wine Institute represents the Canadian industry proactively with all levels of government and their agencies, especially on such issues as standards, market access, and health.   L.F.B.

Aspler, A., *Tony Aspler's Vintage Canada: The Complete Reference to Canadian Wines* (Whitby, Ontario, 1995).

Statistics Canada/Canadian Wine Institute.

Canandaigua, second largest wine company in North America, headquartered in the FINGER LAKES region of upstate NY, where it originally became famous for a fortified pink wine called Richards Wild Irish Rose blended from American hybrids and CA Thompson Seedless. By no coincidence the head of the company, and son of founder Marvin Sands, is Richard Sands. For decades, well into the 1990s, Finger Lakes vineyardists resisted any conversion to vinifera varieties, which were proving so artistically and financially successful for their Canadian counterparts on the Niagara Peninsula, because Canandaigua offered NY growers a risk free, albeit paltry outlet for their winter-hardy, disease resistant, labrusca based varieties.

Established in 1945 as a bulk wine house, Canandaigua soon bought wineries in VA, NC, and SC focusing on the distinctive labrusca and Muscadine flavors. As the fortified wine category (cf Mogen David, Thunderbird) declined in the US, however, Canandaigua embarked on an acquisition campaign, beginning with Guild winery in LODI, CA. Today they compete for supermarket shelf space across many different categories with the giants of American mass merchandising. Almaden is their BAG-IN-A-BOX brand going head to head with WINE GROUP's Franzia boxes. Other important

(tectonic) plate; not the North American plate, upon which the other three regions sit. As a result most of the Central Coast soils are marine sediment, which seems to confer a softer, more relaxed texture and style in the wines.   B.C.C.

Central Delaware Valley AVA, district on either side of the DELAWARE RIVER between NEW JERSEY and Southeast PENNSYLVANIA. This AVA is used by Sand Castle Winery in PA, and Del Vista, King's Road, and Poor Richard's wineries in NJ.   R.G.L.

Central Valley, historically the engine of CA's hegemony in North American viticulture, yet a region so thoroughly imbued with the *jug wine image that no winery wants to use the name on a label. Hence Central Valley is probably the most widely employed place name in the wine industry which is not an approved AVA. The Central Valley covers one-sixth of CA and is big enough to swallow the entirety of the East Coast's APPALACHIAN MTNS.

The region puts graphic immediacy to the phrase 'Agribusiness.' After the Second World War, the Central Valley Project, the most intricate and extensive irrigation system man has ever built, transformed the area. Along with the Great Wall of China, it is one of the only man-made structures that can be seen with the naked eye from space. It made agriculture the biggest sector of CA's economy, and would place CA's agricultural output among the top five for *nations* in the world. Within the Central Valley grows every species of temperate-zone or subtropical fruit, vegetable, and field crop known to man, with the lone exception of tobacco. The valley is America's pre-eminent producer of fruits and nuts (despite San Francisco's reputation), second only to FL in citrus, and second only to TX in cotton. In 1997 when CA led the US in cash farm receipts for the 50th consecutive year with $26.8 billion, nearly double second place TX, dairy products were the most valuable CA commodities accounting (with beef and hay) for 22% of gross farm income, even though CA produced more than half of the fruits, nuts, and vegetables grown in the US that year. By comparison grapes moved up in 1997 to capture second place among CA farm crops with $2.8 billion in gross revenue, and finished wine sales were worth $5.9 billion to the CA wineries. Remarkable what deep topsoil and a ten-month growing season can produce when you deliver to it a reliable supply of water. These cornucopia statistics also help explain why Central Valley farmers get taxpayer subsidized water

at $10 per acre-ft which actually costs $100 per acre-ft to deliver once the full cost of the dams and canals are factored in.

It is instructive to try to imagine how the Central Valley must have looked 200 years ago. Each spring most of the precipitation which has fallen on CA is captured in the center of the state in a big bowl between the Sierra Nevada and the coastal mountains. Prior to the damming of all those rivers to impound that water for future irrigation, the Central Valley would have been a huge, frenetically fecund marsh every year from Feb through June. Elk and pronghorn antelope were as numerous as the buffalo further east. Grizzly bears were so abundant they were named the State Mammal. For an example of this dramatic, but normal, ebb and flow between the wet and the dry consider the winter of 1861–2. So much rain fell the Central Valley was again converted to an inland sea, 300 mi long, 60 mi wide, and 40 ft deep in places. Hundreds of thousands of cattle drowned. The rangeland then bloomed the following summer and surviving cattle feasted. Then came two years of severe drought. Livestock loss from starvation was estimated to lie somewhere between 200,000 and a million head.

Things did not change much until the 1870s, when the transcontinental railroad had been completed and farmers began arriving in large numbers. From 1870 to 1910 the railroad aggressively advertised in East Coast newspapers offering land inexpensively. Setting the stage for the concepts of agribusiness and immigrant labor (see Labor essay, p 49) which would persist into the 21st century, Southern Pacific Railroad was the biggest private landowner in the state thanks to a government gift of alternating sections along the right of way. A section is one-quarter of a sq mi, or 160 acres. In those years Southern Pacific owned more than 5% of CA's 100 million acres. In the 1880s the Sacramento Valley was the site of the largest vineyard in the world, railroad baron Leland Stanford's 5,000-acre ranch in Tehama Co south of Redding. Quality was not particularly good. Stanford built a 2 million gal winery, then became the world's largest brandy distiller. Today there are less than 150 acres of vines in Tehama Co. Immigrant farmers originally came to the Central Valley to plant wheat. Then the Depression era of the 1930s saw a huge migration of refugees fleeing prolonged drought and wind erosion in the PLAINS states. The Okies' imprint on CA's Central Valley remains today in religious, political, and cultural institutions transmogrified by three generations of agricultural development.

The northern half of the Central Valley, ie *Sacramento Valley, is the middle of the Pacific Flyway. Ducks and other migratory waterfowl stop to feed on their journey from Canadian breeding sites to Mexican winter vacations. The spring runoff exits CA through the DELTA and San Francisco Bay on its way to the Pacific Ocean. By the end of the summer though, all the wetlands in the southern half, or *San Joaquin Valley, would have become parched. Bakersfield is by definition a desert, with only 6 in rainfall a year. The Delta, in the middle of the Central Valley, is the most interesting section from a wine quality standpoint. It is bounded on the east by the prolific grape growing region of *Lodi, and by two deep water ports, Sacramento (the state capital) on the north and Stockton on the south.

Today the northern portion of the valley is America's rice bowl. Flowing lines of irregularly shaped fields, and varied hues of blue and green as the rice plants mature, are visually engaging, distracting one from the oppressive dry heat. The town of Red Bluff really marks the northern end of the flat Central Valley, but cone shaped Mt Shasta (north of Redding, near the town of Weed) is the emphatic visual terminus, rising 5,000 ft above anything for 50 mi in any direction. It is easy to see why Shasta is considered by some 'the most psychic, occult and mystic' wilderness location in the US. Scientifically Shasta is a volcano, 14,160 ft high including a fair sized glacier. Its last eruption, in 1786, was seen 100 mi away by a French ship passing along the CA coast.

UC *Davis is located in this northern portion of the Central Valley, just southwest of Sacramento. CA's other Enology and Viticulture school, CA State Univ at Fresno (ie Fresno State) is located in the southern portion. The Sacramento Valley was only able to become a major rice producer once scientists at UC Davis developed a strain of rice which ripens a couple of weeks early, allowing harvest before the migrating ducks arrive. The discovery of *gibberellins, growth-regulating hormones isolated at Davis in 1941 from a rice fungus, doubled the productivity of table grapes in CA. In 1995 geneticists at Davis succeeded in splicing a gene into rice plants (and having future generations of those plants spontaneously reproduce that gene) which makes them resistant to bacterial leaf blight, one of the most devastating diseases worldwide in a crop which is the major food source for half the human race. On the downside, Davis detractors love to point out styrofoam-textured tomatoes found in many US grocery stores, developed at UC Davis to withstand a 13 mph impact from a mechanical harvester.

Most of the grape growing is now in Yolo Co west of Sacramento between the towns of Winters and Woodland. Winters sits in the middle of a floodplain where El Río de las Mil Putas used to descend from the mountains which separate Napa Valley from the Central Valley. The River of a Thousand Whores used to flood frequently, but a dam was erected in 1958 and the name of the waterbed changed to Putah Creek. This Yolo Co grape growing region is only 35 mi from the center of Napa Valley; however, it is very warm. Gravelly hillsides are the best sites and irrigation is important. **Dunnigan Hills** AVA, the only approved viticultural area in the Sacramento Valley, is located here. Petite Sirah would be indicated, but a lot of Chardonnay destined for supermarket bargain shelves has been planted since 1990.

The southern portion of the Central Valley, from Stockton to the Tehachapi Mtns south of Bakersfield, is the larger of the two portions and contains most of the vines. It is home to 300,000 acres of table grapes and some of the world's largest wineries, including *Gallo, the world's very largest. In most instances the wineries are not well known, because they sell in bulk rather than through brand names of their own. Sierra Wine Company, Di Giorgio, and Bear Mountain were once names of multi-million gal facilities capable of producing everything from grape concentrate to high-proof distilled spirit. These refineries still operate, but they do not give tours. The culture is professional managers, contract labor, and absentee owners. Tejon Ranch is a good example. With its 7,000 acres of grapes on the northern slope of the Tehachapi range, it is owned by the Chandler family, until 2000 publishers of the *Los Angeles Times*.

Except for two artisan producers of fortified wine and a couple souvenir shops, the San Joaquin Valley is strictly a commodities game. It is often compared to the *Languedoc in France. Sometimes the only way to connect a brand to a company is to note the name of the town where the wine was bottled (which appears in small print on every US label). There are two approved AVAs: **Madera**, where the single winery which applied for the appellation has since gone out of business; and **Diablo Grande** in Stanislaus Co, which was approved in 1999 at the behest of a new tiny operator. Modesto, where Gallo is headquartered, is in Stanislaus Co, but do not expect to see Diablo Grande AVA on any Gallo labels.

Understandably, the calling of the viticulture and enology school at Fresno State is volume production. In the Central Valley a shift of pennies per gallon in the market price can move hundreds of thousands of tons of grapes from fresh fruit to raisins, to concentrate, to wine, or to brandy. One year a big portion of the crop may go into flavoring and sweetening designer-bottled waters; the next year it may go into 5 l BAG-IN-A-BOX wines.

NOTABLE PROPERTIES

Delicato. The Indelicato family owns the 13,000-acre San Bernabe Ranch (8,000 acres planted to vines) in Monterey Co just south of King City, so they certainly have one foot in a higher priced market, as well as one in the commodities end of the business. They were able to make the San Bernabe purchase in 1988 because of their success producing White Zinfandel for Sutter Home's label. They began with a crushing plant in Monterey, and eventually built a full winery there. The combined operations produced 100 million gal in 1998, although a large proportion was made under contract for other wineries. Monterey accounts for about 10% of the production. Settler's Creek is a second label. This is the sixth largest US wine company and growing.

Ficklin, third generation grape growing family, CA's oldest repository of classic Portuguese grape varieties: Tinta Madeira, *Tinto Cão, *Sousão, and *Touriga. All were recommended for the Ficklin's Madera location by UC Davis right after the Second World War. Every year a ruby-style *port is produced, called Tinta Port, which amounts to most of the 10,000-case production. Nine times in the winery's half-century of operation (1951, 1953, 1957, 1980, 1983, 1986, 1988, 1991, and 1996) special lots of about 1,000 cases each have been bottled as vintaged port types. These are given two years of barrel age and five years in bottle before release. Starting in 1993 a 10-year-old average, solera process, tawny-style was introduced. The grapes used for the vintage dated port types have changed over the years, moving from a predominately Tinta Madeira and *Alvarelhão (since pulled out) blend to one primarily of Sousão and Touriga with 5% Tinto Cão. It is a noticeable change because the Sousão is quite dark, with a lot of flavor depth, and the Tinto Cão has a subtle floral perfume. Both vines are low producers.

Fiddlehead. Kathy Joseph is a unique concept, a commuting winemaker. Her office is in Davis, but she makes her wine in CA's Central Coast and in OR's Willamette Valley. That is 900 mi between fermenters.

Pinot Noir is her passion. She chose the two regions specifically for the *terroir of the vineyards she uses. Next she arranged with Talley Winery in San Luis Obispo Co and with Yamhill Winery near Portland to rent space to her and give her access to equipment. Her office is on the main north–south highway (Interstate 5). Fiddlehead produces about 2,500 cases a year.

Franzia, 50 million gal facility in Ripon owned by the WINE GROUP. This is the top selling single brand in the US due to their bag-in-a-box wines which sell the equivalent of 19 million cases a year, including the trademarked Chillable Red.

Gibson, grower co-op with a facility in Sanger capable of storing 12 million gal.

Giumarra, a Sicilian family which farms 15,000 acres, of which 7,000 acres are table grapes and 3,000 acres are winegrapes. They are the largest packer and shipper of table grapes in the world. Their winery facility in Edison has 16 million gal of storage capacity. Only 250,000 cases a year are sold under the Giumarra label; most of the wine is sold in 18 l and 60 l kegs for restaurants. Breckenridge Cellars is a second label.

Heublein. Based in Connecticut and part of an international conglomerate, this thoroughly modern marketing company is all about *brand building and the apotheosis of *terroir. Their production facility in the town of Madera has storage capacity for 115 million gal. Labels they have acquired elsewhere which now use this pipeline include Blossom Hill, Charles Le Franc, Inglenook Navelle, and Le Domaine.

JFJ Bronco. Cousins John, Fred, and Joseph Franzia sold their family winery and name in 1971. They built a new facility in the town of Ceres, a few miles south of Modesto, which in 1992 had a storage capacity of 43.8 million gal. In addition to their CC Vyds label, Bronco also acquired rights to the Grand Cru, Hacienda, and Laurier brand names during the 1990s. Those properties are in Sonoma Co, but were sold separately to other people with Bronco retaining only the names to use as marketing vehicles. This is the eighth largest US wine company.

Orleans Hill, leading organic wine operation in the US along with Fetzer's Bonterra line and Frey in Mendocino Co. Owner Jim Lapsley runs the wine education programs for UC Davis Extension (see Organic essay, p 59). His 12,000-case winery is west of Sacramento in Woodland. Orleans Hill was originally a partnership between Lapsley, who made the wines, and an organic grape grower named Ken Reiff. In the late 1980s Reiff took a gigantic financial bath in a technically successful, but disastrously marketed, truffle farming venture with an eccentric, elderly Russian mycologist who refused to sell his secret to Campbell's soup and ended up taking the technical secret to his grave. Reiff's bankruptcy threatened the solvency of the Orleans Hill partnership for a few years, but Lapsley soldiered on alone, and the brand has now recovered its financial health. Most of the grapes are now brought in from organic growers on a somewhat cooperative basis. Labeling is whimsical.

See also DELTA, GALLO, R. H. PHILLIPS, QUADY.   B.C.C.

Statistics: www.cdfa.ca.gov

Chaddsford, largest farm winery in PENN-SYLVANIA at 30,000 cases. Located in the town of the same name just above the Delaware border in the Brandywine Valley. Chaddsford was founded in 1982 by Eric Miller, whose family had started BENMARL VYDS in NY. At Benmarl Miller experimented with planting vinifera varieties, and conducting barrel ageing trials with oak from different regions of France and the US. The Millers chose the site for Chaddsford based on their confidence in its climate and soils to produce world-class wines. They refer to their region as the 'Atlantic Uplands.' Their goal is to establish an identity for Atlantic Uplands as a significant American wine district.

Chaddsford owns its own vineyards, and purchases fruit from others in the region. Single-vineyard designations can be found on the Philip Roth Reserve Chardonnay, and Mica Ridge Pinot Grigio. Chaddsford's other premium varietals include Pinot Noir, Cabernet Sauvignon, Cabernet Franc, Johannisberg Riesling, Dolcetto, and Chambourcin. 'Merican' is a proprietary red meritage-style wine. Chaddsford has reputation for Chardonnay. Their Philip Roth is a complex wine heavy in *MLF influence. However, their Pinot Grigio and Dolcetto show surprisingly prototypical flavors and balance, and may lead the way for further plantings of Italian varieties in southeast PA. Chaddsford also makes an innocuous Chenin Blanc-style French hybrid blend called Spring Wine.   R.G.L.

Chalk Hill AVA, district in northern SONOMA CO southeast of Healdsburg and subsumed in the RUSSIAN RIVER AVA. Although it technically overlaps the highway, a fair practical representation would be to say it is the area east of Hwy 101 from about River Rd to just south of Healdsburg. Or, call it the district from the Santa Rosa Plain east up into the hills past the 1,400 ft summit north of Mark West Springs Rd. The

mountain for which the AVA is named, incidentally, is composed of light colored volcanic ash; not some seabed carbonate.

The lower elevations can be argued as quite good for a whole marketbasket of different grape varieties precisely because conditions are changeable from one vintage to the next, depending on how aggressively the maritime influence is drawn up the Russian River to impinge upon the Chalk Hill AVA. Over a ten-year period growers can claim top prizewinners in a couple of vintages each for Pinot Noirs, botrytized Rieslings, Chardonnays, Zinfandels, Petite Sirahs, and Meritage blends. But the award winners will be from different vintages depending on the variety. At higher elevations the growing conditions will be much more consistent, tending toward warmer climate varieties like Cabernet and Sauvignon Blanc, or Chardonnays made in the more voluptuous styles.

NOTABLE PROPERTIES

Chalk Hill, luxurious estate winery in the hills at 300–700 ft elevation owned by successful lawyer Fred Furth. Few expenses have been spared. Artistic success eluded Furth until 1990 when Dave Ramey was hired as winemaker following a noteworthy run at Matanzas Creek. Ramey set the style for rich, creamy Chardonnay which prevails today, and has allowed the winery to grow to 70,000 cases, 70% of it Chardonnay. In 1996 Bill Knutell was hired from Saintsbury to take over from Ramey.

Christopher Creek, winery which is not technically in the AVA, but which shares the hillside east of Hwy 101 with it. Started in the mid-1970s as Sotoyome Winery, named for the area's Spanish landgrant, it was purchased in 1992 by John Mitchell, a former history professor from Oxford, who changed the name. He set the winery on a successful course, in no small part by hiring Paul Brasset (now at Pezzi-King) to be winemaker. Wineries, however, can be holes in the ground into which one must shovel money. In 1997 Mitchell capitulated, selling to Fred Wasserman, a retired real estate investor specializing in health and racquetball clubs. The strength of the line is in Syrah and Petite Sirah.

Fisher, started in 1973 and another winery not in the AVA, only in this case much further up into the hills which separate the Santa Rosa Plain from Napa Valley. In fact Fisher is within a couple miles of the ridge which denotes the county line. Fred Fisher, whose family is famous for automobile bodies, makes 7,500 cases total of Chardonnay and red Bordeaux blends based on

Cabernet Sauvignon. All the Chardonnay comes from up in the mountains; some of the red Bordeaux varieties come from vineyards they own on the Silverado Trail in Napa Valley. Fisher is a vigorous proponent of WILD YEAST fermentations, although he prefers to call *his* operatives 'tame yeast.' He refers to the alternative as 'industrial yeast.' Fisher has been using the ambient *yeast in his vineyard for 100% of his fermentations since 1992. He has not had any significant problems, but in 1999 he did dig a 500 ft cave as an addition to his Bill Turnbull designed winery, which is made out of redwoods cut when Fisher cleared land for vineyards on his mountain property. Fisher thinks one advantage of the cave will be somewhat warmer ambient temperatures in midwinter to ensure his tame yeast are always able to finish their task. Interestingly, he also notes that his vineyard yeast have been subject to the same increase in alcohol conversion rates (see Winemaking essay, p 35) observed for commercial yeast strains in CA over the last two decades.   B.C.C.

Chalone, a one-vineyard AVA. Also a winery, which is part of a publicly traded conglomerate, held in significant measure by the *Lafite-Rothschild interests from France. The Chalone group of wineries include CARMENET in Sonoma, Edna Valley Vyds in San Luis Obispo, Acacia in Napa, and Canoe Ridge in WA. Chalone is a valuable brand name. In the 1970s the Chalone property itself, near Pinnacles Natl Monument in the Gabilan mountains east of MONTEREY Co's Salinas Valley, was widely regarded as a shrine. It was one of the six pioneering micro-wineries which helped launch CA's wine boom by creating an air of exclusivity, discovery, and return-to-the-land craftsmanship. (See HANZELL, MAYACAMAS, STONY HILL, MT EDEN, RIDGE.)

The mystique of Chalone derives from its origin during Prohibition. A Frenchman named Tam had noted limestone deposits on this ridge 1,800 ft above the town of Soledad and began planting Chenin Blanc vines in 1919. Warm and arid, this site requires irrigation during the summer. Tam hauled water from the Salinas River all the way up Stonewall Canyon on mules to keep his vines from drying up and blowing away.

A succession of owners added Pinot Noir, Chardonnay, and Pinot Blanc vines to the property in the 1940s, but when it was purchased by a couple of amateur hobbyists in 1965 the vines had been untended for years and were barely alive. Dick Graff had a graduate degree in Music from Yale and a working knowledge of Burgundian winemaking techniques. His first task was to resuscitate the vines by driving a water truck back and forth from Soledad to the vineyard eight times a day. As Graff struggled to produce wine in a converted chicken shed on the Chalone property, he paid his personal bills by drawing a salary to perform as winemaker at Mt Eden Vyds too. In 1969 the first Chalone wines were released, in minute quantities, and generated the definitive CULT WINE following.

First, the flavor intensity from these older vines which had gone fifteen years without adequate water was quite remarkable. Second, Graff's style of *barrel fermented, *sur lie aged white wine with complete (and probably spontaneous) *MLF was quite unlike anything anybody else was making, with the obvious exception of Mt Eden and their Santa Cruz neighbor David BRUCE. Lastly, the physical isolation of the Chalone property, which was then the only winery in Monterey Co, pretty much guaranteed that any visitor who had actually set foot on the site was likely to become an enthusiastic supporter.

In 1974 a modern winery facility was built. In the 1980s Graff's financial partner Phil Woodward took the very bold step of a public stock offering. Over the years tens of thousands of Americans have purchased 100 shares each just to be eligible for the annual shareholders' meeting which features library selections of wine with great food. Direct sales to shareholders comprise a significant percentage of the company's distribution each year. Corporate capitalization allowed Chalone to build underground caves in 1984 and to expand the vineyard to a total of 187 acres in 1989. One unfortunate aspect of the caves project was the surprise discovery of geothermal hot springs on the property. The caves now require an air-conditioner to maintain 55°F cellar temperatures.

Chalone Vyd produces around 40,000 cases annually with more than half being Chardonnay. The low-end range is called Gavilan, which does not necessarily come from the estate. The high-end range, called Reserve, is rarely encountered in the public marketplace. The Estate range is the one most often seen. The best Pinot Noirs are ripe, earthy, and tannic. They are fermented with WILD YEAST and a small percentage of stems. Chardonnay can be the best of the lot, but vintages vary. Most are huge, alcoholic, and very woody, but with a mineral backtaste and very full, concentrated flavor profiles. Some older examples have completely oxidized; others are clean and balanced through their twenty-fifth birthday. Cool vintages are best. Texture is the

Chalone signature. Remarkable vintages include 1975, 1985, 1986, and 1992.

Dick Graff was tragically killed in a light plane accident in 1997.   B.C.C.

champagne, word used generically, and legally, in the US as a synonym for sparkling wine (see *Champagne and US LABEL REGULATIONS), to the great annoyance of Francophones and European wine purists everywhere.

There are three price categories into which US wine labeled champagne will fit. The bottom range is under $6 a bottle at retail. That category is populated by brands using high yield grapes and the *Charmat bulk process of production. When demand is high in CA more than 200,000 acres of Thompson Seedless vines may be diverted from table grapes, or soft drinks, or raisins, or brandy production into the white wine crush. There is a federal EXCISE TAX on sparkling wine, originally levied as a 'luxury tax' during the Second World War, of 70¢ a bottle. It costs in the order of $1.15 per bottle to put anything in a bottle with a nice label and a cork. Those costs of production, and remember one has yet to add in profit, will be marked up by the THREE-TIER DISTRIBUTION system at least two and a half times, especially if any advertising is involved, before arriving at the retail sales price. You do the math. Under $6 is a decidedly mean category for champagne.

The second category is between $6 and $10 per bottle. If there are bargains to be found, they will be in this middle range, usually using a blend of grapes such as Chenin Blanc and Riesling, and often making large quantities with the *transfer technique of production. The third category will be labeled MÉTHODE CHAMPENOISE, will predominantly use Pinot Noir and Chardonnay grapes grown in cool districts, and by necessity will cost over $10 a bottle. Some very fine wines are found in this third range. Many of them, however, will not use the phrase champagne on the label.

Beginning in 1973 seven French champagne houses came to CA to set up subsidiary businesses: Dom Chandon, owned by Moët-Hennessy; Dom Carneros, owned by Taittinger; Mumm Napa Valley, owned by Seagram; Roederer Estate; Maison Deutz; Piper Sonoma, owned by Piper Heidseick; and Pommery bought Scharffenberger (now called Pacific Echo). Two Spanish *cava houses came as well: Gloria Ferrer, owned by Freixenet; and Codorníu. None of these companies will ever use champagne on one of their labels. Since 1995 Piper Heidseick and Deutz have withdrawn, how-

ever, having discovered the sausage was being sliced into so many pieces their share was too thin to live on.   B.C.C.

Charlottesville, city in the center of the MONTICELLO AVA in the Upper Piedmont. Forty per cent of the 50 wineries in VIRGINIA lie within an hour's drive. Charlottesville is home to two legacies of Thomas *Jefferson: his home, Monticello; and the Univ of VA. The Monticello Wine Festival takes place here annually on the first weekend of Oct.

                R.G.L.

Ch Chantal, drop-dead-beautiful winery and get-away resort in the OLD MISSION PENINSULA AVA of northern MICHIGAN. Bob Begin bought a cherry farm on the peninsula in 1983 to begin his vineyard plans. Ten years later he opened the winery and has not looked back since. The winery's bubbly, a blend of Chardonnay with the Pinots Noir and Meunier, is dependable. So is the sweetish Select Harvest Riesling. Experiments with Cabernet Franc and Merlot have been promising.   P.W.F.

Ch des Charmes. In the mid-1970s, a time when scientists at the local research station were strongly advising against planting vinifera, fourth generation French enologist (Univ of Dijon) Paul Bosc defiantly planted 60 acres of Chardonnay, Aligoté, Auxerrois, Pinot Noir, and Gamay Noir. By 1994 his NIAGARA-ON-THE-LAKE, Ontario winery had grown sufficiently to open a new C$6 million facility on a nearby site and to plant an additional 190 acres in the shelter of St David's Bench on the NIAGARA ESCARPMENT. The tourist-friendly château was designed to capture Canada's French and English architectural legacy as exemplified in the towers and mansard roof design of the nation's familiar Canadian Pacific Railway Hotels. With this expansion the winery has been able to establish markets in Japan, Taiwan, the UK, US, and every province across Canada. Bosc's son, Pierre-Jean, also an enology graduate from the Univ of Dijon and currently winemaker, continues his father's focus on premium varietal Chardonnay, Cabernet Franc, Riesling, and Cabernet Sauvignon. Eldest son, Paul Bosc, Jr, Vice President of Marketing, and Bosc senior's wife, Andrée Bosc both continue to play significant roles in the winery's growth. The 100,000 cases they produce each year receive significant recognition in all styles, including a Riesling ICEWINE which sells on the export market for C$80 per 375 ml.

Since the early 1990s Dr John Paroschy, a research scientist employed by Ch des Charmes, has played a lead role exploring transgenic grapevines, a technique of DNA transfer whereby it is hoped the cold hardiness of vinifera can be improved for growth in more extreme climates.   LFB

Ch Elan, established by Dr Donald Panoz in 1982 in Braselton, 30 mi north of Atlanta, GEORGIA, rivals the BILTMORE ESTATE in NC as a large winery with Southern grandeur and style. Ch Elan features 200 acres of vineyards and a 3,100-acre resort in three counties with hotel, convention center, golf course, gift shop, restaurant, and residential community. Dr Panoz once enquired of local Muscadine growers why vinifera wines were not cultivated in GA. He was told outright it could not be done. Ch Elan was established to realize Dr Panoz's dream that good quality vinifera wines could be made in GA. The château's first wines were released in 1985. They have won 253 awards since then, indicating that at least some show judges agree with the good doctor's vision.

To adapt to the challenges of growing vinifera successfully in the humid SOUTH, Ch Elan adjusted its viticultural techniques to include high training of the cordons, special cover crops, and precise measurement of grape chemistry for punctual harvesting. Today, Ch Elan produces seventeen wines from vinifera, French hybrid, and Muscadine grapes, including Chardonnay, Riesling, White Zinfandel, Merlot, Chardonnay, and Chambourcin. They also make sherry and port. As is the case with many Southern wineries, Ch Elan supplements its own vineyards with grapes obtained out of state. However, they remain committed to the pursuit of the Panoz ideal with such wines as an estate-grown Meritage called Essence de Cabernet, whose 1995 vintage has a fine bouquet but on the palate there is more than a suggestion of over-extraction. A more successful example of winemaking at Ch Elan is Summer Wine, a blend of three bronze-skinned Muscadine grapes, Scuppernong, Carlos, and Magnolia, with natural peach extract. The grapes were harvested at 16° Brix, with 3.2 pH and 0.88 TA. The resulting fresh character, low alcohol, and ample acidity shows the potential of Muscadine wines, the peach extract being highly compatible with the base wine. This wine has won multiple awards, and was voted Best Local Wine by *Atlanta* magazine. Summer Wine was the eighteenth largest selling wine in the Atlanta market in 1998, of all brands domestic and imported, demonstrating regionally distinctive wines can capture detectable market share at home. Ch Elan's Georgia Port has also been a medal winner. Although the port is based on Zinfandel

grapes from CA, the remaining 30% of the blend is made from Touriga grapes grown at the estate which bring some of the smoothness, spice, and fruit integration typical of genuine port. Ch Elan's total production is 30,000 cases.   R.G.L.

Ch Grand Traverse, an aggressive winery in MI's OLD MISSION PENINSULA AVA. Ed O'Keefe began buying CA grapes from Santa Barbara, Monterey, and San Joaquin counties in the late 1970s. He performed the vinification in MICHIGAN and made passable wines. He had already, however, begun to make acceptable if leaner varietal wines from local Chardonnay and Riesling grapes. Since that time, O'Keefe's son, Ed Jr, has joined the team. Local fruit is now *de rigueur*, except for some Zinfandel grapes they still import. Standouts from a wide range of wines include the fine, old-fashioned Chablis-like Chardonnays, their Select Harvest Dry Rieslings, and the sweeter models, including their icewines. In very ripe years, they make Cabernet Francs and Merlots that are *cru bourgeois bordeaux tastealikes.   P.W.F.

Ch Montelena, one of the northernmost wineries in Napa Valley, located on Tubbs Lane north of CALISTOGA. So awash in fascinating storylines is it, writers often forget to mention the wines. The property is a photographer's dream: a medieval fortress built in 1882 for the winery; two suits of armor guarding the vineyard; and a Chinese garden with hemispherical footbridges to pavilions on islands in the irrigation pond where swans and ducks provide picnic companionship. The stone winery was built by Alfred Tubbs himself, a successful 19th-century entrepreneur who was already experimenting with *phylloxera resistant rootstock in Napa Valley in 1887. The Chinese motif dates to the early 1960s when the property was purchased by Yort Wing Frank. Modern history at Ch Montelena received a jump start in 1976 when its 1973 Chardonnay, made by Mike GRGICH won the SPURRIER TASTING in Paris. (That wine actually had a large proportion of grapes grown at Hafner Vyd in Alexander Valley.) The attendant publicity put Ch Montelena on the map, but none of those factors are in play any longer. The star of the winery's current range is their estate Cabernet, the first of which came out in 1978. Bo Barrett, the current winemaker and son of the lead investor who salvaged the property in 1972, took over in 1982. Bo Barrett's wife Heidi is a pretty fair winemaker herself, responsible for such CA CULT WINES as Grace Family, Vyd 29, and

Screaming Eagle. Ch Montelena's Estate Cabernet has a marvelous track record, standing as a premier example of the chewy, dense flavor profile one might predict for this northern nook about as far away from the cooling influences of San Pablo Bay as one can get in Napa Valley. Perhaps converse to expectations though, Barrett's very best vintages are the ones such as 1987 and 1990, which are very concentrated elsewhere, because in years such as those he lightens up on the *extract, allowing his Cabernet to speak softly without resorting to the big stick it always carries.

Ch Ste Michelle, is part of the Stimson Lane holding group (in turn a subsidiary of US Tobacco) which produces over 2,000,000 cases, sells nearly 90% of all the wine made in WASHINGTON, and owns 1,280 acres of vineyards in the Columbia Valley. It is something of an understatement to say President Allen Shoup has provided valuable guidance to the WA wine industry with his extensive marketing credentials. Stimson Lane began right after Prohibition as two wineries, Pommerelle and Nawic, who merged in 1954 to form American Wine Growers. In 1967 Ste Michelle emerged with their first varietal table wines. Ch Ste Michelle became their brand name in 1976 at the same time Stimson Lane was formed. The other large Stimson Lane brand is Columbia Crest.

Ch Ste Michelle is located on lumber baron Frederick Stimson's grand estate in Woodinville, a suburb of SEATTLE. Over a quarter of a million visitors come to the winery annually, either to tour and taste, or to attend the spectacular summer concerts on the lawn. Winemaker Mike Januik, who left in 1999 to start his own winery, oversaw winemaking at Ch Ste Michelle as well as at Canoe Ridge Estate Winery in WALLA WALLA AVA. White wines are produced at the Woodinville site with most grapes crushed and pressed near the eastern WA vineyards and juice trucked to western WA, while red wines are processed at Canoe Ridge Estate. At Columbia Crest, Doug Gore aims for more keenly priced wines. Columbia Crest winery is located in the southeast corner of HORSE HEAVEN HILLS, overlooking the Columbia River in eastern WA near Paterson. Both winemakers have a wide range of vineyards with which to work as Stimson Lane purchases many grapes to supplement their own large acreage. Prime vineyard holdings include Cold Creek, Horse Heaven, and Canoe Ridge, plus grapes they purchase from Indian Wells on the Wahluke Slope. Ch Ste Michelle is also releasing a collaborative effort with Tuscan Piero *Antinori to be called Col Solare, a blend of Cabernet Sauvignon, Merlot, and Syrah grown at Canoe Ridge Estate.   R.A.I.

Ch Woltner, fine Chardonnay producer in the HOWELL MTN AVA of CA's Napa Valley. The essence of the place, however, lies in the pedigree of its owners Francis and Françoise Dewavrin-Woltner. She is the daughter of Henri Woltner, legendary winemaker whose half-century of vintages at Ch La Mission Haut-Brion in the *Pessac-Léognan district of Bordeaux brought that winery back to prominence. After his death in 1973 Ch La Mission floated aimlessly until it was sold in 1983 to the American owner of Ch Haut-Brion across the street. The Dewavrin-Woltners decamped for CA with every intention of pursuing Cabernet, as one might expect. When they bought a ghost winery and 56 acres in Howell Mtn, the reputation of the AVA was based on reds such as Cabernet and Zinfandel. The newcomers absorbed more than their share of chuckling about aristocratic incompetence when they decided to put in Chardonnay exclusively. But they were right, and their detractors were wrong. Howell Mtn has revealed itself during Ch Woltner's tenure to be a much cooler growing location than conventional wisdom of the mid-1980s allowed. The Dewavrin-Woltners hired American Ted Lemon away from a Guy Roulot in *Meursault to be their winemaker and he responded with some of the most distinctive Chardonnays in CA, wines that demand extended bottle age. Vine yields at the 1,700 ft elevation in Howell Mtn's barren soils are always under 2 t/a. Ch Woltner does not put its wine through *MLF. The wines stay in French oak for a lengthy time, but only 20% of the barrels are new. The resulting style is taut, acidic, minerally flavored, and completely unforgiving for several years after release. In short, European. There is a value-priced release without these characteristics, but the three single vineyards (Frederique, St Thomas, and Titus) and the estate blend are all very serious wines, priced accordingly. Total production is only a bit over 10,000 cases.

Chelois, French hybrid also known as *Seibel 10878 which can make fruity, medium-bodied red wines in the East and Midwest when ripened fully.

Chesapeake Bay, largest tidal estuary in eastern North America, and source of the famous soft shell crabs which molt in June each year. The Bay contains over 6,500 mi of tidal shoreline. The upper half of the Bay is encompassed by MD, while the lower half lies within Tidewater VA. The DELMARVA PENINSULA separates the Bay from the Atlantic Ocean. Chesapeake Bay provides a moderating climatic influence on viticulture in DE and the adjacent Tidewater regions of MD and VA, as well as for southeast PA. While summer humidity is high in the region, the Bay breezes help reduce *fungal diseases. They also reduce the risk of winter injury.   R.G.L.

Chicago, the Windy City, has evolved from its 1800s meat packing reputation, and its Prohibition era gangster image, into one of America's great cultural, economic, and political centers. With 2.8 million people it is the largest city in the MIDWEST region, indeed half the population of IL lives in the contiguous three-county area. A vital wine and spirits center for the US, Chicago ranks highly for gross number of cases sold, including #1 for cognacs and brandies, and #2 for champagnes and sparkling wines. One of the city's great strengths historically has been the strong independence of its retail stores, and the influence these retailers have been able to exert over wholesalers, resulting in a breadth of selection most knowledgeable people outside of New York City believe is unmatched anywhere in the US. In 1999 however, an import house named Judge & Dolph induced the IL legislature to pass a bill making IL a FRANCHISE STATE, which would seriously undermine the vigorously competitive nature of Chicago's traditional marketplace. Challenged in court by KENDALL-JACKSON, the future of that legislation is uncertain.   P.W.F.

Clarkesburg AVA, see DELTA.

Clearwater River, section of ID historically devoted to grapes and wine. Although not an approved AVA, it is considered an excellent site for future plantings. Average *degree days between 2,500 to 3,000 depending on elevation. This could be an excellent Chardonnay site with about 1,000 plantable acres.   R.A.I.

Clinton Vyds, small Seyval Blanc specialist tucked in rolling hills of NY's HUDSON RIVER Valley. Established in 1972, Clinton is one of the valley's veterans. It grows and makes only Seyval but in half a dozen permutations: still, sparkling, and fortified. The principal release is a light, tart, bone-dry table wine setting the fresh, edgy house style. No oak or *MLF in this cellar. Spring frost sometimes nips the vineyard, resulting in uneven production between 1,000 and 3,000 cases annually.   R.F.

Clore, Walter J., acclaimed viticulturist at the WA State Univ-Prosser Irrigated Agriculture Research Extension Center (IAREC) from 1937 to 1976, considered the father of the WA wine industry. He initiated WA variety and winemaking trials in 1964, and maintained an experimental vineyard at the center. He worked closely with WSU Food Scientist Dr Chas Nagel, and Research Center winemaker George Carter.   R.A.I.

Coastal Plain, low lying geologic zone in the MID-ATLANTIC and SOUTH regions, running between the Atlantic Ocean shoreline and the interior bedrock, consisting of accumulated sedimentary deposits eroded from inland hills and from marine deposits laid down over eons.

Colio Estates, the largest of four wineries located in southwestern ONTARIO at 200,000 cases per year. It is within the LAKE ERIE NORTH SHORE VA and produces a wide selection of premium varietal and sparkling VQA wines. In addition to distributing through LCBO, Colio Estates own and operate fourteen retail stores throughout the province of Ontario which handle 36% of sales. The winery was built in Harrow in 1980, the same year as their first vintage. In 1998 they opened a new barrel room to house their ultra premium Cabernets and Chardonnays.   L.F.B.

Colobel, red-fleshed *teinturier French hybrid also known as Seibel 8357.

Colorado, state in ROCKY MTN region where cool climate grape and fruit wines are produced in some of the highest vineyards in the world. Most of the 21 currently bonded wineries are clustered in the GRAND VALLEY AVA.

Viticulture began on both sides of the Rockies at the turn of the last century. Italian immigrants tended their vines after returning from a hard day's work in the coal mines near Cañon City, southwest of Colorado Springs. Some 100-year-old vinifera vines still dot backyard gardens in the area. The Grand Valley, in western CO, was first explored by prospectors, hunters, and traders in the 1880s. The region has been renowned for fruit production ever since. Governor George Crawford planted 60 acres of grapes and other fruit in 1890, near Palisade. By 1899, the US Dept of Commerce reported CO's grape harvest at over 250 tons, with wine production at 1,700 gal. By 1909, those figures rose to 500 tons from a quarter-million vines, with another 100,000 vines in the ground. One thousand farmers had planted grapes.

Prohibition put a stop to this exuberance. There was no more activity until 1968, when Dr Gerald Ivancie opened his eponymously named winery. While waiting for his own vines to mature, Ivancie purchased wine and grapes from CA wineries such as Parducci. In 1974, 5 acres of vinifera and hybrid grapes were planted at CO State University's agricultural research station at Orchard Mesa. The following year, the University funded a grant for viticultural study. The first new winery, Colorado Mtn Vyds, was bonded in 1978, by Jim and Ann Sewald. In the following two decades, over twenty wineries were bonded. The expanding industry received a huge boost in 1990, when the CO Legislature approved funding for the CO Wine Board. The current budget of $350,000 amply provides for research and advertising. This funding is partially paid by CO wineries, plus a penny per gallon assessment on every one of the 4.4 million cases of wine sold in the state, most of which is imported from CA and overseas.

Grapes are harvested from 225 acres, 95% of which are vinifera located on the Western Slope, the area of CO west of the Continental Divide. Three-quarters of the producing acreage is located in the Grand Valley AVA. The North Fork area, in Delta Co, near the towns of Paonia and Hotchkiss, accounts for 21%, and discussions are under way proposing North Fork as the state's second AVA. That area is bisected by the North Fork of the Gunnison River. At high elevations it receives less than 2,000 *degree days a year. Soils are mostly silt on top of gravel, and the 50 acres of vineyard receive 15 in of precipitation annually.

CO has the highest average altitude in the US. Grand Valley is 4,800 feet high. A commercial vineyard and winery in Paonia is one of the highest in the world, higher than any in Europe, South Africa, or Australasia, at 6,400 ft. Only Latin America and the Canary Islands have commercial vineyards any higher. Killing *frost is predicted to occur only once every 25 years. Snow cover offers protection. In 1989, however, overnight temperatures reached −22°F, knocking 99% of the vines in the entire Grand Valley back to the ground. The vines are mostly planted on their OWN ROOTS because it was erroneously thought too cold for phylloxera to survive. Rainfall on the Western Slope is rather meager, at just over 9 in, of which 3 in are snow melt. For comparison, the Front Range—Fort Collins in the north, through Denver, to Pueblo in the south—receives 17 in of total moisture, of which 11 in is rainfall. It is too cold for *Pierce's disease, although cold temperatures do spawn *crown gall.

Chardonnay and Merlot are the most heavily planted grape varieties, each accounting for about 25% of acreage under vine. Riesling is the next most planted, at about 8%; and Cabernet Franc, Cabernet Sauvignon, and Pinot Noir account for another 6% each. Of the remaining 23%, Viognier is a favorite new planting. Riesling, Chardonnay, and Merlot seem to yield the best wines. Cabernet Sauvignon will ripen to 24°B, but usually produces less than intensely flavored wine. In 1997, Colorado wineries crushed over 750 tons of grapes, yielding approximately 45,000 cases of wine. In-state tank capacity is capable of handling four times that volume. Fifteen per cent of the crush is presently sold out of state.

Tourism figures heavily in the Colorado economy and wineries on the Western Slope have relied on tourists to sell a good portion of their wines. Acceptance of these wines on the Front Range and in the important resort areas has been less enthusiastic. Vail is a predominantly CA wine market, as much as 70% or so over the entire year, but import sales go up there in winter because of skiers from other countries. Sixty per cent of the rare, high demand wines go to the mountains, because those areas supported those brands first, but the Front Range is demanding an increased share.

CO operates under the THREE-TIER system, but wineries below 200,000 cases annual production can sell their wares directly to consumers, as well as obtain a wholesale license for selling to retailers and restaurateurs. In 1998 the population of CO was just under 4 million. Of that number half live in the Front Range. Historically many CO residents drank no alcohol at all, and despite the immigration of nearly 50,000 Californians annually, with their higher per capita wine consumption, it is still estimated that nearly half of the CO population are non-drinkers.

NOTABLE PROPERTIES

Carlson, opened in 1988 by Parker and Mary Carlson. Vinifera and hybrid production, including Chardonnel, is 6,000 cases made from 4 acres of owned vineyards plus purchased grapes. They also make a variety of tasty fruit wines, particularly plum, from fruit purchased in Grand Valley. Chardonnay shows promise.

Canyon Wind, bonded in 1996 by Norm Christiansen, who produces all his 4,000 cases of very promising Chardonnay, Cabernet Sauvignon, and Merlot, from 20 acres planted on a 50-acre ranch. Californian Robert Pepi is the consulting enologist.

Grande River, Steve Smith owns 50 acres of vinifera which comprise the largest vinifera

planting in CO. Production is 5,000–7,000 cases, entirely from estate grapes, notably Chardonnay and Meritage red wines.

Plum Creek, opened in 1985 by Erik Bruner, makes 8,000 cases of vinifera. Eighty per cent is from estate grapes co-owned with Doug and Susan Phillips. Half the estate grapes are from vineyards in Palisade, Grand River AVA; the remainder from their vines in the North Fork area. Older barrels were French oak, but Bruner is switching to Hungarian oak coopered in MO. Bruner makes solid Riesling, a Cabernet Franc/Merlot blend, Sangiovese, and a Chardonnay called Redstone.

Trail Ridge, winery located in Fort Collins, on the Front Range. Opened in 1994 producing 2,000 cases of hybrids and vinifera. Good examples of CO Riesling, Merlot, and Cabernet Franc.

See TERROR CREEK.   R.T.S.

Columbia Valley AVA, broadest appellation in WASHINGTON, encompassing YAKIMA VALLEY AVA and WALLA WALLA VALLEY AVA, and extending across the border into OR. It is a vast drainage system created by the Columbia, Snake, and Yakima Rivers. Shaped like a Chinese dragon facing east, it is about 110 mi wide by 90 mi tall. It is widest at the confluence of the three rivers: the eastward-flowing Yakima and the westward-flowing Snake as they empty into the south-flowing Columbia; just before the Columbia takes a sharp right turn west towards the Pacific Ocean. Its geologic features are a direct result of massive floods that occurred over the millennia, but in particular 12,000 to 15,000 years ago when a series of floods were caused by the break-up of ice dams in the ancient Lake Missoula. The flow of the water as it roared across ID, and much of central and eastern WA towards the Pacific Ocean, was equal to all the flows of all of the world's modern rivers combined. The result was an unbelievable carving of the land.

Because the CASCADE RANGE blocks rain clouds, the region is a semi-arid desert, barren of natural trees. Rainfall ranges between 7 and 12 in. All vineyards are irrigated, using overhead, ditch, or the preferred *drip irrigation. Sophisticated irrigation experiments are being conducted by WA State Univ through their Irrigated Agriculture Research Extension Center (IAREC) in Prosser under the direction of Dr Sara Spayd and Dr Robert Wample. Both continue pioneering research work begun by Dr Walter CLORE. Soils range in depth from a few inches to many feet. Soils are generally sandy and of igneous origin. In some places they are very light and fluffy; in others a bit grainier, especially in areas above the Missoula floodlines. Seventeen and a half hours of sunlight in June at this 46° to 48° latitude provide 1,800 to 3,500 *degree days even though the season is not as long as that found in more southerly maritime climates. Landscapes have an inspirational feel with unobstructed horizons, riverbeds chiseled out of broad valleys, skies wide and domed, usually without clouds. It is truly a big, wide-open country.

To the north are the Okanagan Highlands; to the west the eastern flanks of the Cascade Range; and to the southeast the Blue Mtns. Within the Columbia Valley are numerous basaltic uplifts, where cracks in the earth's mantle have allowed molten rock to intrude near the surface forming solid masses which do not erode easily. Tectonic pressure pushes these up through softer, more easily eroded sedimentary rocks. These basaltic uplifts tend to run east and west here. They allow cold air to flow downhill away from the vines, and also provide southern exposures to catch rays of the sun at a more direct angle in this northern latitude. Most notable are: the HORSE HEAVEN HILLS that run parallel to the Columbia River; the Rattlesnake Hills in the middle of the Yakima Valley that taper off into Red Mtn and Badger Mtn; then the Yakima Ridge; and finally the Ahtanum and Umtanum Ridges. The most northerly ridge is the Saddle Mtns, from there the Wahluke Slope slants south to the Columbia River. Each of these uplifts allows for gently slanting south-facing slopes, interspersed with broad basins where cold air tends to pool, and plateaux where topsoil tends to be scarce. The area is a cornucopia of fruits, vegetables, and crops. Growing alongside apples, peaches, and cherries are potatoes, alfalfa, wheat, mint, onions, asparagus, and melons.

NOTABLE PROPERTIES

Balcom & Moe, winery producing an excellent Merlot from grapes grown north of Pasco on the Columbia Basin bench in their 106-acre vineyard. Winemaker/owner Maury Balcom was one of the first to plant vinifera grapes in the modern era in 1981.

Barnard Griffin, winery owned by Rob Griffin and Deborah Barnard makes a wide assortment of wines from numerous vineyards. Their specialty is crisp *Fumé Blanc, but they produce excellent red wines, notably Merlot. They also produce a rare Zinfandel sourced from Pines Vyd in the Hood River Valley of OR.

Gordon Brothers, winery established in 1983 and, now owned by Jeff Gordon, makes

delicious wines which speak to their vineyard site high above the Snake River. French winemaker, Marie Giles, captures this seductive full flavor with an accompanying mouthful of round fruit. Excellent Merlot, a very good Cabernet Sauvignon, and an interestingly tropical Chardonnay.

Hedges, winery run by Tom Hedges which set the stage for Red Mtn grapes. It employs vineyardist Fred Artz, who also oversees the Klipsun Vyd. Hedges' first wine was an inexpensive red, a blend of Cabernet Sauvignon and Merlot, that appealed to the pocketbook of red wine consumers. His vineyard has expanded considerably to include reserve-styled Bordeaux blends.

Kiona Vyds, winery and also a very prestigious grower selling grapes to other wineries. Scott Williams produces outstanding wine from their Red Mtn vineyard for the Kiona label.

Klipsun Vyds, outstanding Red Mtn vineyard owned by Patricia and David Gelles of West Richland with 120 bearing acres. Managed by the incomparable Fred Artz, who also has a vineyard of his own on Red Mountain.

Sagemoor Farms, includes the Bacchus and Dionysus vineyards located contiguous to Sagemoor vineyard itself 6 mi north of Pasco along the eastern side of the Columbia River. Including holdings on the Wahluke Slope, over 750 acres of prime vineyard are managed. Sagemoor, planted in 1972 by the late Alec Bayless and partners Win Wright and Albert Ravenholt, was the initial grape source of the many Pacific Northwest pioneer wineries.

See also CH STE MICHELLE, COLUMBIA WINERY, QUILCEDA CREEK.   R.A.I.

Columbia Winery,

workmanlike operation outside SEATTLE in Woodinville, WASHINGTON, which has recently created a new corporate moniker, **Corus Brands**, to help consolidate the numerous wines they produce. In addition to Columbia, Corus Brands owns Covey Run, Paul Thomas, and Cascade Ridge, as well as Pintler Cellars in IDAHO where there are plans to plant 600 acres. Columbia started as Associated Vintners in 1962, a corporate partnership of five Univ of WA professors and five businessmen led by the late Dr Lloyd Woodburne and Cornelius Peck, Dean of the UW law school.

Columbia Winery purchases grapes from some of the best vineyards in WA: Sagemoor Farms in the Columbia Basin, Otis Vyd in the mid-Yakima Valley, and Red Willow Vyd in the western Columbia Valley AVA. They own Alderidge Vyd in the HORSE HEAVEN

HILLS. David Lake, who began at Columbia in 1978, became their winemaker in 1979 and now oversees all winemaking, is Canadian born, raised in Britain, educated at McGill Univ in Montreal, and apprenticed in the British wine trade, where he became a *Master of Wine. His heart seems to be in Bordeaux varieties, followed closely by a Syrah from grapes grown at Red Willow which is brimming with notes of cherry and warm chestnuts.   R.A.I.

competitions.

Prizes won at competitions in North America (see Commentators and Media essay, p 14) need to be evaluated in the light of three factors: how comprehensive was the field; how rigorous were the procedures; and who were the judges.

It is axiomatic about wine competitions in North America that the vast majority of really good wines do not enter. If a wine already has a reputation, and is going to sell out easily anyway, why should the winery pay an entry fee and pay the cost of shipping four to six free bottles? A few top wineries, operating on principle, will enter a couple of selected competitions because they think the show circuit is worth supporting, but in the very best levels of quality that practice would be the exception, not the rule. Moreover, there are a great many competitions every year, ranging from tiny county events to big international ones. A Double Gold at the Winnamucca Open is not the same as a Gold at INTERVIN. The **CA State Fair** is a big event with more than 2,000 entries every year, and stiff competition because there are 750 wineries in CA paying attention. But the CA State Fair is open only to wines from CA. The **Indiana Fair** is a big event because it is organized by Richard Vine, who buys wines for United Airlines, and because it attracts some important wine writers from major Midwest markets as judges. But very few noteworthy CA wines bother to enter.

Different procedures are used at different competitions. When the Beverage Tasting Institute in Chicago was running its self-styled world wine championship, it had a good reputation among wineries because there were at least five people on a panel tasting only seven wines per flight, and never tasting more than 75 wines in a day. The CA State Fair by comparison asks judges to taste as many as 150 wines for two days running. Some competitions take each judge's score individually and average the results by panel. Other competitions require the panel to confer and reach a forced consensus. No system is perfect, but as with both legislation and sausage, one is better off not knowing how panel consensus results are reached.

Some competitions use winemakers and/ or winery owners as judges. They are frequently faulted by detractors for having a 'house palate,' which means they are so used to drinking their own wine, they cannot abide anyone else's. Equally problematic is the common procedure of asking prominent writers or distributors to be judges. Distributors become prominent by being aggressive salesmen; not by judicious selection of delicious wines. Writers become prominent because of their facility with the language; they rarely have to bet their own money on a wine's quality. The CA State Fair asks judges to qualify by taking a taste examination, but there are health club instructors serving as judges whose exposure to the wine styles of the world is pretty minimal. The Australian wine show circuit has very professional judges who have come up through the ranks judging at shows for many years as apprentices ('associate judges' whose scores are not counted) before they accede to fully-fledged status. Senior Australian judges are remarkably reliable, in that they will give a wine the same score one day and then again two weeks later. The problem with Australian judges is homogeneity; they all come to agree on a narrow standard which penalizes innovation. In the end, there is no single correct answer for choosing judges, but analysis of competition results should always take into account who the judges are. B.C.C.

consultants, winemaking guns for hire. There are three components to winemaking: expertise; name recognition which will help sell the wine; and grunt labor to move materials around. The first two are hard to acquire; the third takes all the time. People with the first two attributes are expensive. Paying them to perform the third function is not cost efficient. Moreover it takes just about the same amount of expertise to make 500 cases of a wine as it does to make 50,000 cases. In this situation it is understandable that individuals with expertise and name recognition would be vigorously recruited by multiple vineyard owners and small wineries to spend brief periods strategizing, answering questions, and supervising the grunt labor performed by others.

The rise of *custom crush facilities in CA has served to accelerate this trend. A consultant can visit a vineyard a few times, help make the decision about when to pick, then prepare written work orders for the custom crush crew, visit the crush facility a couple of times to taste the *must, get lab reports over the phone, taste the wine in barrel a few times, decide on the final blend, then

pick a bottling day. Total involvement: 20–50 hours. The brand owner needs no investment in facilities, equipment, or payroll. Just a per case cost from the custom crush facility and a retainer bill from the consultant. The brand owner does not even need to own a vineyard; the consultant can recommend a grower and negotiate the grape contract. Is it art? Maybe, after a fashion, but it makes brand performance about as reliable as the quality of a Major League baseball team in a small market.

Another form of this winemaking with mirrors was pioneered by gypsy winemakers from Australia who were dubbed *flying winemakers because they would commute between jobs in both hemispheres. In CA the genre was created by André *Tchelistcheff who took consulting positions with as many as fifteen wineries a year from WA to Los Angeles while in his eighties. Dropping his name into conversations sure helped to jump start the sales efforts for a lot of wineries. Today there are perhaps 20 consultants in CA with the reputations to get wineries off the ground. Inevitably some of them have achieved icon status as painfully small lots of very good wine to which they have lent their name move into the marketplace and receive rave reviews from opinion leaders (see Commentators and Media essay, p 14). A comparison can be drawn with celebrity chefs whose name is often attached to five or six restaurants in different cities simultaneously. B.C.C.

Contra Costa, district named for the CA county east of the Oakland Hills and south of Suisun Bay in the DELTA. It is technically part of the San Francisco BAY AREA mega-AVA approved in 1999. More specifically, the grape growing district is the northern slope of Mt Diablo. Wind, sucked from west to east by the bellows of the Central Valley, is a distinct feature of the area, and DIURNAL TEMPERATURE FLUCTUATION is large. Vine rows planted parallel to the wind flow help. The lower elevations are called Oakley. They have a very deep, almost beach-like, sandy soil. Going down nearly 50 ft, it is not highly prized by gardeners, but it does produce magnificent Zinfandel. The older vineyards, some of them as much as 80 years of age, are *head trained, planted on their OWN ROOTS, and virtually *virus free. Higher elevations, called Brentwood, have much more clay, more humus, and less sand, producing a loam named for the district. Vines grown on Brentwood loam have prettier views, but much more vigorous growth.

The human population of this district has quadrupled since 1970, thanks to com-

muters who work over the hills in Berkeley and Oakland. Housing tracts threatened to end the 120-year history of viticulture in the area as grape prices declined below production costs in the 1980s. But *White Zinfandel saved some vineyards, and by the late 1990s local growers were looking to expand, based on newfound artistic acclaim for wines made from their grapes. B.C.C.

Corison winery in Napa Valley with new premises near ST HELENA in 1999. Diminutive Cathy Corison has cut a substantial figure in Napa Valley for more than 20 years. She was winemaker at Chappellet half that period, and married for a while to prominent winemaking consultant Tony Soter of Etude. Her winemaking helped launch Staglin, which many hold in high regard today, and she currently makes the wines for York Creek Vyd (see SPRING MTN). Corison is a busy woman. Remarried, she has two young children and an impressive second winery project called Long Meadow Ranch where she has also made her own wines for the last three years. Long Meadow is 800 ft high in the mountains west of St Helena. The magnificent rammed-earth winery was architect Bill Turnbull's (best known for Sea Ranch on the Sonoma coast) final project. In addition to wine, Long Meadow is reinvigorating 100-year-old olive trees found on their property and producing olive oil using a granite stone mill.

Cathy Corison sources Cabernet grapes for her own label from several vineyards on the westside bench running from Oakville to St Helena. She makes 2,000–3,000 cases a year, does all the sales work in CA herself, and exports 15% of her production overseas. Corison's Cabernet, notably her well-judged 1995, can withstand comparison with some of the world's finest. It is well balanced, with a nose that announces fine Cabernet and none of the overt reliance on wood to which more expensive wines often stoop. The Corison label features a 7,000-year-old graphic symbol for life based on an impression of rain. B.C.C.

Cornell, see GENEVA EXPERIMENT STATION.

Corus Brands, see COLUMBIA WINERY.

cotton root rot, vine disease caused by the soil-borne fungus *Phymatotrichum omnivorum* which attacks some 2,000 types of plants. Soils derived from calcareous clay loam with a high pH (over 7.5) in areas with hot summers, such as parts of TEXAS and the DESERT SOUTHWEST, are common breeding grounds. The disease kills quickly and usually attacks in mid- to late summer, harvest time in the Southwest. The first sign is yellowing of leaves, followed by leaf wilt within 48 hours, and vine death within a few days. A look inside the taproot just below the soil line will show a reddish rotten area extending up from the roots to the stem and light brown strands of rhizomorphs, or fungal threads, extending from the roots. The only known control is using a resistant rootstock, such as 5bb or Champanel, and avoiding planting in fields that have a history of the fungus. L.A.O.

CQA, Carneros Quality Alliance is the big brother of wine trade organizations in CA such as ZAP and CAL-ITALIA CONSORZIO. The development of the CQA represented the first time in 70 years that CA wineries were able to suppress their brand name mentality in order to cooperate with growers for promotion of a special regional character in their wine. Since the mid-1980s CQA has been highly successful, in part because it assesses its 65 grower and 30 winery members a relatively high fee, calculated on tons either grown or crushed. In this case money translates into influence and continuity. CQA has abandoned consumer promotion in favor of educational initiatives for their members, including commissioning a field guide on the Carneros region. www. carneros.com B.C.C.

craftsman-sized wineries, phrase denoting artisanal operations generally run by a family or a set of partners where all the work is done by one or two principal owners. These wineries rarely produce more than 10,000 cases a year for to do so would require hiring help either in the winery, in the vineyard, or with sales. As a general rule of thumb, paying for that help usually means a winery must expand to about 20,000 cases. It is worth noting that wineries frequently start at this small size, then outgrow the definition when they achieve public acclaim and/ or receive some form of capital investment.

Nevertheless they often persist in referring to themselves as 'small' wineries and encourage their supporters to do so as well. JORDAN and RIDGE were known as BOUTIQUE WINERIES, because they cultivated an air of exclusivity, well after they had grown to 40,000 cases and beyond.

cryoextraction, technique used in the US to make sweet, concentrated, liquorous wines by freezing the must and then filtering out the frozen water. This is similar to an old backwoods tradition in which fermented apple cider would be left outside overnight in winter. The fraction which did not freeze was sweet, flavorful, much higher in alcohol than normal cider, and called applejack.

The phrase *cryoextraction has a more technical connotation in Europe. In Canada it is a call to arms, a clear affront to the integrity of Canadian ICEWINE. US wineries produce cryoextracted dessert wines and routinely give them names such as Vin d'Glacière or even *Eiswein, a labeling practice sure to make German producers almost as furious as Canadians are when US producers call their cryoextraction products icewine.

cult wines, phrase used to describe wines produced in very small quantities which garner enthusiastic support from a (necessarily) narrow segment of the wine buying population. In years past the phrase was usually applied to styles of wine considered somewhat eccentric, such as late harvest Zinfandel, and it implied an evangelic winemaker/ promoter around whose personality acolytes could bond. Celebratory events were a fixture of the connotation then, but high prices were not. Kinship among adherents was based on some sense of a shared secret.

In the 1990s, however, this connotation has changed as the phrase has been co-opted by wine journalists referring to wines produced in tiny quantities and sold at as-

tronomical prices, often in AUCTIONS (see Auctions essay, p 32). These wines are frequently made by prestigious CONSULTANTS, often in borrowed or *custom crush facilities, on behalf of wealthy vineyard-owning clients. They receive extensive publicity because of the prices they command from a small group of well-heeled patrons, but they are not generally subject to peer review because they are not really available on anything one might fairly term a commercial basis and they are never entered into any competitions. The degree of publicity these wines enjoy, and their prices, make them considerably different from cult wines of yore. Thus they might more accurately be called 'celebrity wines.' However, the fact they do successfully command three-figure prices from willing buyers in an open marketplace such as a non-charity auction, makes them increasingly difficult to dismiss as vanity wines. See also *California cult. B.C.C.

Cumberland Valley AVA, one of MD's three AVAs, lying in western MARYLAND between the Catoctin hills of Frederick and the Appalachian Mtns. Ziem Vineyards, near the Potomac River south of Hagerstown, is located in this AVA. R.G.L.

Cuthills Vyds, owned by Ed Swanson, a former AZ distributor, and his wife Holly. He is a self-taught winemaker. Located in Pierce, northeast NEBRASKA, 120 mi northwest of Lincoln. Cuthills produces a total of 4,400 gal from 4 acres of owned vineyards, planted on sand/clay loam soils, including an excellent LACROSSE and fine DE CHAUNAC. R.T.S.

Cynthiana, promising dark-skinned hybrid of several American species which some claim is identical to NORTON, others that it ripens slightly earlier and makes less tannic reds.

D

Dallas Morning News International Wine Competition, and its sister event, the Dallas *Morning News* Wine & Food Festival, were founded in 1985 by Rebecca Murphy in conjunction with the city's largest newspaper. The annual competition was originally only for American wines, but broadened its scope to include wines from around the world in 1999. The first competition garnered 582 entries and had grown to 1,783 entries by 1999. Murphy puts together an impressive group of judges each year, which has propelled the competition into the top ranks in North America. The Wine & Food Festival is a four-day event open to the public each spring that features wines from the competition at seminars, tastings, and dinners.   L.A.O.

Dalla Valle, winery whose 25-acre vineyards straddle the boundary of the OAKVILLE AVA on a ridge in the eastern foothills of Napa Valley. Deserving of CULT WINE status for its 500-case production of Maya, a Cabernet Sauvignon and Cabernet Franc blend named after Naoko Dalle Valle's daughter. Total production is about 5,000 cases, made under the supervision of consultant Heidi Peterson Barrett. The wines are extremely powerful. The Cabernet has a mouthful of tannin, while the Maya is noticeably softer and more fragrant.   B.C.C.

D'Angelo, located in Amherstburg within the LAKE ERIE NORTH SHORE VA of ONTARIO, the winery was founded in 1983 by owner/winemaker Sal D'Angelo. His specialties are Vidal Icewine, Marechal Foch, and Cabernet Sauvignon. He plans to expand and move his present 5,000-case facility to a new site in nearby Colchester Hamlet, adding 26 acres to his present 50 acres. Plans are to plant with Cabernet Sauvignon, Cabernet Franc, Merlot, and Chambourcin. When the new lakefront facility is completed, it will supplant PELEE ISLAND as the most southerly winery in Canada.   L.F.B.

Davis Mtn AVA, see TEXAS DAVIS MTN.

De Chaunac, early ripening, productive, disease resistant, dark-skinned French hybrid, Seibel 9549, widely planted in the FIN-GER LAKES and ONTARIO in the 1970s and subsequently made into a wide range of wine styles and colors. Even the Canadian winemaker after which it is named though, was said to have preferred CHELOIS.

Delaney Vyds, new TEXAS winery. Jerry Delaney began growing grapes in 1986 with 43 acres in Lemesa on the TEXAS HIGH PLAINS. The vineyard has subsequently grown to 100 acres planted to Chardonnay, Cabernet Sauvignon, Cabernet Franc, Sauvignon Blanc, Petit Verdot, and Merlot. Winemaker Jacques Recth, a Frenchman now living in VA, spends an average of two weeks a month in Lemesa overseeing the vineyards and production. The Lamesa winery has a total capacity of 60,000 gal a year.

Delaney opened its French château-inspired 'Dallas palace'-style winery and tasting room in GRAPEVINE in 1996. The fully operational winery is surrounded by 10 acres of vines which were originally planted in 1992 with Chardonnay, Cabernet Sauvignon, and Merlot. They were able to make wines in 1995, 1996, and 1997 from the vineyards before the onset of *Pierce's disease. The vineyard is now partially planted to Seyval Blanc and Vidal Blanc with plans to plant the rest to Chambercin and Cynthiana. The 5,200 sq ft barrel room, with 40 ft ceilings, along with a patio which is actually the crush pad during harvest, is popular for weddings and receptions. What is not sold at the tasting room is self-distributed through most of the state.

Of particular interest is their 1997 TX High Plains Sauvignon Blanc, a well made dry wine with just enough grassy notes under the grapefruit and cantaloupe nose to remind one that TX is a great place to grow Sauvignon Blanc. Their 1995 TX High Plains Cabernet Sauvignon, redolent of ripe black cherries, smoked bacon, and olives, is notable for its well-balanced tannins.   L.A.O.

Delaware, small state on the northeast corner of the DELMARVA Peninsula, with a coastline on the Delaware Bay and the Atlantic Ocean. The only commercial winery in Delaware at this time is Nassau Valley Vyd in Lewes, near Rehobath beach. Peggy Raley is the proprietor; Joel Werni the winemaker. Raley acquired her knowledge of wine in Europe, and learned winemaking hands on with the assistance of others in the trade, especially Eric and Lee Miller of CHADDSFORD.

Nassau Valley owns 7.5 acres, first planted in 1987 and now growing Chardonnay, Seyval, Cabernet Sauvignon, Chancellor, Chambourcin, and Foch. They also purchase fruit from VA, especially INGLE-SIDE PLANTATION. The five mainstay wines are a light Chardonnay (barrel aged for less than six months); a red Meritage blend; Laurels Red (all Chambourcin, light and not barrel aged); a sweet white French hybrid blend of Seyval and Villard called Meadows Edge (35 g/l RS); and Cape Rosé, a semi-sweet rosé from STEUBEN (15 g/l RS). Tourbus visitors tend to favor the sweet Peach Ambrosia line which includes all-peach wines, a Baco Noir, and a Delaware.

Raley finds vinifera varieties resist rot better than hybrids in her location. Ocean breezes from the Atlantic less than 5 mi away moderate temperatures and lower the risk of most fungal diseases, although black rot can threaten in cold, wet springs. Nassau Vyds is DRY FARMED, and vines are trained on a traditional French low trellis with a non-divided canopy. When HURRICANE Bob came in 1996, the fruiting canes were strapped down and suffered no damage. Nassau's sandy soils and long growing season are particularly good for Cabernet Sauvignon, and Chardonnay is also strong. Seyval has the most pronounced regional style, with a heady grapefruit finish, in contrast to the usual bland character of the grape. Production is 3,000 cases per year.   R.G.L.

Delaware River Valley, which defines the boundary between PA and NJ, has a moderating influence on the region's climate and allows viticulture to flourish in the Central Delaware Valley AVA, found in both states.   R.G.L.

Delmarva, large peninsula in the MID-ATLANTIC region which derives its name from three states: DE, from the northeastern corner south to the middle of the peninsula along the Atlantic coast; MD, which defines the western half to the Chesapeake Bay, and the entire mid-section of the peninsula below Delaware; and VA, whose Eastern Shore is the southern 40 mi of the peninsula on both the Chesapeake and Atlantic sides. There are commercial vineyards in all three areas of Delmarva, with the VA section noted for the quality of its Merlot.   R.G.L.

De Loach, winery in Sonoma Co's RUSSIAN RIVER AVA begun in 1975 by a retired fireman and his wife. Today they control over 800 acres and produce nearly 200,000 cases annually. Their reputation was built on Chardonnay. In a period when big name competitors came from Napa Valley, De Loach Chardonnay garnered attention for its citrus-accented fruit and lengthy, refreshing acid in contrast to more wood-dominated wines. Having led this charge successfully, De Loach soon found the style category crowded with followers. In the late 1980s De Loach was very successful with another style of Chardonnay, one which exasperated purists: intense Pippin apple flavors and very high acid, achieved by picking their cool climate grapes early, and then balanced with a subthreshold (3–4 g/l) smidgin of sugar. As Robert Frost said about the poetry of e e cummings, 'It was like playing tennis with the nets down.' Nevertheless this Chardonnay style was a delicious drink, and American consumers flocked to buy it. In recent years some of the most noteworthy wines from De Loach have been their small lots of single vineyard Zinfandels sourced from ancient vines owned by their third and fourth generation Italian neighbors. Top-end items throughout the De Loach range are labeled OFS, officially meaning Our Finest Selection, but ubiquitously referred to in the trade as Out-F***in'-Standing.
                                    B.C.C.

Delta, regional description for the center-piece of the natural hydrology whereby the Sierra Nevada and the CENTRAL VALLEY conduct water out of CA through San Francisco Bay to the Pacific Ocean. In deference to the mighty Mississippi River, perhaps this region should be called the CA Delta, or the Sacramento Delta. But it never is. Nor is it an approved AVA, although it contains several of them. To Californians the phrase Delta is just the most effective general description for an area with unique characteristics. It is in the Central Valley, but it is neither as hot as the northern and southern sections of the Central Valley, nor does it give the visual impression of dry farmland

stretching to the horizon. The Delta is different because it is a maze of waterways. They are called sloughs (pronounced 'slews') and represent the historical topography, ie a giant marshy lake. The parcels of land surrounded by these sloughs have all been diked, with levees around their perimeter, and the marsh water pumped out, much like the reclaimed land of the Dutch *polders*. Although farming on these islands can be very productive, winter storms perennially threaten to rupture the levees. Road building in this environment is very difficult, which contributes to the Delta's sense of separateness. Most Californians know where it is, but very few have actually been through it.

People are surprised to learn that the Central Valley cities of Sacramento and Stockton are deep water ports. Today ocean-going vessels reach them via dredged channels. In 1850 it was easy to sail right through the Delta. So Sacramento and Stockton grew large as natural points of disembarkation and resupply for prospectors. A majority of the great fortunes of that era were made in those cities from the provision and transportation businesses; not in the mines. But one of the unique inventions of the *gold rush changed the Delta dramatically before being outlawed in 1870. Placer mining was the technique of impounding water high in the mountains, then dropping it hundreds of feet to a decreasing diameter nozzle in order to form an amazingly powerful instrument of hillside destruction. In one day two men using a cradle in a stream might wash about a cubic yard, say one ton, of gravel in order to extract the gold flake. Those same two men, using a nine-inch nozzle which passes 30,000 gal of water per minute, could drive 1,500 tons of gravel through a sluice box each day. 600 ft deep valleys a mile wide exist today in the Sierras which were not there until the hydraulic gold miners created them. The amount of material washed out of the mountains raised the normal level of the Sacramento River 7 ft and ended natural navigation beyond the Carquinas Straits. Sacramento, CA's state capital, has an attractive city center with massive Sycamore trees shading historic districts, but it is in serious danger of flooding whenever CA gets more than average rainfall.

Roughly defined by Sacramento on the north, Stockton on the south, the Carquinas Straits at Benecia on the west, and the Sierra Foothills on the east, the Delta receives cooling marine airflow through the Golden Gate along its low waterways. It is more humid than most CA grape growing districts, which means *fungal diseases can-

not be effectively controlled by weekend farmers. Soils are often peaty, and it is not hard for vine roots to reach the water table.

CLARKESBURG AVA
The center of northern Delta grape growing is at Clarkesburg. It completely encloses Merritt Island AVA, which has no good reason to exist separately. Both can be thought of as tracts of land in the Sacramento River's geological channel. Productivity is very high in these clay soils with their peat-like, high organic content. Growers here have the opposite of an irrigation problem. The water table is so high, they must imbed tile drains in the vineyard. Then, when they want the grapes to ripen up quickly, they pump water *out* of the vineyard.

Chenin Blanc and Petite Sirah are two varieties which achieved artistic notoriety here in the 1980s, but were overwhelmed in the marketplace by *fighting varietal Chardonnays and Cabernets. The fruity aroma of Clarkesburg Chenin Blanc was unusually pronounced. Noted wine journalist Gerald Asher (*Gourmet* magazine) called the region 'California's *Vouvray.' Bogle is the only winery still operating in the AVA, but the best example of Clarkesburg Chenin Blanc is made by Dry Creek Winery from Sonoma. Other islands in the geographic center of the Delta, such as Bethel and Mandeville, have historically produced high quality grapes, but none are approved AVAs and their relative values are a trade secret among the large producers in Lodi.

SOLANO & CONTRA COSTA COUNTIES
The hills bordering Suisun Bay in the western Delta have been grape growing districts for 150 years. On the northwest side they are Solano Co; on the southwest side CONTRA COSTA Co. Suburbanization just about ended viticulture there in the 1980s, but pockets of ancient Mourvèdre, Grenache, Zinfandel, and Carignane vines survived. Planted on well-drained, piedmont soils, these grapes can produce intense, long-lived wines. In Solano Co two approved AVAs exist: Suisun Valley AVA and Solano Green Valley AVA (there is also a Green Valley AVA in Sonoma County). As a practical topographic matter a third approved AVA should be included in this group. Wild Horse Valley AVA overlaps part of Solano Green Valley AVA, but sits entirely inside the county line for Napa Co so those grapes are allowed to go to market as NAPA VALLEY AVA. Suisun Valley, Solano Green Valley, and Wild Horse Valley are all separated quite clearly from the actual Napa River watershed by the Vaca Mtns. Nevertheless, they have somewhat similar climate and soils to those of the Napa Valley, and

---

facing: Unlike most European examples, North American labels are usually designed to make customers turn their heads and look while walking down the aisle of a retail store.
overleaf: The intrusion of marine **fog** into CA's coastal valleys is an important determinant of mesoclimate.

historically most of their grapes were sold to Napa Valley wineries. There are but two wineries within all three AVAs. Wooden Valley, owned by opera singer Mario Lanza's family, has 500 acres. Quail Creek is the other.

The southern side of Suisun Bay, on the northern slopes of Mt Diablo looking out across the oil refineries at the mothballed fleet of Second World War era Navy ships, is a district capriciously called Oakley or Brentwood. It too had its day as a fine region for Zinfandel and promiscuously interplanted Rhônish red varieties sold by Italian stallions in value sized containers. In fact Ernest *Gallo began his career during Prohibition sourcing grapes in Oakley to sell to home winemakers in Chicago. Only one winery exists today in Contra Costa Co: Viano in the town of Martinez. Cline Cellars (see CARNEROS) was located there and still sources some grapes in the area. ROSENBLUM though, champions the region and has done most to resurrect its image as a quality viticultural district with three separate Zinfandels made from ancient vines.

LODI AVA

The eastern part of the Delta is the approved Lodi AVA centered around the sleepy valley towns of Woodbridge and Lodi, and the Mokelumne (pronounced *moh KELL hum neh*) River. During Prohibition Lodi was the most prosperous grape growing district in the US due to the brilliantly colored Flame Tokay table grape, which never achieved the same color intensity anywhere else. The key was a site on a particular soil series deposited by the river and known as Hanford clay loam. Seedless grape varieties were the competitive end for Flame Tokay and it is rapidly disappearing.

Today there are over 600 grape growers in the Lodi region farming 45,000 acres of grapes for sale to very large producers. These growers are noteworthy in the absentee owner-, agricultural syndicate-dominated environment of CA's Central Valley because they are mainly small acreage, hands-on, mixed crop farmers. They average less than 100 acres apiece, making a living on cherries, almonds, row crops, and grapes. Dating back to the 1880s, they traditionally formed themselves into cooperative wineries. The consolidation of distribution channels in America, and the need for innovative marketing, rendered the co-ops obsolete by the end of the 1970s. Gallo bought the Liberty Co-op, Robert MONDAVI bought the Cherokee Co-op, SEBASTIANI bought the Woodbridge Co-op, and CANANDAIGUA bought the Guild Co-op. East-Side, with their Oak Ridge and Royal Host brands, is the only co-operative left in the AVA.

Lodi is best known for Zinfandel. In the late 1960s and early 1970s RIDGE VYDS and David BRUCE brought considerable attention to the Lodi area by making massive Zinfandels which beat consumers about the neck and shoulders with opulent, ripe berry fruit. The wines were too alcoholic and extractive to appeal to a mass audience, but nobody who tasted one ever had any trouble recognizing Zinfandel aroma afterward. The gargantuan structure of those wines accurately reflected the stature of the vines themselves. Trunks with 30 in circumference are common. Zinfandel comprises 35% of the planted acreage in Lodi, but most of it goes into *White Zinfandel these days. In the 1990s a great deal of acreage was added in the AVA with grape varieties such as Chardonnay and Merlot. Producing up to 10 t/a, these vines make reliable commercial wine.

NOTABLE PROPERTIES

Diablo Vista Vyds, long time grower in Oakley section of CONTRA COSTA Co who specializes in Zinfandel and Petite Sirah. The DRY-FARMED vineyard is at 82 ft of elevation which puts it right on the edge of the deep sandy soils. Recent quality recognition for wines from his grapes has induced Dwight Meadows and his son to acquire and plant more land in the district, contravening conventional pressure toward housing tracts. They are using budwood from PRE-CERTIFICATION CLONES of Zinfandel found in Sonoma and Napa. Most of Diablo Vista's grapes go to Rosenblum and Star Hill Winery in Napa.

Quail Creek, production facility in the Solano Green Valley AVA for Rutherford Benchmarks, an investment group that owns the Quail Ridge and Monterey Peninsula brands as well. They source some Merlot from Ben Volkhardt's vineyard surrounding the winery site, which was formerly Ch de Leu. The 1990 vintage of those Merlot grapes won Best of Show for Ch de Leu at the CA State Fair.

See also CANANDAIGUA, CONTRA COSTA, KAUTZ, LODI AVA, MONDAVI, SEBASTIANI.

B.C.C.

Denver, largest metropolitan area in COLORADO, the geographical center of the US, and its highest major city. In 1998, excise taxes collected on spirits rose 5.4%; on wine 4.5%; and on beer 4.9%. Most of these increases are due to a rise in population. The spirit market seems to be going in only one direction: higher prices for premium and super-premium brands. Dollars are up, and volume is down all over the state. Big beer brands pay for promotions in ski areas to keep their products visible. On the Front Range (ie the big cities north and south of Denver on the east side of the ROCKY MTNS), micro beers are losing popularity. Wine volume has steadily increased for 25 years with CA wines maintaining a strong portion of the market. Visitors to ski resorts tend to seek out higher priced wines, especially in restaurants. But the resort market is prone to fluctuation. When tourism drops, perhaps due to a substandard year for snow conditions, so do wine sales. In years past, the mountain market received the highest allocations of expensive and rare wines, but Front Range restaurants and retailers are now successfully acquiring a bigger share.

R.T.S.

Desert Southwest, region comprising four arid states west of the Rocky Mtns and east of the Sierra Nevadas: NEW MEXICO, ARIZONA, UTAH, and NEVADA. Cold winters are followed by hot summers and there is good potential for vinifera vines. AZ, NM, and UT are basically rectangular shaped states which all meet at one point along with CO. A now-defunct cooperative commission for the Four Corners deserves credit for advancing each state's wine industry as far as they have all come in the last two decades.

The development of civilization in the southwest is irrefutably linked to the availability of water: who has it; who controls it; and who wants it. By definition a desert is any region which receives less than 10 in of precipitation per year. Portions of all these states qualify. Which is why rights to the Colorado River are such a hotly contended issue. Arising in Rocky Mtn Natl Park, about 35 mi from Denver, the Colorado River then drains the Western Slope before flowing south through Moab, UT, to form the Grand Canyon in northern AZ. So much water is taken out for irrigation, the river is just a trickle by the time it becomes the border between CA and AZ, and then expires exhausted into the Gulf of California.

At the end of the 19th century, NM and AZ claimed substantial wine industries. But Prohibition, natural disasters, and the emergence of the CA industry eradicated most traces of the vine in the Southwest. Today, AZ and NM contain the lion's share of re-emerged wineries. But vineyard plantings are expanding in NV and UT, despite restrictive legislation in the latter.

Though winter temperatures can dip quite low, especially in the mountainous regions, WINTER KILL is generally not a threat to vines in the Desert Southwest. Warm

---

previous page: Monticello Vyd, VA, was the home of Thomas Jefferson, second US President and an avid oenophile.
facing above: British Columbia's **Okanagan Valley** is the northernmost American viticultural region, further from the Equator than all but a handful of German vineyards and those of a few plucky eccentrics in Britain.
below: The Mississippi River drains almost all of middle America from the Rocky Mtns to the Appalachian Mtns. Native American grape species such as the **Muscadine** varieties grow prolifically in the river's rich, humid southern districts.

spells in the spring, followed by *frost are a much more serious cause for concern. Vine pests and diseases are also quite rare, because of low rainfall and low humidity. Most vinifera vines are on their OWN ROOTS. Acids are usually adequate. French hybrids in the northern areas occasionally require *chaptalization.

R.T.S.

Diamond Creek Vyd, park-like winery with an enviable reputation created entirely by the indefatigable Al Brounstein. Established in 1968, it is one of the premier examples of how different soil types intrude small areas throughout CALIFORNIA's coastal geology. Brounstein had previously owned a pharmaceutical distribution business, and bought his 80-acre parcel 600 ft up a canyon on the westside slope of Napa Valley south of CALISTOGA without having a vision of its wine potential. He cleared and planted three separate parcels using budwood from several *first growth vineyards in Bordeaux. He named the parcels after their soil characteristics: 8-acre south-facing Volcanic Hill; 7-acre north-facing Red Rock Terrace; and 5-acre Gravelly Meadow in the flat bottom of the canyon. Using outdoor wooden fermenters Jerry Luper, Diamond Creek's first winemaker, vinified the parcels separately. They soon became classic CULT WINES. And they are magnificent, but it would be erroneous to imply that Diamond Creek rose to fame while Brounstein dawdled. In fact he personally called on hundreds of retailers a year for nearly 20 years, and has barely slowed down recently even after the onset of Parkinson's disease in 1990.

All the wines are labeled Cabernet Sauvignon, although Brounstein has been gradually introducing a few *field blended Merlot and Cabernet Franc vines. All the wines share a family resemblance in that they are dark, tannic, broodingly closed in youth, and often show a rustic complexity. Side-by-side the separate vineyard plots do, however, show distinct personalities. Volcanic Hill is the hardest edged and most powerfully flavored. Red Rock Terrace is the most refined and the most likely to show berry nuance in the mouth. Gravelly Meadow has more mineral flavors and length. A fourth vineyard plot called Lake is just 1 acre in a cool section at the back of the property. It is not always bottled separately but when it is, the wine shows more green bean nuance than its brothers, and sells for as much as $250 a bottle simply because production is extremely limited.

B.C.C.

Diamond Mtn, district in the western mountains of NAPA VALLEY southwest of Calistoga and north of SPRING MTN, although not yet an approved appellation. The ridgeline which serves as county boundary between Napa and Sonoma is lower here than it is further south, and the mountain range is narrower, allowing cool breezes to sneak through from the Russian River and Chalk Hill districts on the Sonoma side. Sites above the inversion layer are much cooler than sites on the Napa Valley floor near Calistoga. Soils are hard to typify due to their intruded and folded nature, but most have volcanic antecedents. There are hot springs, geysers, and even a petrified forest in the district. The raised pH effect found on Spring Mtn, however, is not found on Diamond Mtn.

NOTABLE PROPERTIES

Schramsberg, winery built by German barber Jacob Schram and well known before Robert Louis Stevenson began visiting in 1880, eventually to commemorate those days in his book *Silverado Squatters*. The historic property had marvelous caves impressively dug by Chinese coolies whose every pick mark remains in the walls today. In 1965 the derelict winery was brought back to life by Jack and Jamie Davies and given a new mission: sparkling wines. Their *méthode champenoise wine received an exponential boost in 1972 when US President Richard Nixon took it with him to China to toast the first Sino-US rapprochement since 1946, a public relations coup even the Davies had not anticipated. One year later Moët-Hennessey began the wave of CA investment by influential French champagne houses when they broke ground for Dom Chandon in Napa Valley and started to compete with Schramsberg. Jack Davies died in 1998. The winery produced 40,000 cases that year, sold nationally and exported to more than 30 countries. Cuvée Schram is their top end; Mirabelle is their second label.

Von Strasser, small winery purchased in 1990 by Rudy Von Strasser and his wife Rita. Formerly Roddis winery, it had the odd distinction of being planted by a very energetic paraplegic who did most of the work in a wheelchair. Von Strasser has expanded the vineyard and doubled the density by putting a second row of vines on each terrace. His wines are bold and firmly structured. Among the rarest in CA is a unique, 100% Petit Verdot sold to an exclusive mailing list in a thick, black, liter bottle that must weigh 5 pounds.

See also DIAMOND CREEK VYD. B.C.C.

Dijon clone, catch-all phrase referring to *clonal selections of Chardonnay (primarily #76 and #95) and Pinot Noir (primarily #667 and #777) originating in Burgundy and made available through authorized nurseries in North America beginning in the early 1990s. They contrast with selections made from early plantings of these varieties in CA which typically have far fewer Burgundian characteristics.

See ENTAV. B.C.C.

dining habits, North America. After the Second World War America experienced several changes which had a noticeable impact on attitudes to dining. Many soldiers returned from Europe having had their first encounters with wine, for example. At home, the technological revolution produced frozen food, a concept which was pushed very hard in the media (both print and the then new television). Homemakers were inundated with messages about how fashionable it was to employ the new convenience of 'fresh' frozen food products.

In the late 1960s when the feminist movement took hold and American women began entering the workplace in large numbers, going out to eat became increasingly common nationwide. Household incomes rose because of women in the workforce, and food prices dropped because of greater farm productivity. While in 1940, 21% of Americans' disposable income was spent on food, that figure was 14% in 1970, and had fallen to 11% by 1995. And Americans spent 15% of their food dollar away from home (in restaurants, carry-out, and fast food chains) in 1940; 26% in 1970; and 40% in 1995.

The relationship between fine dining and fine wine (see Wine Service essay, p 28) is most finely drawn in the San Francisco BAY AREA because of its *gold rush history as a restaurant town, its proximity to wine producing regions, and its access to year-round fresh produce, which made it somewhat resistant to the nationwide 1950s media blitz designed to popularize frozen food. Alice Waters opened Chez Panisse, her justifiably famous Berkeley restaurant in 1970. Ms Waters has always executed her concept brilliantly, but the question remains, 'Did she found California Cuisine, or did it seek her out?' Either way, the Bay Area has since become a destination for creative chefs, more of whom are women than anywhere else in the world. It remains to be seen whether San Francisco's location at the intersection of wine culture with traditionally non-wine drinking societies, such as those of Asia and Latin America, will produce notable new classics in wine/food pairings or whether it can catalyze the custom of regular wine consumption amongst Oriental and Latino populations.

B.C.C.

direct shipment, the sale and delivery of wine from winery straight to consumer at some distance (as opposed to CELLAR DOOR) in contravention of the THREE-TIER DISTRIBUTION system common throughout the US. When said transaction crosses state lines, a practice analogous to mail order sales of thousands of other products, myriad legal questions are raised. How strictly the widely varying laws in any particular state are likely to be enforced is anybody's guess.

Further complicating matters, MARK-UPS on expensive wines are proportionally more than on cheaper ones, for essentially the same service. For example, a distributor normally receives about $16 per case for its middleman role in selling and delivering a wine which retails for $7 a bottle; but $80 a case to perform that same function on a wine which retails for $35 a bottle. That is why producers of limited volume wines which are in very high demand would like to be able to deal with their customers directly. Moreover, wineries which put a lot of effort into entertaining customers at their hospitality facilities, then sell them a few bottles, would like the ability to contact these customers three months later to ask if they want another bottle or two.

This issue has intensified in the US since the mid-1980s due to technological advancements in desktop publishing and printing. Some state legislatures (eg KY) have made direct wine shipments a felony. The practice is likely to increase (see Cybersales essay, p 24) due to Internet commerce. Distributor trade groups such as the Wine & Spirits Wholesalers' Association (WSWA) officially lobby against direct shipment. At the same time, consolidation in the wholesale segment of the wine industry makes it harder and harder for small and new wineries to gain representation in many markets.

Fourteen state governments have created a legal relationship with CA agreeing to allow direct wine shipments between the two states. These are called 'reciprocal states.' Other state governments have enacted statutes outlawing direct shipping, and there have been lawsuits by KY and FL against direct shippers as states begin for the first time to actively enforce these statutes. In 1995 FL filed suit in federal court against seven wine clubs, alleging they violated state law by selling wine directly to FL consumers by mail order. Justifications for the suit given by FL officials were that out-of-state retailers cheated the state of its rightful share of taxes and fees, that legally licensed FL retailers (including native wineries) were put at an unfair competitive standing, and that 'there is no way of knowing whether underage persons in Florida are receiving wine shipments.' Defendants stated that the Interstate Commerce clause of the Constitution takes precedence over the 21st Amendment, in which authority for local control of alcoholic beverages was given to state governments. FL's case in the 11th US Circuit Court of Appeals, however, was dismissed. The appeals court noted that nothing prevents states from prosecuting such cases in state courts. Attorneys for FL replied they needed federal enforcement, because defendants' attorneys have claimed the sales actually took place in the states of origin. FL then took the case to the US Supreme Court, which refused without comment to hear the case in 1998.

B.C.C. and R.G.L.

diurnal temperature fluctuation, average difference between high temperature in the day and low temperature at night. The importance of this climatological indicator is a contentious issue, often blurring the distinction between wine style and wine quality. One advocate for the advantages of minimal fluctuation is academician Dr John Gladstones from *Western Australia. His position is that enzyme activity leading to flavor development will occur at an optimum rate when diurnal temperature variation is minimized in a range approximating 70°F. In Gladstones' opinion, hot days alternating with cold nights produce too much alcohol and not enough flavor. CA's CENTRAL VALLEY has hot days and fairly balmy nights during the summer. Since 1960, as CALIFORNIA vineyards moved to districts in the coastal mountains and up to higher elevations in the Sierras, the beneficial results in wine quality were often attributed by growers and winemakers to cool nights, which they said helped retain acid in the grapes and slowed ripening down, increasing hang time. CA growers argue that if Gladstones were correct, the Central Valley would produce better wine than districts such as PASO ROBLES, SANTA CLARA VALLEY, and EL DORADO Co where temperature fluctuation is quite dramatic. Since Margaret River, the closest fine wine district to Gladstones' home in Perth, is famous for having one of the world's least fluctuating diurnal temperatures, CA winemakers sometimes rush to question the good Doctor's objectivity. This controversy has a long run ahead of it though. As CA vineyards move further into low lying coastal valleys where both days and nights are cool, Gladstones may yet accumulate some endorsements from CA winemakers.

See *temperature variability.   B.C.C.

Gladstones, J., *Viticulture and Environment* (Adelaide, 1992).

Dom Carneros, sparkling wine producer in the CARNEROS district of Napa Valley. Owned by the Taittinger family from *Champagne, who also control several hotels and an extensive collection of luxury brands throughout the world. The eye-catching Napa winery is modeled after Taittinger's château in France (although solid stone masonry was not a CA option) and is extensively landscaped befitting its position as one of the first wineries encountered on the drive into Napa Valley on the Carneros Hwy. The delicacy of Taittinger's house style is rigorously maintained in their CA sparkling wines under the direction of general manager Eileen Crane, making Dom Carneros the most reliably elegant CA fizz. Capitalizing on this, a *tête de cuvée called Le Rêve (The Dream) was released with the 1992 vintage.   B.C.C.

Dom Drouhin Oregon, (DDO), owned by Joseph *Drouhin of Burgundy, the first French investor in OR wine. The firm purchased a major vineyard plot in 1988 and originally planted it using established OR vineyard techniques near EYRIE VYDS in the RED HILLS OF DUNDEE. Robert Drouhin recognized immediately the differences between OR and Burgundy, and these have been accentuated to produce rounder, fuller Pinot Noir in OR. Winemaking is overseen by Veronique Drouhin, Robert's daughter, at the gravity fed winery. Currently 82 acres are planted at 3,000 vines to the acre. Laurène is a second, high-end label. A limited amount of Chardonnay is produced from 6 acres of DIJON CLONES. Initially DDO planted available clones of Pinot Noir, but recently they have added a mix of Burgundy clones sold through OR State Univ.   R.A.I.

Dominus, venture started in the early 1980s as a partnership between Christian *Moueix of Pomerol fame and the descendants of Inglenook founder John Daniel (see NIEBAUM-COPPOLA). In 1995 Christian Moueix bought out Daniel's daughters Robin Lail and Marcia Smith and set about building a stark modern winery on the Napanook vineyard site, which is technically just outside the OAKVILLE AVA boundary on the westside bench to the south. Despite their impeccable pedigree, the Dominus red Meritages from 1983 through 1994 could be more accurately described as implacable. Unyielding tannins have been much more evident than any fruit component, and to some CA palates the distinct odor of Brettanomyces (see Microbiology essay, p 39) and a bitter finish have been the most striking characteristics of this controversial wine. Europeans found the wine more familiar, and noticably drier than the CA norm. More recent vintages have been more obviously opulent, however. B.C.C. and J.R.

Dos Cabezas, winery located in Kansas Settlement, ARIZONA, 90 mi east of Tucson and named for the Dos Cabezas Mtns. What are now AZ's oldest vinifera vines were planted in 1985. The site is 4,300 ft high in the SULPHUR SPRINGS VALLEY. The winery has 40 acres, all from the original planting, and is owned by a group of wine enthusiasts. They produce aromatic Pinot Gris and Viognier. R.T.S.

dram shop insurance, liability coverage that servers of alcoholic beverages, ie ON-PREMISE license holders, need to have against the possibility of being named in a suit for damages by an individual who has consumed alcohol in their establishment and then injured himself or others.

dry, quasi-legal term used in the US to describe some geopolitical unit, such as a county or even something as small as a voting precinct, where local option has made it illegal to sell alcohol. This does not preclude residents from buying wine elsewhere and consuming it in the privacy of their home or workplace, although it does preclude package stores, grocery stores, and restaurants from selling wine. Cf *dry as a description for wines without any appreciable sweetness.

Dry Creek AVA, useful appellation in northern SONOMA CO. It has almost as much as SONOMA VALLEY AVA's 6,000 acres of vines planted, but Dry Creek's vines are all in one-third of its total surface area: the narrow valley floor and adjacent hillsides along the creek itself running southwest from Warm Springs Dam (built in 1985) to its confluence with the Russian River immediately south of Healdsburg. The remainder of the AVA, upstream from the dam and the mountainous area west of the valley, is almost entirely devoid of paved roads and people, as well as of vines. The planted area of the AVA is about 12 mi long and never more than 2 mi wide. Rising sharply from the creekbed, 1,500 ft mountains lie within a mile or two on the western side. On the eastern side a 600 ft ridge separates Dry Creek Valley from ALEXANDER VALLEY.

From an image standpoint Dry Creek Valley is virtually synonymous with Zinfandel. One cannot claim to fairly evaluate that grape variety without including at least one example from this appellation. Growers and wineries are trying to expand their reputation by planting and promoting other grapes. Zinfandel was linked to Dry Creek Valley by Italian immigrants who settled here from the 1870s on. They knew how to choose vineyard sites. Zinfandel is a thin-skinned berry with compact clusters which ripen late in the season. Dry Creek Valley is smack in line for the first storms spinning out of the Gulf of Alaska each fall. Valley floor vines, high in vigor, would ripen last, likely to catch rain during harvest which would cause rot in tight Zin clusters. So the Italians DRY FARMED their Zins on the steep hillsides and the porous benches. The most desirable sites feature a soil so particular it is called Dry Creek Conglomerate. Its coin-sized gravel allows rapid drainage, but the unique characteristic is an admixture of geologically older, red metamorphic soil with a modestly clay-like texture. Locals call this soil *volcanic* because of its iron oxide color, but it is actually weathered in place and unrelated to either lava or to volcanic ash.

Zinfandels from the western hillsides of Dry Creek Valley are somewhat lighter bodied and less prone to the jamminess often found in their eastern hillside cousins. The distinction is one of style, not quality. Claret style on the west; traditional style on the east. Eastern foothill versions can be more voluptuously scented and friendlier on the palate if the winemaker refrains from harnessing donkeys to the press. Unfortunately for students of these matters, few Dry Creek Valley Zinfandels make it to market in site designated form. Most are blended from several vineyards to achieve complexity and balance.

Valley floor vineyards, especially along the creekbed in the southern half of the valley, tend to be alluvial, sandy soils. They are generally planted to white varietals. Sauvignon Blanc is most common although some Semillon has been introduced in the last fifteen years. Heat summation is substantially lower in the southern third of the valley. At that point confining hills drop away, and the mouth of the valley opens onto the RUSSIAN RIVER AVA. Conceptually, it is accurate to imagine foggy maritime weather moving 20 mi from west to east along the river and not having much impetus to make the 120° left turn in order to blow with any impact or regularity northwest up the Dry Creek Valley. The middle third of Dry Creek Valley is Zinfandel heaven. The upper third is warm and features several exciting investigations into Rhône and Italian varietals. Barbera grown by Lou PRESTON in flatland plots north of Yoakim Bridge Rd is one of

CA's three best, and has been extremely reliable over fifteen vintages.

NOTABLE PROPERTIES

Collier Falls, grower at the very terminus of West Dry Creek Rd with beautiful bench vineyard. In fact the falls come over the bench in spring. A superb Zinfandel is produced for him under his own label.
Duxoup, tiny winery making dark-hued, effusively fruity Gamay and Syrah in a style which defines *New World. There is no reason to wait on these wines. Corks are printed *Facilis par Duxoup* ('as easy as ...').
Dry Creek, first winery to open (1972) in the district since Prohibition. Voluble David Stare had come from the East Coast, where his father taught at Harvard, and David led the education of American consumers in introducing Sauvignon Blanc. Today the winery makes well over 125,000 cases which are distributed internationally. Of particular note is their Chenin Blanc sourced from Clarksburg in the DELTA.
Lytton Springs, fabulous pre-Prohibition Zinfandel and Petite Sirah vines in 50-acre vineyard on a plateau above the east side of the valley. RIDGE VYDS has bought grapes here since the 1970s and now owns the winery too.
Michel-Schlumberger, very upscale operation nestled into the foothills on the west side of the valley emphasizing Cabernet and Chardonnay. Begun by Jean-Jacques Michel of Swiss banking giant Paribas in 1979 after a conversation with Tom JORDAN. After several uneven years, a majority interest was purchased in 1993 by Jacques Schlumberger, whose family is one of the bigger vintners in *Alsace and who has now taken over day-to-day operations. Presently making 25,000 cases.
Pezzi-King, formerly the William Wheeler property high on the southern lobe of the western mountains above Dry Creek Valley. Purchased by the Rowe family from San Francisco, flush from their international construction finance business in 1993. Outstanding Zinfandel and noteworthy Cabernet. They also own a tasteful facility in the valley floor which used to be the Robert Stemmler winery. 25,000 cases in 1997; due to be 40,000 soon after the millennium.
Rafanelli, third generation Italian-American family with 60 acres of vineyard on the west-side of the valley making 6,000 cases of clean, yet formidable Cabernet and Zinfandel.

See also GALLO SONOMA, FERRARI-CARANO, NALLE, PRESTON. B.C.C.

dry farm, American phrase, used as a verb, to describe the decision to raise vines without added irrigation water. The term would be virtually meaningless in France where rain falls throughout the summer. In the arid American west, it implies vines forced to struggle for survival. See *dryland viticulture.

Dufour, Jean-Jacques, industrious Swiss-born pioneer vine grower, who eventually went under the Americanized first and middle names John James. It is no wonder this man brought up surrounded by vineyards on the north shore of Lake Geneva took a love and a knowledge of wine with him when he went to America in the spring of 1796. After scouting out the few worthwhile vineyards in the East, he moved to Lexington, KY, where he attracted investors such as Henry Clay and established the KY Vyd Society, a stock company with winegrowing as its goal. In 1799 he planted his First Vyd on the Kentucky River southwest of Lexington. Most of the vines he planted had been purchased from Pierre Lagaux of Spring Mill, PA, who had established his own, less successful company, a vineyard, and a nursery as well. Along with other varieties, Dufour got the Alexander grape from Legaux, who claimed it was the grape that was used in the famous *Constantia wine. In fact it was often called the Cape grape.

After a few good seasons, the vineyard developed various diseases, probably *black rot, and the decimated vineyard was abandoned in 1809. The Alexander did survive. When Dufour moved his family and friends to their new home at 'Vevay' (American spelling) in far southwest IN along the Ohio River, he took it with him. Dufour promoted the hardy grape as a vinifera. He more or less had to, since he considered all other species of grapes to be unworthy of winemaking (Lucie Morton describes Dufour as 'the world's first grape-variety '"racist," but not the last'). In any event, it seemed to survive the local conditions and to make at least passable wine.

After a lengthy stint in Europe, during which time his family and neighbors tended the New Switzerland vineyards and spread the wine word, Dufour returned to IN and began to write *The American Vine Dresser's Guide,* probably the first wine book in the US. He died in 1827 shortly after the book was published. He did not live to see the New Switzerland Vyd abandoned in 1835, victim of any number of pests and diseases.

P.W.F.

Dunn, winery on HOWELL MTN in Napa which pretty much launched the concept of CA CULT WINES in the mid-1980s. Randy Dunn had reached the ABD (all but dissertation) stage of an entomology doctorate at UC Davis when he was bitten by the winemaking bug. He became the first winemaker at CAYMUS in 1972 and stayed twelve years, gaining celebrity status in the process. But Randy Dunn does not enjoy the spotlight; he would rather be flying airplanes or riding motorcycles. He never cultivated the icon image; it just followed him. He had moved with his wife and young daughters to a small vineyard and 100-year-old house on Howell Mtn in 1979. He brought out his first Cabernet, the 1979, under his own label in the early 1980s and was soon besieged, and mildly annoyed, by wine hobbyists desperate for a few bottles no matter what the price.

He retired from Caymus in 1984 to take consulting positions with Livingston, Pahlmeyer, Grace Family, and La Jota, some of which he maintained until the early 1990s. Meanwhile he developed his own 5-acre vineyard, had 500 ft of caves dug into the hill behind his property, and purchased the old 15-acre Park Muscadine Vyd on the red soil slope behind his house. Fertility and water retention are so low in these rocky soils he has to irrigate several times a month in summer. As he has for 20 years, in 1999 Dunn made 2,100 cases of his Napa Valley Cabernet which is blended from his own grapes and fruit purchased in the valley floor. His Howell Mtn Cabernet comes entirely from his own vineyards and amounts to 1,900 cases. Half the wine is reserved for his fanatical mailing list. Unlike other cult classics, he releases the other half to the trade, including 400 cases for export. Dunn Howell Mtn Cabernet is one of America's first growths, very consistent from year to year, with solidly wrought structure framing cassis and leather notes which persist full strength for decades. One of the most valuable CA wine items that can appear at auction would be any of the original 53 impériales (6 l) bottled from Dunn's 1979 vintage. They are all from Howell Mtn, yet say Napa Valley on the label because BATF had not yet approved the appellation and would not permit Dunn to use it.

B.C.C.

earthquake, massive earth undulations caused by shock waves when two sides of a fault slip against each other either horizontally or vertically. They are common at tectonic plate boundaries, such as the west coast of North and South America, but usually in such low magnitudes as to be virtually unnoticed by human inhabitants. During the 1906 earthquake that pulverized San Francisco, one 45-second jolt moved the granite outcrop of Pt Reyes 20 ft further up the Sonoma coast on its slow trip toward Alaska. At one time that granite had been part of the Tehachapi Mtns in southern Santa Barbara Co. In 1971 the San Fernando earthquake raised the San Gabriel Mtns behind Los Angeles 6 ft in about fifteen seconds. It is an ongoing process. Pressure on massive sections of the earth's crust may be smooth and steady; movement is not. On average Pt Reyes progresses toward Alaska two or three inches a year, but does so in steps every several decades. Wave-like movement of the ground may damage structures and cause suspended objects (such as stacked barrels) to fall, but it is of minor consequence to a person or a vine standing in an open field. Modern building codes which require structures to be connected in an integrated manner, and designed flexibility which allows tall office buildings to sway several feet in any direction, have considerably reduced the potential for catastrophic damage in CA compared to places like Iran and Ecuador. Still, one will never see stone châteaux in Napa such as are typically found in Bordeaux. Historic stone 'ghost' wineries in CA, and unreinforced masonry buildings in San Francisco, can be readily purchased for very little money because legal occupancy will require a seismic retrofit more expensive than building a new structure from scratch. This economic consideration is one reason caves, dug by a machine similar to the one that created the Chunnel between France and England, have become so popular in Napa. They are no more expensive than freestanding, insulated, air-conditioned buildings.   B.C.C.

Eastern Shore, as seen on wine labels, refers to the MD part of the DELMARVA Peninsula in VA.

Eastern Wine Competition, Intl, a North American judging in which Mid-Atlantic, other Eastern, and Canadian wines are well represented. Held annually since 1976 near Watkins Glen, NY. Wines compete in grape variety or class categories. As a practical matter, this competition highlights Eastern wines of quality. In 1999 the best white wine was judged a FINGER LAKES Riesling (1998 Lakewood).   R.G.L.

Edelweiss, white American hybrid bred in Minnesota in the 1960s making wines which taste strongly of its *labrusca antecedents.

Edna Valley AVA, district in the southwestern, maritime portion of SAN LUIS OBISPO CO. Contiguous with, but much more homogeneous than ARROYO GRANDE AVA. Edna Valley looks northwest along the line of the coastal mountains, past the earnest college town of San Luis Obispo to Estero Bay. It has nearly 2,500 acres of grapes, mostly planted in rolling former cattle pasture. The AVA itself is a bowl that would have formed a seasonal marsh each winter. Soils are black, with lots of humus and lots of clay. Chardonnay has comprised two-thirds of the acreage ever since Paragon Vyds pioneered the region by planting 650 acres right down the center of it in 1973. Paragon has now grown to 1,000 acres. Although the configuration of Edna Valley resembles a smaller version of SALINAS VALLEY 100 mi north, the soils are quite different and so are the wines. Chardonnays from Edna Valley have a grapefruit-like intensity and lower pH. Consistent cloud cover gives them a large *malic fraction to their total acid, often as much as 4.5 g/l, so 100% *MLF can make them smell like butterscotch.

One difficulty experienced in Edna Valley which is not common in CA is humidity. Frequent fog, combined with minimal DIURNAL TEMPERATURE FLUCTUATION, means spraying against *powdery mildew is often required. Likewise *botrytis can get out of hand quickly. The season is extremely long, with budbreak sometimes occurring by the end of Feb, harvest often continuing into Nov, and winter *dormancy not the automatic assumption it is elsewhere.

NOTABLE PROPERTIES

Claiborne & Churchill, small winery operated by Clay Thompson and Fredericka Churchill, who also teach Germanic Languages at CA Polytechnic Univ in San Luis Obispo. They have successfully carved a niche for themselves among knowledgeable restaurateurs by producing dry, food enhancing Rieslings, Gewürztraminers, and Muscats in the style of *Alsace. Unlike many CA aromatic whites, these wines age quite well. They have good acid tension and grape flavors, but little of the mineral character found in Alsace wines. Grapes come from Mosby Vyd in Santa Ynez Valley and from Ventana Vyd in Monterey. Half their 5,000-case production is Gewurz, aged 4–6 months in neutral *barriques. Occasionally a Cuvée Fredericka is made with WILD YEAST from Mosby Vyd grapes. In 1996 the Thompsons and their friends raised the walls on a winery building constructed out of 16 in thick blocks of bundled rice stalks. This natural insulation keeps the normal inside temperature between 58°F in winter and 65°F in summer.

Edna Valley Vyds, winery which is part of the CHALONE group. Started as a partnership with Paragon Vyds, Edna Valley Vyds takes more than half of Paragon's 600 acres of Chardonnay. Production is large at 120,000 cases, all but 5% Chardonnay, but few expenses are spared in an effort to make rich, toasty wine. It is all *barrel fermented, with a quarter of the barrels bought new each year, and aged *sur lie. All the Chardonnay is started through MLF, then some lots are stopped by chilling, sulfur dioxide, and filtration. The result has always been a reliably buttery bouquet aimed at one's primitive instincts. Priced under $15, these Chardonnays deliver a lot of French oak and winemaking procedure for the money.

MacGregor Vyd, hillside location facing southwest run by conscientious former engineer in part responsible for design of the Apollo moon rocket. Quality Chardonnay grapes are vineyard designated on many top labels dating back to 1980. Andy MacGregor's daughter Cathy is a UC Davis-trained winemaker who worked for several wineries before launching her own operation called **Windemere**. She now has a small facility in Edna Valley specializing in wines from her father's grapes.

Tolosa, custom crush facility near the airport with some adjacent vineyards owned by a partnership which includes local lawyers who also have a large residential development further south in the valley with extensive vineyard plantings.

See also ALBAN.   B.C.C.

El Dorado, county and AVA in the SIERRA FOOTHILLS which represents an intersection of high elevation viticulture/winemaking with CALIFORNIA's capital, expertise, and marketplace. An acre of plantable vineyard land in Napa Valley cost anywhere from $40,000 to 80,000 in 1998. At the same time good vineyard land in the Sierra Foothills could have been purchased for $5,000 an acre. Clearly the mountains are where younger, less well-heeled, more radical winemaking types are headed. For every thousand feet of elevation, the temperature cools 4°F. El Dorado Co already has several vineyards over 3,000 ft and one at 3,600 ft. These elevations may sound paltry by the standards of CO, NM, or Mt Tupungato in Argentina, but El Dorado has access to resources likely to drive the pace of vinous development much faster than in other, more extreme locations. In 1998 there were 1,250 acres planted, up by a third in two years, primarily owned by family smallholders. There were eighteen wineries at that time, with another ten rumored to be in the planning process. Three-quarters of the county's grapes are used in the county.

Placerville, the main town of El Dorado, is located a bucolic hour's drive north along Hwy 49 from Plymouth in AMADOR CO or south a little longer from NEVADA CITY. Placerville is the junction of Hwy 49 with Hwy 50, the major thoroughfare from CA's state capital Sacramento into the recreation area at the south end of Lake Tahoe. Almost all El Dorado vineyards are sited above 2,400 ft. Anything above 2,000 ft is no longer in a Mediterranean, two season climate; four separate seasons start to appear. El Dorado vineyards see snow for brief periods every year, but frost protection in the spring is not a concern because *air drainage down the steep slopes is quite efficient. Soils are usually thin and quite acidic, being composed of weathered granite with most organic matter, other than conifer duff, quickly eroded away. Rainfall increases in direct proportion to altitude. A good 12 in more per year fall at 3,000 ft than at 1,500 ft. Thin, infertile, acidic soils enforce their own production limitations on vines, helpful

in this climate which naturally slows ripening.

Delicately scented Rieslings are produced here on land which previously supported apples. Moreover, these Rieslings age well and never require *acidulation. Zinfandels from El Dorado are always lighter colored, lighter bodied, and more strawberry scented than their Amador neighbors. Cabernet Franc from El Dorado is often noteworthy by itself, and always adds a grace note to meritage blends. Syrahs, Barberas, and Petite Sirahs from El Dorado have drawn critical acclaim precisely because of their high-toned complexity, making low elevation examples seem ponderous by comparison. *Tannin management is the challenge in red wines for El Dorado's young entrepreneurs. They are going to have high acid levels, and the acid component of the structure is going to push the tannins forward—making them more obvious than they would be in higher pH reds from Napa or Santa Maria. El Dorado reds show bright fruit character, especially if crop loads are minimized, but they are often hard and impenetrable in youth. There are not yet enough examples of high altitude Viognier to draw conclusions, but stylistically the potential would seem enormous.

El Dorado is seen by locals as two districts, the distinction having more to do with driving convenience than with any difference in growing conditions. Wineries and vineyards are more or less equally split between them. The portion they call North County is in the immediate vicinity of Hwy 50 with its public creature comforts which, incidentally, include a 200 sq ft dive named Poor Red's BBQ which sells more Galliano liqueur than any other bar in the US. The second area, FAIR PLAY or South County, is about half an hour south by car. It contains a wonderfully congenial accretion of small wineries with unique, sometimes eccentric personalities, arrayed along a 10 mi circular road through very pretty country.

NOTABLE NORTH COUNTY PROPERTIES
Boeger, charming historic site just outside Placerville. In fact the colloquial and descriptive *gold rush name for Placerville is employed for Boeger's second label, Hangtown Red. Greg Boeger grew up in Napa Valley, related to the Nicholinis, one of the fourth-generation winemaking families there. Greg matriculated at UC Davis and no doubt got an earful about winery cleanliness before he graduated. Boeger's wines have nothing in common with the Italian immigrant, primitive style of Nicholini Winery. In 1973 Boeger opened the first winery in El Dorado Co since the repeal of Prohibition.

He restored buildings dating back to the 1850s and planted 60 acres of grapes at about 2,000 ft of elevation. From the late 1970s until the early 1990s, Boeger consistently produced the most technically correct, persistently enjoyable wines in the Sierra Foothills. Since then, his performance has not waned, but other wineries have begun stepping up to provide more competition.

Merlot is conspicuous amongst Boeger wines because it has always been quite good, and when they first brought it out at the end of the 1970s, few other wineries in CA produced a varietal Merlot. The most noteworthy red, however, is Barbera. It is made from Ritchie Vyd grapes purchased at slightly lower elevation. With the possible exception of PRESTON in Sonoma Co's Dry Creek Valley, Boeger Barbera has the most reliable, long-standing record for quality with Barbera in the US. The wine always has a meaty nose with sweet fruit that reminds one of Moo Shu Pork with Plum Sauce. The tannins are exceptionally well integrated, giving the wine a dense but smooth *mouthfeel. Keeping up with developments in the rest of the Sierra Foothills, in the early 1990s Boeger planted an acre each of Syrah, Grenache, Mourvèdre, Viognier, Sangiovese, Nebbiolo, and Refosco. The Syrah and the Nebbiolo, at this cool elevation, hold particular interest.

Madroña, winery named because Dick Bush believes that tree is an indicator of good growing regions for winegrapes. On average over 3,000 ft, his vineyards are the highest in CA. Bush has a PhD in Materials Science from Stanford. His shy academic demeanor disguises a fundamental confidence and excitement he finds in his own analytic ability. In 1972 Bush and his wife Leslie planted their 35-acre vineyard 6 mi east of Placerville in a district considered extreme by grape growing standards of that era. The next year, while waiting for the vines to come into full production, they departed with their four young children for a Peace Corps assignment in what was to become Zaire. Today the Bush children have bought 250 acres at 3,600 ft and are planting a vineyard they call Sumu Kaw (local Indian name meaning 'lone Sugar pine'). Most interesting is their collection of Syrah clones. One they call Espiquette came from Estrella River Vyd near PASO ROBLES. Probably the first modern importation of Syrah cuttings into CA, made by Gary Eberle in the early 1970s, it has large clusters and requires fruit thinning to give top quality. Another Sumu Kaw clone is from Australia and gives a white pepper spiciness. A third clone came from France via UC Davis and is reputed to have originated on the hill at Hermitage. It shows a definite roast meat nose and structural density. Bush's son Paul describes the fourth clone as 'proprietary,' which implies it arrived taped to somebody's thigh after an overseas trip.

Riesling was the first grape from Madroña to deserve artistic attention, and it remains noteworthy because it is so unlike others from CA. In a vertical tasting of their off-dry versions going back fifteen years, there are dramatic differences between vintages, but all the wines share a low pH backbone which gives refreshing rigidity to even the oldest wines. That acid more than balances the 12 g/l RS with which most of them are finished. Even 5-year-old Madroña off-dry Rieslings will have barely begun to move toward yellow tones from their natural green tint, and they rarely have a pH much above 3.1. *Botrytis occurs irregularly in Madroña's vineyard, allowing for occasional production of some of CA's best dessert wines. They exercise care and expertise not always found in CA during harvest to select certain bunches over a period of weeks using a Mexican crew that arrives every year at the behest of Madroña's Mexican vineyard manager, who is a year-round employee.

See FAIR PLAY, LAVA CAP, SIERRA VISTA.

B.C.C.

Enological Society of the Pacific Northwest,

the largest wine consumer society in US. Begun in 1975 providing wine education, tastings, and seminars, it holds the Northwest Wine Festival annually at the end of July to judge and showcase PNW wines.

R.A.I.

ENTAV, Établissement National Technique pour l'Amélioration de la Viticulture, official organization in charge of the French viticultural gene pool. After ENTAV's work on virus status and *clonal selection, approved cuttings are released to nurseries. In the mid-1990s agreements were signed with certain North American nurseries to begin importing these clonal selections.

The nomenclature by which clones are identified is absolutely stupifying in its confusion and variability. Sometimes different names are the result of political mergers or dissolutions amongst organizations involved in clonal research. Sometimes it is French bureaucracy run amok. Sometimes the differences are a result of an organization getting clonal material from another and then assigning a new number after they perform some manipulation, such as heat treatment to remove virus. Sometimes names are just applied colloquially which subsequently become popular. Often FIELD SELECTIONS are

made in a famous vineyard, say Ch Beauzeau, then inaccurately called the Beauzeau Clone, when they really are not a clonal selection at all.

To illustrate this naming confusion, there is a single clonal selection of Chardonnay which researchers in France called ENTAV #199. After it was approved for nursery distribution, the CTPS (Comité Technique Permanent de la Sélection) assigned it a new number, #75. It came to be known in the US as the Dijon clone #75 because another French agency ONIVINS (Office National Interprofessional des Vins), which provides the tags used by nurseries when they multiply the grape stock, has an office in Dijon. The origin of the material was the Côte d'Or just south of Dijon, but the research was actually performed at Domaine de l'Espigette, an agricultural station in southeastern France. Once that clonal material was given to FPMS, they assigned their own record keeping number, #55. Meanwhile the French equivalent of the US Dept of Agriculture is called **INRA** (Institut National de la Recherche Agronomique). At some point they probably worked with the same clone and assigned their own number to it as well. Similar acronym madness applies to German, Italian, Eastern European, Australian, South African, and Latin American clones being internationally disseminated.

B.C.C.

Eola Hills AVA, area located in the north WILLAMETTE VALLEY section of OREGON. The hills begin 10 mi south of McMinnville and extend south about 10 more. Soils, called Nekia, are primarily basalt based silt and sand, with a rocky matrix and less clay than further north. Grapes here ripen two weeks ahead of neighboring RED HILLS OF DUNDEE.

NOTABLE PROPERTIES

Amity Vyds, owned by Myron Redford in the Eola Hills near the town of Amity. Redford is a tireless promoter of Oregon wineries in general. His own wines have lacked the consistency of the top producers, but he has had his share of winners. Although noted for Pinot Noir, he produces excellent Rieslings and Gewürztraminer, especially LATE HARVEST versions, and helped pioneer OR Pinot Blanc.

Bethel Heights Vyd, established in 1984 by winemaker Terry Casteel and his twin brother Ted who manages the 51-acre vineyard near the south end of Eola Hills. Pinot Noirs are linear and crisp, rather than soft and plump, with good *acidity and healthy amount of wood tannin to promote longevity. They also produce a vineyard designated Pinot Gris from Freedom Hill Vyd outside of

Monmouth in the facing Coast Range foothills.

R.A.I.

Estancia is a brand. **Pinnacles** is a 600-acre vineyard originally planted by the Paul Masson winery on the eastern slopes of the Salinas Valley of MONTEREY Co just east of Soledad along the road which leads up into the eastern mountains where Chalone is located. Currently owned by the FRANCISCAN Estates fine wine division of CANANDAIGUA, Estancia is a mid-market label for Cabernet from Alexander Valley in northern Sonoma and for Chardonnay and Pinot Noir from Monterey. Estancia Chardonnay is a reliable, single digit priced wine emphasizing bright papaya and apple flavors framed in good acid. 300,000 cases of Estancia were produced in 1998.

B.C.C.

Etude, the personal NAPA VALLEY brand of winemaking consultant Tony Soter, whose credentials were established as winemaker for Spottswoode during its first years in the 1980s, and whose current clients include such CULT WINES as Viader and Moraga. Soter produces about 7,000 cases for Etude with a well-respected Cabernet and one of the better early versions of Pinot Gris in CA. His best item, however, is a reliably seductive Pinot Noir from grapes sourced in CARNEROS. Since 1990 Etude Pinot Noir has been among the top three wines from that district, distinguished from its competitors by the lush elegance of its texture and aromatic qualities that bespeak the way sophisticated women apply perfume to themselves. In 1999 Soter announced he was going to move his winemaking operation to Oregon.

B.C.C.

excise taxes, fees collected by a state or by the federal government based on a volume of wine. These taxes are paid to the federal government by the producer when the wine leaves the premises bonded under the producer's license. They are collected by state governments from the business entity which holds the wholesale (ie distributor) license based on the amount of product they bring into the state. These tax records form the basis for most accurate statistics on wine production and sales. **Sales taxes** are different. They are a percentage on the retail price of the wine, and are collected by the retail store or restaurant on behalf of the state and local governments. **Import duties**, various **license fees**, and **label registration fees** are additional forms of taxes levied on wine. Label registration fees can be a significant barrier to entry for small production wineries wishing to send a few cases, either by request or as an introductory gambit, to some limited number of stores or restaurants in those states that impose significant label registration fees. $100 per label is nothing if a winery is sending pallet-loads, but it might double the retail price if only a few cases are involved. DIRECT SHIPMENT is significantly complicated by the existing welter of aforementioned fees and taxes on wine in the US.

Eyrie Vyds. David Lett is Papa Pinot to most OREGON wine fanciers. He planted the first modern era vinifera in WILLAMETTE VALLEY in 1966. His 1975 South Block Pinot Noir shocked the wine world when it scored well in *Gault Millau*'s 1979 follow-up to the SPURRIER TASTING in Paris. His Pinot Noir is definitely old school, in its lighter crisper fashion, but it is also proven. He produced America's first Pinot Gris, a fine wine which always rewards a little bottle age. Lett's Chardonnay is a great wine, with its refined yet forceful fruitiness and its demonstrated ability to mature. It is made from Draper Selection clones which seem to include a touch of toast and almost hazelnut flavors. Eyrie also produces one of America's rare Pinot Meuniers. R.A.I.

F

Fair Play district in EL DORADO Co of CA's SIERRA FOOTHILLS AVA, equidistant, about a half-hour on backcountry roads, between Placerville and the winegrowing districts of AMADOR CO. Not yet an approved appellation, it is called South County by locals. Almost all of the dozen or so wineries in the district are arranged along the circular path of Fair Play Rd, making visitation quite convenient once one devises a strategy for ingress, and for safe egress after alcohol consumption. Wine quality is well above average and value is exceptional given the CRAFTSMAN-SIZED nature of the wineries and the isolation of the district.

NOTABLE PROPERTIES

Chas Mitchell, winery whose namesake must have some circus blood. He is such an entertainer it is easy to overlook the fact he puts out very artistic wines every now and then. Best results so far have been with Bordeaux blends.

Fitzpatrick, bed & breakfast with a view, Irish ploughman's lunch, laps pool, and an organic vineyard. Don't forget to try the wine.

Latcham, also *Granite Springs*. Les and Lynne Russell pioneered El Dorado as a wine region along with Dick Bush at Madroña and Greg Boeger. The Russells named their place Granite Springs after dynamiting through ten solid feet of stone while excavating a hillside for their winery. Over the years they made wine for six or seven start-up ventures while those newcomers built their own facilities. After Lynne's tragically early death, Granite Springs was sold to the Latcham family, a successful lawyer and his children who had moved to El Dorado and become growers. Latcham maintains both labels, and there are separate properties, but Craig Boyd makes the wine for both brands at the Granite Springs facility while the Latcham property has become the hospitality center. Total production in 1998 was 16,000 cases, and they expect to grow to 22,000 in the succeeding five years. Premier under the Granite Springs label is Petite Sirah. The 1983 vintage was chosen American Champion in a taste-off conducted by

Wine & Spirits magazine of Gold Medal winners from various competitions in 1986. It has been very good every year since. Star of the Latcham line is a medium-bodied Cabernet Franc, fragrant with floral notes.

Perry Creek, large winery well staffed by district standards. Owned by a well-heeled former haberdasher, it plays to the poseur wine crowd with a cigar lounge, but has a talented winemaker producing impressive Zinfandel.

Windwalker, winery with a graphically compelling label and a sincere young owner/winemaker whose technical expertise puts him well up the local totem pole. Barbera is excellent; Orange Muscat too.   B.C.C.

Fall Creek Vyds, pioneer winery in TEXAS. On a cattle buying trip to France in 1973 rancher and businessman Ed Auler and his wife Susan first noticed what they considered to be the similarities of some of the French winegrowing regions to the Auler family's ranch near Lake Buchanan in the TEXAS HILL COUNTRY. Two years later, in 1975, they planted their first vines at Fall Creek Vyds, a 65-acre site on the shore of the lake. Using a borrowed wine press in a renovated garage, they pressed their first grapes in 1979, becoming convinced they were on to something.

Full-scale planting was begun, and by the late 1980s they were producing quite respectable wines. Then disaster struck. Mother Nature hit the Hill Country full blast: first with several days of 12°F temperatures in the winter of 1991, destroying most of the vineyard; then with the entirely unexpected arrival of *Pierce's disease in 1992, necessitating a complete replanting of the vineyard. Of the winery's original 65 acres, 5 are now planted to Chardonnay, 5 to Sauvignon Blanc, 4 to Cabernet Sauvignon, 3 to Chenin Blanc, 3 to Semillon, 1 to Merlot, 1 to *Carnelian, and 1 to Malbec. All varietals are planted on either 5BB or 5C *rootstock. One section, on a slope facing the lake, has proven to be in a peculiar freeze zone and will not be replanted. The remaining area will be planted over the next few years.

Auler, who has resigned himself to losing about 5% of the vineyard each year to Pierce's as a cost of doing business, is concentrating on perimeter management as the best-known defense. Auler hopes to source his grapes exclusively from his vineyards and from the 300 growers in the Hill Country in the future. Bought-in grapes are transported blanketed with dry ice which releases carbon dioxide, preventing *oxidation.

Fall Creek's vineyards begin about 75 yards from the shores of Lake Buchanan. The 15,000 sq ft winery was designed by Susan Auler and a group of Austin-based architects to evoke the charm of an old Hill Country ranch home while providing the latest in modern winemaking equipment. The three-sided, grey stucco structure has a tasting room on one side, guest quarters across a courtyard opposite the tasting room, and a lab, barrel room, and stainless steel storage tanks between the two. The antique doors to the vaulted barrel room are from the stables of the Pasteur Laboratory outside Paris. Total storage capacity is 65,000 gal. The growing season is relatively short, from Apr to late-July/mid-Aug and occasionally through early Sept. The average high temperature is in the mid-90s to low 100s, and lows from 65–70°F from June through Aug are offset by the prevailing winds off the lake, which provide rapid nighttime cooling. Without the breeze, the 13–15 hours of daylight combined with high temperatures during the growing season would certainly have an adverse affect on the vines. As if Pierce's, the unpredictable winters, and scorching summers were not enough to scare the Aulers off, there is always the possibility of hail, floods, and tornadoes, along with pesky raccoons, birds, and, occasionally, deer.

Soils vary in depth from 3 to 6 ft of light brick-red to almost-black clay and sandy loam with an abundance of limestone rock and gravel. Soil pH levels are between 7.0 and 7.2. Vines are trained on an old *lyre trellis with 8 × 12 ft spacing using HEDGING along the top catch wires for canopy management. An average annual rainfall of 22 in (which falls mostly in Sept, Apr, and May) has induced Auler to install *drip irrigation. He says he usually applies 1 gal per day per vine.

Annual production at Fall Creek is about 30,000 cs. Fall Creek's 1998 Sauvignon Blanc is one of the best among a varietal that does very well all over the state. It is dry, crisp, with lots of mineral and grapefruit aromas and great acidity. It is early to judge the reds since most of the vines are less than 5 years old. Promising, though, is Fall Creek's first super-premium cuvée, Meritus, a blend of Merlot (54%), Cabernet Sauvignon (40%) and Malbec (6%).   L.A.O.

Fall Line, geologic dividing line between the PIEDMONT and the COASTAL PLAIN. In the MID-ATLANTIC and the SOUTH regions, many older cities were built on the fall line because it was the limit of river navigation from the coast. The higher, rocky Piedmont created rapids where rivers met the Fall Line. Some of these cities include: PHILA-DELPHIA; WASHINGTON, DC; Richmond, VA; Raleigh, NC; Columbia, SC; Columbus, GA; Montgomery, AL; and Jackson, MS. Interstate 95, the major north–south highway on the East Coast, largely follows the Fall Line through the Mid-Atlantic and the Carolinas.   R.G.L.

Farrell, Gary, one of the top artisan winemakers in CA's RUSSIAN RIVER district. From the early 1980s Farrell pursued an eminently reasonable plan for a talented young winemaker without recourse to family money. He was employed as winemaker at Davis Bynum winery, and they allowed him to make small lots in their facilities for his own label. He bought his own barrels and sourced his own grapes from a few selected and assiduously cultivated growers. There is nothing wrong with the Bynum wines, but the Gary Farrell label has risen since 1985 to superlative status. It began with Pinot Noir, which Farrell purchased from ROCHIOLI Vyd and the contiguous Allen Ranch. Farrell won the Sweepstakes Award at the CA State Fair in 1992 for his Pinot Noir from Allen Vyd. Today Farrell is always in consideration for CA's best Pinot Noir and his offerings compete effectively on a worldwide standard. More parochial perhaps, but equally delicious, he has produced magnificent Zinfandels from older Russian River vineyards since the early 1990s. He completed a very rare double when his 1995 Russian River Zinfandel (mostly Collins Vyd grapes) won for him a second Sweepstakes Award from the CA State Fair.

In 1999 Farrell announced a deal whereby he would sell 20% of his company to Bill Hambrecht, a San Francisco venture capitalist who founded Hambrecht and Quist.

With cash from the sale, Farrell and his wife are building a winery on Westside Rd about 3 mi west of the Bynum winery. They now own about 40 acres of their own grapes which will begin bearing soon. 'But I'm not committed to using them,' Farrell says. 'If they don't come up to the standard we've set over the years, I'm happy to sell them.' Farrell makes about 12,000 cases.   B.C.C.

Favorite, Texas version of LENOIR grape making less tannic wine.

Fenn Valley Vyds, established in 1973 in Michigan, this is the sole winery of FENN-VILLE AVA. Winemaker/owner Doug Welsch's early efforts centered upon *fruit wines as well as Vidal Blanc, De Chaunac, and Foch, but he has expanded into other French hybrids as well as vinifera. Long a hands-on farmer, he is also a good businessman. Of their 55 acres, three-quarters are French hybrids: Vidal, Seyval Blanc, Chardonel, Chancellor, Chambourcin, and others. The other quarter are vinifera: Riesling, Chardonnay, Pinot Gris, Pinot Noir, and Cabernet Franc. His hybrid whites, in particular Chardonel, are noteworthy. The reds, Chancellor and Chambourcin, are reminiscent of *Loire Pinots. His Brut sparkling wine is an excellent aperitif.
                                      P.W.F.

Fennville AVA was approved in 1981 as the first AVA in MICHIGAN. Located in Van Buren and Allegan counties in southwestern MI, its boundaries are the Kalamazoo River on the north and the Black River to the south. The western boundary of this AVA is the eastern shore of Lake Michigan, and the AVA amply demonstrates the GREAT LAKES EFFECT upon viticulture. Here the average winter temperatures are 2°F warmer, and the average summer temperatures 2°F cooler, than the surrounding countryside. Additionally, it sports 184 *frost free days while rainfall is 35 in annually. Average snowfall is about 100 in per year. Of the 75,000 acres in the AVA, approximately 4,500 are under vine. Most of that is Concord and is used for non-wine purposes. Winegrape production is a function of the only winery in the AVA, FENN VALLEY VYDS.
                                      P.W.F.

ferment on premise, a do-it-yourself retail service whereby the space, raw materials, and advice are provided to amateur wine (and/or beer) makers to enable them to make their own product for personal consumption. By paying a slight fee to the government, the proprietor is permitted to assist at various steps in the process such as fining, filtering, clarifying, and stabilizing

the product. The customer is responsible for starting and finishing it, ie adding yeast and bottling.   L.F.B.

Ferrari-Carano, showplace winery at the northern end of CA's DRY CREEK Valley with opulent decor and vigorously maintained gardens. It is an easy target for detractors who point to the Caranos' background as successful partners in the Eldorado and the Silver Legacy, glitzy hotel/gaming houses in Reno, NV. What the winery's ostentation often disguises is the impressive quality of its wines. Now owners of more than 1,250 acres throughout Sonoma Co, Ferrari-Carano produces 150,000 cases a year over a broad range of varieties. The wines are fat, vinous equivalents of a bearhug from a portly, but much loved older relative. For folks who think big oak and big fruit are the CA style, these Chardonnays provide ample evidence. Sauvignon Blanc (they call it Fumé) is similar, although nicely balanced with a long earthy finish. Their 200 acres of new mountain vineyards on a 1,000-acre property 1,300 ft high in the very southern end of the ALEXANDER VALLEY AVA began producing reds in 1996 which will be bottled in small quantities with the Tre Monte designation.   B.C.C.

Fess Parker, winery in the Santa Ynez AVA of SANTA BARBARA CO. Parker is the actor who played both Daniel Boone and Davey Crockett, near-mythical characters from the American frontier, on US television in the 1950s and early 1960s. These characters were romanticized as homespun, self-sufficient fighters against vague but omnipresent dangers, usually portrayed as Indians, bears, or Mexicans.

In real life Parker proved to be a savvy investor in southern CA real estate and Red Lion hotels. He began work on his winery in 1987 and installed son Eli as winemaker with Jed STEELE as consultant. Tastefully employing a modicum of Boone/Crockett memorabilia, the visitors' facility has been a rapid success. The wines have as well. Pinot Noir and Chardonnay buttress the argument that Santa Barbara Co is a premier region for those grapes, although the Chardonnay has a little baby fat to it, and the Pinot Noir's tannins are a bit obvious. Less appreciated by the tourist traffic, but more gustatorily accomplished are Riesling and Syrah. The first is a shameless crowd pleaser whose strength lies in fresh apricot aroma and solid acid balance to keep the sugar from cloying. The Syrah is a revelation, thickly textured and deeply scented, with hints of white pepper when young, but only in the finish.
                                      B.C.C.

Fetzer, winery brand formerly synonymous with CA's MENDOCINO CO, but broadened somewhat since 1992 under ownership of distillers Brown-Forman. Fetzer is the sixth largest premium winery in the US making 3.35 million cases a year, a quarter of which are sold overseas.

Barney Fetzer had been a local lumber executive who bought his first vineyard property in 1958 with the goal of keeping his eleven children busy selling grapes to home winemakers. The family began commercial wine production in 1968. They bought a place for their toe in the big pool around 1975 when they released 1,500 cases of an excellent quality 1973 Cabernet Sauvignon for $3.50 a bottle. Notably, that wine had lots of extract, but very soft tannins. The national trade press sat up straight and started to pay attention. In 1974 they produced five times as much.

Barney Fetzer died in 1981. The winery was then producing 200,000 cases a year. Obviously he was a salesman of mythic proportions, and he set a high standard for what his family calls the 'road hounds' who followed him. Nevertheless the family succession at Fetzer Vyds was quite remarkable. Ten of Barney and Kathleen Fetzer's children took over and made a conscious decision to grow the business enough to accommodate all of them and the families they soon expected to have. They built a hospitality center in an old high school gymnasium at Hopland. Son John became CEO responsible for financial strategy. He had gone to a couple years of college. Son Jim became Chief Roadhound. Daughter Mary, with her high school education, became Sales and Marketing Director. She was about 30 years old at the time. Paul Dolan, a Fresno State graduate had joined the winery in 1977 as winemaker. He married daughter Diana in 1982. The Fetzer image as friendly farmers dressed in jeans and flannel shirts, making good value wines, was honed to perfection. They threw parties at the Big Dog Saloon, and grew the company to 2.2 million cases a year farming 1,400 acres.

Their first maneuver (1982) was to segment the line by launching Sundial Chardonnay. It became their *fighting varietal. Today it sells 850,000 cases a year. Next came Bel Arbors, named after the street on which their Redwood Valley winery was located, designed for competition at the lowest end of the cork-finished 750 ml market. The *White Zinfandel boom was an inviting opening for the Bel Arbors, and the Fetzer kids drove a convoy of trucks through it. Then came vineyard designated Zinfandels from ancient vines grown on benchland

properties, often by third generation Italian immigrants with names like Riccetti who were proud to see their name on a label in prestige retail stores. Then came the Barrel Select series of reds aimed at the upper segment in the value market. Finally, the top segment was redefined around 1990 by introducing more French oak barrels and parlaying that investment into a line of Reserve wines priced over $20.

In 1992 John Fetzer accurately interpreted the US economic recession. He had foreseen the consolidations occurring throughout the wine business. He did not want to be in a leveraged position in that environment. The Fetzers sold their brand names, the winery facilities, the inventory, and some 400 acres of grapes to Brown-Forman for a figure rumored to be over $80 million. They signed an eight-year non-compete agreement and an eight-year exclusive contract to supply grapes from the 1,000 acres on which they retained ownership (now called Kohn Properties).

Since the sale, Brown-Forman has continued to take advantage of adroit business decisions initiated by the family in the mid to late 1980s. Prominent among these is unequivocal espousal of *organic viticulture begun around 1985. They added an organic vegetable garden near the tasting room in Hopland and a separate hospitality center with celebrity chef John Ash. They have an organically grown brand of wine called Bonterra. They also have their own *barrel operation employing Master Cooper Keith Roberts to bring oak stave wood from France and from MN for seasoning in Mendocino, then to produce *barriques using the traditional fire coopering techniques. It is important for America's export image that her large wineries have a top quality segment. Fetzer complies admirably.   B.C.C.

field selections (see *mass selections), technique to acquire cuttings for planting or grafting a vineyard which is different than using *clonal selections. Clones all come from the same mother plant and therefore have identical genetic complements. Field selections are taken from many different plants, and so *may* have somewhat different genetic complements. Field selections are usually taken from plants identified for specific characteristics the grower seeks, such as a particular flavor, or small clusters, or healthy growth. If the grower takes a field selection from a vineyard with similar soil and climate conditions to the vineyard in which the new vines will be grown, there is every reason to suspect the characteristics for which the cuttings were chosen will, in

fact, emerge in the new vineyard despite some degree of genetic variability. Clonal selections offer genetic integrity, but the growing conditions which helped to bring out, or express, the characteristics for which the clone was selected may not be duplicated in the new vineyard. Many people think the same clone on three different soil types will give bigger differences in wine than three different clones on the same soil type. (See Vine Family essay, p 54.) That is why some CA growers, for instance, question the advisability of planting ENTAV clones in CA which have presumably been selected in France for their ability to ripen quickly and to drop acid.

This whole field of inquiry is so new it often raises more questions than it answers. One school of present thought maintains that certain virus suites in any given plant may be a major cause of clonal variation. That is why the FPMS assigns a new clone number to any genetic specimen from which they eradicate viruses before they release that clone to nurseries for distribution. By way of illustration, a vineyard in CA which claims to have the Wente clone of Chardonnay probably did not get a clone at all, but rather was planted with a field selection taken from Wente's vineyard. One of those vines in Wente's vineyard would have supplied the cuttings which FPMS heat treated to remove viruses and then released as FPMS Chardonnay Clone #5. Is there a genetic relationship between Clone #5 and the vines in the vineyard the grower calls Wente clone? Yes. Are they identical? No.
        B.C.C.

Finger Lakes AVA, largest wine district in eastern North America (in sq mi and cases produced), located in the west-central part of NEW YORK state. As a practical matter this appellation denotes wines grown within an area of slightly over 4,000 sq mi encompassing all or part of ten counties. In 1996 the Finger Lakes had slightly over 10,000 acres of vineyard and 55 wineries. Nearly all cluster along the shores of four lakes: (from west to east) Canandaigua, Keuka, Seneca, and Cayuga.

These are the largest of more than a dozen long, narrow lakes that streak NY's western plateau, resembling the imprints of fingers. For many millions of years this region lay under a shallow inland sea collecting layer upon layer of sediment in runoff from ancient Adirondack Mts. The sediment compacted into thinly layered, fractured shale that underlies the Finger Lakes area. The sea eventually contracted into a river system draining south. When glaciers advanced through the area, they carved deep channels in the river valleys, which then filled to create parallel lakes. Glaciers also smeared the larger valleys with limestone from calcium deposits along the northern edge of the ancient sea.

Because of their extraordinary depth but narrow surface area, the Finger Lakes act like much larger bodies of water to create powerful mesoclimates on surrounding hillsides, delaying vine budbreak until the threat of spring *frost has passed and extending the fall ripening season. In winter the larger lakes rarely freeze, radiating stored heat that protects bordering vineyards from the damage of low temperatures elsewhere in the region. This is particularly true for the two biggest lakes, Seneca and Cayuga, where most cold-tender varieties are planted. (See *lake effect.)

Fruit growing around the Finger Lakes pre-dates European settlement, when Iroquois Indians tended huge orchards. In 1829 an Episcopal rector planted Catawba and Isabella grapevines in his Hammondsport garden on Keuka Lake and began distributing cuttings to parishioners. Hammondsport quickly became the region's early hub of grape culture. By this time the Erie Canal connected the Finger Lakes to NEW YORK CITY and other East Coast markets, opening a huge fresh fruit market. Vineyards spread rapidly. Wineries began to appear in the 1860s to absorb overproduction in bumper-crop years.

The first wineries hired French vintners from the foundering enterprise of Nicholas Longworth in OH, giving the Finger Lakes a running start and an early focus on sparkling wine. By the turn of the century there were 20,000 acres of vineyards rimming Keuka, Canandaigua, and Seneca Lakes, supplying more than 50 wineries. National Prohibition closed most of them and consolidated the rest into a handful of larger firms led by the Taylor and Widmer families. They dominated NY wine until passage of the state's farm winery law in 1976 initiated a renaissance of CRAFTSMAN-SIZED wine estates. As more small wineries opened, the large producers coalesced into one mega-firm: CANANDAIGUA Wine Company.

The area's well-drained, shaley slopes proved ideal for grape culture. More acidic soils along the western lakes favored the early cultivation of labrusca grapes on Canandaigua and Keuka Lakes. Gold Seal Vyds introduced French hybrid varieties in the 1930s in pursuit of a more international wine style. Gold Seal also introduced vinifera varieties to the Finger Lakes and to eastern America with the experiments of Charles

FOURNIER and Konstantin FRANK in the 1950s. The proliferation of vinifera grapes pushed the locus of Finger Lakes viniculture eastward to the lower lying, warmer mesoclimates of larger sized Seneca and Cayuga Lakes and their generally higher lime content soils. Half of the region's wineries encircle Seneca Lake.

Only a few Finger Lakes wineries produce more than 50,000 cases, and most make less than 10,000. In their product lines they tend to group into two categories. One celebrates the extraordinary diversity of the area's vineyards with a selection of labrusca, French hybrid, and vinifera wines. The other purposely breaks with the region's past to focus on drier-style vinifera wines.

Catawba, Delaware, Niagara, Elvira, Ives, and Isabella are the chief survivors among American hybrid varieties. The French hybrids with the most acreage are Aurora, Baco Noir, DeChaunac, and Seyval Blanc; but Cayuga, Vidal, and Vignoles (the latter usually for late-harvest styles) make better wines. Most new plantings are in vinifera varieties. Riesling stands apart as the area's best and most consistent wine from year to year and lake to lake, developing the acid structure and bright fruit definition critical to this varietal. Chardonnay is more variable but does find a Burgundian environment in parts of the Finger Lakes that produce wines in a leaner style than CA Chardonnays. Gewürztraminer shows promise with the right clones.

Growing conditions have favored sparklers since the first days of Finger Lakes wine, and the introduction of classic champagne varieties has produced inspiring examples, but the high costs of sparkling winemaking and a tough market have frustrated production. Limited capital resources is a nagging problem in this upstate outback.

Although the Finger Lakes has traditionally been a white wine district, more interest and effort has recently turned to red varieties, which can do well in the warmest sites. Pinot Noir is well established for sparkling wine and has made exceptional reds in warmer vintages as growers address viticultural challenges, such as selecting the right clones and controlling bunch rot. Cabernet Franc also shows promise and is easier to grow.

NOTABLE PROPERTIES

Fox Run Vyds, small winery working to parlay its high lime content site at the north end of Seneca Lake into exceptional Chardonnay and Pinot Noir. About 60 acres of estate vineyards surround the winery on a gentle slope almost at the lake's edge. Chardonnay

dominates, produced in both a stainless-steel fermented model and a barrel-fermented Reserve. The Pinot Noir is the Finger Lake's best. Fine Riesling is made incorporating grapes purchased from Seneca Lake's oldest vinifera vineyard planted by Charles Fournier. First opened in 1990, Fox Run produced 12,000 cases in 1998 with an eventual goal of 20,000.

Hermann J. Wiemer Vyd, winery that has set the standard for the region's benchmark wine: Riesling. It is no happenstance. Hermann Wiemer grew up in Bernkastel, Germany, where his family had made Riesling for 300 years. He was lured to NY by Walter S. TAYLOR in 1968 to help launch BULLY HILL VYDS. Wiemer established his own vineyard on the east shore of Seneca Lake in the mid-1970s, including a nursery that has grown to a 500,000-vine operation supplying new vineyards throughout the US. The estate vineyard totals 60 acres. They produce 16,000 cases. From the first vintage in 1979, Wiemer has been one of America's top proponents of *dry Riesling, made in a style which combines floral delicacy and restraint with a steely, mineral edge. Chardonnay and Pinot Noir are also among NY's best, with the pure fruit focus one might expect from a Riesling specialist. The wines are distributed in six eastern states.

McGregor Vyd, craftsman-sized estate on Keuka Lake planted to vinifera varieties in the early 1970s. Wine production began in 1980 with Chardonnay, Riesling, Gewürztraminer, and Pinot Noir, which remain mainstays of the 5,000-case output. Recently a new standout has emerged called Black Russian, made from a blend of the eastern European varieties Seperavi and Sereksia. Most of the wine is sold CELLAR DOOR and through an active club named, inevitably, the Clan.

Taylor, largest selling wine brand from NY. Company was originally established in 1880 in Hammondsport by a cooper, Walter Taylor, who began shipping wine in barrels to New York City merchants. His five children helped build the business selling grape juice during Prohibition, then took over three neighboring wineries by the early 1960s to form the largest winemaking complex outside CA, fed by more than 300 growers. They were best known for vividly grapey labrusca sparklers. Coca-Cola bought the company in 1977 and ratcheted up production, trying to blend French hybrids with CA wine for a more broadly popular style, but ultimately failing. CANANDAIGUA now owns the brand.

Widmer, rare survivor from more than 50 wineries operating in the district in the 19th century. Founded in 1888 at the southern end of Canandaigua Lake by Swiss immigrants, then flourishing after Repeal when second generation Wil Widmer took over after studying at *Geisenheim. He recognized the potential from *botrytis which is common in the Finger Lakes and began producing wines with *Spatlese and *Auslese on his labels. He also help pioneer varietal labels in the 1940s in conjunction with Frank *Schoonmaker using grapes such as Niagara.

Widmer is best known for its sherry-style wines, matured in a field of barrels that cover the winery's roof through the warm summers and frigid winters. This exposure and long ageing is credited with transforming Concord base wines into something approximating a very fruity, simple version of the Spanish role model. Canandaigua bought Widmer in 1987. Half of the winery's 2 million-case output receives the Widmer label; the other half is Canandaigua's Manischewitz KOSHER brand.

See CAYUGA LAKE, GLENORA, FRANK, TAYLOR. R.F.

Firelands, winery in OHIO whose name recalls the burning of the local dwellings by the British during the Revolutionary War. Located in Sandusky in the LAKE ERIE AVA, this Paramount Distillers-owned winery produces the gamut of Midwestern flavors (fruit juices, American hybrid, and French hybrid wines). It has, however, evolved into a first-rate producer of the lean-and-mean vinifera school sourcing its fruit primarily from the North Bass, or ISLE ST GEORGE, island in Lake Erie. As of now the reds seem pedestrian, but the whites Chardonnay, Pinot Grigio, and Gewürztraminer have the zing and cold climate *typicity one expects from these grapes. P.W.F.

Flora Springs, winery on the westside bench in the RUTHERFORD AVA, although the Komes family is much more significant in Napa Valley as growers than the size of their 50,000-case winery would suggest. They started in 1978 when Jerry Komes retired as President of Bechtel Inc. Not just any suit, Jerry Komes had risen to become head of one of the world's largest engineering and construction companies without benefit of relatives who owned the joint and without a college diploma. His children, John and Julie, took to the wine game immediately. Flora Springs is located in an 1888 ghost winery, and a home where Louis M. MARTINI had lived in the 1930s. Today they own some 700 acres in eight locations throughout Napa ranging from Carneros to Pope Valley. They sell 70% of their grapes. Their Home

Ranch around the winery is 325 acres with 110 acres of vines. *Wine Spectator* writer James Laube considers Flora Springs' rich and creamy Chardonnay to be one of the very best produced in CA. The Reserve Cabernet is also exceptional, as one might expect given the selection of grapes from which winemaker Ken Deis can pick.

B.C.C.

Florida, southernmost state in the SOUTH region. The history of winemaking in the contemporary US dates to the Huguenot settlement near Jacksonville in the mid-16th century. Prior to Prohibition, over 4,000 acres of vineyards were planted in FL but, being mostly non-MUSCADINE, they did not survive long. Since 1923 the Univ of FL at Gainesville's Center for Viticultural Science and the agricultural research station in Leesburg have helped pioneer new hybrids of Muscadines which will not only thrive in the Deep South but will ideally produce vinifera-like wines. The market potential for native FL wines, sold in-state to residents and hordes of annual tourists, is impressive. As is the case elsewhere in the South, there is a natural inclination toward sweet and fruity wines, which will help the market response to FL's fruit and Muscadine wines.

The semi-tropical growing season in FL ranges from 240 to 365 days annually, with 52–8 in of annual rainfall. Only Muscadine grapes and their hybrids will thrive in the hot, humid climate, although citrus wines are a local specialty. Current farm winery production is 115,000 gal annually.

Seven of FL's counties are DRY; six of which are in the traditionally conservative northwestern panhandle. No other unusual restrictions apply to the sale of wine. State wineries and licensed wine distributors must pay the state excise tax on alcohol, ranging from $2.25 to $3.50 per gallon, depending on alcohol content. Half of the revenues collected from native wineries are deposited in a Viticulture Trust Fund.

See SAN SEBASTIAN. R.G.L.

Foch, common US shortened name for the grape *Marechal Foch.

fog, unique climatological feature of the CALIFORNIA coastline north of Pt Conception in Santa Barbara Co. It forms when warm air blows across the Pacific through the tropics picking up moisture, then meets the cold Humboldt Current, ocean flows running down the Pacific coast from Alaska and up from Antarctica. During the summer, cold upwelling water along the coast condenses the moisture-laden air from the tropics to form fog. The intrusions of this

marine fog into CA's winegrowing districts are a function of hot air rising from inland valleys during the late summer, and cool ocean air being drawn in to replace it. Marine fog is not commonly encountered in the cold months of winter or even the moderate months of spring.

Marine fog is not the same as what Californians call **tule fog.** Marine fog comes from the ocean, is most common in summer, and flows like water in discrete currents. Tule (pronounced *TWO lee* by locals) fog is caused by air temperature dropping below the dew point, is most common in CA in the Central Valley in winter, and becomes gradually thicker over wide areas as the air temperature keeps dropping lower. Smart and Dry use relative *humidity (measured at 9 am each day during the growing season) as one index in their viticultural area classification, primarily related to potential for fungal disease. Gladstones argues afternoon humidity is also a factor in yield and in plant metabolism. It is hard to apply these considerations to CA. Marine fog is quite high in relative humidity, but it is also cold, which means the absolute amount of water saturating the air is much lower than the amount the air could carry at a higher temperature. Marine fog flows into CA's inland valleys, but it does not flow back out in the manner of riptides on a beach. Each morning it dissipates in place as the air and the land heat up under the sun. Californians say 'the fog burns off.' What they mean is the air's carrying capacity for water goes up as the temperature rises, and the fog just disappears. Overall CA has very low humidity. B.C.C.

Gladstones, J., *Viticulture and Environment* (Perth, 1992).

Smart, R., and Dry, P., *Australian Grapevines and Winemakers* (Adelaide, 1980).

Fournier, Charles (1901–84), expatriate French winemaker who guided NY's FINGER LAKES region in a transition from 19th-century reliance on American hybrids to the international arena of vinifera wines. In 1934 Fournier left his position as chief winemaker at the prestigious *champagne house Veuve Clicquot Ponsardin to rehabilitate the Urbana Wine Company, one of the Finger Lakes' oldest and largest wineries. Disturbed by the grape jelly flavors of Urbana's wines, but warned that grape varieties he worked with in Champagne would not grow in NY, Fournier introduced French hybrid vines. Using yeast cultures from Veuve Clicquot, he began producing the region's first top quality sparkling wines. Charles Fournier Brut won the only Gold Medal awarded to a sparkler at the 1950 CA State Fair.

In 1953 Fournier hired the Russian émigré Konstantin FRANK to help him experiment with vinifera varieties. Within a few years Fournier's Gold Seal winery was making eastern America's first commercial vinifera wines. After researching mesoclimates and soil profiles, Fournier planted upstate NY's first large scale vinifera vineyard on Seneca Lake. R.F.

FPMS, Foundation Plant Material Service, repository of the viticultural gene pool at UC *Davis. Responsible for identification and selection of vine clones, indexing for virus diseases, and certification of stocks free from graft-transmissible diseases. Various other research institutions have at one time or another also been active in this field, but there is a natural ebb and flow from one location to another as interest and funding wax and wane. In the last quarter of the 19th century TX was an active center. In the late 1980s OR State Univ imported many clones from France. OSU is still involved in research, but no longer imports plant material directly. In MI and ONTARIO, Canada research is focused on German genetic material. GENEVA is particularly active with French hybrids. MS State Univ is a current center for research on Muscadine varieties. B.C.C.

franchise states, is a legal term in the US denoting a procedure whereby certain states require brand owners (ie wineries or importers) to designate a single distributor in that state as the franchise holder for the brand. Designed as a mechanism to identify a single in-state legal entity from which the state can collect EXCISE TAXES, the practical effect of these laws is to give distributors monopolistic veto power over brand owners' ability to market within that state. If a brand owner grants a franchise to a distributor who fails to perform, the brand owner has absolutely no leverage to improve the situation, and may need an act of God (or at least an act of the court) to regain control over their brand in that state. B.C.C.

Franciscan, winery in the RUTHERFORD AVA of Napa Valley, sold in 1999 to CANANDAIGUA, and now part of their **Franciscan Estates** portfolio which includes Simi Winery in northern Sonoma, a new 600-acre purchase east of PASO ROBLES, and Veramonte in the Casablanca Valley of Chile's coastal mountains.

Franciscan was originally established in a prime Hwy 29 location in 1972, and owned from 1975 to 1979 by Justin Meyer (now of SILVER OAK). Despite some excellent vineyard sites in Rutherford and Alexander Val-

ley, it floundered as it went through a series of unfocused corporate ownerships in the early 1980s. In 1985, Augustin Huneeus was invited to join Franciscan on a partnership basis with the Eckes family of Germany and assumed executive control, achieving a rapid turn-around of the winery's fortunes. The Huneeus family had owned Concha y Toro in Chile during the 1960s in partnership with the Guilisasti family. Disenfranchised following socialist Salvador Allende's popular election as president there in 1970, Augustin Huneeus emigrated to take hired postions with Seagrams and Ch Souverain, and later became proprietor of Concannon.

In addition to Franciscan's 240-acre Oakville Estate vineyard, the company owns the Mt Veeder winery and 35 acres 1,000 ft up on MT VEEDER, as well as 300 acres in the Alexander Valley and over 700 acres in Monterey which are used primarily for the ESTANCIA label. In 1998 they produced 150,000 cases under the Franciscan label. Three-quarters of the Franciscan production is red wine focused on Cabernet and Meritage blends. Their most unique wine, however, is a Chardonnay fermented with WILD YEAST which they have made since 1990 called Cuvée Sauvage. It is a deft interplay between the full-bodied, pear-like flavor notes of Napa Valley fruit and the toasted nut esters derived from apiculate yeast. Given three years of bottle age after release, the wine gains complexity unusual in CA. B.C.C.

Frank, Dr Konstantin (1899–1985), Russian viticulturalist almost as well known for his gnarly personality as for his seminal work which revolutionized eastern American wine by introducing and vehemently promoting VINIFERA varieties. He was also the founder of **Konstantin Frank's Vinifera Cellars** and the patron spirit of his family's **Ch Frank** sparkling wine house in the FINGER LAKES district.

Dr Frank managed collective farms and taught viticulture and enology in the Ukraine before the disruptions of the Second World War brought him to NY in 1951. Making his way to the nearest agricultural research station at GENEVA, but unable to speak English, he spent two years working at menial jobs. A chance encounter with Charles FOURNIER gave Frank a chance to vent his frustrations in broken French. He berated the station and local growers (including Fournier) for planting French hybrids, which he believed to be poisonous. Although vinifera vines had failed in commercial plantings in eastern states for 300 years, Frank insisted that based on his ex-

perience in the Ukraine, he could succeed. Fournier hired him. The two men scoured the countryside for rootstocks that would permit grafted vinifera to weather sub-zero winters. Their first Chardonnay and Riesling were released in 1960.

Two years later Frank opened his own winery and nursery on the western shore of Keuka Lake, pointedly calling it Vinifera Wine Cellars. Today the 60-acre vineyard run by his son and grandson includes substantial acreage of Pinot Noir, as well as the mainstays Chardonnay and Riesling. There are smaller blocks of Cabernet Sauvignon, Cabernet Franc, Gewürztraminer, Muscat Ottonel, Rkatsiteli, and Sereksia. Wine quality was wildly uneven under the founder's hand, but since the late 1980s his offspring have consistently made wines among NY's best; an achievement made more impressive by the vineyard's location in one of the region's coolest mesoclimes. Low yields certainly play a role. Old vines and winter low temperatures typically approaching −22°F trim the crop level to an average 2 t/a. To fully ripen red varieties another half-ton is culled at *veraison, contributing to the surprising richness of the Pinot Noir and Cabernets. Production was 20,000 cases in 1998.

Ch Frank is located next door to the Vinifera Wine Cellars and shares family ownership. It is the only sparkling wine house in the Finger Lakes, a region once known as America's champagne district. Other NY wineries make sparkling wine, but Ch Frank does it exclusively, by the MÉTHODE CHAMPENOISE from classic varieties. Twenty-eight acres of estate vineyards on Keuka and SENECA lakes produce the fruit to make four sparklers. Brut is the flagship, a wine displaying the angular refinement of its cool climate, but also layered flavors of partial barrel fermentation and ageing in *tirage for 6–8 years. A sparkling Riesling called Célèbre is a specialty in a lighter vein. The first vintage was 1985. Annual production is 3,000 cases. R.F.

Franus, high quality NAPA VALLEY winery run by the quietly well-spoken Peter Franus, who had been winemaker at Mt Veeder Winery for ten years before embarking on his own venture. Franus makes fine Cabernet, but is best known for Zinfandel sourced from several vineyards including vineyard designated lots from Brandlin Vyd and George Hendry Vyd in the MT VEEDER AVA. All Franus Zins walk a tightly restrained road reaching to one side for fruit intensity, but leaving behind its fleshy companions, and reaching to the other side for claret-like balance, but not settling for the thin flavor profile that style often implies. B.C.C.

Fraser Valley VA, area immediately east of VANCOUVER in the broad flood plain at the mouth of the Fraser River in BRITISH COLUMBIA. The growing district has less than 50 acres planted which are sited on deep fertile soils. It is best known as the home of ANDRÉS, one of the largest wineries in CANADA. Begun in 1961 Andrés' success was based on its Baby Duck sparkling wine. VQA wines are produced under the Peller Estate and Bighorn brands, utilizing grapes from Inkameep Vyd in Oliver at the southern end of the OKANAGAN VALLEY.

Near Andrés in Langley, Dom de Chaberton, owned by Claude and Ingeborg Violet, produces a full complement of wine including grapes grown at the winery as well as some purchased from Okanagan. R.A.I.

French hybrid, also referred to as **French-American hybrids** or **European-American hybrids**, are those varieties whose parents have one foot in the vinifera species and one in a North American species. Seyval Blanc and Chancellor are fairly well established examples while Cayuga, Chardonel, and Traminette are more recent introductions. Although American horticulturists such as Jacob Rommel and Hermann Jaeger in MO or T. V. *Munson in TX had long tinkered with such crosses, the *phylloxera and mildew crises of Europe in the latter part of the 19th century spurred serious transatlantic efforts. Not content with exporting bug and mold resistant native grapes such as Jacquez, Herbemont, and Noah from North America into European vineyards, hybridizers such as Albert Seibel, Maurice and François Baco, Bertille Seyve, Eugène Kuhlmann, Pierre Landot, and other Frenchmen sought to create new varieties. Their intention was to develop grapes that would carry both a resistance to the problems mentioned above and fruit flavors which more closely resembled those of vinifera varieties. These grapes were planted in great numbers in France to take the place of the dying vinifera. However, once the concept of *grafting vinifera scions onto resistant American rootstock be-

came the standard way of dealing with phylloxera, these grapes were summarily banned for *appellation contrôlée wine production.

In America French hybrids were slow to catch fire. Not until after the Second World War were they commonly accepted, in no small part due to the efforts of Philip Wagner at BOORDY VYDS in MD and in a more informal fashion by Elmer SWENSON in MN. Today, although widely planted in the American East and Midwest as well as in Canada, they still make up only 2% of the American vineyard. However, the trend in these areas seems clear. French hybrids represent a significant and growing proportion of the grapes used to make wines. Curiously, 60% of all the French hybrids grown in the US are planted in CA. These are primarily Rubired and Royalty, which are employed as blending grapes treasured, especially in Central Valley reds, for their color. P.W.F.

Frey Vyds, the genuine article in CA's ORGANIC WINE movement, located in the Redwood Valley district of MENDOCINO Co. They have gone from downplaying their organic practices in public, for fear of being dismissed as kooks when they were struggling to sell 5,000 cases a year in 1986, to selling 38,000 cases in 1998 easily and struggling now to keep up with demand. They own 75 acres of vineyard at their winery and 15 acres in Potter Valley AVA. Two-thirds of their wine is red, and the majority is sold through health food stores. All of it is sent to the BATF lab for sulfur dioxide analysis. Usually about half qualifies for a label reading, 'Contains no detectable sulfites. No sulfites added.' The rest gets a label saying, 'Contains naturally occurring sulphites. No sulphites added.' Every Frey wine is labeled, 'Grapes grown organically.' If they were only going to be sold in CA, they could also say, 'Certified organic processor,' but the federal government has not caught up with CA on that issue yet.

A prototype extended family operation, Frey looks like a hippie commune, but the entire clan is exceptionally well educated and incredibly self-sufficient. Situated at 1,000 ft of elevation on a bench in the northern end of the Russian River watershed, the

vineyard is on shallow, but well-drained, sandy soils delivered by an adjacent creekbed. They began planting Cabernet grapes in 1966. Many producing springs on the property give it an abundant water supply even in drought years, which is important even though the vineyard is DRY FARMED because wineries use a tremendous amount of water cleaning equipment. The grapes are LONG PRUNED as their only form of frost protection. Redwood trees mark the eastern boundary of the coastal fog which comes through the mountains at a gap near Willits.

Jonathan Frey, oldest of the second generation and now in charge, attended UC Santa Cruz, then apprenticed himself to British organic horticulturalist Allan Chadwick. More pragmatic than fanatic, the Freys read voraciously to stay current. Their interest in organic viticulture is as much a matter of economics as it is a philosophy or a marketing tool. As an example, wetable sulfur is approved for certified organic use (since it comes out of the ground) against mildew. The Freys prefer to spray a tea leached from compost and mixed with silica rock. They read about it in a German journal which said the yeasts in the compost would act as competition for the mildews.

In the late 1970s Jonathan Frey and his brother Matthew built a 6,000 sq ft winery out of wood salvaged from a ghost winery in Ukiah. They welded their own stainless steel tanks and achieved temperature control by wrapping them with plastic irrigation tubing. They bought used barrels which they scraped and retoasted themselves. They have been expanding this facility piecemeal ever since. They have also paid off their entire start-up debt. Their wine style emphasizes grapier, juicier characteristics best suited to early drinking. 'We want accessible wines,' Jonathan Frey says. 'Not using SO_2 means ageing ability is not going to be a factor for us in the marketplace.' They never make sweet wines; they sterile filter; and their prize possession is a zero oxygen bottling line. B.C.C.

Frontenac, dark-skinned grape variety developed in Minnesota from American *riparia* vines and LANDOT 4511.

G

Galena Cellars was established in 1985, the latest in a triad of Lawlor Family wine enterprises. Others were in IA and WI. Galena was built at the intersection of the Mississippi and Galena Rivers in northwestern ILLINOIS upon a 19th-century granary, which is now a historic site. The wines are made by Christine Lawlor and include the typical small winery range of fruit wines and sweetish grape wines. Many of these are made from grapes grown in other states as IL grape growers are just beginning a rebirth. The home grown Léon Millot, however, is worth a search.   P.W.F.

Gallo, E & J, the world's largest winery and still a family owned company. Gallo makes and sells just under 40% of the wine produced in CA (70 million cases; $1 billion in sales annually), which extrapolates to well over a quarter of all wine sold in America.

Headquartered in the CENTRAL VALLEY town of Modesto, which is one of the gateways to Yosemite, *Gallo's influence is often hidden, if not often subtle. As powerful as they may be, historically they have been distinctly averse to publicity. They are the largest employer in Modesto, but there is not one sign announcing the identity of their headquarters. It is hard to miss though, with a 45-acre air-conditioned warehouse storing 12 million cases at any given time, and glass-making furnaces working 365 days a year. Ernest Gallo did not give his first official press interview until he was 82 years old. But that is not because he is shy, or lacking opinions.

Throughout the wine business executives invoke the name Gallo in conversation when they wish to imply a sense of weight, much like 16th-century Russian peasants must have employed the name of the Czar. The tone of such remarks is always tinged with various proportions of respect, fear, and mystery. Ernest and Julio Gallo got (what is reputed to be) a rolling start in 1933 when Prohibition ended. Older brother Ernest had been very active while still in his late teens and early twenties during the last years of Prohibition, traveling to sell railcars of Central Valley grapes through brokers to

home winemakers in eastern cities such as CHICAGO. It was legal during Prohibition for households to make 200 gal of wine a year tax free and the fresh grape market each fall was massive. The sales experience Ernest gained, and his contacts with the brokers who went on to operate as wine distributors after Prohibition ended, are the sometimes misunderstood engines which drove this company's phenomenal development in the subsequent 60 years. Aggressive, indefatigable, Ernest Gallo was, until nearly his 90th birthday, the robust sales and marketing arm of the family business. Gentler, more thoughtful Julio Gallo was, until his 1993 death in a tractor accident, the production arm.

Several sensationalist books have been written about the Gallo family. One of the implications made by all Gallo detractors is that the company historically engaged in unfair, even ruthless, practices to gain advantages in the marketplace. It should be pointed out that the competitive environment of the US alcohol beverage business from Prohibition until the Second World War was not exactly populated by choirboys. Criminal elements had a virtual monopoly on alcohol sales from 1918 until 1933. Those individuals did not magically disappear when Repeal was passed. Ernest Gallo's accomplishment during the period from 1933 through the 1950s deserves to be cast in a more noble light than it frequently is. He competed successfully without becoming obligated or otherwise entangled with the former criminal element. As entities ranging from the US Teamsters Union to various governments such as Italy, Mexico, and Columbia have learned, this feat is exceedingly difficult.

The first of three segments explaining Gallo's history is the part responsible for much of their image today, as well as for their incredible volume. In 1933 the two brothers had relationships with growers throughout the Central Valley because they had been successfully selling those grapes in the East to home winemakers. Ernest Gallo also had the building blocks of a sales network for wine through the grape brokers in

those cities. Besides distribution, the major accomplishment of this period was Julio Gallo's ability to produce huge quantities of wine inexpensively, which were also free of the spoilage and defects which characterized so much homemade wine and so much of the competition's wine. The most visible solution to this technical problem was screw caps instead of corks. Screw caps gave a reliable seal, while corks tended to overly expand and contract in the extreme temperature conditions to which bottles were subjected by naive distributors and retailers in various corners of the US. Another Gallo tenet became strict avoidance of microbial contamination which was commonly harbored in wooden fermenters and wooden storage casks. Less visible were advances in wine chemistry such as *acidifying musts prior to fermentation, use of *sorbic acid to keep sweet table wines from refermenting in the bottle, and various hot/cold *stabilization procedures. On the sales side, Ernest Gallo and an army of his lieutenants created from whole cloth the procedures and organizations which reached out from the winery to speak to consumers through individual retail wine stores. SHELF TALKERS, bin end displays, depletion monitoring; so many of the techniques commonplace throughout American retailing today took root in the wine business because of the drive and determination of Ernest Gallo.

Numerous famous brands, and their accompanying apocryphal stories, date from this era. Carlo Rossi was an in-law whose demeanor perfectly captured the ethnic culture which had been the primary home winemaking market during Prohibition. So Ernest Gallo turned his name and image into a brand. Prior to 1960 the majority of wine sold in the US was fortified. White port was the cheapest alcohol on the market, but drunks found it too sweet so they always cut it with lemon juice. Bingo: Thunderbird, a product of market research. Night Train had 18% alcohol; Night Train Express had 20%. Pink Chablis was made for the female market with a sweet tooth. Spañada was an adaptation for the American market of the wonderfully appropriate *sangria concept.

In the 1960s surplus pears and apples ended up in Boone's Farm flavored wines which were precursors of the Bartles & James wine coolers in the late 1970s with their innovative television advertising. Red Mountain jug wines became so common in the smoke-filled rooms of the hippie generation that bumper stickers appeared on cars advising 'Stop tooth decay: fluoridate Red Mountain.' Somewhat lost amongst all this noise is the fact that by 1970 Hearty Burgundy represented one of the best conveniently available wines for the money (under $3 per 1.5 l at the time) anywhere in the world.

The second part of the Gallo saga began in 1974 when they introduced their varietal wines on national television. By this point they owned their own bottle manufacturing plant and had begun to edge away from their 'screw-tops are cleaner' mantra. When Gallo made their first cork purchase, it was so large the price of corks rose 60% worldwide overnight. When the wine boom of the early 1970s collapsed, Julio Gallo stepped in and shored up grape prices in CA's coastal valleys by signing long-term contracts. By 1980 Gallo was taking 40% of the grapes grown in Sonoma and 20% of the grapes grown in Napa. In 1975, 32% of the grapes crushed for wine in CA were Thompson Seedless. Gallo has not used any Thompson Seedless in their table wines since 1973. The current wine boom in America is not driven by an increase in per capita consumption. It is being driven by the conversion of consumers from inexpensive jug wines to higher priced, cork finished varietals. From a standing start, that transition has (since 1985) made huge players out of brands like GLEN ELLEN, FETZER, Sutter Home (see ST HELENA AVA), KENDALL-JACKSON, MONDAVI Woodbridge, and others. Gallo certainly does not get all the credit, but they were decades ahead of the wave, and they did a lot to deliver the message to Joe Sixpack America. Gallo is the leading seller of cork finished, varietally labeled wine in the US today.

The third part of the story is just now unfolding. Very late in life, Ernest and Julio Gallo clearly took a decision to create an incontrovertibly upmarket legacy for themselves. They had grown to manhood in the Central Valley, both as neighbors and almost exact contemporaries with Robert Mondavi. It cannot be too great a stretch of the imagination to suspect the Gallos might have long wanted a wine on the market to compete with OPUS ONE. They began in the 1970s purchasing land in Sonoma Co. Today that project is in the hands of their grandchildren and called GALLO SONOMA. Few people in the CA industry doubt Gallo's

ability to produce a top rank wine. They have expertise. They have virtually unlimited capital. And they have a huge resource of grapes from which to select. Nobody doubts Gallo's ability to sell tens of thousands of cases of wine in an ultra-premium price category. The fascinating, and perfectly understandable, wrinkle is the decision the Gallo brothers apparently took before Julio died, to market their top shelf competitor under the Gallo label rather than under a brand name free of *jug wine connotations. B.C.C.

Henderson, B., *Our Story* (New York, 1994).
Oral History Project, *Interview with Charles Crawford* (Bancroft Library, UC Berkeley).

Gallo Sonoma, upmarket winery located in the DRY CREEK Valley and run by two of Julio Gallo's grandchildren, winemaker Gina Gallo and Gen Mgr Matt Gallo. Producing 2 million cases in 1999, and the largest vineyard holder in Sonoma Co with 5,000 planted acres, this operation still represents only 3% of the Gallo Wine Company annual output.

Julio Gallo had been acquiring grapes in northern Sonoma Co for decades when he and his brother took the decision to acquire property there. The first purchase was 625-acre Frei Ranch in Dry Creek Valley. The biggest area during this initial phase was in the ALEXANDER VALLEY: 100 acres called Lyeth Vyd; 100 acres called Chiotti Vyd; and 600 acres around the tiny town of Asti. When they first began work at Frei Ranch, they bought earth moving equipment that had become surplus after completion of the Alaska Pipeline. They then proceeded to roll back the topsoil, smooth out the underlying terrain into undulating hills and terraces, then replace the topsoil evenly. Consistent ripening was the goal. This heavy-handed approach was balanced by Julio Gallo's aesthetic sense about the vineyard sites. He commanded a one-to-one ratio of wildland preservation acres to planted acres. Julio's influence was never more clear than when Ernest Gallo paid architects to design a hospitality center on an eastern ridge of the Dry Creek Valley overlooking the winery site, only to have Julio veto the building because it would require removal of 'too many trees.' Once the groundwork had been established, the founders cast it upon the future by deploying their most talented progeny.

Conspicuously unlike the previous two generations of Gallos, the third generation ('G3s') running the Sonoma operation today are remarkably open and candid. Carolyn Bailey is Julio's oldest grandchild, and currently in charge of international marketing

for the Gallo Sonoma family of brands. In 1998 she had been in wine sales for fourteen years. Citing the traditional view of gender roles in Italian-American communities and her great-uncle's larger-than-life reputation, she was once asked to describe the experience when first she made a sales call on their Chicago distributor. 'The Romanos?' she asked. 'No problem. They are always interested to meet a new Gallo.' A new Gallo! The phrase refers to many aspects of Gallo Sonoma.

To begin with, it is a complete reversal of Gallo's historic *brand-over-*terroir attitude. A good example is the 360-acre Laguna Ranch Vyd. It is in the cold southern end of the RUSSIAN RIVER AVA, surrounded by names such as KISTLER, Iron Horse, Dehlinger, and SONOMA-CUTRER. No surprise then that the Gallos grow Chardonnay there. When they bought the land in 1977, it was an apple orchard. The interesting part is they put the name of the vineyard on their label. It is also noteworthy the 1994 Gallo Sonoma Laguna Ranch Chardonnay took top prize for white wine at the 1996 San Francisco International Wine Competition, which numbered Michel Bettane (Editor of *Revue du vin de France*) among those judges who voted to give it a Gold Medal.

Second, the Gallo Sonoma operation is experimental. They have the big tanks, and a barrel room covered with sod upon which the Latino employees can field two full-sized soccer games simultaneously, but Gina Gallo also has her collection of 300 gal baby tanks in a separate section of the winery where she can ferment individual lots from specific blocks in any vineyard. Laguna Ranch is not even the viticultural fringe for Gallo Sonoma. Stony Point Vyd is a 260-acre parcel planted in 1997 outside the boundaries of both the Green Valley and the Russian River AVAs south and west of Santa Rosa. Locals call the place Petaluma Gap, because the elevation of the hills is minimal all the way to the Pacific Ocean, allowing fog to pour in each afternoon then linger until mid-morning the next day. They have installed a $100,000 radio telemetry system to assess and compare individual blocks of Pinot Noir clones, on different hillside exposures, every fifteen minutes.

Another recent acquisition is Twin Valley Vyd. It is a 1,600-acre property nestled into the redwood trees at Porter Creek, about as far west along the Russian River's meander to the coast as any vineyard site in Sonoma Co. Matt Gallo is planting Viognier, Pinot Gris, and Sauvignon Blanc, citing the award winning *Sancerre style of ROCHIOLI Sauvignon Blanc as an influence on this decision.

'Diverse climate is important to us,' he explains. 'We want to give Gina a full range of blocks to play with.'

The third generation all grew up in Modesto, and attended public school there. They prefer pick-up trucks to Italian sports cars; jeans to tuxedos. Net worth aside, they have little in common with the growing number of wealthy recent entrants to the wine scene around Healdsburg. Of course they are much younger. What they do have is a strong desire to carve an indelible place for their family at the artistic end of the worldwide wine spectrum. That, and some awfully big shoes to fill. B.C.C.

Geneva Experiment Station, sometimes known simply as **Geneva**, the principal vinicultural research center of the eastern US, is located in the FINGER LAKES region and associated with a special publicly funded section at Cornell University. Geneva was established in 1882 as the New York Agricultural Experiment Station. Today it includes one of North America's primary repositories of grapevine genetic material. Viticultural research focuses on clonal trails and an active breeding program that has released a number of commercially successful new varieties, notably CAYUGA WHITE. The Experiment Station is known internationally for the work of Dr Nelson *Shaulis and the *Geneva Double Curtain trellis system he developed there specifically for cool climate viticulture.

Cornell's Cooperative Extension program operates satellite vineyard research facilities in the LAKE ERIE and the LONG ISLAND districts as well. There are outreach programs in viticulture and enology from the Experimental Station, but Cornell offers no viticulture nor enology degrees. Related courses are embedded in the horticulture and food science departments. Cornell does have one of the top Hotel Management schools in the US. R.F.

Geneva White, see CAYUGA WHITE.

Georgia, state in the SOUTH region, in which ATLANTA is located. GA is currently host to eight wineries, although the rate of new vineyard plantings is among the highest in the East. B&B Rosser was GA's first post-Prohibition winery, opening in 1978. Half of GA's wineries, those in the cool northern PIEDMONT region, grow at least some vinifera. State production is 115,000 gal annually. GA requires just 40% native fruit be used in wines labeled as GA produce. Precipitation ranges from 43 to 52 in annually and the growing season ranges from 140 days in the cool northeast, to 240 days in the central Piedmont, to 270 days on the COASTAL PLAIN.

The best markets for GA wines are in-state, with most sales taking place at the winery. The next best market is in retail stores, while the least promising are upscale Atlanta restaurants. GA wines seem to be gaining favor and market share as more native wineries open. Many regional wine festivals are held throughout the state.

NOTABLE PROPERTIES

Habersham Vyds was established in 1983 in northeastern GA and has been winning impressive awards recently for vinifera and hybrid wines, including Chardonnay and a 'port.' Lighter than most ports, the Creekstone Chambourcin Port has a rich bouquet of vanilla, nutmeg, cherry, and coriander. Other wines produced include: Merlot, Cabernet Sauvignon, Sauvignon Blanc, Riesling, Seyval, and Vidal. In addition to their primary vineyard called Stonepile, Habersham acquired Mossy Creek Vyds in 1994, adding 10 acres of Chardonnay, Merlot, and Cabernet Sauvignon grapes. Production is 15,000 cases.

See also CH ELAN. R.G.L.

Geyser Peak, winery in northern Sonoma's ALEXANDER VALLEY. The property's long history is highlighted by a period following Prohibition when the Bagnani family made their well-known Four Monks vinegar there. The commercial associations many consumers assign to the Geyser Peak name stem from the period in the 1970s when Schlitz Brewing built the modern facility which sits on the site and produced 2.4 million gal of *jug wine a year under the Summit brand. Never adequately profitable, the winery was sold in 1982 to Henry Trione, whose family already owned 1,000 acres of nearby vineyards and was active in real estate finance. The Great Leap Forward, however, occurred in 1989 when Trione sold a 50% interest in the winery (not the vineyards) to *Penfolds of Australia. As part of the deal, Penfolds sent winemaker Darryl Groom to CA to manage production. For the previous five years Groom had been responsible for Penfolds Grange, the most expensive and internationally famous wine in Australia. Fortunes at Geyser Peak began to improve immediately. Two years later Penfolds sold their interest in Geyser Peak back to Henry Trione. They also tried to reclaim their talented young winemaker, but he chose to stay in CA.

Geyser Peak is a large winery, producing 400,000 cases a year, with a broad range of wines. Since Groom's arrival, quality has been good across the board and exceptional in the bordeaux reds and Syrah. Merlot, Cabernet Sauvignon, Cabernet Franc, and red Meritage all display soft ripe tannins and clean, aromatic fruitiness. The wines have been consistently fine for a decade. They are readily available and, although much more expensive than before Groom's arrival, they represent honest value for the price. The Syrah may be the best of the bunch. Grange is a Syrah, but Groom's Geyser Peak versions (there is both a standard and a Reserve model) are by no means as idiosyncratic. Geyser Peak Syrah is round and reminiscent of the intersection between raspberry and chocolate. Canyon Road is the winery's second label and the name of their tasting room in Geyserville, located in the old Nervo stone winery building. B.C.C.

ghost wineries, phrase used particularly in CA to imply relic, unoccupied buildings which at one time housed wineries. There are a great many of these properties in the US because of the massive die-off of wineries during the Prohibition era. In CA many of these historic buildings are constructed of stone, and thus remain unoccupied because modern building codes would require them to be brought up to a level of seismic safety which is much less expensive to achieve with new construction.

glacial till or moraine is geological detritus left behind when a glacier stops advancing and retreats. During periodic ice ages, the last of which ended in North America 10,000–13,000 years ago, glaciers carved the land as they grew south. Their margins continually melt and refreeze, one of the most powerful erosion forces known. When warmer temperatures return, the rocks are dumped in place. A moraine is the large deposit bulldozed at the front of the glacier; till is the smaller material pulverized along the glacier's path. In the northern winegrowing districts of America, glacial till represents an opportunity for well-drained soil consistency.

Glen Ellen, brand now owned by United Vintners and Distillers, in a portfolio that includes BEAULIEU VYDS, Blossom Hill, MG Vallejo, and the imported Croft port. Glen Ellen was started by Bruno BENZIGER in 1980, and deserves credit for pioneering the *fighting varietal category in the US. Benziger had already had a successful career in New York as a national distributor with lines such as Parke-Benziger Scotch. His national distribution contacts made development of a volume brand a natural concept for him to pursue. The little town of Glen Ellen in Sonoma Valley was already famous as the country retreat where Jack London moved after he finally achieved financial success. Benziger set up his family winery in Glen Ellen, but the property never had more than an illusory relationship to the brand. Benziger's son Mike, and winemaker Bruce Rector, rapidly mastered the art of having wine made to their specifications at CENTRAL VALLEY processors such as Delicato, or buying wine on the bulk market and blending it to meet the seemingly insatiable demands of Bruno Benziger's national distribution network. Benziger truly had the common touch. He called wine trucked up to Sonoma from the Central Valley 'Private Reserve' and sold it for a price everyone could afford every day. The year he died (1989) Glen Ellen sold over 3.5 million cases. In 1993 the family sold the brand—no vineyards, no facilities, no sales staff; nothing but the name—to Heublein (now UDV) for $80 million.   B.C.C.

Glenora, one of the standard bearers in the 1970s renaissance of New York farm based wineries. The first modern winery on Seneca Lake, Glenora was well positioned to foster the spread of premium grape culture eastward in the FINGER LAKES district to more vinifera-friendly mesoclimates. An initial focus on Riesling and Chardonnay has survived many changes in winemakers and owners. Together the two wines account for about half of the winery's 30,000-case production. Glenora's Riesling style amplifies bright fruitness with a counterpoint of frisky acidity and residual sweetness (even in the 'Dry' bottling). Chardonnays also tend to highlight fruit character; most of the barrels used are older French. A stylish Pinot Blanc follows a similar path.

Sparkling wine took over much of Glenora's production in the 1980s but has receded back into a line of two dozen table wines, fruit-flavored pop wines, and 'port.' Still Glenora is one of only two Finger Lakes wineries putting a serious effort into sparkling wine; a sad commentary on a region with great potential. The Brut (65% Pinot Noir) and Blanc de Blancs follow the house style emphasizing fruit character over yeastiness or malolactic tones. Neither is truly dry.

Glenora's white and sparkling wines originate in a 200-acre estate vineyard directly across the lake from the winery and from other nearby growers on Seneca Lake. Grapes for a smaller line of red wines—Bordeaux varieties and Syrah—come from growers in the Finger Lakes, Long Island, and CA. Seventy per cent of the winery's production is from vinifera grapes. The rest is primarily Cayuga White and Seyval Blanc as varietals or in blends. The wines reach a half-dozen northeast and Midwest states, but most stay in NY, and a new inn and restaurant at the winery aims to increase CELLAR DOOR sales.   R.F.

GM, prefix for vine varieties bred at *Geisenheim in Germany, typically for cool climates. The following are grown in Ontario and were bred from *Chancellor and the Geisenheim clone #239 of Riesling. **GM 311–57** is grown to a limited extent for blending. **GM 311–58** is more commonly planted and may be bottled without blending. **GM 322–58**, also called Hibernal, is grown to an even more limited extent than GM 311–57, and there are also a few acres of a Muscat-like vine **GM 324–58**.

Governor's Cup, name of top award given to a wine in a competition managed by the native state's wine industry. Sometimes used to refer to the competition itself, the term is common throughout the East. VA, MD, PA, and NJ all have Governor's Cup competitions, named in honor of the state governor for his or her symbolic support of the state's native wine industry. The results of the competition are usually publicized at a gala media event with winemakers, growers, and state bureaucracy officials present.   R.G.L.

GR 7, winter-hardy, vigorous, productive French hybrid bred in NY and now producing simple red wine in Ontario.

Grand River Valley AVA. Approved in 1983, this district lies within the larger, multi-state approved appellation of LAKE ERIE AVA. Grand River Valley is located just south of Lake Erie at the eastern edge of OHIO near Ashtabula. It holds 125,000 acres within its boundaries, but vineyards account for perhaps 200 acres. The AVA's riverine aspect lends the vineyards increased potential for air and water *drainage.   P.W.F.

Grand Valley AVA is COLORADO's most recognized district, on the western slope of the ROCKY MTNS near Grand Junction. Approximately 200 acres of vinifera and hybrids are grown on sedimentary rocks of Mancos Shale from the core of Grand Mesa, the largest flattop mountain in the world, overlaid by river-borne gravel deposits and sandy loam benches. Although 4,800 ft high, the area is surprisingly warm, with 3,500 *degree days, but it only gets 8 in of precipitation each year.   R.T.S.

Grapevine, the TEXAS city just north of the international airport between Dallas and Ft Worth, which serves as host for the annual **GrapeFest** and New Vintage Wine & Arts festivals. The TX Wine & Grape Growers' Association is also based here. Trading on its name and the native MUSTANG grapes that grow there, Grapevine has reinvented itself as the Wine Capital of TX. With the passage of legislation in 1999, referred to locally as 'the Grapevine Law,' the city managed to make itself the only place in TX where a winery permit allows a winery to sell wine both for ON-PREMISE and for OFF-SALE consumption.

With 5 million people in the sixteen counties surrounding Dallas and Fort Worth, and the huge annual convention business in Dallas, it is an ideal location for marketing TX wine. CAP*ROCK, DELANEY VYDS, LA BUENA VIDA VYDS, Homestead Winery, and Northstar Vyds have tasting room/wineries in Grapevine. La Bodega Winery is actually in the airport, which serves as a hub for several airline carriers and the headquarters for American Airlines. Because state law requires a winery to actually make wine on premise, La Bodega produced their first wine at the airport in 1999.   L.A.O.

Great Lakes Effect. The largest bodies of fresh water in North America are five interconnected lakes which separate the US MIDWEST from ONTARIO, Canada. From west to east they are: Lake Superior, north of WI; Lake Michigan, which separates MI from WI and upon which CHICAGO is located; Lake Huron, to the northeast of MI; Lake Erie, north of OH and upon which Cleveland is located; and Lake Ontario, north of NY, upon which TORONTO is located. These lakes act as buffers against severe cold weather in these areas. They store summer heat and sometimes give grapevines an extra bit of autumn mildness needed to develop ripeness and its sidekick, fruit flavor. Conversely, in the spring the cool of winter stored in the lakes prevents grapes from initiating *budbreak too soon, which might otherwise result in *frost damage. In these regions *flowering often occurs in late June. An added fillip is snow cover: annually from 30 to 240 in. Cold, dry Arctic air blows in a prevailing southeasterly direction over the lakes, picking up moisture as it warms over the water, then dumping precipitation when it reaches colder land. This natural insulation dramatically affects vines. Air temperature above the snow may be −20°F, while vines buried below live in temperatures 40–50°F higher. Without this protection, most vinifera and many French hybrids would die.   P.W.F.

Greenwood Ridge, tasting room in the ANDERSON VALLEY with the winery and vineyard a 20-minute climb by car up the steep southwest side of the valley to the ridge which overlooks the sleepy town of Elk on the Mendocino coast 1,500 ft below and about 6 mi away as the crow flies. Mild mannered Allan Green bought his 700-acre former sheep ranch in 1971. He has planted 16 acres of Riesling, Cabernet Sauvignon, and Merlot, all on their OWN ROOTS. His soil, albeit high in clay, is very shallow, necessitating frequent summer irrigation. Access to water limits how much he can plant. There is plenty of winter rain, but everything he needs for summer must be captured and maintained in a runoff pond. Moreover all his grapes have to be netted. 'Quail eat a lot,' Green says. 'As a chef I specialize in Riesling-stuffed quail.' He says this quietly. Quail are the official CA State Bird.

In the 1990s Greenwood Ridge has made a number of spectacular wines including an Estate Merlot turned from tannic and herbaceous to amazingly plush by retraining on a *Geneva Double Curtain trellis and serious yield reduction. Other reliable winners are their flinty Sauvignon Blanc from purchased grapes, and one of the top ten Zinfandels in CA from grapes purchased at Scherrer Vyd in Alexander Valley. Much less appreciated, but unique in CA and a very good representative of growing conditions in his vineyard, is Green's Riesling. The wine is Germanic in style: tightly wound, delicately scented, tense acid to sugar balance, light bodied, slight mineral flavor, possessor of an extremely long and productive life expectancy. That is neither an easy wine to make nor to sell in CA. In a 1996 vertical tasting going back to the 1983 vintage, the wines showed an ability to gain not only some honeyed bouquet in the nose, but also an intensified peach/apricot slurpiness which made them simultaneously luscious and refreshing. When first released, on the other hand, the wines are hard and spare, despite 15 g/l of residual sugar. They often come in under 3.1 pH. They have more sense of place than 99% of the wines made in CA.

Allan Green may live in a remote location, but he is a creative guy with several novel approaches to marketing. He is the disc jockey for a weekly rock and roll show on local radio. A few years ago he commissioned a series of paintings and musical compositions by various artists as their impressions of three particular wine varietals. Then he took that show on the road. Since 1983 the vineyard on the ridge has been host to the annual CA Wine Tasting Championships held the end of July. Instead of wines competing, tasters do, in novice, amateur, and professional categories with flights for both singles and doubles. The contest draws several hundred contestants and an equal number of party-minded onlookers.　　B.C.C.

Grgich-Hills, premier winery in the RUTHERFORD AVA of Napa Valley, owned and operated by the colorful Croatian Miljenko (Mike) Grgich in partnership with Austin Hills, third generation heir to a coffee fortune. Grgich came to the US in 1958, working at Souverain, Beaulieu, and Mondavi before vaulting to celebrity status by making the 1973 Chardonnay at CH MONTELENA which won the SPURRIER TASTING in Paris. Grgich-Hills opened for business the next year in 1977. Grgich himself cultivates an image which is almost a throwback in science-and-society oriented Napa Valley. One comes away thinking he is part imp and part magician. He claims all his winemaking decisions are based on innate feel, and that he does not even own a pH meter. His poetic wine descriptions are inevitably laced with double entendre. The experience of tasting wine with him would be reminiscent of a visit with a gypsy fortune-teller were it not for the fact the wines are always the exact opposite of his flamboyant personality: always technically precise, carefully honed instruments.

Of course Chardonnay commands most of the media attention, and it deserves to. Most of the grapes are sourced south of Yountville and into Carneros. Grgich eschews *MLF, although he does barrel ferment and work the wine up with extended lees contact. The result is simply elegant, restrained by CA standards, but harmonious and able to develop over time, be that time 45 minutes in the glass or ten years in the bottle. Perhaps less widely recognized, but no less remarkable, is the Sauvignon Blanc (labeled Fumé). For ten vintages it has been among the five best in CA. It is not overtly *methoxypyrazine-driven or grassy in the style of NZ. Nor is it unctuous and melon-like in the manner of many CA examples. It is flinty, with long, clean flavors that invite one to return again and again. It also ages flawlessly for 6–8 years. Grgich-Hills owns 240 acres in Napa Valley and produces 70,000 cases a year, half of it Chardonnay.　　B.C.C.

Gristina Vyds, small winery on NY's LONG ISLAND North Fork, producing about 6,000 cases from 32 acres of estate vineyards. An elevated 8-acre parcel called Andy's Field, prepped with truckloads of gravel before the vineyard was planted in 1983, produces the ripest fruit for Gristina's high-end wines. Chardonnay leans toward a soft, seductive style with *barrel fermentation in French oak and 100% *MLF. Riesling, labeled Avalon, is made from Finger Lakes grapes. Andy's Field Merlot and Cabernet Sauvignon ferment with WILD YEAST, producing some of Long Island's most interesting red wines, but personnel shifts and vintage variations have created unevenness. Production was scheduled to double around the turn of the century.　　R.F.

Groth, architecturally priapic winery in the center of Napa Valley in the OAKVILLE AVA. Started in 1982 by high-tech entrepreneur Dennis Groth following his success at Atari Computers. The winemaker who established Groth was Nils Venge, now proprietor of his own Saddleback Cellars. Groth's reputation is solidly built around Cabernet Sauvignon from their 110-acre Oak Cross Vyd at the winery. Sited in close proximity to the historic drainage of Conn Creek (see CAYMUS, which is about 2 mi upstream), Groth has a silty gravel soil which delays ripening compared to most Napa Valley Cabernet producers. Hence Groth Cabernet Sauvignon tends to do better than most Napa Cabs in the warmest vintages, and may be overly green bean scented in the coolest ones. Although it is true their most famous wine, recipient of Robert *Parker's first 100-point Score, was their 1985 Reserve Cabernet, a cool but long growing year.　　B.C.C.

Gruet, owned by Laurent Gruet and Farid Himeur, whose families have owned Gruet Fils, in *Champagne, France, since 1952. The NEW MEXICO winery was founded in 1987. It produces 45,000 cases of outstanding sparkling wines, including: Blanc de Noirs, Brut, Vintage Blanc de Blancs, and only 80 cases of a highly sought Rosé, as well as 2,000 cases of still Chardonnay. Chardonnay and Pinot Noir grapes are grown on the 85-acre estate, perched 4,200 ft high, on crusted calcium carbonate called caliche and sandy soils, near Elephant Butte Lake, 150 mi east of Albuquerque. Because of the quality and value of their wines, Gruet has been very successful in establishing out-of-state markets, which account for 70% of sales.　　R.T.S.

Guenoc and **Langtry,** very large estate and AVA primarily located in CA's LAKE CO. The Magoon family had been involved in Hawaiian cattle ranching for generations when, in 1963 they swapped 23 very well-located acres in Honolulu with the US government for these remote 23,000 acres. The Honolulu property became a campus for the Univ of Hawaii. When Orville Magoon arrived in CA he did not realize the historical significance of his property. His mother Genevieve discovered the property included six separate GHOST WINERIES, and one, Lillie Langtry's estate, had been the most prominent winery in Mendocino and Lake counties prior to Prohibition. This association fit the charmingly eccentric Magoon personalities like a glove. Langtry was a Victorian actress infamous in London society for her 'close association' with King Edward VII. In 1888 Langtry bought a 4,200-acre Guenoc Valley ranch which included vines that had been planted as early as 1854 by Lansing Musick. She even imported a winemaker from Bordeaux.

Magoon applied for and received the first single proprietor AVA in the US in 1981. Guenoc Valley summer temperatures regularly go over 100°F around 2 pm each afternoon, and Guenoc Estate is always one of the first wineries in Alta CA to begin harvesting grapes. They started picking Chardonnay in 1994 on Aug 9. One factor modifying the midday heat, however, is Guenoc Valley's 1,000 ft elevation and an extremely wide DIURNAL TEMPERATURE FLUCTUATION. There can be a 50°F shift between 2 pm and dawn the next day. Guenoc Valley AVA is entirely owned by the Magoons, but their property covers much more land than the AVA itself, including land in Napa Co. Magoon legally, and enthusiastically, calls the vineyards on his property in Napa Co by the Napa Valley appellation conferred by BATF, although normal semantics would imply these vineyards are in Pope Valley; not the watershed of the Napa River.

Befitting his engineer's background, in 1980 Magoon built a state-of-the-art 54,000 sq ft winery with fermentation capacity for 200,000 gal. Operations are highly computerized, and temperature control can be exercised from the moment grapes arrive until finished goods leave the premises. Producing vineyards on the property currently total 340 acres and include small plots of such exotic varieties as St Macaire, Gros Verdot, and Carmenère. Tephra Ridge is the highest point in Guenoc Valley, and Magoon has a plot of Cabernet there.

The place may be isolated, but it never wants for lifestyle. In 1987 Magoon married Karen Melander, a native of Dubuque, IA,

who had enjoyed an extensive singing career in Austria and Germany. Today she is Guenoc (pronounced *GWEN ahk*) Winery's Director of Marketing. They have a big staff and sell over 100,000 cases a year. Contrary to climatic expectation their Genevieve Vyd Chardonnay is often quite good, in a very CA sort of way, densely packed with ripe papaya and pumpkin flavors which more than hold their own against the rich, toasty oak and *MLF treatments. The Langtry Meritage wines get a lot of attention, but the most reliable performer in the stable is Petite Sirah. Since 1980 it has always been among CA's top five because of its dark, opulently chewy fruit. Modestly priced, it can be drunk young too. Some vintages shine after extended bottle age, but waiting on Petite Sirah hoping for elegance is like marrying a stripper in the hope of witty conversation in old age.   B.C.C.

Gulf of Mexico, northern portion of the Caribbean Ocean which borders on the SOUTH from the Florida Keys to TEXAS. Famous for its shrimp harvest, the Gulf is also a source for both HURRICANES and the warm, moist air which contributes half the cause of TORNADOES. The Gulf's hot and humid climate enables hardy MUSCADINE grape varieties to thrive, but precludes French hybrid and vinifera cultivation in the COASTAL PLAIN.

Gundlach-Bundschu, historic vineyard and family winery, dating from 1858 but reopened in 1973, which is southeast of the town of Sonoma in the SONOMA VALLEY AVA. Bavarian immigrant Jacob Gundlach arrived in San Francisco with the *gold rush, but had the good sense to open a brewery instead of heading for the hills. He was soon able to buy and plant the 125-acre Rhinefarm Vyd which remains in the family today (Charles Bundschu was his son-in-law), albeit expanded to 400 acres. The original winery was destroyed by the 1906 San Francisco EARTHQUAKE.

Since the 1980s the winery has been a relaxed, innovative performer known best for its marketing techniques, but well ahead of the curve on several good wines including:

Merlot dating from the very early 1980s; a nice Rhinefarm Cabernet Franc dating from the late 1980s; and an excellent Batto Ranch Cabernet Sauvignon, which shifted in 1985 over to winemaker Lance Cutler's own label.

Through the 1980s the Sonoma Valley Wine Patrol, composed of owner Jim Bundschu, Lance Cutler (who also writes books under the *nom de plume* Jake Lorenzo), and Marketing Manager Jim McCullough, fairly terrorized respectable wine society in southern Sonoma. There was the annual harvest party where gumboots were required for entry. There were the pilgrimages to NEW ORLEANS, still the winery's best out-of-state market. Then there was the time they hijacked two busloads of Virgin Atlantic employees bound for DOM CARNEROS and diverted them to a pig roast at Gundlach-Bundschu. Each year they dressed up in costume to produce a humorous poster, until the one titled *A Bottle A Day, That's All We Ask* finally got them in trouble with the local School Board. To this day a very valuable collectors' item at charity wine auctions is a rare copy of their poster which used a name for Sonoma Valley popularized by Jack London as its title: Valley of the Moon. It showed the lunar orb rising over the hill behind the winery, and, if you looked very close, the Sonoma Valley Wine Patrol bending over on the porch with their pants around their ankles.

At present much of the marketing has been taken over by Jim Bundschu's Gen X son Jeff. The Gundlach-Bundschu winery produces 50,000 cases a year. They also manage a very impressive stable of Pinot Noirs made under the **Bartholomew Park** label at the Sonoma Valley Wine Museum which was the original vineyard for Agoston *Haraszthy's Buena Vista Viticultural Society. The 1920s building was once a hospital, then purchased (sight unseen) at auction in 1941 by Frank Bartholomew, at the time Chairman of United Press Intl. He sold the Buena Vista name and caves, but retained the fine old vineyard and building. It operated as Hacienda Winery until 1992, when that name was sold to JFJ Bronco in Lodi for use as a marketing brand.   B.C.C.

Hamptons, The, see LONG ISLAND.

Handley Cellars, excellent ANDERSON VALLEY winery on the ocean side of the coastal mountains in CA's MENDOCINO CO. Milla Handley sprang onto the CA wine stage in the mid-1980s with a string of Show awards, first for Chardonnay and a short while later for her sparkling wines. At that time Anderson Valley was largely a trade secret visited only by flannel shirted romantics hoping to get their dates far enough from the Bay Area to necessitate overnight accommodation.

Handley's great-grandfather was Henry Weinhard, founder of a famous beer brand in the American west. She sources one of her Chardonnays from her father's 20-acre vineyard in southern end of Sonoma Co's Dry Creek Valley AVA. The other comes from 25 acres on a south-facing slope at their winery, the last one in Anderson Valley on the drive to the Mendocino coast. They are the coldest vineyard in the valley, but not the last to pick. They thin their crop, which allows them to pick a week or two earlier than they would otherwise. Handley uses a vertical trellis and rows running north–south. They pull leaves to open up the canopy, but only on the eastern side, which helps avoid sunburn. They have not used herbicides or pesticides since 1990. In a mesoclimate as cool as hers, Handley finds she has to pick grapes based on acid rather than on sugar. Her dad's grapes become physiologically ripe at different sugar level than hers do. 'We develop the same translucency of skin a couple weeks behind him,' she says, 'and 2°Brix lower. It is a rare vintage we do not get at least one rain before the Chardonnay is picked.' Since 1990 Handey has been using an *MLF culture called Inobacter, which works at pHs below 3.0 and does not produce the butterscotchy smells common to Chardonnays with large malic acid fractions.

Production is about 12,000 cases after Handley downsized slightly in order to avoid having to deal with large distributors. Half their production is sold CELLAR DOOR in their handsome tasting room and gardens, elaborately festooned with a collection of primitive and folk art from around the world. Designated drivers (ie non-drinkers) are drawn by freshly brewed, locally roasted Kona coffee, the only coffee grown in the US (Hawaii). On the first weekend of each month appetizers are served as well. Between the two Chardonnays, the Dry Creek is a fatter style with more oak. For those who believe the meat is sweeter closer to the bone, the Anderson Valley Chardonnay would be the choice. It is also the better ageing candidate.

Handley's sparklers always finish near the top in blind tastings. At her end of the valley, the Blanc de Blanc is a bit severe, but the Brut is world class. She also makes an inexpensive Riesling/Gewürztraminer blend for the tasting room called Brightlighter. That is the *boontling* (local patois) word for people from the big city, in case there is any doubt about the wine's purpose.　B.C.C.

Hanzell, tiny winery in SONOMA VALLEY on a hill just north of the town of Sonoma. In a lovely building modeled after *Clos de Vougeot in Burgundy are separate one-ton stainless steel fermenters which produce about 3,000 cases a year. It was established in 1952 by James Zellerbach, part of the family that owned Crown Zellerbach paper and eventually the US Ambassador to Italy. Hanzell was the prototype BOUTIQUE CA winery. Several techniques, which were seminal in CA, date from those first years when R. Bradford (Brad) Webb was the winemaker. Fermenting in temperature controlled stainless steel was one, but introducing French cooperage was much more important. Chardonnay has always been the standout wine. It is not a particularly cool growing site, and the Chardonnays are not worked up with *barrel fermentations, *sur lie ageing, or *MLF. They are sort of simple when young; their attractiveness develops over time in the bottle. Several fifteen-year-old examples have proved marvelously pleasurable with a bouquet like green apples baked in a nut crust. Pinot Noir was James Zellerbach's passion, and the early vintages developed very complex bouquets over time. More recent vintages, however, have seemed to carry a stewed fruit note. The site may be a little too warm for top shelf Pinot Noir.　B.C.C.

Hecker Pass, the single remnant of SANTA CLARA VALLEY's viticultural heritage. Not an approved AVA, it lies west of Morgan Hill and Gilroy about 20 mi south of San Jose. Most of the six wineries in the district do not care about appellations because they sell everything CELLAR DOOR. The present-day Gilroy Garlic Festival celebrates this area's most important modern crop (computers do not grow on trees), and also harks back to the days when immigrant Italian winemakers dominated this market. Then, they sold their wines directly to restaurateurs who drove up with 17 gal demijohns in the back of their pick-up trucks. Tasting rooms consisted of a plank between two barrels. Bottles with bar spouts dispensed samples into shot glasses. Most of the wines were generics, but quality could be very high because the sources were ancient vineyards of Carignane, Grenache, Mourvèdre, Petite Sirah, and Alicante Bouschet. Soon these grandfathers will retire and sell their vineyards to programmers from the nearby IBM facility whose adolescent daughters wish to keep horses.

NOTABLE PROPERTIES
Sarah's Vyd, in many ways an anomaly for the district, because it is a very upmarket operation, but this winery does share an otherworldly charm with its neighbors. Marilyn Clark is two of the best interviews in the wine industry. Marilyn holds certain opinions. 'Sarah,' her alter ego, also holds definite opinions, usually contradictory and always quite colorful. Marilyn is a premier member of the region's entertainment class which includes Randall Grahm at BONNY DOON over the hill in Santa Cruz and Dr David BRUCE. Both Sarah's and Marilyn's opinions come from one mouth, but it is always good fun. The grapes and yeast talk to Sarah. Marilyn maintains a personal relationship with the wines, which she always refers to in the female gender. Of the Ventana Chardonnay, for instance, 'She is for men who like boobs and hips. She has to be

restrained. I started to pick her progressively earlier back in the mid '80s just to get a grip on the reins.' While the Estate Chardonnay, 'comes out of the bottle slowly,' Marilyn says. 'She holds back, waiting for maturity on your part.' Buying these wines is like asking the Mayor's daughter for a date. You expect to be quizzed about job prospects. Then there is the intrigue. Marilyn makes a mystery red blend called Sarah's Affair. 'But I don't do it every year,' she points out coyly.

The 10-acre vineyard was planted in 1977. The winery is compact and scrupulously clean, with fresh flowers, candlelight, and classical music. Guests receive a generous slice of Sarah's personality. 'The winery is Sarah's doll house,' says Marilyn enthusiastically. The label is made with a die sculpted by an engraver from Smith & Wesson, a well-known American gun manufacturer. It is printed by Jeffries Bank Note Company on paper normally reserved for wedding invitations. The estate Chardonnay comes in a hand-blown Demptos bottle with raised indicia. Sarah's Vineyard presently makes about 2,000 cases a year, including an excellent Merlot purchased from Radike Vineyard near Paso Robles, and a new infatuation with Pinot Noir, which Marilyn describes as 'a typical redhead.' The Pinot Noir grapes were planted on the estate in 1989.

Sarah has recently gone completely biodynamic in the vineyard. They do not give the wine away, but most bottlings are extraordinarily fine quality, a discovery that amazes most people who have caught Marilyn's show. Of course, if you have not met Sarah, you only got half your money's worth.
B.C.C.

hedging, mechanical canopy trimming. Grape clusters usually form at the second and third nodes along a growing *cane. Thus growth beyond the fifth or sixth node can be safely cut to open up the canopy, allowing more sunshine to reach next year's buds and allowing air to circulate more freely, which reduces risk of bunch rot and fungal diseases. On deep, fertile soils with plenty of water available and lots of sunshine, the tips of canes will continue to grow all summer, sometimes so vigorously they block the rows between vines. In that case mechanical hedging is almost a requirement prior to harvest. Hedging is widely practiced in CA.

*Mechanical pruning is a different matter, albeit using a similar machine. Pruning occurs in the winter when vines are dormant and leafless. Mechanical pruning shortens canes, usually back to a single bud, but it does not eliminate any canes. Hence vines that are mechanically pruned look like a

hedgehog after a few years because of the great number of spurs left each winter. It is popular in Australia, but mechanical pruning is rarely seen in CA. (See Labor essay, p 49.)

Heitz, winery located in a pocket canyon of the hills immediately east of NAPA VALLEY about as far north as ST HELENA. Joe Heitz is the man who started the winery in 1961, a giant in the CA wine industry. Heitz had taught enology at Fresno State before moving to Napa Valley. Subsequently recognized for his superb palate, his start in the trade came when he purchased at auction two vintages of HANZELL Chardonnay and Pinot Noir to bottle under his own label. His financial partner in that venture was Dr Barnard Rhodes, one of America's top wine connoisseurs (see Auctions essay, p 32). About this same time Rhodes and his wife Belle began planting a vineyard on the westside bench immediately north of the Oakville Grade Rd. They subsequently sold that property to Tom and Martha May. Today it is called Martha's Vyd. Rhodes and May became investors in Heitz Winery. The vineyard at Rhodes house is called Bella Oaks. From 1966 to the end of the 1970s Heitz Martha's Vyd Cabernet Sauvignon was an absolute icon, a CULT WINE before the term existed, one of a handful of CA wines with a truly international following. Heitz Bella Oaks Cabernet has proved a worthy stablemate since 1976. In the 1980s and 1990s Heitz Cabernets have not run as far ahead of the pack as they did earlier, but they have nevertheless been very fine wines.

Joe Heitz began turning over the reins of the business to his son David as winemaker in the mid-1980s, and to his daughter Kathleen for marketing. They continue to make Grignolino from very old vines surrounding the property they also own on Hwy 29 just south of St Helena, and the quality is unique. Angelo *Gaja imported it to Italy for a while. They have added a Cabernet Sauvignon to the stable called Trailside from a vineyard they own on the valley side of Silverado Trail in the Rutherford District. They have also purchased a large tract of land on the eastern side of Howell Mtn facing Pope Valley where they are planting 100 acres of Zinfandel and Cabernet. These new contributors have helped keep total production fairly level at about 50,000 cases a year even though Martha's and Bella Oaks vineyards needed to be replanted due to phylloxera beginning in 1992.

Heitz Martha is an exceptional Cabernet Sauvignon because it combines innate

power with modulated presentation. All the actors who have played James Bond have adequately portrayed him as a refined gentleman, but only Sean Connery simultaneously portrayed a visceral sense of actually being dangerous. Heitz Martha is the Sean Connery of Cabernets. It has deep color, the purple scent of currants, and a signature ethereal note some writers euphemize as mint. It is not mint; it is eucalyptus, and anyone who has worked in a grove of eucalypts knows the difference. Heitz Martha dazzles with complexity in the mouth, while clearing one's sinuses to a point clear back behind the eyeballs.

In 1997 Joe Heitz suffered a stroke of modest severity. He does not attend public wine events much anymore, and the CA wine community cannot help but be diminished when a personality as forceful as his no longer takes the stage.
B.C.C.

Henry of Pelham. Henry Smith of Pelham, ONTARIO, built an inn and toll gate in 1842. Smith's relatives of a century and a half later built a winery adjacent to the inn and planted a vineyard on the 75-acre farm. Today, the sixth generation Speck brothers operate the winery with Ron Geisbrecht as winemaker. Geisbrecht, with his Univ of Guelph degree in microbiology, is best known for Barolo-sized Baco Noir and creamy Chardonnay, both *barrel fermented and *sur lie aged. In 1998 the Specks expanded their winery by 18,000 sq ft of additional space, which allows them to age wines longer before release. In the vineyard, now grown to 225 acres, they work closely with CCOVI experimenting with *pheromones to control berry moth, and with different *trellising systems aimed at achieving greater fruit ripeness.
L.F.B.

Hermann AVA, second approved appellation in MISSOURI, located nearly equidistant between the state's capital at Jefferson City and St Louis in northern Gasconade and Franklin counties just south of the Missouri River. It occupies 51,200 acres with almost 200 acres under vine. One-quarter of this is Norton with about 10 other acres of American hybrids. The rest is overwhelmingly French hybrids including Seyval and Vidal Blanc, Vignoles, Cayuga, and Chambourcin. Bounded by rivers—the Gasconade, First Creek, Big Berger, and the Missouri—the vineyards are on slopes the earliest German settlers occupied a generation before the Civil War. Named after the German barbarian hero Arminius who fought the Romans, the whole area reflects its Germanic background, not only in the names of its surrounding towns—Rhineland, Frankenstein,

Berger, Starkenburg, Holstein, etc—but also in its topographical situation. The confluence of the rivers and the hilly nature of the land afford excellent air and water drainage.   P.W.F.

Heron Hill Vyds, one of the wineries most responsible for NY's FINGER LAKES district's establishing a reputation for exceptional Riesling. Beginning with the first vintage in 1977, Heron Hill Rieslings have displayed racy, flowery fruit with very bright acidity and varying degrees of honeyed *botrytis. There is a recent effort behind DRY Riesling, but the traditional German model has generally prevailed here with all whites. Located on Keuka Lake and working primarily with grapes from cooler areas of the Finger Lakes, Heron Hill whites tend toward lighter, lively-acid styles with a place for some residual sweetness. Chardonnay is fermented in French and American barrels with care to preserve delicate fruit. The 20-acre Ingle Vyd on Canandaigua Lake is the estate's prime property. An exceptional site on a lake marginally suited to vinifera, it produces intriguing single-vineyard Riesling and Chardonnay. Upland air drainage through the 15-acre vineyard at the winery makes it one of the coldest in the Finger Lakes, often trimming the crop, which is supplemented with grapes purchased from growers on three lakes. Pinot Noir and a Cabernet Franc-dominated Bordeaux blend called Eclipse are more recent efforts. Production of 12,000 cases in 1998 is increasing.   R.F.

Hess, winery and extensive modern art collection in a facility on MT VEEDER west of the town of Napa. The buildings were once the Christian Brothers' Mont La Salle winery. Donald Hess is Switzerland's largest distributor of bottled water. He owns some 300 acres of Cabernet, Chardonnay, and Merlot on Mt Veeder, and another 300 acres in Monterey. He also imports the wines of Glen Carlou in South Africa in which he has a stake. Randle Johnson has been the winemaker at Hess for nearly two decades. His previous experience in the district at MAYACAMAS taught him that mountain grown grapes, particularly Cabernet, are always going to have plenty of flavor and color. The key to success is to avoid extracting excess tannin. He uses open topped fermenters and a mechanical *punch-down device. His style produces a reliably good bargain in the Hess Collection Cabernets, even at $20. The second label, Hess Select, uses Monterey fruit.   B.C.C.

Hibernal, see GM 322–58.

Hidden Cellars, see PARDUCCI.

High Plains AVA, see TEXAS HIGH PLAINS.

Hill Country AVA, see TEXAS HILL COUNTRY.

Hillebrand, large Canadian winery best known for its Trius (they pronounce it *TREE us*) brand representing the best of what they produce in Chardonnay, Riesling, Cabernets/Merlot, and a sparkling wine made in the traditional *méthode champenoise. Their VQA wines are the most awarded in ONTARIO. Loire-born and University of Bordeaux-trained winemaker J. L. Groux also makes an unfiltered series of wines, in limited quantities, which are recognized as some of the finest in Ontario. His 1995 Unfiltered Cabernet Sauvignon received a Grand Gold at VinItaly in 1999. Owned by ANDRÉS Wines, Ltd, Hillebrand sources grapes from its own NIAGARA-ON-THE-LAKE vineyard for reds, and from 25 growers throughout the NIAGARA PENINSULA. Varietal wines in the Trius line are vineyard designated, thereby offering an interesting comparison of different characters emerging from grapes grown in various sub-appellations of the Niagara Peninsula VA. Hillebrand is a medium-sized winery at 300,000 cases a year. With its regional restaurant, it is tourist friendly, offering several events and vineyard activities throughout the year.   L.F.B.

Hogue Cellars, WASHINGTON winery established in the YAKIMA VALLEY in 1982 by a successful asparagus and mint farming family from Prosser. It produces and sells worldwide an array of consistent red and white wines ranging from inexpensive table wines to artisan specialties. Upmarket label designations include Barrel Select and Genesis. Of particular interest are their Bordeaux varieties, both red and white, especially Merlot. It also produces an excellent Lemberger.   R.A.I.

Hopkins Vyd, in the hilly northwestern quandrant of CT, an eighth generation Yankee family farm that has followed the latest twist in NORTHEAST region agriculture. Too far inland to benefit much from the maritime warming that defines SOUTHEASTERN NEW ENGLAND AVA, the 35-acre vineyard was first planted to hardy French hybrids in 1979 emphasizing Seyval Blanc and Vidal for light, fresh, country wines. But Chardonnay and Cabernet Franc have been added and done well. They use a mix of American and French oak in the cellar with restraint to produce lively, fruit forward wines.   R.F.

Horse Heaven Hills, a 70 mi long basaltic uplift, running east–west and rising between the Columbia River to the immediate south and the Yakima River to the north. It contains some of the top vineyards in eastern WASHINGTON. 500–1,100 ft high, it acts as a buffer sheltering Yakima from the wind. There is a lot of room for expansion, especially on top where Mercer Ranch (also called Champoux) is located. There, soils are clay undisturbed by ancient floods, resulting in softer, rounder wines with broader flavors than further down the south-facing slope. Canoe Ridge, and their new partnership with *Antinori, as well as Horse Heaven Vyds are located on the slope at a lower elevation, where they produce brighter flavors. They also get some weather moderation benefits from the river. In 1996 when vineyards on top of the ridge froze, those lower on the slope were covered in a protecting fog.   R.A.I.

Horton Vyds, nationally recognized winery in Orange Co, central VIRGINIA just north of the Monticello AVA, located on Rt 33 between Barboursville and Gordonsville. Dennis and Sharon Horton, along with Joan Bieda, are the proprietors. **Montdomaine Cellars** was a winery acquired by the Hortons in 1991. By 1990 Montdomaine had made a reputation for producing fine red Bordeaux varietals. In 1991 Dennis Horton used the Montdomaine winery to crush his first crop of Vidal grapes while his own winery was being built. He was impressed with the quality of the Montdomaine reds, and purchased existing stock and leased the brand.

When Horton Vyds released the first VA Viognier in 1992, it caused a stir in the industry. His 1993 Viognier won more awards than any other American Viognier at the time, and gained national attention for VA wine. His iconoclastic line of vinifera wines includes varietal Marsanne, Syrah, and Mourvèdre, as well as variety of blends. Horton's 1995 Vintage Port and Dionysus wines are largely based on Touriga Nacional. The Montdomaine 1990 Cabernet Sauvignon (made by ROCKBRIDGE VYDS owner Shep Rouse) won the 1992 Governor's Cup. The single-vineyard Ivy Creek Vyd Chardonnay under the Montdomaine label was often the most awarded Chardonnay in the state. The Montdomaine brand and winery were auctioned and acquired by Shep Rouse of Rockbridge Vyd in early 1999.

Horton has 100 acres of vineyards. Much credit for the winery's success goes to Sharon Horton, the vineyard manager, and to Alan Kinne, consultant winemaker, who have worked closely with Dennis in his innovations. The Viognier is trained quadrilaterally with an open-lyre trellis which, though labor intensive, is necessary for the best quality. The impact of Horton's Viognier extends through the product line, being blended with some red wines such as the Stonecastle Red and the Côtes d'Orange, a *Châteauneuf-du-Pape style wine, and as a varietal it is made in regular, reserve, and dessert styles. In 1999 Horton even released a Sparkling Viognier. The grape has figured strongly in Horton's awards, with many Viognier-based Horton wines winning medals in state and national competitions.

Dennis Horton grew up a block away from the Stone Hill Winery in MO, where the Norton grape is still cultivated. Horton Vyds has now reintroduced the Norton to VA, where it was first discovered in the 1820s. Consistently good Horton wines besides the Ivy Creek Chardonnay and Viognier have included Cabernet Franc, Vidal (especially late harvest), Marsanne, Mourvèdre, and Montdomaine's red Heritage blend. A recent Horton innovation includes a sparkling wine made with a cuvée of Marsanne and Rkatsiteli. Horton is unusual for a Mid-Atlantic winery in that 80% of production is sold through distribution, 30% of that outside the state. Annual production of the Tudor-style stone castle winery is 45,000 cases.   R.G.L.

Howell Mtn AVA, district in the mountains east of Calistoga which is also part of BATF's inclusive NAPA VALLEY appellation. Elevation defines the AVA: the boundary basically follows the 1,400 ft contour line around a cigar shaped, flat topped, 25 sq mi mesa approximately 8 mi long and 3 mi wide. The 1,400 ft contour was chosen because it represents the ceiling above which fog rarely rises. As a result, vineyards on Howell Mtn warm up earlier most mornings than vineyards on the valley floor. Equally important, they are above the inversion layer which traps heat in the valley during the day. They receive a cooling breeze early each afternoon which serves to smooth out their DIURNAL TEMPERATURE FLUCTUATION and keep overall *degree days much lower than in the valley. Consistency is the hallmark of Howell Mtn. Historically, going back to the 1880s, the most important grape variety was Zinfandel. Howell Mtn Zins were typified by a black pepper note (which generally indicates cool growing conditions). Beatty Ranch is a modern era grower whose grapes serve as an illustration. Two soil types separate Howell Mtn into northern and southern zones. In the north the soils, called Aiken

series, are rocky and red. In the south the soils are light grey and more friable, dusty even. The back side of Howell Mtn descends into Pope Valley, a hot, enclosed, inland valley whose grapes can legally go to market with Napa Valley appellations on their labels. Land prices in Pope Valley are one-third those in the actual Napa River watershed. Many good sized vineyards have been planted in Pope Valley since 1985.

The community resident on Howell Mtn is about 10 mi by car from St Helena, but they have an air of isolation about them. One of the reasons is the 1909 acquisition of the mineral hot springs resort at Angwin by the Seventh Day Adventist Church for their Pacific Union College. Seventh Day Adventists are a particularly abstemious bunch. Not only do they not smoke or drink, they do not allow the sale of condiments in the convenience store on campus. Nor can any business be conducted on Saturday. In the local elementary school, where Seventh Day Adventist kids rub shoulders with the children of winemakers, tensions are never far below the surface. A second fascinating feature of the community is its heating system. In the 1920s Pacific Union College sank geothermal wells into the hot springs which are used even today to run radiators in the school's buildings.

NOTABLE PROPERTIES

Bancroft Vyd, long-time grower with 130-acre vineyard in the southern half of the appellation on the light grey TUFA soil which is the source of Beringer's excellent vineyard designated Merlot.

Burgess, historic property several hundred feet up the slope toward Howell Mtn, but not high enough to be in the AVA. The property was first used as a winery in 1884. From the 1940s until 1972 it was Lee Stewart's Souverain Cellars, maker of some of Napa's best Cabernets in the 1960s. Airline pilot Tom Burgess bought the winery in 1972. There are 105 acres of grapes with the largest contingent in Chardonnay. The best wine, however, is the Vintage Select Cabernet Sauvignon which ages well to give a smoky, savory bouquet after ten years.

La Jota, ghost winery from 1895 in the southern extreme of the AVA. Acquired in 1974 by Bill Smith, who has always produced grainy, hard-edged Cabernets which stay dried out and earthy even after extended bottle age. Viognier has gotten some attention for its perfume, but can seem phenolic.

Lamborn, small winery and vineyard at the northwest end of the AVA looking back into Napa Valley. Owned and run for more than ten years by a retired private detective once

hired by the Hearst family to investigate their daughter Patty's kidnapping. Bob Lamborn produced medium-bodied, well-concentrated, bramble berry Zinfandels with just a hint of pepper. Since 1996 Lamborn has employed wine consultant Heidi Peterson Barrett.

Summit Lake, craftsman-sized winery in the northern half of the AVA contiguous with Lamborn and Beatty Ranch. Bob and Susan Brakesman own 2 acres of DRY FARMED Zinfandel vines from the Farrazzi Vyd planted in 1920. In total they have 14 acres, several planted more recently to cuttings from the old Farrazzi vines. They make about 2,000 cases a year.

Viader, not part of the AVA: 18 acres on a steep west-facing slope just out of Napa Valley toward Howell Mtn. Delia Viader is the daughter of a diplomat, and was married to the scion of France's Sequin-Moreau coopers. In 1987 she planted the hillside to Cabernets Franc and Sauvignon. Tony Soter is her winemaking CONSULTANT.

See also CH WOLTNER, DUNN.   B.C.C.

Hudson River, one of the oldest wine districts in the US, surrounding the river valley north of NEW YORK CITY. There are records of 17th-century vineyards planted along the lower river and at New Paltz by Dutch and French Huguenot settlers; some sites have been continuously planted in vines for more than two centuries. But wines were homemade and grapes were grown primarily for fresh fruit until the first commercial winery opened on Croton Point in 1827. The valley's proximity to New York City has ironically limited its development as a wine district; first by making the fresh fruit trade more lucrative, and more recently by soaring taxes and property values from commuter-suburban sprawl. The latter has elbowed most of the region's vineyards and 28 wineries back from the river into surrounding hills where the effects of moderating maritime weather, funneled upriver from the Atlantic, quickly dissipates. The river itself typically freezes north of Poughkepsie, limiting its ability to temper extreme winter low temperatures (−30°F at vineyards near Poughkepsie in 1994). Cold-tender vinifera varieties are more at risk here than in NY's other wine districts. French hybrids have proven more reliable, led by Seyval Blanc. The region's once extensive American hybrid vineyards are mostly gone. Geologically and topographically the Hudson region is very complex. Soils derive from bands of schist, slate, and limestone, and abruptly undulating terrain creates a labyrinth of mesoclimates. The vinicultural possibilities are intriguing but the challenges daunting. Total vineyard acreage was at an historic low of about 650 in 1996.

Notable properties

Millbrook Vyds, the most dynamic wine estate in the region, converted from a dairy farm in the Berkshire foothills a dozen miles east of the river. An experimental planting of 30 varieties in 1981 has been winnowed down by steely winters to a focus on Chardonnay, Pinot Noir, Cabernet Franc, and a surprising Tocai Friulano. The undulating site presents a palette of soil types to influence flavors, but short crops after hard winters have prompted purchase of grapes from other regions as well. Reserve is the name on a label which indicates exclusively estate grapes. Chardonnay is fleshed out with full *MLF and barrel fermentation, but the use of new oak is limited to keep the focus on fruit character. The citrusy, tropical Tocai sees no oak. Reds are admirable in good vintages. Owner John Dyson also operates WILLIAMS SELYEM, plus the Mistral and Vista Verde vineyards in CA, and a wine estate Villa Pillo in Italy.

See BENMARL, BROTHERHOOD, CLINTON.

R.F.

Hunt Country, see MIDDLEBURG.

hurricane, a large, rotating cyclone of tropical origin, noted for its strength and violence. It may span 300 to 500 mi in width. Tropical storms which develop into hurricanes have wind speeds ranging from 73 to over 150 mph, while forward movement is relatively slow; from 5 to 15 mph. Hurricanes are also characterized by torrential rains, averaging from 3 to 6 in during the course of a typical storm.

Along the Atlantic seaboard of North America the season for hurricanes is from June through Oct, although they do occur occasionally in May and Nov. The average number of tropical storms in the North Atlantic strong enough to be classed as hurricanes is five per year. Due to the prevailing westward trade winds, the storms normally track west from the tropics. In the late summer, however, hurricanes often track northwest or north from the tropical latitudes, frequently threatening coastal areas of the SOUTH and MID-ATLANTIC regions. Because this period coincides with the beginning of harvest in the Mid-Atlantic, late season hurricanes can cause considerable damage, even far inland due to warm, protracted rains which create optimum conditions for *fungal growth and grape rot. This was a major factor in the poor quality of the 1996 vintage due to two harvest season hurricanes. Vineyards in coastal areas can also suffer physical damage from high winds.

R.G.L.

Icewine. Standards for the production of Icewine in CANADA are the most stringent in the world, which is why the phrase has been trademarked by VQA under Canadian law, and US practitioners of CRYOEXTRACTION are viewed in a very dim light by Canadians. This proud protectionism makes sense. Icewine is the jewel in the crown of the Canadian wine industry, routinely selling for C$50 per 375 ml bottle.

In Canada regulations have been set on the temperature at which Icewine can be harvested (–8° C/18° F maximum), and the minimum sugar level of the *must, with strict recording of amounts of grapes pressed, processed, and sold. Before the regulations were put in place bottles labeled *icewine* were arriving on Canadian shelves from producers who simply froze the grapes at harvest and later pressed them, thus bypassing the risk of losing crops to birds, an uneven winter, and the high cost of winter labor. By artificially refrigerating grapes they also compromised flavour, yet charged the same price as icewines made in an authentic style.

When grapes are allowed to undergo the concentration of their sugars by weathering early winter temperatures, they develop a gentle mellowing of flavors caused by variation in temperatures that freeze and melt the grapes, thus initiating a gentle oxidation that results in an intense tropical character in the wine. Icewine grapes must be picked after this process occurs, and only at temperatures that sustain frozen crystals of water during pressing in order to avoid dilution of the pressed juice. Unfrozen sugar concentrate percolates through the frozen crystals, leaving a block of ice in the press and a golden nectar in the fermenter. Sugar level must be at least 35°B in Canada. The sugar level requirement for *Eiswein is lower in Germany (28.5°B) and Austria (29°B). Those regulations equate Eiswein *must weights to *Beerenauslesen, whereas the Canadian requirement for Icewine would equate to German and Austrian requirements for *Trockenbeerenauslesen.

Beginning with the 1997 vintage, all grapes used in the production of VQA Icewine must be processed by VQA member wineries or Ontario grape growers who have registered as VQA Icewine grower/processors. All Icewine processors are required to verify such details of production as the temperature at which grapes were picked, acreage and tonnage of each given crop, volume of each must as delivered, *Brix levels, harvest date and time, and Icewine pressing capacity. Processors must agree to random analyses of juice, must, and wine designed to detect any illegal additions such as sugar or *grape concentrate. Auditors appointed by VQA have the authority to visit sites, to check harvest timing against temperature data and to 'take whatever measures are necessary to assure appropriate quality control.'

All Icewine must be made as a varietal wine, and from vinifera grapes with the exception of the French hybrid Vidal. Grapes must be grown and pressed within a recognized Viticultural Area (VA). Residual sugar at bottling must be at least 125 g/l. No addition of *sweet reserve is allowed.

With increased recognition of Canada as the foremost maker of Icewine in the world, demand has swelled. Canadian production increased from 8,000 cases in 1993 to over 30,000 cases in 1997, then exploded to 160,000 cases in 1998. Producers of particular note internationally include KONZELMANN, CH DES CHARMES, INNISKILLIN, and Reif Estates; the last, for instance, recognized by *Decanter* Magazine as 'the greatest sweet wine in the world.' Exports to international markets such as Asia have increased considerably, although for technical/protective reasons the wines were still not legally allowed into Europe in 1999. In 1997, Ontario wineries accounted for 90% of the 13,500 cases of Icewine exported from Canada to fifteen countries including the US, Japan, China, and Taiwan.   L.F.B.

Idaho, state famous for potatoes and huntin' and fishin', which guards the eastern flank of the PACIFIC NORTHWEST region. ID is contiguous with the entire eastern borders of OR and WA. The main wine country is predominantly found in the SNAKE RIVER VALLEY just outside Boise, the state's capitol and hub of economic activity, just south of the 44th parallel, comparable to the middle of OR or the middle of MI. Rising in the Rocky Mtns near Yellowstone Natl Park, the Snake was a major thoroughfare for white explorers seeking passage from the Continental Divide to the Pacific Ocean. It travels westward across southern ID, then north forming the state border as it flows through the 6,600 ft high walls of Hells Canyon, eventually meeting the CLEARWATER RIVER at Lewiston, where it turns west again into WA to join the Columbia. Limited vineyards are located along the Clearwater, but they offer promising sites for quality grapes. Unfortunately those choice sites are in competition with vacation homes. There are presently no approved AVAs in Idaho.

Although grapes had been planted along the Clearwater in the late 19th century, it was less than 20 years ago that Bill Broich lifted ID back onto the Northwest wine map. And he did that at STE CHAPELLE Winery west of Boise in the Snake River Valley. Ste Chapelle Chardonnays were stunning mouthfuls of fruit flavors. Today ID's sixteen wineries have slightly over 560 acres of planted grapes. CORUS BRAND's recent purchase of Pintler Cellars will double the ID acreage if they fulfill stated plans to plant 600 acres of vineyard. This commitment has infused enormous excitement into the previously stagnant ID wine industry. It validates past efforts, and arouses hope for the future.

Riesling and Chardonnay are currently the two most widely planted grape varieties. New plantings will concentrate on red wine varieties. All ID vineyards are planted on their OWN ROOTS. To date *phylloxera has not threatened. Most growers feel the light, well-aerated soils offer some protection, and cold winter temperatures will act as a further line of defense. Along the Snake most vineyards are at an altitude of 2,900 ft. Ripening is not a problem; long, warm summer days combine with cool nights to provide fine sugar/acid balance. About one year in ten a crippling *winter freeze will cause significant bud damage or kill the vines back to the ground. These events drastically reduce crops and the vineyardist must retrain suckers that grow up out of the vine's trunk, another reason to abjure grafted vines (see Viticulture essay, p 44).

The wine industry is represented by the ID Wine Commission, which must battle against the entrenched dairy and agricultural interests in the state legislature. Wine is tolerated, but its position appears fragile in a freedom-loving, conservative state that ironically constantly threatens wine commerce with higher taxes, or further restraints. Wine is regulated by the ID State Liquor Dispensory, which sells all spirits and wines over 16% alcohol. Retail wine stores must purchase through a licensed wholesaler. Prices are regulated but discounting is allowed.

NOTABLE PROPERTIES

Indian Creek. Bill Stowe, as co-owner and winemaker, makes one of the best Pinot Noirs in the Pacific Northwest. His vineyard in Kuna Butte, outside Boise, produces wines with a cranberry flavor and color, with smooth *mouthfeel, that are light bodied but expansive and complex.

Pend d'Oreille, in Sandpoint, ID, purchases both WA and ID grown grapes to make full-flavored reds.

Stephie Martin, an excellent winemaker, formerly of Rose Creek Vyds, is trying to re-establish herself at Carmelle Vyds, at Glenns Ferry considerably east of Boise.

Vickers Vyds produces estate-grown crisp, focused Chardonnays on a very limited basis.

See also STE CHAPELLE.   R.A.I.

Illinois, state in the MIDWEST region south of Lake Michigan. Curiously, a mixture of Utopians and Mormons helped the early winegrowing in the state. In the 1830s Joseph Smith, the Mormon Prophet, had fled with his band to Nauvoo in Hancock Co at the most western spot in the state along the MISSISSIPPI RIVER. After some ugly disagreements, which ended in the death of Smith among others, the Mormons headed west to UT. In their place, in 1849, came a communal sect known as the Icarians, led by Étienne Cabet, a Burgundian-born writer, teacher, and lawyer. His plans also failed; he and part of his flock moved on to establish other colonies in IA and CA. But some of them stayed, planted vines, dug cellars, made wines, and established Nauvoo as a leading wine center of the time. They along with settlers of Irish, German, and Swiss backgrounds planted 600 acres of vines in the area. Among them was Emile Baxter who planted his first vineyard in 1857. Today, even though many of the cellars dug now provide ageing homes for the local

cheeses instead of wines, BAXTER'S VYD, the state's first and oldest, is a remaining testament to that time.

IL is plagued by harsh winters and 2, 4-D. Still, it is interesting to note that as recently as 1930 there were over 1 million vines in the state, the equivalent of about 2,200 acres. Currently the state has fourteen very small wineries, over half in the southern tip of the state southeast of St Louis, between the Mississippi and Ohio rivers. The rest are scattered along the state's western and north-central periphery. There are about 175 acres of grapes, almost all being used for wine making, about 80% of which are French hybrids with Chambourcin, Vignoles, Seyval Blanc, Foch, and Chardonel the leaders. The rest are planted to American hybrids. Vinifera varieties remain in an experimental stage. This mix is admittedly chump-change to a Californian, but the complete switch from Concords to more wine-friendly French hybrids in the last few years marks a turning point in IL wine fortunes. Furthermore in 1997 the state legislature created an IL Grape and Wine Council with initial funding of $200,000.

CHICAGO is the 800-pound gorilla in the equation, the city and suburbs representing over half of the state's 12 million population. On the one hand, it is one of the nation's best-stocked wine cities, offering thousands of relatively familiar vinifera wines to compete with home-grown French hybrids. On the other hand if local wine became fashionable, Chicagoans could consume IL's entire current production on a festive weekend.   P.W.F.

Indiana, basketball-mad, corn-producing farm state in the MIDWEST. Situated between MI to the north, OH to the east, IL to the west, and KY to the south. IN's wine-growing scene began with Swiss settlers such as Jean-Jacques DUFOUR in the early 19th century. By 1820 his estate at Vevay had grown to production of 12,000 gal annually, but was ultimately abandoned fifteen years later because of grapevine diseases, most notably black rot. Later settlers took Dufour's beloved ALEXANDER grape and others westward along the OHIO RIVER VALLEY past Cincinnati. There they established an IN industry that became second only to OH's by the mid-1800s, only to succumb to a similar fate within a short time.

Today most of the winegrape acreage is still located in central and southern IN, where the greater abundance of forests, combined with the smaller size of grain farms, lessens the danger from 2, 4-D. IN's current wine scene was jump started by the

enactment in 1971 of the Small Winery Act which allows the present nineteen wineries to sell directly to consumers. This spurred the inevitable change in grape plantings which result in today's collage. There are now about 250 acres of grapes in the state with 60% planted to American hybrids, overwhelmingly Concord for Welch's grape juice. One-third is represented by French hybrids. Seyval and Chambourcin are the white and red leaders, followed by Vidal, Vignoles, Chardonel, Foch, and De Chaunac.   P.W.F.

Inglenook, see NIEBAUM-COPPOLA.

Ingleside Plantation Vyds, one of the oldest wineries in VIRGINIA and the only one currently in Northern Neck George Washington Birthplace AVA (in VA's upper Tidewater, and for typesetting reasons the nation's least likely to appear on wine labels). Ingleside's 50 acres also make it one of the largest estate vineyards in VA. The plantation house is an official Historic Landmark.

The story of how Ingleside Plantation became a leading VA winery is one of the local industry's most colorful. In 1979, proprietor Carl Flemer decided to start a commercial vineyard and winery on the estate. A year later Belgian enologist Jacques Recht, a protégé of Émile *Peynaud, retired from the Univ of Brussels and, with his wife Lillian, sailed a catamaran across the ATLANTIC and up CHESAPEAKE BAY. He arrived on Northern Neck as Flemer and his son Doug were beginning their initial crush. Recht was impressed by the resemblance of Northern Neck to the Bordeaux estuary. So when the Flemers implored Recht to assist them with their first wine, he agreed. Originally intending to stay only a short while, Recht and his wife are still in VA, having contributed significantly to the evolution of the nascent wine industry as *consultants.

With Recht's Bordeaux experience, he was able to help the Flemers establish Ingleside as a producer of quality Cabernet Sauvignon. Ingleside is currently the only VA winery to have won that state's GOVERNOR'S CUP three times (in the 1980s; twice for Cabernet Sauvignon and once for Chardonnay). While other VA Cabernet producers made great strides in the 1990s, Ingleside is still a consistently good producer. They also make a fresh Merlot with 20% Malbec, which has surprising mint and berry flavors, and a smooth, supple Cabernet Franc for which they win awards. The Grand Reserve Cabernet Sauvignon is bordeaux-like in its subtle, skillful integration of fruit and oak.

Ingleside's regular and Reserve Chardonnay continue to win competition medals both in and out of the state. Moving with the times they have also released a Sangiovese and a Viognier, adding breadth to a solid vinifera line-up. The historic estate house in Oak Grove adds a unique attraction to a winery tour. Production is 15,000 cases. Stephen Rigby is the winemaker. R.G.L.

ingredient labeling for wine was a controversial issue in the US during the late 1970s and into the 1980s which deepened the divide between CRAFTSMAN-SIZED wineries and the very large wine producers, who dominated trade organization decision-making by virtue of their much larger financial contributions. The federal Food & Drug Administration was beginning to require labels on foods which would specify what the packages contained. Small wineries saw no reason to oppose ingredient labeling since their labels would in most cases simply say, 'Grapes, yeast, sulfites, and (maybe) tartaric acid.' Big wineries were concerned about engaging the federal bureaucracy at all. At least one of them argued the ingredient statement would be a financial burden to print because it would have to be so long, raising the curiosity of smaller producers who wondered what that winery could possibly be doing to their wines. In the end, sulfite and health warnings were mandated for wine labels. Small wineries were incensed, but big wineries were fairly passive on the issue because in the legal climate of that era it was thought that health warnings on cigarettes would insulate big companies against health-related class action lawsuits, a high priced strategy subsequently shown to be wrong. B.C.C.

inner stave, technique whereby the flavoring function a barrel contributes to a wine can be continuously renewed even in old barrels by simply inserting some matrix of fresh wood inside the barrel. Inner staves may be made from any sort of oak, eg French or American, and the surface can be *toasted to whatever degree a winemaker chooses. Since most barrels give up the majority of their available flavoring constituents over a year-long period with wine in them, most wineries have a regimen of replacing barrels every 3–5 years, or of shaving their inner surface to reveal fresh wood. Inner staves are a much less expensive alternative, although considered by many winemakers with the same distain that *oak chips receive.

See also *barrels, OAK and AMERICAN OAK. B.C.C.

Inniskillin led the way in the revolution of the modern wine industry in ONTARIO. In 1974, co-founders Donald ZIRALDO and Karl Kaiser were the first since Prohibition to be granted a new license to make and sell wine in Ontario. When Inniskillin tried to export wine to France in the early 1980s, they could not prove to the satisfaction of the French that their grapes were actually grown in Ontario, as opposed to transported from some warmer clime. That imbroglio prompted Ziraldo to initiate and drive the creation of the province's first appellation system, VQA.

In 1991 Inniskillin was the first winery in Canada to capture the Prix d'Honneur at the international trade show VinExpo in Bordeaux, for their 1989 Icewine. That event reverberated throughout the Canadian industry as an encouraging bell-wether of potential for Ontario wines. Best known for their Pinot Noir Founders' Reserve, Icewine, and Chardonnay, Inniskillin also produce varietal wines from Gamay Noir, Viognier, and Pinot Gris. In 1992, Inniskillin became a wholly owned subsidiary of Canadian-owned VINCOR, fourth largest wine company in North America. L.F.B.

International Pinot Noir Celebration, world-famous annual fest for lovers of this tantalizing grape held on the Linfield College campus in McMinnville, OREGON since 1987. Growers, winemakers, consumers, and distributors converge from all over the world (notably Burgundy) on the state's wine country to taste, discuss, and learn. This July event, which has arguably become more famous than Oregon's wines, is usually preceded by a technical conference held at Steamboat Inn south Oregon for growers and producers only. Both events are handled by the Oregon Wine Advisory Board. www.oregonwine.org

InterVin International, wine competition founded in 1985 by Andrew Sharp (Ontario) and David Male (NY). Judges, who come from all walks of life and are from a cross-section of major markets across North America, must pass a three-phase, three-hour test that evaluates consistency, ability to recognize wine faults, and ability to identify wine components at varying levels of intensity. Wines are not segregated by price. Gold medals require two judging panels to confirm. Results at www.intervin.com L.F.B.

Iowa, farm state in the MIDWEST south of MN and across the MISSISSIPPI RIVER from IL. The Amana colonies, a local Amish sect, off Hwy 149 in the heart of the Hawkeye state still produce wine. Today though, if it is not made from grapes purchased elsewhere, it is the traditional Piestengel, or Rhubarb wine. Grain fields and the concomitant vinous misery caused by 2, 4-D, as well as low rainfall and harsh winters, have so far successfully stymied vineyard growth. Still, there are 150 acres of grapes in the state and ten wineries, including the seven Amana wineries. Two-thirds of the acreage is planted to Concord and Niagara for table and juice purposes. The remaining third is given over to French hybrids, some of which are also raised for table fruit. P.W.F.

Island Belle, an American hybrid grape variety named by Adam Eckert, early nurseryman on historic Stretch Island in PUGET SOUND, sometime around 1910. It was the most widely planted red grape in WA at that time, and became the major grape variety for wines produced immediately following Prohibition. A light fruity version continues to be made by Hoodsport Winery. R.A.I.

Isle St George, established in 1982, is an AVA within the larger LAKE ERIE AVA located entirely on a small island just south of the Canadian border opposite Sandusky, OHIO, in the middle of Lake Erie. Half of the AVA's total of 640 acres (the whole of the island) are under vine, most of which are vinifera, and almost all of which go to either Meier's or FIRELANDS, two OH wineries owned by Paramount Distillers. Benefiting heavily from the GREAT LAKES EFFECT, the AVA has a frost free growing season of 206 days. The AVA is very similar to the nearby Canadian Viticultural Area on PELEE ISLAND. P.W.F.

Jackson Triggs, see VINCOR.

Jade Mtn, Rhône variety specialist which leases space east of Napa, but owns 22 acres on MT VEEDER. Douglas Danielak buys grapes in CONTRA COSTA Co, CARNEROS, and northern ALEXANDER VALLEY, near Cloverdale. Production is small and quality is superb, placing Jade Mtn on the fringe of impending CULT WINE status. The Syrah made from Hudson Vyd grapes in Carneros would be in every critic's top five for CA if only there were enough to let a quorum of critics taste it.   B.C.C.

Jefferson Vyds, formerly Simeon Vyds until 1993, located on historic Colle, the farm on which Thomas *Jefferson's Italian friend Filippo Mazzei planted vinifera vines in the early 1770s. It is just down the road from MONTICELLO itself, and located in the AVA of the same name.

The arrival of Beaune-educated winemaker Michael Shaps in 1994 enabled Jefferson Vyds to rise to the top rank of VA wineries. His Burgundian training shows in his Chardonnays. The elegantly complex Thomas Jefferson Signature Reserve and the Fantasie Sauvage (fermented with WILD YEAST) have performed well in national competitions and in wine press reviews, and Cabernet Sauvignon and the Signature Reserve meritage-style blend have been consistently good. 1997 Estate Reserve with 17% Malbec is particularly impressive, and cask samples of the 1998 reds show that these may surpass Shaps' fine 1997 wines. Jefferson has also won many awards for its 1997 CRYOEXTRACTION Vidal and is experimenting with a blend of Alsace varieties. Jefferson controls 50 acres and produces 6,000 cases annually.   R.G.L.

J. Lohr, large CA winery with a production facility in San Jose, but extensive vineyard holdings in MONTEREY, PASO ROBLES, and Clarkesburg in the DELTA. Begun as a vineyard partnership in 1971 between two Silicon Valley developers, this vertically integrated business has grown steadily and avoided the excesses which brought down many of its contemporaries. The first investment was a 280-acre vineyard near Greenfield in the Salinas Valley during the rush to accumulate tax advantages. Seeing the writing on the wall as that era ended, the partners bought the defunct Fredericksburg Brewery in 1974 near downtown San Jose and converted it to an industrial-sized winery. Their next door neighbor is the Santa Clara Co Alcohol Services Dept, responsible for alcohol abuse rehabilitation and intervention. In the mid-1980s Jerry Lohr bought Bernie Turgeon out of the partnership and began expanding his vineyard holdings. Today Lohr makes 400,000 cases a year and owns nearly 1,400 acres of grapes.

Lohr makes good quality, everyday wines with a couple of items deserving special attention. The *fighting varietal line is called Cypress. The Paso Robles Cabernets are called Seven Oaks; Merlots called Los Osos; Syrahs called South Ridge. They stylistically reflect the soft, approachable texture of the Paso Robles region and always balance their oakiness well with fruit. The Monterey Chardonnays are called Riverstone. They share the softness of their Paso stablemates.

The big winners though, both come from Greenfield: Gamay and Riesling. The Monterey Rieslings are called Bay Mist. There is a standard bottling with about 2% RS and occasionally a late harvest model with about 10% RS. Both are currently the best examples of ARROYO SECO AVA Rieslings commonly available. Both Lohr Rieslings have the district's characteristic nectarine nose and an acid flavor more like lime than apple, which balances their sweetness. That lime note is particularly useful in the botrytized version of the Riesling because its honeyed overtones are even more unctuous than the RS.

Lohr's 'Gamay' is a remarkable wine. Recognizing the true identity of the grape known as Napa Gamay, BATF forced Lohr to change the name from Wildflower Gamay in 1998 to Valdiguié. This was most unfortunate for the Lohr marketing department because no American wine drinker has ever heard of it, and no American wine writer alive can spell that grape name without resorting to one of Jancis Robinson's reference books. Lohr's track record with this wine goes back a decade and never falls below impressive. They make 13,000 cases and sell it in supermarkets all over the US for $6.99. Okay, the wine is simple. Simple like minimalist art, or a child's smile. Perfectly balanced, it is a pure expression of the brightest fruit imaginable. Five years in a row the wine finished in the top five for Sweepstakes Award at the CA State Fair. It never won, because none of the 40 judges could bring themselves to vote a $7 wine as Best in CA. And they all recognized the wine, even blind, because nobody else in CA makes anything quite like it.

                B.C.C.

Jordan, winery in CA's ALEXANDER VALLEY AVA in northern Sonoma Co which most effectively demonstrated the use of tuxedo marketing during the 1980s. Sales grew to 55,000 cases of Cabernet Sauvignon by 1998, a feat which makes Jordan the most widely sold CA Cabernet priced over $25 per bottle, an ironic statistic when one considers the exclusivity aspect inherent in tuxedo marketing. The winery also produces 20,000 cases a year of Chardonnay from a total of 275 owned acres in the valley floor; it is the winery that is on the hill. The brand *J is not technically part of Jordan. It is owned separately by Tom Jordan's daughter Judy, and operates out of a different facility, the former Piper-Heidseick winery in Windsor. J produces 20,000 cases annually of sparkling wine and another 8,000 of still Pinot Noir and Pinot Gris.

Tom Jordan brought his oil and gas exploration fortune to Sonoma from DENVER in 1972 when he and (then) wife Sally were thwarted in their attempt to buy one of the *first growth châteaux in Bordeaux. They spent a reputed $20 million building a showplace winery and French styled residence in a region which until then had been more attuned to grape farmers driving old pick-up trucks with dogs wearing bandanas in the back. One of Jordan's best moves was to hire a young winemaker named Rob Davis, who had just finished working at Ch *Lafite. Davis brought a couple of barrels back with him from Lafite, and was technically savvy enough to culture the malo-*lactic bacteria out of that wood. From the beginning Jordan Cabernets have been designed for the restaurant trade. They are silkier and lighter bodied than most top-of-the-line CA Cabernets, almost like a light-bodied Merlot. They also receive two years in barrel and two more in bottle before release, which makes them ready to serve the minute they arrive in a restaurant. In cool years, Jordan's vigorously growing Cabernet vines, planted in the flood plain of the Russian River, tend to have an overly vegetal quality which only intensifies with age. Warm years, however, produce elegant, finely textured Cabernets which develop a wonderful bouquet over 10–12 years in the bottle.   B.C.C.

JS 23–416, pink-skinned old French hybrid developed by Johannes Seyve. Imported into Ontario from Maryland in 1947 and now more common as a parent of newer hybrids such as TRAMINETTE than as a producer of slightly bitter white wine.

K

Kanawha River Valley AVA extends across 64,000 acres mostly in the southwest part of WEST VIRGINIA but also in OHIO. Only about 100 acres are under vine: 80% French hybrids; 10% American hybrids; 10% vinifera. It differs from OHIO RIVER VALLEY AVA, of which it is a part, in that most of the vineyards are planted on ridges above the river. Thus the latter's moderating influence is slightly less; but the elevation of the vineyards is favored more by the prevailing wind which lessens (but does not obviate) a need for anti-fungal applications.   P.W.F.

Kansas, state in the PLAINS region. KS has a rather uniform *continental climate throughout the state, with cold winters and hot summers. Severe weather may take the form of freezing temperatures, *hail storms, and TORNADOES.

In the late 1800s, KS had a thriving wine industry, but cellars were drained in 1880 when state Prohibition was introduced 40 years before national Prohibition took effect. When the next crush occurred, in 1988, there were only 10–15 acres of producing vineyards. A farm winery law was passed, due largely to the efforts of Dr Robert Rizza and James Fair. Shortly thereafter Fair opened the first modern winery, Fields of Fair. In the 1990s, seven more wineries were bonded. Most of the wineries are located in the northeast part of the state, and all are east of the north/south midline. Currently, there are about 65 acres under vine yielding 200–250 tons annually. Of these, the majority are winegrapes, almost all hybrids. In 1995 there was a single aggregate acre of Chardonnay, Riesling, and Cabernet. The remaining acres are table grapes, or are used in the production of juice and jelly. Fruit wines are also produced by several wineries.

Grapevines struggle in this climate. Wild fluctuations in the weather, both in summer and winter, sweep across this relatively flat landscape. Night temperatures in summer can be above 75°F, and daytime as high as 100°F. If fruit is in the final stages of maturity, acids drop, and sugar will not rise. Precipitation in the northeast averages 30 in a year, often occurring as thunderstorms or hail. There is seldom any need to irrigate, but well water is readily accessible because the water table can be as high as 20 ft from the surface. Ample conditions exist for the proliferation of a number of vine pests and diseases. Snowfall averages 15 in annually, which can provide some vine insulation in winter. Late frosts occur regularly. Soils are generally loam/sandy loam, or clay.

Changes to the current legislation are being addressed. The original farm winery bill did not allow for fortified wine production. Presently KS wineries can sample and sell their wares at the winery, but not at trade shows. There are no DRY counties, but 33% of KS counties do not allow liquor by the drink. State population is about 3 million. Regulations require wineries to use 60% KS grapes, but enforcement is not rigorous. KS State Univ maintains an agricultural research station at Haysville.

NOTABLE PROPERTIES

Fields of Fair winery in Paxico is the state's largest, producing 13,000 gal a year of hybrids from owned and purchased grapes, the majority of which are in-state.

Wildwood Cellars, winery in Mulvane, in south-central Kansas making some wine from grapes and excellent fruit wines, including an oak-aged mulberry wine, and a cinnamon-flavored elderberry wine. Napa Valley's Michael Martini acts as consulting enologist because the owner's wife is Martini's wife's best friend from college.

R.T.S.

Kautz (Ironstone Vyd), destination edifice in CA's Calveras Co on the road to Yosemite Natl Park's northern entrance in the SIERRA FOOTHILLS. The Kautz visitors' center is seven stories high and covers 70,000 sq ft of floor space. It features a 42 ft blue marble fireplace and an on-premise kitchen capable of feeding 1,500 guests at one time. There is an art gallery, a 60 ft waterfall in the underground caves, an outdoor theater, a helicopter to move journalists conveniently from San Francisco, a demonstration kitchen for cooking classes, the largest crystalline gold nugget ever found (about 3 ft high), and an organic garden. Kautz also owns the hotel dating from 1858 in nearby Murphys. They have planted 72 acres of grapes at the winery. In 1998 they produced 350,000 cases, ten times more than they made in 1995. They export 30% of it.

John Kautz is not a farmer; he is a businessman in the farming game. He controls 5,000 acres in CA, including 1,800 acres of grapes around LODI. At one point he was president of the state Board of Food & Agriculture. Kautz traces his heritage back to Bavaria. His immediate family moved from NE to a 38-acre Lodi farm in 1923. After high school, Kautz made his fortune raising canning tomatoes. Then he extended it into cherries, and by getting himself in front of the *fighting varietal wave when he planted Chardonnay and Cabernet Sauvignon in Lodi ten years before the huge wineries got around to doing the same thing. 'Success,' Kautz says, 'is not accomplished sitting on a tractor.'

Oh, and the wine ... Ironstone Vyds grows Chardonnay, the red meritage varietals, Syrah (they call it Shiraz after touring Australia), and highly aromatic Symphony. Estate vines are trained to a *Geneva Double Curtain and cropped at 6–8 t/a. You can take the man off the farm, but you can't take the farmer out of the man. The wines are competently made by Steve Millier, who spent eight years at local competitor Stevenot. The estate grapes are blended with fruit from Kautz's Lodi vineyards 'to make the wines more accessible.' They generally sell for under $10 and are generally competitive with other commercial wines from Lodi, although the estate Cabernet Franc has shown an impressively perfumed nose, and an aftertaste long enough to indicate intriguing potential at the 2,400 ft winery vineyard site. In 1998 Kautz purchased the 8-million-gal capacity Bear Creek Winery in Lodi (previously owned by Almaden). They spent $10 million modernizing the processing equipment, including new 75 ton rotofermenters. Most of the capacity is currently used for custom crushing.

B.C.C.

Kay-Grey, hybrid table grape bred by Elmer SWENSON.

Kendall-Jackson, K-J, very important name in the recent history of the CA wine industry, now moving onto a world stage (see *Kendall-Jackson). Beginning with a LAKE CO pear orchard in 1974, San Francisco lawyer Jess Jackson has parlayed the phenomenal market success of Chardonnays, blended during the 1980s from several coastal regions by superstar winemaker Jed STEELE, into an empire even his own PR staff cannot keep track of. Since 1987, he has simply bought everything in sight. Jackson's deal-making gene excited the competitive urge in others of his ilk, and launched a 1990s acquisition mania in CA (not unlike that in Australia) which saw several score of the state's most prestigious labels subsumed into corporate umbrellas, such as CANANDAIGUA, BERINGER Wine Estates, ALLIED DOMECQ, Brown Forman, etc. The collective name for Jackson's portfolio is ARTISANS & ESTATES (A&E). Technically K-J and A&E are two separate companies, but Jackson owns them both, they share much the same distribution network, and wine made at certain A&E facilities in excess of their requirements no doubt flows naturally downhill toward the sea of K-J bottlings.

An engine driving the business early on was an understanding of what would be necessary to command attention from the rapidly consolidating wholesale tier of the US THREE-TIER DISTRIBUTION system. A brand name was crucial, and it had to have a reputation for Chardonnay. Steele provided the ideal product: aromatic lushness from the Central Coast; acid and length from Sonoma; toasty sophistication from barrel fermentation of ripe Napa grapes. Moreover he produced a seemingly unlimited stream of this elixir at a very attractive price. The 1982 K-J Vintners Reserve Chardonnay won the first ever Platinum Award (ie 95 points, see Commentators and Media essay, p 14) from an ambitious outfit in Chicago calling themselves the American Wine Competition. Within weeks that score was on SHELF TALKERS and table tents in fifteen major markets. Once K-J Chardonnay had collected top prizes in several national shows, Jess Jackson found he could get any distributor sales manager in the country on the phone any time he wanted. By the mid-1980s an $8 bottle of Kendall-Jackson Chardonnay was synonymous with white wine in the minds of 21–35-year-olds having wine-by-the-glass in bars throughout America. Steele was pumping out 800,000 cases of

*barrel fermented Chardonnay a year, no small physical feat.

In 1987 Jackson acquired half (700 acres) of the critically acclaimed, but financially bankrupt, Tepusquet Vyd in SANTA MARIA. That acquisition is instructive because it set the stage for Jackson's flurry of activity in the 1990s and for the long-term potential success of A&E. Tepusquet (pronounced *teh poos KAY*) was one of the first large plantings in the Central Coast. Located on a sandy bench running up a canyon in the cool Santa Maria district, Tepusquet had always been a gamble. It was planted by a man named Louis Lucas who made a lot of money betting on quarterhorse races. Quarterhorses are faster than thoroughbreds for a quarter-mile, and they run for huge stakes in wild west venues. Tepusquet sold grapes to a lot of wineries, and before long it became obvious to industry insiders that many previously mediocre wineries were turning out truly superior wines from Tepusquet fruit, especially aromatic white varieties and Chardonnay. One of the distinquishing features of those wines was great acid and delicacy due to the long growing season. When the Lucas house of cards finally tumbled in 1985, Jackson and his second wife Barbara Banke, a land-use attorney, stepped in. They quickly segmented their line by creating a separate winery called Cambria. They hired talented young winemakers away from successful wineries and gave them free rein. They identified special blocks in the vineyard and designated those on labels as Julia's Vyd and Katherine's Vyd (two of Jackson's daughters). They embarked on these high-end sorties confident that any wine unused by those programs could find a home in the river of wine going to market under the K-J label. Moreover, they could now begin to participate in the pricing gamesmanship so beloved by large US distributors called PROGRAMMING. They would get the attention of distributor sales staffs by offering volume discounts on K-J, while gradually inserting new brands such as Cambria and the vineyard designated wines into the limited volume slots at the top of the distributors' catalogue.

Other vineyard acquisitions, brands, winemakers, winery facilities, and segmentations have followed with mind-numbing rapidity. The overall strategy is so successful, it is almost impossible to evaluate any of the individual parts, or even to tease them out of the swirling mix at all. In northern Sonoma Co brands include Hartford Court, La Crema, Stonestreet, and Legacy. Verité is in Sonoma Valley. Pepi, Cardinale, and Lokoya are in Napa. Carmel Road is in Monterey.

Cambria and Kristone are in Santa Barbara, along with Camelot, although that brand has been declassified to CA appellation status and moved to the K-J side of the ledger. Edmeades is in Mendocino Co. Internationally, Tapiz is in Argentina, Calina is in Chile, and Villa Arceno is in *Tuscany. Then there is the joint venture with the stave mill in France's Vosges forest providing wood for the cooperage Jackson has bought in MO so his winemakers can have French oak barrels made to the precise specification of *toast level they may desire. In 1999 Jackson began casting about for a château in Bordeaux as well. In 2000 he bought MATANZAS CREEK.

One is tempted to predict Jess Jackson will overreach at some point, but as of the end of the 20th century that point had not yet occurred. In addition to his general strategy, Jackson has been adroit at hiring clever, creative people, then letting them perform. The environment seems to burn many of them out after a few years, but if there is one thing the organization is able to handle it is change and rollover. Another gigantic plus is the quality of several of the vineyard acquisitions. The Gauer Ranch mountainside vineyards high above ALEXANDER VALLEY may well turn out to be some of the finest vineyard sites in CA. Likewise A&E's new Sonoma Seaside plantings west of the Russian River AVA look enormously promising.

B.C.C.

Kentucky. The KY Vineyard Society's First Vyd, established by Jean-Jacques DUFOUR in 1799 a few miles southwest of Lexington along the Kentucky River, was among the handful of successful commercial wine-growing establishments of the 18th-century US. (It was revived in 1981 and still flourishes.) Dufour's first attempts with the Alexander and with a grape he called the Madeira were successful, although the vineyards were eventually abandoned in 1809. KVS did not give up because of the climate, but because of disease problems (rot, virus, and phylloxera) which could then not be countered. Wine may well take a seat next to bourbon and thoroughbred horse studs in the moderate climes of the Bluegrass state.

In 1976, KY passed a law to permit wineries a legal existence. At the time, most of the grapes in the state went for juice or the table. Shortly thereafter the federal TN Valley Authority and the Univ of KY began working with prospective grape growers in the western part of the state. Today, KY boasts six grape wineries (and one black-berry winery) and just over 200 acres of vines. Of this, 70% are French hybrids with American hybrids accounting for 20% and vinifera the balance. Clearly, with tobacco's fortunes fading, other cash crops such as grapes have the field open to them in the state. Native wineries also enjoy the rabid protection of a legislature which voted in the late 1990s to make DIRECT SHIPMENT of wine to KY residents a felony.   P.W.F.

killer yeasts are yeasts that have the capacity to produce a protein or glycoprotein that can kill other yeasts. It has absolutely no effect on humans or bacteria. All of the commercial starter yeast strains for wine are killer yeasts.

More than ten different killer systems have been identified in *Saccharomyces and other wild yeast species. About a third of the yeasts found in nature are killer yeasts. Unfortunately the Saccharomyces killer strains kill mostly wild Saccharomyces and have no effect on many other spoilage yeasts, many of which can kill wine yeasts.

If a wine yeast strain is not a killer, it is sensitive to the killer toxins produced by wild yeasts. Sensitive strains may be killed off and the fermentation continued by wild yeasts. Most wild yeasts are not ethanol tolerant so after taking over the fermentation they fail to survive and the winemaker is left with a slow or stuck fermentation. Most commercial wine yeast strains are killer strains and a genetically engineered strain of wine yeast has been developed that contains two different killer systems to extend the range of immunity (see Microbiology essay, p 39). The killer toxin is not very stable and does not persist after the fermentation. Research is presently under way to develop wine yeast killer toxins that will be stable in 14% alcohol to kill off spoilage yeasts such as *Brettanomyces that grow after the fermentation.

See also WILD YEAST.   R.S.

King Estate, became the largest winery in OREGON almost over night when it opened in relative isolation on top of a ridge in the Lorane Valley, southwest of Eugene in the south of the state. Below the sprawling faux château of a winery are 825 acres owned by this aircraft millionaire from KS, of which 350 are vineyard. Will Bucklin is director of winemaking; Brad Biehl is director of viticulture at this estate noted for its vineyard nursery Lorane Grapevines. King produces soft, carefully rendered Pinot Gris and improving Pinot Noir and Chardonnay which exhibit a similar level of technical sophistication. Because this unusually (for OR) slick operation is located 5 mi south of the border of the Willamette appellation, all of the wines carry the Oregon appellation.   R.A.I.

Kistler, certainly one of CA's top five Chardonnay makers. Steve Kistler and Mark Bixler's workmanlike winery is in the RUSSIAN RIVER district of northern Sonoma Co, but they source grapes for vineyard designated wines from SONOMA VALLEY as well. They currently farm about 150 acres and produce about 25,000 cases, half of which is sold to their mailing list (mostly the vineyard designated Chardonnays and the small amount of Pinot Noir they make). Five per cent is exported.

Kistler and Bixler are mildly edgy guys. They exhibit several personality characteristics one associates with creative individuals tired of explaining themselves. The wines are edgy too. That is what has always made them noteworthy. Kistler Chardonnays began with the 1979 vintage. The wine was wonderful, and every retailer they showed it to wanted some. Not being overly enamoured of cold call sales visits, they asked for 20-case orders with a portion of the price payable on delivery. Retailers were infuriated. But the wine was *very* good, so they went along. When the 1980 vintage was released, the edge upon which Kistler had been tip-toeing crumbled. It is important to any understanding of Kistler Chardonnays to appreciate this point and how disproportionate the marketplace's reaction was compared to the severity of the infraction. Their 1980 Chardonnay had a *reduced character, with distinct notes of hydrogen *sulfide in the nose. A subthreshold amount of this characteristic adds tremendous richness and complexity to Chardonnay, but Kistler's 1980 Chardonnay crossed the line of recognition for many retailers, who were only too happy to extract retribution for what they perceived as an attitude problem the previous year. A very promising start was throttled in its crib. It took four years for the Kistler brand to recover.

To their credit, Bixler and Kistler persevered. Moreover, they did not waver from their artistic vision for the wine. Today they continue to walk that edge of richness and complexity that others find too risky. Seventeen years later, most critics would aver that Kistler has achieved solid control over their technique. Steve Kistler has even become confident enough to speak in public about 'good sulfides.' They maintain their own crew of year-round vineyard workers, which allows them to drop excess crop and to be very selective during harvest. They like a PRE-CERTIFICATION CLONE of Chardonnay which they isolated from Larry Hyde's vineyard in Carneros because of its small berries and cluster size averaging about 170 g each, preferring it to the newer DIJON CLONES of Chardonnay. They *barrel ferment, but do so in small, cold rooms, so that the ambient air temperature will slow down the fermentations. Then they rigorously barrel select their wines for the vineyard designated labels. As an example, the 1996 crop was very small, and the 1997 crop much larger in CA. Nevertheless, the amount of each Kistler vineyard designated Chardonnay from each of those years is approximately the same. The repository of wine not selected for vineyard designation is a Chardonnay they label Sonoma. In 1996 there were 7,000 cases of Kistler Sonoma Chardonnay; in 1997 there were 16,000 cases.

The hallmark of the Kistler Chardonnays is the manner in which luxuriant nutty, buttery bouquet from the winemaking process is juxtaposed with tense, focused structure that lasts long after one has swallowed the wine, and the concentrated taste of pears and Pippin apples that expands like an afterthought from somewhere inside the core of the wine as it warms in one's mouth. There are nuances of flavor difference between the designated vineyards, but it is perhaps more remarkable how consistent and similar the eight different wines can be. Kistler Estate Vyd in the mountains east of Sonoma Valley is the most intense, almost strident of the wines, while McCrea Vyd on Sonoma Mtn on the west side of Sonoma Valley is more pliant, with the texture and flavor of a Comice pear. Dutton Ranch, in the southern Russian River AVA is the most tart and slow to evolve, hence the most Burgundian in its homage.   B.C.C.

Knights Valley AVA, obscure appellation in CA's northern SONOMA CO west of Mt St Helena, north of Napa Valley, east of ALEXANDER VALLEY and contiguous with Lake Co. There are 1,000 planted acres, half of which are owned by BERINGER. Its warm, inland climate and fertile, volcanic soils produce vigorous vines much beloved by bankers. Cabernet Sauvignon is the best grape variety so far. Sauvignon Blanc is grown in several vineyards, but none has distinguished itself.

NOTABLE PROPERTIES
Peter Michael, the only winery in the AVA is an 85-acre vineyard owned by a British based computer entrepreneur. While waiting for his own vineyard to mature, Michael purchased Chardonnay grapes on HOWELL MTN in Napa and from the former Gauer Ranch mountainside plantings above Alexander Valley (see KENDALL-JACKSON). Those wines were made each year under the supervision, and definitely in the style, of celebrity CONSULTANT Helen Turley who left after the 1990 vintage. Unctuous, dripping with ripe

fruit and new wood, they created quite a stir among wine buyers more accustomed to underripe European Chardonnay. Recent years have continued the style in a Chardonnay called Mon Plaisir which continues to be sourced from the former Gauer Ranch grapes on a long-term contract. Less successful are the estate-grown Chardonnays called Belle Côte and La Carrière, although the estate red blend called Le Pavots can be rounded and nicely fruity in cool vintages. A Pinot Noir from Monterey is in the works.

B.C.C.

Konzelmann. Fourth generation winemaker/proprietor Herbert Konzelmann moved to ONTARIO from Germany in 1984 to open his family winery on the shores of Lake Ontario. With an annual production of 33,000 cases, Konzelmann is well known mainly for Riesling in a range of styles, plus tropical Chardonnay, fruity Pinot Noir, and lush Vidal ICEWINE.

L.F.B.

kosher wine is made according to prescribed methods especially for use on the Jewish sabbath and holy days. Although there is a long history of commercial *kosher wines in Europe, in early 20th-century North America the only way to obtain kosher wine was to bring a jug to the local synagogue. The influx of Jewish immigrants in the early 1900s spawned several small wine cellars in New York City's Lower East Side, precursors of today's multimillion-case kosher wine industry. Kosher wines were among the first successful American wine exports.

Several religious groups administer differing guidelines for the processing of kosher foods and other products, including wine. Their stamp of approval is either a K or U, the latter denoting the stricter standards of the Orthodox Union of Jewish Congregations. It requires that only observant, orthodox Jews be involved in the winemaking process from the point at which grapes are crushed to when the wine is poured, unless the product is cooked or, in effect, pasteurized, after which it can be handled by non-Jews. All equipment used must be dedicated exclusively to the kosher process or sterilized after any other use, and any ingredients, additives, filter media, etc must also be kosher. Since the crush and winemaking process occur during the late fall, simultaneously with the high holidays, it is difficult and expensive for small wineries to get a representative from their local Rabbinical Council out to oversee the winemaking operations. CRAFTSMAN-SIZED CA kosher wine producers estimate this supervision adds $2 to the cost of a bottle.

The association of kosher with sweet, *foxy Concord wine derives only from the happenstance that Concord grapes were available to New York City immigrant winemakers. Dry vinifera table wines and sparkling wines have since joined the ranks of American kosher wine. Some, such as Napa Valley's Hagafen and Sonoma Co's Gan Eden, are made to a very discerning level of quality, as is the Baron Herzog line produced in Monterey Co as part of the 650,000-case portfolio of the ROYAL KEDEM WINE COMPANY of NY.

R.F.

labrusca or **Vitis labrusca**, native American species of the *Vitis* genus of vines whose grapes, juice, jelly, and wine have a very distinctive flavor commonly called *foxy. Grape leaves are leathery, with a tomentous (hairy) underside. Berries have a slip skin. Concord is the best known labrusca grape.

La Buena Vida Vyds, one of the first wineries of the TEXAS revival. Dr Bobby Smith, a family practitioner, bought 50 acres of old dairy farm in Springtown, 45 mi northwest of Fort Worth in 1972 and planted his first vineyard; 25 acres are now under vine, planted to Chambourcin, Pinot Noir, Pinot Blanc, and Johannisberg Riesling. As a follower of natural gardening guru J. Howard Garrett, Dr Smith has practiced ORGANIC viticulture for the past decade, believing that healthy grapes come from healthy soil. To combat fungus problems he uses a topical spray mixture of baking soda and liquid soap or vegetable oil mixed with water. His son Steve attended UC *Davis, studied winemaking in Bordeaux and Dijon, and is now the winemaker. They sell 90% of the 8,000 cases a year they bottle through their tasting room in GRAPEVINE, including 2,000 cases of Chilean Merlot and Chardonnay they import in bulk containers and bottle under the name La Buena Vida Vyds.

The wines from their TX vineyards are bottled under the **Springtown** label and include Sauvignon Blanc, Muscat Canelli, Johannisberg Riesling, a White Merlot, and a *blush wine called Mist, which is a blend of Zinfandel, Cabernet Sauvignon, Chenin Blanc, and Johannisberg Riesling. They make 'ports' under their Walnut Creek Cellars label. Muscat Dulce is a trademarked name they use for a fortified dessert wine made from Muscat Canelli. It is a heavily perfumed wine with notes of peaches and pears, a big full *mouthfeel, and sufficient acid to avoid being cloying.   L.A.O.

L. A. Cetto, Mexico's largest winery making 1.1 million cases, 70% of which is sold domestically. The remainder is shipped both in bulk and bottle to Europe. The winery owns a bottling facility in Mexico City which is used for bottling fruit juice blended with wine as a 'cooler.' The functional winery in the Valle de Calafia section of VALLE DE GUADALUPE 16 mi east of Ensenada in Baja California is distinguished by its bullring in the vineyards. The vineyard is distinguished for having 50-year-old vines of the La Mura clone of Nebbiolo brought from *Piedmont by L. A. Cetto himself. Later attempts to import Italian cuttings have not yielded the same intensity of flavor. Among the wide range of inexpensive wines on offer, the Nebbiolo and the Petite Sirah stand out. The latter wine is lighter in structure than one might expect, but redolent of beetroot on the nose and long in the finish. The Nebbiolo has huge body, dark color, earthy flavor, and a doughnut structure, ie definite entry and finish, but a hole in the center.
                                          B.C.C.

LaCrosse, white French hybrid not unlike a slightly grapier *Seyval Blanc, from which it was bred by Elmer SWENSON, but with very much better cold resistance.

Lake Co, inland district in CALIFORNIA, immediately east of Mendocino Co, but actually more closely associated historically with Napa Co from which it was geopolitically split before the end of the 19th century. The Pomo Massacre, in which 130 Indians were slaughtered by US Army troops while fishing in Clear Lake, took place here in 1850. The first vineyards were planted in 1857. By 1884 there were 600 acres of grapes in Lake Co. By the early 20th century 36 wineries were in operation and nearly 5,000 acres of grapes had been planted. This wine industry development paralleled the growth of hot springs health spas and bottled mineral waters from the region. But Prohibition and the American Medical Association (which was trying to popularize newly discovered antibiotics) brought it all to an end, in part because Lake Co wineries never developed any brand or regional identity for themselves in the broader marketplace. No wineries and few vineyards survived the 1920s.

Resurgence began in the 1970s when Mendocino's Parducci Winery was sold to the California Teachers' Association (union) pension fund, and John Parducci moved much of his considerable talent and energy across the border to Lake Co. At this same time San Francisco lawyer Jess Jackson (see KENDALL-JACKSON) purchased 600 acres, initially as a holiday retreat, and Orville Magoon began developing his GUENOC property. Today the number of acres of grapes in Lake Co has climbed back to almost 5,000 and ten wineries have opened.

Clear Lake is the largest body of fresh water (Salton Sea is saline) entirely in CA (Tahoe is partially in NV). The social flavor is encapsulated by powerful boat engines throbbing and whining as they pull water skiers and paragliders up and down the lake all summer. Seven miles across at its widest point, the lake is more than 20 mi long. Its watershed occupies half the surface area of Lake Co. It is well respected for bass fishing, and walnut groves occupy dramatic slopes on 4,300 ft Mt Konocti right at the midpoint. Nightlife consists of high stakes bingo at the Indian reservation, dinner buffets at a resort owned by the Plumber's Union of San Francisco, and stock car racing at Lakeport's tight oval on Saturday evenings. Aesthetic attitudes run to cigarette boxes rolled up in men's sleeves, tattoos with military heraldry, and deeply tanned women in tight jeans with bare midriffs. Fifteen years ago, any man drinking wine in this milieu would have been immediately dismissed as a sissy. Today wine-drinking strangers are more likely to be offered sincere recommendations on local winery tasting rooms worth visiting.

Clear Lake AVA surrounds the lake and encompasses most of the watershed draining into it. Almost all the grapes are planted in an area called Big Valley on the southwest side of the lake. Zinfandel does particularly well in the upland hills west of Big Valley's flattest portions, which are really reclaimed marshland. The water level of the lake rises seasonally, so *flooding can be a problem. After the heavy rains of spring 1995, water levels rose nearly 15 ft. The lake moderates temperatures in bottomland vineyards, but overall *degree days in the region are quite high. BUENA VISTA Winery has made a series of Sauvignon Blancs from Lake Co fruit which emphasize the melon-like, fragrant side of the Sauvignon Blanc spectrum. They leave 0.5% residual sugar in those wines to guarantee no one will miss the point. Semillons grown in the district are much more attractive.

Guenoc AVA is outside the Clear Lake AVA and warmer. Benmore Valley AVA is a pointless appellation, just over the county line into Lake from Mendocino, of 170 acres owned by the Trione family who also own GEYSER PEAK winery. The only other grapes in Lake Co are on the northern slopes of Cobb Mountain and Mt St Helena in a band above 1,200 ft in a district settled at the end of the 1800s by Swiss, Austrian, and German immigrants who planted stonefruit orchards. By virtue of their elevation they are 10°F cooler than Clear Lake and Guenoc. They are frost free because of air drainage down the hillsides. Their permeable volcanic TUFA soils are a contrast to the heavier clays found near the lake. The best present example would be 400 acres, including Barbera, owned by Louis MARTINI Winery at 2,000 ft on Big Canyon Rd, not far from the New Age, get-naked-get-spiritual destination resort at Harbin Hot Springs.

NOTABLE PROPERTIES

Wildhurst, winery owned by the Holdenreid family, third generation pear growers from the district. Located south of lake. Best wine has been moderately priced Chardonnay with well-integrated vanilla notes, cunning fruit backdrop, and lots of refreshing acid.

See also STEELE. B.C.C.

Lake Erie AVA, approved in 1983, is a vast multi-state appellation spreading along the southern edge of Lake Erie from Toledo, OH, to Buffalo, NY, and includes the far northwestern tip of PA. The AVA covers 2.2 million acres but currently has about 29,000 acres of vines planted. Just over 60% of the vines are in NY, about 35% in PA, and the balance in OH. The great preponderance of grapes are American hybrids with less than 5% of the total represented by French hybrids and vinifera.

The GREAT LAKES EFFECT applies throughout the AVA with the warmth of summer retained and radiated back by the lake's waters. This allows for a growing season of anywhere from 173 days in western NY to just over 200 days on ISLE ST GEORGE in OH. Conversely, the cool of winter retards budbreak until about early May, neatly avoiding most frost problems. Further, the winds off Lake Erie onto the nearby vineyards keep fungal problems to a minimum. Clearly, this is not a Mediterranean region; hence alcohol is lower and *acidity higher than for wines produced in CA or some other western and northwestern states. P.W.F.

Lake Erie North Shore VA, designated appellation in ONTARIO, Canada, located on the northern shore of Lake Erie in the southwestern part of the province bounded by the counties of Essex, Kent, and Elgin (excepting a portion lying north of the Thames River). It runs west from the town of Amerherstburg to Leamington. Although the region is approximately on the same latitude as northern CA and the *Chianti region of Italy, and it enjoys some moderating effects from Lake Erie during the summer and fall, this shallowest of the Great Lakes freezes over in winter forcing winegrowers to take special precautions to help the vines survive. L.F.B.

Lake Michigan Shore AVA, approved in 1983, is a 1.3 million acre tract of land in southwest MI's Berrien, Van Buren, Allegan, Cass, and Kalamazoo counties. The bulk of the state's grapes are grown in this AVA. It is also a district whose beaches attract a lot of tourists from CHICAGO, many of whom own second homes there. For the most part it is Concord country, but its French hybrids, which represent most of the winegrape acreage, and vinifera varieties, are experiencing a renaissance. The GREAT LAKES EFFECT plays a less dramatic role here than it does in the LEELANAU and OLD MISSION peninsulas to the north, yet still affords a longer growing season than in the center to eastern half of the state. Rot is more of a problem here than in the north, especially for vinifera, but conscientious, undoubtedly dogged, growers find the fight worth the effort. P.W.F.

Lakeview. Ever since 1986 winemaker/founder Eddie Gurinskas has specialized in long, cool fermentations of whites and elongated *maceration of reds at his winery located on the BEAMSVILLE BENCH district in the NIAGARA PENINSULA of Ontario. His wines are recognized for their deep concentration and rich extract. The 11,000-cases production focuses mainly on Cabernet Sauvignon, Chardonnay, Baco Noir, and Vidal ICEWINE. L.F.B.

Lake Wisconsin AVA, appellation approved in 1994 is WISCONSIN's only AVA so far. Located in Dane and Columbia counties in the south-central part of the state, it comprises 28,000 acres of land but has less than 50 acres of vines. The AVA is bounded by the Wisconsin River and the lake that resulted from the latter's damming, Lake Wisconsin. It was Agoston *Haraszthy who in the late 1840s first planted winegrapes in the area before the cold winters drove him to CA. His successors dug out the caves currently employed by the WOLLERSHEIM, the AVA's sole winery. Reposing between 800 and 900 ft elevation, the AVA sports well-drained (air and water) sites for grapes that cannot be found just north or just south on higher or lower land, respectively. Conditions in the AVA keep frost and rainfall to a minimum, while the river and lake help to moderate winters which are often harsh in other parts of the area. P.W.F.

Lamoreaux Landing, in NY's FINGER LAKES district, grew out of one of the area's oldest family grape farms which was for many years a supplier to wineries in NY and other states. Only about a quarter of the 130-acre vineyard on the east side of Seneca Lake feeds the winery, established in 1991. Its all-vinifera vineyard resources and viticultural expertise have helped propel Lamoreaux Landing to prominence among a wave of small wineries springing up around Seneca Lake in the 1990s. A high profile winery structure has also helped. Lamoreaux Riesling and Chardonnay are often among the district's best, and burst into the spotlight when both won top honors in the New World Wine Competition (see LAS VEGAS below) shortly after the winery opened. Riesling is made in various sweetness levels. Both the regular and reserve Chardonnays display plenty of (American) oak influence from barrel fermentation and aging (9 months to more than a year in barrel is high for Finger Lakes Chardonnay). The reserve undergoes full *MLF. Red wines, representing about half of production, have been overshadowed by the whites. Pinot Noir may benefit from more clonal diversity's being introduced in the vineyard. Total production in 1998 stood at half of the long-term plan for 18,000 cases. R.F.

Lancaster Valley AVA, one of three approved appellations in Southeast PENNSYLVANIA. It is a subset of the Susquehannah Valley AVA, along the river of the same name, in the center of the region south of Harrisburg. NISSLEY VYDS near the Susquehannah is located in the Lancaster Valley AVA. R.G.L.

Landot Noir, or Landot 4511, dark-skinned French hybrid named after its early 20th-century creator Pierre Landot.

Las Vegas, the twinkling light of the NEVADA desert, has grown rapidly in recent years to a population of 1 million. It is noteworthy for both the glamour of the new properties being built, with their high-end restaurant trade, and for the fact it is the second largest convention destination in the US. At the Bellaggio Hotel, the sommelier in Julian Serrano's exquisite Picasso restaurant has a difficult time keeping wines priced at four figures in stock. No other restaurant in North America outside of Manhattan can fairly make that claim. But Picasso serves 200 meals a night. The Bellaggio serves 5,000 meals each day.

By comparison, Reno has half the population of Las Vegas, but is more of a resort town, similar to Aspen or Vail, albeit with the biggest bowling alley in America. San Francisco is only 200 mi away from Reno, so overall the area is more wine knowledgeable than Las Vegas. Syndicated wine columnist Jerry Mead (d. 2000) moved to Reno in the early 1990s, taking his annual New World Wine competition with him.   R.T.S.

late harvest, legally undefined term allowed on US labels. It usually implies sweet, dessert-style wines made from grapes left on the vine beyond the normal harvest date. Unfortunately no distinction is drawn between wines made from *botrytized grapes and wines made from merely overripe grapes which may well include *raisins. In the former instance, *noble rot concentrates the grapes' acid as well as the sugar and flavor to produce a *balanced sweet wine. In the later instance, acid levels fall and a flabby, alcoholic wine with carmelized smells may result.

Laurel Glen, inspirational winery in Sonoma Mtn AVA overlooking the town of Glen Ellen in SONOMA VALLEY. Patrick Campbell has a Masters in Philosophy and Religion from Harvard, three grown daughters, and ten years under his belt holding down a union viola chair with the Santa Rosa Symphony. He personally farms 34 acres of hillside Cabernet Sauvignon with the help of one full-time worker. He makes 4,000 cases a year from his own property himself with only the part-time help of Ray Kaufman. He writes regular political action pieces and plays an active role in trade organizations lobbying on behalf of CRAFTSMAN-SIZED family wineries. He manages a large *négociant program importing wine from Chile and making wine from purchased grapes for his lower echelon labels. He exports nearly 20% of his own production. It is a lot of work. To Campbell, who had polio as a child and performs these labors on crutches, it is just a way of life.

Laurel Glen Vyd is on an east-facing slope of the mountain. The vines get full morning sun, but only oblique rays in the afternoon, which gives them a very even ripening day.

Campbell has tried Cabernet Franc, Merlot, Malbec, Petit Verdot, and even Tempranillo in small blocks of his vineyard since first planting in 1972. None of them remain. 'I didn't like them in the blend,' he says. 'I didn't like them because they didn't grow well.' Laurel Glen has thin top soil and needs vigorous vines. Everything is planted on St George rootstock. 'I give other varieties a seven-year trial on about 150 vines,' Campbell explains. If they add a positive dimension to Counterpoint, his second wine, he will consider them for Laurel Glen. If not, 'I give 'em the hook,' he states pragmatically. Laurel Glen's size and Campbell's prestige in the industry make them a prime candidate for CULT WINE status, but Campbell's mild socialist leanings militate against it. He does not believe one should have to pay three figures for good wine. Hence he has resolutely held the line on his own prices. His successful export program has also benefited in Europe from the style of Laurel Glen Cabernet. Campbell's wines are medium bodied, and tightly wound around an acid axle which is higher than most CA Cabs. This structure gives them good bottle ageing potential.   B.C.C.

Lava Cap, fine winery in the Apple Hill district just north of Placerville in CA's EL DORADO AVA. True to its name (the owner is a geologist) the 30-acre vineyard sits at 2,600 ft on extruded volcanic soils loaded with minerals. They produce about 20,000 cases a year. One of their best wines is Petite Sirah. The Muscat Canelli is delicious too, but their most exceptional wine is Zinfandel from the warm vintages. In normal years at this elevation Zinfandels are crisp, Claret-style models with medium to light body and cherry-like fruit. Lava Cap's 1993, however, combined nuances from *all* the great Zinfandels. First it gave peppery spice in the nose wrapped up in boysenberry jam. Then there were layers of quince and sesame. In the mouth the wine was medium bodied, but it took the restraint of the normal El Dorado style and infused it with a smoldering intensity. There was a rich raspberry flavor robe, with just a hint of briar, and no bitterness or astringency in the finish at all. If more Zinfandels came up to this standard, native-born Californians, instead of French waiters, would be the ones with arrogant attitudes.   B.C.C.

LCBO, Liquor Control Board of Ontario. During the decade after the Temperance Act of 1916 was passed it became apparent that Prohibition was causing more problems than it was intended to address in CANADA. Consumption of wine soared, boot-

legging was rampant, and respect for law enforcement was negligible. The quality of products being sold by many newcomers to the industry was not only wretched in taste, from being pressed, stretched, and adulterated, much of it was dangerously unfit for human consumption. It was not unusual to find wine had turned to vinegar, or to discover an unseemly black sludge at the bottom of a bottle, often accompanied by foreign bodies such as spiders or flies. Public antipathy towards Prohibition rose. A new Canadian federal government was formed in response to strong public sentiment in favor of Prohibition's repeal.

Prohibition in the US would not be repealed until 1933. During that time smuggling and underworld production of substandard product would become widespread. By the middle of the 1920s the provincial government in ONTARIO was looking for ways to bring order out of an industry run amok. They explored the feasibility of establishing a system for retail sale of liquor under the exclusive control of the government. On Dec 1, 1926 the conservative leader, Howard Ferguson, went to the people of Ontario with an election platform of repeal and the establishment of government controlled alcohol sales. He won by a large majority in an election difficult to second-guess today. If there had been no Prohibition then, would there be a government controlled system now?

The Liquor Control Act was passed in the spring of 1927. Other provinces soon followed with similar patterns establishing provincial control. By 1933 the LCBO's mandate was expanded to include not only the distribution and sale of beverage alcohol, but what at the time was seen as the regulation of quality as well. In hindsight this attempt seems laughable. The new regulations set standards such as a maximum 250 gal of wine per ton of grapes, where previously as much as 640 gal had been produced per ton. The implicit aim of this regulation was to limit the amount of water that could be added; today, more than 200 gal of wine from a ton of grapes would imply what CA vintners privately call 'the Black Snake treatment.' LCBO's 1933 rules even purported to set standards for cleanliness in winemaking: they fixed the permissible level of *volatile acidity at 4% (about 30 times what European regulations specify today).

As a further maneuver in this perceived drive to improve wine quality, the Dept of Health set up a wine school. It lasted for two years, then interest faded. All products sold through the LCBO had to be tested though. Gradually, as poorer products were refused listings at the provincial liquor stores, the ambitions of many fly-by-night winemakers evaporated. More reputable companies, such as Bright's and Jordan, were encouraged by the government to buy up existing licenses that remained in business in order to own other retail outlets off their main winery premises. The number of wineries was eventually scaled down from an all-time high of 67 at the height of Prohibition, to six. No new licenses to manufacture and sell wine would be granted for the next 47 years.

Since then, LCBO has grown to become the largest single retailer of beverage alcohol in the world. They buy wine, spirits, and beer from more than 60 countries and operate 598 stores across Ontario, offering a range of 5,000 products. They also regulate the sale of products through 428 Brewers Retail stores, 36 on-site brewery stores, 335 winery stores, three distillery stores, and eleven land border-point duty-free stores. They conduct approximately 200,000 tests on 11,000 different alcoholic beverages yearly in a quality assurance program. They employ nearly 5,500 people, and in fiscal 1997–8 paid a C$745 million dividend to the provincial government. Privatization proponents in Ontario have a tough row to hoe.   L.F.B.

Leelanau Peninsula AVA was approved in 1982 as MI's second AVA (after FENN-VILLE). Leelanau AVA comprises just over 200,000 acres of land in the northern part of the state less than 150 mi from the Canadian border. Bounded on the west and north by Lake Michigan, and on the east by Grand Traverse Bay, it currently sports about 200 acres of winegrapes equally split between French hybrids and vinifera. The GREAT LAKES EFFECT plays its most significant role here, and in the OLD MISSION PENINSULA across Grand Traverse Bay. It provides both a late start to a season that would otherwise be frost prone in the spring, and a harvest much later than normal for this 45°N latitude. It also provides 200 in of snow cover annually, insulating the vines and mitigating against vine damage in the winter.   P.W.F.

Lenoir, name used in TEXAS for a hardy, dark-skinned American hybrid known variously as Jacquez, Jacques, and Black Spanish. It was taken from GA to France in the mid-19th century where it was noticeably phylloxera resistant but was finally banned in France in 1934. Its resistance to *Pierce's disease makes it popular in Del Rio, TX. See also FAVORITE.

Lenz, second wine estate to be established on NY's LONG ISLAND, in 1979, known for a cellar in zealous pursuit of a defining Long Island style. Estate vineyards total 70 acres of Bordeaux, Burgundy, and Alsace grape varieties, located at the center of the North Fork vineyard district.

White and red wines are equal players at Lenz. The reserve (Gold Label) Chardonnay sets the house style: French-oak fermented, 100% *MLF, with almost no stirring during lees ageing and no fining or filtration, aiming for a *reductive, even slightly cheesy, complex but still fruit-driven style. Pinot Gris, Pinot Blanc, and Gewürztraminer are experimental releases (there are no unadventurous wines here) and there is a fine, very dry, Pinot Noir dominated Brut sparkler made in cooler years. Cool fermentations are used for red wines as well as whites to amplify fruit character. Lenz Merlot and Cabernet Sauvignon show very soft tannins and reductive, mushroomy notes. Estate bottlings spend a year and a half in barrel and another year bottled before release, emerging with a seductive early maturity. All reds are unfiltered. Total production is about 10,000 cases, mainly distributed on Long Island and in NEW YORK CITY.   R.F.

Leonetti, winery in the WASHINGTON section of the WALLA WALLA AVA begun in 1978 by winemaker-owner Gary Figgins, who has shown consistent ability to produce wonderfully rich and powerful red wines. This track record, combined with limited production, make Leonetti WA's most collectible wine and it commands CULT WINE prices at auction. The Merlot in particular strides between lushness and balanced structure, with layered flavors of ripe berries and oak. Various Cabernet Sauvignons are equally outstanding: some vineyard designated, others appellation specific, with an occasional reserve bottling. Occasionally Figgins produces a Meritage blend called Select Walla Walla Valley Red Table Wine, and in the late 1990s he released a Sangiovese.   R.A.I.

Léon Millot, very early ripening red French hybrid, sibling of *Marechal Foch, particularly useful for regions with short growing seasons such as MINNESOTA or ONTARIO.

Linden Vyds, small but prestigious winery in VIRGINIA in the BLUE RIDGE foothills near Interstate 66 in Fauquier Co. Although Linden was not established until 1985, owner Jim Law had already been apprenticed at VA wineries when he opened his own winery, and from the start, Linden offered stylish, elegant, and polished wines from vinifera and French hybrid grapes. While Seyval Blanc often resembles an unremarkable ersatz Chardonnay, Linden's is skilfully made in a light, crisp, white Bordeaux style. The Riesling/Vidal blend combines the best of both grape varieties in a fruity but balanced wine while Chardonnay tends to richness and weight. Their luscious Late Harvest Vidal brought Jim and Peggy Law their first VA Governor's Cup in 1994 and continues to garner awards.

Linden reds also perform well, and are some of the last to be released on the market by a VA winery, allowing them to develop in the bottle. Following the Bordeaux model, Law likes to blend his red Bordeaux varieties in proportions appropriate to the flavors of the vintage. His Cabernet is mostly a blend of the two Cabernets, but he is one of the few East Coast growers to include Petit Verdot in his blend. In a tasting for *Vineyard & Winery Management* magazine, Law brought barrel samples of his 1996 Cabernet Sauvignon and Petit Verdot, harvested on the same day. The tasting panel was struck by the contrast in styles. The Cabernet was typically lean and closed, while the Petit Verdot was rich, explosive, and lush. 'Petit Verdot provides some fat middle palate concentration. Cabernet Sauvignon provides structure, but lacks some middle palate,' Law explains. Production is 5,500 cases.

R.G.L.

Linganore AVA envelops the Linganore watershed which flows west from a high north–south ridge in the PIEDMONT section of central MARYLAND. Moderate elevation, good air and water drainage, and shaly loam soil make this area favorable for viticulture. The district's three wineries (Elk Run, Lowe, and Linganore) are located north and west of Mt Airy.   R.G.L.

liqueur wine is a legal phrase used in CANADA to describe grape wine with an alcohol content greater than 14.9% but not greater than 20% by volume. No spirit may be added. The designation 'natural' may be applied to the label if any residual sugar results exclusively from the sugar of the grapes.   L.F.B.

Livermore Valley AVA, district east of the hills which bound San Francisco Bay which is technically part of both the Central Coast mega-AVA and the newer San Francisco Bay AVA. Livermore Valley itself is shaped like a 'T' lying on its side with the tail pointing east. The approved Livermore AVA is in the middle where a lagoon would historically have formed before creeks out of the surrounding hills were dammed. Walnut Creek and Danville (where Eugene O'Neill spent his last years) are the north end of the crossbar. Immediately east of them is 3,500 ft Mt Diablo. North of them is CONTRA COSTA Co and the DELTA. Because it is linked by light-rail transit with San Francisco, urbanization is a constant threat to viticulture. A picturesque route west through the hills takes one past Palomares Canyon, where Charlie Chaplin made movies prior to the ascendancy of Hollywood, and where three wineries opened in the 1990s. By far the biggest employer in Livermore is Lawrence Radiation Laboratory, developer of some of the modern era's most fearsome weaponry.

Livermore Valley is separated on its eastern side from the San Joaquin Valley by a line of hills which are breached through the Altamont Pass. Rock music fans of a certain age will recognize Altamont as the place where Hell's Angels snuffed out the spirit of Woodstock at a free Rolling Stones concert by stabbing a man to death in front of the stage. Today the district's otherworldly feel is accentuated by row upon row of Christoesque windmills. As the San Joaquin Valley heats up during the day, a concentrated flow of cooler air is sucked across the Livermore AVA and through this pass, driving the wind farms, a weirdly technical gash set in an otherwise implacably pastoral landscape. Soils in the valley are clay on the hillsides, sand in the former lagoon, and 2 in pebbles strewn along former creekbeds. Most vineyards are on one of the latter two.

The first vines were planted in Livermore in 1844 by an English sailor who gave the place his name. Charles Wetmore, however, thrust the district into the limelight 25 years later and created a Bordelais imprimatur for it (much as Paul Masson created a Burgundian imprimatur for the SANTA CRUZ MTNS), by traveling to Ch d'*Yquem with an introduction from his neighbor Louis Mel, whose wife happened to be a friend of the owner. Wetmore returned with cuttings of Semillon, Sauvignon Blanc, and Muscadelle for his Cresta Blanca Vyd. This coup, and his relentless orations, garnered for Wetmore the position of CA's Viticultural Commissioner. He and Mel planted their cuttings on the gravel benches. The result was a wine which won the Grand Prix (out of 17,000 entries) at the 1889 Paris International Exposition.

James Concannon was able to prosper in the district during Prohibition by carefully cultivating a relationship with Archbishop Alemany of the Catholic Church in San Francisco. But this heritage and the old Semillon vines with which it began must now go to heroic lengths to avoid disappearing under the tracks of the developers' bulldozer. Kalin, Ahlgren, and Rosenblum wineries all make very fine Semillons, well

worth bottle ageing, from Louis Mel's old vineyard, and CA's only response to the classic aged *Hunter Valley Semillons of Australia. Unfortunately selling these wines is difficult in Chardonnay-obsessed America, and Livermore Semillons have an air of nostalgic reliquiae about them. Ruby Hill, the most famous of several late 19th-century Zinfandel vineyards in the district which produced excellent Zinfandels through the 1970s, is a further example. Sold to a computer retailer who wanted to construct a headquarters on the property, the vineyard was grubbed out in 1983. Subsequent financial reversals by Computerland resulted in building plans being scrapped in 1985, but it was too late. The property has since been sold to WENTE and replanted to young vines for white grapes, a pyrrhic victory. At present Wente owns 1,300 of the 1,600 planted acres in the Livermore Valley AVA.

People who looked at Livermore soils in the past and saw only white Graves were too parochial. Stones everywhere, wind, and a warm climate should remind them of Hermitage. By far the best wine Concannon produced during their last fifteen years of independent existence in Livermore was a wonderfully earthy, long-lived Petite Sirah grown right next to the winery. If the Wentes can succeed with their countywide planning strategy to set aside areas reserved for agriculture, the district may rise again as a prestige producer. There is both a past and a future; the only dismal part is the present.

NOTABLE PROPERTIES

Murrieta's Well, owned by Wente, but a separate winery and a stand-alone brand featuring the grapes and property of the old Louis Mel winery, which was called El Mocho. The names are references to a period after the gold rush when a Mexican with predominantly Indian blood named Joaquin Murrieta gained a Robin Hood-like reputation in CA. The creek, flowing into the Livermore lagoon out of a canyon in these southern hills, upon which Wetmore and Mel sited their vineyards, was called Arroyo del Mocho. Murrieta was thought to have used the canyon as a staging area for stolen horses prior to driving them south for sale to the Mexican army. El Mocho was the colloquial nickname of the 'short' Chinese-Indian mestizo who managed Murrieta's affairs in the canyon.

Sergio Traverso, the polo-playing Argentine winemaker at Murrieta's Well, specializes in Bordeaux blends called Vendemia. The red is a perfectly nice wine, but it is the white which distinguishes the winery. *Barrel fermented, figgy flavored Semillon,

blended with a backbone of minerally flavored Sauvignon Blanc makes a wine ideal for matching to root vegetables and Szechuan-style cuisine.

Westover Vyds, winery established in 1984 in the Palomares Canyon by the grandson of a North Coast logging family who a century ago owned the forest which is now the Bohemian Grove in western Sonoma. Westover Vyd is not in the Livermore AVA, it is in the hills west of it. Their broad range of wines are very good quality, and sold primarily CELLAR DOOR at attractive prices through a unique tasting room which features various kid-friendly diversions such as a pillow fight arena.

See WENTE. B.C.C.

Llano Estacado, best known of the TEXAS wineries, located in the TEXAS HIGH PLAINS AVA. The name Llano (pronounced *YAWN oh*) Estacado means 'staked plains' in Spanish. Legend has it that while searching for gold in 1541, explorer Francisco Vázquez de Coronado and his men drove stakes into the ground to mark their way in order to avoid becoming lost in the flat, endless sea of prairie grasses on the Great Plains. However, writings from Coronado's expedition speak of using 'piles of bones and cow dung' as markers rather than stakes. More than likely the name derives from the appearance of the Mescalero Escarpment near present-day Cuero, NM, described by Coronado and other early European explorers as having the appearance of 'palisades, ramparts, or stockades,' thus giving rise to the idea there is a geologic origin to the name.

Building the highways of TX in the 1950s often meant uprooting native grapevines, some of which made their way to Robert Reed's patio in Lubbock. Reed, a Texas Tech Univ horticulturalist, intended to use the cast-off vines as part of his landscaping scheme. As the vines began to produce, Reed's interest turned from landscaping to winemaking. In the early 1970s, Reed joined forces with Dr Clint McPherson, a Texas Tech chemistry professor, to plant an experimental 10-acre plot with over 100 grape varieties. He wanted to find out what would grow best in the sandy loam of the High Plains.

In 1976 the two professors joined forces with a group of investors, which included Jean Dorn and her son-in-law Dick Gill, who were later part of the original group (SGRC: Sanchez, Gill, Richter, and Cordier) that started STE GENEVIEVE winery in partnership with Univ of TX. They founded Llano Estacado Winery as a privately held corporation with the intention of producing the first commercial wines from the area. In 1977 they released their first 1,300 cases, named Cibola Blanca and Cibola Rioja, sourced from growers in the area around Lubbock. Llano's first commercial vinifera vineyards were planted in 1978. Dr McPherson's son Kim, who had studied at UC *Davis and worked at TREFETHEN, came home in 1978 to act as winemaker for the new winery. Kim would leave in the mid-1980s for stints at other TX wineries and eventually become the inaugural winemaker at CAP*ROCK. In 1986 Llano became the first TX winery to win a medal in a national competition, taking a Double Gold at the San Francisco Fair for its 1984 Chardonnay.

In 1985 Walter Haimann, formerly president of Seagram Distillers Company, joined the winery as a sales and marketing consultant. He would eventually buy into the company and take over day-to-day operations in 1990. CA native Greg Bruni, whose family started the San Martin Winery in the SANTA CLARA VALLEY and who had been the winemaker at Arciero, Byington, and Bandiera wineries in CA, came on board in 1993. After a few years at Llano, he became a confirmed believer in the feasibility of making quality wines from the grapes of the High Plains AVA. Though yields are low, averaging less than 2 t/a, what is harvested is of good quality. Dealing with the climate is the toughest part of growing on the High Plains AVA. Helicopters and smudge pots are not adequate for *frost protection because of the incessant dry, cold winds. Llano tries to combat the heat at harvest with night picking and refrigerated transport for bought-in grapes.

Llano currently produces about 80,000 cases annually, making it the second largest winery in TX. Most of the wines are made from the 1,000 acres of vineyard owned by Llano in the High Plains AVA. They also have a long-term contract for grapes grown at Californian Dale Hampton's MENARD VALLEY VYDS in the TX Hill Country. Reflecting the difficulty of growing grapes here, Llano's High Plains vineyards produced only 1,170 tons of grapes in 1998: primarily Zinfandel, Cabernet Sauvignon, Sauvignon Blanc, and Chardonnay.

Chardonnays are barrel fermented and, like Cabernet Sauvignon, Merlot, and Sangiovese, aged in medium *toast French oak. Heavy toast American oak is used for Zinfandel, Nebbiolo, and Signature Red, a proprietary blend of Cabernet Sauvignon with Cabernet Franc and a small amount of Merlot.

Across the board, Llano's wines are well made and show what is considered standard varietal character. There is no 'pretty good wine for something from Texas' about them. Llano's 1996 Texas Zinfandel, from the Mont Sec Vyd in the Guadalupe Mtns which are in the TRANS-PECOS on the border with NM is a big fat Zin with lots of blackberry, chocolate, mint, and a nice spicy finish. The sharp, clean 1997 Signature White, a blend of 60% Sauvignon Blanc, 30% Chenin Blanc and 10% Chardonnay has lots of citrus, melon, and apple character.

TX's first super-premium wine was Llano Estacado's Viviano Noble Cepage Texas 1994, a blend of Cabernet Sauvignon, Merlot, Cabernet Franc, and a little Carignan. It has withstood blind comparison with some of Bordeaux's and California's best.

L.A.O.

Lodi AVA, eastern portion of the DELTA in CA's Central Valley. The whole Delta is climatologically similar, and distinguished from the northern and southern sections of the Central Valley by cooler and more moist air. Lodi is distinguished from the diked islands surrounded by waterways in the western Delta by its sandier, more stable soils. Interstate 5, the major traffic artery running north through the middle of CA from the Mexican border to Vancouver, Canada, marks the dividing line between these two soil profiles, as well as the western boundary of the Lodi AVA. Highway engineers did not want to build on the spongier peat soils that typify the central Delta. Some areas around Lodi have soils infused with round stones the size of a man's fist, reminiscent of the *galets* found in parts of *Châteauneuf-du-Pape. These are 'tailings' washed out of the Sierra Nevada by placer miners between 1850 and 1870. Historically farmers in Lodi eschewed such rocky soil, preferring the easier-to-work Hanford loam. Recently vineyardists, perhaps taking a cue from southern France, are beginning to plant on these rocky sites hoping for the quality that often accompanies vine struggle.

NOTABLE PROPERTIES

Mondavi Woodbridge, production facility responsible for 5.5 million cases in 1998, 80% of which was sourced in the Delta. A refinery appearance masks the expertise this winery contains. Unlike many of his commodity *négociant neighbors, Brad Alderson sees his mission as that of a producing winery, doing vineyard research and working hand in hand with growers to create an artistic product, albeit in vast quantities. Starting in 1999 the 150,000 cases of Woodbridge Zinfandel have carried a Lodi appellation, and a tasting room is being opened in which

to sell items such as an $18 bottle of Woodbridge Zinfandel sourced from their best old vine vineyards. Half the winery's production is currently Chardonnay, but the quality prize really belongs to Sauvignon Blanc. In export markets such as Europe and Canada, Woodbridge Sauvignon Blanc outsells their Chardonnay. It is an excellent value.

See also CANANDAIGUA, DELTA, MONDAVI, SEBASTIANI.   B.C.C.

Long Island, extends 120 mi into the ATLANTIC OCEAN east of NEW YORK CITY and contains a small but dynamic new wine district. The island's East End splits into North and South Forks separated by Peconic Bay. Both forks have vineyards and wineries and approved appellations (North Fork of Long Island AVA and The Hamptons AVA), but the North Fork is the island's principal wine district centered around the town of Cutchogue. There the area's first commercial wine vineyard was planted in 1973. A quarter-century later Long Island has 1,500 acres of vineyard supporting 20 wineries, with both figures steadily growing. Visitation by New York City residents has helped create good marketing opportunities in the metropolitan area for Long Island wineries.

Chardonnay is the most planted variety accounting for two-fifths of total acreage and responsible for launching Long Island's reputation as a quality wine producer. A second wave of planting in the 1990s shifted toward the varieties Merlot and Cabernet Franc, reflecting an affinity felt by island winemakers for the wine culture of Bordeaux and a mentoring relationship between the two regions. Other prominent varieties are Cabernet Sauvignon, Sauvignon Blanc, Gewürztraminer, Riesling, and Pinot Noir.

Long Island's frost free growing season averages 210 days on the North Fork and 190 days on the South Fork, where fog and Atlantic breezes create a cooler mesoclimate. Wines from the North Fork tend to show slightly denser, richer fruit character, but both area's enjoy the insulating effect of surrounding water, minimizing winter injury to vines and *frost damage to crops. Winter low temperatures rarely dip below 5°F. This is the NORTHEAST region's warmest wine district, but not without its hazards. It lies directly in the path of HURRICANES. High humidity and warm nights also put more disease pressure on Long Island vineyards than on inland vineyard districts.

Sandy loam soils predominate, typically well drained but low in pH, requiring a regimen of lime application to grow vinifera grapes. Low fertility with little organic matter produce modest crop yields of 2.5–4 t/a.

Hargrave Vyds, the pioneer with the region's first vineyard planted in an erstwhile potato farm in 1973. Early vintages probed uncharted territory. Chardonnay and Sauvignon Blanc were successes and have remained the winery's most consistently stylish wines, the latter now a barrel fermented Blanc Fumé. Reds have been more variable, but Hargrave Cabernet Franc and Merlot are often among NY's best, displaying a particular attention to acid structure and ageing ability. More than any of the area's other wineries, Hargrave also pursues the holy grail of Pinot Noir, albeit in very limited production, with a selection of ENTAV CLONES added to the 84-acre estate. Annual production is 8,000 cases.

Pindar Vyds, largest producer on the island and one of the oldest, established in 1979. Estate acres number 300 on the North Fork, producing fifteen varieties for the winery's 60,000-case output which is supplemented by sources outside the area. The range includes sweet generic blends and a much praised red meritage called Mythology, as well as sparkling wine, port, and icewine. Pindar prides itself on leaving no palate unpleased. Aggressive marketing has propelled Pindar into the broadest regional distribution of any Long Island label. **Duck Walk** is a satellite operation on the island's South Fork.

Sagpond Vyds, one of the few wineries located in the trendy Hamptons AVA. From the first vintage in 1992, Chardonnay has excelled, with brighter fruit character than is typical of wines from the neighboring North Fork. The house style plays leesy, barrel fermented textures against lively acidity. Sagpond's stylish Merlots show a similarly leaner, brighter profile than North Fork competitors. Labels use the **Wolffer** brand name after the winery's owner. Production is 10,000 cases.   R.F.

See BEDELL, GRISTINA, LENZ, MACARI, PELLIGRINI.

long pruning, a technique that involves leaving portions of cane on the vine until buds start to burst in the spring, then pruning those portions away to shock the vine into another 2–3 weeks of *dormancy in an attempt to avoid spring frost damage.

Loramie Creek AVA, an OHIO appellation approved in 1982. Located entirely within Shelby county in the west central part of the state between Lima and Dayton, it encompasses 3,600 acres of land but today sports no operating wineries. When the AVA was approved, it had two wineries with less than 20 acres of vines.   P.W.F.

Los Angeles, for all intents and purposes a single megalopolis covering the entire region which runs more than 100 mi down the southern CALIFORNIA coast from the Santa Ynez Mtns in Santa Barbara Co to the Mexican border south of San Diego. Taken as one market it would have more than 20 million people, but marketing executives usually think of it as five separate districts because travel between them is so difficult on the clogged freeways: San Diego; the Inland Empire, from Riverside to Palm Springs; Orange Co; Los Angeles, from Pasadena to Santa Monica; and the Valley, meaning San Fernando Valley and implying business north through Ventura.

The region is arid, receiving 12–18 in of rain a year, but almost all of it in Jan and Feb. Hence it never had the indigenous hunter-gatherer population of northern CA, and almost all the development has come with interwoven political implications. European settlement began with the era of the Californios at missions in San Fernando Valley and San Diego. Secular winegrowing commenced in 1832 when an appropriately named *Graves native (Jean Louis Vignes) left his wife and children at age 47 to sail around the Horn. A cooper by trade, he arranged for the importation of French vine varieties which he used to replace wild *Vitis californica* vines he found growing along the Los Angeles River. That location was within sight of the Spanish Presidio, which became the city center, and it is today a couple of blocks from the architecturally triumphant Union Train Station. To put LA development in perspective, note that Vignes sold his 100-acre vineyard to his nephews in 1855 for $42,000, the biggest commercial transaction southern California had yet seen. At the same time millions of dollars, much of it extracted from northern mines, was being spent on vineyards and other forms of real estate in the San Francisco BAY AREA.

Population growth in the Los Angeles Basin did not become extreme until the 1920s when real estate speculators brought water by pipeline from the Owens Valley on the eastern slope of the Sierra Nevada, and a combination of defense industry jobs and Hollywood entertainment industry glamour created a magnet for Americans throughout the Midwest. By this time the wine industry in Los Angeles had already gone through a boom and a bust. *Pierce's disease destroyed most of the vines planted in the 1860s along the Santa Ana River which had grown into a large industry in the late 19th century as European vineyards were devastated by *phylloxera.

Unlike other parts of the US though, Prohibition did not finish the job Pierce's started. There was much more than a remnant wine industry left baking under the unrelenting southern CA sun in a district called Cucamonga near present-day Pomona. The district gets about 4,500 *degree days annually. Grapes had been grown there since the Spanish Land Grant property had passed into the hands of Tiburcio Tapia in 1839. A facility on his property was approved by the US government as Bonded Winery #1 under the name Thomas Winery (now J. Filippi). They proceeded to produce millions of gallons of sweet, tasteless, fortified headbuster annually through the 1950s. Their big competitor was the Guasti Winery which had 4,000 acres in 1917. In all, Cucamonga had 20,000 producing acres throughout Prohibition, twice the amount of Napa Valley. The downfall of Cucamonga and San Bernardino was a simple matter of poor quality and rising land prices versus grapes grown in the Central Valley.

The northern edge of the LA megalopolis is a remarkably fertile agricultural region formed by the confluence of the Ventura and the Santa Clara rivers flowing out of the mountains which make up Sespe Condor Refuge. Historically, this district produced a large portion of the vegetables which fed Los Angeles. It still produces a huge citrus crop, but much of the land, especially along the coast, is now succumbing to the ravages of housing development and strip shopping malls. There are no approved sub-AVAs in the Ventura or Santa Clara River watersheds. Technically the district is just another part of the Central Coast mega-AVA. There are not many vineyard acres, but there are several wineries. Old Creek Ranch near Ojai makes a sensuous Merlot with pillowy texture and plummy fruit. Further south there is an approved district level AVA called **Malibu-Newton Canyon** which illustrates how different mesoclimates can be in this region. Rosenthal, the AVA's only vineyard and winery, is 500 ft above the chic oceanfront homes of tv producers and rock stars at Hwy 1 along Malibu beach. Numerous creeks drain these friable seabed soils in deeply eroded east–west running canyons which end right at the shore. There is very little coastal plain. Rosenthal Vyd grows Cabernet Sauvignon which makes a tannic, somewhat abrasive young wine.

The LA Basin itself has warehouse wineries, but not much left in terms of visible vineyards. Cucamonga claimed 16,000 acres in 1960; 2,000 in 1980; and 1,000 in 1990. A casual search for any of these acres in 1992 revealed not one, although BATF did grant

Cucamonga Valley an approved AVA in 1995. More interesting by far are a couple of tiny, hobbyist-sized plantings in the San Gabriel Mtns which rise behind Pasadena. Rhône varieties were planted there in the mid-1990s.

Retail wine sales in Los Angeles range from highly sophisticated specialty stores in the wealthy districts west of the city center to vast stretches of less affluent residential neighborhoods with few wine outlets other than chain grocery stores. Some of the best wine retailers in the Los Angeles market are upscale independent gourmet grocery stores.

NOTABLE PROPERTIES

Ojai Vyd, winery owned by former AU BON CLIMAT partner Adam Tolmach on a family estate in the Ventura River watershed. Only about 5,000 cases are made annually, but the quality has always been very good and on occasion it has been brilliant. Unfortunately Pierce's disease has decimated the estate vineyard and it may not be replanted. Nevertheless Tolmach is a supremely competent judge of vineyards who will surely source fine grapes elsewhere. Chardonnays from various designated sources have shown a deft hand with oak, making them adroit companions for most food courses. Another fine offering has been Viogner with a delicate, blossom-like fragrance, no phenolic cling, a long finish, and just a bare hint of wood complexity. No one would ever call Tolmach 'flash.' What he does have is a truly gifted palate.

Moraga, 7-acre steeply terraced backyard vineyard in Bel Air looking west across the Interstate 405 freeway at Gehry's new Getty Museum and Art Restoration Campus. Owner Tom Jones is a retired engineer, who also happened to be CEO of Northrup Aviation and largely responsible for America's Stealth Bomber. The vineyard is in a district where $3 million homes sit on quarter-acre lots. Jones lobbied the city to get his parcel rezoned as an agricultural trust, so that it could not be subdivided for residences after his death. That environmentally motivated maneuver decreased the value of his property by eight figures. He does not care. He feels an obligation to preserve this estate in its entirety, having bought it in 1959 from Victor Flemming, producer of *Gone with the Wind* and *The Wizard of Oz*.

In 1978 Jones began planting the shale hillside above his house quite densely, 1,600 vines to the acre, with a mix of 80% Cabernet Sauvignon, 15% Cabernet Franc, and 5% Merlot. Tony Soter of ETUDE was hired as the winemaking CONSULTANT. The wines are physically made at SANFORD in Santa Barbara Co under Jones' and Soter's close supervision. Less than 1,000 cases are made. It is expensive but barrels are rigorously selected. This CULT WINE is medium bodied and sinewy, but is strongly flavored and possesses an earthy-tobacco bouquet. Wood notes are clear, but not dominant, and tending toward cedar. Everything is sold to a waiting list.

San Antonio, 1,500,000-case winery located in the barrio about a mile and a half from downtown Los Angeles. A deli-style restaurant in the winery does many hundreds of sandwiches on Friday afternoons. Grapes come from all over the state including owned property in Monterey and Napa. Most of the volume is sold in private labels bottled for restaurants. Top of the range is a brand called Maddelena. It represents extraordinary value, particularly the clean, flavorful, well-balanced Chardonnay.   B.C.C.

Louisiana, westernmost state in the SOUTH region encompassing NEW ORLEANS and the mouth of the MISSISSIPPI RIVER. Louisiana has one approved appellation, the MISSISSIPPI DELTA AVA, and four wineries: Casa de Sue in the Delta AVA; Feliciana; Hungarian Harvest; and Pontchartrain Vyd. Total annual wine production in LA is 20,000 gal.

LA State Univ's Agricultural Station in Hammond contributes to Southern viticultural research. They report their French hybrid seedling known as Q21B#17 is very resistant to *Pierce's disease and anthracnose, yields well, and produces good red wine.

Of LA's 64 parishes (counties elsewhere in the US), roughly one-third (20) have some form of restrictions on the sale of alcohol. As elsewhere, the situation is confused by some wards within a parish having restrictions while others do not. Aside from being totally DRY, jurisdictions may allow only the sale of beer, for example. Native wineries may sell on both wholesale and retail levels.

          R.G.L.

Loyalist, phrase used in CANADA to indicate both a period in history and a form of political patronage. From the late 1700s until about 1815 (following the War of 1812 with the US) it was common for the British government to give land in exchange for services. These Crown Grants would have been similar in concept, albeit much smaller in size, to the Spanish land grants of the same period in CA.

Lynfred, winery in Roselle, IL, almost an hour's drive west of CHICAGO. It has no vineyards, yet founder Fred Koehler manages to turn out often spectacular wines from grapes he has purchased from MI, WA, CA, and elsewhere in his 20-year dance with wine. He had learned his craft and was making acceptable fruit, hybrid, and vinifera wines when one day he struck gold. In 1985 his 1983 Chardonnay made from grapes grown in the Pope Valley district of NAPA VALLEY AVA took top honors at the New World Wine competition in Reno, NV. Today, he continues to prove that award was no fluke as he turns out very passable wines from all the sources he used before.

          P.W.F.

Macari Vyds, major estate appearing in the surge of growth experienced by NY's LONG ISLAND wine district during the 1990s. Planting began in 1994 on the northern edge of the island's North Fork, backing up a slight south-facing rise to bluffs along Long Island Sound. Acreage in 1998 stood at 140, headed toward 200. Principal varieties are Chardonnay, Sauvignon Blanc, Merlot, and Cabernet Franc. The tightly spaced vineyard follows practices of *organic viticulture including an ambitious on-farm composting operation, a sensible response to sandy soils very low in organic matter. Macari's early Chardonnays showed impressive style and complexity for such young vines.   R.F.

Magnotta, one of the few wineries in ONTARIO to sell predominantly through their own outlets rather than through the LCBO. The Magnotta line is based on both NIAGARA PENINSULA vineyards and imported wines blended and bottled in Ontario. Magnotta was the first to produce a sparkling ICEWINE, although that term and Magnotta's relationship to VQA is a matter of some legal contention.   L.F.B.

Malivoire. Special-effects film producer Martin Malivoire and his partner Moira Saganski opened their BEAMSVILLE BENCH winery in 1999 dedicated entirely to ultra premium wines, most notably Gewürztraminer, Pinot Noir, Pinot Gris, and Chardonnay.   L.F.B.

Manischewitz, one of the leading American brands of KOSHER WINE, made from Concord grapes. The wine's beginnings can be traced back to Prohibition, when Jewish synagogues could legally sell kosher wine. Leo Star, the son of a Polish cantor, began supplying synagogues with sweet Concord wine he bottled on New York City's Lower East Side. After Repeal the wine turned up on store shelves and sales took off. Star contracted with a well-known kosher food company to put the name Manischewitz on the label, although it turned out many of his customers were not Jewish and often asked store clerks for 'Massachusetts wine.' A new winery in Brooklyn in 1938 accommodated

production that had increased to 3 million gal by 1970, including drier table and sparkling wines added in the 1960s. CANANDAIGUA acquired Manischewitz in 1986 and moved production to Naples, NY. The product line was pruned back to a dozen traditional, sweet, Concord-based wines. Annual production totals 1 million cases.   R.F.

Marcassin, the supreme CA CULT WINE. Made by mega CONSULTANT Helen Turley for a 1,200-cases label she owns with her husband John Wetlaufer. They also own 5 acres each of Pinot Noir and Chardonnay on the Sonoma Coast near the old Russian fur station at Ft Ross. Chardonnays are worth their weight in gold, and taste like the concentrated essence of butterscotch, pear liqueur, and honey. They are a ripe, very obviously unfiltered, mouthfilling, sensory overload which sticks to the back of your palate for days, and to your credit card statement for months.   B.C.C.

Markko Vyds, in the far eastern section of the LAKE ERIE AVA in OH, was established by Arnulf (Arnie) Esterer in 1968. This all-vinifera winery takes the tried and true approach to their Cabernets, Chardonnays, Pinots, and Rieslings: low yields, minimal handling, and ample bottle ageing before release. These are not flashy wines. They get lost in the fruity crowd. They are, however, complex, integrated, lingering wines made by people who love what they do and enjoy talking with people about their wines.   P.W.F.

mark-up, the amount a price is raised over purchase cost to cover expenses and profit. Similar to profit **margin,** but calculated differently. If a bottle of wine costs a retail store $10, and they sell it for $15, the profit margin is 33% ($5 profit divided by $15 sale price), but the mark-up is 50% ($5 profit divided by $10 cost of goods).

Martinelli, old-time grape growers from the western reaches of the RUSSIAN RIVER AVA. In fact every third mailbox on Martinelli Rd seems to belong to a member of this extended family of blue-eyed, dark-haired Italians. Their best-known vineyard is called

Jackass Hill, and it is instantly recognizable to anyone driving along the canyon where it is located because it is one of the steepest vineyards in CA, with some of the oldest vines on it. The name derives from the tale that only 85-year-old Leno Martinelli was 'jackass enough' to drive a tractor up that slope to cultivate each year. Zinfandel from that property is majestic. It is made in the traditional style with well over 15% alcohol, deep purple color, aroma like boysenberry brandy, and a jammy/tarry finish. It is a wine normally served after women and children have left the table.   B.C.C.

Martini, Louis, third generation winery symbolizing CA's NAPA VALLEY in the middle of the 20th century before tuxedo marketing overtook the valley in the late 1970s. Louis M. Martini moved his family to St Helena from the Central Valley right after Prohibition. His son Louis P. Martini was an industry and community leader until his death in the mid-1990s. Granddaughter Carolyn has run the winery for the last 20 years and grandson Michael is the winemaker. They currently produce 200,000 cases a year and maintain the same high traffic tasting room they always have on Hwy 29.

The Martini's operation's most valuable asset is a collection of often high quality vineyards amounting to 550 total acres. The best known is Monte Rosso 1,000 ft high in the eastern mountains above SONOMA VALLEY. Equally wonderful grapes come from Los Vinedos del Rio in the RUSSIAN RIVER AVA, source of Martini's best wine Reserve Merlot. Varietally labeled Merlot was inaugurated in CA by Martini in 1970. Over a quarter-century the styles have fluctuated a little, but a track record for fine ageing potential has been established. Their Merlots from the 1990s have been particularly choice with a middleweight structure, plumskin flavor, and deeply commingled wood/fruit smells.   B.C.C.

Maryland, state ranked fourth in MID-ATLANTIC wine production, with 32,000 gal produced in 1997. MD has three AVAs: CATOCTIN and LINGANORE in the Blue Ridge foothills of central MD and CUMBERLAND

VALLEY west of Frederick. The state's geography ranges from the APPALACHIAN MTNS in the western panhandle to the PIEDMONT of central MD, to the Eastern Shore of the CHESAPEAKE BAY. French hybrids and vinifera varieties are cultivated in MD with Chardonnay the most widely planted vinifera variety, followed by Cabernet Sauvignon and Riesling. Seyval, Vidal, and Chambourcin are the most common hybrids. Chambourcin and Cabernet Sauvignon show particular promise for reds.

With its German heritage, MD is better known for beer than wine. However, MD has played a major role in the revival of the Eastern wine industry. Philip *Wagner introduced French hybrids to the East at BOORDY VYDS in the 1930s and 1940s, whence they were introduced throughout the East. Hamilton Mowbray pioneered vinifera plantings in the Mid-Atlantic at Montbray Vyds in the 1960s. Unfortunately, there is no state funding for research and marketing of MD wine, and the MD Alcohol Control Board, in its zeal to crack down on illegal DIRECT SHIPMENT of wine in 1997, prohibited state wineries from even shipping samples to regional wine competitions that year. The famous wine critic and Maryland resident Robert *Parker was also required to visit the state capitol to prove his wine expertise in order to receive wine shipments to his home. The MD wine industry does not have a strongly supportive native consumer base, as its neighbor VA does. Nor does MD have a concentration of wineries near high volume tourist attractions. However, the quality potential for MD wine is impressive, and the wines of Boordy, Elk Run, and Fiore Vyds bear witness to this fact. If the state government were more supportive, the quality and recognition of MD wines could be significantly advanced.

MARKETPLACE

The majority of native winery sales occur CELLAR DOOR or at state wine festivals. MD has three major festivals: Wine in the Woods takes place in mid-May in Columbia; Chesapeake Celebration of Wine & Beer is in Middle River in Sept; and so is the MD Wine Festival in Westminster. The spring wine festival draws 15,000 people, and the fall events often get 20,000 combined.

Boordy Vyds is the second biggest winery in the state at 10,000 cases. Approximately 60% of Boordy's revenue is in direct sales, representing approximately 40% of inventory sold. They have even sold some wine futures. The remainder is in wholesale distribution, with the ratios for revenue and inventory reversed. The wholesale sector grew by 16% in 1998 for all MD wines sold in the state. Boordy's restaurant sales have grown across the board, from mid-priced tourist menus to the finest restaurants. A very small amount of MD wine is sold outside the state, mostly in Washington DC.

NOTABLE PROPERTIES

Elk Run, winery in the Linganore AVA which has made a name for itself with vinifera wines, garnering several awards for Riesling, including an icewine-styled Vin de Jus Glacé. Other wines include dry Riesling, Chardonnay, and Cabernet Sauvignon. Production is 3,500 cases.

Fiore, winery located in northeast MD on the Mason-Dixon Wine Trail shared with wineries in neighboring PA. Proprietor Michael Fiore has been making wine in MD for many years. He is particularly adept at, and enthusiastic about, Chambourcin with which he has won the MD Governor's Cup. The 1995 Fiore Chambourcin was fermented with Barbaresco yeast, yielding an impressively northern Italian style. Total production is 6,000 cases.

Linganore Cellars and *Berrywine Plantation*, MD's largest winery, founded and run by the Aellen family. The first vines were planted in 1972 and the winery was established in 1976. As the names imply, a wide range of *fruit wines is made, as well as dry to sweet French hybrids and a Cabernet Sauvignon. Over 30 labels are produced with an annual production of 50,000 cases. Expanded in 1999, the winery has the capacity to produce 200,000 cases. The fruit wines are clean and fresh and a dry, barrel aged blueberry is particularly interesting. Linganore's strongest offerings among table wines are a full-bodied Chambourcin with smooth fruit, and a lighter oak aged Cabernet Sauvignon with mild tannins and good varietal character. See BOORDY VYDS.   R.G.L.

Marynissen. Veteran grape grower John Marynissen established his NIAGARA PENINSULA winery in Niagara-on-the-Lake in 1990. He is one of the pioneers in growing vinifera varieties in Canada, and has the oldest Cabernet Sauvignon vines in ONTARIO. He and his daughter also make robust, ripe Merlot and Cabernet Franc. He has two vineyards: 27 acres on sandy clay loan; and 42 acres on stony gravel. In each he achieves ripe fruit in a mesoclimate protected by the Niagara river and the influence of nearby Lake Ontario.   L.F.B.

Matanzas Creek, one of the best wineries in CA, located in Bennett Valley, a subsection of the SONOMA VALLEY AVA. The remarkable wrinkle about the winery's consistent quality since 1977 is the way owner Sandra MacIver seems to change winemakers on a four- or five-year cycle and yet never misses a beat. She started with Merry Edwards (author of the Winemaking essay, p 35), a crackerjack technician who isolated the strain of lactic bacteria today widely used in CA to force low pH wines through *MLF out of the old concrete floor in the milking barn they were using as the winery then. It is called the MCW (Matanzas Creek Winery) strain. Edwards won the Sweepstakes Award at the San Francisco Fair twice in a row for Matanzas Creek Chardonnay. This accomplishment generated extraordinary publicity, in no small part because Edwards was followed by a documentary film crew from the local PBS station throughout the entire week of the second competition. When her wine won the Sweepstakes Award, the excited cameraman lost his ability to hold the camera steady.

Success notwithstanding, MacIver decided to make a change, and brought in the then unknown Dave Ramey to replace Edwards. He maintained the very high quality of the Chardonnay and moved the winery's Merlot into the top ranks as well. Then he was replaced, moving on to Chalk Hill, then a year at Dominus. Susan Reed and Bill Parker currently occupy the winemaking job. Throughout these transitions the quality of the wine has remained superb. There are even two special bottlings made in good years from a rigorous barrel selection called Journey, both a Merlot and a Chardonnay, selling for $125–150 a bottle. Standard Matanzas Creek Chardonnay is good value, always cunningly wooded, with apple crisp aroma and smooth texture, but none of the puppy dog sloppiness that attends big-bodied CA Chardonnay. Matanzas Creek Chardonnays are focused in the mid-palate and slowly yielding in the finish, every year. The winery is engaging to visit. They farm lavender, and have wonderful large sculptures placed around the property. In 2000, the winery was sold to Jess Jackson. B.C.C.

Mawby Vyds, L. in MI is owned and operated by the eponymous Larry Mawby, one of the wine industry's true characters in the most positive sense. He planted his first vineyard on LEELANAU PENINSULA in 1973 and made his first wine five years later. He utilizes both vinifera and French hybrids from 12 acres under vine in 1999 and plans six more. Production is 2,000 cases annually. His MÉTHODE CHAMPENOISE sparkling wines, especially the Talisman, are solid.

His Reserve Vignoles is a weird cross between a crisp German-style Riesling and a barrel aged Chardonnay.   P.W.F.

Mayacamas, winery in the MT VEEDER AVA west of NAPA VALLEY which helped launch the CRAFTSMAN-SIZED winery movement in CA. Highly regarded in the 1970s for its limited volume, blockbuster-style mountain Cabernets, the winery has been bypassed in the last decade by more finely tuned styles of wine. This diminished current role in no way compromises the crucial contribution Mayacamas made to the CA industry by inspiring an entire generation of artisan winemakers, and in several instances supplying them with their original Cabernet vine cuttings.

The stone winery was originally built at the top of Lokoya Rd in 1889 at about 1,600 ft of elevation. It was resurrected in 1941 by Jack and Mary Taylor, then sold in 1968 to Bob Travers. Commentators such as *Wine Spectator* columnist Jim Laube rank Mayacamas Cabernet in the top vintages of the 1970s as 'among the best from CA.' Everyone assumed their uncompromisingly tannic style would age very well. It did not. At fifteen years the wines were as dry and dusty as an attic bookshelf. No trace of fruit remained, but the bitter residue of their phenolic youth was clearly present. Those wines were made in a labor-intensive manner using equipment which would be deemed primitive today. Current releases are too. As admirable as the physical effort and the lifestyle may be, it has taken on a Calvinist stubbornness which is reflected in the narrowness of the wines.   B.C.C.

meets and bounds, surveyors' technique for narratively describing an enclosed geographic area by sequentially connecting boundary points around the perimeter which may be found on a prescribed map. It is the technique demanded by BATF of petitioners for AVA approval in the US. Boundaries may follow roads, or streams, or contour lines. They may also proceed in straight lines drawn between two points, such as the summits of two peaks. If one is able to obtain a copy of the prescribed map(s), narratively described topographic features are relatively easy to identify. The difficulty for laymen in this process occurs when a boundary point is defined in whole or part by an artificial surveyors' grid which divides the map into numbered 'Sections' using axes of township and range. For this reason the precise boundaries of many AVAs are complete mysteries to all but professional cartographers in the US.   B.C.C.

Melody, relatively recent hybrid developed from *Seyval Blanc at GENEVA and now grown in MISSOURI.

Menard Valley Vyds, planned as a large, high quality commercial vineyard beginning in 1995 by CA grape grower Dale Hampton on 891 acres near Menard, in the far northwestern edge of the TEXAS HILL COUNTRY AVA. The vineyard is managed by Jim Collins, who had worked with Hampton in CA. As all the Californians working in the TX wine industry have come to realize, it is a different ballgame in TX. Expecting to find wineries willing to commit to long-term contracts with a reputable grower, Hampton discovered to his chagrin that in TX wineries want to wait until their own harvests come in, then buy what they need from an outside source. Only LLANO ESTACADO would step up to the plate with a twelve-year commitment. At this time only 216 acres have been planted, with the entire production destined for Llano.

A third of the vineyard is planted to Cabernet Sauvignon, a quarter to Chardonnay, another quarter to Zinfandel and Merlot, with the rest planted to Sauvignon Blanc, Chenin Blanc, Gewurztraminer, Johannisberg Riesling, Syrah, and Pinot Noir. *Mechanical harvesting is used throughout, and all grapes are sent to Llano's facility near Lubbock in refrigerated trucks for crushing and fermenting. Vines are planted on a three-wire vertical trellis with 6 × 10 ft spacing. Soils are sandy loam to clay loam on an elevated river bench sloping down to a riverbed. High acidity in the soil keeps COTTON ROOT ROT away while the semi-arid climate holds fungal problems to a minimum. Water for irrigation comes from the nearby San Saba River and from a well on the property. Overhead sprinklers are in use now and drip irrigation will be added over the next few years, although the sprinklers will be retained to combat spring *frost. Collins is also prepared to call in helicopters in case of a hard frost. Unlike many vineyards in Hill Country, Menard Valley had not been affected by *Pierce's disease by 1999. As a precaution against insects carrying Pierce's bacteria, and to keep the abundant deer population out, the entire vineyard is fenced with a clear-cut area 300 ft from the vines to the fence.   L.A.O.

Mendocino, county and approved AVA north of Sonoma on the CALIFORNIA coast approximately 125 mi north of San Francisco. Pounding ocean combers staging a timeless battle with 300 ft cliffs up and down Mendocino's fog-shrouded coastline have long attracted artists. Writers and folks

for whom even San Francisco may not be tolerant enough routinely seek refuge on this soulful coast. But wine tourists understandably find it difficult to ignore the more convenient blandishments of Sonoma and Napa in favor of a forced march into Mendocino. Nor are most wine writers immune to the easier distractions, which is one very good reason wines from Mendocino command significantly less money than do their closer-in cousins. Nobody commutes to work in San Francisco from Mendocino Co. The cost of land in Mendocino Co is approximately one-fifth of the cost of similar land in Napa Valley. Vintners and growers in Mendocino do not enjoy the sales and marketing exposure in the urbanized BAY AREA that Napa and Sonoma do, but neither do they have to surmount the massive financial barrier to entry posed by land prices.

HISTORY
The economy of Mendocino traditionally relied on timber. Russian seal and otter hunters established semi-permanent encampments along this coast during the 18th century, but once they had depleted their seaborne resource, they moved on. The *gold rush created demand for lumber. One of the two or three oldest living things on earth is the redwood tree. Displayed in several North Coast parks are cross-sections with growth rings marked halfway to the center of the tree with a tag saying 'Birth of Christ.' Lumber companies were the largest employers in Mendocino Co until the early 1980s. Then the County Agricultural Commissioner began reporting (unofficially) that high grade Sensimilla (seedless marijuana) had replaced lumber as the most valuable crop.

There had been 5,800 acres of bearing grapes in 1910, and nine wineries producing a total of 90,000 gal annually. Almost all of those wineries disappeared during Prohibition. In 1967 PARDUCCI was the only winery operating in Mendocino Co. FETZER was bonded the following year. At that time the county had less than 3,000 acres of grapes, most going into bulk wine. Twice as many acres were planted to red varieties as to whites. Thirty years later the plantings have quintupled to more than 15,000 acres and the ratio has reversed to twice as many acres in white varieties as there are in reds. In fact, there are more acres of Chardonnay alone than there were total acres of all grapes in 1967.

CLIMATE AND TOPOGRAPHY
Mendocino is the northernmost important grape growing region in CA. Arguable

159

exceptions to that qualified claim include a pretty good winery outside Eureka in Humboldt Co called Fieldbrook, but they get the grapes for their best wines in Mendocino. There is also a tiny, interesting operation 2,700 ft high in the Trinity Alps called Alpen Cellars growing 15 acres of cool climate grapes and making 2,000 cases a year. Two approved AVAs do exist north of Mendocino, but they are both ridiculous. There are many more fly fishermen than vines in either AVA. **Willow Creek** is lost in the mountain wilderness near the juncture of Trinity and Humboldt counties along the Trinity River. Technically the most northerly grapes in CA are 2 acres in Siskiyou Co on the Klamath River east of Happy Camp at 1,700 ft. That official AVA is called **Seiad Valley**, but the vineyard is functionally abandoned. It is a safe bet no BATF official has ever laid eyes on either of the aforementioned AVAs.

As with many counties along CA's Pacific shore (see SAN LUIS OBISPO), Mendocino Co sports two extremely different grape growing conditions depending on which side of the coastal ridge a vineyard may be located. Mendocino is one of the largest counties in CA. The Mendocino AVA is confined to the southern third of the county, yet it still comprises 430 sq mi. Because it encompasses both the ANDERSON VALLEY on the west, or ocean, side of the coastal ridge, and the extremely different Potter Valley, Redwood Valley, and McDowell Valley areas strung out from north to south along the Russian River on the east, or inland, side of the coastal ridge, the Mendocino AVA is not of any great usefulness to consumers when cited on a label. The entire Mendocino Co is included in the approved appellation North Coast AVA.

On the inland side of the coastal ridge, Hwy 101 runs up the Russian River north out of Cloverdale in northern Sonoma Co. Here the river forms a rocky gorge which distinguishes the districts of eastern Mendocino from Sonoma Co's ALEXANDER VALLEY. The first town encountered is **Hopland**. By then drivers will have passed 5 mi of lush vineyards running from the hills on the west to their irrigation source at the river. Hopland is the centerpiece of Fetzer's empire. It sits in the middle of a broad expanse where the mountains widen to form a fertile valley with deep alluvial soils. Properly the district is called Sanel Valley, although no one has applied for AVA status. A right turn in Hopland on Hwy 175 toward Clear Lake takes one in about 4 mi to the McDowell Valley AVA, a pocket-sized district nestled into the hills. Rhône varieties grown there do exceptionally well.

Further north along Hwy 101 and the south-flowing Russian River, the mountains pinch more narrowly, then widen again into a much bigger expanse surrounding the city of **Ukiah**. This is the agricultural center of Mendocino Co. Like Hopland, it is quite warm. Although it receives 12 in more rain a year than does St Helena in the Napa Valley, it is in the rain shadow of the coastal mountains and thus somewhat protected from the path of storms. The Ukiah Valley has many pear orchards and has long produced hearty red wines bound for Italian family-style restaurants. Again, no one has applied for AVA status. The noteworthy topographical feature of the Ukiah Valley is a series of high benches 200 ft above the river on the eastern side. These well-drained sites grow outstanding Zinfandel and feature a number of individual vineyards with ancient vines. The names are not well known in the marketplace because the grapes have historically gone to factory-sized wineries where their identity was submerged in generic red blends. Chardonnay and Sauvignon Blanc are grown successfully in this district, usually on the bottomlands closer to the river. Both white varieties here tend to a riper, more full-bodied, somewhat simpler character than their higher priced competitors from cooler parts of California.

North of Ukiah, past Lake Mendocino and Hwy 101's junction with Hwy 20, is the last widening of the mountains which line the Russian River before one ascends out of the valley to the source of the river. This appellation is called **Redwood Valley**, and it was granted AVA status in 1999. Redwood Valley is slightly cooler than Ukiah or Hopland. It is several hundred feet higher, with most of the vineyards planted on sites 800–1,000 ft above sea level, and it receives a stiff breeze every afternoon through a gap in the coastal mountains near the town of Willits. This increased degree of marine influence is clearly demonstrated by the name. Redwood trees imply fog arriving during dry summer months. Cabernet Sauvignon and Barbera seem to do particularly well in the Redwood Valley, taking on nuances of flavor complexity which are often missing in the same varieties ripened past peak perfection in the Ukiah or Hopland districts.

A unique district is the approved **Potter Valley AVA**, directly east of Redwood Valley. Potter Valley is a good sized, but sparsely populated, region at a 200 ft higher elevation even than Redwood Valley. Virtually surrounded by mountains, Potter Valley is in the Eel River watershed along a canal which delivers water from the Eel River to Lake Mendocino, and thus into the Russian River for irrigation purposes. Potter Valley gets very hot at midday, but downright cold at night. It also has a very high water table, which in turn produces botrytis fairly regularly. Potter Valley is not well known because it has no wineries. Some 1,000 acres are under vines at present, which makes Potter Valley almost as big a growing district as Anderson Valley. Potter Valley's true claim to world class status, however, comes from *botrytized Semillon, Riesling, and Gewürztraminer.

Cole Valley AVA is a pointless appellation west of Hwy 101. **Yorkville Highlands AVA** is a new appellation with a few small vineyards just past the summit on Hwy 129's route from Cloverdale to the Anderson Valley.

NOTABLE PROPERTIES

Dom St Gregory, series of small volume labels made by Greg Graziano, first in a converted hop kiln near Ukiah, then since 1995 in the former Hidden Cellars facility (see PARDUCCI) in Talmadge. The Italian varietals program from Lowell Stone's Fox Hill Vyd go to market under a Monte Volpe brand. These include Nebbiolo, Sangiovese, Dolcetto, and Malvasia. Pinot Blanco, Muscat, and Barbera are sourced elsewhere. The Dom St Gregory brand includes Chardonnay and Pinot Noir. The top-end range is offered under a Martin Ray label, the rights to which were purchased from Martin Ray's heirs in the SANTA CRUZ MTNS. Although a connection to the historical significance of Martin Ray's name is completely fallacious, these wines are very good quality.

Gabrielli, multi-family CRAFTSMAN-SIZED partnership in the Redwood Valley making very good quality Zinfandel in the traditional style. It shows intense berry fruit mingled with black pepper flavor and dried heather notes. The wine lacks the astringency and alcohol burn which can mar the variety when made by others in this style. Syrah is also well made.

Kohn Properties, the Fetzer family vineyards retained after sale of the winery and name to Brown-Forman. Kohn is Kathleen Fetzer's maiden name. About 1,000 acres are certified as *organic viticulture. The family's eight-year non-compete agreement with Brown-Forman ended with the new millennium.

Lolonis owns 300 acres dating back to 1920 on a beautiful bench northeast of Ukiah and some wine is made under the Lolonis label. Tremendous track record for Chardonnay.

McDowell Valley Vyds. The story began when the Keehn family purchased 375 acres in 1970, much of it planted to old vines. They

Although still a relatively young man, **Donald Ziraldo** was a pioneer in the renaissance of the Canadian wine industry.

Über **consultant** Helen Turley's name alone has been enough to catapult numerous small production CA wines into the rarified air of three-digit auction prices and **cult** status.

has operated continuously since 1864. In southern NJ there is a city named Vineland where the Delaware grape was discovered in 1849, and where Thomas Welch launched America's grape juice (he called it 'Unfermented Wine') industry after the Civil War. Rapid expansion of vineyards was followed by a blight of vine disease that sent Welch packing for western NY. Nearly all the rest of the wineries have opened since farm winery legislation in 1982. Total production in 1998 was about 175,000 gal, made from 450 acres of grapes. Forty per cent of the production came from Tomasello winery in the state's southern fruit belt. NJ's ranking in total wine bottled dropped from fifth to fifteenth in the US over the last quarter of the 20th century as some of the big companies stopped importing CA bulk wines.

NJ's topography and climate define two distinct wine districts, divided by a northeast–southwest line from Trenton to Raritan Bay. The southern, warmer half of the state contains the Pine Barrens and the Warren Hills AVA on the east side of the Delaware River. Further south the land is relatively flat, with light, sandy soils and a frost-free season of well over 200 days due to moderating effects from the encircling waters of the Atlantic Ocean and Delaware Bay. Annual rainfall there averages 40 in. Wineries dot the marketing corridor between Philadelphia and the lavish casinos in Atlantic City. This is NJ's older winegrowing area, although not an approved AVA. This sparsely populated district includes Vineland and Egg Harbor, and Cape May where the Delaware meets the Atlantic. *Fruit wines are particularly fine in NJ, and some producers are making fruit-flavored grape wines.

The hillier northern half of NJ has heavier, more *calcareous soils with annual rainfall averaging 51 in and a notably shorter growing season. A newer crop of small, farm-based wineries has grown up on hillsides near the Delaware River, in the CENTRAL DELAWARE VALLEY AVA, where mesoclimates allow a slightly drier, longer season than immediately adjacent districts. French hybrid varieties predominate throughout the state. Rutgers Univ in the state's northern half is NJ's research facility, with experimental plantings of a dozen cool climate vinifera varieties from northern Italy.

Wine is marketed through the THREE-TIER DISTRIBUTION system. Retail wine-liquor stores are licensed according to a formula based on population density. About 8% of the jurisdictions are DRY. Native wineries may have licenses to sell from premises other than their production facilities. NJ authorities have seized trucks containing DIRECT SHIPMENT wine, and a bill has been introduced to make it a felony to ship any alcoholic beverage directly to a consumer. Debate on this bill will be politically entertaining considering the number of fine wine customers who regularly drive into NJ from PA (see PHILADELPHIA), the MONOPOLY STATE across the Delaware River, to make purchases.

NOTABLE PROPERTIES

Cream Ridge has set the standard for quality fruit wines, not only in NJ but in the whole Mid-Atlantic region. Tom Amabile made his first Ciliegia Amabile, a light semi-sweet cherry wine, for Buffalo Valley Winery in PA in the early 1980s. The same wine made under his own label won the NJ GOVERNOR'S CUP in 1990 and 1995. The wine has 60 g/l RS balanced with 10 g/l TA. Amabile produces 450 gal of Ciliegia Amabile annually, with a small batch being fermented *dry and aged in oak for ten months. The wine's fruit aroma can be overwhelming. There are also two raspberry wines in these respective styles, a plum wine, and a cranberry wine.

Sylvin Farms, almost experimental in size, is a 7-acre all-vinifera vineyard established in 1976 and bonded in 1985 by Frank Salek, a local college professor. The 70 ft elevation in Atlantic Co in south-central NJ helps minimize frost damage while benefiting from southwest breezes which reduce the threat of rot. Influenced to plant vinifera by the work of Russian immigrant Konstantin FRANK in NY's FINGER LAKES, Salek has won the NJ Governor's Cup five times since 1988: for Pinot Noir, Cabernet Franc, sparkling Rkatsiteli, sparkling Muscat Ottonel, and Merlot. His 1995 Cabernet Franc recalls both Rhône and Loire elements with an explosive, pure varietal character and peppery finish. Other varieties include Cabernet Sauvignon (which Salek considers the best variety for the region in the long run), Pinot Grigio, Pinot Blanc, Sauvignon Blanc, Chardonnay, Riesling, Malbec, Gamay Noir, and Muscat Blanc. Production is all of 700 cases annually.

Unionville Vyds were established in 1993 and quickly moved to the forefront of NJ winemaking. John Altmaier was nominated by his industry peers as Winemaker of the Year in the trade publication *Vineyard & Winery Management* for 1997. Unionville has a reputation for impressive barrel fermented Seyval. The white wines, particularly the Riesling and Seyval, have a certain creaminess of texture with good varietal character. Production is 7,000 cases.

R.F. & R.G.L.

New Mexico, historic, sparsely populated, high elevation state in the DESERT SOUTHWEST region, bordering MEXICO with 20 wineries mostly scattered from north to south along a midline irrigated by the RIO GRANDE. There are currently three approved AVAs: MIDDLE RIO GRANDE VALLEY, MESILLA VALLEY, and MIMBRES VALLEY. Extensive plantings of vinifera begin at the town of Truth Or Consequences and extend south. North of Santa Fe, the climate is too cold for vinifera, and hybrids dominate the plantings.

NM is the oldest vinifera growing and winemaking region in the US. In order to protect valuable Old World trade routes, Spanish law during the Age of Discovery prohibited raising grapes in the New World. The oligarchy living in Mexico could afford to pay for imported Spanish wine, but priests charged with saving heathen souls in remote locations needed a more reliable source for sacramental wine. This problem was particularly acute as colonization moved north into the southwestern parts of what would become the US. It was a 1,000 mi journey of six months to the source of supply in Old Mexico. There are reports of smuggled European vines being cultivated in the Mesilla Valley, in southern NM, as early as 1580. A breakthrough occurred in 1629 when two monks, a Franciscan named Fray Gracia Zuñiga and a Capuchin named Antonio de Arteaga, brought vinifera cuttings to an Indian pueblo south of present-day Socorro. These vines, which came to be called the *Mission grape, are thought to have originated from a Sardinian grape called Monica, which can still be found growing in NM. Wine was first produced from these plantings in 1633. By the 1880s, NM was the fifth largest wine producing area (it did not become a state until 1912), with over 3,150 acres of vines. Production yielded over 900,000 gal, which was double what the state of NY was doing at the same time.

In 1885 there had been ten wineries in Albuquerque, but as CA's wineries expanded, competition proved too fierce. From nearly a million gal in the late 1880s, production dropped to 300,000 in 1890, 30,000 gal in 1900, and only 2,000 gal in 1910. By 1920, no commercial wine production was recorded in the state. The Rio Grande flooded in 1926, damaging many vineyards. After Repeal, a dozen wineries reopened. Production rebounded temporarily. But the Rio Grande overflowed its banks again in 1943, the greatest NM flood of the century, ruining any hopes of a revival by washing away vines planted next to the river.

In 1972, the NM Wine & Vine Society was instrumental in orchestrating a government-

---

previous page: In America's arid west, vine growth and flavor development can be manipulated by adjusting irrigation during the growing season. This tensiometer measure moisture in the soil.

sponsored study which led to major plantings of mostly French hybrids, but by 1977 only three wineries were still open. Then in 1980, 1,200 acres were planted north and west of Las Cruces by European investors, although most of this acreage died over the next decade thanks to mismanagement and COTTON ROOT ROT. By 1990 production in the state had risen to 100,000 gal. Today there are 500 acres of vinifera, and about 50 acres of hybrids, with more than 20 wineries. In 1997 200,000 gal were produced. Most wineries in NM are small, under 2,000 cases. Most of those in the cooler north are vinifying hybrids. The larger wineries, GRUET and St Clair, for instance, work primarily with vinifera.

The winegrowing areas north of Santa Fe are wetter than the others in NM, but higher and colder too. (See altitude versus latitude theory in ROCKY MTN entry.) Santa Fe is 7,000 ft high. These districts can receive 14 in or more precipitation in a year. Some vinifera are planted (on their OWN ROOTS; *phylloxera has not yet been reported), but hybrids are more commonly planted at this 5,800 ft average altitude. *Winter freeze can be an issue, with temperatures dropping as low as −20°F, as in 1972. The growing season is short. *Frost can occur as early as Oct 1, and as late as June 1. In the Española Valley frost has been recorded as early as Sept 7. Despite the overall arid climate, significant *powdery mildew occurs statewide, because of MONSOONS.

In the middle regions around Albuquerque the last spring frost occurs by May 5, and the first fall frost arrives around Oct 15. The southern regions, from Socorro south, are the most arid, averaging less than 10 in per year of precipitation, of which only about 3 in occurs as snowfall. Temperatures can reach 100°F for much of the day in summer. The last frost occurs Apr 15; and in Demming, west of Las Cruces and also the state's most prolific district, frost dates are Apr 1 and Nov 15. In 1994 Cabernet Sauvignon, Merlot, and Chardonnay were newly planted near Las Cruces, where the Rio Grande meets the TX border, the lowest point in the state at 2,800 ft. Here *acidification is necessary. It is not uncommon for pH in red wines to rise to 4.0.

There are also some plantings, and one winery, in eastern NM, on the Pecos River (see TRANS-PECOS) which rises near Santa Fe then flows south past the UFO capital of America at Roswell and on into TX. This area is really a continuation of the Staked Plains, or Llano Estacado, shared with northwestern TX (see TEXAS).

NM operates under the THREE-TIER DISTRIBUTION system. Most wineries sell a substantial percentage of production at the winery; out-of-state sales are rare. NM only has a million residents, but receives 2 million tourists per year, mostly for the history in Santa Fe and the skiing in nearby Taos.

NOTABLE PROPERTIES

Anasazi Fields. High elevation winery north of Albuquerque specializing in wood aged, dry, fruit wines, which are uniquely and surprisingly serviceable with food.

Casa Rondena. As a classical guitarist, John Calvin spent many years in the Andalusian region of Spain. Now he designs Moorish styled buildings, and has one of the best two or three wineries in New Mexico. His Cabernet Franc is especially good.

Il Santo. John Balagna was one of America's brightest and youngest scientists when he went to work for Los Alamos Labs under Robert Oppenheimer during World War II. Now in his 80's, he has retired to his spectacular 7,000 ft high home/winery overlooking the caldera in which Albuquerque sits. Labels such as La Bombe Grande and Dago Red demonstrate his puckish good humor.

Jory. Californian Stillman Brown makes very impressive Zinfandel from grapes grown near Deming in the sourther part of the state.

Ponderosa. Henry Street aims for the tourist trade, but his winery and vineyard an hour northwest of Albuquerque is one of the few on soils with a significant clay content, which allows him to retain much better acid than most.

St Clair Vyds, part of the winery group managed by the Lescombes family's New Mexico Wineries Inc, which also manages Blue Teal Winery and Mademoiselle de Santa Fe. Theirs is the group responsible for the defunct investment scheme near Las Cruces now being litigated in the European Courts. A 100,000 gal production facility exists, but its equipment today sits largely idle.

See also GRUET.   R.T.S.

New Orleans, major international port in LA almost on the GULF OF MEXICO which has been the most conveniently accessible trading depot to Americans from the center of the continent for nearly 300 years. Built on a bend in the MISSISSIPPI RIVER, it is widely known as the Big Easy for its bawdy lifestyle, lack of regulation, and soporific climate. New Orleans was founded in 1718 by the French, was ceded to Spain in 1763, then back to France in 1800, and finally became part of the US in 1803 as part of the Louisiana Purchase. In the latter half of the 19th century it imported as much CA and MO wine as did New York City. The rich blend of French, Spanish, and African cultures of the early LA settlers followed by Italian and Irish immigrants gives the city an exotic appeal not to be found anywhere else in the US. French-Canadian immigrants called Cajuns developed their own subculture in the surrounding swamps (bayous), including zydeco music, beginning well before 1800. The famous French Quarter (Vieux Carré) with its Spanish-French inspired architecture is the center of the enormous Mardi Gras celebration that takes place just before Lent each year. Dixieland, or New Orleans-style jazz, was born in the Black Storyville district here in the early 20th century and is still synonymous with the city's image. New Orleans cuisine, with its traditional Creole and Cajun ingredients, is highly regarded throughout North America, which helps make the city an outpost of fine wine consumption and availability not to be found in many other places in the SOUTH region. A population of 500,000 is supplemented by the very large tourist and convention business.   L.A.O.

Newton, steep hillside vineyard and winery in the SPRING MTN AVA of CA's Napa Valley. It is owned by Peter and Su Hua Newton, he the lead investor in a group who founded STERLING Vyds; she a 6 ft tall Asian former model with a degree from the London School of Economics who has brought considerable attention to CA wine worldwide. The vineyards were planned by Ric Forman (see NAPA VALLEY), and they are visually striking. Cabernet and Merlot both have extensive reputations for elegance. They certainly have noteworthy complexity, with tarragon, allspice, and chocolate notes, but they also reflect the struggle these vines must undertake on the steepest portions of the vineyard, often exhibiting a meager flavor profile and an astringent finish.
                                        B.C.C.

New York, most populous state in the eastern US and also the region's largest producer of wine. The state's 8 million gal of annual wine production ranks second in the nation (well behind CA). However, 65% of the NY grape crop goes to the juice market and most of the wine emanates from one very large producer (CANANDAIGUA Wine Co.) using substantial quantities of bulk wine from out of state (mainly CA) for blending. As a producer of wine from its own 31,400 acres of grapes, NY ranks third in the nation behind fast-charging WA. Eighty-three per cent of NY's grape acreage is in labrusca varieties (mostly Concord). The rest is roughly evenly divided between vinifera and French hybrid varieties.

There are four distinct, geographically separated wine districts: along LAKE ERIE in the state's western extremity; around the FINGER LAKES in a west-central area; in the HUDSON RIVER Valley north of New York City; and on the eastern end of LONG ISLAND which juts into the Atlantic from New York City. Long Island and the Finger Lakes are the significant districts, accounting for two-thirds of the state's 125 wineries. There were only nineteen wineries when a Farm Winery Law passed in 1976, cutting small-producer regulations and licensing fees.

Most of NY's soils originated with the last glacial advance and what it left behind, predominantly gravelly or slatey silt loams in the grape growing districts, with some heavier clays in the Finger Lakes and sand on Long Island. Soils tend to be acidic except for a band of limestone arcing east–west through the state's midsection. NY's humid *continental climate is unusually diverse for a state its size, shaped by complex topography and many bodies of water. Influxes of cold, dry air from the northwest spar with warm, humid weather from the ATLANTIC OCEAN's Gulf Stream. Annual precipitation ranges from 30 to 50 in. The frost free season along Lake Erie and in the Finger Lakes district averages 180–200 days, depending on mesoclimates, while the season extends to 220 days on ocean-insulated Long Island. Long Island is warmer but also somewhat more humid, with slightly higher fall precipitation due in part to coastal storms and HURRICANES.

The state's viticultural history began with 17th-century Dutch and Huguenot vineyards in the Hudson Valley. Commercial wineries did not appear until the early 1800s, and somewhat later along Lake Erie, but it was the Finger Lakes that became the center of NY's wine industry by the late 19th century.   R.F.

New York City, largest city in the US or Canada (greater metropolitan population of 16.6 million), although slightly smaller than Mexico City with an extremely diverse population. It is also the most influential wine market in North America because it is the center of publishing in the US, including most wine-related publishing. It is also an important AUCTION market with a lively trade in rare wines, and a particularly important restaurant market, in no small part because of the financial, advertising, and entertainment institutions which make Manhattan America's premier location for the sale of expensive bottles ON-PREMISE. Popu-

lation diversity and wine influence notwithstanding, New York City is a European-oriented market, dominated by a limited number of distributors, and it has been a challenging arena for America's own producers. France, Italy, and Australia run aggressive, well-financed promotional offices in Manhattan and even New York state wines (particularly from upstate) can find it hard to make friends here.   R.F.

Niagara Escarpment, a 575 ft scenic ridge winding for 550 mi from Queenston, ONTARIO near Niagara Falls to Tobermory in northern Ontario, where it progresses underwater to Manitoulin Island and into the US forming the Michigan Basin. The ridge developed first as a delta from deposits of eroding ancient mountains 450 million years ago, then became the bottom of an immense sea. Its composition is layers of shale, sandstone, limestone, and dolostone including sea fossils. Rivers, creeks, and streams tumble over the edge flowing north into present-day Lake Ontario, eg Niagara Falls. Because of its numerous rare species of plants and animals, restrictions on urban development along the Escarpment are being studied.

In the Bench part of the NIAGARA PENINSULA, during *frost conditions, the Niagara Escarpment serves as a backboard against which winds off Lake Ontario bounce into a circulating pattern thus creating the active airflow which prevents dangerous pockets of frost from settling in the vineyards.   L.F.B.

Niagara-on-the-Lake, subdistrict in ONTARIO's NIAGARA PENINSULA VA at the mouth of the Niagara River as it empties into Lake Ontario. First settled during the 1760s as a British fort. European settlement began during the American Revolutionary War with farmers and refugees. At one point it was the capital of Upper Canada. Then it was a very popular summer retreat for wealthy Americans. Its Victorian legacy is reflected in the intact architecture of its stately homes and picturesque streetscape. It is also home to the Shaw Theatre, which has helped attract visitors to this Canadian wine country. Soils in the district are sandier and more low lying than those on the BEAMSVILLE BENCH.
L.F.B.

Niagara Peninsula VA, designated appellation in ONTARIO bounded by Lake Ontario on the north, the Niagara River on the east (which includes Niagara Falls and is the Canada/US border), the Welland River on the south, and Hwys 56 and 20 on the west. This single appellation accounts for 80% of

CANADA's grape growing volume. Throughout the year the NIAGARA ESCARPMENT is a passive barrier against continental winds, while Lake Ontario acts as a moderating influence on temperature, raising winter temperatures and lowering spring temperatures so that the development of fruit buds is held back until the danger of late spring *frost has passed. The lake cools summer air so that grapes do not ripen too quickly, then keeps the fall air comparatively warm so that the first frost is delayed and the growing season extended. Most of Ontario's wineries are located is this appellation.   L.F.B.

Niebaum-Coppola, the historic Inglenook winery in the RUTHERFORD AVA of CA's NAPA VALLEY, now owned by movie director Francis Ford Coppola (*The Godfather*). The property was first planted in 1871 by George Yount's son-in-law (see YOUNTVILLE AVA), then sold eight years later to Gustave Niebaum, a Finnish sea captain who had made considerable money in the fur trade. The winery was built ten years later by the giant among all Napa architects Hamden McIntyre. Niebaum's most important contribution to CA wine was the introduction of bottling and marketing by the winery rather than by *négociants. Estate bottling and labeling was a gambit he initiated after his spectacular winery had been built and all the producers in CA had begun to be squeezed by their brokers in San Francisco (see SANTA CRUZ MTNS AVA, History). Following Niebaum's death in 1908, the winery was only marginally active until after Prohibition. In 1939 it was taken over by the son of Niebaum's niece, John Daniel Jr. From then until 1964 Daniel and George Deuer produced a series of magnificent Cabernets with specific cask numbers which rapidly accelerated the accession of Napa Valley to recognition among wine connoisseurs throughout the US.

The next 30 years were a sad commentary on US-style marketing. Inglenook was sold to the Allied Grape Growers, which eventually became part of Heublein. To exploit the value of the venerable name, Heublein attached the name Inglenook to a line of jug wines, which eventually sold 4 million cases a year, but bled any connotation of quality out of the brand. This attitude could not have been more clearly demonstrated than when the brand managers at Heublein's CT headquarters decided to raise a modern tilt-up warehouse on the Napa property, and chose to place it squarely in front of the monumental stone winery building such that the landmark could no longer be seen by the millions of tourists who visit the valley each year and drive by it on Hwy 29. Coppola purchased the Niebaum home and vineyard in 1975. In 1994 he was able to purchase the historic winery as well.

The flagship for Niebaum-Coppola is their Meritage red Rubicon. It is tannic and dense, but rarely bitter or astringent. Eight years of bottle age barely starts to open it up. By age 12 the bouquet has evolved enough for one to confidently remark that the wine is impressive, and to start wondering if one will live long enough to enjoy it at its peak.

B.C.C.

Nissley Vyds. Established in 1977 in the LANCASTER VALLEY AVA on the Susquehannah River in PA by J. Richard Nissley, this winery swept the EASTERN INTL WINE COMPETITION in 1998 with thirteen awards. Nissley winemaker William Gulvin demonstrates that skillful wine production can make French hybrids stand on a par with their vinifera counterparts. Only two of Nissley's medals in the 1998 competition were for varietal hybrids; most were proprietary house blends. Nissley also has a track record for award-winning cherry wines. Annual production is 12,500 cases.   R.G.L.

North Carolina. The state where English settlers first reported native Scuppernong grapes growing wild offers viticultural opportunities from Muscadines in the COASTAL PLAIN, to French hybrids and vinifera varieties in the upper PIEDMONT and select locations in the Blue Ridge and Appalachian Mtns. Where there was once a boom in Muscadine cultivation, the focus in viticulture has shifted to quality hybrids and vinifera. Total state production was 300,000 gal in 1998.

NC features two of the SOUTH region's leading wineries, and the state government has declared its support in assisting the industry in competing with its well-established neighbor to the north, VA. As newly planted vinifera vineyards in cool climate locations mature, new and existing NC wineries will have increasing opportunities to prove the potential of the state for producing fine wine. Six of NC's eleven wineries produce some vinifera wines. All of the NC wineries are able to wholesale their wines to retailers and restaurants even if the wineries also use a distributor.

NOTABLE PROPERTIES

Duplin, located in Rose Hill, in NC's central Coastal Plain. Established in 1972, Duplin is an example of a successful mid-sized Southern winery specializing in Muscadine products, which include table wine,

sparkling wine, dessert wine, and non-alcoholic wine. David Fussell Jr is president. Production is 30,000 cases.

See also BILTMORE ESTATE, WESTBEND.

R.G.L.

Northeast, region slightly larger than Italy, encompassing the six New England states (CT, RI, MA, VT, NH, and ME) plus NY and the northern half of NJ. All these states produce wine except NH, but only NY produces a large quantity. Only two of the region's 200-odd wineries are major producers with international or even national distribution. Few of the rest venture near the 100,000 gal mark. Most sell primarily direct from the winery into local markets with limited but increasing amounts of wine crossing state borders.

Although the Northeast's first vineyards were planted in the early 17th-century colonies of MA and New Amsterdam, and the first commercial wines date back to the early 1800s in the HUDSON RIVER Valley, the region's present-day wineries rarely pre-date the last quarter of the 20th century. There is no winegrowing history in New England, and in NY progressive winemakers often attempt to distance themselves from a history of sweet, grapey wines made from labrusca grapes.

The humid *continental climate of the Northeast averages 40–50 in of precipitation annually, evenly distributed throughout the year. Cold winters and relatively short growing seasons have always been the limiting factors in Northeast winegrowing. While the area's latitude is lower than Bordeaux, winters are generally colder than any western European wine district, with temperatures typically falling to 0°F or below throughout most of the region. Early winemakers responded by relying on hardier fruits (notably apples) and grape varieties bred from wild vines attuned to the region's climate. Vineyards are only commercially viable in coastal areas from Cape Cod south, such as the approved AVAs WESTERN CONNECTICUT HIGHLANDS, **Martha's Vyd** (an island just south of Cape Cod), and SOUTHEASTERN NEW ENGLAND, or near inland bodies of water large enough to have a temperate effect such as the FINGER LAKES and Hudson River. Informed site selection has played the major role in the emergence of fine vinifera wines in the Northeast, but more astute vineyard management and even the apparent selective adaptation of vines to local conditions have also been key factors. The most favorable sites are planted to vinifera varieties while cooler locations are generally given to French hybrids or, in the older districts, left

to the labrusca. Most new plantings for wine are vinifera.

Recognizing that their climate resembles northern Europe far more than even the coolest reaches of America's West Coast, Northeastern winemakers look to France and Germany for vinous models. With neither an indigenous school of enology nor the cachet to attract trained winemakers from other regions, the Northeast has struggled to grow its own talent in the cellar. This and minimal interaction between the half-dozen scattered northeastern wine districts tends to emphasize their separate identities and wine styles.

The region's major markets, notably NEW YORK CITY and BOSTON, are strongly European-oriented and have paid scant attention to the development of wine districts in their backyards. But the increasing market penetration of high-end West Coast estates has paved the way for what sometimes seems an almost grudging recognition of some Northeastern wines, particularly LONG ISLAND wines in metro-New York. And progressive restaurants are beginning to embrace the concept of local wine along with locally grown produce. The region presents a patchwork of state distribution regulations from MONOPOLY STATE (NH) to allowing wine to be sold through food stores (ME).

R.F.

Northern Neck George Washington Birthplace AVA. One of six approved appellations in VIRGINIA, the Northern Neck is a peninsula defined by the Potomac and Rappahannock rivers in VA's upper Tidewater. To date, the AVA is only found on the labels of the region's single winery, INGLESIDE PLANTATION.   R.G.L.

North Fork of Long Island, see LONG ISLAND.

North Fork of Roanoke AVA. One of six approved appellations in VIRGINIA, this small district encompasses the North Fork of the Roanoke River southwest of the city of Roanoke, as it descends from the Appalachian Plateau to the Valley of Virginia. Viticulture has been recorded in this region since colonial times, in a temperate, sheltered river valley. While it features some vineyards, there are no wineries currently operating in the AVA.   R.G.L.

Norton, high quality all-American red winegrape whose origins are obscure. This hardy vine is well suited to humid areas and thrives in the Midwest where it produces deep-coloured, full-bodied wine with no shortage of assertive character and not a hint of *foxiness. It was the mainstay of the important 19th-century AR and MO wine industries. It is named after the VA nurseryman credited with introducing the vine in the 1830s. Norton can be difficult to distinguish from CYNTHIANA in the vineyard.

Nova Scotia, north Atlantic island province of CANADA better known for its fishing fleets than its vineyards. Four stalwart wineries, however, are holding the banner for a small, but proud industry.

HISTORY

No winegrapes had been grown on a commercial scale in NS until the late 1970s. Chipman Wines, founded in 1941, produced only *fruit wines from local apples, blueberries, cranberries, and cherries. In 1965 ANDRÉS built a bottling plant in Truro, but planted no vineyards. Table grapes were viable, but only the most hardy varieties. Then Roger Dial, a political science professor from CA joined the faculty at Dalhousie Univ in Dartmouth, NS, in 1967. Dial had been a partner in newspaperman Davis Bynum's winery in Berkeley before it moved to Sonoma Co. Today Roger Dial is considered the father of the NS wine industry. His enthusiasm for wine defied local wisdom, so when he arrived he persuaded a university colleague, who had table grapes in his well-sited property at Grand Pré, to plant some winegrapes. First they tried winter-hardy Russian varieties, Michurinetz and Saperavi Severny. Encouraged, they extended their ambitions to include some vinifera, which were nearly obliterated the very next year by an extremely harsh winter. In 1980 Dial took over the property and established a winery. Other growers in the island planted vineyards to supply Dial. By 1982 there were enough growers to form the Wine Growers' Association of NS with Dial as Chair and Hans Jost from Malagash on the Northumberland Straight as Vice Chair. Jost opened the second NS cottage winery in 1984.

In 1984 the province passed a Farm Winery Act allowing Dial and Jost to sell their wines directly to restaurateurs, a supportive move that would take Ontario thirteen more years to emulate. Grand Pré by any standards was successful. By 1987 Dial had 200 acres and annual sales of C$11.2 million. But the combined blows of the Oct 1987 stock-market crash and the subsequent free trade legislation put Grand Pré into receivership. Swiss interests bought Grand Pré in 1994 from a couple who had tried, unsuccess-

fully, to restructure it. With a million-dollar renovation and replanting project, Swiss owner and former banker Hanspeter Stutz is taking a serious run at winegrowing in NS.

CLIMATE

Although located on the sea, the NS climate is a combination of both *maritime and *continental. Storms are more frequent throughout the year than in any other part of Canada. Two viticultural growing regions offer sufficiently long growing seasons: the coast along the Northumberland Strait and the Annapolis Valley. Northumberland Strait features the warmest salt water north of the Carolinas because it is shallow and sheltered, warming up more in summer than other coastal areas and thus providing ample autumn heat. Winter ice in the strait delays early spring bud break. The 25 sq mi Annapolis Valley is sandwiched between an escarpment on the north and a second set of mountains on the south that shelter this lowland and provide the warmest temperatures and second lowest precipitation totals in NS. This district has the greatest number of frost free days in NS. Annapolis Valley *degree days range from 1,400 to 1,650 (using °F calculation as elsewhere in this book), with annual winter low temperatures averaging –15°C/2°F, and –20°C/–2°F being very rare.

VITICULTURE

There are 26 NS growers managing 325 acres. Only 10% of the province is arable, much of it slate and rock, the deposits of a receding Ontario glacier. Grapes include Marechal Foch, Michurinetz (although diminishing), Pinot Noir, Seyval Blanc, NY Muscat, L'Acadie (a hybrid developed in Ontario), and several Geisenheim clones. To protect the vines, most growers practice MOUNDING, which in NS involves pruning the vines, bending them over, then covering the entire plant with soil or straw. Some growers, such as pioneer Wayne MacDonald, are experimenting with varied spacing and vertical shoot positioning. Soils range from sandy loam of the Annapolis Valley, which often requires lime to reach proper pH levels, to loam with more clay in the Malagash area further north on the Northumberland Strait.

REGULATORY ENVIRONMENT

There are three types of NS winery license: commercial, farm winery, and estate winery. Farm wineries must make wine 100% from

grapes sourced in NS. Commercial licenses allow imported juice to be bottled as Product of Canada (as practiced by Andrés in Truro). Estate wineries can bottle wine made both from imported juice and from local grapes. The provincial liquor authority (NSLC) has a monopoly on retail sales, other than CELLAR DOOR sales by farm or estate wineries. Estate wineries are allowed to sell about three times as much wine as they grow, however the Farm Act stipulates that over an eight-year stepwise program, the 35% local content requirement will be increased to 75% in 2005. NS winegrowers are negotiating with the VQA to join the national appellation system. Issues such as which hybrids they can and cannot employ are contentious, but they are all very much in favor of joining.

NOTABLE PROPERTIES

Grand Pré, built on an elegant 1826 home near the historic village of Wolfville, once a LOYALIST settlement. Hanspeter Stutz has introduced lower training systems and added a Swiss-influenced restaurant. He wants to eliminate Michurinetz entirely and concentrate on Léon Millot and L'Acadie Blanc, from which he intends to make a sparkling wine. A distillery was planned for 2000.

Habitant Vyds, opened as an estate winery in 1998 on the shore of the Bay of Fundy in the Annapolis Valley. Wayne MacDonald and Laura McCain have 30 acres planted in 1986, including Chardonnay and Pinot Noir, as well as French hybrids. They make 12,000–15,000 cases.

Jost Vyds, on the shore of the Northumberland Strait, was where Rhine Valley émigré Hans Jost settled in the early 1970s on 600 acres of farmland. In 1984 he built an estate winery and when Jost Sr died in 1988, his son Hans Christian took over, expanding the winery as he went. He manages their 45-acre Malagash vineyard, a 22-acre vineyard in Gaspereau Valley, and another 45 acres contracted in Annapolis Valley. Varieties are mostly French and German hybrids, producing 35,000 cases.

Ste Famille, in Falmouth, the gateway to the Annapolis Valley, was founded in 1989 by Suzanne and Doug Corkum on an old Acadian village site settled in the 1680s. They have 30 acres on south-facing slopes, and make 6,000 cases annually.   L.F.B.

Dzikowski, P., *The Nova Scotia Agroclimatic Atlas* (Truro, Nova Scotia, 1984).

O

Oakville AVA, a cross-section of NAPA VALLEY from the 600 ft contour line on either side, and 2 miles thick from just north of the Yountville Hills to its border with RUTHERFORD AVA. It is more or less the geographic center of Napa Valley, a position reflected in its wines. Chardonnay does well here, although it is susceptible to criticism for its blowsy, Californicated style which gets judges' attention in blind tastings but overwhelms many dishes at the dinner table. Sauvignon Blanc is perhaps the better choice from Oakville, if only because it produces a nicely balanced centrist style composed of flinty flavors rather than the herbal or melon notes of more extreme climates. Sangiovese seems to indicate good potential, but the acknowledged king is, and will continue to be, Cabernet Sauvignon.

On the west side of the valley, the southern end of the undefined 'bench' has certainly proven itself one of the premier Cabernet sites in the world with names such as HEITZ Martha, MONDAVI To Kalon (a portion of the vineyard famous since 1870 when it was first planted by Hiram Crabb), and BEAULIEU Vyd #2. Deep soils washed out of the mountains, composed of large particles which drain readily, provide a natural balancing mechanism between vine growth, crop size, and grape ripening. In other districts growers need expertise to produce high quality. On the Oakville Bench, all one needs is the price of admission. The difference between Cabernets grown on the Oakville Bench and those grown on its contiguous twin to the north, the Rutherford Bench, are very subtle. While both are round and concentrated, Oakville will produce the slightly fruitier, more refreshing midpoint; Rutherford the more powerful, more earthy center with a slightly dusty finish.

NOTABLE PROPERTIES

Cosentino, mildly eccentric winery which buys most of its grapes for a 15,000-case production of a broad range of small lots. Best are two red Meritage wines named The Poet and M. Coz, which rely on a stabilizing contribution from an owned 4-acre Merlot vineyard surrounding the winery on the west side of Hwy 29. M. Coz is the the woodier of the two; The Poet more austere in structure, but plummier in flavor. Both age very nicely to produce expansive bouquet after eight years.

Far Niente, beautifully restored stone winery with a million-dollar copper roof smack in the center of the Oakville Bench. The Chardonnay received enormous attention in the early 1980s because its embossed gold leaf label cost about 10¢ rather than the then CA standard of about 1¢ each. Still, it is curious the winery would have any reputation for Chardonnay at all given its location. By all rights their Cabernet should be their main claim to fame.

As a sidelight, and in a separate location on Spring Mtn, they produce a *botrytized Semillon/Sauvignon Blanc blend which they call Dulce, from grapes grown in an owned vineyard east of the town of Napa. Very expensive, it has managed so far to capture the *volatile acidity of *Sauternes without much of the taut acid, compressed fruit, or elegant length. Neither does it age particularly well, although it is extremely sweet.

Harlan, one of the best of the CA CULT WINE Cabernets. Owned by former Pacific Union Real Estate Co. executive Bill Harlan, who is also one of the owners of Meadowwood CC, the 25-acre hillside property is behind Martha's Vyd (see HEITZ) above the bench. Michel Rolland is the CONSULTANT. Less than 2,000 cases are made. Wine takes several years to develop in the bottle. It is finely structured: full, with a slippery texture, but also a backbone and plenty of focus.

Paradigm, a cultish red meritage blend grown on a 50-acre property planted in 1975, and now owned by prominent Napa Valley grower Ren Harris. Wine is made by Heidi Petersen Barrett. It is round and full of blackberry scents beautifully integrated with wood. Although the vineyard is 60% Cabernet, the wine seems dominated by Merlot.

Robt Pepi, winery purchased in the mid-1990s by Jess Jackson's ARTISANS & ESTATES and subsequently renamed **Cardinale**. The attractive stone building is perched on one of the knolls which pop abruptly from the center of the Napa Valley floor. Construction was continuous for five years after the purchase as the property headquarters for A&E's Napa Valley operations. Eventually separate facilities will be built. Top wines are: the Sauvignon Blanc, which former owner Robert Pepi's son pioneered on a trellis system he called Two Heart; and the Italian grape variety program currently under elaboration by Marco DiGiulio, whose Sangiovese has shown considerable weight in the mid-palate compared to other CA examples.

Cardinale is a red Meritage being afforded top status position within the A&E hierarchy. Charles Thomas was hired away from Robert Mondavi to be *über* winemaster within Jackson's empire, and to take personal responsibility for Cardinale. As of 1999 the wine had not yet attained these lofty ambitions, being routinely upstaged by stablemates such as Stonestreet Legacy from A&E's more mature Alexander Valley operation.

See also DALLA VALLE, GROTH, OPUS ONE, SILVER OAK. B.C.C.

Oakville Ranch, winery and 60-acre vineyard 1,000 ft high in the eastern mountains of NAPA VALLEY above the contour line which marks the boundary of Oakville AVA and higher up the hill than, although a neighbor of, DALLA VALLE. The estate was built by Bob Miner, who founded the computer software company Oracle, and is run by his heirs. Oakville Ranch produces 50,000 cases total with fine performances by Chardonnay and Merlot in big, luxuriously oaked, plush styles. *Très Californien*. B.C.C.

off-sale, license to sell wines to consumers for consumption elsewhere, ie a retail store, as opposed to *on-sale* or ON-PREMISE which would be a restaurant or tasting bar.

Ohio, state in the MIDWEST region. At the beginning of the 19th century, the young Nicholas Longworth had come along the OHIO RIVER VALLEY to what is now called Cincinnati. He developed into a very good lawyer and land speculator which gave him the capital and time to exploit his developing hobby, grape growing. By that time, grape growing had been started to the east on the Ohio River by Jean-Jacques DUFOUR. In 1823 Longworth planted his own vineyard, experimenting until he finally settled on the grape he considered most suitable, the Catawba he had obtained from John Adlum's collection in MD. He planted and promoted it, not only as a grape for making table wine but one which could be turned into America's first 'champagne.' Confident in his mission, he imported experts from France to apply the MÉTHODE CHAMPENOISE. Longworth and other winegrowers prospered until a combination punch of politics and fungal diseases brought them to a standstill. First, *black rot hit the area, decimating vines in an era before the discovery that copper sulfate handily controls the fungus. Second, the onset of the Civil War in 1861 demonstrated wine was not as valuable as grain, guns, or soldiers. Many producers moved either north to LAKE ERIE or west to IL, IN, and MO.

Lake Erie had already been exploited by grape growers as early as the 1830s. They took advantage of the milder macroclimate caused by the GREAT LAKES EFFECT, and did not experience as much black rot because the breeze off the lake minimized fungal infestation. In a generation and a half, wineries along the lake had re-established OH as a major eastern wine producing state. Then came Prohibition. As in neighboring MI to the north, demand for grapes for juices or for home winemaking escalated and acres upon acres of easy-to-grow Concord vines were planted. This was a two-edged sword. It certainly helped the economic situation of the grape growers during these hard times, but it also destroyed OH's fine wine image. Only in the past generation has this situation begun to rectify itself.

Currently, OH is planted to just under 1,600 acres of vines. Predictably, the category leader is American hybrids with 83% of the total. Concord is tops in this category with just over three-quarters, while Catawba and Niagara fill in the gaps. These varieties declined as a category by 22% from 1994 to 1999. Surprisingly French hybrids also declined, albeit at a slower rate. They currently account for 9% of total acreage. Vidal and Seyval Blanc lead white varieties, while Chambourcin, DeChaunac, Baco Noir, and Foch are the heavy red hitters, in that order. Vinifera varieties experienced the greatest gain from 1994 to 1999 with a 38% increase, to weigh-in currently at just over 8% of the total vineyard plantings. White Riesling, Chardonnay, and Pinot Gris are the leading white vinifera varieties, while Cabernet Sauvignon, Pinot Noir, and Cabernet Franc lead the reds. Whites predominate in acreage with 75%.

NOTABLE PROPERTIES

Chalet Debonué Vyds, begun in 1916 when Anton Debevc, a Slovenian, planted vineyards near the Lake Erie shore just east of Cleveland, then accelerated in 1971 when his son and grandson opened a winery in Madison and a bed & breadfast on the estate. They make a light, but well-balanced Chardonnay, a very nicely dry Pinot Gris, and a Rhônesque if tart Chambourcin.

Klingshirn, started as a juice business during Prohibition, but expanded with a winery in 1935 a few miles west of Cleveland in the Lake Erie AVA. DeChaunac and Cabernet Sauvignon are light but solid examples. A specialty called Glaciovinum is a standout icewine, made of equal parts Delaware and Vidal Blanc grapes.

Meier's, OH's largest winery, was founded in 1895 as a juice producer then transformed into a winery emphasizing Catawba after Repeal. Although located in Cincinnati on the Ohio River in the far south of the state, most of the grapes come from Lake Erie AVA and especially ISLE ST GEORGE. Owned by Paramount Distillers who also own FIRELANDS, Lonz, and Mon Ami wineries. Over the wide range of products fortified dessert types are the best, particularly the generically labeled No. 44 Cream Sherry and Three Islands Madeira.

Valley Vyds, winery in the Ohio River Valley AVA run by Kenny and Dodie Schuchter on 20 acres planted in 1970. Dry Seyval and Vidal Blanc wines are quite good, while a Vidal icewine produced in 1997 from grapes picked at 37°B was quite remarkable, and unusual for the AVA.

See MARKKO.　　　　　　　　　　P.W.F.

Ohio River Valley AVA. Comprising 16.6 million acres over four states, it is the largest AVA in the country, although that boast belies the fact that fewer than 500 acres of grapes grow within its sprawling boundary, a zone that covers the western edge of WEST VIRGINIA through KENTUCKY, OHIO, and INDIANA running along the river. It is a relatively warm area for the MIDWEST region with 180 to 200 frost free days. It was along this valley that the first colonists heading west staked their claim and placed their bets on vinifera grapes. Sadly black rot did them in, and many of these disappointed pioneers moved north to the Lake Erie area or further west to MO. Today, the vineyard is primarily planted to French and to American hybrids.

　　　　　　　　　　　　　　P.W.F.

Okanagan Valley VA, the slender, 100 mi long, lake filled valley which is the heart of the BRITISH COLUMBIA wine industry. It is also a popular vacation playland offering water sports in summer and skiing in winter. Vines were first planted near Kelowna in 1860 by the Oblate Mission of Father Pandosy. The first winery opened in 1930.

Nearly 3,000 acres are planted to grapes with over 30 wineries stretched from the northern tip of Okanagan Lake, past Penticton at the southern tip, ending in Oliver and Osoyoos, within 10 mi of the US–Canada border. The Okanagan Valley is a northern finger of the Great American Desert, in many ways a continuation of the COLUMBIA VALLEY in WA but with a greater contrast in geography. It is wedged between the foothills of the ROCKY MTNS to the east, including the Okanagan Highlands, and to the west the CASCADE RANGE. Rainfall is a meager 6–16 in annually. Hills are topped by forests. Vineyards along the lake tend to cling to benchlands composed of gravelly soils. By contrast, vineyards in the south near Oliver are planted in softer, sandy soils more like those of the Columbia Valley.

Hindsight and continuous varietal experimentation is showing there are two different growing regions in the Okanagan. The district south of the lake is capable of producing consumer popular red wines such as Cabernet Sauvignon and Merlot. Even three cool wet vintages in a row from 1995 to 1997 could not extinguish the enthusiasm of wineries and growers there. The hot dry summer of 1998 rewarded most wineries with big, rich, flavoured red wines. The Western Piedmont slopes here are called The Golden Mile. Exciting vineyard developments on the Eastern Piedmont slopes are called Black Sage Bench. They include Osoyoos Indian land, a broad sandy basin along the east side of the Okanagan district where soon nearly 1,250 acres will be in production.

The northern district is an area around the lake starting at Okanagan Falls, and running to the town of Vernon. Here the geography changes abruptly from an open valley to mountainous hillsides. The north region includes the narrow bench at Naramata, a modest-sized vineyard community on the east hillside of the lake where vineyards sprout out of hillside granite. Here Pinot Noir, Pinot Blanc, and surprising Syrah vines cling to protected sites. Directly across the lake on the westside are Summerland and Peachland. Summerland is the home of the Summerland Research Center, funded by Agriculture Canada to conduct agricultural and viticultural research. It is also the site of VQA tasting and testing.

Burrowing Owl Vyds, up-and-coming winery with a large, newly planted, 290-acre vineyard located on the Black Sage Bench. Excellent Chardonnay, Pinot Gris.

Gehringer Brothers, located in the south Okanagan, producing Germanic-styled wines in a spectacular setting looking east at the Black Sage Bench. Walter Gehringer produces delightful Riesling and Ehrenfelser and phenomenal ICEWINE.

Gray Monk is among the world's most northerly vineyards. It sits high above the northern end of Okanagan Lake and is owned by the Heiss family. They produce Germanic wines including successful Pinot Gris, Pinot Auxerrois, Riesling, and Ehrenfelser.

Inkameep Vyd, owned by Osoyoos Indians and a grower for several wineries. In partnership with VINCOR they have planted 500 acres to Cabernet Sauvignon, Merlot, and Syrah, employing Osoyoos Indians for vineyard work and mechanically havesting.

Inniskillin Okanagan is, like INNISKILLIN Ontario, owned by Vincor. Bordeaux varietals and blends are produced from grapes grown at Inkameep Vyd (above) and their own Dark Horse Vyd in the Golden Mile, also known as the Oliver Bench.

Mission Hill, winery on the west side close to Kelowna, resurrected in 1981 by negociant Anthony von Mandl, and now extensively expanded with an elaborate new architectural vision. John Simes is the winemaker. Relying on their 225-acre vineyard in the south, they produce Chardonnay, Pinot Gris, and a Merlot-Cabernet Sauvignon blend. Superb view.

Nichol Vyd. Alex and Kathleen Nichol produce interesting reds including a light cranberry-like Pinot Noir and an excellent Syrah from vineyards carved out of the granite in the hills of Naramata.

Quail's Gate, located across from Kelowna on the westbank in the northern section. Pinot Noir, a dessert wine from *Optima, and a Riesling Icewine are excellent. Australian winemaker.

Sumac Ridge, 50,000-case winery located in Summerland. Started in 1980 by Harry McWatters, a tireless promoter of BC wines. In addition to his own 8-acre vineyard, McWatters is developing a new vineyard and winery called Hawthorne Mtn Vyds specializing in Pinot Noir, Chardonnay, and Riesling. McWatters is also active in the 115-acre Black Sage Vyd, a new development in the south with plantings of Merlot, Cabernet Sauvignon, and Cabernet Franc. R.A.I.

Oklahoma, state in the PLAINS region best known for oil production. There were several wineries as late as the 1890s, but the bullet of Prohibition proved fatal here as well as in most other parts of the territory. In 1970 the OK Office of Economic Opportunity attempted an innovative project. They planned to settle 10 families on 12-acre parcels of proposed vineyard land at Caney in the southeast part of the state. Initially 20 acres of vines were planted, but a philosophical change at administrative level ended the project. Those original plantings, plus 20 more acres, are now owned by Dwayne Pool of Cimarron Cellars. A severe cold snap in 1988 reduced the acreage to about 20. Cimarron's annual production is 2,000 cases.

Oklahoma seems to have more favorable conditions for the survival and proliferation of the vine than any other Plains state. Annual rainfall is a moderate 17 in, mostly falling in the winter. Summers are hot and windy. The area near Enid, in the northwestern part of the state, has similarities to the TEXAS HIGH PLAINS AVA around Lubbock. Elevation is over 1,300 ft, and rises even higher west into the Panhandle where there is a vineyard planted to Pinot Noir and Gewürztraminer. A line running north–south through the middle of the state at about Oklahoma City divides it according to winter temperature. In the lower elevations east of that line, temperatures fall below 0°F, thus making most sites unsuitable for vinifera. Vines planted at Enid just west of the line go dormant early and stay dormant until at least Apr 10, and there is no problem with trunk splitting during the winter. Nor does *frost cause much damage. Near Oklahoma City, however, *budbreak can occur in late Mar, and vines are susceptible to late cold snaps. Grapes near Enid are picked in late July, or early Aug. Vines tend to produce vigorously, so some spring frost damage to primary buds is no disaster; secondary buds provide ample yields. In the southeast part of the state trunk splitting does occur, although it is less of a problem with hybrids. The severe winter of 1988–9 wiped out all vinifera, and they were not replanted. Summer temperatures can reach 100°F, and rainfall is plentiful. The OZARK MTN AVA extends into the northeastern corner of OK from AR. There are several planted vineyards, and two wineries were bonded in the late 1990s.

OK operates under the THREE-TIER system, but wineries may sell directly to consumers. A recently proposed law, establishing a small winery license which would permit wineries to sell directly to restaurants and retail stores, had not been passed at time of writing (mid-1999). Currently the majority of the winery production in OK is sold at the wineries. There are 40 DRY counties in OK where alcohol cannot be sold by the drink for ON-PREMISE consumption, although package stores may sell it 'in original containers at room temperature.' These dry counties also allow bottle clubs where individuals pay a membership fee for the privilege of bringing in their own bottles of alcohol and pay to have drinks mixed and served to them by the licensee.

Bartunek, winery in Enid, 80 mi northwest of Oklahoma City. Production is 2,000 gal, including Cynthiana. All 4 acres must be netted to keep birds away. R.T.S.

Old Mission Peninsula AVA, approved in 1987, is a slip of land lying in MICHIGAN's Grand Traverse Co just east of the LEELANAU PENINSULA. It displays a similarly strong GREAT LAKES EFFECT, especially with respect to snow cover, which affords not only protection against WINTER KILL, but often provides an interesting setting for the icewine harvest. Pickers, many of them just arrived from sunny Mexico, digging through the snow to find the grapes, have never looked so bewildered. The AVA includes nearly 20,000 acres but is planted to just over 200 acres of vines. The vast majority of vineyards are vinifera vines used for wine. P.W.F.

on-premise, license to sell to consumers for immediate consumption in the establishment, a restaurant or tasting bar. It is uncommon for US states to grant both on-premise and off-premise (ie OFF-SALE) licenses to the same establishment.

Ontario, most populous province of CANADA, and the one that extends furthest south, which helps explain its dominant position in the Canadian wine industry. It includes TORONTO and the federal capital at Ottawa and comprises the northern border of all the Great Lakes. Vine growing, however, is largely confined to a strip, vigorously contended during the war of 1812 between Britain and the US, running from about Detroit, MI, to Niagara Falls just outside Buffalo, NY.

There are 20,000 acres of winegrapes currently under vine in Ontario. A diminishing proportion are devoted to grapes for juice. Winegrape growing is concentrated on sites closest to Lakes Ontario and Erie in three designated VAS: the northern part of the

NIAGARA PENINSULA; the southern part of western Ontario called LAKE ERIE NORTH SHORE; and PELEE ISLAND in the middle of Lake Erie. These appellations sit between 41° and 44°N, about the same latitude as Bordeaux and Burgundy in France, Oregon, and the southern tip of Washington's Yakima Valley in North America.

HISTORY

Wine has been produced commercially in Ontario for over 150 years. Before the mid-1970s, the industry was based predominantly on American varieties and hybrids made from LABRUSCA grapes such as Delaware, Concord, Isabella, Clinton, and Dutchess. It was not for lack of trying that the better vinifera varieties were not part of this early industry. Vinifera vines proved to be vulnerable to low temperatures and to diseases to which native vines are resistant. After 100 years of experimentation, interspersed with political and social forces that militated against their growth, it seemed as though the finer European varieties would not survive in Canada. By the early 1960s however, with improved clones, more appropriate rootstocks, advances in vineyard management practices, and a changed political climate, a few pioneering growers challenged the prevailing wisdom to take another chance at growing vinifera.

CLIMATE AND TOPOGRAPHY

The moderating presence of the GREAT LAKES EFFECT helps to provide a humid temperate continental climate for all three of Ontario's growing areas. Each, however, has significant topographical features that influence growing conditions. The Viticultural Areas (VAs) of Ontario are part of a zone called the Carolinian forest, named after the same vegetation zone found in North and South Carolina in the southern US, which flourishes in the shelter of Lakes Ontario, Erie, and Huron. The region is considered a Canadian national treasure containing more than half of the 139 species of Canada's rare, threatened, and endangered plants and animals. Nowhere else in Canada can one find the Carolinian flora and fauna, though many of them exist in NC.

The main topographical feature in the Niagara Peninsula is the NIAGARA ESCARPMENT running east and west across the region and rising sharply to 175–185 metres (610 ft) above Lake Ontario, 2 to 8 miles from shore, which acts as a backboard against which winds off the lake circulate. Distance from either of the lakes or the Escarpment causes significant variations in the rate of spring warm-up, the frequency of spring and fall frosts, maximum tempera-

tures in summer and minimum temperatures in winter, and amount of snow cover. In central Niagara the Escarpment forms two broad terraces called the BEAMSVILLE BENCH that slope gently up to a cliff. Vineyards are located on these prime growing sites. The St David's Bench is about 7 km away.

Most soils in the winegrowing regions are composed of GLACIAL TILL or of sediments left in glacier-carved rivers and lakes. Many older vineyards on the Niagara Peninsula were established on clay-loam soils near the Escarpment. These have almost all been drained with buried tiles. New vineyards have favored sandy loam sites once predominately occupied by tender fruits such as peaches and pears. New producers are aware that they must choose their sites judiciously, matching each variety to an appropriate *rootstock. Some rootstocks such as SO4, once touted as among the better choices for Niagara, are proving to be too vigorous for the soils.

The length of the growing season is variable and unpredictable. Defined by the number of *frost free days, it can range from as few as 139 to as many as 231. For grape growers, the period from budbreak to harvest must accommodate that somewhat elastic window. Surrounded by water and the southernmost point in all of Canada, Pelee Island is likely to have the longest season, perhaps beginning as early as Apr with harvest extending to the end of Nov. The vineyard sites with the longest season are those closest to the Lakes. *Heat summation for Niagara Peninsula has ranged from 2,000 degree days in the coolest vintage to 3,000 in the warmest (expressed in °F as elsewhere in this book). The warmest month is July with a mean temperature of 21°C (72°F). The growing season in Niagara is similar to the FINGER LAKES district in NY with budbreak occurring on average from late May to early June.

The severity of winter also varies considerably, but the predictability of conditions conducive to the production of ICEWINE is one of the Canadian industry's great strengths. The coldest month is usually January with a monthly average temperature around −5°C (22°F), although the moderating effect of the lakes is significant. In winter, Lake Ontario releases close to shore the heat it has absorbed and stored throughout the summer months. Even during a severe winter, only 25% of the lake will have ice cover. Lake Erie, a shallower body of water, cools much faster and freezes over regularly, surrounding Pelee Island with ice in midwinter. On the Niagara Peninsula temperatures have been recorded as low as −25°C

(−13°F), but these incidences are few. Lake Erie, on the other hand, has little moderating effect, either in North Shore vineyards or in Harrow, on the mainland near Pelee Island, where the temperature falls to −25°C every two to three winters. Annual precipitation throughout the three designated VAs ranges from 816 mm to 890 mm (37 in), including rain and snow.

VINTAGES

There were at least five excellent vintages in Ontario in the 1990s: 1991, 1995, 1997, 1998, and 1999. All had *degree days significantly above the 30-year average of 2,480 (expressed in °F). More challenging vintages occurred in 1992 (the worst year on record) and 1996 when cold and rainy weather characterized short seasons, although the white varieties in 1996 have held their own fairly well. In 1993 a relatively mild winter ended with record low temperatures in Mar resulting in spring frost which reduced the crop. Sept was not much better, recording the coldest harvest since 1975, but the wines had concentrated sugars and better acidity than the salubrious larger crop in the warm vintage of 1991. Although the 1997 harvest was later than usual, and yield was down due to heavy rains at harvest that followed on the heels of an Aug drought, the fruit came in ripe and in good condition. The 1998 vintage had an edge from the start. Buds peeked out early due to a warm, frost free spring. By June the vines were 2–3 weeks ahead of other seasons. This lead time allowed the grapes to achieve greater maturity. 1999 appears to be an outstanding year marked by unusually warm weather.

COLD WEATHER PRACTICES

The main criterion for choosing a site in Ontario is its history of cold temperatures. Growers on the Niagara Peninsula have been encouraged to locate their vineyards on at least 3% slopes to achieve some air and water drainage. Clay soils are avoided since poor drainage causes soils to remain cold longer. Most of Ontario's growers choose grape varieties that bud late (to avoid spring frost) and mature by mid-September such as: Riesling, Chardonnay, Auxerrois, Pinot Gris, Gamay Noir, Pinot Noir, and Cabernet Franc.

Vine management practices are designed to encourage *photosynthesis and also enhance winter hardiness. Trellis techniques such as variations on the Pendlebogen system (low cordon, spur trained) and Scott Henry are becoming popular. LONG PRUNING is frequently practiced. Mechanical HEDGING is commonly used to remove excessive summer vegetative growth. *Cover crops are often employed between rows, causing vines to compete for nitrogen and water. In view of the harsh winters, many growers have adopted practices such as using multiple trunks instead of a single one; retaining extra buds and removing them if no damage has occurred; and hilling or MOUNDING soil around the base of the trunk to protect the graft scar and root system from winter damage.

RESEARCH

Better ways to address winter hardiness for vinifera in Canada were given deeper urgency when winter temperatures dipped below –24°C (–11.2°F) in 1992/3. Using government funds Dr John Paroschy, a research scientist employed at CH DES CHARMES, and an interdisciplinary team from the Univ of Guelph headed by Prof Bryan McKersie took an innovative, thoroughly late 20th-century approach to the problem. They inserted a gene from a wild relative of broccoli (*Arabidopsis thaliana*) into the DNA of Cabernet Franc vines. Evaluation as to improved winter hardiness, and whether or not the broccoli gene affects wine flavor, are still ongoing.

Next the team looked at a RIPARIA vine that can withstand temperatures as low as –40°C(–40°F). After isolating 200 genes that were different from vinifera's, they chose eight they thought might have an impact on winter injury. In order to place a riparia gene into the vinifera plant, they first put it into a disarmed Agrobacterium. Normally, Agrobacterium causes tumors (see *crown gall) on grapevines, but once the gene that produces gall is omitted from the bacterium, the *disarmed* bacterium can carry the new gene into the vine as if it were invading the plant cell and injecting its own DNA. When the tumor-forming gene was replaced with a winter-hardy riparia gene, it became a natural vehicle for the gene transfer. It is unknown whether wine from the resulting plant will taste of the vinifera or of the *foxy riparia.

See *winter protection, LCBO, VQA. L.F.B.
Gayler, H. J., *Niagara's Changing Landscapes* (Ottawa, 1994).

Opus One, seminal winery venture begun in 1979 pairing CA's Robert MONDAVI with Baron Philippe de Rothschild of Bordeaux's Ch *Mouton-Rothschild. While the cooperative aspects of the 50 : 50 partnership are remarkable, and the architectural design and lavish furnishings of the $20 million, 20,000-case winery built in 1992 at Hwy 29 and Oakville Cross Rd in NAPA VALLEY are wondrous to behold, the most profound impact of the venture was a wholesale, virtually overnight switch in attitude toward CA Cabernet wine. In the space of five vintages preferences went from 100% Cabernet Sauvignon ripened as much as possible, to Meritage blends made in leaner, more deftly balanced styles. The prestige and promotional acumen of the Opus One partnership far outweighed the amount of wine made in the early years.

In fact the monumental difficulties encountered in the early years of producing Opus One would long ago have sunk less buoyant participants. The venture owns 75 acres surrounding the winery, densely planted at 2,200 vines to the acre. But they are in the center of the valley, not on the Oakville Bench nor in the gravel deposits by the river. Half of the vines were replaced in the early 1990s to reorient the direction of the rows for better air circulation and in Opus One's first decade and a half none of the wines used any of the grapes from the vineyard owned by the venture. The concept of a winery buried in such a way as to minimize disruption to sightlines is laudable, but the projected cost doubled during construction because underground thermal springs made the barrel cellar too warm and cooling equipment had to be installed in the walls.

These obstacles aside, Opus One has been very fine wine indeed, right from the beginning. It is often closed with little nose when young, but always possesses smooth tannins and a supple *mouthfeel. After 8–10 years it begins to unfold a bouquet which represents its great strength, a smell of toasted almonds and seared lamb (appropriate considering the Mouton connection) that announces itself well before one's nose arrives at the glass. B.C.C.

Orange Co Fair, annual wine COMPETITION run by a 900-member consumer club, the Orange Co Wine Society, in conjunction with the county agricultural fair in Costa Mesa, CA, south of LOS ANGELES. Noteworthy among US competitions for the manner in which it is structured. No entry fee is charged, but entering wineries must submit six bottles of each wine. The organizers also maintain a budget to buy from retail stores in Orange Co a few bottles each of 40–50 high profile CA wines which are not entered. After the judging, all the wines in the competition are then poured at a public tasting booth during the seventeen days of the Fair for a charge of $4 for 6 ounces of a non-award winning wine; $1 for a 1-ounce sample of an award winning wine. B.C.C.

Oregon, state in the PACIFIC NORTHWEST region with over 120 wineries in 1999, but only 7,500 acres of vinifera vines, thus more or less defining itself as an ultra-premium producer and ceding the value end of the industry to its neighbors CA and WA. In OR 62% of all sales of OR wines are of red wines. There are five discrete viticultural zones. Most important is the WILLAMETTE VALLEY which runs from PORTLAND on the Columbia River border with WA south for 100 mi. In the southern portion of the state are the UMPQUA and the ROGUE viticultural areas which lie along rivers running to the ocean. OR also has a small share, with WA, of the two eastern viticultural areas of COLUMBIA VALLEY and WALLA WALLA VALLEY.

Winegrapes first arrived in OR in 1847 with Henderson Luelling, whose partner William Meek won a gold medal for his white Isabella wine at the 1859 CA State Fair. Other late 19th-century wineries existed until their will was finally broken by Prohibition. Wineries which started up after Prohibition were squeezed out of the marketplace in the 1950s by cheaper CA wines, which may explain why OR is dominated today by CRAFTSMAN-SIZED wineries. They are primarily located in the Willamette Valley within easy access of its urban population and the cultural center of PORTLAND. A broad expanse between the Coast Range and the Cascade Mtns, the 40 mi wide Willamette Valley is often thought of as two areas: north Willamette directly southwest of Portland; and south Willamette from the EOLA HILLS down to Eugene. Soils are mostly GLACIAL TILL, layered with red volcanic soil. Some soils are deposits of rich topsoils washed from eastern WA over the millennia by massive floods. Based on the period 1961–90, the north Willamette annually receives 40 in of rain with 2 inches falling in Sept and 3 falling in Oct. Every vintage in the 1990s, except for 1992, 1994, and 1998, was harvested in cool, damp conditions producing restrained flavors and high *acidity. Further south, in the Umpqua and Rogue wine regions, soils tend to be drier and more sandy. Rainfall drops appreciably towards the south. In the Umpqua annual precipitation is close to 32 in; in the Rogue it varies from 19 to 26 in.

The north Willamette has grown quickly as a wine district, almost doubling in size from 1994 to 1999, partly because local wine folk are both stubborn and clever. OR producers chose a narrow path and stuck to it, pursuing and taming the elusive Pinot Noir variety. No other goal would have generated as many headaches, nor as much publicity and international interest. The region includes a great mix of wineries who specialize in estate bottling alongside those who purchase grapes. Vineyard owners often live and work in nearby Portland and produce grapes as a sideline, emphasizing the artistic aspect of grape growing—less farming than vine rearing. Few vineyards are larger than 40 acres. Few wineries make more than 20,000 cases. The Willamette Valley's success with Pinot Noir has attracted substantial investments from sophisticated vintners in France, CA, and elsewhere. This investment pushed up land prices significantly, which helped catalyze developments in the south Willamette, the Umpqua, and the Rogue.

The few wineries located outside the five recognized viticultural areas include the state's biggest, KING ESTATE in Lorane Valley southwest of Eugene. Hood River Vyds and Flerchinger Vyds are located in the Hood River Valley in the center of the state where there is talk of a new AVA called Columbia Gorge that would encompass the Hood River Valley and continue across to the WA side.

Over the vigorous objections of CA vintners, OR Pinot Noir has achieved a public image as the American standard of this finicky variety. OR winemakers recognized a cooler climate's ability to provide favorable growing conditions early in the game. David Lett planted EYRIE VYDS in 1966 and blazed a trail with his light, oaky, ephemeral wines that somehow aged gracefully, broadening in their development. Through his leadership new OR producers stayed the course and staked their claim to be America's answer to Burgundy. It was a risky strategem as Pinot Noir had a limited consumer share and OR was isolated from established markets. In essence they put all their grapes in one basket.

But the Siren's call of Pinot Noir is compelling, and Willamette Valley's success has summoned a world-class roster of new investors: Gary Andrus of PINE RIDGE and William Hill, both from Napa Valley, opened Archery Summit and Van Duzer (now owned by Carl Thomas) respectively; Tony Soter came from Napa as well; Australian Brian Croser of Petaluma Winery has opened Argyle; and the *Drouhin family of Burgundy set up DOM DROUHIN OREGON. Even pre-eminent US wine critic Robert *Parker became an investor with his brother-in-law in Beaux Frères.

Along with recognition, has come a new attitude. Winery owners of the past were committed visionaries working on a shoestring, scraping together just enough money to buy bottles. Frequently today new wineries are well financed and staffed with separate marketing, hospitality, and production

personnel, in sharp contrast to their counterparts of 20 years ago whose owners did everything themselves. Big new wineries change the rules. They offer more money for the best grapes from proven vineyards, and they even shape the marketplace by producing wines that drink earlier and easier, wines that highlight softness and fatness over structure.

Changes are being made with both Pinot Noir and white varieties, notably Pinot Gris. The buzzword is *clonal selection. OR State Univ at Corvallis has a Clonal Selection Program which was very active in the late 1980s importing vine specimens for testing in OR vineyard conditions. Much of the early Pinot Noir was a clone from *Wädenswil in Switzerland. More recent Pommard clones have added complexity to the wines. And now one can expect very much more exciting Chardonnays as new clones are planted. Currently the DIJON CLONES which give wines a more distinctive middle palate with a more concentrated, complex flavor are preferred, although Eyrie Vyds has also had great success with the Draper Selection of Chardonnay clones. Much of the Chardonnay currently in production is UC *Davis clone #108, developed for CA conditions to prolong the growing season. In OR this has resulted in less than ripe fruit in too many years, creating wines that are dominated by simple lemon fruitiness, although occasionally in hot years complete ripeness has produced beautiful wines.

Pinot Blanc is a bone OR is eager to pick with CA. The clone widely planted throughout OR came from the INRA (see ENTAV) agricultural station in Colmar, Alsace. OR generally does not age Pinot Blanc in oak, instead aiming for more crisp, more delicate fruit flavors with hints of Casabah melon, mineral, and a touch of anise. OR State's Clonal Selection Program is also working to acquire some examples of Pinot Bianco from Italy.

Further strides are occurring in vineyards with better cultural practices that include denser plantings, reduced crops, and *leaf removal. In the winery winemakers are decreasing stem contact, doing more *whole bunch fermentations, and pressing more gently. Some red wine producers choose to cold soak the juice with the skins prior to fermentation in an effort to extract more color and flavor, hopefully without vegetative flavors or harsh tannins.

While north Willamette has been distinguishing itself with Pinot Noir, the areas in the south have had to battle isolation and lack of varietal identity. South OR has long produced a mix of wines: Merlot, Cabernet

Sauvignon, Syrah (often planted next to Pinot Noir), and Gewürztraminer. Mesoclimates vary greatly as most of the vineyards are located in mountainous regions along narrow river valleys. The Umpqua and the Rogue River valleys are slightly warmer than north Willamette, although site selection is an important variable.

REGULATORY ENVIRONMENT
As early as 1977 OR winegrowers drew up regulations which were much more strict than federally mandated US LABEL REGULATIONS. OR required varietally labeled wines to be made 90% from the stated variety, and they did not allow generic names such as Burgundy or Chablis. The Oregon Liquor Control Commission (OLLC) handles all licensing of wineries and administration of rules and regulations. The OLLC is overseen by five volunteer commissioners. All sales must be purchased COD through a licensed wholesaler without quantity discounts.

Wine and beer may be sold through private retail licensees in OR. A unique, and not widely known feature of the law, however, is a provision called 'dock sale,' wherein consumers may buy wines directly from the wholesalers, at the same price that retailers must pay. Minimum dock sale purchase is two cases of an item.   R.A.I.

organic wine. All over the world political efforts are under way attempting to both define, and to enforce restrictions on the use of, the phrase 'organic' when applied to wine. While regulations exist in the US for defining and enforcing who may or may not use the phrase *organically grown*, no such regulations exist to define *organically produced*. Hence grapes grown without herbicides, pesticides, and inorganic fertilizers may be subject to unlimited chemical assault in the winery and still bear something of the imprimatur of organic-ness. The US Food & Drug Administration has tried to write regulations concerning *organic wine production, but their first attempt was withdrawn in 1999 in the wake of extensive public protest over the allowed inclusion of irradiated foods, foods grown in fields to which grey water and sludge from waste treatment plants had been applied, and genetically altered organisms. One of the biggest debates specific to wine concerns whether or not added *sulfites will be permitted. In Europe the phrase *biologique* carries the same connotation as organic does in the US, but European organic wine activists do not view SO_2 with the same alarm mustered by their US counterparts. Hence 'biologique' is allowed on European labels even though no universal standard for allowable added sulfites has been agreed upon.

Wines which are not sold across state boundaries in the US may bear label phraseology which is approved by their state. An organization named California Certified Organic Farmers (CCOF) is approved by CA's state government to inspect and certify both vineyards and wineries. A grower must pass their inspection three years in a row before they can call themselves certified. See FREY VYDS. A similar organization exists in OR called Oregon Tilth. Both are members of IFOAM, an international organization attempting to bring uniformity to varying standards used by different trading partners. See also Organic essay, p 59. B.C.C.

own roots, phrase used in the US for vinifera grapevines that have not been grafted on to rootstock of another species but are planted on their own, vinifera roots. The implication is that they are therefore suscept-ible to *phylloxera. In Europe such vines are described as un*grafted, but CA vine-yardists have been so quick to *T-bud vine-yards over to new varieties since that technique became widespread in the mid-1980s, that it would not be clear whether the graft in question involved phylloxera-resistant rootstock or a move to a more fashionable *scion.

Ozark Highlands AVA, a 1.3 million-acre land area in Phelps and Crawford counties, MISSOURI, about 100 mi southwest of St Louis. Known as the Big Prairie, it is on a plateau above the Missouri River valley. Vineyards are on ridges with efficient *air drainage of cold air in spring. While most of the surrounding land is chalky, the AVA is primarily a clay-loam soil. Within it are planted 200 acres of grapes, at least half of which belong to the AVA's leading winery, St James, which is also the largest vineyard holder in the state. Of the AVA's 200 acres, the majority is planted to American hybrids.

Over a third are Concord, but there is also some Catawba, Delaware, and Norton. The balance is planted to French hybrids such as Vignoles, Rougeon, and Cayuga.

P.W.F.

Ozark Mtn, a mega-AVA approved in 1986. It covers the southern half of MISSOURI, including all or parts of 53 counties, the entire northwestern quarter of ARKANSAS, impinging on 29 counties, and seven counties in northeastern OK. The total land mass within this AVA is just over 3.5 million acres, making it the fifth largest AVA in the country. The number of acres of vines, however, does not exceed 5,000. Bounded by the Mississippi, the Missouri, the Osage, the Neosho, and the Arkansas rivers, it is considered an upland plateau with varying macroclimates depending upon exposure and elevation. Within the mega-AVA are the following sub-AVAs: in AR, ALTUS and ARKANSAS MTN; and in MO, AUGUSTA, HERMANN, and OZARK HIGHLANDS. P.W.F.

Pacific Northwest, region comprising the northwest corner of the contiguous US and including BRITISH COLUMBIA, Canada's most westerly province. The region begins with the CA border on the south at the 42nd parallel. To the north it runs over the 51st parallel, approximately 110 mi from the US–Canada border. Its westerly border faces the Pacific Ocean and includes the western states of OREGON, and WASHINGTON. The eastern border runs through the middle of IDAHO.

It represents an extremely diverse geographic area, captivating in its variety and magnitude; from the 6,600 ft drop into Hell's Canyon, ID to towering, snow-capped 14,000 ft Mt Rainier in WA's CASCADE RANGE. This virtual rectangle, 500 mi wide by 600 mi high, is over 300,000 sq mi and comparable in size to an area that includes all of France, Germany's southern wine regions, and Italy's northern provinces. This geographic mélange affects an already dynamic climate, influenced foremost by low pressure systems of southeasterly moving marine air from the Pacific Ocean in the southwest, often in conflict with more extreme temperatures in the continental air arriving from the north and from the east. The Jet Stream blows rainy weather fronts into the Pacific Northwest with regularity which is why WA's Olympic Peninsula is one of the wettest regions on earth, a spectacular temperate climate rainforest one hour's drive from SEATTLE. However, the modest hills of the Coast Range and the much more substantial, volcanically built mountains of the Cascade Range act as a weather buffer to these storms from the west. Eastern WA and OR are in a RAIN SHADOW and almost qualify as deserts. The entire Pacific Northwest region is bisected by enormous rivers draining large areas of mountains which have accumulated snow. The granddaddy of these watersheds is the Columbia River. The Yakima, the Snake, the Okanagan, the Willamette, the Deschutes, the Umpqua, and the Rogue rivers are smaller (all but the last two are tributaries of the Columbia), nevertheless each is larger than any river in CA save the Sacramento. These systems help moderate climate. In winter they drain away the cold winter air and in summer they cool the surrounding landmass baking under the sun.

Driving over the Cascade Range at Snoqualmie Pass demonstrates the abrupt weather change between the west slope of the Cascades and the eastern slope. Forests of giant Douglas fir give way to a mix of fir and Ponderosa pine. Within 20 mi of the summit trees become sparse. Twenty miles west of Snoqualmie annual rainfall is above 50 in a year; 20 mi east annual rainfall is close to 10 in. Snow accumulations average about 10 ft along the crest of the Cascades. In 1999 Mt Baker recorded its highest snow accumulation in history at nearly 93 ft.

Vineyards comprise only a small fraction of the arable land in the Pacific Northwest, covering less than 40,000 acres. Almost all of it is vinifera. Amazingly, almost all of these vines were planted since 1980. In 1970 there were less than 1,000 acres. The growth has been remarkable, but the surprise is that it took so long to happen. Wine is not new to this region; its roots can be traced to the first planting of vinifera grapes along the banks of the Columbia River at Fort Vancouver in 1825. The region's history of wine and grapes parallels the rest of America. Where there were immigrants there was wine. The early history of wine in the Pacific Northwest is shared by Germans, French, Italians, Croatians, and other European immigrants.

While volume production in the Northwest today is dominated by a few large wineries, there are in total more than 250 wineries dotted throughout the region. WA leads in vineyard acreage with its productive vineyards in the irrigated Columbia Basin. OR boasts the most wineries, consisting mainly of CRAFTSMAN-SIZED operations nestled in the Willamette Valley. BC is the newest region, and the most visually stunning.

OR's vineyards are located primarily on the western flanks of the Cascade Mtns, with only the diminutive parallel Coast Range for protection in an annual battle with the caprice of Pacific Ocean storms. In the northwestern corner of the region plucky winemakers try to carve a niche for cool climate grapes out of WA's Puget Sound, or BC's Fraser Valley and Vancouver Island. ID's vineyards are much like the irrigated vineyards of WA, although at a slightly greater risk of frost damage from cold continental air settling in vineyards. In BC most of the recent plantings have occurred on slopes above the lake and river in OKANAGAN VALLEY, five hours' drive east of VANCOUVER, where semi-arid conditions mimic those of the COLUMBIA VALLEY to the south.

Wines of the Pacific Northwest offer a rich geographic smorgasbord. At their best they can offer intensely flavored and layered Cabernet Sauvignon or plummy Merlot from WA; silky smooth and juicy Pinot Noir from OR; bright, yet softly rendered Pinot Gris, and subtly fruity Pinot Blanc from OR; beautifully balanced Germanic wines of the Okanagan, such as Ehrenfelser, Kerner, Riesling, and sublime icewines from those grapes; uniquely herbal Semillon and Sauvignon Blanc from WA; the intensely flavorful Riesling or Chardonnay from ID. Wines of the western slope can be too thin, too light, and perhaps too acidic in less-than-ripe vintages. Some might criticize wines of the eastern slope for being too intensely fruited, or too herbaceous. Yet, in these 'faults' can be found their unique personalities. Western slope wines can be delicate, subtle, less alcoholic, with lingering flavors. Eastern slope wines can be more fully flavored, richer on the palate, bolder, and fully ripened. R.A.I.

package store sales, category of retail wine sales in between large grocery supermarkets and specialty wine merchant shops. Package, or convenience stores, generally have small inventories of mass market brands and do a much brisker trade in lottery tickets and soda pop than in wine.

Palmer Vyds, one of the older, larger, and most aggressively marketed wineries on NY's LONG ISLAND, has played a key role in raising the region's wine profile. The winery and a 50-acre estate vineyard lie on the western edge of the island's North Fork district, tucked against a low ridge rimming Long

Island Sound. Cooling breezes off the Sound make this site particularly favorable for white wine varieties. Palmer's top-of-the-line Chardonnay, consistently one of the island's most elegant, has experimented with WILD YEAST fermentations, spending a moderate 6–8 months on the lees in French oak barrels with 100% *MLF. Pinot Blanc is more purely fruit oriented. Sauvignon Blanc shows grassy intensity.

A second estate vineyard a few miles east in slightly warmer Cutchogue contributes to Palmer Merlot, a solid, middleweight wine spending just over a year in French and older American oak. A Reserve appears only in better vintages, as does a Cabernet Sauvignon-dominated blend, Select Reserve—both wines in the top ranks of Long Island reds.

The wines reflect vineyards with some age, mostly planted in the mid-1980s. Wine production began in 1986. New plantings are expanding production from 20,000 cases in 1998. Palmer is the most widely distributed of Long Island brands, going to 23 states from coast to coast and exported to Europe and Asia.   R.F.

Parducci, historic winery located just north of Ukiah in MENDOCINO with good consumer name recognition in the modest price ranges. It was sold by the Parducci family in 1973 to the CA Teachers' Union Pension Fund, then purchased in 1997 by Carl Thoma, a venture capitalist from Chicago, who has made significant upgrades to the facility. About 300,000 cases of pedestrian wine are produced annually for the Parducci label and the company owns 250 estate acres of vineyard. The Cellarmaster Petite Sirah has been their best item, but in the future grapes for the Parducci label will not be exclusively sourced from Mendocino.

The portfolio of small, upmarket brands which will comprise Thoma's better Mendocino wines include Zingaro and Sketch Book. In 1999 Thoma also acquired **Hidden Cellars**, a 25,000-case brand run by Dennis Patton, one of the CA wine industry's most entertaining personalities. Patton had made wines himself in the district since 1981, but always chafed under the perception he needed to be a seller of 75,000 cases to get distributor attention in other states. 'It is like tending 32 small fires on foot with each being a mile apart,' he explains. 'You can show up and put wood on one fire at a time, but you cannot move fast enough to keep them all burning at once. You have to get big enough in each marketplace that the damn distributor thinks it is in his own interest to occasionally throw a log on the flames him-

self.' Being part of the Thoma stable may solve Patton's dilemma. It will also help him maintain the loyalty of his growers in the face of grape price increases due to 'poachers' (big wineries from outside the county bidding up the price of Mendocino fruit).

During the 1980s *botrytized Rieslings and Semillons from Bailey Lovin's vineyard in Potter Valley were Hidden Cellars' claim to fame. They were spectacular, with intense citrus peel notes in the botrytis Semillon proprietarily named Chanson D'Or. Although drought conditions from 1990 through 1994 threw a dry blanket over botrytized wine production at Hidden Cellars, Semillon continued to be important to them in a Meritage blend proprietarily called Alchemy which is 80% Semillon. Patton discovered he could get some hazelnut character into this wine by *barrel fermenting all of it, then leaving it on the lees for an entire year, stirring every ten days.   B.C.C.

Paso Robles AVA, large regional appellation on the inland side of the coastal mountains in CA's SAN LUIS OBISPO CO running from the foothills of the coastal mountains all the way to the northern and eastern county boundaries, more or less a rectangle 35 mi wide by 25 mi high that is very different from the coastal sections such as EDNA VALLEY. The coastal ridge runs diagonally through the county from southeast to northwest separating the maritime quarter, which has more in common with SANTA BARBARA CO, from the northeastern three-quarters around Paso Robles, which composes the headwaters of the Salinas River and topographically is an extension of the southern reaches of the MONTEREY AVA.

The town of Paso Robles (passageway of the oaks) is little more than a rural farming center, but it is as close as one gets to a population center on this side of the coastal mountains. Conventional nomenclature divides Paso Robles AVA along the line of brightly flowered, drought-resistant, 15 ft tall oleanders which run down the middle of Hwy 101. There is the Westside, then there is all the rest, which stretches nearly 30 mi to the east. The highway parallels the bed of the Salinas River. West of the highway average daily temperatures grow cooler toward the foothills of the coastal mountains. Moreover, the famous carbonate based *chalkrock* of the district is predominantly situated west of the highway. Traveling east, one enters a large open plain, historically employed by alfalfa farmers drawing water from the Estrella River (pronounced *ess-TRAY-ya*) and other tributaries to the Salinas. These eastern sections have hot climate, deep topsoil,

high fertility, and very little of the alkalinity found in soils west of the highway. This eastern plain, out to the post office/convenience store at Cholame, odds on bet to be the epicenter of CA's next big EARTHQUAKE and also the place James Dean wrapped his sports car around the only tree in sight in 1958, has seen a great many vineyard tracts of 500 to 1,000 acres planted—first in the 1970s as tax shelter investments, and again in the 1990s to take advantage of demand for varietal wines. Wines from this eastern section are softly fruity, full bodied, inexpensive, ready to drink immediately, and relatively successful in their commercial niche.

The Westside of Hwy 101 is much more interesting territory. It does not get FOG cover and midday temperatures can go well into the 90s. Ocean breezes blow over the ridge in the evening, however, dropping temperatures by 40–50°F. Almond and walnut orchards have been mainstays of the economy for a long time, and pistachios have entered the scene in a big way since 1970. Pianist and Polish statesman Ignace Paderewski had an estate and grew grapes here during the first part of the 20th century. Some interesting full-bodied Pinot Noirs and Chardonnays have come out of these hills over time, replete with limestone resumés, but ancient, DRY-FARMED Zinfandel vineyards deserve the most attention. The Italian immigrant community was as well established here as it was in AMADOR CO and in the Healdsburg area of northern SONOMA CO. Well-made, technologically modern wines sourced from old Westside Paso Robles Zinfandel vineyards are truly world class. They have texture, concentration, and length. They often have a pepper grinder aroma. In fact this character is noticeable enough to engender superstitious conjecture: one traditionalist winemaker claims it comes from walnut leaves in the soil.

A more painstaking analysis of the Paso Robles AVA than the simplistic highway divider technique reveals that actually the coolest section is 5 mi south of the city, on both sides of the highway, around the village of Templeton. Low points in the coast range allow breezes from Estero Bay to blow into Templeton, creating beneficial combinations of sunlight candlepower with reduced ambient air temperatures and less DIURNAL TEMPERATURE FLUCTUATION. Several nondescript wineries have made wines considerably finer than is their wont by purchasing grapes in this as yet undefined district in the path of the breeze. Particularly noteworthy have been Merlot, of which JanKris Vyd (formerly Ceres) is a good example.

Contiguous with the western border of the Paso Robles AVA is a small sub-appellation tucked into the eastern slope of the coastal ridge called **York Mountain AVA**. It makes eminently good sense, even though it only contains a single, tiny winery, because it represents a district of vineyards at higher elevation where temperatures are much cooler, annual rainfall is greater, and topsoils are less deep.

NOTABLE PROPERTIES

Castoro, modest sized winery not well recognized either in the marketplace or by critics. That is a clear oversight. Prior to launching his own venture Neils Udsen developed and standardized the procedures for producing J. LOHR's Wildflower Gamay. Castoro makes a *nouveau style wine of their own which is quite good, but their very best, and the finest value is Zinfandel. A claret style, it carries as much flavor complexity on its light frame as many of the best monster versions. Udsen knows old, shy bearing, dry-farmed vines do not require extract to deliver taste.

Dusi Vyd, actually two vineyards. Dante Dusi's comprises 85-year-old vines planted adjacent to Hwy 101 on the east side opposite the Hwy 46 exit to Cambria. Those grapes are sold to several wineries, but have been vineyard designated by RIDGE for a quarter-century. The other vineyard is owned by Dante's cousin Benito Dusi. Both are dry farmed and *head trained low to the ground in the classic Italian-American immigrant style. Grapes from both growers make wonderfully dense, spicy wines with bright boysenberry surprises popping out at the most unexpected times.

Eberle, winery with 35 acres on the main highway 2 mi east of Paso Robles. Gary Eberle took a Zoology degree at Penn State while playing defensive line for their nationally ranked football team. He is one of the top technical wine people in the region, and one of the largest. He is also something of a philosopher. Asked once if he agreed when winemakers spoke of their wines as their children, he replied, 'No. I'm a father, and I know it is possible to sit down and have a serious discussion with a bottle of Cabernet.'

Eberle came to Paso Robles in 1977 to design the Estrella River Winery (now MERIDIAN) after helping them to plant their vineyard, and being credited with one of the first importations of Syrah into CA. Fittingly, Eberle's best wines are Syrah. He buys grapes from Fralich Vyd and produces dense, fully packed wines. He also does well with Zinfandel which he buys from the old

Sauret Vyd. That one satisfies the baser tendencies of individuals who like a little roughhouse.

Justin. Located some 12 mi west of Paso Robles, the 75-acre vineyard is actually 4 mi outside the western boundary of the Paso Robles AVA in rolling oak woodland tucked into the lee of 2,500 ft high coastal mountains. The vineyard itself extends from 1,100 ft at the base to 1,700 ft at the top. It has very alkaline soils and gets a lot of rain. Vines are traditionally dry farmed here, but still tend to be quite vigorous. It is a fairly warm climate, especially in mid-afternoon. In addition to 20 acres of Chardonnay, they have 25 acres of Cabernet Sauvignon, and 10 acres each of Merlot and Cabernet Franc. The Cabernet Sauvignon tends to the chewy, chocolatey end of the spectrum, but the Cabernet Franc is wonderfully fragrant with blueberry aromas and medium to light body. Justin and Debbie Baldwin's best wine is Isosceles, a Meritage with equal proportions of the three principal Bordeaux grapes. It is deeply concentrated in low tonnage vintages such as 1987 and 1990. Another offering with good potential is a Cabernet Franc-Merlot blend named Justification, although it occasionally shows too much weedy, over-cropped Merlot flavor.

Martin Bros, winery with a flair for Italian varietals on 80 acres just east of Paso Robles. Begun in 1981 by Nick Martin, whose roommate at UC Santa Cruz had been Dave Ramey (winemaker for Matanzas Creek, Chalk Hill, then Dominus). Martin's style was for crisply *acidified wines, in particular one of CA's most fragrant, well-balanced Chenin Blancs with 30 g/l RS and 3.1 pH. A light-bodied but varietally true Nebbiolo dates from 1985. A 12-acre vineyard on the Westside, which came into production in 1996, is planted exclusively to the Lampia clone of Nebbiolo while the winery site Nebbiolo is the Michet clone. A 7% alcohol, slightly *frizzante Muscat is the hands-down favorite of tasting room visitors. Dessert wine offerings include an Aleatico and a *vin santo made from Malvasia Bianca.

Peachy Canyon, a decade-old label, primarily making Zinfandel, but a winery with colorful, CRAFTSMAN-SIZE antecedents. The wines today are twice as expensive, but still worth every penny. They come in many different incarnations each year: Estate; (Benito) Dusi Ranch; Eastside; Westside; Leona's; and sometimes Late Harvest. Dusi is the best. Westside and Leona's are very good.

See also WILD HORSE, TABLAS CREEK.

B.C.C.

Patz & Hall, small NAPA VALLEY Chardonnay producer making top rank wine from Caldwell Vyd east of the town of Napa and from Hyde Vyd in CARNEROS. The style is big and boisterously Californian, with full *MLF and *sur lie treatment, but always reliant on a pear and citrus zest fruit component rather than the wood. They are among the best Chardonnays in Napa because the flavors are plush in the middle, not tense and dried out in the way many of their local competitors finish. B.C.C.

Paul Masson. Sold by Seagram to CANANDAIGUA in 1987, this sister facility of Monterey Vyds in Gonzales produces 5 million cases of *jug wine annually under the Paul Masson, Masson Vyds, and Taylor California Cellars labels.

The Paul Masson name is all that remains of one of CA's most important wineries, started by an immigrant Frenchman at Saratoga, east of San Jose, in 1852. It really is a SANTA CLARA VALLEY story, although the original, historical winery in the SANTA CRUZ MTNS won international awards at the turn of the century and attracted stars of the theater, a few of whom added to the place's notoriety by indulging in champagne baths in their dressing rooms. For decades after the Second World War the mountain winery, by then turned into a museum, hosted well-attended classical music concerts all summer long. Rising land values and a volume production mentality forced the agricultural part of the business to move south in the 1960s. Seagram acquired 4,500 acres in the Salinas Valley and, at one time, reached 8 million cases of annual sales. Quality never again approached the reputation enjoyed prior to Prohibition, but marketing creativity did. A man named Stanford Wolfe accounted for much of Paul Masson's supermarket sales in the 1960s by packaging their wine in reusable carafes which could be opened with a bottle cap lever, perfectly designed for Middle Americans. Wolfe had the common touch. He once proposed naming a wine Fun Red and Fun White so he could go on television with advertisements saying, 'Have a little fun with your wife tonight.'

B.C.C.

Paumanok Vyds, small wine estate on the western edge of NY's LONG ISLAND North Fork viticultural district. Paumanok is the Indian name for Long Island. White wines are important here. Family roots in Germany encouraged the owners to plant a quarter of their 50-acre vineyard to Riesling, a curious effort in a district hanging its hat on Merlot. It is picked early to retain acidity. More recent plantings of Chenin Blanc are also unusual but perhaps more promising. Paumanok Chardonnay is a reliably stylish, mostly French oak-fermented wine, 100% MLF, spending eight months on the lees. Sauvignon Blanc is also made, but Cabernet Sauvignon has earned the winery's highest accolades for its muscular, tannic style; Paumanok believes this variety outperforms Merlot in the North Fork's best vintages. All red wines are bottled unfiltered.

Established in 1983, Paumanok's vineyard is one of the island's veterans and the first to employ the dense vine spacing that has become standard practice. On this very sandy, exceptionally dry site, yields of only 2 t/a have built intensity into the wines but have also encouraged the introduction of irrigation to boost yields. This and modest vineyard expansion is projected to increase Paumanok's total output from 7,000 cases in 1998 to a 10,000-case target.   R.F.

Pelee Island VA, once the site of CANADA's first winery in the 1860s (Vin Villa), it is today the location of 600 acres of vineyards owned by Pelee Island Winery. This designated ONTARIO appellation is a small island in Lake Erie 11 mi south of the shoreline, and the southernmost point in Canada. It is very close to Isle St George AVA, an approved US appellation also on an island in Lake Erie. The growing season on Pelee is 30 days longer than that of the Canadian mainland, but because of the cold winter winds off the ice, growers have to take special precautions with their vines. Drained marshlands in the center of the island provide grapes for the Pelee Island winery on shore. Although the winery is recognized for lighter styles of Chardonnay, Pinot Noir, and Gamay Noir, they are turning their focus to fuller-bodied styles of Merlot and Cabernet Sauvignon. Soils are mainly clay with some sandy loam. Production at Pelee Island winery is 150,000 cases.   L.F.B.

Pelligrini Vyds, on the North Fork of NY's LONG ISLAND, released its first wines in the early 1990s and quickly elbowed its way into the top echelon of East End wine estates. An Italian villa-style winery sits in one of the island's most densely planted vineyards; new vines are packed 2,500 to the acre in Pelligrini's attempt to concentrate fruit flavors from small vines. A second estate vineyard several miles east in Southold brings the total acreage to 78.

Pelligrini focuses 75% of its 10,000-case production on Merlot, Cabernet Sauvignon, and Cabernet Franc. Top-of-the-line Vintner's Pride bottlings, selections of the best barrels only in the better years, receive a generous two years in a mix of French and American oak; Pelligrini's elegant cellar contains 650 barrels. A percentage of each of these wines is partially barrel fermented and even lees stirred to bring in an earthy, peat-mossy undertone. Varietal Merlots and Cabernet Sauvignons always include some small percentage of the other Bordeaux varieties, while Cabernet Franc tends to stand alone. A stylish Bordeaux blend called Encore has shifted from being Cabernet Sauvignon dominated toward Merlot, and includes Petit Verdot. All reds are bottled unfiltered, including Pelligrini's basic every-vintage estate wines and a more moderately priced East End Select line from purchased grapes.

Pelligrini makes the same three tiers of Chardonnay. The Vintner's Pride and Estate Chardonnays ferment in puncheons, twice the size of regular barrels, to limit oak influence while the wine ages on the lees for up to eighteen months. Extended barrel time, without loading wines up with oak, is a key part of Pelligrini's elegant style. All estate-bottled Chardonnays go through 100% *MLF; the Vintner's Pride is unfiltered.

The wines are distributed throughout NY and in scattered markets across the country.   R.F.

Peninsula Cellars, winery on the OLD MISSION PENINSULA of MICHIGAN. The Cabernet Franc and Merlot grapes are purchased from Raftshol Vyds on the peninsula, and the wines are worth searching out.   P.W.F.

Pennsylvania, Southeast, the most densely populated quarter of this state and home to PHILADELPHIA as well as the state capital Harrisburg. It is well suited to draw both local and tourist traffic due to a location halfway between Baltimore/Washington DC and New York City on Interstate 95, the primary north–south highway of the East Coast. The rural charm of the Pennsylvania Dutch countryside of Amish and Mennonite farmers, centered in Lancaster Co, brings considerable tourism to the area.

Bounded by the Blue Mtns of the Allegheny range to the north and west, the Maryland state line to the south (also known as the Mason-Dixon Line), and the Delaware River to the east, Southeast PA has been home to viticulture since the 1700s. While the bulk of the state's grape and wine production shifted west to the Lake Erie district in the last century, its viticulture has rebounded since the 1960s, despite political resistance from state alcohol regulation authorities. Southeast PA is the second largest wine producer in the MID-ATLANTIC, after VA, with roughly 200,000 gal produced in 1997. The first Farm Winery law in the East was passed in PA in 1968.

Southeast PA is currently home to nearly 30 wineries. The region features three AVAs: CENTRAL DELAWARE VALLEY in the east, along the Delaware River; and LANCASTER VALLEY and the Susquehannah Valley on either side of the Susquehannah River, in the south/central region. Roughly half of the region's wineries are in the Central Delaware Valley, most of which are in Bucks Co, bordering the Delaware River. An unofficial region called Atlantic Uplands lies above the DELMARVA Peninsula. Atlantic Uplands is championed by CHADDSFORD, a leading local winery. Another unofficial but viticulturally distinctive region is the Lehigh Valley, in Lehigh and Northampton counties at the northern range of Southeast PA. Elevation and its effect on the length of the growing season, cool night temperatures, and the complex shale-based soils produce wines with fresh varietal flavors and acidity. The best varieties are late ripening ones such as Chambourcin and Vidal. In fact the region has become a little pocket for Chambourcin.

The region has a mild climate due to the influence of CHESAPEAKE BAY to the south, and the Susquehannah and Delaware rivers. Peaches are grown in parts of the region, with warmer winters than areas further west at the same latitude. The region is also somewhat sheltered from tropical storms in the Atlantic, and by cold air masses in winter, by the Blue Mtns. French hybrids are successfully cultivated, and fine fruit wines are also made. In the 1990s, vinifera plantings outstripped hybrids, with Chardonnay the most widely cultivated variety followed by Cabernet Franc and Cabernet Sauvignon. In addition, Italian varieties are now being cultivated, with Pinot Grigio and Dolcetto examples from Chaddsford showing great potential. Viognier is made by some wineries, and while some Pinot Noir is being planted from DIJON CLONES, it remains to be seen whether the region is cool enough for successful Pinot cultivation. With the high humidity of the East Coast, Pinot Noir tends to rot before it fully ripens.

NOTABLE PROPERTIES
Blue Mtn Vyds. Just south of Allentown on Rt 9, Blue Mtn began with 5 acres as a vineyard operation in 1986. Proprietor Joseph Greff expanded his 'hobby' to include winemaking in 1993. The vineyard has since expanded to over 80 acres, and produces 4,000 cases annually of estate bottled wines. Varieties include: Chardonnay, Cabernet Sauvignon, Cabernet Franc, Merlot, Riesling, and

Syrah. Awards in 1998 included gold medals for a 1996 Meritage and a 1996 Cabernet Franc. Greff is also championing a regional quality alliance.

Buckingham Valley Vyds, located north of Philadelphia in the Central Delaware Valley, and noteworthy as one of the oldest wineries in the state, established in 1966. The winery is a paragon of a successful, small, family operation. All adult members of the Forest family are partners: founder Jerry Forest is winemaker; his wife Kathy is operations manager; brothers Jon and Kevin are purchasing manager and vineyard manager respectively; and daughter-in-law Pauline is sales manager. The Forest family was recognized by trade magazine *Vineyard & Winery Management* in 1998 as 'Outstanding wine family of the year' for their contribution to three decades of Eastern wine industry. Most wines are French hybrids, but a semi-dry Riesling is quite commendable. Annual production is 12,500 cases.

Calvaresi, located 10 mi northwest of Reading, and established in 1981 by owner and winemaker Tom Calvaresi. This winery brought home four gold medals in 1998 for a 1997 'Autumn Gold,' a 1996 Cabernet Franc, a 1997 Cayuga, and a 1997 Vidal.

French Creek Ridge Vyds, new winery north of the PA Turnpike and south of Reading producing a range of vinifera varietals, notably a fine, dry Gewürztraminer, a delightfully fresh, focused Viognier with nuances of peach, and awards to its credit, and a rich, intensely flavorful Vidal icewine, also an award winner. Fred and Janet Maki are the proprietors.

Naylor Vyds, in the rolling hills near the Mason-Dixon line east of Interstate 83, the winery was established in 1978 by Richard and Audrey Naylor in a former potato cellar. The winery's success has enabled the Naylors to expand to a 50,000 gal capacity facility. Richard Naylor grows and purchases mostly French hybrids but also works with some vinifera. He is a noted champion of the Chambourcin grape, of which he makes several styles, from Beaujolais-like to a premier reserve Rioja-style to a dessert wine. Aware of consumers' ignorance of French hybrid varieties, Naylor successfully markets them with descriptive, proprietary names such as Seductivo and Perfection. Gold medals in 1998 included Intimacy, a 1997 Riesling, and the 1995 Essence of Chambourcin, a dessert wine. Annual production is 9,000 cases.

Slate Quarry, winery located in the Lehigh Valley which began as a vineyard and is now 13 acres. Proprietor Sid Butler is noted for developing and registering a trademark for the rootstock SQR. When Professor *Galet,

the French ampelographer, visited the vineyard with viticulturist Lucie Morton in 1980, he recommended grafting vinifera to the local wild riparia rootstock. From three initial selections, the best performing one was identified after ten years. Butler reports his Pinot Meunier has greatly improved on SQR, and his Cabernet Franc on SQR has performed well in competitions. Mr Butler states that SQR improves winter hardiness while reducing vigor and improving fruit set. Slate Quarry has also produced an impressive natural Vidal icewine, with final RS ranging from 380 to 420 g/l. Annual production is 900 cases.

Twin Brook, winery east of Lancaster, south of Rt 30, established in 1989 by the Caplan family. Richard and Theresa Caplan are co-presidents, and daughter Cheryl heads operations. Chardonnay, Cabernet Sauvignon, and Pinot Gris are made as well as hybrids Chancellor and Chambourcin. Twin Brook's 1995 Pinot Gris won a gold (90 points) in a national competition.

See also NISSLEY.   R.G.L.

Philadelphia, major port near the mouth of the Delaware River. It is where the Declaration of Independence was signed in 1776, and is a region more likely than almost any other in the US to have 250-year-old buildings incorporated into daily life. It is surrounded by well-bred, well-educated, wealthy residential communities, but never even thought of as a wine market because PA is a MONOPOLY STATE. Unlike certain Canadian provincial alcohol monopolies such as the LCBO, PA's bureaucracy has never bothered to develop any fine wine expertise. The net result of this situation has been the development of several world-class retail wine stores along the banks of the Delaware River, but on the NJ side in tiny hamlets such as Lambertville.

Despite this surrealist scenario, Philadelphia is still able to boast several dynamic restaurants. The sole exception to the wholesale wine market monopoly is native state wineries, so this protectionist environment provides a good opportunity for local producers. CHADDSFORD, a winery located in the greater metropolitan area, reports their average visitor from the city is likely to dine out three to four times weekly. Nevertheless worldly Philadelphia consumers look for vinifera varietal labels such as Chardonnay and Merlot, and are hesitant to try local hybrid wines.   R.G.L.

Phoenix, largest and fastest growing metropolitan area in ARIZONA, built at the confluence of the Salt, Verde, and Gila Rivers on a site first settled in 300 BC. The

local Native American culture reached its peak in AD 800 having developed I-beam construction for multi-room dwellings, as well as a technique for etching shells using the acidic juice of the saguaro cactus 300 years before etching techniques appeared in Europe. Hohokam civilization abandoned this site around 1350. Modern Phoenix began its emergence in 1867 when a prospector discovered the ancient irrigation canals still worked. He immediately began leasing farmland and selling water rights. Today the irrigation network called Salt River Project virtually duplicates a map of the Hohokam system built more than a millennium ago.

Twenty palatial resorts dot the Scottsdale/Phoenix area accounting for a large portion of fine wine sales in the conurbation. CA is the dominant category, although affordable Australian and Chilean wines are making strides. French wines are only found on about 20% of wine lists. Price is not the determining factor though, as high priced CA wines sell briskly, along with some high ticket Italian wines. At the retail store level, big brands dominate the chain market, although a couple of small, nichemarketers offer a wider selection.   R.T.S.

Piedmont. Literally meaning foothills, this phrase is used to describe the swath of land along the Atlantic seaboard which sits between the low lying COASTAL PLAIN and the higher elevations of the APPALACHIAN MTNS. The Piedmont is the favored region for winegrowers in the MID-ATLANTIC region. VA viticulture advisor Dr Tony Wolf has noted that risk of spring *frost is greater at elevations below 800 ft, due to cold *air drainage, than at 800–1800 ft. This elevation also protects against extreme heat in the summer. The Piedmont offers well-drained soils and a variety of site *aspects and slopes.   R.G.L.

Piedmont Vyds, one of the oldest wineries in VIRGINIA with 30 acres of vineyard near MIDDLEBURG and a house on the US Natl Historic Register. Since the state's first commercial Chardonnay vines were planted here in 1973, Piedmont Vyds has been a leading producer of this variety. The first VA vinifera wine sold outside the state was Piedmont's 1977 Chardonnay, for which the winery's founder Elizabeth Furness was honored by then-governor James Dalton.

Piedmont's signature wine is a complex, *barrel fermented Chardonnay, and this wine won VA's first Governor's Cup in 1982. Piedmont's Chardonnay evolved in the 1990s, with the introduction of the Native Yeast Unfiltered label. Produced under the supervision of winemaking CONSULTANT Alan Kinne, this wine is made only in dry, hot years where the grapes achieve full ripeness with minimal risk of rot. With careful monitoring the ambient *yeasts produce flavor complexities not found through fermentation with conventional yeasts. The 1995 vintage of this Chardonnay has scored highly in national competitions.

Also of note is Piedmont's Special Reserve Chardonnay, the founder's reserve blend of Semillon and Sauvignon Blanc made in exceptional vintages, and impressive recent progress with Cabernet Sauvignon, for which the 1995 vintage won one of six gold medals in the 1998 Virginia Governor's Cup. R.G.L.

Pillitteri controls 110 acres of Chardonnay (their flagship wine), Cabernet Sauvignon, and Merlot. All are grown on the sandy loam soils of NIAGARA-ON-THE-LAKE in the Niagara Peninsula of Ontario. Notable is their Riesling ICEWINE and a full-bodied Cabernet Franc. Their first vintage was in 1991 when grape grower Gary Pillitteri decided to produce wines of his own. The family runs the winery while Pillitteri fulfills his obligations as a Member of Parliament. Production is 20,000 cases. L.B.

Pine Ridge, winery in the STAGS LEAP AVA of Napa Valley with vineyards planted on some of the most gravity-defying slopes in CA. Partially owned, and fully operated, by Gary Andrus, nephew of a former US Secretary of the Interior. In addition to the vineyards at the winery, Andrus and his corporate partners also own another 150 acres in Carneros, and on the bench in Oakville and Rutherford. Total production of nearly 100,000 cases a year includes large quantities of Chardonnay and Chenin Blanc, but the very best offerings are cleanly made, precise bottlings of Cabernet Sauvignon, usually with a small proportion of Merlot. The Andrus style of Cabernet is understated by CA standards, relying on balance rather than heft. In this manner it makes a marvelous comparison medium between the districts of Rutherford, Stags Leap, and Howell Mtn, where they purchase grapes. They have Cabernets each labeled with specific AVA designations. All the Cabernets are well made, but the Stags Leap is particularly fine, emphasizing as it does the heavily perfumed fruit which is the AVA's signature. B.C.C.

Plains, grassland region east of the Rocky Mtns consisting of five states: NEBRASKA, OKLAHOMA, KANSAS, North and South Dakota. These states share severe winters, hot summers, and moderately high precipitation. Vinifera vines survive only in the western parts of OK. The survival of hybrids is mostly confined to the eastern edges of these states, along a north–south corridor.

One of the geological characteristics which define the Plains is the immense layer of hardpan on which they sit. Once one travels off the edge of the hardpan, the landscape immediately becomes more varied, ie trees and abrupt changes in elevation appear. The Plains themselves are characterized by rolling grasslands, the American steppe, with few topographic barriers. In the early 1800s, an estimated 60 million bison mowed the Plains acting as manure spreaders. In some places ancient buffalo dung has decomposed into topsoil 30 ft thick, providing remarkably fertile growing conditions for crops like wheat, corn, and alfalfa. Grape growers, however, would prefer to deplete this soil.

Man and Mother Nature conspire against the grapevine in these Plains States. Prohibition eradicated a nascent wine industry, and the herbicide 2, 4-D virtually precluded its revival in favor of omnipresent grain crops. Horrendous cold snaps cause concern every year. Unpredictable storms in TORNADO Alley are capable of destroying a vineyard in seconds. The mid-continent climate is much too generous: too much rain, too much wind, too much heat. But the vine is tenacious. Farmers and hobbyists have planted hundreds of acres, mostly hybrids. Vinifera suffers, but perseveres in a few pockets. A wide variety of *fruit wines have gained local following. All the winemaking operations are quite small.

Winter temperatures on the Plains can dip to –50°F. Summer temperatures always reach well into the 90s, with overnight lows often well above 70°F. Still, even Meriwether Lewis and William Clark on their 1804–6 expedition, mapping the territory west of the Mississippi River acquired from France in the Louisiana Purchase, noted hundreds of acres of native grapes in SD. In 1953 the Agriculture Research Station at Brookings, SD, initiated a grape breeding program to develop table and/or juice grapes favorably adapted to the region's relatively short growing season. Dr Ron Peterson engineered various hybrid grapes, including in 1967 Valiant, a cross of the labrusca variety Fredonia pollinated by a riparia variety called South Dakota. Initial testing proved favorable, and in the winter of 1983–4 Valiant survived –45°F. In 1996, Eldon Nygaard wrote SD's Farm Bill. A year later, he opened the doors to the state's first winery, Valiant Vyd, at Vermillion. Today, not counting Nygaard's 2 acres, there are 26 additional acres of hybrid vines scattered over a dozen vineyards in the southeast part of the state. White grapes include Kay Gray, LaCrosse, and St Pepin. Frontenac and St Croix are planted red grapes. Raspberries are the primary fruit used in wine production, although chokecherries also make good wine because of their high acidity.

SD production is expected to reach 3,000 cases in 1999. *Winter freeze is the main threat. Vines must be dropped from the trellis to the ground each fall and covered with grass. The length of the growing season is always a concern: *budbreak occurred on 30 May in 1998, after grapes had been picked at 23°B in Aug 1997. Soils in the southeast part of the state are very well drained GLACIAL TILL. This is critical because that part of the state can receive 25 in of rain in the summer.

No wine is produced commercially in North Dakota.

NOTABLE PROPERTIES

Valiant Vyd, located near the Missouri River in the southeast corner of SD not far from Sioux Falls. Two wines stand out. The most typical is Valor, a blend of Valiant and two other hybrids, which does have a *foxy nose, but also has a fine fruity flavor and long finish with good acid. The most unusual is the 1997 Wild Grape. It has no foxiness, but instead a mix of bush berries and beefsteak in the nose, with great balance and length. An extremely interesting and surprising wine, bringing to mind nothing more appropriate than pemmican, winter staple of the Lakota. R.T.S.

Pollux, hybrid with mainly American but some Gamay genes.

Ponzi Vyds, Dick and Nancy Ponzi consistently make the best Pinot Gris and dry Riesling in OREGON. Their wines are bright and fresh with great focused fruit and nut flavors. They have 12 acres in the north WILLAMETTE VALLEY and produce something under 10,000 cases annually by supplementing their vineyard with purchased grapes including Medici Vyd production. Today the wines are made by daughter Louisa, while her brother and sister run marketing and vineyard operations. Louisa is producing two Italian varieties, Arneis and Dolcetto. R.A.I.

Portland, major urban center and port for ocean-going vessels located on the Columbia River at the mouth of OREGON's Willamette Valley. This proximity has greatly enhanced the local winegrowing efforts over the last twenty years. Portland is a town of considerable middle-class wealth, and growth, with 1.5 million people in the larger metropolitan area who like to dine out and drink wine. Portland patrons support a large and sophisticated blend of restaurants. Portland has led the nation in controlling urban sprawl through strident zoning laws, thereby protecting some farmland to the immediate south and west. Oregonians have tended to be highly provincial, supporting their fledgling wine industry with pride and passion. It helps that Nike's corporate offices are located nearby and that the thriving hi-tech industry has adopted this city.   R.A.I.

Potomac River. The river divides into two forks, the North Fork which delineates the north–south line between the MARYLAND and WV panhandles, and the South Fork, which flows northeast through WV's Eastern Panhandle. The Potomac moderates the climate in these cool Appalachian regions, as well as in MD's Cumberland Valley and Montgomery Co, and VA's Loudoun Co. Further south as it enters the CHESAPEAKE BAY, it provides a maritime mesoclimate for VA's Northern Neck and for southern MD.   R.G.L.

Potter Valley AVA, see MENDOCINO.

pre-certification clones, cuttings taken from vines planted before UC *Davis began their program to select, clean up, and propagate certain clones of the major vinifera varieties. CA has some of the oldest vines in the world. Probably because of Prohibition and the fact that wine production then sank into such an uneconomic trough, there was no incentive to replant in order to keep yields up. In the 1960s UC Davis began a concerted effort under the auspices of Dr Austin Goheen to eradicate *leafroll virus in CA. They identified attractive clones of important grape varieties, killed any virus in the sample specimens by holding the cuttings at 120°F for several weeks, then planted and reproduced the vines several times to make sure the virus would not reappear. These *certified* clones were then distributed through authorized nurseries. By the turn of the millennium more than 85% of CA's fine wine vineyards were planted to virus free, heat-treated, certified clones. Detractors of the program point out that most of the clones were selected for their generous production, and that many clones producing high quality wine were excluded.

Preston, homespun winery at the far northern end of DRY CREEK AVA. Lou Preston maintains the image of a dirt farmer in suspenders riding his tractor to town, but he ac-

tually has an MBA from Stanford Univ. The give-away is his insatiable curiosity. Farming 120 acres since 1973, he moved rapidly in the 1980s to plant Rhône varieties. He created a marketing stir with a *Châteauneuf-du-Pape type blend he called Faux-Castel, until asked to desist by the owners of Ch de Beaucastel in Châteauneuf. Preston's Marsanne has plenty of the sage honey and smooth texture one would hope for from that variety. His best wine, for fifteen years, has been his Barbera however. It bubbles over with berry fruit aroma and finishes with a tartly refreshing acid nudge—definitely a drink-now wine. The winemaker at Preston since 1989 has been Kevin Hamel. Under his own label he makes a very limited quantity of superb Syrah from grapes sourced in the Russian River AVA. Hamel Syrah is dark and spicy, with a core strip of flavor much like tamarind beef jerky.   B.C.C.

Prince Michel Vyds, second largest winery in VIRGINIA at 35,000 cases, which also produces the **Rapidan River** label. Prince Michel was established in 1983 by Jean Le Duq, Parisian chairman of the Ellis Group, a multinational industrial French laundry. Prince Michel began by offering a line of French varietals, including a regular and a reserve Chardonnay, Cabernet Sauvignon, and Merlot. Prince Michel also has one of the largest vineyard holdings in VA at 150 acres.

With the acquisition of Rapidan River Vyds, Prince Michel diversified its product line with dry and semi-dry Riesling and Gewürztraminer. In the 1980s, the Prince Michel label was known for consistently good Chardonnay, as was the Rapidan label for Riesling and Gewürztraminer. Joachim Hollerith, Prince Michel's winemaker until 1990, then CONSULTANT winemaker through 1997, brought the winery its first VA Governor's Cup in 1988 for its 1986 Gewürztraminer.

Prince Michel's performance has been less consistent with red wines, but is improving. Their ultra-premium Cabernet Sauvignon Le Duq was at one time a blend of grapes from VA and a Napa Valley vineyard owned by the winery. Today Le Duq is 100% Napa wine from a 35-acre vineyard just north of St Helena. In 1999 the 1994 vintage was called Blockbuster Wine of the Year by trade magazine *Vineyard & Winery Management*. Prince Michel's Reserve VA Merlot/Cabernet Sauvignon has performed well in competitions, especially the 1997 vintage. The regular Cabernet Sauvignon and Merlot de Virginia carry an American appellation (see US LABEL REGULATIONS, geographical).

Prince Michel also offers visitors a convenient location on Rt 29 between Culpepper and Madison, a self-guided winery tour, a wine museum, lodging, and a four-star restaurant. *Vineyard & Winery Mgmt* made Hollerith's replacement, Tom Payette, their Winemaker of the Year in 1999.   R.G.L.

programming is the phrase US distributors use to describe the manner in which they sequentially allocate attention to the various brands in their portfolio in exchange for discounts and ancillary sales tools generated by the producers. A brand *on program* for the month will usually send a representative from the winery to address the distributor's sales staff and spend a few days visiting accounts with salesmen. The winery is expected to cooperate in tasting events, as well as to provide promotional aids such as SHELF TALKERS and table tents. Most importantly, the winery is expected to offer the distributor various volume discounts for purchases made during the *on program* period so the distributor can offer special discounts on the brand to retailers and restaurateurs in order to get advantageous displays in stores and featured wine-by-the-glass placements. It should be no surprise that most of the distributor's purchases from wineries occur during the one or two months each year those wineries are *on program* with the distributor. The expense and complexity of managing these relations in a large number of separate states is the single greatest incentive wineries have to grow to certain threshold sizes.   B.C.C.

proprietary label denotes a name made up by the winery to identify a wine. Thus it is not a *varietal label subject to regulations pertaining to the percentages of grapes which may be included. Nor is it an appellation subject to regulation as to where the grapes were grown. Nor is it a *generic label which presumably customers might recognize. Proprietary labels, such as Phelps (see NAPA VALLEY) Insignia or ROSENBLUM Ch La Paws, confer on the winery the advantage of being able to put any grapes from any place they want into the wine. And the further advantage of being able to change that blend from year to year depending on weather conditions, market conditions, or simply their whims. The disadvantage for the winery in a proprietary label is that it must be explained to each and every customer. Hence it costs a great deal of time and money to create widespread consumer recognition for the name. That is the reason proprietary names may be legally protected as exclusive rights for their originators. That right must, however, be enforced by the entity holding it, sometimes in costly court battles. See US LABEL REGULATIONS. B.C.C.

Puget Sound AVA, new appellation approved in 1995 for WASHINGTON in one of the state's oldest grape growing districts with vines planted as early as 1872 on Stretch Island by Lambert Evans, a Civil War soldier from the Confederacy. Located about an hour southwest of SEATTLE, Stretch Island became the center of WA's wine industry following Prohibition based on the historic American hybrid ISLAND BELLE.

Puget Sound reflects its maritime location. Vineyards and wineries are dotted along the numerous islands of this inland sea. The Puget Sound appellation reaches to the north and includes Whatcom County and south to the state's capital, Olympia. Prime growing regions appear to be Bainbridge Island and Whidbey Island with their protected climate in the lee of the dramatic 8,000 ft Olympic Mtns to the west. Soils are alluvial sand, the result of glacial retreat over much of the Puget Sound region. Although annual rainfall is plentiful, ranging from 30 to 60 in, most of the rain falls between Nov and Apr.

Sunshine hours during the prime growing season are long. *Degree days are less than in eastern WA, but ripening occurs into late Oct routinely, and into early Nov some years. Germanic varieties are preferred, although recently French varieties made popular in Oregon are finding a place in the vineyard. Recent plantings include Pinot Noir, Chardonnay, and Pinot Gris. Also grown are Island Belle, Chasselas, Madeleine Angevine, Madeleine Sylvaner, Müller-Thurgau, and Sieggerebe. Wines tend to be light and crisp with a corresponding delicacy, and long, lingering aftertastes. Thus they are very distinct from the wines of eastern WA, and even OR.

NOTABLE PROPERTIES

Andrew Will, winery begun in 1989 by owner/winemaker Chris Camarda and wife Annie on Vashon Island west of Seattle. They produce some of the most lush Merlots in WA, benefiting greatly from the recent popularity of Merlot. They rely on grapes shipped west from Pepper Bridge, Ciel du Cheval, Mercer Ranch, and Klipsun Vyds in the Columbia Valley AVA and often produce vineyard designated wines, as well as a reserve. Excellent Cabernet Sauvignon is also made.

Bainbridge Island, winery established in 1982 by Gerard and JoAnn Bentryn, tireless promoters of sustainable agriculture who argue vineyards are an appropriate mechanism of saving green space in the highly urbanized western WA. They have planted about 7 acres, including Müller-Thurgau, Madeleine Angevine, Pinot Gris, Pinot Noir, and Sieggerebe. Wines are well made and the Germanic whites seem best with a balancing touch of RS. Pinot Noir shows good promise.

DeLille, winery begun in Woodinville near Seattle in 1992 as a partnership of Charles Lille and his son Greg, with marketer Jay Soloff and winemaker Chris Upchurch. They currently produce blends of Bordeaux varieties: the reds Chaleur Estate and D2; and a fine white blend. Grapes come from Columbia Valley AVA.

Hoodsport, winery started in 1978 by Dick and Peggy Patterson, making a complete palette of wines using grapes from eastern WA. Of special interest is their Island Belle.

McCrea, winery located in western WA near the state capital at Olympia, although grapes come from east of the Cascades. Founded in 1988 by Doug McCrea, McCrea produces noteworthy Syrah based wines and soft, full-flavored Chardonnays, including one from Celilo Vyd perched 1,000 ft above the Columbia River in the Columbia Valley AVA's most western section near The Dalles. McCrea also makes a richly flavored Viognier.

Mt Baker Vyds, begun in 1982, pioneered the Nooksack Valley, near the Canadian border at the base of Mt Baker. Today new owners utilize the original vineyards to produce very good Pinot Noir, Chasselas, Madeleine Angevine, and Sieggerebe. This location definitely qualifies as the margin of grape growing conditions. R.A.I.

Quady innovative dessert wine and vermouth producer in the Madera AVA of CA's CENTRAL VALLEY. Andrew Quady is a good spokesman for American wine, promoting in several export markets with a unique story. In the late 1960s he took his degree in chemical engineering to work for a fireworks company. Apparently it was not as exciting as it sounds. He moved on to the wine business and found himself in 1981 experimenting with a batch of seeded table grapes called Orange Muscat, which were dying out under the onslaught of seedless varieties. The name derives from their orange blossom aroma, which Quady found he could intensify by putting them in cold storage. Also, they started to ferment very slowly because they were so cold. Thrilled with the sense of invention, Quady stopped the fermentation after 2% alcohol had formed by adding enough distilled spirit to raise the alcohol to 14.5% leaving 140 g/l RS. He called the wine Essensia, put a brilliant orange Ardison Philips painting on the label, and never looked back. His sales of Essensia now approach 10,000 cases a year worldwide and account for half his production. It comes vintage dated, and the honeyed, penetratingly floral, citrus jolt that makes it special only fades with time, so fresher is generally better.

The Quady line includes a 4% alcohol afternoon delight called Electra. Also a port type he calls Starboard, so he can legally export to Europe, made entirely from Tinto Cão and Tinta Amarela. His newest venture is a pair of high quality vermouths made with a proprietary secret concoction of herbs called Vya. But his item clearly unchallenged for world supremacy is a Black Muscat called Elysium. It smells like rose petals and tastes like wild blueberries. A singular experience, with 4% less alcohol than most *fortified wines, Elysium is brilliant with cake-like desserts that have sweet milk chocolate in them, but no one ever turns it down by itself.   B.C.C.

Quebec. Eastern province in CANADA encompassing the St Lawrence Seaway and contiguous with Ontario as well as with the northern boundaries of four New England states. As quixotic as it sounds, there are 32 wineries in Quebec, which is situated entirely above 45°N latitude. And these wineries produce wines from locally grown grapes. Three factors make it possible to grow grapes in this marginal region: well-chosen pockets of mesoclimates warmed by a tempering body of water (Lake Champlain, the St Lawrence River) or protected by mountains (the Laurentians, Appalachians); labor-intensive viticultural practices using winter-hardy hybrids; and the fascinating cultural passion, bordering on a fine madness, of the vignerons of Quebec who are determined to have an indigenous wine industry to go with their French language. Wine country in Quebec is accessible from both MONTREAL (an hour by car) and from the US border in either NY or VT.

HISTORY
Explorer Jacques Cartier in 1535 recorded riparia grapes growing on an island near Quebec City. The first determined Frenchman to grow better varieties was Samuel de Champlain, who in 1608 attempted to grow vinifera grapes. It simply could not be done at that time in this merciless climate. Like many other North American regions, a small industry based on American hybrids evolved in the 19th century; then declined during Prohibition, reducing vineyards from 70 to two by 1939. Experimental plantings returned in the 1970s. As consumers' tastes changed the provincial liquor authority (Regie des Alcools, des Courses, et des Jeux) loosened restrictions on wine sales, allowing wine to be sold in food stores, a first in Canada. With the introduction of better French hybrids, growers lobbied for licenses to open wineries. By 1979 they had formed a political organization, Association des Viticulteurs du Quebec, and in 1985 they convinced the government to issue permits to allow them to produce and sell wine on a commercial scale. Five permits were issued that first year.

CLIMATE
The people may be hospitable, but the climate of Quebec is not. Winter is long and cold. The growing season is short, with only about three-quarters the number of sunshine hours (1,150) that Bordeaux enjoys (1,450). Arctic-like winters can plunge temperatures as low as –35°C (–30°F), with 4–5 ft of snow burying vineyards for eight months of the year. *Frost can come as late as June. Three areas, however, have comparatively mild pockets. One is located along the US border near Lake Champlain. That is where most of the wineries are located. Another is along the St Lawrence River, and the third is south of Montreal in the foothills of the Laurentian Mtns.

VITICULTURE AND PRODUCTION
A French film producer from Arles, Christian Barthomeuf, helped relaunch Quebec viticulture in 1979 near the LOYALIST village of Dunham in the Eastern Townships. The site had a shallow layer of topsoil over permeable slate. Unlike the NY practice of burying *canes, which most Quebec growers had done as well, Barthomeuf used no trunk. He left fruiting buds within a foot of the ground in a *gobelet system similar to the vineyards of his native Provence. He left 10 ft spaces between rows to allow a V-shaped machine he had imported from France to move the dirt from the center of the row to the base of the plants where the vines were mounded with 15 in of earth. This hilling or MOUNDING was able to protect vines from temperatures as low as –30°C (–20°F). Most vineyards in Quebec now follow the same procedure.

Soils vary from sand and sandy loam, to mixed clay and silt, shale, slate, and gravel. Vineyards total 300 commercial acres: Seyval (70% of whites); Cayuga White; several Geisenheim clones (see GM); Marechal Foch (40% of reds); plus De Chaunac, Chancellor, Sainte-Croix, Gamay, and Baco Noir. Total annual production amounts to 1.5% of Canada's total volume, approximately 25,000 cases per year, not including the commercial wineries' output using imported material. White wines provide 52% of volume, reds 22%, with digestifs, sparkling, and ICEWINES providing the balance.

REGULATORY ENVIRONMENT
There are two types of licenses in Quebec: farm winery and industrial. A farm winery

license may be granted to a grower who has at least 5,000 grapevines planted, with a minimum of 2,500 in production. Applicants are asked to demonstrate grape growing and winemaking expertise. Unlike in other provinces in Canada, farm winery licensees can make wine only from their own vines. Another constraint is the Société des Alcools du Québec (SAQ), the authority with monopoly control over distribution of wine and spirits in Quebec. Because of purchasing quotas and mark-up policies, a farm winery licensee currently finds it a practical impossibility to sell through SAQ outlets. Originally sales were restricted to CELLAR DOOR facilities, which forced growers to invest in tasting rooms and tourist accommodations. Since July 1996 they have been permitted to sell directly to restaurants. This change has eliminated the SAQ handling charge of 140%; however, the Quebec wine industry is still very tourist dependent.

The second, industrial type of license does not require that wines be made from local product. Those operating (Paul Mason, VINCOR, and ANDRÉS) are permitted to buy juice, wine, or concentrate from suppliers outside Canada and sell the bottled product through SAQ outlets and grocery stores. Despite the constraints, the young Quebec industry is thriving. Returns are modest, but respect amongst the Quebecois is a form of compensation. The vignerons are negotiating to join VQA and working through a number of issues such as autonomy regarding acceptable grape varieties.

NOTABLE PROPERTIES

Dom des Côtes d'Ardoise, in Dunham a few miles from the US border, was the first vineyard planted by Christian Barthomeuf. In 1985 Montreal plastic surgeon Jacques Papillon joined Barthomeuf and expanded the 16-acre vineyard of hybrids to include some vinifera (Riesling and Gamay) on their slatey slopes. Barthomeuf left in 1991. Patrick Barrelet has been winemaker ever since. A tasting room and restaurant overlook the Appalachian foothills. Production is 1,700 cases.

Vignoble de L'Orpailleur, also in Dunham, is the largest winery in Quebec. It was first planted in 1982 by Hervé Durand, a winemaker from France who studied in Dijon. Three other men, intrigued by his operation, joined him: impresario Frank Furtado, publisher Pierre Rodrique, and French winemaker Charles-Henri de Coussergues. Saying, 'Making wine in Quebec is like panning gravel for nuggets of gold,' Durand named the winery accordingly. They have 24 acres producing 7,000 cases of mostly Seyval Blanc, a sparkling wine from Seyval, and a fine dessert wine from Cayuga Muscat.

Vignoble Dietrich-Jooss, owned and operated by Alsace-born Victor Dietrich and wife Christianne Jooss, opened at Iberville in 1986 in the Richelieu Valley. They experiment with nearly 60 different grape varieties in their 14-acre vineyard, producing a wide range of table wines totaling 2,000 cases. They also make an Icewine that complies with VQA standards.

Vignoble Les Arpents de Neige, which means 'a few acres of snow,' as one of King Louis XIV's advisors described Canada when England and France were at odds over the region; 'not worth fighting for,' the advisor concluded. But vigneron Giles Séguin, a restaurateur and former VP at Labatts Brewery, thought differently when he bought the 5-year-old operation in 1993. With the help of French winemaker Jean-Paul Martin, the winery produces a very fine rosé and a well-structured Seyval Blanc. Séguin's 18th-century farmhouse is now the winery, tasting room, and restaurant. Séguin is also president of the Vignerons du Quebec, an organization formed in 1988.

Vignoble Morou, in Napierville, is 30 mi south of Montreal and close to the head of Lake Champlain. It was founded in 1987 by chemical engineer Etienne Héroux and his wife Monique Morin. Among several styles produced, their barrel aged Clos Napierois is particularly interesting: a complex white that has received several awards across the US.   L.F.B.

Dubois, J.-M., and Deshales, L., *Guide des vignobles du Québec: sur la route des vins* (Quebec, 1997).

Quilceda Creek, one of the top three Cabernet producers in the PACIFIC NORTHWEST and among the best in America. The winery is located in Snohomish, just north of SEATTLE. Alex Golitzen is the nephew of CA legend André *Tchelistcheff and began Quilceda (pronounced *kil SEE da*) in 1979. He buys all of his grapes from top vineyards throughout eastern WA, including: Klipsun, Kiona, Champoux (of which he is part owner) and Ciel du Cheval Vyds.   R.A.I.

Qupé, a Chumash Indian name for the prolific CA state flower, the Golden Poppy. Bob Lindquist is a founding member of the *Rhône Rangers. Syrah has been his passion from the beginning in 1982 when both the grape and the winery were struggling for American recognition. Today both are firmly established, and Lindquist looks like a prophet for having said then, 'I feel the evolution of the US wine drinkers' sophistication will soon rank Syrah as a dominant red varietal.'

Lindquist began grafting vines to Syrah in the eastern canyons of SANTA BARBARA CO in 1985. He wanted to test the effect of cool climate on the variety because his only sources at the time were in warm regions such as Estrella Vyd east of PASO ROBLES, Phelps Vyd halfway up NAPA VALLEY, or McDowell Valley on the inland side of the mountains in MENDOCINO CO. All those areas are considerably hotter than Los Olivos in the eastern half of the Santa Ynez AVA or any of the Santa Maria AVA. The results of Lindquist's seminal work are threefold: critical acclaim for Qupé Syrahs; an explosion of Rhône variety plantings in this district, which had lots of vineyard investment from the middle of the 1970s on, but few Rhône varietals until the 1990s; and a flying winemaker position for Lindquist who has now been hired to make the Ch Routas wines in Provence as well as his own in CA. Not a bad tribute to a guy who took ten years to work up to 10,000 cases of production.

Qupé Syrahs may be productively compared to see the effect of climate. Those labeled Bien Nacido Vyd come from the cool Santa Maria AVA. Those labeled Central Coast include grapes from warmer areas like Paso Robles. Critics disagree as to which is best. Rough-and-tumble guys like Robert *Parker and influential *Wine Spectator* columnist James Laube prefer the Central Coast version citing its uniformly ripe, raspberry fruit, and generous tannins. They are wrong. The Bien Nacido version always offers spicier overtones, brighter acid balance, and more layered evolution as it airs in the glass. Lindquist sees little reason to take sides, although it should be observed the Central Coast comprises 40% of his sales volume and the Bien Nacido is a relative specialty item at less than 700 cases.

Lindquist also makes limited volumes of Viognier, Marsanne, and Roussanne. None are breakthrough wines. The white mainstay of his range is Chardonnay, which is built like the proverbial brick outhouse. Both the standard and a Reserve version can be recognized from 2 ft away by the full blown, voluptuous, heavy toast oak. In the mouth the Reserve is the more ripe, pumpkin-like, palate-coating of the two, but neither would ever be called shy and retiring. Rather than expressing a sense of place, Qupé Chardonnays suggest an expression which is recognized the world over, 'Hey, sailor, looking for a date?'   B.C.C.

R

rain shadow, land area behind mountains relative to the prevailing movement of storm clouds which is broadest behind the highest peaks. When moving clouds encounter mountains, they rise. Gaining elevation cools them 4°F for every 1,000 ft of elevation, condensing the water, which then falls on the mountains. After passing the mountains the clouds have less moisture, and they warm as they descend, which increases their capacity to carry what moisture they do have. On the west coast of North America the Jet Stream blows clouds in from the west. The highest elevations in the coastal mountains get the most rain, and inland valleys are often in rain shadows, as witness the Mojave Desert lying east of the 10,000 ft San Gabriel Mtns behind Los Angeles, or the fact ski resorts in UT boast dry, powder snow compared to the damp snow which falls in the Sierras at Tahoe, eventually to irrigate CA, but not NV.

Ravat, breeder of French hybrid vines. **Ravat Noir** makes red wines which display some of the character of its parent Pinot Noir (and its low yields). Its other parent is Seibel 8365. See also VIGNOLES.

Ravenswood, winery in CA's SONOMA VALLEY which started in 1976 with something of a cult following for its boldly flavored Zinfandels sourced from old, DRY-FARMED, head-pruned vineyards, fermented with WILD YEAST and *punched down by hand in open topped wooden fermenters. The winery's pagan aesthetic was neatly captured in the logo designed for it by Berkeley artist David Lance Goines: a Celtic circle of three symmetrical ravens joined in the middle by their feet. It is CA's most easily recognizable label.

Today the winery has outgrown its early position, if not its mildly bohemian attitude. It has floated a public stock offering and used those funds to expand in size to 100,000 cases a year, including Merlot, Cabernet, and Chardonnay. The vineyard designated Zinfandels, however, continue to rule the roost. Most come from Sonoma, and they are all exceptional, but the very best comes from a Napa vineyard in the westside hills

north of St Helena owned by long-time supporter Bill Dickerson, a Marin Co psychiatrist. Ravenswood's Dickerson Zinfandels have a textural advantage over their other wines, an elegance to the rampant flavors of berry and heather. It is still traditional, and far from Claret-like, just more composed than the other Ravenswood Zins. The other Zins make people want to leg wrestle.

B.C.C.

Rayon d'Or, or Seibel 4986, French hybrid grown in Eastern and Midwestern states whose wine is spicy, white, and relatively alcoholic.

Red Hills of Dundee, center of OREGON's north WILLAMETTE VALLEY, situated about 20 mi southwest of Portland along Hwy 99W heading to the ocean. Turkey farms and hazelnut orchards once dominated this area. David Lett of EYRIE VYDS planted OR's first vinifera since Prohibition here in 1966. Soils are red and are classified as Jory, a mix of deep soils with high iron content over basalt and volcanic outcroppings. A higher proportion of clay, compared to districts further south, delays ripening in some vintages. Wines tend to be lighter in color with delicate fruit aromas and flavors, although they can age well, especially in vintages with slightly higher *acidity.

NOTABLE PROPERTIES

Argyle, above average size winery making 25,000 cases in Dundee under joint ownership of Petaluma from Australia (in which *Bollinger of Champagne has an interest) and Cal Knutsen of Seattle. Winemaker Rollin Soles dedicates half his production to a well-respected sparkling wine made from Pinot Noir and Chardonnay. New releases will include extended *tirage and vineyard designated sparkling wines.

Cameron, Dundee winery owned by John Paul producing opulent, attention-grabbing wines led by a full-bodied Pinot Noir. Good Chardonnay and a fruity item labeled Pinot Bianco also use grapes from partner Bill Wayne's notable property, Abbey Ridge Vyd.

Erath Vyds, pioneer winery just outside of Dundee started in 1972. Himself a large

man, Dick Erath produces contrastingly sharp, more acidic versions of Pinot Noir than his neighbors, but always with a wonderful length of flavor. R.A.I.

Redwood Valley AVA, see MENDOCINO.

Reif. Chardonnay, Riesling, and Vidal Icewine provide the basis for the top three varietal wines produced at this NIAGARA-ON-THE-LAKE, Ontario estate. *Geisenheim-trained Klaus Reif also produces an ultra-premium Meritage called Tesoro and crisp Sauvignon Blanc. He bottles different clones of Riesling (Alsace, Geisenheim, Mosel) from the same vineyard separately using the same winemaking style but resulting in notably different profiles. L.F.B.

Renwood, also **Santino,** makers of hearty wines from old vines in CA's AMADOR CO. In 1984 Scott Harvey had the good fortune to purchase John Downing's Zinfandel vineyard, which at the time was nearly 120 years old. Harvey sold some of those grapes, made wine at Santino from a portion of the crop, and started calling the vineyard Grandpère. In 1991 Harvey launched his own brand, Renwood, which he made at Santino in conjunction with his winemaking job there. In 1994 Harvey put together a deal with a venture capitalist from Boston to buy Santino. At of the end of 1995 Robert Smerling, the venture capitalist, announced he was going to take over Renwood/Santino. Harvey continues to own Grandpère Vyd and has now become the winemaker at Folie à Deux in the Napa Valley.

Gordon Binz, ex-RIDGE, was hired as winemaker at Renwood/Santino. Production is being increased from 40,000 cases in 1995 to a goal of 100,000 in 2000. Exports account for 10% of sales. While there have been certain cosmetic changes, such as a significant increase in the amount of White Zin produced and the introduction of Smerling's subsidiary company's Dominican cigars into the tasting room, the overall quality of the wines has remained high. The roster of old vine Zinfandels, Syrah, and Barbera are as butch as ever. The two stars of the line-up are Zins from Jackrabbit Flat

Vyd and d'Agostini Vyd. A blend of Zinfandels from different vineyards, which they proprietarily name Grandmère, is more impressive than this game of label Three Card Monte would normally predict. The Syrah is dark, alcoholic, heavily wooded, and tarry flavored, albeit not nearly as astringent as one might assume from looking at it in the glass. In the past these Syrahs have aged like Barolo. Renwood owns a total of about 30 acres of vineyard in Amador Co. A wine to watch from them will be their Linsteadt Vyd Barbera, which delivers rusticity in the finish softened by a round berry middle that is quite intriguing.   B.C.C.

R. H. Phillips, owned by the Giguiere family, whose third generation own a huge agricultural business based in CA's Coast Range foothills northwest of Sacramento near the town of Esparto. They were solely responsible for the Dunnigan Hills AVA application. The Giguieres only got into grape growing as a diversification crop in the 1970s, then warmed to the venture and built a winery in 1983. Their view of farming is to think in terms of sections, not acres. Today their 1,600 acres of vines and 425,000-case production is still a minor part of the family's total agricultural enterprise.

These value priced wines are noteworthy for two reasons. First, their quality is a distinct cut above other CENTRAL VALLEY producers, and they draw attention to at least one of the techniques responsible with a series called Night Harvest. These are wines such as Sauvignon Blanc, Chardonnay, and Chenin Blanc which compose the bulk of the business. Mechanically harvested at cool nighttime temperatures under lights, these grapes come in at much better pH than one might expect from a region which is so hot during the day. The second distinguishing mark of the line is the extremely dramatic packaging applied to their entrepreneurial effort with Rhône varieties. Not only are Syrah, Grenache, and Mourvèdre well suited for this location, the wines come in 500 ml Italian designer bottles with clear capsules, riveting graphics, and, if you please, wooden boxes—quite a handful for $7.   B.C.C.

Ridge Vyds, icon of CA winemaking located in the SANTA CRUZ MTNS AVA, although owned today by Otsuka, a Japanese pharmaceutical company. Management decisions remain in the extremely capable hands of Paul Draper, who provides leadership worthy of this property's long and storied history. Ridge is the crowning glory of Montebello Ridge, and site of high-level, artisan winemaking since 1870. Many successful

vintners operated on the eastern slope of this ridge, but two stand out. Pierre Klein came to CA from Alsace in 1875 and opened the Occidental Restaurant in San Francisco. The sheer quality of his wine list earned for him the position of manager for the tasting room at the CA Board of Viticultural Commissioners. In 1888 Klein purchased 160 acres on Montebello Ridge and opened Mira Valle Winery growing Cabernet Sauvignon, Merlot, Cabernet Franc, and Petit Verdot. In 1900 he took a Gold Medal at the Paris Exposition. A portion of Klein's vineyard survives today and goes to market as the Jimsomare Vyd designated wines from Ridge. The top of Montebello Ridge was purchased in 1885 by Osea Perrone, a San Francisco physician. He built a lucrative winery and a beautiful summer home. The cellars were constructed of limestone quarried nearby. It is in that facility, at 2,600 ft of elevation, where the Ridge Vyds wines are made today. In 1960 the property was purchased by a group of engineers from Stanford Univ looking for a place in the country to exercise their children on weekends.

The first Ridge Zinfandel was produced in 1964 from nearby Picchetti grapes. In 1966 the first Geyserville designated Zinfandel was produced from old vines growing on the Trentadue Ranch in northern Sonoma. Sinking cap *maceration techniques, WILD YEAST fermentations, and seeking out old, dry-farmed vines quickly created Ridge's reputation as a front rank specialist in macho, palate shaking, long-lived Zinfandels, Petite Sirahs, and Cabernets. Those wines seemed to arrive in a muscle car with a pack of Camel cigarettes and a subscription to *Soldier of Fortune* magazine. The labels had informative paragraphs about the vintage and varietal make-up on the side, and the silver capsules were half-length so connoisseurs could see the business end of the cork. Supporters could also pick out the Ridge bottle in any group of wines from 50 yards away.

Paul Draper came to Ridge in 1969. During the 1970s Ridge expanded their very successful program of buying grapes from old, dry-farmed vines anywhere they could find them. Great Zinfandels were made from Dante Dusi Ranch in PASO ROBLES, Eschen Vyd in AMADOR CO, Lytton Springs in DRY CREEK Valley as well as from LODI and from the slope of Montebello Ridge. Petite Sirahs from the York Creek Vyd on SPRING MTN in Napa were also excellent. The Cabernets from atop Montebello Ridge continuously vied for the state's best scores among international critics. By 1980 Ridge was making 25,000 cases; half of it Zinfandel and another 40% Cabernet.

Today Ridge makes more than 60,000 cases and they own the Lytton Springs winery in Dry Creek. The line-up of wines is much broader, but quality remains excellent, and the overall style remains true to its rustic, intense antecedents. The Cabernet Sauvignon from Montebello should be considered the centerpiece because it has been made continuously from the very beginning at the home estate. It contains 10–15% Merlot in most years. Funky and brash, it nevertheless ages like a well-crafted violin. Many critics get most worked up over the warmest vintages because the 2,600 ft ridge top is a moderately cool location and cold vintages show some herbaceous notes in their youth. It is easy to disagree. Warm vintages also accentuate the rusticity factor, which is a mild *Brettanomyces element, well controlled and fine as a complexing agent (see Microbiology essay, p 39). The best Montebello Cabs are the cool vintages because of their sense of restrained power, and the afterthought of flavor that shows up like a shadow in the finish. Ridge wines never need to prove their strength; it is their civility one should worry about. Greatest recent vintages would be 1985, 1990, 1994, and 1995. Best bargain would be 1989 because it was a poor vintage elsewhere, but the rains did not come south of San Francisco.   B.C.C.

Rio Grande, river originating in southwestern CO, and bisecting NM, then flowing into TX to form the southern edge of that state, and finally draining into the Gulf of Mexico.

riparia or **Vitis riparia,** native American species of the *Vitis* genus of vines commonly used for breeding *American hybrids and *rootstocks, particularly for its cold hardiness.

Rochioli, winery and vineyards in the RUSSIAN RIVER AVA of CA's northern Sonoma Co. Maker of an excellent Zinfandel, as well as one of CA's top five Sauvignon Blancs (twice the State Fair Sweepstakes winner), but internationally recognized as CA's finest Pinot Noir vineyard extant.

Joe Rochioli (pronounced *roh kee OH lee*) started in the late 1930s managing farmlands along the Russian River. Eventually he bought 120 acres for himself to grow string beans and hops. His son Joe went to college at Cal Poly in San Luis Obispo, then returned to the family property. In 1958 he planted some of the first Sauvignon Blanc vines in the area. They are on sandy soils near the river and only bear a couple t/a now that they are in their forties. These are the source of Rochioli's exceptional Reserve Sauvignon Blanc, a *Sancerre style wine quite unlike any other in CA. It has more *methoxypyrazine character than most except SANFORD or BABCOCK, but those capsicum notes are woven throughout a gravel, flint, and redwood smoke core in such a way they do not draw attention. Moreover, the wine ages magnificently, retaining the central flavors while adding a baked crust note in the bouquet.

Tom Rochioli grew up like many third generation Italian-Americans working in the vineyard and drinking wine with meals every evening. After college he went to work for Bank of America, but found himself managing loans to wineries. In 1982 he rejoined his father on the farm, and they decided to begin making wine on a commercial basis to better represent their grape growing business. Since then Tom Rochioli's winemaking skills have improved every single year. A third of Rochioli's property is on sandy soil near the river. Another third is on a bench above the river. The final third is on a south-facing hillside. Over 20 years Tom Rochioli has identified at least two separate clones in his older Pinot Noir vines and planted a couple of newer ones as well. Pinot Noirs sourced from the Rochioli Vyd but made by WILLIAMS SELYEM, Gary FARRELL, and by Rochioli himself have all either won the Sweepstakes Award at the State Fair, or been *Wine Spectator*'s Top Pinot Noir of the Year. It is an amazing accomplishment. In several instances, the grapes were picked in alternating rows by the three different wineries. Rochioli's own Reserve Pinot Noir is deep and extremely well integrated. Nothing hangs over its belt. The black cherry aroma is taut and the flavor concentrated. It has good color, good acid, smooth tannins, no leafiness, and a stable finish upon which the wood and yeast notes can play themselves out.   B.C.C.

Rockbridge Vyds, winery located in the SHENANDOAH VALLEY. Shep Rouse won more awards than any other winemaker in the 1997 VIRGINIA Governor's Cup, not only for his winery but as a CONSULTANT winemaker. Having trained at both UC *Davis and the German *Geisenheim institute, Rouse had already made a reputation for himself in the 1980s as winemaker at Montdomaine Cellars, at the time VA's leading red wine producer. After leaving Montdomaine, Rouse introduced his own Rockbridge Vyds, but continued to consult, most notably for Oakencroft Vyds in Charlottesville where the wines subsequently achieved a noteworthy rise in quality.

Rouse devotes as much attention to value-priced French hybrid blends as he does to vinifera wines. He works skillfully with Vidal and Chambourcin, using Vidal in two proprietary house wines as well as in two dessert wines. His 'Cabernet' is a blend of the two Cabernet grapes. His regular Chardonnay is one of the most subtle and smooth, and the Riesling is *Kabinett-like in ripeness and texture. Rouse won the VA Governor's Cup for his 1994 CRYOEXTRACTION icewine-type made from Vidal grapes. His Dashiell label is reserved for ultrapremium barrel fermented Chardonnay, unfiltered Merlot, and impressive Pinot Noir. Production at Rockbridge is 4,000 cases.
                    R.G.L.

Rocky Knob AVA, one of six approved appellations in VIRGINIA, a small region on the eastern slope of the BLUE RIDGE MTNS near Meadows of Dan on the south side of the Smith River. The AVA is seen on some wines from nearby Ch Morrisette, notably their Pinot Noir and Chambourcin, but is not otherwise notable.   R.G.L.

Rocky Mtn, region of three states (COLORADO, MONTANA, and WYOMING) which share high elevation and proximity to the Continental Divide. Although agriculture here is marginal, all three states have the ability to grow pitted fruit, which is a positive indication for the production of winegrapes. Large DIURNAL TEMPERATURE FLUCTUATIONS yield wines with good sugaracid balance.

In terms of climatic conditions, each gain of 1,000 ft elevation is equivalent to moving 2° of latitude, or about 120 mi, further from the Equator. Thus a corridor of relatively similar growing conditions starts in WA, and meanders through western ID, western MT, western CO, east-central NM, western OK, and terminates in TX. This description accounts for the ability of vinifera to survive in such apparently diverse situations. The band of tolerance for vinifera, however, can be quite thin. In the North Fork area of CO the corridor is only a couple of miles wide, while the Sonoita AVA in AZ fans out over 160 sq mi. Where vinifera fail, hybrids survive on the shoulders of the corridor. Most vinifera are planted on their OWN ROOTS in the Rocky Mtn region because of the sandy eroded soils, and the prevailing theory that phylloxera can not survive the winters.

Precipitation (a portion of which is snow) is quite low, between 6 and 18 in. Expanding population in most Rocky Mtn states will no doubt precipitate ugly battles over water. More is needed to maintain a winery than to grow a sizeable vineyard. Water conserva-

tion concerns have induced most growers to adopt drip irrigation. Though winters can be severe, snow cover does afford some protection for vines against the cold. *Frost dates are generally May 15 and Sept 15. Judging from results so far, it would not be presumptuous to assume this region is capable of producing world-class wine. A valid comparison of the state of the industry could be made with the wines that were produced in WA and OR in the early 1970s.   R.T.S.

Roederer Estate, the best producer of sparkling wine in CA, in no small part because of a decision Jean-Claude Rouzaud, head of the Roederer champagne house in France, took to eschew the society intrigues of Napa Valley in favor of a backwoods location in Mendocino's ANDERSON VALLEY. Rouzaud and his uncle André spent two years looking at property and made a production choice, not a marketing one. The makers of Cristal wanted growing conditions as much like home as possible.

The temperature gradient from the 800 ft elevation northwestern end of Anderson Valley to the (relatively) warmer, 1,300 ft elevation southeastern end also provided an opportunity to plant for diversity in blending lots. The estate owns 125 planted acres in the coolest end of the valley, where the winery is located, plus 160 planted acres in the middle around Philo and 117 planted acres in the warmer end near Boonville. This is the only French-owned producer of CA sparkling wine to grow all its own grapes, currently making 60,000 cases a year, but growing enough grapes to make 75,000 and owning plenty of land for future vineyard expansion. The winery property is a 580-acre ranch. The Philo property could add another 100 acres of vines, and the Boonville property could add another 65.

Among Roederer's Anderson Valley holdings are 175 acres trained on an open *lyre trellis, which consists of posts driven into the ground at an angle to form X-shaped supports. The advantages of this system are two canopies for each vine, and increased yields. The disadvantages are a huge capital requirement in the beginning, and a lot of maintenance work each year. This long-term view was a hallmark of the Champagne houses' diversification into the *New World. Although of the seven original French ventures into CA, two have retreated, and a seminal exploratory effort by Charbaut into NY in the early 1990s came to naught.

Winemaker Michel Salgues has a doctorate in enology from *Montpellier and previously served as a professor at Institut de la Recherche Agronomique (INRA). The style of his Roederer Estate Brut is firm acidity, which identifies its cool climate origins, but with nothing delicate or shy about the flavor profile at all. It has complexity, especially in the middle, and it has length. The most striking feature is its combination of tautness and weight. Roederer is one of the more difficult pairings of a CA sparkler with its parent company's French counterpart (in this instance, Prestige Brut v. Anderson Valley Estate) for most people to tell apart in a blind tasting—which makes the Estate Brut a very good value. In 1998 there was more premium quality sparkling wine en *tirage in CA than the entire US sparkling wine consumption for a year at all price categories. That is why CA sparkling wine in general is such an excellent bargain.

Roederer also makes small quantities, about 3% of their total production, of a vintage dated premium blend called L'Ermitage. It is very fine and provides a marvelous stylistic comparison with DOM CARNEROS' delicate Le Reve bottling. The characteristic which sets L'Ermitage apart from the crowd is its ability to accentuate complexity and let its sinewy texture carry that complexity further and further into the finish. It is an insistent wine. The wine demands one's attention. America should be proud of it, even if it took the Rouzauds' vision and Dr Salgues' expertise to make it.   B.C.C.

Rogue Valley AVA, remote appellation approved in 1990 which is, surprisingly, home to one of the larger wineries in ORE-GON, Bridgview Vyds. It helps that the winery is located on the entrance to the Oregon Caves Natl Monument. Rogue Valley is chiseled out of mountain ranges twisted askew by the pressure of tectonic plates. This set of interlocking mountains and river valleys causes a great range of *meso-climates. Forests of fir and madrone cover the hills. *Frost and WINTER KILL are a real danger where moist marine air collides with low mountain temperatures. Sandy, lighter soils can help by draining moisture away from the vines. The AVA is nearly square in shape, about 70 mi wide by 60 mi long. Eight wineries currently operate out of this area with easy access to Grants Pass, Medford, and Ashland; and in close proximity to the CA border. *Degree days vary between between 2,300 and 2,500, generally increasing as one moves eastward toward Ashland, home of a lively Shakespeare festival and theater.

Within the Rogue AVA are three rather distinct river valleys, from west to east: Illinois Valley; Applegate Valley; and Bear Creek Valley. Annual rainfall goes from 60 in at Illinois Valley to less than 20 in at Bear Creek Valley. Cool climate varieties, such as Pinot Noir, Pinot Gris, Gamay Noir, Gewürztraminer, Riesling, Chardonnay, Pinot Blanc, and Early Muscat, are grown in the Illinois Valley and give way to warmer climate varieties in the Bear Creek Valley, such as Cabernet Sauvignon, Merlot, Cabernet Franc, Syrah, Chardonnay, and Malbec. The Applegate Valley weather is somewhere in between and is planted to Chardonnay, Cabernet Sauvignon, Merlot, and Zinfandel.

NOTABLE PROPERTIES

Bridgview Vyds in the Illinois Valley offers OR's best value in Riesling and Pinot Noir. Both wines sell well in PORTLAND restaurants and are quickly finding a national market, especially for their distinctive bright blue bottled Blue Moon Oregon Riesling. Bridgview sold 30,000 cases of Riesling alone in 1998.

Foris Vyds, planted in 1976 by Ted and Meri Gerber, has prospered under the winemaking of Sarah Powell. The winery is committed to sustainable agriculture in the Rogue Valley through their various vineyard contracts. Powell works with a wide range of grapes secured from all three sub-valleys of the Rogue. They were the first to use the DIJON CLONE of Chardonnay. Impressive Gewürztraminer, delicious Chardonnay, piercing Pinot Blanc, bright full-flavored Pinot Noir, and excellent Merlot are made. The winery plans to expand its offering of Bordeaux varietals while continuing its success with Burgundian ones.

Valley View Vyds, located 15 mi from the CA border in Applegate Valley near Jacksonville, on a site where Peter Brit originally established OR's first winery in 1850. Currently owned by the Wisnovsky family, who replanted in 1972. They have consistently made excellent wines from Bordeaux varieties, and have produced Zinfandel and Chardonnay.   R.A.I.

Rosenblum, CA WAREHOUSE WINERY located in naturally air-conditioned Alameda, between San Francisco Bay and Oakland, which has been very successful since 1978 at sourcing old, DRY-FARMED, virus infected, hillside vineyards in many locations to make an extensive roster of wines with particular emphasis on Zinfandel. It is an oversimplification to say, as many people do, that CA's best Zinfandels are made by the Three Rs, but if go down that road we must, Rosenblum is one of the three (Ravenswood and Ridge would be the other two).

Amiable is a good word to describe Kent Rosenblum. Called at work, he often comes on the speaker phone to calmly chat while he 'finishes up a client.' He is a veterinarian, and the client is usually a cat undergoing surgery. Rosenblum knew his winemaking activities would produce emergencies just like his vet practice. He did not want to make wine in the country and commute to his office in Alameda. So, Rosenblum Cellars was launched in one of the liveliest parts of West Oakland, across the street from the railroad station. Grapes were crushed in the former Dead End Bar of the 1880s. 'Neat spot,' Rosenblum avers. 'We were between a soul food place and a brothel. What with the girls, and the gambling, and the players driving up in fancy cars, our neighbors saw nothing strange about a bunch of people crushing grapes in the middle of the night. We were just part of the action.' The winery quickly outgrew those 600 sq ft quarters, affectionately known to loyal customers as the Cat House. Rosenblum Cellars now occupies a former railroad repair barn in what used to be the Naval Air Station.

Stylistically Rosenblum Zins are clean, concentrated, and well extracted, but not astringent. They fall more into the Claret category than into the traditional, or Italianate category, but they are the polar opposites of the washed out, simple quaffers that industrial/commercial producers offer. In 1998 there were seventeen Rosenblum Zins on offer. Hendry Vyd, from the southwestern hills in Napa, is usually lighter bodied than Rosenblum's others, with high acid and long ageing ability. Brandlin Vyd is riper with more of a dark fruit, plum sauce nose. The Contra Costa vineyards tend to have the roughest tannic edges. Sauret Vyd, from PASO ROBLES, is full bodied and the only one anybody would call rustic. Samsel and the Sonoma Old Vines bottling are the most fruit forward and lushly textured. If ability to age well in the bottle is a criterion for Zinfandel, Rosenblum and STORYBOOK MTN are by far the best two brands to consider.

Today Rosenblum makes nearly 65,000 cases a year. He still maintains his feline clientele, but he has a full staff at the winery including winemaker Jeff Cohn. They make a Semillon from the old El Mocho Vyd in LIVERMORE, and a rock-solid Petite Sirah from very old, head-pruned vines at the northern end of the Napa Valley. Extraordinarily dark colored and dense, the wine has mouth-stuffing body, but very soft and pliable tannins. It develops more sophisticated flavors over 8–10 years in the bottle, but is actually most impressive when 3–4 years old because the texture is so unusual. It makes one think pork ribs.   B.C.C.

Rosette, or Seibel 1000, an early French hybrid short on yield and color but still sometimes used to make pink wines.

Rougeon, or Seibel 5898, French hybrid valued for its deep colour but cursed for its erratic yields.

Royal Kedem Wine Company, the largest producer of KOSHER wine in North America, with wineries in NY and CA. Royal is a family-run business of the Herzogs, who opened their first winery-distillery in Czechoslovakia in the early 1800s. When the communist regime took over in 1948 the family emigrated to America and joined a small kosher wine cellar on New York City's Lower East Side, the Royal Wine Company. Soon the firm's prime movers, they introduced the Kedem label for sweet Concord wine and expanded production with CA wines in less-sweet styles. In 1965 production shifted to a new winemaking facility in the HUDSON VALLEY at Milton, closer to grape sources. Ten thousand tons of Concord and Niagara grapes are crushed annually from contract growers in upstate NY.

In 1985 Royal took American kosher wine in the new direction of dry varietals from CA, opening Baron Herzog Wine Cellars in San Martin. Recent vintages have been well received by wine critics, particularly Chenin Blanc. Royal took another step into the premium market with the purchase of Weinstock Cellars in Healdsburg. The parent company also sells grape juice and imports, with annual sales over 1 million cases in sixteen countries.   R.F.

rupestris or **Vitis rupestris,** native American species of the *Vitis* genus of vines commonly used for breeding *American hybrids and *rootstocks, particularly for its phylloxera resistance. St George is the name of the most widely known rootstock.

Russian River AVA, approved appellation with 30% of the grapes in CA's SONOMA CO. Located in the western part of the county, the region is in large part a series of low hills through which the Russian River meanders on its way to the ocean at Jenner. The AVA is an area around a stretch of the river running from the town of Healdsburg west about 12 mi to the town of Guerneville, then south to Sebastopol.

HISTORY
Prior to 1982 the image of the district was not one of great artistic wine quality. Dairy farming, sheep ranches, and apple orchards have been staples for a hundred years. The local apple, a specialty cultivar called a Gravenstein, has a particularly pronounced,

somewhat floral scent. As the apple market has been crushed by WA, and the third generation scions of dairy farmers opt for lifestyles with less persistent demands on their time, landowners have begun looking at alternatives. The region currently sends tens of thousands of ducks to Chinese markets in the Bay Area each month and lately even started to sell high quality *foie gras*. Much of the top-end exotic produce (think baby arugula) which shows up in San Francisco's best restaurants is grown on contract in western Sonoma Co.

There have always been plenty of older hillside vineyards, but they were primarily owned by third generation Italian-Americans who sold their grapes to large wineries where they disappeared into generic blends. The image of the district was one of recreational outings, such as canoe trips on the river, followed by huge family style meals in one of the three Italian restaurants in Occidental, each of which would serve hundreds of meals each evening. Since the mid-1980s everything has changed. Rising housing prices closer to San Francisco have driven commuters further and further north, focusing more attention on the visual attractiveness of the district. Spectacular vineyard designated wines from the region made by CRAFTSMAN-SIZED wineries have won competitions, energizing connoisseurs to embark on exploratory quests. Finally, high land prices for vineyards in Napa and Sonoma valleys, and a shift in overall attitude about wine styles in the direction of more cool climate approaches, have combined to give the Russian River district considerable cachet.

CLIMATE AND TOPOGRAPHY
The defining characteristics of the Russian River district are redwood trees and FOG. A vineyard site in Guerneville might have the same *heat summation as a site in Carneros, because the temperature at 2 pm and the overnight low would be the same, but the Guerneville site is likely to see six fewer hours of sunshine four days out of seven in July and Aug because of fog cover. The role of this fog in the Russian River appellation is crucial, but it varies from site to site and year to year. Picture the fog as you might the tide, rolling in and out on a regular cycle, but coming further up the shore some days, and not so far on others. How far up the river the fog travels in any evening or late afternoon is a function of how hot the inland valleys (such as ALEXANDER VALLEY) have gotten. Guerneville always gets a lot of foggy hours. The vineyards around Healdsburg, however, are on the fringe. Some years they get much more than in other years.

North of the river mountains rise abruptly to 1,500 ft. They are largely unpopulated, with few paved roads and fewer vines. West of the approved appellation, especially on the ridges of the mountains north of the river, there are two or three noteworthy Pinot Noir vineyards. The middle of the Russian River appellation southeast of the river itself was once a low lying lagoon. In spots the lagoon soils are dense, water-retentive adobe clay. Along the river's present course and its tributaries deposits of eroded, fist-sized gravels can be found. In between the prehistoric lagoon and the present river, gentle hillsides often sport well-drained sandy loams infused with smooth, pea-sized quartzite pebbles, which would have washed out of the igneous rock formations in the mountains.

Directly south of the river, and almost entirely encompassed by the Russian River AVA, is another approved appellation called **Green Valley AVA**. The name usually has Sonoma appended to it somewhere to discriminate it from a Green Valley AVA which was also approved in Solano County (see DELTA). Green Valley Sonoma is a neatly homogeneous appellation of more than 1,000 acres and among the coolest growing areas in CA. Pinot Noir and Chardonnay are the main grapes and many of them go into sparkling wines. Most of the vines were planted in the last 20 years, replacing apple orchards or dairy farms. Dutton Ranch is the best-known grower in the AVA, selling to a wide range of wineries for vineyard designated still wines.

Russian River Pinot Noir has blackberry-like fruit aromas. It also has more weight in the middle than CARNEROS Pinot Noir. Whether one finds that weight ponderous, as opposed to deftly concentrated, is a function of personal taste *and* of how much fog cover the particular vineyard site received in that vintage. Chardonnay from the Russian River has more fruit stuffing than does Chardonnay from Carneros, but the focus goes toward lemon peel rather than toward the more exotic fruits suggested by SANTA MARIA Chardonnay.

NOTABLE PROPERTIES
Dehlinger, reclusive quality-oriented winery growing 45 acres of grapes since 1975 on the south side of Vine Hill and making 12,000 cases a year. Tom Dehlinger has always been more interested in working his vineyard than in schmoozing through sales exercises. Many commentators have opined it is not enough in CA to merely make great wine, but Dehlinger in the 1990s is a rock solid rebuttal of that position. His top rung

Chardonnay is good, but his top Pinot Noir is great. By manipulating his trellising technique to match the vigor of vines in different sections of vineyard, Dehlinger has succeeded in producing the richest, most dense fruit flavors in the district. His Pinot Noirs are ripe, plush, darkly colored, and immensely satisfying.

Gan Eden, 25,000-case winery making very good quality KOSHER wines in the Green Valley appellation, although it owns no vineyards and sources grapes widely throughout Sonoma Co. Cabernet is the strength of the line. Winemaker Craig Winchell had worked for several wineries when, in 1985, he became Sabbath observant, and thus unable to drink non-kosher wines. Starting his kosher winery was the logical next step.

Hop Kiln, restored hop drying building overlooking the river. The winery produces 10,000 cases a year in a broad range aimed at sales in the tasting room. The best item is a Zinfandel labeled Primitivo from vines at least 50 years old. Made in the traditional style, it is alcoholic, extractive, and face-slappingly aromatic, with just enough *volatile acidity to bring the berry fruit up where no one can miss it. Marty's Big Red is a bargain priced generic made in the style of the district's old Italians who planted several varieties in each field to give both complexity and insurance against ripening problems from any single variety. Big Red apparently never has a problem getting any of its components ripe.

Iron Horse, winery in the cool Green Valley AVA west of Forestville with 240 acres of vineyard planted to Chardonnay and Pinot Noir used for sparkling wines. The winery also owns 45 acres in Alexander Valley used for still wines bringing the total to 40,000 cases. Joy Sterling, the Yale-educated daughter of the owners, is the sales manager and author of two well-received books on wine country life and hospitality. At present Iron Horse shares with J (see JORDAN) the mantle as best American-owned producer of sparkling wines in CA. Several different cuvées are made, but the most attractive is the vintage dated Brut Vrais Amis. It gains texture from time on the lees and has a solid center of flavor. There is enough acid to be refreshing, but none of the tart bitterness and citrus rind flavor often found in cold climate grapes.

J. Swan, winery on Vine Hill started by retired airline pilot Joe Swan in 1967. His cult following during the 1970s put his wines in the same class as the best of the artisan winery pioneers, allowing him to sell everything to a mailing list by sending a postcard once each year saying, 'Your 3 bottles are ready.

Please call to let us know when you want to come by to pick them up.' Everyone complied. Joe Swan's Zinfandels were so intensely colored, they stained glasses when swirled. Swan's acolytes included Jerry Seps (STORYBOOK MTN) and Joel Peterson (RAVENSWOOD) among many others.

Rod Berglund was a butcher turned winemaker who founded La Crema Vinera winery in Santa Rosa in the 1970s. Berglund sourced Chardonnay and Pinot Noir grapes from cool climate areas long before it became fashionable. Moreover he wantonly employed the 'filthy French' techniques of skin soak, barrel fermentation, and aging on gross lees at a time when they were considered marginal lunacy by mainstream CA winemakers. La Crema Vinera was ahead of its time, and like the first soldier on the beach, it took an arrow in the neck. Berglund, however, married Joe Swan's daughter Lynn, and is now the keeper of the Swan flame. Under a now older Berglund the Swan wines are much more restrained. They rely on wood/fruit balance in the nose, and their structure is more firm than effusive.

Korbel, pedestrian producer of 1.7 million cases best known for sparkling wines priced under $10 and for brandy. Owned since 1991 by Anheuser-Busch, which has expanded this foothold in the wine business by acquiring Kenwood and Valley of the Moon in Sonoma Valley. Lake Sonoma Winery in Dry Creek Valley at the entrance to the recreational lake behind Warm Springs Dam was also acquired with the intention of combining that tasting room with a microbrewery, but county planners have yet to grant a permit.

The Korbel Estate on River Rd in western Sonoma is noteworthy for several features other than the wine it produces. It was founded by three Czech brothers in 1886. Francis Korbel was the Austrian consul in San Francisco. Like several operations in the SANTA CRUZ MTNS, Korbel began by harvesting old growth redwood timber. Once they cleared the land around the mill, they started planting grapes. The picturesque location right on the Russian River and the historic buildings are well worth the trip. It is CA's best spot for a photograph of vines and second growth redwoods in the same frame.

Marimar Torres, winery owned by the sister of Miguel A. *Torres, head of Spain's renowned producer in *Penedès. The 60-acre Russian River vineyard is about as far west as any in Sonoma Co, and is planted evenly to Chardonnay and Pinot Noir making a total of 15,000 cases. The Pinot Noir is a little too dill scented, but the Chardonnay is a very precise lemon drop packaged in

caramel oak with rich texture. It makes a wonderful match for Petrale sole from the Sonoma coast.

See DELOACH, FARRELL, KISTLER, MARTINELLI, ROCHIOLI, SONOMA-CUTRER, WILLIAMS SELYEM, WINDSOR VYDS.   B.C.C.

Rutherford AVA, district on the NAPA VALLEY floor north of OAKVILLE and south of ST HELENA. Best known for Cabernets, primarily because of the Who's Who list of vineyards located along the westside bench: Sycamore; Bella Oaks; Inglenook; Beaulieu #1; Bosche; and Livingston Moffat. Because of its deep, well-drained, but not particularly fertile soil profile, the bench naturally restricts crop load and vegetation. Cabernet ripens two weeks earlier on the bench than in the silty soils of the valley floor. It also gets 1° Brix riper. Rutherford Bench Cabernets are round, and complex with earthy flavors, but fully packed with fruit. The fruit does not dominate in the nose, it fills the mouth and evolves slowly in the finish. No other single district in CA has as enviable a track record for 100% Cabernet Sauvignons worth bottle ageing.

The other Rutherford district of note is the area between the Napa River and Conn Creek on the east side of the valley. There the gravel deposits washed out of the eastern mountains provide equally fine natural sites for Cabernet. In total there are 5,000 acres of vines in the Rutherford AVA.

NOTABLE PROPERTIES

Frog's Leap, whimsically named winery started on an old frog farm in the early 1980s. A small operation then, it made marvelous Sauvignon Blanc and sold out quickly each year to a clientele who loved to show guests the 'ribbettt...' printed on each cork. In 1994 the partners split, with Larry Turley keeping the farm (see ST HELENA) and winemaker John Williams keeping the name. Williams moved to his new location on Conn Creek Road and now produces 50,000 cases annually, half of it Chardonnay. Grapes for the Chardonnay come from CARNEROS producing a clean, apple flavored wine. Sauvignon Blanc is also nice with a tart, earthy flavor.

Mumm Napa Valley, joint venture between Seagram and the Mumm champagne house from France begun in 1986 by Guy Devaux who came from the FINGER LAKES region in NY, and who is commemorated today in their *tête de cuvée DVX. Seagram also owns the Winery Lake Vyd in Carneros, allowing Mumm Napa Valley to produce a vintage dated, vineyard designated Brut cuvée. Both of those items are very good quality. The Winery Lake is the most pointed of the offerings, with the freshest and longest flavors. DVX is broader, toastier, and a bit more expansive in the nose. Winemaker Greg Fowler produces 200,000 cases a year, largely without direction from France.

Raymond, winery and vineyards started in 1971 on 90 acres in the center of the valley when Roy Raymond and his wife, the granddaughter of Jacob Beringer, sold BERINGER to Nestlé. Their sons expanded the operation to 250 acres of vineyard, then stayed on to manage after selling a majority interest to Kirin Brewing of Japan in 1988. Extra capital enabled them to purchase an additional 300 acres in Monterey whence come most of the grapes for Chardonnay, which makes up the lion's share of production, and also the second label Amberhill. The winery currently produces 300,000 cases. Napa Valley appellation bottlings of Cabernet are good value, well made, and consistent.

Staglin, well-financed winery and Italianate showplace estate on the bench at the southern end of the appellation with 50 acres of Cabernet, Chardonnay, and Sangiovese, producing 3,000 cases a year of expensive bottlings. The Cabernet has strong fruit behind it and plenty of new oak. The Sangiovese is much oakier than most in CA and could use more fruit intensity for balance. There is good potential as the vines mature.

Swanson, winery on the bench with some of their 160 acres in the middle of the valley owned by the heir to a frozen TV dinner fortune. Good Sangiovese is made by winemaker Marco Capelli who worked two vintages in Tuscany before moving to Napa but the best item is a Syrah from a 13-acre vineyard on the bench in Oakville acquired in 1992 which had previously been the source of Sean Thackrey's Orion. Total production is 25,000 cases.

ZD, winery begun almost as a hobby in 1969 with a focus on Pinot Noir from the Madonna Vyd in Carneros, then gradually expanded to a 30,000-case facility and 33 acres on the Silverado Trail, with the second generation taking on almost all of the responsibilities for winemaking, sales, and marketing. Pinot Noir is still well made, but the best current item is Chardonnay. Extensive barrel testing has convinced the deLeuze family to age their Chardonnay in air-dried, fire-coopered American oak. The result is a coconut nuance to nicely complement the pineapple character of the ripe, full-bodied ZD Chardonnay.

See also BEAULIEU, CAKEBREAD, CAYMUS, FRANCISCAN, GRGICH-HILLS, NIEBAUM-COPPOLA, ST SUPÉRY. B.C.C.

S

Sacramento Delta, see DELTA.

St Croix, relatively successful hybrid that withstands extremely low temperatures and makes soft red wine.

Ste Chapelle, named for a little chapel built on a hill overlooking the vineyard, and for 20 years the dominant wine producer in IDAHO with a noteworthy commitment to quality. Its owners are envied for their marketing acumen. The winery is located in the Sunnyslope region near Caldwell, not far west of Boise and vineyards are planted along a gentle hillside on the east side of the Snake River. Ste Chapelle has produced wonderful Rieslings and Chardonnays in a variety of styles.

In the mid-1980s there was a controversial and explosive shake-up between Bill Broich, the pioneering winemaker, and the owners, the Symms family. Local newspapers polarized the community and pitted conservative US Senator David Symms against everyone else, which left the tiny wine community fractured and confused for many years. The winery, through its new winemaker, the alliteratively named Mimi Mook, changed its style of wines. Fresh fruit qualities were emphasized, making the wines more food friendly, but not nearly as much fun as the fat, toasty Broich Chardonnays of the past. Today Ste Chapelle is again causing major ripples. The 130,000-case winery was purchased in 1997 by CORUS BRANDS, owners of COLUMBIA WINERY in WA. Winemaker Kevin Mott (who married Mimi Mook and succeeded her as winemaker) continued the style of winemaker Mook and in 1999 turned over the winemaking to Steve Roberta, formerly of Robert Mondavi's Woodbridge winery (see LODI). Mimi and Kevin Mott were set to open a small winery of their own along the banks of the Snake River in late 1999.

R.A.I.

Ste Genevieve, TEXAS' largest grower and producer of wines bottling 330,000 cases a year for sale exclusively in TX, and located in the Escondido Valley AVA near Fort Stockton in the TRANS-PECOS region. Owners

*Cordier of Bordeaux, via affiliate Cordier Estates Inc, ships varietal wine in bulk from France's *Languedoc, which is bottled at Ste Genevieve under the brand name L'Orval and sold throughout the US. About 275,000 cases of L'Orval are bottled each year. There is 1.5 million gal of storage space at the winery.

The Ste Genevieve vineyard is on 1,016 acres leased from the Univ of TX Lands System as part of the Permanent Univ Fund. This fund owns 2 million acres in west TX, the income from which provides endowment funds for the whole Univ of TX system. The fund also receives a percentage of the gross income of the winery. Cordier Estates, along with three other investors, took over the vineyard from the university in 1987. Cordier Estates is now the sole owner of the property. Leonard Garcia is president and Frenchman Jean-Louis Haberer is the winemaker.

The mesas surrounding the winery are limestone mountains topped with sandstone which has eroded over the years to cover the desert valley with calcareous soil and clay loam. A substratum of gravel for drainage, long days of sunlight, an elevation of 3,000 ft, and calcium-rich underground water combine to provide fine growing conditions. If the weather would cooperate, everyone would be happy. Lack of rain and unpredictably late *frost have forced Ste Genevieve to employ some innovative techniques. Temperatures in summer range from 100°F to 110°F at midday, then drop to the high 60s at night. Winds up to 80 mph can do serious damage to the vines. A two-pronged attack toward late frosts every spring has kept the winery in business. They import 5 ft horizontal heaters powered by natural gas that do not emit smoke from apple orchards in WA for the ground war, and they launch a fleet of helicopters in an aerial assault attempting to find warm air pockets aloft which can be driven down to the vineyard. Drip irrigation is required because what little rain may fall in the summer evaporates before it hits the ground. Ste Genevieve uses a computer controlled *fertigation program for adding nitrogen, potassium, and

phosphorus fertilizers to the irrigation water they draw from 22 wells before it is sent to the vines. They are also able to add micronutrients such as iron and zinc at a mixing station for site-specific irrigation needs.

The winery has 930 acres under vine, most of which were planted in the early 1980s. The vineyard is planted to Chardonnay, Chenin Blanc, Sauvignon Blanc, Muscat, Cabernet Sauvignon, Merlot, Ruby Cabernet, Gamay Noir, Pinot Noir, and Zinfandel. Unlike in TX's other major growing district, the TEXAS HIGH PLAINS, Ste Genevieve achieves substantial yields: 8 t/a for the Chenin Blanc and Ruby Cabernet, 5 t/a for Cabernet Sauvignon, Sauvignon Blanc, Zinfandel, and 3 t/a for the Pinot Noir and Merlot. Vine spacing is currently at 12 × 8 ft, but a program of interplanting has begun on 200 acres of Chardonnay and 80 acres of Merlot that will cut that in half. Yields on the interplanted acreage are expected to increase by 40%. They have an option on another 1,000 acres of land adjacent to the current site, but have decided that interplanting will be more efficient than managing additional acreage.

French and American oak barrels are used for ageing the Chardonnay, Cabernet Sauvignon, Merlot, and Pinot Noir. All their other varietal wines are produced entirely in stainless steel. Ste Genevieve is a reliable and very popular source of inexpensive, grocery store wines in TX. They manage to make a very good $3.50 bottle of non-vintage Sauvignon Blanc and have also introduced a new label, Escondido Valley, which features mid-priced ($8/bottle) Cabernet Sauvignon and Merlot. Judging from barrel samples of the Cabernet, the new range looks quite promising.

L.A.O.

St Francis, winery with 90 acres of vineyard near Kenwood in the center of CA's SONOMA VALLEY. Vines were planted in the early 1970s; the winery constructed in 1979. Half of the 100,000-case production is Cabernet and Chardonnay, but the winery's claim to fame is Merlot, much of it planted at the winery. The Reserve version is one of CA's best. The success of the variety in their location induced owner Joe Martin to graft over all the Riesling, Gewurz, and Pinot Noir he had to Merlot. The key to the wine's attraction is its weight combined with remarkably soft tannins. Fruit aromas are not as prominently in play as wood and depth. Old vine Zinfandels have gained favor in some circles, but their alcoholic style is not for everyone.   B.C.C.

St Helena AVA, appellation approved in 1995 in the northern half of CA's NAPA VALLEY. The AVA runs from Zinfandel Lane in the south to Bale Lane in the north, and up the sides of the valley to about the 400 ft contour line. The little town of St Helena has long been the cultural center of the valley. It has the best restaurants and the most of them. It is the home of the Napa Valley Wine Library Association. Many of the businesses and offices are in 100-year-old buildings.

The town is at the apex of a configuration in the valley where the surrounding hills pinch together. The result is that sites south of town are cooler than sites north of town. The other difference is that south of town there is a westside bench, whereas north of town the prominent westside Cabernet vineyards are very close to Hwy 29, but on relative steep slopes. Because Napa is actually a pull-apart basin (see CALIFORNIA, geology) rather than a true valley, it stands to reason it would parallel the San Andreas Fault, running westnorthwest. That produces more rain at the northern end of the valley than in the south and St Helena averages 34 in annually compared to 25 in at the city of Napa. Fluctuation is greater as well. St Helena received 70 in during the *El Niño winter of 1982/3, then 12 in during the drought of 1975/6.

NOTABLE PROPERTIES

Casa Nuestra, tiny winery on the Silverado Trail specializing in Loire-type wines such as Chenin Blanc and a very high quality Cabernet Franc made in the fruit forward style of a Loire red. It is owned and run by a Harvard-trained lawyer who abandoned the Bar to become a gentleman farmer and folk music impresario.

Crocker-Starr, winemaking operation begun in the mid-1990s as a joint venture between Pam Starr, formerly winemaker at Spottswoode, and Charlie Crocker, great grandson of the man who engineered and built the western half of the first railroad across America. Crocker's 70-acre vineyard in the center of the valley includes an historic stone winery building in which he and his wife have built their house. The Crocker-Starr wines are based on Cabernet Franc, with small admixtures of Merlot or

Cabernet Sauvignon. The first release in 1996 was light in color, but loaded with black stonefruit smells. Its style was to float and move; not sit and ponder.

Duckhorn, winery on the Silverado Trail, just north of Lodi Lane, begun in 1976 by then banker Dan Duckhorn. Well known for Merlot, particularly the vineyard designated version from Three Palms Vyd, which is located further north in the center of the valley. The vineyard is owned by a Duckhorn investor and shared with STERLING. The style of this wine has always been forceful, carried by alcohol, and designed to impress in blind tastings. Since the early 1990s grapes have also come from two owned vineyards on HOWELL MTN: 28-acre Candlestick Ridge and 40-acre Stout Vyd. Those grapes are red Bordeaux varieties, primarily split between Cabernet Sauvignon and Merlot. Tom Rinaldi has been winemaker since the winery's inception.

Folie à Deux, winery acquired by Dick Petersen in the mid-1990s and currently undergoing an impressive renaissance. Petersen was a prominent winemaker who worked with André *Tchelistcheff at BEAULIEU before moving to MONTEREY Co to help lead the viticultural surge beginning there in the mid-1970s. Petersen returned to Napa Valley and eventually played a central role in the establishment of ATLAS PEAK Vyd. A friendly and generous man, Petersen is arguably doyen of a Napa Valley dynasty: one of his daughters is married to Tim *Mondavi and another, Heidi, is married to the scion at CH MONTELENA and winemaker for a string of cult Cabernets including Grace Family and Screaming Eagle. The winemaker at Folie à Deux is Scott Harvey, who previously engineered the artistic success of RENWOOD before falling out with that investment group. The name Folie à Deux is a clinical term for a shared delusion. It was chosen by the winery's founders, a psychiatrist and his psychologist wife, who fell apart when he was successfully sued for improper physical relations with one of his patients, a young female from the local religious college.

Grace Family, tiny winery and 3-acre Cabernet Sauvignon vineyard, half of which was out of production in the middle of the 1990s for post-phylloxera replanting. This is definitely a CULT WINE with bottles selling for nearly $200 each to a mailing list, then showing up a few years later at auction for twice that amount. The vineyard is on a westside slope just north of Deer Park Rd. Dick Grace, a former stockbroker, is an evangelical Buddhist, and non-drinker, who donates much of his production to charity auctions. His wine is made by top CONSULT-

ANT Heidi Peterson Barrett. She also uses the cozy production facility at Grace to produce equally small quantities of Barbour Vyds Cabernet for Grace's vineyard manager, and Vyd 29 for Grace's neighbor Tom Paine, whose vineyard is actually located at 2929 Hwy 29. The Grace Cabernet is built around the concept of balance. It is not particularly powerful, concentrated, or fruity. It simply has all the elements in place, neatly harmonized with cedary wood overtones. The wine's charm emerges slowly in the glass, indicating good downstream potential. Of the other wines in the barn, the Vyd 29 is the more fruit driven, and the Barbour is the more ripely punchy.

Chas Krug, winery in the center of the valley north of St Helena producing 1 million cases annually from 1,000 acres in Napa and another 900 in Yolo Co (see CENTRAL VALLEY). The lion's share of the production goes to market under the CK Mondavi line of jug wines. German émigré Charles Krug began making wine in Napa Valley in the 1850s. The winery went dark during Prohibition, and was then purchased by Cesare *Mondavi in 1943 when he arrived from Lodi with sons Peter and Robert. Their winery was notable in the 1960s for an excellent, fruity, off-dry Chenin Blanc made with cold temperature, stainless steel fermentation techniques which were then new to the industry. Cesare died in 1959. Robert and Peter Mondavi disagreed about the positioning of the company: Robert advocating vigorous and expensive promotional campaigns linked to top quality and an upmarket image; Peter preferring a budgetary emphasis in production and a marketing strategy built around lower priced, volume products. In 1966 Robert left to open his own winery Robert MONDAVI, but retained his financial stake in C. Krug. Continuing altercations over Krug's management came to a head between the brothers shortly after their mother Rosa died, and in 1976 Robert brought a legal suit demanding to be cashed out of his equity share. The court set a fair market price for the winery at $45 million, which was interesting in light of the sale that same year of Ch *Margaux for $12 million. Peter Mondavi was required to shoulder a substantial debt in order to compensate his older brother while retaining ownership of Krug. That debt burden hampered Krug's ability to modernize for nearly a decade, but in the 1990s they have grown considerably. Among their quality wines Sangiovese stands out.

Merryvale, winery started in 1983 by partners from the extraordinarily successful Pacific Union real estate company in San Francisco (at one time owners of the Pebble

Beach CC) and Robin Lail, daughter of former Inglenook proprietor John Daniel (see NIEBAUM-COPPOLA). It has since been sold to the Schlatter family of Switzerland. Since 1986 the winery has occupied the old Sunny St Helena winery building on Hwy 29 just south of the town, which includes a banquet room lined with 2,000 gal wooden casks and a tasting area inside a 22,000 gal wooden tank. Merryvale is highly regarded for a dense, oaky Chardonnay. The red Meritage called Profile is elegantly balanced, with an insistent black tea bouquet evolving after five years of bottle age. Production is 50,000 cases.

Rombauer, *custom crush facility owned by a former airline pilot which also makes about 20,000 cases a year for its own label. Rombauer does own some vineyards, and the staff are of course intimately acquainted with the fruit from many others.

St Clement, lovely restored Victorian home on a westside hill north of town. The winery was developed around fine Cabernets by eye surgeon William Casey, then sold in 1987 to Sapporo, the Japanese brewer. St Clement owns 38 acres in Carneros, the source of the Chardonnay. Cabernet grapes come from the few acres at the winery plus top vineyards further south on the bench. The Cabernets have become increasingly impressive every year for the last ten. They accomplish a seemingly contradictory feat of being sinewy in the mouth but expansive in the nose. They also age very well, dropping astringency and producing more plum flavors after 6–7 years in the cellar. Total production is around 15,000 cases, one-third Cabernet.

V. Sattui, premier CELLAR DOOR seller in Napa Valley. Darryl Sattui had the eminently good idea in 1974 of bringing his grandfather's wine business back to life, and was able to get a loan from the bank by the simple expedient of pointing out he would be the first winery in the valley on the right-hand side of the road (as drivers came into St Helena) to have picnic tables, lawn, and shade trees. He also proposed to sell sandwiches, fruit, and cheese as well as wine. So successful was this approach, he quickly repaid the bank loan, rebuilt the winery building, and has now even purchased winery property in Italy. Sattui owns 60 acres in Napa and sells 40,000 cases a year, at full retail. One thing Sattui does do which other top producers eschew is enter competitions, and he frequently wins. His Preston Vyd Cabernet is particular fine. It is medium bodied and smoothly round, with spiced plum flavors and wood really only apparent in the finish.

Spottswoode. These respected grape sellers with 40 acres right on the edge of the houses west of St Helena brought out their own wine in 1982 and now make 8,000 cases a year. Sauvignon Blanc is crisp and mineral flavored. Cabernet is too, medium bodied with earthy flavors and mild astringency. The winery is now just up the street in an old ghost building dating from 1884.

Sutter Home, winery named for its location on Hwy 29 south of St Helena which was a house owned at the end of the 19th century by a man surnamed Sutter. Purchased in 1950 by the Trinchero family, it became a purveyor of reputable jug wines for many years until stepping briefly into the limelight with a 1974 Zinfandel from Deaver Vyd in AMADOR CO. While that wine and a few successors from old Zinfandel vineyards in Amador were remarkable, the essence of the winery evolved in the mid-1970s when a few small batches of the curiosity White Zinfandel proved to be big hits in the St Helena tasting room. Mrs Trinchero did not raise any fools. Sutter Home today owns 5,500 acres, mostly in the CENTRAL VALLEY and sells nearly 7 million cases a year, much of it White Zin. This is one of the 20 largest wineries in America, based largely on a wine no one in the world, except Americans, drinks. In 1988 the Trincheros bought Montev)ña winery in Amador Co to pursue their higher-end ambitions.

Turley, small winery on Hwy 29, a little bit north of Lodi Lane, with an interesting history and a big reputation. Larry Turley was for 25 years an emergency room physician. He and John Williams started Frog's Leap Winery (see RUTHERFORD) at this spot, which used to be a frog farm, in the early 1980s. That partnership ended in 1994. Larry's sister Helen is one of the most sought-after winemaking consultants in California, responsible for a couple of cult Cabernets, including Bryant Family, and for her own label, Marcassin, which focuses on Chardonnay. Although Helen made the 1993–5 Turley wines, she is no longer involved. The Turley label, which no doubt gets a continuing boost from the family name, then moved into the very capable hands of Ehren Jordan, a superstar in his own right, for four years. Jordan produced 5,000 cases a year of single vineyard cult Zinfandels and Petite Sirahs for the Turley label. They are expensive, but never disappointing. Always known for massively dense fruit, the wines under Jordan retained that signature while whittling away some of the ponderous extract to present a more elegant, refined finish.

See also BERINGER, FLORA SPRINGS, HEITZ, MARTINI. B.C.C.

St Julian, winery in Paw Paw, MICHIGAN, in the southwest grape belt of LAKE MICHIGAN SHORE AVA. It is the state's largest, producing 65,000 cases of wine as well as 225,000 cases of sparkling grape juice. They own no vineyards but have contracts with about 90 growers in the region, 12–15 of whom specialize in grapes for the more interesting wines. The winery's origins began in 1921 in Ontario when the Meconi Wine Cellars were established by Mariano Meconi. At Repeal, he moved the winery to MI, settling in Paw Paw in 1938. Today his grandson, David Braganini is the president.

Winemaker Chas Catherman did what many might call a reverse move in that he started in CA at Giumarra Vyds in 1976 but came to MI a year later to be hired by Paul Braganini, David's father. With more than two decades of harvest under his belt, he has helped guide the winery to both commercial and critical success for his wines. Aside from a likeable collection of sweet table, fortified, sparkling, and fruit wines, St Julian turns out a very respectable line of French hybrid wines, as well as a small amount of viniferas. Of the former, the barrel fermented Vignoles and the Chancellor are consistently good and solidly made. The Chardonnays and Rieslings are typically light but seem to do well with some bottle age, while the Cabernets, Franc especially, and Merlot, score well in ripe years. The sparkling raspberry wine is particularly delicious. P.W.F.

St Pepin, one of Elmer SWENSON's later hybrids: a winter-hardy vine producing ordinary wine.

St Supéry, winery in the RUTHERFORD district of CA's NAPA VALLEY owned by the Skalli family, France's largest pasta purveyor. The winery is run by Michaela Rodeno, one of the CA wine industry's most capable executives. Their visitor center is a special experience including a nose-on display of typical wine aromas called Smellavision and raised relief maps of the area. Most of the grapes come from 450-acre Dollarhide Ranch in the Pope Valley. The best item, Sauvignon Blanc, belies its origins in this warm eastern valley by being sharply acidic and very full flavored with a clean, gun metal finish that surprises like a splash of cold water in the face. The winery has grown to 175,000 cases from a standing start in 1982. They also make a value priced line called Bonverre with wines from both CA and from the Skalli's *Pays d'Oc operation in the south of France. For a while they even made a KOSHER wine called Mt Maroma. B.C.C.

sales tax, percentage added to the price of wine which is collected by the retail store or restaurant and forwarded to the state, usually for the benefit of local jurisdictions such as counties and municipalities. The percentage differs by location, but can be over 8% in large cities. It can therefore be of considerable consequence when it is not collected on DIRECT SHIPMENT sales made in the gray legal arena of lax enforcement.

Salinas Valley, 100 mi long agricultural wonderland in CA running southsoutheast through MONTEREY Co from Monterey Bay past the SAN LUIS OBISPO CO northern border almost to PASO ROBLES. Watered by the Salinas River, which flows underground for much of its length, the valley is home to vast truck farming enterprises. It produces much of the lettuce grown in the US. The name is not an approved AVA, but it is almost synonymous with the Monterey AVA. B.C.C.

San Benito Co, located in CA's CENTRAL COAST mega-AVA, and topographically a southeasterly extension of the SANTA CLARA VALLEY. The Gabilan Range is west of San Benito, separating it from the Salinas Valley. CHALONE (both winery and AVA) is on the southwestern slope of the Gabilans in Monterey Co but outside the Monterey AVA, while CALERA winery in the Mt Harlan AVA is on the northeastern slope, in San Benito Co but outside the San Benito AVA. Got that? The only point worth remembering is that Calera and Chalone share a mountain range. The Gabilans are on the Pacific plate; the eastern half of San Benito Co is on the North American plate. The San Andreas Fault runs right up the northeast side of the Gabilans through the heart of San Benito Co and underneath the sleepy little farming village of Hollister, which is as close as the county comes to having a real town. Put Hollister in your top three choices when making bets about where the epicenter of the next big EARTHQUAKE in CA will be located. Two landscape features of the Gabilans reflect their tortured position on the cusp of two colliding tectonic plates, and reveal why grapes grown here can be dramatically different in sites right next to each other. First is Pinnacles Natl Monument just over the ridge crest northeast of Chalone as one drives from Monterey Co into San Benito Co. Pinnacles is a natural wonderland of vertical basalt spires, six-sided columns of magma that have cooled in distinctive crystalline shapes then resisted weathering better than the softer rocks surrounding them. Finding enough topsoil for vines to survive is difficult on any site with basalt underpinnings. And finding geothermal steam is

easier than finding liquid water for irrigation. The second feature found in the Gabilan Range is large sections of limestone-like, carbonate, 'chalk-rock' which has obvious sedimentary seabed origins. These limestone-like soils drain pooled rain or irrigation water away from the vines, but retain it evenly, and release it to the roots in a gradual manner so that dry farming is possible even in these arid mesoclimates.

Demonstrating the lack of consequence in many approved AVAs, there is only one winery in San Benito Co and less than 2,000 acres of vines, but no less than five AVAs. Almaden planted 3,500 acres of vines in the 1970s, then virtually abandoned them when the brand name was sold to Heublein in 1983. **Mt Harlan AVA** is defined by the 1,800 ft contour line, and separate from the **Cienega Valley AVA**, which is defined by the 1,200 ft contour line in some places and by the 1,600 ft contour line in other places. That is correct. These two AVAs parallel each other with 200 to 600 ft of elevation between them undefined in terms of viticultural appellations. Mt Harlan is cooler, because of its elevation, and it receives more rain. The other approved appellations in San Benito Co are: **Lime Kiln AVA**, which partially overlaps Mt Harlan AVA and also Cienega Valley AVA; **Paicines AVA** in the valley floor; and San Benito AVA which totally encompasses Cienega Valley AVA and Paicines AVA, plus some additional valley floor land to the north. B.C.C.

Sanford, winery with a slightly eccentric wine style, located in the western portion of SANTA YNEZ AVA in CA's SANTA BARBARA CO. The most compelling story of viticultural passion in this district belongs to Richard Sanford and Michael Benedict, who began planting a vineyard in 1971 on a long slope with a north-facing aspect, but sheltered from winds off the ocean by a fold in the Santa Rosa Hills immediately to the west. All the road cuts in the area are composed of fractured shales and sandstones; there is a commercial diatomite mine within sight of the property. Sanford and Benedict lived in a one-room cabin on the property without electricity for five years while they planted 112 acres of vines. It was the first cold climate, seriously coastal Pinot Noir venture in CA, pre-dating similar moves by other radicals in Sonoma and the Santa Cruz Mtns. The conventional wine industry was skeptical but curious. Winemaking commenced in 1976 in an old barn on the property, still without electricity. Initial reviews were mixed. These first Pinot Noirs had great depth of flavor, but Michael Benedict's

purist attachment to primitive Burgundian techniques left him open to criticism about microbiological spoilage. Reasonable people can disagree where the line between defect and character lies, but Benedict's prickly relations with the public only exacerbated the situation. In 1980 Sanford left the partnership to start his own winery. Benedict retained the vineyard, but also took over the need to service the debt. For ten years the place struggled. Wineries such as AU BON CLIMAT purchased grapes and made stunning wines which sold briskly for ultra-premium prices, but Michael Benedict's own winemaking remained controversial to say the least, and his inclination toward congenial sales and marketing functions remained non-existent.

Richard Sanford on the other hand is Mr Personality. He had looks good enough to land him a job on a Santa Barbara television news program, and was well connected in the community. He began making wines in 1981 in leased industrial space near Buellton. He purchased grapes from such top Santa Maria AVA vineyards as Bien Nacido and Sierra Madre. In 1983 he hired Bruno D'Alfonso as his winemaker. The style of the Sanford wines has always been recognizable for its leesy, feral, diacetyl-laden richness. Sanford Chardonnays are ripe, pineapple scented and full bodied, but the grape component is still subservient to the toasty bouquet that points in the direction of onions frying in butter, without going quite that far. The best ones are called Barrel Select.

A similar, and in this case much more fascinating style is applied to Sauvignon Blanc. Few other Sauvignon Blancs are ever treated in this fashion. *Barrel fermented, put through *MLF, and sometimes left with a hint of RS, these wines are nothing if not distinctive, which provides a counterpoint to their extreme *methoxypyrazine or green chiles aroma. Strange, yet artistically persuasive. By comparison to neighbor BABCOCK's Eleven Oaks Sauvignon Blanc, Sanford is an elephant on roller skates, ie much less rigidly structured.

Sanford's reputation rests on Pinot Noir even though it accounts for only 20% of production. The untamed smells and the morel mushroom character of the Sanford style are just perfectly suited to all the taboo-tweeking implications of Pinot Noir bouquet. 'This wine slips your socks off,' as one wag put it. The Barrel Select Pinot Noirs justify their increased price over the two lower tier models. The Pinot Noirs have more finesse than the Sanford Chardonnays, always with a band of raspberry fruit and often a dusting of dill.

In 1990 Michael Benedict gave up. Harried by creditors, he sold the Sanford & Benedict Vyd to Robert and Janice Atkins of London. Throughout the 1980s Benedict had stubbornly refused to sell any grapes to Richard Sanford. Little did he realize that Sanford was lobbying behind the scenes with the new potential buyers. When the deal closed, Atkins appointed Sanford as manager of the vineyard, and Sanford was once again united with the vines he had helped plant nearly two decades earlier. Meanwhile Sanford and his wife purchased a 738-acre property in the Santa Rosa Hills called Rancho El Jabali and constructed their own winery. B.C.C.

San Francisco, see BAY AREA.

San Luis Obispo Co, the middle of CA's CENTRAL COAST mega-AVA, equidistant from San Francisco and Los Angeles, about four hours by car either way. Beef has been king in the region since 1772 when Junipero Serra chose it as the site of the second Spanish mission in Alta California. Alfalfa and almonds were bigger crops than grapes, but that changed in the 1990s. Tourism is growing as well. Hearst Castle draws millions of visitors each year.

Viticulturally SLO Co separates into two distinctly different climatic zones. La Cuesta Grade, the steepest piece of state highway in CA, is the dividing line. The city of San Luis Obispo sits at a few hundred feet of elevation. Driving north on Hwy 101 out of San Luis Obispo one gains nearly 2,000 ft of elevation in barely 2 mi of distance on the Grade, often emerging from the fog covered valley into bright sunlight at the crest. The city and cool coastal districts are represented by EDNA VALLEY AVA. The warm inland section, called North County, is represented by the PASO ROBLES AVA. Both parts saw a rapid expansion of vineyard planting in the 1990s. Total county acreage went from 6,500 in 1989, evenly split between reds and whites, to 15,000 acres in 1998 with twice as many reds as whites. Cabernet and Chardonnay account for half the plantings, evenly split between the two. Even more significant than the increased grape acreage is the fact that production facilities are beginning to open in the region. Unlike the 1980s, few SLO grapes leave the county for processing anymore. From the beginning of 1996 to the middle of 1999, 48 winery projects were approved by the county, ranging from garage conversions to the 700,000 sq ft expansion at MERIDIAN and a 540,000 sq ft winery being built by the Villa Mt Eden brand (sold separately from the property

upon which it started in Napa Valley) east of Paso Robles.

ARROYO GRANDE is another AVA in the county, fairly large physically, but accounting for only 3% of the grapes, and stretching over both extremes of climatic condition.

NOTABLE PROPERTIES

Seven Peaks, brand co-owned by *Southcorp, Australia's largest wine company, and the Niven family who own Paragon Vyds in Edna Valley. The Nivens also own 100 acres in Paso Robles, and Southcorp is developing 400 acres in the flatlands east of that city. A tasting room for the brand has been opened in San Luis Obispo, and the brand name is a reference to a line of cone shaped peaks (called *morros*) rising abruptly out of the valley floor that runs from the town of San Luis Obispo to the ocean at Morro Bay. Fruit for the brand's Chardonnay and Pinot Noir is sourced in Edna Valley, while Cabernet, Merlot, and Syrah (they call it Shiraz) come from the new Paso Robles plantings. Wines are presently made at the Tolosa *custom crush facility in San Luis Obispo. Production of the reds from Paso Robles will stay at Tolosa for awhile, but production of Pinot Noir and Chardonnay will move to a new winery the Nivens are building in Edna Valley. Ian Shepard has been sent from Oz to oversee wine production. He brings with him techniques such as the use of *rotofermenters and *barrel fermentation towards the end of red wine fermentations. B.C.C.

San Pasqual AVA, see TEMECULA.

San Sebastian, winery located in St Augustine, FLORIDA, demonstrating the potential from well-made Muscadine wines. **Lakeridge Vyds** in Clermont is owned and operated by the same management, Seavin Inc. San Sebastian features 39 acres of hybrid grapes, with expansion to 55 acres in the works. Wines offered include a wide range of proprietary and generic blends (including a 'sherry') based on Muscadines and vinifera imported from CA. Lakeridge winery has 45 acres of FL grapes currently planted, with expansion planned to 60 acres. A wide range of wines are made from both grapes and citrus.

The San Sebastian/Lakeridge operation demonstrates the versatility of style available to vintners in the SOUTH region with Muscadine, the new hybrids, and fruit wines. San Sebastian Stover Reserve resembles a Cayuga with a slight Muscat hint, and is dry and refreshing. The Lakeridge Chablis, although a bit low in acidity, is fresh and clean, with a flavor reminiscent of the Dutchess grape from NY. The 100% Noble grape Vintner's

Red, though an intensely fruity and sweet wine, has won awards in many national competitions. Those who are not fans of Muscadine table wines might be more impressed with San Sebastian winemaker Jeanne Burgess' skill in making fortified wines from native grapes. The 'cream sherry,' a blend of three-quarters Niagara and one-quarter Carlos grapes, is a wine of compelling smoothness and finesse. The 'port,' made entirely of Noble grapes, does not have the balance of the sherry, being low in acid and intensely fruity. San Sebastian/Lakeridge is setting a standard for varietal, blended, and fortified Muscadine grapes and hybrids and will be a Southern wine operation to watch in the next decade. Production is 25,000 cases.
R.G.L.

Santa Barbara Co, region two hours by car north of LOS ANGELES, and culturally wedded to it. As a practical matter, Santa Barbara Co is the southern end of the CENTRAL COAST, although technically the Central Coast AVA extends clear into Los Angeles. Southern California is distinguished from the Central Coast and from the CENTRAL VALLEY by a somewhat anomalous range of granitic mountains called the Tehachapis (pronunciation emphasis at the second syllable) in its eastern portion of the range, and the Santa Ynez Mtns in its western section. The anomaly is that their ridge tops run east–west, rather than northwest–southeast parallel to the coast and to the San Andreas Fault as do the Sierra Nevadas and the Coast Ranges. The reason for this anomaly is indicated by a careful examination of a CA relief map. As the Pacific plate has moved northwest grating against the North American Plate for tens of millions of years, it has *turned* the southern extremity of the Sierra batholith, dragging it into its present position. In fact, the Pacific plate ripped off a portion of the batholith and transported that granite outcrop 325 mi north along the coast to where it currently resides as the Point Reyes Natl Seashore in Sonoma Co.

The distinction between the Central Valley, Central Coast, and LA Basin is as dramatic for the traveler on the ground as it is from space or for the observer in an airplane. At the western tip of the Santa Ynez Mtns in Santa Barbara Co the coastline of CA abruptly changes direction, altering climate, lifestyle, and grape growing conditions. The twin promontories demarcating this place are called Point Arguello and Point Conception. North of Pt Arguello the coastline runs more or less north–south. A cold ocean current running forcefully down the coast from

Alaska produces FOG and air temperatures in the 50s°F. It also makes sailing from Los Angeles to San Francisco much more difficult than a sailing trip in the opposite direction. A day at the beach north of Pt Arguello requires a sweater. Wind from the ocean creates huge sand dunes. Nobody goes in the water for more than a couple of minutes without a wetsuit. But the current does not make that hard left turn around Pt Conception. Below Pt Conception the coastline turns east–west. Most people think of Los Angeles as 100 mi south of Santa Barbara. Actually it is 100 mi almost due east. The climate becomes borderline tropical. Citrus and avocado trees, which cannot survive any frost, blanket the hillsides. A day at the beach means scanty clothing, sunscreen, and fun in the waves. The city of Santa Barbara is on the southern side of the Santa Ynez Mtns; the winegrowing districts of Santa Barbara Co are on the north side. Specialized farms south of the mountains grow orchids, exotic bananas, cherimoya, and star fruit. North of the mountains Santa Barbara Co is the world's biggest producer of strawberries, grown year round.

SANTA MARIA AVA is the approved appellation at the county's northern boundary. The one running along the northern side of the mountains, but well south of Santa Maria, is called SANTA YNEZ AVA. In the western portions of both these appellations, the areas closest to the sea, temperatures are consistently moderate and fog cover is frequent. Two things are different than in CARNEROS or RUSSIAN RIVER though: (1) it rarely rains until the end of Dec, so grapes can stay on the vine a very long time; and (2) this entire Central Coast region is on the Pacific tectonic plate. Soils in Santa Barbara Co are marine sediments on top of the ophiolitic series spreading out from a mid-ocean ridge, ie sand, shale, diatomes, and much higher pH than Russian River or Carneros.

The result is fruit weight and concentration from long hang time, but softer texture, with a more lifted fragrance in Santa Maria Pinot Noir and a more papaya-like fruit nuance in the aroma of Chardonnay. Coastal Santa Barbara grape regions are cold. Sauvignon Blanc from the Russian River has grassy hints, while Sauvignon Blanc from sites west of Hwy 101 in the Santa Ynez Valley has a militant jalapeño chiles character.

A district currently not proposed for AVA status, yet logically demanding such attention, is conventionally called **Los Alamos**. It sits between the two approved AVAs, sharing climate characteristics with Santa Maria and the western portion of Santa Ynez, but soil characteristics with the eastern portion of Santa Ynez. Los Alamos has 3,000 acres of grapes (50% more than Santa Ynez), including 1,900 which go to MERIDIAN winery near PASO ROBLES where they make an extraordinary contribution to that brand's excellent value Chardonnay. AU BON CLIMAT winery began its climb to international acclaim working with Pinot Noir and Chardonnay grapes from a large vineyard in Los Alamos which was subsequently sold to a massive Central Valley marketing company, where those grapes are currently blended into oblivion. Los Alamos is a virtually unpopulated buffer zone between the small, but toney, enclaves of Santa Ynez and the sprawling tract homes which surround the agribusiness city of Santa Maria. Los Alamos was the last telephone exchange in CA to abandon operator placement of phone calls and two-party lines.

The wineries of SAN LUIS OBISPO CO, Santa Barbara's neighbor to the north, are not really practical candidates for a day trip from Los Angeles, but those in Santa Barbara Co are. That simple fact changes the demographics of the ownership cohort. Just as Napa Valley is the playground for San Francisco society, and its owners are older, wealthier, and more likely to vote Republican than are the winery owners in Mendocino, a similar claim can be made of Santa Barbara compared to San Luis Obispo. In Santa Barbara Co, vineyards share vast vistas with exotic thoroughbred racing studs. The cost of fencing alone around these irrigated paddocks would support most craftsman-sized wineries. The biggest employer and landholder north of the mountains, however, is Vandenberg Air Force Base, where many US satellites are launched.

The Santa Ynez Valley has been threatening for a decade to explode into southern California's rendition of Napa Valley. The one-street village of Los Olivos is strangely reminiscent of ST HELENA in the 1960s with its boutique shops and museum-like air. But at present there are only a tenth as many wineries, and all of Santa Barbara Co only has half as many acres of vines as the much smaller Napa Valley has. Resort hotels, upscale restaurants, and golf courses are still clustered south of the Santa Ynez Mtns around the city of Santa Barbara; not in the wine districts where the horsey set flaunt their cowboy boots and put on rural airs. Fashion-conscious Angelenos still dote on Napa's reputation when they make wine selections in a see-and-be-seen restaurant. But proximity exerts an inexorable influence. The undeniable quality of Santa Barbara Co Pinot Noirs, Chardonnays, and Syrahs must surely wean Los Angeles consumers progressively away from the status quo and toward greater appreciation of their own backyard.

NOTABLE PROPERTIES

Santa Barbara Winery, located in the city of Santa Barbara, most critics dismiss this 30,000-case winery as little more than a tourist trap. It does sell most of its production directly to tourists in tasting rooms strategically located to accomplish that goal. Its history goes back to 1962, when all its effort was devoted to dessert wines. Since the late 1980s though, various high quality elements have emerged. Seventy-five acres were planted in 1972 in the Santa Ynez Valley well west of Buellton, almost as far toward the coast as Sanford & Benedict Vyd. The Cabernet from that vineyard is nothing to write home about, but the 500 cases of Reserve Chardonnay are good and the 500 cases of Reserve Pinot Noir are great: finely aromatic, flecked with hints of sage and heather, beautifully integrated with heavy toast French oak.   B.C.C.

Santa Clara Valley AVA, the broad savannah south of San Francisco Bay which was once home to as many CA wine industry pioneers as Napa or Sonoma. Today it is home to Silicon Valley, centerpiece of the US computer industry. The single remnant of the valley's viticultural heritage is a district called HECKER PASS, although several wonderful vinous practitioners do still operate in the contiguous SANTA CRUZ MTNS AVA to the west.

HISTORY

Mission Santa Clara was begun in 1777. That is the same year the first civil settlement was established in Alta California, El Pueblo de San Jose. There was never any question among the settlers that grapes would do as well in this region as they had in the best parts of Spain. Indigenous *Vitis californica* vines climbed trees in all the creekbeds flowing into Santa Clara Valley. Native grapes were so prolific in the Hecker Pass area the Franciscan padres named the place Uvas. Once the necessities of survival had been seen to, the planting of Old World grape cuttings became a passion, although practical expertise was sorely missing. Charles Sullivan's research of mission records indicates the first successful vineyard was planted at Santa Clara in 1798. A Russian visitor to Mission Dolores in San Francisco in 1806 wrote that the wine there, which had been imported from Baja California, was awful, but that the wine from Mission Santa Clara was sound and sweet, 'resembling a Malaga.' It is likely this product was CA's first real contribution to winemaking, a beverage called Angelica. It was made by adding grape spirit to unfermented grape juice. This process preserved the finished product and avoided the flavor problems inherent from fermenting in cowhide vats.

Vinous advancements in the Santa Clara Valley owe a great deal to a series of French expatriates. Antonio Maria Suñol was born in Spain, but served in the French Navy. He jumped ship in 1818, married into a land-owning family, and was selling wine in San Jose by 1823. Suñol's daughter married Pierre Sainsevain, who had come to CA in 1839 to help his uncle, Jean Louis Vignes, in LOS ANGELES. Sainsevain was making sparkling wine on his father-in-law's vast rancho east of San Jose by the mid-1850s. In 1851 the French consul estimated there were 25,000 of his countrymen in CA. Many came for gold. Others came to escape the political upheaval in France between 1848 and 1850. Those that did not settle in San Francisco, or remain at the diggings in the Sierra, came to San Jose. They knew what good wine tasted like, and they wanted nothing to do with the old Californio era vinestocks. Between 1853 and 1856 4 million gal of wine were imported into CA, and 3 million gal of brandy. The French community in Santa Clara Valley quickly set about acquiring cuttings of better winegrape varieties. The first of these came around the Horn from New England and included labrusca varieties such as Catawba and Concord. Nevertheless these first shipments also delivered vinifera varieties like Black Hamburg, Muscat Frontignan, Zinfandel (originally called Black St Peter's), Malvasia, and Chasselas. The master of this endeavor was Antoine Delmas who convinced British sea captains to bring him equipment and cuttings directly from Europe. His French Garden nursery in 1857 advertised Cabernet, Merlot, Meunier, Gamay, Pinot Noir, Folle Blanche, Colombard, and Tokay. By 1863, Riesling and Melon Blanc had been added via the nursery run by Louis Pellier, and newspapers were saying the viticultural collection in San Jose could 'not be exceeded on this continent.'

The patriarch of fine wine production in Santa Clara Valley was Charles Lefranc. He brought cuttings (including Malbec) which he claimed were 'from the most celebrated vineyards in France,' then grafted single buds onto V. californica vines in order to quickly propagate his New Almaden Vyd. From the 1850s until his accidental death (trying to stop a runaway horse and wagon) in 1887, Lefranc's wines dominated the com-petitive show circuit in CA. Lefranc's daughter Louise married a young Burgundian named Paul Masson. In 1892 Masson released his first sparkling wine in CA. It was made from the still wines of New Almadén, for whom he worked as a marketing manager. By the turn of the century Masson had purchased property in the hills, planted imported cuttings of Pinot Noir and Chardonnay on resistant rootstock, begun employing the MÉTHODE CHAMPENOISE, and even introduced the use of pure strain yeast cultures into the western hemisphere. Five years later the PAUL MASSON Champagne Company brought out Oeil de Perdrix made from the grapes he called 'Petite Pinot' and turned it into the single most successful CA wine produced prior to Prohibition. In fact, the most fabulous collectors' item amongst CA wine labels is probably Masson's 1929 Oeil de Perdrix which he produced during Prohibition using his thoroughly legal permit to make 'champagne for medicinal purposes.'

These strong antecedents led to a vigorous Santa Clara industry which lasted well into the 1960s, but after the Second World War high technology innovations of many sorts began spinning out of Stanford Univ. The valley floor districts from Palo Alto to San Jose and up into the Santa Cruz mountains at that time were mixed-use agricultural land just beginning the transition from stonefruit orchards to residential neighborhoods, with their associated retail centers, and to the industrial parks of the computer industry. Wine production was one of the most important local industries. In other words it was very much like Sonoma and Napa are 50 years later.

CLIMATE AND TOPOGRAPHY

There are two approved district-level appellations which lie more or less within the confines of Santa Clara Valley. **Pacheco Pass AVA** is of little use. It sits astride Hwy 152 running east to the Central Valley, with steep hillsides and topsoil so thin it barely functions for rangeland. The more interesting appellation is **San Ysidro AVA** south of Hwy 152 nestled into the eastern foothills near the southern boundary of Santa Clara Co. In general, Santa Clara Valley is moderately warm. It is common for high summer temperatures in San Jose to be 20°F above those in San Francisco. San Ysidro AVA, however, sits directly opposite the lowest spot in the coastal hills looking due west at the center of Monterey Bay. The crescent shape of the topography around Monterey Bay funnels a narrow blast of cold air through this gap to hose down the single vineyard located in San Ysidro AVA. There are no wineries there, but several very high quality wines have been made from grapes grown in Le Mistral Vyd. It is an unrecognized resource.

NOTABLE PROPERTIES

Kathryn Kennedy, winery and philosophical statement of a vineyard, located in the low foothills on the west side of the valley in Saratoga directly beneath MT EDEN, except at 300 ft of elevation instead of 1,800 ft. The place has the look of a large residential garden. Nonetheless the neighborhood's viticultural resumé sparkles clear back to the 1880s. Mrs Kennedy found herself with 10 acres of property in 1971 after a divorce. The adjacent farm had just been turned into 30 homes. Kennedy planted vines because she thought the houses were ugly. Her accountant might feel differently. Two more homes were built on property adjacent to their vineyard in the late 1980s. The land alone for each one cost $285,000 then and would cost twice as much today. They are built on quarter-acres.

The vineyard is entirely Cabernet Sauvignon planted on its OWN ROOTS from cuttings taken in one of David BRUCE's original mountain vineyards. No irrigation is used. The winery was bonded in 1979, and Kathryn's son took over as winemaker in 1982. The estate Cabernets are expensive and prone to wide vintage fluctuations. By far the best years are the coolest ones, although all the wines are medium bodied and never prone to extractive structure. The wines age very successfully, developing expansive cigar box bouquet by their eighth birthday and continuing to evolve long afterward.

Mirassou. The Evergreen district, or eastern foothills of the Santa Clara Valley immediately south of downtown San Jose, was once an integral part of the prestige enjoyed by this whole region. William Wehner planted 175 acres of vines there in 1887. At the turn of the century Wehner's Highland Vyd was producing white wine that the top winemakers in both Sonoma and Livermore pronounced 'the finest in California.' It never competed in the Paris Exposition because, like most CA wines of the time, it used a French place name as its generic label, in this case Sauterne (*sic*).

The Mirassous like to trace their CA wine heritage back six generations. Their starting point is Pierre, younger brother of the nurseryman Louis Pellier, who arrived in the 1850s from La Rochelle, France. Pierre Pellier maintained an important collection of vinestocks, and made wine, on property in the Evergreen district until his death in

1894. More interesting is the fact that when his son died in 1874, Pierre took his 14-year-old daughter Henriette into the winery and taught her the business. In 1880 she married the recently immigrated Pierre Mirassou, with whom she had five children. Mirassou died in 1889, and when Pierre Pellier died five years later, Henriette was left with a huge debt still owing on the property and a large pre-adolescent family. She remarried a man named Thomas Casalegno and the three Mirassou boys gradually grew to take over the winemaking operations.

They split up during the difficult years before the First World War and all ceased making wine during Prohibition. Peter Mirassou retained 100 acres in the Evergreen district, and in 1937 he built a 130,000 gal winery with his sons Norbert and Edmund. Perfectly suited to the role of patriarch, with his twirled mustache and resplendent wardrobe (one of the few men ever known who could wear an ascot without looking ridiculous), Edmund Mirassou successfully expanded the business as a supplier of bulk wine. But it was the fifth generation of four sons and a son-in-law who formed a corporation in 1966 and borrowed the money to expand the winery into THREE-TIER DISTRIBUTION under the Mirassou label. In 1960 the winery sold only 1,350 cases under its own label, all cellar door. In 1980 it sold 1 million cases under the Mirassou label nationwide.

That was the zenith. They presently only sell about 125,000 cases a year. Although they have kept their production facilities in Evergreen, they bought 650 acres in the Salinas Valley and moved almost all of their grape growing interests to Monterey Co. It was a long learning curve, particularly with the reds. Much of Mirassou's image problem can be traced to the phenomenon of vegetal flavors which dominated those wines for a decade, and to the dissembling the Mirassou marketing apparatus did trying to explain the problem away. The bottom line was that consumers did not care whether it was caused by previous asparagus crops in the ground, mechanical harvesters that took leaves as well as grapes, or overproduction due to irrigation. They just stopped buying. When an entanglement with a national distribution company unfortunately turned sour, the bubble burst for Mirassou and they had to retrench. Their best items today are a fruity bargain priced Riesling, a nicely mace scented Chardonnay, and clean sparkling wines which represent good value.

B.C.C.

Sullivan, C. L., *Like Modern Edens* (Cupertino, 1982).

Santa Cruz Mtns AVA, large region in the BAY AREA including the spine of the peninsula south of San Francisco almost to Monterey Bay on both sides of the coastal mountains above the 400 ft contour line. At its midpoint the appellation is 30 mi wide with mountains 2,200 to 3,400 ft high in the center. There are only about 300 acres of vineyard in the appellation, partly because the steep slopes limit suitable sites, partly because *Pierce's disease seems to be harbored in the native vegetation, but mostly because proximity to the Bay Area makes land too expensive. It was not always so.

HISTORY

At the beginning of Prohibition there were 1,600 acres and 39 wineries in production. Prior to the financial crash of the mid-1890s, when SF wine merchants Koehler and Froming tried to corner the market, there had been 4,000 acres of vines. The explanation concerns transport. In the latter half of the last century, moving bulky products like wine in anything other than a boat was a difficult proposition. This region's proximity to the Bay Area marketplace represented a considerable advantage then. At the same time, the region's biggest industry was timber. Logging companies built a web of strong, good-sized roads throughout the mountains in order to get at the virgin redwood groves. They also built railroads to haul out sections of tree trunks that might be 20 ft in diameter. Then they clearcut entire hillsides. Once the timber was removed from a show, the lumbermen's rapacious attention turned elsewhere. They were more than happy to give, or lease, these denuded parcels and use of the adjacent dirt roads to vineyardists and orchardists for very little money. Land speculators and developers swarmed into the area. Several wineries opened in partnership with lumber mills.

For nearly two decades starting in the mid-1870s California enjoyed a wine boom at the expense of French vineyards devastated by *phylloxera. North of San Francisco Bay the land was still considered frontier, with bloody Indian wars commonplace and title to property frequently in dispute. The South Bay was considered secure and civilized by comparison. Ethnic groups tended to congregate together: the French in Santa Clara, the Germans in Napa, and the Italians in northern Sonoma. Huge vinicultural ventures sprang up in the South Bay during this boom period, but sales outside the local area (mostly to New Orleans and to the East Coast) were made through San Francisco *négociants who finished the wine, blended it to their own specifications, and bottled it

under their own labels. By 1896 production far exceeded demand. Growers were completely at the mercy of the San Francisco brokers, who forced prices lower and lower. Since the rigors of living and producing a crop in the mountains were high, even without a mortgage, many of the growers in the Santa Cruz Mtns gave up.

Phylloxera had also come to CA during this period, but its spread was much slower than in Europe. It is thought dry summers hampered the development of the winged, above-ground stage in the females' life cycle. So infestations remained localized. At the same time, land promoters went to great lengths to minimize publicity about phylloxera in CA during the boom in order to better capitalize on France's misfortune. This rush-to-riches attitude in the 1880s exacerbated the bust of the late 1890s when French production began returning to historic levels and many CA growers could not command prices high enough to justify replanting on resistant rootstock. Large wineries that farmed in the more economical Santa Clara Valley and had been able to gain control of their marketing or brands survived. Most of the wineries and vineyardists of the Santa Cruz Mtns did not.

CLIMATE AND TOPOGRAPHY

A dramatic weather phenomenon common to this region is late afternoon FOG in July, Aug, and Sept flowing over the ridgeline then tumbling wave-like down the inland slope. The warmest sections of the AVA are on the inland side of the mountains at the lower elevations. In fact turn-of-the-century wine merchants in San Francisco referred to those inland, east-facing slopes from about 400 ft to about 1,200 ft of elevation as the Chaine d'Or. The coldest sections of the AVA are on the coastal side of the mountains at the lower elevations where fog cover is most frequent. Rain is most prevalent at the highest elevations on the coastal side of the ridgeline. Hence mountain weather stations above the city of Santa Cruz at the southern (highest) end of the range report 60 in of precipitation annually, while Woodside on the inland slope at 500 ft of elevation toward the northern boundary reports less than 30 in a year.

Soils in most locations above the piedmont are thin, due to the steep gradients. The San Andreas Fault runs right up the eastern side of the AVA, so the mixture of soil components is a hopeless tangle. These are young mountains, still growing. All things being equal, one would expect the Santa Cruz Mtns AVA soils to be as alkaline as those of the CENTRAL COAST, in which it is technically included. Weather patterns, however, deliver a lot more rain here. Hence leeching of carbonates occurs faster here than it does in the Central Coast. Also the duff from conifer forests is quite acidic, which helps explains why azaleas and other rhododendron species flourish in these areas.

A road called Skyline Drive runs north–south along the ridge crest of the mountains. It is a favorite weekend rendezvous for bond traders from San Francisco on expensive motorcycles with their latest gymnasium acquaintance in the passenger seat. In several spots on this road at the northern end of the AVA one can simultaneously see the ocean and the bay. Looking west, the view is decidedly rural. It is too cold and windy for grapes. In fact the wind is so strong, one of the world's top three big wave surfing beaches (Maverick) lies barely north of the AVA. It is so unpopulated that Carl Djerassi, developer of the birth control pill, put his 2,000-acre artists' retreat there. On this coastal side of the mountains, elevation is a crucial factor in viticulture. Below 1,000 ft the fog will make ripening all but the earliest varietals next to impossible. Pinot Noir can be brilliant in these lower locations, but Chardonnay must be planted higher up to ripen. The best-known vineyards are close to the summit, or at least above 2,000 ft. Being above the fog, they can even ripen grapes like Cabernet, and they derive intense flavors since their sparse topsoils result in low vigor vines. There is a potentially very useful district-level approved appellation called **Ben Lomond Mtn AVA** encompassed by this coastal portion of the regional Santa Cruz Mtns AVA but few wineries use it on their labels because there are not enough grapes grown in the district to generate name recognition by consumers. Too bad. There have been several extraordinary vineyards at various times. McHenry Vyd, planted by the former Chancellor at UC Santa Cruz, produced several of the best Pinot Noirs in CA during the late 1980s. Those wines combined clear varietal aroma with a structural firmness and a forest floor finish that no one else in CA quite duplicates. The viticultural problems are unrelenting though. Deer and bird damage is always extensive, and *Pierce's eventually spelled the end of McHenry Vyd in this location.

Looking from Skyline Drive to the east one sees a completely different story. From the foothills to the bay lies a district which has been highly prized for 150 years. Robber baron Leland Stanford could have had any property in CA, and this is the place he chose. He does not deserve credit for initiating winegrowing in the area, but he did plant 158 acres of grapes on 'the Farm' which eventually became the university. He died in 1893 and his widow promptly stamped out any association between the school and alcohol by hiring a Prohibitionist as president and banning 'spirituous beverages' from the premises in her will. Meanwhile, immediately next door in the town of Woodside, Dr Emmett Rixford was busy creating one of CA's finest artisan quality wines. He planted his vineyard to the red Bordeaux varieties in exactly the same proportion as at Ch *Margaux, a wine he greatly admired and from which he had obtained cuttings. The list of awards won on both sides of the Atlantic by Rixford's La Questa Cabernet was extensive. One acre of the original vineyard still exists (and produces wine) today, surrounded by multi-million dollar homes on land which sells for seven figures an acre.

Stylistically, wines made from the few grapes now grown in this locale demonstrate the relatively cool climate of the district and the importance of a favored site. Woodside Vyds, a hobbyist-sized winery that receives the La Questa grapes, makes a very complex wine which is too tight to be pleasurable in youth. After fifteen years in bottle, the wine develops insistent, expansive bouquet, but only in warm vintages is that enough to overcome the thinness of the flavor profile. Hard, metallic flavor elements make the wine more reminiscent of St Estèphe than of Margaux. Still, the finish is usually pronounced and the nose is always quite sophisticated. If these ancient vines were not being treated as *objets d'art*, it might be possible to coax more fullness into the wine's texture. Another example comes from grapes grown on the opposite side of the university in Los Altos Hills. Same land value situation, only this time it is a 2-acre Chardonnay vineyard planted in the early 1980s by a retired woman who likes to garden. She sells her grapes to her neighbor, Page Mill Winery. The wine always shows an extraordinary natural acidity and a fairly conspicuous lack of fresh fruit aroma. It does develop bouquet nicely over 5–6 years in bottle.

NOTABLE PROPERTIES

Ahlgren, winery in the basement of a home built in 1973 on 26 nearly vertical acres close to Boulder Creek. Val and Dexter Ahlgren still only make about 2,000 cases a year and sell most of it to a loyal mailing list. They use basket presses and rarely get more than 135 gal per ton. Their Cabernet from Besson Vyd is worth a search. Sited on a lowland bench in the HECKER PASS section of Santa Clara Valley, it is softly structured and brightly fruity, but draws as well on a layer of mild herbaceousness, and can be counted on for expansive bouquet capable of charming anyone. Ahlgren's Chardonnay from VENTANA VYDS has also been noteworthy since 1976. It is pleasant, but a little dumb, when first released. Then long after flashier competitors have gone to their grave, Ahlgren's Ventana is still coasting on great structure and a perception of cantaloupe sweetness in the finish which is unlike aged Chardonnay from any other place.

Bargetto, destination tasting room on the Soquel River in Aptos. Occasionally worthwhile Chardonnay and Gewürztraminer, but the true star is the Ollallieberry *fruit wine bottled under the Chaucers label. It is a Thanksgiving dream, absolutely the purest expression of that genetic cross between blackberries and Jung berries imaginable. Served with a piece of plain cheesecake at dinner it earns a guaranteed standing ovation.

Cinnabar, named for the blood red ore that yields mercury, and which 13th-century alchemists hoped would yield silver, this winery is 24 acres of Chardonnay and Cabernet on a 1,600 ft high ridge top above Saratoga. MT EDEN and RIDGE are, respectively, the next two ridge tops in succession to the north. Unlike his more illustrious mountain top neighbors, Tom Mudd's property did not come with a history. He had the vineyard put in from scratch during 1983. It was a very expensive undertaking. The road alone, to reach the hilltop, must have cost more than three-quarters of the wineries in CA. Since the earth-moving equipment was there anyway, they excavated the peak, built a three-story winery with tunnels, and covered it all back up.

The Chardonnay cuttings came from Mt Eden, and thus lay claim to being a clone which originated at Corton Charlemagne. Cabernet cuttings came from La Questa in Woodside, hence tracing their parentage ultimately back to Ch Margaux. Yields on the mountain top are meager, and Mudd is never shy with new oak. As a result the Chardonnays are dense and very powerful. If picked a little earlier, they could step up into a very high rank indeed. The Cabernets are not of the same style at all. Lighter in body, they can be overrun by significant oak treatments except in the most concentrated years.

Cronin, basement winery restricted by zoning ordinance to 2,000 cases a year, but very high quality nonetheless. Chardonnay is the best item, made in the big, rich, flamboyant style which gains immediate attention from both critics and consumers. Unlike less sophisticated purveyors of this style though, Cronin Chardonnays always have a nice backbone of acid, and the track record for longevity that goes with it. Beyond those similarities, the Chardonnays from different vineyard sources have distinctly different layers of flavor. The Santa Cruz Mtn exhibits the most mineral character, especially in the finish. The Alexander Valley is the most expansive, rounded, and nutty. The Ventana is the most subtle, with shimmering fruit notes throughout. Moreover the Ventana never fails to show up with bells on when a 10-year-old bottle of it is opened.

Fogarty, Thomas. Any surgical supply catalogue in America will have several pages devoted to the inventions of Dr Thomas Fogarty. He grew up in Cincinnati, where at age 13 he invented a clutch for the Cushman scooter, a vehicle used today by practically all the parking enforcement officers in the US. Fogarty came to Stanford Univ in the late 1960s to work with Norman Shumway pioneering heart transplants. He also had the foresight in 1968 to purchase 300 acres running from the ridge of the Santa Cruz Mtns down the eastern slope into Portola Valley. The view from Fogarty's entertainment deck, which is regularly rented out for weddings, commands the entire southern half of San Francisco Bay.

In 1980 14 acres of Chardonnay and half an acre of Pinot Noir were planted at the top of the property near the 1,700 ft elevation. Wines from the Fogarty Estate Vyds dramatically demonstrate the cold climate characteristics of the site along with the uncertainty that fog cover can introduce from vintage to vintage. Winemaker Michael Martella cites harvests which have been completed in Sept followed by harvests which have not begun until Nov. Fogarty always puts the estate Chardonnay through complete *MLF, but even so the acid rarely drops below 9 g/l. The Chardonnays are heavily oaked (believe me, the cost of new barrels is not a factor here), but need more fruit weight in the middle to balance heavily toasted wood.

Storrs, winery located in a small artists' enclave in downtown Santa Cruz. Enthusiastic advocates for the Santa Cruz Mtns appellation, they make Chardonnay from at least three single vineyards in the AVA every year, and their results argue persuasively for the value of cold climate grapes in the hands of talented winemakers, especially if those wineries are small enough to allow extensive hand operations. Storrs uses lots of new French oak, induced MLF, selected 'cock-

tails' of different yeast strains introduced at different points in the fermentation, and long periods of lees contact. Their Chardonnays are cleanly balanced on the palate, faintly green apple in the finish, but rich with toasty, nutty smells throughout.

Sunrise, living museum in a restored 1880s historic winery. Soon after he arrived in CA in the 1870s, the Church helped Vincenzo Picchetti obtain some property halfway up the slope of the Chaine d'Or. By the time the 1880s Wine Boom started, the Picchetti brothers had dug a road several miles into the hills and established the first winery on Montebello Ridge. Soon others joined them. Jimsomare Vyd was established by one of the most celebrated winemakers of the period, Pierre Klein, and Pirrone Winery was built at the top of the hill on property now owned by Ridge Vyds. The Picchettis were virtually self-sufficient, with 500 acres of vines, pears, and apricots along with pigs, chickens, and cattle. San Francisco wine merchants would drive wagons fitted with redwood tanks through the hills to the winery to purchase wine in bulk for their blends. The Picchettis lived on the ranch, making wine and grappa until 1975, when the property was sold to the Mid-Peninsula Open Space District, part of a 400 mi continuous hiking trail proposed to circle the Bay on publicly owned lands.

In 1984 Ron and Rolayne Stortz negotiated a 25-year lease with the Open Space District on the 6 acres of Picchetti buildings and 3 acres of 80-year-old Zinfandel vines. The property is part of the US Natl Registry of Historical Sites, and the Stortzs were charged with renovating it. One interesting wrinkle of the restoration process is temperature control. Modern standards for fine wine production require it, but air conditioning is not historically accurate for the Picchetti era. So they use various passive solar techniques. The Zinfandel from the shy-bearing, old Picchetti Vyd is as focused as one might expect, but often cranky and brooding. It is not made in an overtly extractive manner, despite the historical technique of using wooden screens to hold the skins submerged in the fermentation tank, yet the flavors are hard and more in line with mineral descriptors than with any sort of ebullient fruit.   B.C.C.

Adams, L. D., *The Wines of America* (Boston, 1973).

Sullivan, C. L., *Like Modern Edens* (Cupertino, 1982).

Santa Maria, largely homogeneous appellation in the northern part of SANTA BARBARA CO. Of the 5,000 acres of grapes in the Santa

Maria AVA, more than half are contained in three large vineyards: Bien Nacido, Sierra Madre, and Tepusquet (see KENDALL-JACKSON). The first grapes grown here since Prohibition were planted in 1964. The Santa Maria Plain is flat to the ocean, sandy, and quite cool; much like the northern half of the Salinas Valley. Similarly, it is a prime area for truck farming. The growing season is very long. DIURNAL TEMPERATURE FLUCTUATION is minimal. Annual rainfall averages 13 in, and overhead irrigation is standard practice. Soils have a mildly alkaline pH. Fragrant White Rieslings, fruity Chardonnays, and black cherry scented Pinot Noirs from these vineyards have developed a huge following. Both CRAFTSMAN-SIZED WINERIES and factory-sized producers throughout the state vie for these grapes, and prices per ton frequently rise higher than those for the same varieties from Napa and Sonoma. The long hang time these grapes undergo gives them concentrated flavor profiles and a slurpy perception of sweetness which neatly counterbalances their high natural acidity to produce splendid early drinkability. Although long periods of bottle age are not necessary, these wines can effortlessly endure them due to their relatively low pHs.

NOTABLE PROPERTIES

Cambria, also *Kristone* and *Camelot*, three brand names, the first two marketed as part of the ARTISANS & ESTATES stable, with Cambria getting a Santa Maria appellation and Kristone a Santa Barbara appellation; Camelot is handled by the Kendall-Jackson sales organization with a California appellation. Cambria is a winery plus 1,400 acres of vines, including 800 acres of what was previously Tepusquet Vyd, and almost all of Tepusquet's Chardonnay, now 670 acres. Katherine's Vyd is a designation applied to 82,000 cases of Cambria Chardonnay. Julia's Vyd is a designation applied to 12,000 cases of Cambria Pinot Noir. Both designations refer to plots of Tepusquet grapes renamed for daughters of Jess Jackson. Camelot used to be a vineyard designation, from a 500-acre vineyard in Santa Maria next to where the Cambria winery was built, but it has since been moved to brand status and is now made at a separate winery facility owned by Kendall-Jackson. Kristone is a sparkling wine brand, made at the Cambria facility, in volumes of a few thousand cases each year by a separate winemaker.

Camelot wines have been routinely adequate. They concentrate on Chardonnay, which does show some of Santa Maria's ripe fruit and racy acid balance, but it is a little washed out in the middle. Cambria wines are rather more impressive, with a couple of vintages of the Katherine's Vyd Reserve Chardonnay moving well up toward the top of the heap due to its smooth texture and seamless integration of modulated oak with a pineapple finish and a well-endowed flavor profile. Reds, including Pinot Noir and Syrah, have been nice enough wines in the sense of being well made, but lacking any notable varietal distinction.

Kristone is controversial. It is made across the three styles of Blanc de Blanc, Blanc de Noir, and Brut Rosé. First of all, it is priced at three times what other CA sparkling wines command, ie $45–60 a bottle. And it was priced like that right out of the box with the first vintage. Given the parent organization's clout with US distributors, they can probably maintain those prices, but the cheek of the maneuver is nonetheless extreme. Second, the wines are made in a manner that renders them completely unlike French champagnes or sparkling wines made by Frenchmen in CA. Kristone wines are barrel fermented and forced through *MLF. The grapes are from a relatively cool area, but they are picked riper than those for sparkling wines elsewhere. The result is bigger body and more complexity than their competitors in the top price brackets. That is the distinction the PR people from Artisans & Estates point to when justifying their decision to 'position' the wine as Most Expensive Sparkler from California. Many reviewers climbed on the bandwagon with gusto. Sales though, were slow. The concept of fuller body and winemaker manipulated complexity may be acceptable as a break with tradition, but the wines are extracted and phenolically cloying. Not what one usually asks of a sparkling wine.

Foxen, launched in 1987 on one of the north–south roads running through the eastern canyons of Santa Maria AVA by a cattle ranching family with a long history in the district and by the former vineyard manager for Chalone. Sourcing Merlot grapes from a particularly advantageous block on a bench high above Rancho Sisquoc, Richard Dore and Bill Walthen burst on the market with more hoopla than a 6,000-case winery can usually muster. They have followed up with a string of red winners and gathered a following based on an ability with Cabernet Sauvignon which seems to bedevil all their neighbors. They do get some of the Sanford & Benedict Pinot Noir each year, but their extractive winemaking style does not suit the variety nearly as much as the Bordeaux reds. In Cabernet Sauvignon their Santa Barbara Co appellation is superior to their Santa Maria one. Both the Cabernet and the

Merlot have a firm but smooth texture and a clever cedar-like polish that seems quite elegant. The Cab is more leafy and tobacco-like; the Merlot is rounder and more like blackcurrants.

See AU BON CLIMAT, QUPÉ.   B.C.C.

Santa Ynez AVA, approved apellation in CA's SANTA BARBARA CO defined by the watershed as the Santa Ynez River runs west from its impoundment in Lake Cachuma to the ocean at Lompoc. In doing so it drops some 800 ft over a distance of 25 mi, draining both the line of the Santa Ynez Mtns on its southside and a series of canyons on its northside. It should be considered a regional designation because there is considerable temperature change and soil variation from the low lying western end of the appellation to the protected canyons and higher elevations at the eastern end. A rule of thumb, useful in many of CA's coastal valleys, applies with precision here: for each mile from the ocean add 1°F to the expected midday high temperature. Once again Hwy 101, through the town of Buellton (famous for its split pea soup restaurant), is a convenient indicator for dividing the Santa Ynez AVA into two more meaningful portions. Romanticists might prefer to use the little village of Solvang, which is 3 mi east of Buellton, since that Danish-theme curio and crème-filled pastry center is so well known to visitors. West of Hwy 101 the Santa Ynez AVA is very similar to the Santa Maria AVA, although mildly more extreme in terms of cold temperatures. Soils are straight seabed composition with visible shells and many diatomaceous deposits. Humidity is somewhat higher than Santa Maria, leading to some beautifully *botrytis concentrated Rieslings and Gewürztraminers. Sauvignon Blanc produced here is intensely packed with *methoxypyrazines and sharply acidic. The first vineyard planted in this district, SANFORD & Benedict, is today one of America's most renowned for the Pinot Noir grapes it grows. That property is halfway from Hwy 101 to the coast, but tucked into a sheltered nook on the slope of the southside mountains.

East of Hwy 101 the Santa Ynez AVA offers a great many sites on well-drained, benchland soils which enjoy warmer temperatures and more sustained sunlight. These sites are 15 mi further from the coast and 600–800 ft higher in elevation than sites west of Hwy 101. Frequently the eastern sites are in water-eroded canyons whose north–south orientation effectively blocks wind and marine weather intrusion. Cabernet Sauvignon and Sauvignon Blanc have

made good quality wines here, albeit in a lean, almost South African style. That is to say the Cabs have some haricot vert aroma and medium to light body. The Sauvignon Blancs are more earthy than grassy, but also medium bodied and certainly not melon-like. Vintages do make a difference, with warmer years being the most noteworthy. Merlot shows fine promise. Unfortunately some of the bigger producers habitually overcrop, and their Merlots routinely end up with nuances that are more vegetative than mulberry-like. These same large producers have had popular success with Riesling, in an opulent, ripe peach, semi-sweet but acid-balanced style. The biggest artistic winner, however, clearly seems to be Syrah. Only planted since the late 1980s to more than experimental acreage, fabulous quality has been achieved overnight. Syrahs grown on the canyon benches have shown monumental depth of flavor, velvety texture, and playful pepper highlights in almost every vintage since their inauguration.

NOTABLE PROPERTIES

Brander, long-time craftsman-sized winery begun in 1975. Fred Brander now makes 8,500 cases a year from his 40-acre vineyard surrounding the winery just east of Los Olivos. A devotee of Bordeaux, Brander began experimenting in the mid-1980s with closely spaced vines pruned very low to the ground, and with severe *leaf removal in his normal height, vertical shoot positioned vines. The results have been impressive. Brander's white Meritage blends of Sauvignon Blanc and Semillon are among the top echelon produced in CA and improving every year. They have a lean structure, but a floral (rather than grassy) nose. Citrous notes in the finish give these wines length. Fred's red Meritage called Bouchet has a healthy slug of Cabernet Franc in with some Merlot and a majority of Cabernet Sauvignon. Despite the large amount of Cabernet Sauvignon, the wine shows cassis *lift above a well-colored, but light-bodied structure. In cool years it can get too herbaceous, but warm years produce finely balanced wines reminiscent of the *Touraine.

Byron. The Zaca Mesa wine academy, which produced so many future stars in the years just before and after 1980, ran under the tutelage of Byron (Ken) Brown, a man who already had a successful business management career under his belt when he returned to college at Fresno State to take a degree in enology. Brown opened Zaca Mesa for Louis Ream and remained its winemaker until 1986. In 1983 though, Brown began working on his own place. It was built just south of Tepusquet Vyd at the mouth of a canyon east of Santa Maria. In 1989 Byron Winery acquired the Nielson Vyd, which had been planted in 1964 and was the oldest vineyard in Santa Barbara Co. Needing a cash infusion, Byron was sold to MONDAVI in 1990. It is run today as an autonomous operation with Ken Brown still in charge of the winemaking. Byron has played a prominent role in establishing the reputation of Santa Maria, particularly with Chardonnays which have mouthfilling texture, with forward pear and peach fruit, plus nicely integrated wood tones. The acid levels are understated, but the wines would rarely be described as broad. The Pinot Noirs are good quality wine, well respected by meat eating critics, but tending to a more extractive, woodier style than is optimal from the fragrantly scented grapes grown in this district.

Firestone, first commercial winery north of the Santa Ynez Mtns in Santa Barbara Co since Prohibition. Brooks Firestone planted 265 acres of grapes on the deep gravel benches of a canyon north of the Santa Ynez Valley in 1972, then built an 80,000-case winery in 1975. Firestone's grandfather, Harvey, was founder of the tire and rubber Company. Brooks Firestone is married to Catherine (Kate) Boulton, former ballerina with London's Royal Ballet. The strength of an extensive roster is Riesling. They sell 35,000 cases a year and are among America's premium priced leaders in the category along with CH STE MICHELLE of WA. Firestone owns 40 acres of Riesling and buys more from their nextdoor neighbor and from the cooler White Hills Vyd west of Los Alamos. Some vintages produce botrytis concentrated Rieslings which Firestone labels Ambassador's Selected Harvest (Firestone's father was US Ambassador to Belgium). Hallmarks of Firestone Rieslings are fleshy texture, ripe Persian melon and Comice pear aromas, refreshing acid balance, and a mild lime juice finish.

Gainey. Daniel Gainey's father was a founder of the Arabian Horse Registry and Gainey Fountainhead Arabians are one of the top pure-bred lines in the world. The 2,000-acre Gainey Ranch is one of the largest diversified farming operations in the Santa Ynez Valley. Grapes only account for 120 acres, but the large visitors' center furnished with 18th- and 19th-century French antiques was designed from the beginning to sell most of each year's 18,000 cases CELLAR DOOR. Gainey is well east of Solvang on a mesa (right next to the airport) which is one of the higher points in the Santa Ynez Valley. Quite hot at midday, DIURNAL TEMPERATURE FLUCTUATION is extreme. Frost

protection is essential because spring temperatures can drop as low as 12°F at night. Best item in the range is Cabernet Franc, a dark, full-bodied example with surprisingly long finish for this varietal, but not at all astringent or bitter.

Zaca Mesa, winery better known for its alumni, which include Jim Clendenen, Adam Tolmach, and Bob Lindquist, than its wines. The winery owns 250 acres of vineyard on a mesa in the canyonlands of the northeastern AVA, where it opened in 1978 with Ken Brown (now at Byron; see above) as winemaker. At its zenith, just before Brown left, Zaca Mesa was producing 100,000 cases annually from nearly 400 acres of estate grapes and a one-third ownership interest in Sierra Madre Vyd in Santa Maria. A downturn in the marketplace, and years of frankly commercial wines, were responsible for consolidation after that. The nadir was in 1994 at 25,000 cases. At that point Dan Gehrs was hired as winemaker to pursue a new direction. Gehrs had a long and enviable record in the Santa Cruz Mtns with a place called Congress Springs before it was sold to a huge British agribusiness company. Gehrs' reputation had been built on turn-of-the-century vineyards he found from library records and then resurrected for use by his winery. As of 1998 Gehrs had raised Zaca Mesa's fortunes at least to 50,000 cases a year.

See BABCOCK, FESS PARKER, SANFORD.

B.C.C.

Santo Tomás, historic bodega which was once the largest in MEXICO, and produces 300,000 cases annually from a magnificent new winery facility 20 mi south of the VALLE DE GUADALUPE in Baja California, selling much of the wine through its world-class restaurant in Ensenada called La Embotelladora Vieja (The Old Bottling Line). The original winery was established in the Santo Tomás Valley in 1888, utilizing vineyard resources begun at the Mission de St Tomás Aquinas but nationalized by the federal government of Mexico in 1857. The winery moved into Ensenada around the turn of the century, then was sold in 1920 to Don Abelardo Rodriguez, who went on to become President of Mexico. In the mid-1960s Santo Tomás was sold to Grupo Pando, a food industries consortium, who hired Dimitri Tchelistcheff, son of André *Tchelistcheff, as winemaker. He stayed nearly 20 years, gradually converting vineyards from mediocre bulk varieties to premium varieties such as Cabernet Sauvignon, Chardonnay, Sauvignon Blanc, Merlot, Sangiovese, Syrah, Barbera, and Tempranillo. He has

since moved on to become winemaker at Jarvis Vyd in Napa Valley. Santo Tomás currently owns 500 acres of vines in the Santo Tomás Valley where their winery is located, 600 acres further south in San Vicente Valley, and 120 acres in San Antonio Valley just east of Ensenada. There are regional differences between these grapes, and they are all cooler climate areas than the more easterly sections of Guadalupe Valley.

The new Santo Tomás winery facility, built under the auspices of General Manager Hugo d'Acosta and costing nearly $10 million including new vineyards, is a spectacular piece of architecture. It is Mexican, in the sense of looking more Aztec than Spanish. Two long sloping ramps for trucks lead up from opposite sides to a stone crush pad on the top, an altar open to the sun where the grapes are sacrificed and the juice runs down inside the pyramid. Outside, below the stone crown, the building is clad in the ochre color of oxidizing iron. Inside, the circular configuration of stainless steel tanks is completely modern and temperature controlled. The new winery has definitely contributed to a vast improvement in the quality of Santo Tomás wines during the 1990s. Barbera remains as a flavorful, if somewhat brooding favorite. Cabernet/Merlot blends show excellent promise. But the star of the line is a Tempranillo with charming strawberry and leather intensity, firm structure, and spotlessly clear finish. Served in their restaurant with a hot dish consisting of beets, calamari, orange slices, and ginger, the Tempranillo sings with the poignancy of a good tenor. B.C.C.

Seattle, economic hub of the PACIFIC NORTHWEST. Built on hills between PUGET SOUND and a large freshwater lake, it has a massive containerized cargo business connected directly to Asian markets. A population base of 2.5 million enjoys more than its share of excellent restaurants with a particular emphasis on seafood such as wild King salmon, Olympia oysters, and a local treat Halibut cheeks. This cuisine helped the PNW get a 20-year headstart on CA with Pinot Gris as a successful wine varietal. Seattle is home to Boeing, Microsoft, and Starbucks. R.A.I.

Sebastiani, for many years the most important name in the town of Sonoma, although now more associated with the JUG WINES procured in the CENTRAL VALLEY and bottled at their facility in LODI under the Vendange and August Sebastiani Country labels. Patriarch Samuele Sebastiani came from Tuscany in 1895 at the age of 21 and developed a thriving business shipping bulk wine to the east, having no trouble switching during Prohibition to shipping grapes. He rolled his profits into Sonoma real estate, buying everything from vineyards to the theater on the city's central plaza. His son August belied these wealthy and influential beginnings by becoming, until his death in 1980, the most frequently quoted vintner in CA—always shown in bib overalls standing in some field, usually with a straw hat on, spinning country homilies about what a lickin' his poor little winery was taking from 'da big boys.' Meanwhile he was selling 2.5 million cases a year. That man could get his picture in the San Francisco newspapers easier than Sharon Stone. Besides his natural gift for publicity, his claim to fame was the introduction of varietally labeled jugs.

When August Sebastiani died, voting control remained with his widow Sylvia, but their oldest son Sam took over management responsibility. It was a transition period for the US wine industry. Cork finished *fighting varietals were just about to start stealing market share from jugs. Consolidation of distributors was beginning nationwide, and big distillers were contemplating the acquisition of wine brands. Sam Sebastiani needed to modernize his facility, and he chose a strategy designed to downsize and move upmarket. Meanwhile, his brother Don (12 years younger) had been elected to the state legislature. Sebastiani was a prominent name, and Don Sebastiani's constituents were prepared to overlook that he was the only legislator to vote against a bill commending Sally Ride as America's first woman in space. 'Well, it's the principle of the thing, isn't it,' said Don by way of explanation to newspaper reporters after the vote. Between 1980 and 1986 Sebastiani Vyds absorbed significant losses attempting to implement Sam Sebastiani's strategy. At that point Sylvia Sebastiani fired Sam and put Don in the driver's seat. He quickly reversed directions by acquiring the facility in Lodi. Today they produce 7 million cases, primarily at the lower end of the price scale. Sam and his wife Vicki have opened their own upmarket, Tuscan-themed operation in CARNEROS called Viansa. The best quality Sebastiani wines come from their 300 owned acres and carry a SONOMA VALLEY appellation.　　　　　　　　　B.C.C.

Seneca Lake, center of NY's FINGER LAKES AVA, encircled by more than two dozen wineries and approximately 2,000 acres of vines. One of the two largest Finger Lakes, Seneca is also the deepest at 632 ft with the greatest heat storing capacity, offering surrounding hillsides the strongest mesocli-

matic benefit. This fact is reinforced by the prevailing wind pattern. Winter lows on the lake's southeastern shore, in the lee of the deepest water, are generally the warmest in the region by a few °F, and vines often ripen their crops there into late Oct and early Nov. Soils are relatively high in lime content; increasingly so toward the north end of the lake where soil pH can range up to 7.5. The lake's first winery was built in 1866, but the wave of winery openings did not happen until the 1980s when the appearance of vinifera varieties brought new impetus. GENEVA EXPERIMENT STATION is located at the north end of Seneca Lake.
　　　　　　　　　　　　　　　　R.F.

Shafer, winery in the STAGS LEAP AVA of CA's NAPA VALLEY tucked into a terraced bowl immediately adjacent to the basalt palisades which give the appellation its name. Planting began in 1972, and the first wine was made in 1978 at another winery. That 1978 Cabernet was absolutely exquisite from age 12 to about age 16. Shafer now consists of some 90 planted acres at the winery, predominantly in Merlot and Cabernet Sauvignon, and about 50 acres in Carneros, predominantly in Chardonnay. The Cabernet and Merlot on the hillside at the winery will become increasingly valuable since, being planted on St George rootstock, they will be 15–20 years older than most Cabernet and Merlot vines in Napa. The Hillside Select Cabernet is always firm and boney, needing six years to become enjoyable. As such it is not really typical of the Stags Leap appellation. The Merlot, on the other hand, is muscular without being rough or flabby. It develops early and has maintained consistently high quality throughout the frenzied years of Merlot popularity when its competitors were apparently being stepped on for extra volume. Firebreak is an interesting, if yet unproven, idea for Shafer: a *Supertuscan concept of Sangiovese with 20% Cabernet Sauvignon.　　　　　B.C.C.

shelf talker, wine trade jargon for small promotional signs hung on retail store shelves next to bottles as a means to catch the eye of customers and distinguish that wine from the herd. Sometimes bright colors are the design goal; sometimes a big Score (see Commentators and Media essay, p 14). Certain wine critics have developed a sensationalist style of commentary knowing effusively laudatory phrases will be excerpted by the wine producers and distributors for use in shelf talkers, along with the critic's name. Sometimes shelf talkers are professionally mass produced, but often distributor salesmen put up hand lettered

signs meant to look as if the store owner were providing an objective, third party opinion. Sometimes hand lettered signs actually are a store employee's opinion.　　B.C.C.

Shenandoah Valley AVA, home to AVAs in VIRGINIA and WV, the Shenandoah Valley is VA's largest approved appellation, extending from the state line in the north to the hills above Roanoke in the south, and from the western slope of the Blue Ridge Mtns to the Allegheny Highlands. The Valley continues north through WV's eastern Panhandle. Despite its size, Shenandoah Valley is the only VA appellation besides MONTICELLO with a distinctive regional character. Due to a cooler, drier mesoclimate than the Piedmont to the east, vineyards in Shenandoah Valley have delayed budbreak, which protects them against spring frost, and yield grapes with refreshing acidity. In addition, the limestone and shale soils of the valley produce high quality Riesling, Chardonnay, and Pinot Noir. Leading area wineries include ROCKBRIDGE VYDS, Shenandoah Vyds, and Landwirt Vyds.

One should not confuse the Shenandoah Valley AVA herein described with the Shenandoah Valley AVA described in AMADOR CO which appears on wine labels as Shenandoah Valley of California. The former was famous as a site of battles in the Civil War; the latter was named by homesick refugees from same.　　R.G.L.

Siegfried(rebe), hybrid with Riesling genes produced at Geilweilerhof in Germany which has produced correct, crisp white wines in the cool conditions of NIAGARA PENINSULA.

Sierra Foothills AVA, sectional appellation in CALIFORNIA running 160 mi from Yuba Co in the north through Mariposa Co in the south along the face of the Sierra Nevada at higher elevation than the CENTRAL VALLEY. The AVA is primarily bordered on the east by a national forest. Winegrowing, however, tends to be clustered in relatively concise pockets. The region is loosely known as the Gold Country, and it is traversed by the aptly named Hwy 49. Towns in the region have names such as Bootjack, Mormon Bar, Dogtown, Ophir, Chinese Camp, and Drytown. Driving times are longer than distances might imply, because 'as the crow flies' is not very meaningful there.

Today mining activity waxes and wanes as inflation manipulates the price of gold. Cattle ranching is more likely to set the social tone in any Sierra Foothills community. Large numbers of retirees have moved to the area to enjoy the ample recreational opportunities and take advantage of real estate prices which are low by CA standards. Hydro-electric power is generated at more than 50 major dams, which regulate flows to maintain white-water rafting on the seventeen western slope rivers until well into Oct. Among the 20 ski resorts in these mountains, Heavenly Valley on the south side of Lake Tahoe, Squaw Valley on the north side (where the 1960 Olympics were held), and Mammoth Mtn on the eastern slope are all world-class locations drawing experts with their 9,000+ ft summits and 3,000 ft of vertical drop. There are 60 small glaciers scattered about the Sierras. Sun and shadow, dancing on the glaciers and bare granite walls, caused John Muir to label these mountains 'The Range of Light.' Nature's cathedrals, such as nearby Yosemite Valley, provide inspiration that might otherwise have to be found at the ballet or opera.

HISTORY

CA's Capitol Building bears the inscription, 'Give me men to match my mountains,' and in 1849 alone the state's white population increased by a factor of ten as loose individuals from all over the world scrambled up into these foothills to seek their fortune. Bret Harte, Ambrose Bierce, and Samuel Clemens (Mark Twain) recorded and embellished their tales. It was a lively and lawless era. Future robber barons like Stanford, Huntington, and Crocker got their start in the dry goods business selling to miners. Hangtown Fry (oysters cooked with bacon, then served in sourdough bread) takes its name from the city, now called Placerville, where justice was freely dispensed without the bother of a trial.

Gold was found during the rush in CA in three ways: originally in running streams using pans; eventually by digging shafts to follow seams or veins; and in-between by using giant hoses to wash gold bearing gravels out of ancient riverbeds that had dried up millions of years ago. These ancient rivers were formed in the Eocene Age long before the Sierra Nevada was uplifted. The rivers flowed from the middle of the North American continent westward across low lying tropical plains while the landmass of CA was still under ocean. When the Sierras rose, these riverbeds were lifted with them.

Grape growing in the Sierra Foothills has yet to reclaim the status it enjoyed during the *gold rush, when more than a hundred wineries vied for miners' attention. All but one of those wineries was out of business by the end of Prohibition. Zinfandel vineyards dating from the late 1800s still exist, but

until 1973 those grapes were sold to bulk producers in the Central Valley. Resuscitation began in 1973 when Greg Boeger purchased a ghost winery built of river rock by Lombardi Fossati in 1872 (with a distillery building erected in 1857) near Placerville in EL DORADO Co. Monteviña Winery was launched by Cary Gott that same year in AMADOR CO and Barden Stevenot established his vineyard in CALAVERAS CO the next year. Today, plantings are increasing steadily throughout the region, and several new wineries open every year. There are some really wonderful wines, and they all tend to be undiscovered bargains because most writers never travel that far.

NOTABLE PROPERTIES

Indian Springs, winery with a tasting room in Nevada City and a 400-acre vineyard north of town making very good Syrah, Sangiovese, and Cabernet Franc. Jed STEELE is their CONSULTANT.

Renaissance, remote, physically spectacular, slightly bizarre vineyard and winery responsible for the North Yuba AVA. Getting there requires a map, and an invitation. Owned and run by the Fellowship of Friends, a group founded in San Francisco during the 1960s to pursue philosophical tenets expostulated by G. I. Gurdjieff, a Russian mystic from the last decades of the Czarist regime. The Fellowship bought 1,400 acres outside the hamlet of Oregon House, on the first ridge rising out of the Sacramento Valley, in 1971. They now have 365 acres planted to vines. 2,000 members donate 10 per cent of their annual income to the Fellowship and are expected to spend at least one month per year working on Fellowship projects. A large percentage of the membership come from outside the US. Basic to the organization is a philosophy that art should be part of life. For fifteen years they had one of the finest Chinese art collections in CA, which they sold in the mid-1990s in order to purchase fine art works in other genres.

The membership has done an incredible amount of hard manual labor to create 100 mi of terraces out of hillsides strewn with boulders. Topsoil was so scarce. 175,000 one-foot deep holes had to be drilled into the granite and filled with compost to accommodate the vines. Deer fencing did not deter bears, who walked right through them. It is a warm location with a median elevation around 1,500 ft. Drip irrigation is necessary to achieve even 2 t/a. On occasion exemplary wines, like their 1985 and 1987 *botrytized Rieslings, have been made. Frequently, the wines have been roughly alcoholic and

under flavored. The original winemaker was Karl Werner, formerly at Schloss Vollrads. Werner died in 1988, and his wife Diana took over without much success. Gideon Beinstock, a French-Israeli painter took over in 1994. He has produced several intensely flavorful Cabernets. They make 30,000 cases a year and export 20% of it.

See FAIR PLAY, NEVADA CITY. B.C.C.

Sierra Vista, high elevation Rhône producer in CA's EL DORADO Co with a magnificent view of the snow capped Crystal Range which separates the Sierra Foothills from Lake Tahoe. John and Barbara MacCready bought 70 acres in 1972. They have planted 28 acres on their own property and lease another 13 acres nearby. Both vineyards are in a band between 2,400 and 2,800 ft. They first planted Syrah in 1979 from cuttings obtained at Estrella River Vyds using a clone reputed to come originally from the Chapoutier vineyard in *Côte Rôtie. It is the same clone Madroña (see EL DORADO) calls Espiquette. All of Sierra Vista's vines are planted on their OWN ROOTS. The estate vineyard runs along a gentle ridge with topsoil 12–15 ft deep. It is a fairly fertile soil and overcropping was a definite problem in the early years. MacCready began using canopy management techniques to control the excess vigor in 1991 and the results were immediately apparent. The 1991 Syrah was darkly colored, with a combination of leather and asphalt in the nose lying behind a flowery cassis aroma, a fairly singular characteristic among CA Syrahs. The wine's best feature was its silky texture. It had high extract, but only moderate alcohol, moderate acid, and no astringency at all.

This single wine is notable because it elevated expectations about Syrah in CA. Prior to 1990 the vast majority of Syrahs had either been overtly fruity for quaffing like dark-colored *Beaujolais, or else heavily wooded and tannic with just the barest complexity to recommend them over well-made Petite Sirahs. The 1991 Sierra Vista Syrah stood out as perhaps the best example of a higher calling to which Syrahs could aspire: fragrant and fruity without becoming fatuous; distinct and recognizable as a variety; voluptuous body without bitterness or astringency. Heeling to their advantage, the MacCreadys are now vociferous that Petite Sirah should not even be mentioned in the same breath with Syrah when discussing Rhône varieties.

Grenache and Cinsault at Sierra Vista are blended into a fine proprietary label they call Fleur de Montagne. They also produce top rank Zinfandel. B.C.C.

Silver Oak, Cabernet winery located in the OAKVILLE district of CA's NAPA VALLEY, although most of their 200 acres of vines are in ALEXANDER VALLEY and those wines are vinified at the former Lyeth winery facility there. Burly co-owner Justin Meyer was an ordained member of the order while winemaker at Christian Brothers, but quit prior to starting his own winery in 1972. He and his wife Bonny own a 4-acre vineyard at their home in Napa which supplies the grapes for the winery's most limited item. The Silver Oak style is ripe, full bodied, smoothly textured, and aged in American oak for the vanilla/coconut perception of sweetness it adds to the chocolate notes of the Alexander Valley grown fruit. Production in 1999 was 50,000 cases.

Similkameen Valley VA. Located west of Okanagan Valley, BRITISH COLUMBIA in steep cattle country, the district is planted to less than 100 acres along the Similkameen River cutting through the Cascade Mtns. There are two wineries, Crowsnest Vyds and St Laszlo Estate, producing Chardonnay, Riesling, Auxerrois, Merlot, and Pinot Noir. R.A.I.

skin soak, phrase used in US for the winemaking technique known elsewhere as *skin contact whereby white grapes are crushed and then allowed to macerate with their skins for some period of time before pressing and the onset of fermentation. The implication is that aromatic constituents will be leached from the mucilaginous layer between skin and pulp, as well as protein constituents which will provide improved body and greater potential for bouquet development. The downside risk is picking up off-smells if there is rot or free sulphur on the grapes, also the potential for protein haze in the finished wine.

Snake River Valley, important watercourse flowing out of the northern Rocky Mtns in MT then through IDAHO, where it is the location of most of the state's vineyards, not an approved AVA though. Further along its course it becomes a tributary of the Columbia River in WA at the Tri-Cities, geographic center of that state's viticulture industry.

Society of Wine Educators, organization begun in 1976, originally with several hundred members who taught classes on college campuses around North America. Wine industry support soon diluted the academic focus while simultaneously broadening the membership and attracting international participation. An annual conference is held in early Aug each year with a week's worth of demonstrations, tours, tastings, and lectures. SWE also offers a syllabus and testing program leading to a Certified Wine Educator (CWE) credential. The distinction between promotion by industry producers, and objective education by third parties without vested interests, is not always clearly drawn, but noteworthy presentations on both sides of the line are always included in the annual conference. B.C.C.

Sonoita AVA. The only approved AVA in ARIZONA, located 50 mi southeast of Tucson. This 160 sq mi district is home to four wineries, and extends in a rough 12 mi radius from the town of Elgin. Soils tend to clay with lots of gravel and rock. They are rich in calcium, iron, and other metals (except zinc) and extremely low in nitrogen and phosphorus. Soil pH ranges from a mildly acidic 6.5 to a very alkaline 8.3. Only about 50 mi from the Mexico border, at 5,000 ft of elevation, temperatures rarely reach 100°F. The DIURNAL TEMPERATURE FLUCTUATION can be as much as 35°F. Last frost date is approximately May 15. First snowfall (but not the first hard freeze) can occur by the end of Oct, but most grapes are picked by then. Precipitation averages 25–30 in per year, with nearly all of that occurring as rain. Some growers do not need to irrigate, but those that do use drip irrigation, drawn from wells that rarely need to be more than 100 ft deep.

All grapes in AZ need plenty of irrigation if growers expect to get anything resembling a crop. Riesling does surprisingly well in this relatively warm, 3,800-*degree-day climate. Most vines are on their OWN ROOTS, but some drought resistant rootstocks, like 5C, are being tried. R.T.S.

Sonoma Co, geopolitical jurisdiction on the CALIFORNIA coast north of Marin Co, south of Mendocino Co, and west of Napa Valley. Speakers on American wine routinely employ the phrase 'Sonoma' without defining whether they mean Sonoma (the town), SONOMA VALLEY, or Sonoma Co. There is a big difference. Sonoma (the town) is a small, historically significant tourist destination in the southern reaches of Sonoma Valley, which opens onto San Francisco Bay. Both the town and the valley have more in common with nearby Napa Valley than they have with other parts of Sonoma Co. Both Sonoma town and Sonoma Valley are important from an image standpoint to Sonoma Co's reputation, but they are small potatoes in the matter of overall wine volume or vine acreage. Sonoma Co covers some 2,600 sq mi, three and a half times as big as Napa Co and ten times as big as the Napa River watershed (which is all wine consumers think of when they visualize NAPA VALLEY, although the approved AVA is much bigger). For viticultural or travel purposes it makes sense to think of Sonoma Co in three different sections: Sonoma Valley has a quarter of the vine acreage; the Santa Rosa Plain, which means most of the lowland districts from Petaluma to Healdsburg and west to the ocean such as the RUSSIAN RIVER AVA, has a third of the vines; the remaining 42% of the vineyards are in the northern and inland districts of the county such as DRY CREEK AVA, ALEXANDER VALLEY AVA, and KNIGHTS VALLEY.

The convenience of the one and a quarter hour drive from San Francisco to either Sonoma town or to Healdsburg in northern Sonoma Co speaks volumes about why so many wineries are clustered in those places. Nevertheless at the end of the millennium Sonoma Co had retained much of its rural flavor. SANTA CLARA Co had a very similar agricultural heritage, but is today the headquarters for more than 200 companies with sales in excess of $100 million per year. None of them is an agricultural company. Sonoma and Napa counties combined have fewer than ten companies that big. But urbanization is a pressing issue. 'Those who cannot remember history,' said the General Antonio López de Santa Anna, President of Mexico as civil war threatened to break out in 1834, 'are condemned to relive it.' Land prices in Sonoma Co, whether for vineyards or houses, are directly correlated with travel time from San Francisco.

Sonoma Co is often viewed as a 'second string' version of Napa. Accuracy aside, that perception is partially due to Sonoma Co's size, which reduces the feeling of specialness, and partially due to the fact Sonoma wineries were later than Napa getting their own name onto labels. In the 1960s great wine was being made in Sonoma Co, but it was not going to market with a Sonoma Co appellation or under a brand name associated with Sonoma Co, it was merely called North Coast. Since Prohibition there has been a boom-bust cycle to CA wine industry fortunes. The cycle has a 10–12 year phase. Napa's turn in the spotlight occurred in the early 1970s. Sonoma was not *discovered* by broad popular acclaim until the next cycle came around in the mid-1980s.

HISTORY
The difference between districts in southern and northern Sonoma Co can be neatly illustrated by tracing their émigré development. Likewise, the overall historic signifi-

cance of Sonoma Co lies in its frontier function. It is the precise place where several cultural vectors drew borderlines, choosing *not* to overlap.

At the end of the 1700s Spanish missionaries were pressing north from Mexico, establishing cattle and farming empires to better utilize the labor of the Indian souls they were so busy saving. Simultaneously, Russian fur trappers were sailing south from Alaska along the coast. The Russians' main quarry were sea otters, whose fur is more dense (hairs per sq in) than any other animal, allowing these playful creatures to spend their entire life in 50°F water harvesting abalone and sea urchins from the kelp forest surge zone along the rocky north Pacific shore. Russian entrepreneurs impressed Aleut Indians to do the actual hunting. They built Ft Ross on the Sonoma coast in 1812. That was the terminus of Russian incursion on the American continent. The terminus of Spanish expansion in CA was Mission San Francisco de Solano in the town of Sonoma, built in 1823. The Russians looked northwest to the Pacific Ocean and pursued a cold climate economy. The hispanic missionaries looked south across San Pablo Bay. They planted olive trees and vineyards. These two frontier settlements were barely 40 mi apart, but they did not mingle.

The wildcards in this hand were hardy, self-sufficient, somewhat rapacious individuals who for one reason or another had minimal ties to polite society, and who came west following the Louisiana Purchase in 1803. The mountain men of the first half of the 19th century were a much different lot than the families of farmers who dominated western migration in the second half of that century. Biographers like to portray these men as giants among their contemporaries and to speak of their activities in Sonoma in the late 1840s as the 'liberation' of CA from Mexico. That sort of romantic misperception is deeply ingrained in the American psyche; the righteousness of the 'can do' spirit. The American mountain men's favorite activities, when they convened for a month each summer to sell their furs and to resupply themselves, were eye-gouging brawls, mortal combat with hatchets and knives, incredible bouts of drunkenness featuring the basest forms of cheap distillates, and the rape of Native American women. By a large margin the most civilized, accomplished person on the scene in Sonoma during this period was Mariano Vallejo. As the military Governor of Alta California he had overseen the secularization of the missions in 1830. General Vallejo and his wife Benecia planted vines at Lachryma Montis, their home in Sonoma, in 1834. They encouraged others to join them in this pastoral life. They even planted cork oak trees.

Vallejo was not particularly distressed when a rabble of mountain men from the Sacramento Valley, and Lake Co, and the northeast section of Sonoma Co staged the Bear Flag Revolt on the plaza at Pueblo de Sonoma in 1846. Proclamations were read, guns were fired in the air, nobody got hurt. Vallejo was no longer Mexico's military comandante, that responsibility had passed to General Castro stationed at MONTEREY. Mexico City itself was about to be invaded by US troops, which would result in a treaty ceding most of the southwest to the US anyway. Then, two years after the Bear Flag brouhaha on the plaza, gold was discovered at Sutter's Mill in the Sacramento Valley, and the face of CA changed forever.

The direct effect growing out of (overland immigration) was to develop traits of character, not in single individuals, but in the entire community. A man coming to California could no more expect to retain his old nature unchanged than he could retain in his lungs the air he had inhaled on the Atlantic shore. The most striking change was an increase in activity with a reckless and daring spirit. Ordinary forms of courtesy were flung aside with a bluntness of good-fellowship. I was constantly reminded of the stout Vikings and Jarls who exulted in their very passions and made heroes of those who were most jovial at the feast and most easily kindled with the rage of battle. Indeed, it required little effort of imagination when rugged gold-diggers, with their long hair and unshorn beards, would revel in the ruddy light of a mountain campfire giving full play to a mirth so powerful and profound that it would not have shamed the Berserkers. I have dwelt with earnestness on these features because I found so much in Nature (here) to admire I am compelled to view Man as he appeared under these new and wonderful influences. (Bayard Taylor, *Eldorado* (1850))

Most of the Bear Flag mountain men rode off to seek their fortune at the 'diggings,' but Vallejo maintained and expanded his position as the most important figure in the southern part of Sonoma Co by inducing talented émigrés to help him create a wine industry. His earliest recruits were Emil Dresel and Jacob Gundlach, experienced German winemakers. When the Hungarian promotional genius Agoston *Haraszthy arrived in 1856, two of Vallejo's daughters married Haraszthy's sons Arpad and Attila. This familial relationship did not stop Vallejo from also employing a French winemaker, Dr Faure, to aid him in his vigorous (and usually successful) rivalry with Haraszthy for honors at the CA State Fair wine competition. Agoston Haraszthy created tremendous attention, but few profits for the San Francisco investors in his Buena Vista Vinicultural Society. In 1869 he withdrew and moved to Nicaragua to establish a sugar cane plantation for production of rum. Legend says he died when he fell from a tree limb while trying to cross an alligator infested stream.

Jack London had grown up penniless on the docks of Oakland. Although popularly known for his Alaskan adventure stories (*White Fang, Call of the Wild*), which he unabashedly wrote 'for money,' he was also one of America's most prominent socialists (*The Iron Heel* published in 1907; *War of the Classes* published in 1904). After achieving commercial success in the literary world, London moved to Glen Ellen in the Sonoma Valley where he spent three years building a magnificent house. The same week it was completed, it burned to the ground. The fire was rumored to be arson perpetrated by disgruntled revolutionaries who felt London had betrayed them by joining the landed gentry. Six months later, in 1916, London died of uremic poisoning, basically having drunk himself to death. London's move to the Sonoma Valley was not some creative sojourn amongst bohemian neighbors. At the time there were nearly 100 wineries in Sonoma Valley, including nearby Madrone Vyd which had been planted to the finest Bordeaux varieties in 1885 by US Senator George Hearst, the multi-millionaire mine owner and father of publishing magnate William Randolph Hearst. US Senator James G. Fair (for whom the Fairmont Hotel in San Francisco is named) had a large vineyard, winery, and brandy distillery in Petaluma. The vineyard adjacent to London's (and now part of Jack London State Park) had originally been established in the 1870s by Charles Kohler and John Frohling, musicians from Germany whose network of wineries throughout CA, along with sales depots in New York City, San Francisco, and the basement of the Los Angeles City Hall, made them the grandest of the early American international wine merchants.

The Italian-Swiss colony began with much more humble ambitions. It was founded a few miles from the northern Sonoma border as a philanthropic venture in 1880 by San Francisco grocer Andrea Sbarbaro. His idea was to place poor immigrant farm families on land where they could support themselves growing grapes. They named their town Asti because it reminded them of the Piedmont region in northern Italy. Under the leadership of Pietro Rossi, a graduate in pharmacy from the Univ of

Turin, the colony eventually prospered. In fact it was deposits from this community, and from the Genoan fishing community at North Beach (now Fishermans Wharf) in San Francisco, which founded the Bank of Italy, today known as Bank of America. This contrast between the social milieus in northern and southern Sonoma Co is offered as an aid to understanding how far apart they were, both topographically and culturally.

Fountain Grove was midway between the two. Fountain Grove Vyd was planted on a west-facing hillside 4 mi north of Santa Rosa in 1875 by acolytes of a mystical prophet named Thomas Lake Harris. He had moved his Brotherhood of the New Life to CA from NY. Within seven years he was shipping wines, 'potentialized with the electro-vinous spirit of joy,' all over the US and on to his original London headquarters. Harris decamped stealthily one night in 1892, awash in scandal concerning free love practices at his utopian community. One of his followers was a Japanese prince. Baron Kanaye Nagasawa maintained the Fountain Grove property and developed a superb quality reputation, especially for Pinot Noir, in the years just prior to Prohibition, foreshadowing the prestige heaped upon Russian River AVA Pinots today. Recognized as a superior wine judge in his own right, Nagasawa enjoyed the inestimable benefit of a close friendship with Luther Burbank who lived nearby in Santa Rosa.

Burbank (1849–1926) was a botanical genius, lionized in his day. Henry Ford, responsible for the concept of the assembly line, and Thomas Edison, credited with thousands of important inventions including the light bulb, both made arduous cross country journeys to Santa Rosa just to meet Luther Burbank. Burbank's work revolutionized thinking about biological classifications by proving separate plant genera could be hybridized. His results ran the gamut from simply whimsical to amazingly utilitarian genetic feats: spineless cactus, thornless raspberries, white blackberries, soft-shelled walnuts, an azalea-flowered nectarine, plumcots, elephant garlic, seedless watermelon, the Burbank potato, the Santa Rosa prune, the Shasta daisy (a new species). All told, Burbank created nearly 1,000 new varieties of plants. He first came to national attention in 1890 when he developed a propagation technique which allowed him to deliver 20,000 plum trees for planting exactly one year from the date he received the order. Mar 7, Burbank's birthday, is celebrated as Arbor Day in CA. It is no small benediction for Sonoma Co agriculture that

a man of his stature would say of the intersecting weather and soil features at Santa Rosa, 'I firmly believe, from what I've seen, that this is the chosen spot of all this earth as far as Nature is concerned.'

CLIMATE AND TOPOGRAPHY
Modern social history does not demarcate the districts of northern, southern, and western Sonoma Co as clearly from each other as do the historical vignettes above. Climatological differences do, and of course those contribute to different wine styles.

There are two approved regional appellations: **Sonoma Coast AVA** and **Northern Sonoma AVA**. Both are pieces of bureaucratic obfuscation pumped through BATF by single wineries whose marketing departments have truly run amok. Northern Sonoma is Gallo's self-serving creation to encompass all their Sonoma Co vineyards. As such, it encircles (with one, slight exception) six other AVAs: Green Valley, Russian River, Chalk Hill, Knights Valley, Alexander Valley, and Dry Creek. Why the appellation Sonoma County is inadequate for Gallo's purposes, one can only guess. Northern Sonoma allows GALLO to blend grapes from the cool Santa Rosa Plain with grapes from the hot northern end of Alexander Valley, so it hardly suggests any *typicity, but it does imply at least a subliminal awareness of the historic distinction between northern and southern Sonoma Co. Sonoma Coast is SONOMA-CUTRER Winery's singular creation, allowing them to blend Chardonnay grapes from the southern end of Sonoma Valley with Chardonnay from the Santa Rosa Plain. Running up and down the entire Sonoma Co coastline and then along the entire southern county border with Marin all the way to San Pablo Bay, Sonoma Coast completely obliterates all the historic precedents, but it does have the virtue of generally outlining the cooler, maritime influenced half of the county's total area. It also performs a service by covering vast amounts of land which are not included in other AVAs at present. If Northern Sonoma AVA were reduced in scope, so it no longer overlapped Sonoma Coast AVA in the cool Russian River district, then these two mega-region appellations would make descriptive sense, at least in terms of climate.   B.C.C.

Sonoma-Cutrer, Chardonnay winery and vineyards just north of River Rd in the RUSSIAN RIVER district of CA's SONOMA CO. Begun in 1973 by Brice Jones, an Air Force pilot with an MBA from Harvard whose maternal grandfather (Cutrer) was once Mayor of Houston, the original investment group

included such luminaries as Robert Noyce, founder of Intel. From the start Sonoma-Cutrer was high end. They brought grapes in and immediately put the trays into a cooling tunnel which brought their temperature under 50°F within minutes. Crushing at lower temperatures resulted in lower natural pH in the wine. One of their three wines comes from the Cutrer Vyd at the winery; a second from the Les Pierres Vyd in southern SONOMA VALLEY on the westside a few hundred yards from the northern edge of the Carneros AVA. Of the two the Les Pierres is the more recognizable with its namesake stony flavors, tight acid structure, and bony hips, it always looks best dressed in fresh oysters. The Cutrer is equally taut, but broader abeam, with more of the pear-like fruit that can give pleasure by itself. The winery owns 650 acres and makes over 100,000 cases. In 1999 it was purchased by Brown-Forman. The signature marketing gambit at Sonoma-Cutrer is a pair of world-class croquet courts at the winery and a croquet professional on the staff.   B.C.C.

Sonoma Valley AVA, called Valley of the Moon by local Indians, is a subsection of CA's SONOMA CO in its southeastern corner, opening on San Pablo Bay and running parallel to Napa Valley, its neighbor on the eastern side of the Mayacamas Mtns. Most of the population in southern Sonoma Co is not in the Sonoma Valley, but rather to the west in the Hwy 101 corridor which runs north through towns such as Petaluma, Cotati, Rohnert Park, Santa Rosa, and Windsor, which have large bedroom communities and relatively little industry. Sonoma Valley is separated from the Hwy 101 corridor both by a ridge of mountains and (today) by a considerable disparity in sensibilities.

Sonoma Valley is far enough east of Hwy 101 that it is actually faster to drive there from downtown San Francisco by going over the Bay Bridge and up the East Bay through Napa than it is to cross the Golden Gate Bridge and drive north on 101 through Marin before exiting east on Hwy 37. In 1850 the tidal zone traversed by Hwy 37 would all have been wetlands, immensely productive of sealife and extremely hospitable to water fowl migrating along the Pacific Flyway. In the 1880s government grants became available to build dikes for the purpose of converting these wetlands into pasture. Historically, this whole region immediately adjacent to the bay was considered too cold for grapes. As attitudes changed in the 1980s away from alcoholic, ponderous wines toward more precision-tooled styles, the advantages of certain upland pockets close to the bay became obvious. CARNEROS AVA is the appellation closest to the Bay in the southern end of both Napa Valley and Sonoma Valley.

Sonoma Valley AVA completely encompasses the Sonoma Co portion of Carneros AVA. The windy stretches of Sonoma Valley lie south of the town of Sonoma. Surrounding the town itself is a moderately cool, but less windblown, district which it is helpful to separate from the more northerly two-thirds of the Sonoma Valley AVA based on temperature. The boundary of the Sonoma Coast AVA (see SONOMA CO) makes a similar, but rather more bureaucratic, straight-line distinction. The topographical feature creating this distinction is 2,500 ft Sonoma Mtn, the main peak in a ridgeline which defines the western side of the valley. Sonoma Mtn is about 8 mi northwest of Sonoma town. Vineyards in the center of Sonoma Valley, around the towns of Glen Ellen and Kenwood, get hotter than those further south because Glen Ellen is in the lee of Sonoma Mtn relative to prevailing weather patterns which arrive from the west (ie Pacific Ocean) after sweeping across the Santa Rosa Plain.

Sonoma is a charming town. It is contiguous with historic vacation hamlets whose names clearly indicate their recreational function: Agua Caliente, Fetters Hot Springs, Boyes Hot Springs. Within a radius of a few blocks from the town plaza, Sonoma retains a village-like atmosphere. No conventional wine district name is attached to the area immediately surrounding the town of Sonoma which lies just north of the Carneros AVA boundary. There are, however, many vineyards in that spot and very clear taste differences between those wines and those of neighboring districts. John Batto is a grower in the flatland just east of town. Cabernet Sauvignon made from Batto Ranch grapes is less herbaceous than Cab grown in Carneros by Buena Vista, fuller bodied and less fragrantly lifted in the middle than Cab grown on (east-facing) Sonoma Mtn, and less muscularly tannic than Cab grown at Monte Rosso Vyd (west-facing in the Mayacamas Mtns which form the eastern edge of Sonoma Valley). Even more distinct for having stepped over a line of climatic demarcation would be the Pinot Noirs from HANZELL Estate grown on a low hillside just north of town. Chewy with flavors which often border on overripe, Hanzell Pinot Noirs are the polar opposites of their Carneros counterparts. And no Pinot Noirs of any particular note are grown further north in Sonoma Valley. Finally, one might consider the Chardonnays produced by

SONOMA-CUTRER Winery from Les Pierres Vyd in the flatland just west of town. Those wines have a structural tautness reminiscent of Carneros, and are obviously less fleshy than Chardonnay from further north in Sonoma Valley, but they also have a mineral aftertaste, not found in Carneros, which harks back to the gravel strewn alluvial soils of this specific site between two creeks draining out of the western foothills.

Only a couple miles further north taste profiles change once again. This time, however, the topography lends itself more readily to visual documentation that differences may be likely. The valley narrows from about 3.5 mi across to less than 1 mi in width. The mountains on either side become higher and steeper. That their eroded upper elevations are included with the dense, deep, fertile soils of the valley floor in a Sonoma Valley AVA points up the weakness of the US appellation system.

On the left as one drives northwest up Hwy 12, **Sonoma Mtn AVA** drapes like an apron around the eastern and northern slopes of that peak's midsection. The lower elevation boundary pretty much follows the 400 ft contour line. The upper elevation boundary moves between the 1,400 ft and 1,600 ft contour lines. The concept of the appellation has something to do with identifying an area above the fog line which will catch early morning candlepower as the sun rises over the Mayacamas Mtns across the valley, but not too high to be out of the reach of accumulated heat from the valley floor once the shade of evening descends. In support of this theory, vineyards in the Sonoma Mtn AVA do have significantly smaller DIURNAL TEMPERATURE FLUCTUATION than those on the valley floor. Vineyards in the Sonoma Mtn AVA, such as LAUREL GLEN, are recognized for Cabernet Sauvignon with high-toned, almost floral notes in the aroma which is quite beguiling and lends itself well to wine styles with finesse. Ham-fisted winemakers lose all the advantages that come with this fruit. It is interesting to compare Cabs from the Sonoma Mtn AVA to those from STAGS LEAP AVA in Napa since they both share a tenuous, fleeting coloration in the nose which separates them from most other CA Cabs. Between the two, Sonoma Mtn is more perfumed; Stags Leap juicier.

Soil may help explain the high note found in Sonoma Mtn AVA Cabs. In most places soils are thin, well drained, and somewhat rocky. Patrick Campbell at Laurel Glen says he tried Merlot on his site. 'It was junk,' is his evaluation. Meanwhile one of the best, and most consistent, Merlots in CA is grown

at St Francis Vyd (outside the Sonoma Mtn AVA) on the valley floor near Kenwood, virtually within eyesight of Laurel Glen, but 800 ft below in deep, denser soils. Pickberry would be an example of a vineyard in the Sonoma Mtn AVA which demonstrates the appellation's signature even when subjected to RAVENSWOOD Winery's take-no-prisoners style of winemaking. Nelson Vyd would be an example of a property there which has done quite well with a varietal Cabernet Franc, even though the owner lives in Seattle and the wine is made for him at a custom crush facility. An exception to the homogeneity of Sonoma Mtn AVA would be Steiner Vyd. It is located on the northern slope of the mountain as the apron of the AVA wraps around so far it becomes directly exposed to cold air blowing across the Santa Rosa Plain. Precipitation there is much higher than in the RAIN SHADOW on the eastern slope. Soils are also deeper and composed of higher clay content, thus retaining more water. In fact Steiner is at the headwaters of Matanzas Creek, which flows northwest to the ocean rather than southwest to the Bay via the Sonoma Valley watershed. Cabernet Sauvignon grapes grown in Steiner Vyd bud at the same time as those on the eastern slope, but ripen three weeks later. Wines made from Steiner's Cabernet Sauvignon are more intense than those BATF calls their siblings in the Sonoma Mtn AVA, more acidic, and much grassier in the nose.

Sonoma Valley AVA completely encapsulates Sonoma Mountain AVA by drawing its boundary in a straight line from the peak of Sonoma Mtn to the peak of Taylor Mtn just south of Santa Rosa. That situation leads to a semantic absurdity, ie should a vineyard be planted at 1,800 ft on the eastern or northern slope of Sonoma Mtn it would not lie within the Sonoma Mtn AVA, but would lie within the Sonoma Valley AVA.

Across the valley from Sonoma Mtn AVA, the Sonoma Creek watershed is defined by the 2,400–2,700 ft ridgeline of the Mayacamas Mtns which separate Napa from Sonoma. The ridgeline, the eastern boundary of the Sonoma Valley AVA, the western boundary of Napa's MT VEEDER AVA, and the county line are (for all intents and purposes) identical. No district level AVA, however, distinguishes west-facing vineyards in these mountains from those on the Sonoma Valley floor as far as US wine labels are concerned. That is a mistake, as anyone who has driven one of the nosebleed paths over these mountains can attest. A challenge to man and machine, Cavedale Rd ascends abruptly. Between 1,000 and 1,200 ft one can see portions of Louis MARTINI's Monte

Rosso Vyd. As the name implies, soils there have a heavy iron content. Vines receive direct rays of the summer sun late in the afternoon while ambient air temperatures are elevated and grape skin turgidity is low. Traditionally these hills have hosted Zinfandels, and made a style of wine Italian men kept for after dinner with pistachios, chocolate, and pinochle. Cabernet grapes grown at Monte Rosso would never be confused with the more delicate, feminine ones grown across the valley at Laurel Glen. Monte Rosso Cabs are tough as woodpecker lips, both in flavor and in structure. They are not necessarily big bodied, but until they are 10 years old the tannins are cinched down tight and a brackish nuance in the finish fairly screams *terroir.

North of the tiny burg of Kenwood, the Sonoma Valley broadens again perceptibly. It also cools a bit as ocean air from the Santa Rosa Plain spills in through mountain gaps. At this point it is easy to cross a few low hills going west into the Matanzas Creek watershed which is called Bennett Valley. Both Bennett Valley and the northern tip of Sonoma Valley terminate in the suburbs of Santa Rosa, Sonoma Co's largest city. But Bennett Valley is much the cooler of the two. Given the amount of fog cover and the temperature change between Glen Ellen, in the lee of Sonoma Mountain, and Bennett Valley, which is really a canyon flowing onto the Santa Rosa Plain, it is easy to understand why MATANZAS CREEK Winery does so well with Chardonnay. Both areas are technically in the Sonoma Valley AVA, but they are certainly not peas in the same pod. Very similar to Bennett Valley climatologically, and sharing a clay-like soil structure with the broad Sonoma Valley floor at Kenwood, but not technically part of the Sonoma Valley AVA (ie outside its northern boundary), is a district of expensive homes in the low hills immediately east of Santa Rosa. The district does not have a conventional designation. The most successful vineyard property there is called Golden Creek Winery, run by a Czech refugee named Ladi Danielik. In fifteen years he has never failed to earn at least one Gold Medal from the two or three county level competitions he enters each year with his Merlot, and with his Merlot stiffened by a little blend of Cabernet. The wine is always cleanly fruity and balanced around strong natural acid rather than tannin. Golden Creek is virtually unknown as a label because Danielik sells exclusively CELLAR DOOR to his friends. He does sell grapes though, and Gary FARRELL makes an award winning red meritage blend designated Ladi's Vyd each year, which sells

out in a matter of weeks at $25 a bottle, several times what Golden Creek fetches from Danielik's buddies.

NOTABLE PROPERTIES

Adler Fels, castle-like building on a hill looking down the throat of Sonoma valley from the north. David Coleman was educated at the Rhode Island School of Design. His creativity shows throughout the operation. Gewürztraminer is beautifully floral. Sauvignon Blanc is flinty and worth twice the price.

Arrowood, high-end winery owned and run by former Ch St Jean winemaker Dick Arrowood, on his own since 1986. Best offerings include a nicely harmonious Merlot, intensely spicy LATE HARVEST Riesling, and fatly luxuriant Chardonnays.

Ch St Jean, winery started in 1973 with Dick Arrowood producing attention grabbing big, rich Chardonnays from vineyards such as Belle Terre and Robert Young in Alexander Valley, and sweet botrytized Rieslings with much higher RS than anyone had thought possible. Sold to Suntory of Japan in 1984, then to Beringer Wine Estates in 1996. Owns 200 acres and produces 200,000 cases.

Kunde, begun in 1884 by German immigrant Karl Kunde who purchased the estate property called Wildwood in 1904. After Prohibition the family put their 750 acres to work raising cattle and went into the nursery business becoming one of the biggest vine suppliers in CA. The winery was reopened in a new building and caves in 1990. They currently produce 100,000 cases a year. Zinfandel from the 100-year-old vines is the most interesting offering.

Landmark, a congenial winery featuring a fly casting pond on the property for guests. It is owned by Damaris Ethridge, heiress to the John Deere tractor fortune. Chardonnay has been the focus since 1990 when super CONSULTANT Helen Turley was hired to advise on style. The result is a line of Chardonnays packed with wood, *MLF smells, and ripe peachy flavors. Seventeen acres are owned and 20,000 cases produced.

See BENZIGER, CARMENET, GUNDLACH-BUNDSCHU, HANZELL, LAUREL GLEN, MATANZAS CREEK, RAVENSWOOD, ST FRANCIS, SEBASTIANI.   B.C.C.

South, the, region comprising the southeastern US with an area of 425,270 sq mi and a population of 47,821,265. Includes NORTH CAROLINA, SOUTH CAROLINA, TENNESSEE, GEORGIA, FLORIDA, ALABAMA, MISSISSIPPI, LOUISIANA, and ARKANSAS. The South as defined here matches the states of the former Confederacy with the exception of VA and TX, and is bounded by the ATLANTIC

OCEAN to the east, the GULF OF MEXICO to the south, TX and OK to the west, and MO, KY, and VA to the north.

Magnolias, palm trees, Spanish moss, and cotton do not seem congruous with traditional grape growing. Yet viticulture is thriving and expanding across the South today. The region offers both opportunity and challenges for a native wine industry. *Pierce's disease and the grape root borer are found in the hot, humid coastal plain where vinifera and conventional hybrids cannot be cultivated. However the native Muscadines such as Scuppernong, Carlos, and Noble are immune to this threat and are grown widely in this region. In the upper PIEDMONT and mountain regions, French hybrids and vinifera have been successfully introduced. Viticultural research has produced new Muscadine hybrids suited to quality wine production in the humid South. As the region's population grows, frequently from an influx of new residents culturally familiar with wine drinking, the marketplace may well become increasingly accepting of the South's native wine industry.

There is a wide diversity of soil types in the South. The COASTAL PLAIN regions include sandstone, marine-derived soils, and alluvial deposits from further inland. The Piedmont soils are a derivative mixture of sedimentary and metamorphic rock, with clay deposits common throughout. In the Appalachian regions of TN, NC, GA, and AL, a mixture of shale, sandstone, granite, and limestone soils are dominant. While much of the South consists of the Coastal Plain, the higher elevations of the Piedmont in the Carolinas, TN, GA, and AL offer opportunities for cool climate viticulture, as do the Ozark regions in northwest AK.

HISTORY

Wine production in the South has a long history, and it is ironic that this tradition has been almost forgotten until recently. The first wine documented to have been produced in what became the US was from Scuppernong grapes, made by French Huguenots near Jacksonville, FL, between 1562 and 1564. In 1584, Sir Walter Raleigh established the Roanoke Island colony of English settlers in the Outer Banks of NC. He brought back reports of a profusion of native Scuppernong vines. Though this original colony vanished mysteriously, one legacy still remains: 'the Mother Vine' on the island of Manteo near the ill-fated settlement. That single vine covers half an acre and is estimated to be over 300 years old.

Four of the most successful American hybrids of the 19th century originated in the

Carolinas: Catawba, Isabella, Lenoir, and Herbemont. General James Oglethorpe, founder of GA, required that grapevines and mulberry trees be planted throughout the colony. In SC, the American hybrids Herbemont and Lenoir were cultivated with success in the early 19th century. In 1813, remnants of Napoleon's defeated armies established a winegrowing colony in AL, which failed because vulnerable vinifera varieties were planted. Viticulture thrived in the South in the mid to late 19th century with American hybrids. In 1880 GA was the sixth largest wine state in the nation, making over 900,000 gal. A Catawba based wine from TN won first prize in the 1875 Louisville Natl Fair. Around 1880, Swiss, German, and Italian immigrants in AK planted vineyards, and by 1925 there were 9,000 acres of vineyards under cultivation there.

The heritage of the Scuppernong grape was celebrated by Captain Paul Garrett of NC, whose proprietary blend of Scuppernong, NY, and CA grapes was named Virginia Dare after the first child born to English-speaking parents in North America. Ironically, he had to move his operations to NY's FINGER LAKES district as NC, then VA, adopted Prohibition. At Repeal, Virginia Dare was the only wine brand available nationally, and its distinctiveness was largely due to its Scuppernong based flavors. His company subsequently became the wine industry behemoth, CANANDAIGUA.

CLIMATE

The South is divided viticulturally by climate as well as by geography. The humid maritime climate of the Gulf of Mexico and the Atlantic Coast prevail in the Coastal Plain, while a continental macroclimate dominates in the Piedmont and mountain regions. *Heat summation ranges between 4,500 and 5,300 *degree days in the Coastal Plain, between 3,000 and 4,600 in the Piedmont, and between 1,500 and 4,000 in the mountains, depending on site and elevation. The growing season can range from 130 days in the coolest sites to nearly 300 days in the Gulf and FL Panhandle regions. Precipitation can range from 42 in annually in the mountains and Piedmont to 70 in annually on the Gulf Coast. Summer heat and humidity can be challenging to vinifera varieties, with temperatures and relative humidity commonly in the 90s (°F) from June through Aug. Harvest is generally from Aug 1–Sept 15 in the upper Piedmont, and can start in July in the Coastal Plain.

VITICULTURE

Since vinifera and hybrid grapes grow in tight clusters, they are referred to in the South as 'bunch' grapes in contrast to the looser berry pattern of the Muscadine grapes, sometimes referred to as 'shot' grapes. While a variety of vinifera and French hybrid varieties are grown in the cooler regions of the South, the most successful of them are the same as are successful in the MID-ATLANTIC: Chardonnay, Riesling, Cabernet Sauvignon, and Cabernet Franc for vinifera, and Seyval, Vidal, and Chambourcin for hybrids. Delaware, Niagara, Concord, and Catawba have a minor presence, and Norton is also grown in AK and TN.

Vinifera and hybrid varieties are grafted onto C-3309, 5C, or 5BB rootstocks. While a variety of training/trellising systems are used for hybrids and vinifera, Vertical Shoot Positioning with movable catch wires is the most popular. Vineyard spacing for vinifera and hybrids averages 6–7 ft between vines and 9–10 ft between rows. Muscadine varieties, due to their excessive vigor, are planted 20 ft between vines and 10 ft between rows. Muscadine yields typically range from 6 to 7 t/a, and can yield up to 9 t/a.

In addition, viticultural research at Southern universities has added new, high quality Muscadine hybrid grapes. The Univ of FL has been breeding new hybrids since 1923. Today the most promising of these varieties include Suwannee, and Lake Emerald. Suwanee is a white grape producing a subtle, slightly Muscat flavored wine. Lake Emerald also makes a white wine, light, clean, crisp, and stylistically versatile. MS State Univ's viticulture research program released a new hybrid in 1982 called Miss Blanc which also makes a crisp, delicate white wine.

Based on 1992 data, MS produced 2,082 tons of grapes, including non-wine varieties. The 1,350 acres of vines in AK produced only 2,000 tons. GA harvested 1,108 tons of grapes in 1992. SC produced over 12 million gal of Muscadine wine from Tenner Brothers winery for wine giant Canandaigua. NC grew to a mid-sized Southern wine producing state in 1998, with 550 vineyard acres and eleven wineries. NC provides an instructive model for the evolution of Southern viticulture. Roughly half the total acreage is in Bronze Muscadines, with Carlos the leading grape at 180 acres. White vinifera grapes represent about 20% of the total, with red vinifera at 15%, Dark Muscadines at 7%, and French hybrids at 8%. NC is expanding new vineyard acreage at a rate of 25–35% annually. They hope to match VA's acreage by 2008.

While Muscadine plantings expanded rapidly in the 1980s, by 1997 nearly 32% of new vineyards planted in NC were red vinifera, and nearly 25% were white vinifera. Moreover, new vineyard plantings in the cool mountain regions in 1997 equaled those of both coastal and Piedmont regions. NC's two leading wineries, BILTMORE ESTATE and WESTBEND, are located in the mountain and upper Piedmont regions respectively. NC's viticultural transition toward cooler growing regions with appropriate varieties deserves a closer examination by other Southern states.

The risks in Southern viticulture vary with the region and species. In the mountain areas spring *frost damage for vinifera varieties is a problem, particularly with the temperature fluctuations and false springs in the Appalachians. Winter damage is a threat at mountain elevations over 2,300 ft and in the high Ozark Plateau of AK. In NC some wineries in the Piedmont and BLUE RIDGE MTNS use wind machines and overhead sprinklers to diminish frost damage to buds in the spring.

As in the Mid-Atlantic, wildlife depredation is a concern. Animals, especially deer, are more of a problem in the mountains and Piedmont, while migratory birds are more of a problem in the coastal regions. Some vineyards employ bird nets, while others employ deer exclusion fences. The grape root borer, Pierce's disease spreading leafhoppers, and Japanese beetles are the main insect pests, the former two found only in the Coastal Plain. Fungal threats abound throughout the hot, humid South for French hybrid and vinifera varieties. Downy mildew, powdery mildew, black rot, phomopsis, and botrytis are the leading fungal diseases. Even in the cooler mountain regions, proper spray programs must be followed to avoid fungal crop loss. Late season HURRICANE and tropical storms are a threat both on the Atlantic Coast and the Gulf Coast.

MARKETPLACE

The South has traditionally been an agricultural economy, and as tobacco's importance continues to fade, state officials are anxious to diversify and maintain the vigor of their agricultural sectors. States such as FL which rely heavily on tourism are discovering the value-added benefits of viticulture and native wineries. A study undertaken for the VA Dept of Agriculture demonstrated that wine-oriented tourists tended to stay longer and spend more money than the average tourist. CRAFTSMAN-SIZED WINERIES sell the majority of their inventory CELLAR DOOR or at regional festivals. Larger volume wineries rely more on distributors. Typically larger wineries in the South make about half of their sales at the winery and half through distribution.

Ch Elan and Biltmore Estate are two examples of major Southern wineries which draw large tourist traffic due to their strategic locations. Ch Elan is located at Interstate 85, 30 minutes north of ATLANTA in the scenic Piedmont countryside. Biltmore Estate is the Victorian-era country estate of the Vanderbilts in Asheville, NC, a popular summer resort area in the Blue Ridge Mtns. Each winery is a tourist attraction in itself, with lavish and stately buildings, and each attracts thousands of visitors annually.

REGULATION AND NEOPROHIBITIONISM

As the South has continued its transition from a rural and agriculturally based economy to more diversity based in cities and suburbs, the political and cultural character of the South has evolved in recent years. Since 1981, when a third of Southern jurisdictions were DRY, per capita wine consumption has more than doubled. BLUE LAWS and other NEOPROHIBITIONIST legislation have steadily dwindled across the South. Protestant Fundamentalism and neoprohibitionism have been closely related, but anti-alcohol sentiment has begun to fade as state governments see the financial benefits of supporting native wineries. In the Deep South, while MS was the last state to repeal Prohibition in 1966, roughly half of its jurisdictions allow the sale of alcoholic beverages today, typical for the South as a whole. TN provides an illustration of the contemporary wine industry in the South. There are fourteen wineries in TN, the most in the South. There is a state Farm Winery law, allowing local wineries to make limited retail sales on-premise. However, wineries may only wholesale to the state monopoly system, and anti-alcohol sentiment is still strong. Per capita wine consumption in Tennessee is still very low.

The hottest alcohol regulation issue in the South, as elsewhere, is DIRECT SHIPMENT of alcohol to consumers outside the THREE-TIER DISTRIBUTION system. States seem to be more concerned about revenue loss than about any moral neoprohibitionist issue. For example, states as culturally diverse as NJ, MD, KY, and FL are leading the case against direct shipping through litigation. FL has attempted to prosecute direct shippers of wine all the way to the US Supreme Court, which refused without comment to hear the case they brought in 1998. By that time though, FL had enacted a law allowing felony charges to be brought against out-of-state direct shippers, the constitutionality of which was subsequently challenged. More than 85% of the wine sold to restaurants in south FL (ie Miami and Palm Beach) is sold by a single distributor, Southern Wines & Spirits. R.G.L.

Southbrook Farms northwest of TORONTO was once the largest cattle farm in ONTARIO. Bill Redelmeier converted first to a farm market, then in 1991 added a winery operation sourcing fruit entirely from Niagara Peninsula vineyards 75 mi away. Notable is Southbrook's Chardonnay called Triomphe, and their Framboise and Cassis dessert wines. Both fruit wines are made in the same manner as *port. They use a short, incomplete fermentation (3–7 days) of fruit from Ontario farms. They stop fermentation by adding 192 proof unaged brandy. Yield is less than one litre of produce per kilo of fruit producing a concentrated fresh fruit flavor. L.F.B.

South Carolina, state in the SOUTH region where secession and Civil War hostilities commenced, at Ft Sumter. French Huguenots in SC cultivated Herbemont and Lenoir grapes in the early 19th century. At the time of the Civil War, the Isabella grape was used to make a claret by the Benson & Merrier winery in Aiken. Today SC's viticultural heritage contributes to the wines of the CANANDAIGUA through the 12 million gal of Muscadine wine produced by Tenner Brothers winery in Patrick. Other SC wineries include Cruse Vyds, growing French hybrids and vinifera in Chester, and Montmorenci Vyds in Aiken. Aside from Tenner Brothers, annual production for SC's other wineries is a mere 5,000 gal annually. The growing season ranges from 210 to 300 days, with between 45 and 70 in of annual rainfall.

SC has no jurisdictions currently exercising an option for the restriction on sales of alcoholic beverages, and native wineries have no unusual restrictions. R.G.L.

Southeastern New England AVA, stretches along the coast of the ATLANTIC OCEAN from New Haven, CT, where Yale Univ is located east along the north side of Long Island Sound through RI, then north past Cape Cod to Plymouth, MA, where the Pilgrims supposedly landed. It extends inland only 15 mi, at which point the maritime influence dissipates into a colder Yankee growing season (see WESTERN CONNECTICUT HIGHLANDS). While the AVA's season averages about 190 frost free days with mild winters throughout the area, soil types range from stony in the west to sandy in the east. Commercial vineyards were first planted in the 1970s. They are widely scattered, favoring the varieties Chardonnay, Vidal, Seyval Blanc, and more recently Cabernet Franc.

The wines show characteristically lean, bright fruit, and vibrant *acidity. The appellation facilitates access by wineries to grape sources in all three states and helps them to cooperatively enlarge the region's wine identity.

NOTABLE PROPERTIES

Chamard Vyds, located on the rocky southern coast of CT in Clinton, is a CRAFTSMAN-SIZED producer of well-regarded Chardonnay, which acounts for three-fourths of the 20-acre vineyard planted in 1980. Bordeaux varieties make up the remainder, augmented with fruit purchased from nearby Long Island. The Chardonnay is *barrel fermented in French oak, given extended *lees contact, *MLF, and minimal filtration. Production is 6,000 cases.

Sakonnet Vyds, the largest winery in New England and a pioneer in the region's modest emergence as a wine producer. Located in the southeastern corner of RI, the 45-acre vineyard produced its first vintage in 1975 with a focus on fresh, crisp, austerely fruity white wines crafted for local seafood. In this style, Vidal Blanc rapidly became Sakonnet's signature wine and a defining example of the varietal. Recently that model has been expanded with a richer, barrel fermented Fumé Vidal. Both Chardonnay and Gewürztraminer are also barrel fermented, but given very little barrel age and no MLF to maintain high pitched fruit. In 1999 an excellent sparkling wine was introduced. Red varieties have a tougher time in the AVA's mercurial weather. Aggressive marketing has created demand which outpaces vineyard resources, so the winery imports wine from the *Languedoc to blend with small proportions of estate grown Vidal and Chancellor. These importations have raised annual production close to 60,000 cases.

Westport Rivers Vyd, a winery devoted to sparkling wine with 75 acres of Chardonnay, Pinot Noir, Pinot Meunier, and Riesling on the southern coast of MA. The vineyard was planted in 1986. Best wine is the genuinely dry, austerely refined, partly barrel fermented Blanc de Blancs. With the largest vineyard in New England, Westport Rivers is influential in the nascent process of defining a regional style closely tied to 'downeast' cuisine. R.F.

Spring Mtn AVA, approved appellation in NAPA VALLEY running from the 400 ft contour line up to the 2,200 ft ridgeline, which marks the Napa/Sonoma county border, west of ST HELENA. Some Rieslings such as Smith-Madrone's do surprisingly well at the higher elevations, proving the effect of the inversion layer which holds heat in the valley while bringing cool breezes from the Bay and from the Santa Rosa Plain. Cabernets in the district are much harder to predict. In some locations the soils produce high pH wines that can be chewy and attractively supple when young, but embarrassed by flabby lack of acid after 7–8 years of bottle age. Other vineyards have hard edges which never soften. The best reds are *Meritage blends.

NOTABLE PROPERTIES

Cain, fabulously expensive winery to build, as the 100 acres of steeply terraced vineyard right at the top of the AVA where one can even look over into Sonoma were to plant. A little over half of the vineyard is Cabernet Sauvignon; a fifth is Merlot. The rest is divided among Cabernet Franc, Malbec, and Petit Verdot. Winemaker Chris Howell produces the top item, Cain Five, using all the varieties, but varies proportions each year at assembly time in an artistic evaluation of what the vintage has produced. The aim is to produce around 6,000 cases a year of the Cain Five, with the wines not chosen for the first string going into a wine called Cuvée, which can be an excellent value in great vintages. Around 8,000 cases of Cuvée are made each year. Cain Five has a lot of things going on in the glass. Howell got a good grip on the reins during the 1990s making a series of smooth, medium weight wines with wonderful interplay of spice, cassis, and tarragon.

Ritchie Creek, CRAFTSMAN-SIZED WINERY in the woods with 8 acres making 1,200 cases, run by Richard (Pete) Minor since 1974. He started with Cabernet cuttings from MAYACAMAS but broke ground in the late 1980s when Ritchie Creek became the first winery in CA to release a Viognier.

York Creek, vineyard well known from 25 years of vineyard designation on RIDGE Petite Sirah. It is owned by Fritz Maytag, whose grandfather founded the washing machine company. His father founded the famous blue cheese maker in IA, and Fritz founded Anchor Steam Beer of San Francisco, the original US microbrewery.

See also NEWTON, STONY HILL. B.C.C.

Spurrier Tasting, blind comparison held in Paris in the US bicentennial year 1976, by British wine merchant Steven Spurrier using prominent French judges. Four CA Cabernets and four CA Chardonnays were matched to four top Bordeaux reds (Chx Mouton-Rothschild, Haut-Brion, Montrose, and Léoville-Las-Cases) and four prestigious white burgundies, including several grands crus. Two features distinguished the tasting and helped it mark the ascension of

CA wine to a world-recognized standard: (1) it was covered by *Time* magazine; and (2) the French judges confidently panned certain wines and touted others by predicting their French origin. Fortunately for CA, the wines most vigorously applauded by the judges for their French breeding were in fact CA wines. The 1973 Stags Leap Cabernet and 1973 Ch Montelena Chardonnay finished first in their respective categories. And five days later *Time* made sure millions of people knew about it. The French judges claimed they had been hoodwinked. In an effort to save French honor, the French gastronomic magazine *Gault Millau* staged a rerun, only to find that the results, while not identical, were remarkably similar.

Stags Leap AVA, approved appellation in the southeastern portion of NAPA VALLEY 6 mi north of the town of Napa. The district runs from the Napa River up the eastern slope of the valley to the 400 ft contour line. In the north it ends at Oakville Cross Rd. The physical formation which gives the district its name is a 1,200 ft vertical basalt palisade which looks like six-sided columns. Rocks eroded out of these hills provide the deep, well-drained, arid soils of the district which produce *budbreak two weeks earlier than elsewhere in the valley. At the same time, cool winds blowing from the Pacific through the low spot at the Golden Gate Bridge, then turning north as they confront the 2,000 ft hills behind Berkeley, arrive in Napa along this east side. Stags Leap ripens fruit more slowly than sites further north in the valley, so other areas catch up and harvest in Stags Leap is about the same time as in Rutherford. The signature characteristic of Cabernet Sauvignon grown in Stags Leap is lighter body, and a more lifted, cherry-like fruit aroma which seems delicate by CA Cabernet standards.

NOTABLE PROPERTIES

Clos du Val, winery started in 1972. For the first decade of operation Bernard Portet was known for being the son of the technical director at Ch *Lafite, but he carved his own reputation in CA. Today the winery owns 300 acres and makes 85,000 cases. The wines are tense. They need to be aged, and ten years barely puts a dent in their potential. One of the best offerings for extended bottle age is the Semillon, which seems light and nondescript in youth, but polished with 8–10 years in the cellar. When well aged the bouquet of the Semillon is like bananas griddled golden brown in butter.

Chimney Rock, Cape Dutch winery building owned by Sheldon (Hack) Wilson, who once had the Pepsi franchise in South

Africa. Winemaker Chris Fletcher has done extensive research on vine spacing and trellis systems, including using a split canopy which is higher on one side than the other in order to even out the sunlight exposure. The result of this research has been to virtually eliminate any grassy, vegetative character in their Cabernet, and instead produce high toned cherry fruit notes which typify the district. Fletcher has not increased yield per acre, but he has doubled the percentage of the crop that qualifies for the best wine.

Silverado Vyds, winery and vineyards owned by Walt Disney's family. There are 340 acres planted around the hill on which the winery perches, about a third Cabernet including a unique clone called See. Jack Stuart was hired as the original winemaker in 1981. His reputation since then has been for wines, totaling 100,000 cases a year, with quality far exceeding their price. The Reserve Cabernet from Stags Leap is not typical of the other Silverado wines. It is big and heavily wooded, but stuffed with the sour cherry fruit of the district.

Sinskey, winery in Stags Leap but drawing heavily on grapes from Carneros to produce their best offering, a Meritage called RSV Reserve which often has majority components of Merlot and Cabernet Franc. The wine tends to feature berry and plum notes when young, then shows more of a leather turn after 6–8 years. Warm years are best.

Steltzner. Top vineyardist who planted and managed properties for other people for many years, Dick Steltzner began his own place in 1967. He was instrumental in establishing Stags Leap as an AVA. In 1990 he sold the land on top of a hill behind his winery, then used the money to dig caves into the bottom of the hill. His Cabernet is a good example of Stags Leap style when young, showing fresh fruit in the cherry spectrum, but evolving after age 8 into a nice roast pork bouquet. He makes about 12,000 cases a year.

See PINE RIDGE, SHAFER, STAG'S LEAP WINE CELLARS. B.C.C.

Stag's Leap Wine Cellars, winery in the STAGS LEAP district of CA's NAPA VALLEY opened in 1972 by Warren Winiarski, a former professor who had taught Greek in the Univ of Chicago's renowned School for Social Thought. Catapulted to prominence by the victory of his 1973 Cabernet in the SPURRIER TASTING, Winiarski then proceeded to start making some of CA's best Cabernets. Amazingly, the wine that won the Spurrier tasting was made from 3-year-old vines grown in the Wild Horse Valley east of Napa. Of course, 1973 was a very good vintage. Winiarski's top wine is called Cask 23, a blend of grapes grown in his own vineyard at the winery, and in the vineyard of his next door neighbor Nathan Fay. It is not particularly typical of the Stags Leap AVA though, in that it does not demonstrate perfumey fruit. What it does show is waves of flavor and infinitely changing nuances in the nose. It is an adroit balancing act between cedary oak, tobacco leaf varietal aroma, and the rustic richness small concentrations of microbiological complexing agents such as Brettanomyces can provide. None of the individual elements stands out; they all push together. The winery produces 55,000 cases of Stags Leap and a similar amount of second label Hawk Crest annually.

Standing Stone Vyds occupy one of the best viticultural sites in NY's FINGER LAKES district, on the eastern shore of Seneca Lake. Thirty acres of vineyard surround a cluster of renovated barns producing 6,300 cases in 1998, scheduled for modest expansion. Most of the vineyard plantings followed establishment of the winery in 1992, but Chardonnay and Riesling blocks date back to Seneca Lake's first vinifera plantings by Charles Fournier for Gold Seal Vyds in the early 1970s. Some grapes are purchased from vineyards close by; Standing Stone is committed to working only with southeastern Seneca Lake fruit. Dry Gewürztraminer is a specialty, and a Bordeaux blend has been successful. All wines are from European vinifera varieties except a popular Vidal Blanc. Standing Stone is one of the Finger Lakes' rising stars. R.F.

Steele, winery in LAKE CO and its owner, CONSULTANT Jedediah Tecumseh Steele, who is named for America's most famous Indian statesman. Steele's wine career began in 1968 as a cellar rat for Fred McCrea at STONY HILL in Napa Valley, one of CA's pioneer BOUTIQUE WINERIES. From 1975 until 1983, Steele resurrected historic vineyards around ANDERSON VALLEY while making wine at Edmeades. His career trajectory, however, achieved earth orbit from 1983 through 1991 as winemaker for KENDALL-JACKSON.

The defining aspect of that work was creation of superior Chardonnay through adroit blending of characteristics drawn from several regions, and the ability to perform that trick consistently in large quantities. He was named Winemaker of the Year by the CA State Fair in 1986, by *Wine & Spirits Buying Guide* in 1989, and by the International Wine and Spirits Competition in London in 1990. These accolades merely echo the

Show prizes won by wines Steele made for Kendall-Jackson during that same period; a period in which he was producing 800,000 cases of Chardonnay annually, much of it barrel fermented.

Steele left Kendall-Jackson in 1992, but remained at the center of wine industry attention due to a court battle he fought with Jess Jackson. The bone of contention was Jackson's seminal legal effort to define Steele's ten-year learning experience as a 'trade secret' and as tangible property owned by Kendall-Jackson Winery. Not only did this concept directly contradict a spirit of open information sharing in which the CA industry took some pride, but it tantalized wine journalists who became eaten up with curiosity about what specific techniques were not being revealed. In the end, Steele got some money, and Jackson got the court's cooperation in keeping Steele from delivering any overt, public exposés. Speculation ran wild.

Today Steele has moved into the winery facility formerly called Konocti. His second label **Shooting Star** is the translation of Tecumseh from Shawnee. Logically enough Chardonnay is the wine for which he receives most attention, although he produces many other wines as well. Of the vineyard designated Chardonnays, the Lolonis is broader and riper, the Durell is woodier in the nose, and the Sangiacomo has more green scents and lighter body. His blended California appellation Chardonnay is the one most indicative of Steele's talent. It shows the very sophisticated French oak treatment melded into the apple fruit of a rather intense nose, crisp acid, and supple mouthfeel. Then the toastiness and fruit return in spades for the finish.

Steele makes 25,000 cases for his own label. His consulting clients include Indian Springs in the Sierra Foothills and FESS PARKER in Santa Barbara. B.C.C.

Sterling, eye-catching white Moorish arch winery on top of a wooded hill in the middle of CA's NAPA VALLEY just south of CALISTOGA. Built in the early 1970s, it quickly became a destination visit complete with aerial tramway to sweep tourists from the parking lot to the hilltop. In 1977 the original investors (see NEWTON) sold out to Coca-Cola, which began development of vineyards at the 1,800 ft elevation on DIAMOND MTN to the west. In 1983 the company was sold to Seagram, which now uses it for their wine group headquarters. Seagram also acquired Winery Lake Vyd in CARNEROS which gave it access to excellent Chardonnay and Pinot Noir grapes. Sterling currently produces

240,000 cases from 1,150 acres. The Chardonnays were pretty good in the middle years, and those made in the 1970s by Ric Forman aged surprisingly well for 10–12 years. In the 1990s the Cabernet Reserve became the best wine. Blending grapes from both Diamond Mtn and the Three Palms Vyd in the valley floor south of the winery produces wine which can deliver flavor without having to resort to heavy extract. B.C.C.

Steuben, dark-skinned hybrid released from GENEVA in 1947 as a table grape whose juice has also been used to make pink, slightly labrusca flavored wine in the east.

Stone Hill, winery established before the Civil War (1847) in HERMANN, MO, just west along the Missouri River from St Louis at a time when the state was the largest wine producer in the country. It closed, of course, during Prohibition and its vast cellars were employed in the storage not of wines, but of mushrooms. In 1968 it was re-established as the first winery in the state since Prohibition. It is now MO's largest at 75,000 cases annually. Owners Jim and Betty Held continue to make wines which win awards not just locally, but nationally. Their Nortons are delicious and dependable. Their Vidals, Seyvals, and Vignoles, including late harvest, are worth the search as well. P.W.F.

Stoney Ridge, located on the BEAMSVILLE BENCH in Vineland, ONTARIO. One-third of the 50,000-case production is devoted to several styles of Chardonnay. Chief winemaker Jim Warren also produces Merlot and Cabernet Franc with approachable softness and forward fruit. Most of their grapes for the Stoney Ridge line are sourced from neighboring vineyards along the Beamsville Bench. When the new 70-acre vineyard is producing, its fruit will be dedicated to an ultra-premium line called Cuesta Estates. Warren also makes specialty wines such as Cranberry (always sold out at Thanksgiving), a port style made from Marechal Foch, and a *solera based fino sherry style. CEO John Belanger intends to build a new facility which will house a fine art gallery and restaurant. L.F.B.

Stony Hill Vyd, one of the original model wineries for what became the artisan winery revolution in CA in the 1970s. The vineyard was started in the 1940s as a weekend hobby by advertising executive Fred McCrea and his wife Eleanor. At its 800 ft of elevation in the western mountains opposite Bale Lane in the SPRING MTN AVA of NAPA VALLEY, cool breezes come across the mountains each evening. Stony Hill is in a similar location to sparkling winemaker Schramsberg (see DIA-MOND MTN), just a mile south. Since the 1950s when they started producing small quantities of wine, Stony Hill Chardonnays and Rieslings have been among CA's most remarkable examples of ageability in those varieties. Neither is fermented or aged in barriques. Nor is *MLF induced. The Chardonnay does see some time in used puncheons. When young, both varieties have the ripped musculature of skinny men devoted to weight lifting. As they age in the bottle, varietal nuances begin to appear. Apple fruit blossoms in the Riesling and grapefruit notes show up in the Chardonnay. After ten years the wines are just hitting their stride and 25-year-old bottles of the Chardonnay are still fully intact with nice hazelnut bouquet and a long mineral finish. In the 1960s and 1970s Stony Hill sold all of the 2,000 annual cases to a mailing list which had ten applicants for every spot that opened up. As such it was a CULT WINE before its time, and today it often represents an excellent bargain in AUCTIONS. The McCrea's son Peter administers the property these days, while winemaker Michael Chelini, who has been in place for three decades, produces 5,000 cases each year.   B.C.C.

Storybook Mtn, northernmost winery in CA's NAPA VALLEY. The winery caves were originally dug in 1883 by brothers Jacob and Adam Grimm (hence the fox and grapes motif on the Storybook Mtn label), whose winemaking roots dated back to 1542 in Germany. In 1976 the east-facing hillside property was purchased by former Stanford history professor Jerry Seps. He devoted his wine passion to Zinfandel, and in the 1980s reversed the downward trend red Zinfandels had been on by producing the prototype claret-style Zinfandel. Seps worked to bring back the PRECERTIFICATION CLONE vines on his steep property, which rises from 400 to 1,200 ft over a small distance encompassing only 36 acres. Where he had to replace vines, he used the Hand clone UC Davis

had chosen for its ability to retain acid. Demonstrating this characteristic, in 1980 several lots Seps picked were 26° Brix, but more than 10 g/l TA and finished in the wine at 3.2 pH. Grapes of this type help Seps stylistically because Zinfandel needs to get fairly ripe to show its boysenberry varietal aroma, but alcoholic, extractive models were ruining the popular market. Seps was able to blend aromatic fruit with less ripe batches to make wonderfully balanced, medium-body wines, elegant from their date of release, and CA's best bet among Zinfandels to still be doing something interesting on their tenth birthday. Today Seps is continuing his pioneer creativity by blending a small admixture of Viognier into his Zinfandels. Now they are not only elegant, but they whisper witty secrets.   B.C.C.

Sulphur Springs Valley, located 50 mi east of Tucson, ARIZONA near Willcox, about 50 mi northeast of the SONOITA AVA, and 50 mi west of the border with NM. The elevation of this region, also called Kansas Settlement, is over 4,000 ft high. It is not an approved AVA. After the Apache were removed from their homeland in the 1890s, a contingent from Kansas settled this valley. It is home to a variety of agriculture, from cotton to pitted fruit to cattle feed lots. There are four wineries including DOS CABEZAS.

Climate is slightly warmer than Sonoita. Soils are terra rossa, an iron oxidized clay. Last frost occurs by the end of Apr, but can cause problems if late, as in 1998. DIURNAL TEMPERATURE FLUCTUATION can be as much as 35–40°F. The first frost occurs around the end of Oct. Slightly warmer than Sonoita, the area usually needs *acidification to balance its wines. Like Sonoita, vines are planted on their OWN ROOTS. The area receives 17 in of rainfall, but can have humidity levels as low as 3%. This low atmospheric moisture, the altitude, and lack of pollution provide more sunlight than anywhere else in the US. There are three wineries in the area.   R.T.S.

SV 23–512, old French hybrid whose limited appeal in ONTARIO lies in its disease resistance and cold tolerance rather than in the quality or quantity of wine produced.

Swedish Hill, ambitious, rapidly growing winery in NY's FINGER LAKES district, drawing upon two dozen growers on four lakes to make a dizzying smorgasbord of the region's wine types. A preponderance of sweet-fruity French hybrid and labrusca wines is driven by one of the area's busiest tourist facilities. Riesling is also an important wine here with more serious aspirations. Swedish Hill's first vintage was 1985. In 1996 it spun off a second winery, Goosewatch, nearby on the shore of Cayuga Lake. Goosewatch specializes in varietal oddities for the area, from Viognier to the native grape Isabella. The two wineries combined produce four dozen wines plus brandy and eau de vie from a resident alembic pot still. The mantra here is something for everyone. Total production in 1998 was 40,000 cases distributed in western NY, but expansion is projected to take the wines into markets in the eastern half of the US.   R.F.

Swenson, Elmer, hybridizer whose initial work centered on trying to create interesting table grape varieties that could withstand the vine-numbing winters of MINNESOTA and the upper MIDWEST in general. Later work resulted in grapes that today's cold climate growers use readily for wines. Working primarily with a super cold-hardy riparia/Concord cross called Beta, created by fellow Midwesterner Louis Suelter in the last century, Swenson went on to release the Kay Gray, St Croix, and Edelweiss grapes. Later crosses included the St Pepin and LaCrosse varieties which were themselves based partly upon the Seyval Blanc, one of the earliest of the successful French hybrids. In 1999 Swenson was in his eighties, living in retirement in WI, and not drinking wine!   P.W.F.

Tablas Creek, vineyard, winery, and nursery operation in the far western section of PASO ROBLES AVA in CA's San Luis Obispo Co. It was begun in 1991 as a joint venture between American wine importer Robert Haas and France's Perrin family, owners of Ch de Beaucastel in *Châteauneuf-du-Pape. The projected size is 15,000–20,000 cases. Although individual varietals are made separately, so special single varietal bottlings are possible, the focus of the winery is a red blend of Syrah, Grenache, and Mourvèdre, with a smaller quantity of a white Marsanne/Roussanne blend. In the beginning Tablas Creek also established a nursery, where French FIELD SELECTIONS of the Rhône varieties were propagated for the Tablas Creek vineyards as well as for sale to other CA growers. As ENTAV clones from France have become more widely available through American nurseries, Tablas Creek has de-emphasized its nursery operation. In the mid-1990s however, the attention Tablas Creek brought to the interaction between clones and vineyard site helped raise the issue in CA, where it is now seen as an exciting opportunity to create individual wines with increased complexity. The Tablas Creek wines are an example. Their red blend in particular is a very attractive value, with many facets of flavor; a wine notable for its subtlety rather than its power. B.C.C.

Tabor Hill, winery in what is now LAKE MICHIGAN SHORE AVA with a checkered career. Established in 1970 in an area that was better known for producing Concord grape juice, Tabor Hill flourished under winemaker Len Olson into a haphazardly successful producer of French hybrid and vinifera wines. After Olson's departure it floundered for a while before stabilizing into a solid and consistent producer of commercial wines, including currently the very respectable Grand Mark Brut sparkling wine. Lean, but well-balanced Chardonnay and dry Rieslings are noteworthy as well. P.W.F.

taxes, see EXCISE TAXES and CANADA: REGULATORY ENVIRONMENT.

Taylor, Walter S. (1931–), grandson and namesake of the founder of the Taylor Wine Company, who is perhaps best known for his battles with this giant producer of NY wine. He joined the family's FINGER LAKES wine firm in the 1950s and began a lifelong crusade for French hybrid wine varieties in 1964 when he and his father pioneered vinification of them in NY as varietals, under Taylor's Great Western label. A history buff, Walter turned his grandfather's original winery into America's first wine museum, filling it with artifacts from a century of winemaking around the Finger Lakes.

As the Taylor winery passed from family to corporate managers in the late 1960s, Walter opposed changes in winemaking practices, particularly the addition of water and CA bulk wine to ameliorate *foxy flavors. Fired from the company in 1970, he set up his own BULLY HILL winery and escalated his criticism of Taylor as a corporate profiteer manipulating grape growers. In this campaign against the mega-winery and his plea for the dignity of growers, and in the immediate success of Bully Hill wines, Walter Taylor set the stage for a renaissance of small Finger Lakes wineries. But his monogamous embrace of French hybrids limited his influence on those wineries, which increasingly turned to vinifera. R.F.

telemarketing, wine, sales technique curiously centered in northern Sonoma Co, and an industry populated by both sincere acolytes and colorful scoundrels. If one put an advertisement in the classified section of any typical US newspaper seeking experienced telephone wine salesmen, even a single response would be unlikely. If one were to place that same ad, however, in the Santa Rosa *Press Democrat*, one might fairly expect hundreds of responses the very first day. There are fewer than ten telephone wine marketing companies in all of America at any given moment, and six or seven of them are located between Santa Rosa and Healdsburg. It is a brutal business. The average tenure of a wine telemarketer is about 60 days.

Temecula AVA, district in CA's South Coast AVA, on the inland side of the coastal mountains in the high desert two-thirds of the way from the outskirts of Los Angeles to San Diego. The soil is large-grained sand, the natural vegetation sparse. North and south of Temecula the general impression can accurately be described as moonscape, interrupted only by succulants such as cactus. Not far to the south is the US Navy's Top Gun flight school for fighter pilots. The approved Temecula AVA, however, has one unique climatic feature, for it sits directly east of a low spot in the mountains called Rainbow Gap, and every afternoon, as temperatures rise in the desert, a funnel of cooler air is sucked through the Gap right across the vineyards and housing tracts which make up the giant real estate speculation called Rancho California begun here in 1964. Pierce's disease became a serious threat in 2000 due to the arrival of a more vigorous insect vector, the glassy winged sharpshooter.

Grapes were first planted at Temecula as a diversion to get travelers to stop long enough to view the model homes in the planned community. Eventually 50-acre 'ranchettes' of producing vines were sold, complete with vineyard management and a winery home for the grapes. As a real estate development, Temecula is an astonishing success. The whole region along Hwy 15 into San Diego continues to grow dramatically, sprouting golf courses and retirement communities on all sides—every one of them dependent on imported water, but awash in the voters necessary to procure it. Financially, fifteen or so Temecula wine producers do alright too, because they can sell most of their production CELLAR DOOR to a local population which has both a curiosity about the product and the time to explore it in the convenient, socially convivial atmosphere of the winery tasting rooms. The wines may be a matter of some local pride, but to outsiders the quality is less inspirational.

Temecula AVA is at 1,400 feet of elevation. It is primarily a mesa, with rolling hills and gullies formed by rapid erosion whenever rainfall creates brief torrents. Cover crops are sowed, then mowed, to help hold vineyard soils in place. The DIURNAL TEMPERATURE FLUCTUATION is large, with 100°F days common and cold nights routine. The growing season starts early, and Chardonnay is frequently harvested during Aug. Temecula lies at 33° 30' latitude. Fruit weight, natural crispness, and flavor concentration are never hallmarks of a Temecula-grown wine. Hence wood aging has had a tendency to overpower vinosity, and today a large proportion of Temecula wines are unwooded whites. Soft textures and early drinkability are important sales tools (20 years of aging potential in the cellar is not a major inducement to a retiree population). Modest price points and a little bit of RS never hurt with the average tasting room customer in Temecula.

San Pasqual AVA is a second viticultural area several miles south of Temecula, approved upon petition by a winery there that subsequently went out of business. The property was dormant for a decade, but was reborn in the 1990s as Orfila Cellars. A couple of old style producers of sweet fortified wines, similar to the Cucamonga habitués (see LOS ANGELES), exist in an area further south called Escondido. They are a cultural slice from the past, and a distinct cut below the quality standard set by Temecula.

Although it is not an approved AVA, the local region which produces the best grapes is the one in the coastal mountains between Temecula and the ocean. Fallbrook is primarily devoted to avocados, but elevations of 2,500 ft, volcanic soils, and cool midday temperatures have produced some very flavorful Cabernet Sauvignon in vineyards there called La Cresta. A more speculative district is 60 mi east of San Diego in the mountains around Julian, where elevations of 4,500 ft are average. There are many stone fruit orchards in the district, snow every year, and even a healthy tourist trade drawn by the old gold mining town and 30 quaint bed & breakfast inns. Menghini Winery has operated in Julian for two decades, but never bothered to grow grapes there. A 4-acre vineyard nearby had not yet come into bearing as of 1999. The Julian district shares many characteristics with the DESERT SOUTHWEST region, including a July MONSOON SEASON.

NOTABLE PROPERTIES

Hart, begun in 1973 when Travis (Joe) Hart and his wife Nancy purchased 12 acres in Temecula next to Callaway Vyds, a convenient commuting distance from their weekday jobs. The winery was built in 1979. They make 4,500 cases a year. Whites are grown in the extremely sandy soils on the property. Various reds were tried there, then grafted over to Chardonnay and Sauvignon Blanc. Since Hart is the first winery encountered by visitors to the Temecula area, it stands as a symbolic bastion against the encroaching development of Rancho California.

Orfila, winery with 32 acres of estate vineyards in San Pasqual AVA and an exclusive contract on 45 acres in Fallbrook; it is the best producer in the San Diego area. Owned by former Argentine Ambassador to the US and Secretary of the OAS, Alejandro Orfila, it is managed by Italian born winemaker Leon Santoro, who previously raised Quail Ridge to some degree of recognition in Napa. Best wines are Syrah, and a Sangiovese with more depth and lavender nuance than any other from CA.

Thornton, winery in Temecula producing 17,000 cases of sparkling wine and 22,000 cases of still wine. Most of the grapes for the sparklers are purchased in the Temecula AVA. In the mid-1980s this winery created some distance between itself and the pack, under the brand name Culbertson. It was reeled back in by the peloton of French champagne houses then opening in CA and has yet to find another breakout niche.

When John Culbertson had the glitzy Los Angeles market all to himself, and a southern CA business address, sales boomed. In 1988 he built a palatial winery/visitors' center on the main road through Temecula. At the time he was selling 80,000 cases a year. Cafe Champagne, the elegant tasting bar and fine restaurant in the facility, is still a big success with tourists. The Culbertson brand, however, faltered. In 1991, investors John and Sally Thornton took over control of the property, put their own name on the line, and introduced still wines as well, mostly sourced outside the district. All the sparklers, under either brand name, have tended to be broad. That is a structural comment.

See CALLAWAY.   B.C.C.

Tennessee, state in the SOUTH region, bordering and sharing many characteristics with KY to the north. Tennessee can be divided both viticulturally and just culturally into three separate areas. Memphis is the centerpiece of the western zone which sits across the MISSISSIPPI RIVER from AR, and is the most similar to the Old South. This western edge of TN along the river includes a piece of the MISSISSIPPI DELTA AVA, is very warm, and does best with Muscadine varieties. Nashville is the heart of country music in America, the center zone of the state, and perhaps most akin to the MIDWEST. French hybrids do best there. Knoxville is the high-tech zone nestled against the APPALACHIAN MTNS in the east, a region historically associated with Daniel Boone's brand of frontier spirit. With its mid-continental latitude and ample cool climate vineyard sites at higher elevations in the hilly section from the Tennessee River in the west to the Allegheny foothills in the East, this easternmost third of TN offers much promise for successful viticulture in the new millennium, perhaps even growing vinifera.

A century ago TN Catawba wines were winning awards in national competitions. However there is still a considerable NEOPROHIBITIONIST sentiment in TN. Lynchburg, the home and headquarters of Jack Daniels Distillery for more than five generations, is in a DRY county. It therefore cannot sell its own most famous product, leaving red-eye gravy (hot coffee poured into bacon grease to be served on biscuits) as the county's most memorable local experience. Limited wine retail sales are allowed at wineries, but otherwise only through state PACKAGE STORES. Wine consumption is considerably below the national average. Nevertheless, TN is currently home to fourteen wineries, the largest number in the South. A 1989 survey of state grape growers showed that the top cultivated varieties at the time were the hybrids Vidal, Seyval, and Cayuga, all Muscadines, and Delaware, Concord, and Catawba. At that time, the volume of vinifera grapes amounted to less than a ton statewide, but growers increased cultivation of Chardonnay and Cabernet Sauvignon in the 1990s. Good quality fruit wines are also produced.

TN has two approved AVAs: Mississippi Delta and TENNESSEE VALLEY. Most farm winery vineyards are in the eastern and central regions of the state, as those sites have the coolest summers. Growers struggle to find a balance between grape varieties which appeal to consumers and also have winter hardiness. A spring *frost in 1989 killed half the state's primary grape buds. The TN Farm Winery Law only requires 75% grapes in a wine labeled as state produce to be grown in-state, and the state growers have largely been able to supply demand to satisfy the law. Total state production is 180,000 gal.

NOTABLE PROPERTIES

Apple Barn, winery located in Sevierville in the Tennessee Valley AVA, specializing in quality fruit wines (80% of production). Despite its folksy name, Apple Barn has been winning numerous national awards for its Vyd Red, White, and Apple Raspberry wines, Mtn Valley Blush, and Collier Reserve. Owners are Bill Kilpatrick and Sandra Collier.

Monteagle, winery established in 1986 in the town of the same name. It does well with Niagara and Cynthiana and also makes Seyval, Riesling, Cabernet Sauvignon, Chancellor, and Merlot. Owned and managed by the Harlow family, it produces 12,000 cases.

Mtn Valley Vyd was established in 1991 in Pigeon Forge by Philip Don Collier. Rick Donley is the winemaker for these 12,000 cases, as well as 6,000 at Apple Barn.

R.G.L.

Tennessee Valley AVA, located in eastern TENNESSEE, southeast of Knoxville and west of the Appalachians. This appellation enjoys the moderating influence of large lakes in the district such as Douglas, Tellico, Watts Bar, and Chicamauga, which were created by the massive TVA (Tennessee Valley Authority) project begun in the 1930s to provide electricity to rural areas by building dams.

tensiometer, device buried, usually 2–8 ft deep, in a vineyard to measure the amount of moisture available to vine roots. When a series of tensiometers are connected to a computer and some profiling software, irrigation management can be raised to a level of sophistication unknown a generation ago.

Terre Rouge, Dom de la, also **Easton,** winery in AMADOR CO whose owner Bill Easton played an active role with the *Rhône Rangers during the 1980s, most of it performed as an influential retail store owner in Berkeley. Easton's store had an active tasting bar, specialized in Rhône wines from France and Rhône varietals from CA, and served an entertaining selection of Mediterranean-style dishes. At the time, the other young Rhônish entrepreneurs (they like to call themselves Rhônigades) were all located in the coastal counties. So in 1983, when Easton decided to make wine, he went to the SIERRA FOOTHILLS.

Easton, a large individual given to cowboy boots and laconic conversation, set himself the task of taking stock of all the old Rhône variety vineyards in the mountains. As a winemaker he is really something of a delicate French aesthete, but you would not know that to look at him. Easton quickly became aware of the role elevation played on mesoclimate, and he has had remarkable success persuading growers to reduce yield in order to concentrate flavor. He buys Grenache from the 60-year-old, sandy soiled Tattersfield Vyd at 800 ft near Loomis in Placer Co, and also from the Marchini Vyd

at 1,500 ft above Coloma in El Dorado Co. At 2 t/a, picked at 24–5°B, and cold macerated without SO_2, both these vineyards give fabulously perfumed, unusually dark wine which is helping revolutionize America's concept of Grenache. Most of the wines are fermented with WILD YEAST. *MLF is extended into the spring to entrain additional complexity.

Terra Rouge is the name of the winery and the brand used for all the Rhône varietals and blends. Easton is the brand used for other varietals such as Zinfandel. The Easton Fiddletown Zin from Eschen Vyd is chewy with dark berry aroma and hints of black pepper in the mid-palate. Its long finish is surprisingly supple for a wine with so much punch on entry, but vintages do make a difference, especially with DRY-FARMED vineyards. There were only 19 in of rain in Fiddletown in 1994, compared to 55 in for 1995 and 32 in as the long-term average.

Easton's 1994 Fiddletown Zin was a wine picked at 24.8° Brix with a pH of 3.35 and 7.2 g/l TA. Numbers as remarkable as this are found only with PRE-CERTIFICATION CLONES on ancient vines, and extensive hand sorting to remove green berries and raisins from each bunch.

B.C.C.

Terror Creek, winery in COLORADO and the highest vineyard in North America, at 6,400 ft, located on Garvin Mesa, above Paonia in the North Fork region of western CO. It is owned by John Mathewson and his wife Joan, who has an enology degree from *Changins, Switzerland. Terror Creek produces some of the finest wines made in CO, including a stunning unoaked Chardonnay made in part from purchased grapes, a stylish Alsace-like Gewürztraminer, a fine Riesling, and some French oak-aged Pinot Noir. Production is only 1,000 cases, from 5 planted acres on the 10-acre vineyard. R.S.

Texas, state with three of the US's ten largest metropolitan markets (Dallas/Ft Worth, Houston, San Antonio), and also the fifth largest wine producing state (1.76 million gal) and the fifth largest consumer of wine (18.9 million gal) in the US. Known for the independent, sometimes flamboyant, attitude of its residents, TX is simultaneously regarded as part of the South (by people in the Far West and the North) and as part of the West (by people in the South). Oil, cattle, cotton, and gridiron football have long been the mainstays of the TX economy and public image. Following the financial busts of the 1980s, the economy has rapidly diversified. In 1980 the notion that TX could

produce well-made wines from vinifera grapes would have evoked disbelief, if not outright laughter. But things have changed and, as with all things Texan, in a big way. Although it is difficult to characterize wines from so vast a region, TX reds, especially Cabernet Sauvignon and Merlot, often have a pronounced nose of ripe cherries and fresh herbs. Texas whites tend to have good acidity, and often a mineral quality from the prevalence of limestone or granite based soils in much of the state.

Even as early as the 1970s the beginnings of a commercially viable wine industry began to take shape when a new generation of TX viticulturists started growing grapes and making experimental wines. Two Texas Tech professors, Robert Reed and Clint McPherson, founded what would become LLANO ESTACADO Winery in Lubbock. As manager of 'surface interest' (as opposed to oil drilling) in west Texas for the University of Texas Lands Department, Billy Carr's enthusiasm for the possibilities of grape growing in TX was the key to the success of the experimental vineyards in Bakersfield that would grow to be the largest vineyard in the state and home to STE GENEVIEVE Wines. Ed and Susan Auler started FALL CREEK VYDS on land near the Auler family ranch in the TEXAS HILL COUNTRY. Dr Bobby Smith founded LA BUENA VIDA VYDS in Springtown, just west of Fort Worth. Robert Oberhelman started his vineyards in what would become the Bell Mountain AVA in the Texas Hill Country. As part of the Extension Services at Texas A&M University (Agriculture & Military) horticulturist George Ray McEachern began experiments in grape research, rootstock selection, and site selection. Along with another dozen or so early vineyardists, these people laid the groundwork for the growth of the industry in the 1990s and found ways to deal with some of the difficulty inherent in growing grapes in a semi-arid climate with unpredictable and at times extreme climatic conditions.

GEOGRAPHY

TX really is big, covering 267,339 sq mi, which makes it larger than France, or Germany, or CA. Residents are fond of saying that if the ice melted in Alaska, TX would be able to resume its position as the biggest state in the Union. The Rio Grande River marks its border with MEXICO, the Sabine River the LA border, the Red River the border with OK, and the Gulf of Mexico the southeast border. The Panhandle on the northwestern side is adjacent to NM where the terrain rises gradually to become the ROCKY MTNS. As far as grape growing is concerned, the state can be divided into four major areas: Southeast, TRANS-PECOS, and North-Central, all of which surround the Texas Hill Country in the center of the state.

The Balcones Fault Zone splits TX in two from east to west. This inactive fault runs from Eagle Pass on the Mexican border, northeast through San Antonio, Austin, Dallas, and through Sherman on the OK border. The Balcones Escarpment breaks through the earth's crust in the Hill Country to create dramatic *limestone hills, giving the region its name. The Llano Uplift, Edwards Plateau, and the Cross Timbers meet in the Hill Country.

The Southeast area takes in the 367 mi of coastline on the Gulf of Mexico, through the Coastal Plains, north through the Piney Woods of east TX to the northeast border with AR and OK, south to the Rio Grande and west to the Balcones Fault Zone. This is the most difficult grape growing region in the state. It is not possible to grow vinifera vines because black rot and Pierce's disease are so widespread. Small lots of LENOIR and FAVORITE are used to produce port-style wines in the region. MUSCADINE varieties tend to grow well in east TX and the Piney Woods.

The Trans-Pecos region lies west of the Balcones Fault, from just north of Austin, northwestward towards the southernmost reaches of the Panhandle and west and south to the borders with NM and Mexico. The area encompasses parts of the Great PLAINS, the Edwards Plateau—the western, elevated section of the Balcones Fault—and the Llano Uplift. The highest elevations in the state can be found here, along with the rich lands of the Rio Grande Valley and vast stretches of desert. Forty per cent of the total winegrape producing acres in the state are in the Trans-Pecos area.

North Central Texas begins north of the Trans-Pecos and west of the Coastal Plains continuing up through the Panhandle to OK and NM. The Great Plains stretch down through the Panhandle and western parts of this region. The Caprock, an impervious layer of caliche which forms a 'cap' over the Ogallala Aquifer in the Panhandle, has given its name to both a town and a winery. The Caprock Escarpment dramatically marks the line between the flat, northwestern part of the Plains and the rolling hills of the southeastern Plains as they begin to blend into the Edwards Plateau. Another 40% of the total winegrape producing acres in the state are in this area.

There are now six AVA's in the state: TEXAS HIGH PLAINS, TX Hill Country, Fredericksburg in the TX Hill Country, Bell Mtn,

Escondido Valley, and TEXAS DAVIS MTNS. In addition a small portion of the Mesilla Valley AVA reaches into TX from NM.

HISTORY

Making wine in TX is by no means a modern phenomenon. The first vineyards were planted in the 1650s at the first permanent Spanish settlement at Ysleta in the present-day town of El Paso. Between 1659 and 1682, four missions were settled by Catholic priests and Christianized Native Americans. Foreseeing the need for sacramental wine, the priests had brought cuttings of Mission, or *Criolla Chica, vines with them from Spain.

The Spanish constructed rudimentary dams on the Rio Grande, from willow branches woven into baskets and filled with stones, to provide water for irrigation. By the 1720s a rather large irrigation system had developed and the area was producing enough corn, wheat, and beans along with grapes to fulfill the needs of the community. Whether or not the wines were any good, by 1853 around 200,000 gal a year were being produced from the vineyards in the El Paso area.

As with the rest of the emerging US, grape growing and winemaking tended to go hand in hand with immigrants from wine producing countries. Immigration from Europe and the southeastern US began in earnest after TX gained its independence from Mexico in 1836. Groups of German immigrants began to settle in the Texas Hill Country in the 1840s. The first Italians arrived in 1879 in Montague Co, on the OK border north of Ft Worth and east of Witchita Falls. Mission grapes, other European varieties, native grapes, and vines ordered from CA were all planted and crossbred over the next 60 years.

The French were interested in grape production in TX at an early stage. Victor Prosper Considérant, a somewhat naive French socialist dedicated to creating a community of cooperative good, brought well-educated professional men and skilled craftsmen to TX to establish a colony to be called La Reunion in what is now the Dallas-Fort Worth area. After seeing the native MUSTANG grapevines and considering the rocky, thin soil, Considérant had thought the area an ideal one in which to produce wine. Unfortunately, the winter of 1856–7 was freakishly cold and wiped out the French vineyards. Add that to the doomed confrontation between socialism and the hard-nosed spirit of capitalism that was the underlying unifier of the other settlers, and La Reunion was soon abandoned.

TX's greatest contribution to the wine industry is the work of Thomas Volnay (T. V.) *Munson. Munson became interested in the idea of improving grapes by cross-breeding from visits to the vineyards of his chemistry professor at Kentucky State College. He initially attempted to establish a research vineyard in NE using 40 varieties of grape clusters from the professor's vineyards. When the droughts of summer and the hard winters took their toll on his vines, he accepted the invitation of two of his brothers to join them in Denison, TX, on the Red River border with OK. Munson later wrote of his arrival in Denison in 1876, 'Here were six or eight good varieties of wild grapes, several of which had not been seen by me previously. I had found my grape paradise!'

His industrial, scientific, and literary work were all carried out in Denison. In 1890 his *Classification and Generic Synopsis of the Wild Grapes of North Americas* was published. His premier work *Foundations of American Grape Culture* was published in 1909 and is still in use today. For the 1893 World's Columbian Exposition in Chicago he prepared the most complete botanical display of the entire grape genus ever made (it is now held by the US Dept of Agriculture). His scientific and horticultural work led him to develop more than 300 distinct grape varieties, the best of which were offered for sale to the general public by Munson Nurseries.

Munson's work in developing disease resistant rootstock rescued the French wine industry from the devastation of the *phylloxera epidemic. Munson worked for four months with vineyardists from Bell to Bexar counties in south central Texas to amass fifteen wagons of dormant stem cuttings of American species that were resistant to the phylloxera louse. These vines formed the breeding stock for the rootstocks that saved the French wine industry. In 1888 he was given the title Chevalier du Mérite Agricole by the French government for his work.

By the end of the 19th century 2,900 acres of vineyards had been planted and some 20 commercial wineries were operating in TX. Most of the vineyards that were planted at that time were in Tarrant, Grayson, and Montague counties in North Central Texas, and in El Paso, far west TX. But the rumblings of Prohibition had been heard since the inception of the Republic of Texas. The Sons of Temperance, a 3,000-member organization that counted Sam Houston (the first popularly elected President of the Republic of Texas) among its supporters, was an early anti-alcohol voice in Texas politics. According to T. E. Fehrenbach, the election of 1911 was fought almost entirely on the alcohol issue, with the brewery industry alone raising more than $2 million in campaign funds in support of pro-alcohol candidates of any party. In 1914, TX Governor James E. Ferguson would be impeached partly as a result of an unrepaid 'loan' from the TX Brewers' Association. By 1920, two years after TX outlawed liquor and one year after joining the US federal government in Prohibition, total acres numbered only 900 and only one winery, Val Verde, was producing wine, that for medicinal purposes. Not until the 1970s would there be any attempt to re-establish winegrape vineyards in the state.

THE MODERN WINE INDUSTRY

By 1999 there were 32 wineries in TX where 1.62 million gal of wine was made from the 7,500 tons of grapes harvested on the 3,200 acres of vineyard planted as of 1997. TX is the fifth largest wine producing state in the US after CA, NY, WA, and OR. Total economic impact from the production and sales of TX wines in 1997 was estimated at $107 million, supporting 2,291 jobs. The industry contributed $19.6 million dollars to payroll and added $9.3 million to the economy through excise and sales taxes. But TX wine is virtually unknown outside the state: 96% of all TX wines are sold in TX; 60% through grocery stores. TX-produced wines represent 7.6% of the total TX wine market.

Most of the state's vineyards are planted to vinifera. Roughly 43% of the acreage is planted to the key grape varieties Cabernet Sauvignon (695 acres) and Chardonnay (664 acres), but Chenin Blanc (305 acres) and Sauvignon Blanc (382 acres) lead in actual tonnage produced. Merlot (199 acres) and Riesling (108 acres) account for another 10% of the acreage. Zinfandel (97 acres), Ruby Cabernet (88 acres), Pinot Noir (74 acres), Cabernet Franc (71 acres), Muscat Canelli (68 acres), and Gewürztraminer (40 acres) make up the majority of the remaining acres. Semillon, Lenoir, Favorite, Muscadine varieties, Seyval Blanc, Vidal Blanc, Chambourcin, and Cynthiana are also grown.

As the economic impact of the TX grape and wine industry has grown, so has the support of the TX Dept of Agriculture (TDA). In April 1995, TDA launched a four-year 'Buy Texas' consumer advertising campaign highlighting products grown, sown, and processed in TX including 'Buy Texas Wines' as part of the promotion. TDA is a sponsor of the annual Lone Star Wine Competition, assists with pest management, legislative guidance, and news releases. October is designated Texas Wine Month.

Texas Technical University in Lubbock is home to the Texas Wine Marketing Research Institute, which compiles industry data concerning the economic significance of the TX wine industry. Grayson County College in Denison, which offers a two-year associate degree and a continuing education program in viticulture and enology, is home to the T. V. Munson Viticulture and Enology Center and to the T. V. Munson Memorial Vineyard.

There are several large annual festivals and competitions in the state, the most significant being the Texas Hill Country Wine & Food Festival; the DALLAS *Morning News* International Wine Competition, and its sister event, the Dallas *Morning News* Wine & Food Festival; Grapefest; Lone Star State Wine Competition; and the Fredericksburg Wine & Food Festival.

Two primary associations supporting the industry are the Texas Wine & Grape Growers' Association (TWGGA) and the Associated Wineries of Texas. TWGGA, headquartered in Grapevine, is a non-profit organization whose membership is composed of wineries and grape growers throughout the state. They offer educational and marketing support along with lobbying for legislation to improve the industry. Associated Wineries of Texas is an alliance of the four largest, most influential, and well-funded wineries in the state: Llano Estacado, CAP*ROCK, Ste Genevieve, and Fall Creek. The sole focus of this political group is on legislation as it pertains to wineries.

The two groups have distinctly different approaches to marketing and selling TX wines. The Associated Wineries are intent on building a viable industry in the state by working within the established THREE-TIER DISTRIBUTION network and have the resources to market their wines through traditional channels. TWGGA members are promoting self-distribution, CELLAR DOOR sales, tasting rooms, wine festivals, and DIRECT SHIPMENT to consumers as a primary means of distribution, growth, and advertising. Ed Auler of Fall Creek states his opinion concisely about the difference between the two groups when he says 'cellar door sales and tasting rooms are the tail on the dog; not the dog.'

Two of the biggest obstacles in marketing TX wines are the long distances between wineries and cities in TX, and the cost of shipping wine from TX to the rest of the world. Llano Estacado and Cap*Rock are now warehousing some of their wines in CA whence shipment to the rest of the US is more economical.

Unlike Napa Valley where one can drive up and down a single stretch of road and hit ten wineries in a day, one has to be dedicated to visit many of the wineries in TX. And only those in the Hill Country could be said to be anywhere remotely touristic. As country singer Mac Davis put it, 'I thought heaven was Lubbock, TX in my rearview mirror.' In order to overcome this problem Cap*Rock, Delaney, La Buena Vida, Northstar Vyds, and Homestead have opened production facility/tasting rooms in GRAPEVINE just north of Dallas-Fort Worth Airport to market and sell their wines. A sixth winery, La Bodega, is actually in the airport. TX law prohibits a winery from having a second location that serves only as a tasting room, but they can have two winery permits. Four of the winery/tasting rooms in Grapevine are equipped to make just enough wine to pass muster, and Delaney has a full-scale operational winery.

DISEASE

*Pierce's disease makes it impossible to grow vinifera in the Coastal Plains or anywhere east of the Balcones Fault Zone. And although west of the fault zone was originally considered free of the disease, there were signs of the disease in the early 1990s in some Hill Country vineyards. TWGGA is discouraging interested newcomers from planting vinifera in the Hill Country at all. Perimeter control appears to be the best way to control the disease at this time. To that end, MENARD VALLEY VYDS has a 300 ft clear space between their deer fence and the vines and insects caught on the property are constantly monitored. Although Hill Country winters from 1991 to 1995 were dangerously warm, freezing temperatures during the winters 1996–8 seemed to halt the spread of the disease.

Fungus diseases (especially *black rot) are widespread throughout TX—except on the High Plains—and necessitate use of fungicides in most vinifera vineyards. *Crown gall is an ongoing problem in all areas of the state and COTTON ROOT ROT is a constant threat except in the acid soils of East Texas and in the High Plains.

And as if all these diseases were not burden enough, the phylloxera louse infested one vineyard in Gillespie County that has since been plowed under. By the end of the century there had not been any signs of phylloxera in any other TX vineyards, but since it is present in vineyards across the Rio Grande in Mexico, it may only be a matter of time. Some vineyards near Lubbock have planted on AXR1 rootstock, but most TX vineyards are planted on their OWN ROOTS because it is less expensive.

THE MARKETPLACE

Ninety-six per cent of TX wines are sold in TX: 60% through grocery stores, 24% through liquor and PACKAGE STORES, 10% through restaurants and bars, and 6% at the CELLAR DOOR. TX wines represent about 8% of the wine sold in TX each year. On a per capita basis, Texans consume 0.61 gal of wine each year (compared to 27.1 gal of beer) representing 5% of the total wine consumption in the US. Total wine consumption in TX, however, has grown 22% over the last decade. Domestic wines make up the majority of the market: 83% of the still wines and 78% of the sparkling wines sold in the state are domestic.

With the consolidation of several mid-size distributors during the 1990s, there are now only two statewide wholesalers in TX: Glazer's and Republic Beverage/Block. There are a number of smaller regional houses that bring in wines from smaller producers, many of whom have accurately concluded they would be lost in the shuffle at either of the big houses. The main drawbacks of these small distributors are small sales staffs and, from a logistical standpoint, it is extremely difficult for them to service the entire state. That means consumers in the Interstate 35 corridor from Denton south to San Antonio, or in the Interstate 45 corridor from Dallas south to Houston, may choose amongst the best wine available in TX. Anywhere else, one's access to fine wines is limited.

Houston, on the Gulf Coast, is the largest city in the state with a population of 3.3 mil in the metropolitan area. It is a far more freewheeling city than its northern rival, the more conservative Dallas (pop. 1.06 million). However both cities lay claim to the title of the city with the largest number of gentlemen's clubs. Fort Worth (pop. 479,000) has retained much of its western, Cowtown feel. The inelegantly named Dallas-Fort Worth Metroplex area has a combined population of about 3.5 million. All three cities boast major cultural attractions such as the Kimbell Art Museum in Fort Worth, the Dallas Opera, and the Houston Alley Theater. San Antonio (pop. 1.05 million), on the southern edge of the TX Hill Country, is the most charming big city in TX. Unlike glitzy Houston or Dallas, downtown San Antonio is filled with restored early 20th-century buildings, park space, understated new buildings, and the Riverwalk, which make it a major tourist destination. Austin (pop. 541,000) is the state capital and easily the most liberal place in TX. The enormous Univ of TX at Austin, along with thriving music and independent film scenes, combined with a lot of ready cash from the high-tech industry have made Austin a very desirable place to live and a good wine market.

REGULATORY ENVIRONMENT

TX is not as restrictive about the sale of alcohol as some of the MONOPOLY STATES in America, but it may take the top prize for confusing legislation passed to benefit special interest groups. The state's Constitution of 1876 allowed communities the right of local option on liquor (and such other matters as fences and carrying guns) which laid the groundwork for the bewildering jumble of wet and DRY areas that is in place today. Every individual precinct has the choice of voting on its wet or dry status. At this time, 184 out of 254 counties are *mostly* wet. Of these, only 37 are totally wet for distilled spirits. In certain instances, the wet/dry line zigzags across the same street. It may be wet for 5 mi, dry for 2, then wet again for beer only. There are five counties in which only alcoholic beverages containing less than 14% alcohol may be sold and eleven where only beer containing less than 4% alcohol may be sold. In all 54 counties are completely dry, mostly in the Panhandle and northeastern regions of the state.

In a strange twist of fate, the vineyards Ed Auler planted at Fall Creek in the Hill Country and Dr Bobby Smith planted at Springtown were in dry counties. They did not realize that meant neither would be able to make wine on their property. This led them to instigate the legislation and passage of the Farm Winery Act of 1977, which allows grape growers to produce and bottle wine in a dry county, but not to sell it at the winery. Their next step was having legislation introduced to make cellar door sales legal in a wet county. Auler was eventually able to garner enough interest to call for a local option election. Thus the precinct where Fall Creek is located is now a wet area.

One exception to the three-tier distribution system, which is otherwise applied to all alcoholic beverages sold in TX, is for holders of a winery permit, who are allowed cellar door sales to consumers, if their winery is in a wet area, and they may ship directly to retailers in TX. They may also ship wines to consumers in the state as long as the consumer arranges and pays for the shipping. There is an annual 25,000 gal cap on the amount of cellar door sales a winery may transact.

For wineries in dry areas there is an annual 25,000 gal cap on the amount of wine they may sell directly to retailers, and they are not allowed cellar door sales. Non-Texans may marvel at the complexity of the following exceptions: if the winery is located in a dry area and in a county with a population of 15,000 or less, in which a majority of the area of the county is dry and in which one municipality is in a wet area; or a county that has a population of at least 20,000, but not more than 30,000, and that borders the Red River and in which a majority of the area of the county is dry *and* the grapes used to produce the wine are grown and harvested in the dry area, then one may apply for a permit to sell wine directly to consumers for seven consecutive days per year! This exception is clearly aimed at wineries in or around Dennison, 60 mi north of Dallas.

A winery permit allows a winery to charge a fee for tasting, but they are not considered to be licensed to sell wine by the glass or bottle for on-premise consumption unless they fall under what is locally known as the *Grapevine Law*. That regulation states, 'The holder of a winery permit may sell wine to ultimate consumers for consumption on or off winery premises, and dispense free wine for consumption on or off the winery premises, if the winery is located in a city that: (1) is located in three or more counties, at least one of which has a population of 500,000 or more; and (2) has within its boundaries all or part of an international airport.' The only place this regulation applies to is Grapevine, Texas. Which is why six wineries have set up winery/tasting rooms there.

Two types of wholesale license exist in TX. Class A wholesalers, such as Glazer's, can only sell to retail stores and/or restaurants and bars in wet areas. Class B license holders are retail stores which also carry a license allowing them to sell wine and beer to *private clubs* and liquor to all restaurants and bars. There is no restriction on total number of Class B licenses allowed in the state.

Private clubs are allowed to sell alcoholic beverages to consumers whether they are located in a dry or a wet area. Restaurants which are open to the public in dry areas are able to sell alcoholic beverages by obtaining a *private club* beverage license. Membership in these *clubs* can be bought on the spot, most charging a nominal fee of $2–10 for a membership. Only the person in the party who is actually paying for the alcoholic beverages needs to be a *member* for everyone in the party to be allowed to drink legally. A Unicard can be purchased which confers membership in the 500 or so *private clubs* throughout TX that honor the card. Country clubs and other types of membership clubs, whether in dry areas or in wet areas, are considered *private clubs* as far as their beverage permits are concerned.

Private clubs, whether in dry or wet areas, must buy their wine, beer, and spirits from a Class B license holder. However, Class B license holders cannot deliver any alcoholic beverage to a *private club* in a dry area; the account must pick up the goods from the Class B license holder themselves. Class B license holders can deliver alcoholic beverages to *private clubs* in wet areas. All ON-PREMISE accounts are required to buy spirits from Class B license holders.

Pricing at the retail level in markets such as Houston, where wine sales are driven by supermarkets working on low margins, tend to be lower than in areas such as Dallas where sales are driven by package store chains. Sam's Clubs, a national chain of discount stores for members, provide TX consumers a source for discount pricing on national brands. This is a bone of considerable contention with other retailers. Any retail establishment with an on-premise beverage permit must include a 14% liquor tax in the price of all alcoholic beverages they sell in lieu of collecting the regular sales tax. Additionally, a $0.01 per bottle tax is added to wine. That revenue goes directly to the TX Dept of Agriculture to fund research on growing grapes and marketing wines in TX.

All alcoholic beverages may be sold in liquor stores from 10 am to 9 pm every day except Sunday. Convenience stores and grocery stores, which may sell only beer and wine, are permitted to sell them every day until midnight, and after 12 noon on Sunday

See individual geographical entries below.   L.A.O.

English, S. J., *The Wines of Texas* (Austin, 1986).

Fehrenbach, T. R., *Lone Star: A History of Texas and the Texans* (New York, 1985).

Special thanks for the technical assistance and cooperation of Tim Dodd at the Texas Wine Marketing Institute, George Ray McEachern at Texas A&M University, and Roy Renfro at Grayson County Community College.

Texas Davis Mtn AVA, a 60 mi U-shaped mountain range extending north and northwest from Fort Davis in the TEXAS region called TRANS-PECOS. With higher average annual rainfall than the rest of the Trans-Pecos (18 in versus 8–12 in) the mountain pines, oaks, and black cherry trees are a welcome change from the surrounding desert. The range was formed by volcanic eruptions about 35 million years ago.

NOTABLE PROPERTIES

Blue Mtn, winery with a 50-acre vineyard at 5,300 ft of elevation, originally planted by Gretchen Glasscock in 1977. The vineyard was bought in 1990 by Nell and Philip Weisbach, and bonded in 1994. Winemaker Patrick Johnson has a Masters in plant botany and worked for GALLO before coming to Blue Mtn.

Blue Mtn has the advantage of being the only vineyard in the state where the temperature drops following *veraison. In June, temperatures normally reach a high of around 100°F in the day, but in July and Aug highs are usually in the low 90s, cooling off to the low 60s at night. Combine that with rocky, gravelly clay soils and almost no disease problems, and one might think the Davis Mtns are the perfect TX location for grapes—except for the *wind, which can blow off shoot tips, and the regular late spring *frosts. Blue Mtn Winery is a low tech operation that is producing truly noteworthy Cabernet Sauvignon and Merlot. Total production is only 1,000 cases a year, but the winery is worth keeping an eye on. Since it is almost exactly in the middle of nowhere, 220 mi southeast of El Paso just outside Ft Davis, and in a dry county, there is no tasting room.   L.A.O.

Texas High Plains AVA includes 12,000 sq mi in the central and western region of the TEXAS Panhandle near Lubbock, and has the potential to produce high quality wines from any vines that manage to survive the extreme weather conditions. Spring frost combined with dry air and constant wind, followed by periods of heavy rain and hail in late spring, precede the 100°F temperatures of July and Aug. Daytime temperatures will climb to 100°F by 1 pm and often not begin to drop again until 6 pm. While there are DIURNAL TEMPERATURE FLUCTUATIONS of 20–30°F in the summer, it is not the sort of rapid cooling that TX grape growers would like to see. Overnight lows in the high 60s are reached after midnight and temperatures begin to climb again by early morning.

Constant dry winds, which often pick up hot sand and create static electricity, can burn shoot tips and flower parts during bloom, but have the positive effect of keeping the area free of mildews, black rot, and other *fungal diseases. The region is unique in TX because it is completely free of *Pierce's disease. There is, however, some risk of TORNADO damage as Lubbock represents the southern end of Tornado Alley in the US.

Average rainfall of 18 in and humidity below 20%, combined with continuous dry wind, produce very high rates of evaporation, making irrigation a necessity. Luckily water from the Ogalala Aquifer is available. The Ogalala Aquifer is one of the world's largest aquifer systems, stretching across eight states from SD to CO and down through the Great PLAINS in TX covering a total of 174,000 sq mi. Vineyards totalling 1,215 acres are planted in the High Plains AVA at elevations of 2,750 to 3,800 ft, placing this region among the highest major growing districts in the US, but the rise is so gradual that everything appears to be flat. Soils are porous, deep sandy loam derived from the decomposed limestone of the caprock over the aquifer. Impermeable subsoil starts between 8 in and 3 ft down.

Cabernet Sauvignon and Merlot tend to grow well in the region. In the hands of talented winemakers such as Kim McPherson at CAP*ROCK and Greg Bruni at LLANO ESTACADO, they have produced some of the best wines to come out of TX in recent years. New plantings of Sangiovese, Nebbiolo, and Viognier may prove to be well suited to the region.   L.A.O.

Texas Hill Country AVA incorporates 15,000 sq mi (larger than the Yankee states of CT and MA combined) in the center of TEXAS, and is the largest AVA entirely in any single American state. It encompasses 22 counties and the sub-AVAs of Bell Mtn and Fredericksburg, although there are only about 500 acres of vineyards in the area. Soils range from sandy loam to clay loam 2–6 ft deep over limestone and granite. The combination of good soil pH between 7.0 and 7.2, an abundance of water for irrigation, and nighttime cooling during the summer make this a prime area for growing grapes in TX. However, problems with *Pierce's disease, COTTON ROOT ROT, *hail, and late spring *frost pose problems to many of the Hill Country vineyards, making it rather less than ideal. A 150 mi stretch of the Colorado River (which rises in TX and flows to the Gulf of Mexico, and therefore should not be confused with the river of the same name which forms the major drainage for the western slope of the Rocky Mtns and flows to the Sea of Cortz off Baja California) flows through the area. It has been dammed to create several large lakes, including Lake Buchanan. The Hill Country boundary runs from San Antonio north to Austin, northwest to San Saba, then southwest to Menard, southeast to Kerrville, and back to San Antonio. The hills, along with the natural springs and man-made lakes in the area, will erase anyone's preconceptions of TX as a great flat desert wasteland. Long a popular destination for deer hunting, boating, fishing, and camping, the area now boasts numerous wineries which have become a destination in their own right.

NOTABLE PROPERTIES

Becker Vyds in Stonewall, the heart of Hill Country, is owned by Dr Richard Becker, a San Antonio endocrinologist, and his wife Bunny. The winery sits on 33 acres purchased and planted in 1992. The vyd is planted primarily to Sauvignon Blanc, Chardonnay, and Cabernet Sauvignon. Becker also purchased a 12-year-old vineyard of 24 acres near Ballinger, 36 mi northeast of San Angelo, in 1997. Half the Ballinger vineyard is planted to Johannisberg Riesling. Total production for 1998 was 6,300 cases, primarily Cabernet Sauvignon, Chardonnay, and Riesling. In 1996 TX's first commercial Viognier was released, but the most promising wine to come out of Becker is their 1997 blend of Cabernet and Cabernet Franc made from St Clair Vyd grapes sourced in the MIMBRES VALLEY AVA of NM. The wine has deep garnet color with scents of black cherry, rosemary, and tar and a full-bodied, well-balanced *mouthfeel.

Bell Mtn, formerly Oberhellmann Vyds, was begun by Robert and Evelyn Oberhelman in 1974. After twelve years of experiments with various grape varieties, they released their first wines in 1984 under the Oberhellmann Vyds label. The name was changed to Bell Mtn Winery after their petition for approval of the Bell Mtn AVA was granted in 1986, making it TX's first AVA. There are 56 acres under vine at the winery, primarily planted to Cabernet Sauvignon, Merlot, and Pinot Noir, on the slope of Bell Mtn northeast of Fredericksburg in the Hill Country at an elevation of 2,000 ft. Soils are well-drained, sandy loam with a pH of 6.5 and good mineral content. Water for drip irrigation is drawn from two wells drilled into the Hickory Sands Aquifer. The winery has an additional 20 acres on Bell Mtn under contract.

Small AMERICAN OAK barrels are used for Cabernet Sauvignon and Merlot; French oak for Pinot Noir. Puncheons (see *barrel types) of Nevers oak are used for Chardonnay and their Fumé Blanc, a blend of Sauvignon Blanc and Semillon. Wines are bottled under two labels: Bell Mtn for wines from the AVA; and Oberhof for a group of specialty wines including non-appellation *blushes and fruit wines. Current production is 11,000 cases per year with the well-regarded Bell Mtn Cabernet Sauvignon the top seller.

See FALL CREEK VYDS, MENARD VALLEY VYDS. L.A.O.

Thirty Bench Vyd, NIAGARA PENINSULA winery established in 1994 with four co-operative but independent-thinking winemakers: a physician, Dr Tom Muckle; a professor, Dr Yorgo Papageorgious; a businessman, Frank Zeritsch; and a viticulturalist, Deborah Paskus. They divide responsibilities according to interest and expertise, each for a different wine. Seventy per cent of their fruit is sourced from the Thirty Bench Vineyard of Riesling, Cabernet Franc, and Merlot. Chardonnays are good; Cabernet blends are better. The 1995 Reserve Blend, which is half Cabernet Sauvignon and a quarter each Merlot and Cabernet Franc, and was harvested in Nov, strode through a line-up of CA's and France's best in San Francisco recently. It was carried by a beguilingly lifted floral overlay to a nose which was otherwise deep and substantial. The wine was light bodied, but had impressive tannin/acid balance and seemingly unlimited ageing potential. L.F.B.

three-tier distribution, system prevalent throughout the US whereby three separate transactions occur in the sale of wine between the winery and the consumer: (1) the winery or importer sells to a distributor in any individual state or market at what is called the distributor' price; (2) the distributor in turn sells to retail stores or restaurants in its territory at what is called the wholesale price; and (3) the store or restaurant sells to the consumer at what is called the retail price or, respectively, a higher restaurant price. (See also DIRECT SHIPMENT and the essays on Distribution and on Cybersales, pp 21, 24).

tied house laws, a generic phrase describing regulations used by most US states to prohibit a single entity from simultaneously owning both a wholesale and a retail license (see THREE-TIER DISTRIBUTION), thus making vertical integration of the US alcohol beverage business virtually impossible. This was exactly the intent of most legislation passed immediately after 1933 relevant to alcohol because of the criminal underworld's success in vertically integrating US alcohol distribution during Prohibition.

tornado, violent swirling storms, caused by cold, dry, arctic air at a high elevation confronting warm, moist, tropical air, usually from the Gulf of Mexico. The warm air wants to rise; the cold air wants to drop. Characteristic dark funnels extend to the ground from cumulo-nimbus clouds associated with swiftly moving low pressure fronts. They may only last for a few minutes. Interior wind speeds can reach 300–500 mph. The effect on agriculture is indiscriminate but devastating, destroying one field and leaving a field only yards away untouched. They have been recorded in all 50 states, but occur most frequently in Tornado Alley: TX, OK, KS, NE, IA, AK, MO, IL, and IN. The TEXAS HIGH PLAINS record the highest number annually, followed by OK. Thus tornadoes pose a threat to winemaking ambitions at wineries such as LLANO ESTACADO and CAP*ROCK. Most tornadoes occur in Apr, although Mar through June is the season, and they have been recorded in all months of the year. They are most frequent between 1 pm and 9 pm, but have been recorded at all hours of the day.

Toronto, Huron for 'meeting place,' is the capital of the province of ONTARIO and is Canada's largest city with 4.7 million people. The greater metropolitan area is the tenth largest in North America, and also host to the Toronto Wine and Food Show, and Santé, a weekend of international wine/food tastings and seminars held on trendy Bloor Street in Mar. L.F.B.

Traminette, crossing of Gewürztraminer and JS 23–416 grown in MISSOURI and MICHIGAN.

Trans-Pecos, non-AVA region in southwest TEXAS. This area is about the size of SC, bounded by the Pecos River to the east, by the Rio Grande border with Mexico to the south and west, and by NM in the north. As the Rio Grande runs southeast from El Paso it winds through the dramatic canyons of Big Bend Natl Park in Brewster Co on its way to the Gulf of Mexico. Much of the area is considered an extension of the Chihuahua Desert with mesas sprouting up in the eastern portion and mountain ranges in the western. The TEXAS DAVIS MTN AVA, where Blue Mtn Vyds is located, and the Guadalupe Mtns, where Llano Estacado has their Mount Sec Vyd, are in the Trans-Pecos. L.A.O.

Trefethen, historic winery property in the YOUNTVILLE AVA of southern NAPA VALLEY. The original winery was called Eschol, after the biblical tale of Jacob's spies who returned from 'the land of milk and honey' bearing a grape cluster so large two men were needed to carry it. Eschol is now the winery's second label. The Trefethens bought the property in 1968 and restored the magnificent redwood, gravity flow winery building, which had been erected in 1886 by the same architect responsible for CH MONTELENA, Far Niente (see OAKVILLE AVA), and the Greystone Winery which now houses the Culinary Institute of America. The Trefethens own 600 acres in the middle of the valley, replete with airstrip down the center. They produce 100,000 cases a year and sell grapes to many other wineries.

The most noteworthy item among the Trefethen offerings is the Chardonnay. Unlike most in Napa, or in CA for that matter, the majority portion of the Trefethen is fermented in *stainless steel, prevented from undergoing *MLF, and then aged only briefly in older *barriques. It is a style of Chardonnay dependent on the grapes, and on the gradual development of bouquet in the bottle. To that end, each year Trefethen holds a quantity back for release at age 5 or 6 under their Library Selection moniker. While applauding the choice this program provides consumers, one wonders if a cooler climate and a less fertile vineyard site which caused the grapes to struggle a bit more might not yield more character in these bottle matured wines. B.C.C.

Treleaven, label for King Ferry Winery, a small Chardonnay specialist on the eastern edge of New York's FINGER LAKES district.

From the first vintage in 1988, Treleaven Chardonnay has settled into a stylish, full *MLF wine exploring the influence of barrels from various American and European regions and coopers. The reserve bottling comprises the best barrels for extended ageing, and a private reserve is released in exceptional vintages. The winery also makes consistently good Riesling from its 17-acre Cayuga Lake vineyard. It buys Bordeaux variety grapes from a Long Island vineyard for red wine. Production in 1998 was 5,500 cases, with long-term projections to double. R.F.

Truchard, vineyardists in the Napa portion of the CARNEROS AVA who in 1991 started their own 10,000-case winery. They own 170 acres though, and continue to sell grapes to many other wineries. The emphasis of the vineyard, as with most in Carneros, is on Chardonnay and Pinot Noir with a smaller specialty in Merlot. The superstar of Truchard's winery offerings, however, is Syrah from a small 4-acre plot on a rocky slope behind the winery. Densely concentrated, with much more weight in the mid-

palate than other varieties grown in Carneros, Truchard's Syrah is a revelation. It is not particularly woody, yet no one would call it *fruit-driven either. The aroma is more like East Indian spices and blackstrap molasses. B.C.C.

tufa, Californians use this term to describe lightweight rock and soils of volcanic origins which are extremely porous and thus well drained. This usage is different from that employed by Europeans (see *tufa).

2, 4-D, introduced in 1947, is the most commonly used herbicide worldwide and third most widespread in Canada and the US. It effectively makes grape growing (as well as cotton, tobacco, and tomato production) impossible. The vine is most susceptible during leaf development each spring. In the grainfields of the MIDWEST in particular it is a considerable deterrent to viticulture. Spray is the most destructive form, but even its granular use can be harmful. Widespread use has diminished since the mid-1980s, allowing the expansion of grapevines into areas once unfeasible. P.W.F.

Ukiah, see MENDOCINO.

umami. Californian Tim Hanni, America's first *Master of Wine researched Japanese studies from the 1930s on umami, out of which developed the monosodium glutamate industry. Hanni says umami is an additional taste sense, like sweet and bitter, but more closely related to the sensation of savoriness. Hanni hypothesizes that glutamates exist at widely varied concentrations in different foods and wines, and that they are potentiated by ribonucleotides, commonly found in fermented products (eg soy sauce, wine), to yield various levels of the umami sensation.   B.C.C.

Umpqua AVA, approved in 1984, and where the OREGON wine renaissance began when Dick Sommers left UC *Davis in 1961 to open Hillcrest Vyds. The AVA runs north to south, about 70 mi long and 35 mi wide, along the middle bar of the Z-shaped river in hilly, lightly forested country. The Umpqua AVA, like its neighbor to the south the ROGUE, is dominated by sub-valley *mesoclimates tucked amongst the northern edge of the Klamath Mountains. The Umpqua River flows from the Cascade Mountains through the Coast Range to the Pacific Ocean, allowing cool marine air to penetrate inland to cool the vineyards in summer, and to provide sufficient rainfall to nourish grapevines. Six wineries are located here along Interstate 5, the main traffic artery from CA to WA. Roseburg is the AVA's economic center. Nearby hillsides rise abruptly to 500 ft on many sides above the valley floor. *Degree days hover around 2,500.

The Umpqua is slightly cooler than the Rogue, but generally warmer than WILLAMETTE VALLEY. Bordeaux varieties are grown as well as Burgundy and Germanic varieties. Recent plantings even include Dolcetto, Syrah, and Tempranillo. Umpqua wines have a touch more ripeness than Willamette wines, highlighting more of the berry flavors.

NOTABLE PROPERTIES
Henry Estate, producer of distinctive, rich Chardonnay and Pinot Noir aged in American oak and home to *Scott Henry, best known for his internationally adopted trellis system which runs a set of canes from one cordon upward and another set downward from a second cordon. The effect is a thin vertical wall with every leaf in the sun and all the fruit positioned about waist high for easy harvest.   R.I.

US label regulations are administered by BATF and apply to all wines shipped across state lines. Individual states may have laws which are more, or less, stringent than those of the federal government. Labels must be submitted to BATF for approval prior to application on bottles. Several humorous instances of BATF disapproval have occurred because regulators thought particular graphics were salacious. The most famous was a *Ch Mouton-Rothschild 1993 label featuring a reproduced painting of a young nude girl. Bottles sold in the US had a blank space where bottles sold in Europe had the picture. Although the blank space bottles are rarer, the naked girl bottles sell for more money at auction.

GEOGRAPHICAL LABELING
For a label to carry an AVA appellation 85% of the grapes must have come from that AVA. To use a country, state, or county name on a US label, 75% of the wine must come from the place named. In the case of varietally labeled wines which also use a place name, 75% of the named grape variety in a bottle must come from the appellation named.

This further restriction was promulgated to stop the following abuse: 60 units of Napa Chardonnay might be extended with 15 units of Fresno Chardonnay and 25 units of Napa Chenin Blanc, then sold for a price 30% less than true Napa Chardonnay. Today that practice would be illegal.

If a vineyard is named on a label, 95% of the grapes must have come from that vineyard, which in turn must fall within the appellation cited on the label, be it an approved AVA or a geopolitical unit such as a county or a state.

The 75% content rule is a federal regulation. That means a wine which is blended half and half from grapes grown in CA and grapes grown in GA would have to use 'American' as the appellation on its label in order to be sold in interstate commerce or to be exported. It would not need federal approval, however, if it were merely going to be sold within the state of GA. The state regulation in GA only requires 40% native fruit. So that same wine could legally say 'Produce of Georgia' as long as it was not sold outside that state's boundaries.

VARIETAL LABELING
A wine must be made with a minimum of 75% of the grape named on the label. This law was changed from 51% in 1983. In 1975 more than 55% of the white grapes crushed in CA were *Thompson Seedless, which led to that variety being known jokingly as the Fresno Chardonnay because it was perfectly legal to call a wine Chardonnay that was nearly half cheap, neutral flavored Thompson. *Varietal labeling was popularized by professors from the Enology Dept at the Univ of CA following Prohibition as a means of inducing growers to plant better quality winegrapes. It had been legal for households to make 200 gal of wine per year during Prohibition. That led to vast plantings, but for the most part these were cosmetically sound, physically tough grapes which made inferior wine. Varietal labeling is a largely New World phenomenon which rapidly improved the mix of grapes in American vineyards in the last half of the 20th century.

ALTERNATIVES TO VARIETAL LABELS
Wines that do not use a varietal label will either use a *generic name for the wine type or a PROPRIETARY name. Generic is deemed in the US to be a name, usually derived from a place, which indicates where a style, not necessarily very close to that of the wine in question, originated. 'Burgundy' is a common US example, but a wine so labeled would be barred from Europe where Burgundy is a controlled and protected appellation. Claret, an English term for red bordeaux, is another example of a generic name used in the US, generally indicating a red wine that is rather lighter and drier than one labeled burgundy. OR state regulations, incidentally, are more restrictive on this

issue than are US federal regulations or CA regulations for they prohibit the use of European place names on labels.

*Champagne is a special instance of the generic label issue. In 1945 all the wine producing countries of the world signed an agreement in Madrid not to use the name 'champagne' generically to indicate sparkling wine and to restrict it to wines made in the region of the same name in northeast France—all except the US. American mass marketers have spent a lot of money connecting the concept of celebration, sparkling wine, and the term 'champagne' in US consumers' perception. Based on this long-term advertising investment, GALLO was able in 1993 to get a US federal court to stop BATF from prohibiting the use of the term 'champagne' as a generic type for US-made sparkling wine. The phrase must be used in close proximity to the appellation, eg California Champagne, and it cannot be in a bigger typeface than the appellation, but it is legal despite the damage it surely visits upon US-French diplomatic relations. No French champagne house operating in CA (see CHAMPAGNE) would dream of putting champagne on the label of sparkling wine they produce in CA.

Fascinatingly, CA law requires 100% of any wine bearing any CA place name to come from grapes grown in CA. Hence, a French wine labeled San Francisco Treat could not be legally imported into CA, although it could be imported and sold elsewhere in the US.

*Port is another instructive case. Like champagne, port is a protected name in Europe and most of the rest of the world where it is restricted to the fortified wines produced in the Douro Valley in northern Portugal. In the late 1980s QUADY winery started using the name Starboard on their Vintage Port so they could export it to Europe. Starboard is thus an example of a proprietary name; a name to which its creator could establish exclusive rights if he wanted to go to the expense and trouble of defending those exclusive rights in court. If Andy Quady were to encourage other CA producers of port-style wines to use the name Starboard, it would become a generic name.

*Blush is a similar example. The first CA winery to use that phrase on a label, as a type name for a very lightly pink wine, was a small operation named Mill Creek Vyd near Healdsburg in northern Sonoma. They chose not to incur the expense of defending their exclusive rights to the name once bigger wineries picked the phrase up. Hence it is now a generic name.

*Sherry may provide an example of how hard it is to put the genie back in the bottle once a name becomes genericized. Sherry is analogous to port, in that it is a corruption of a place name, in this case Jerez, from whence sherry comes in Spain. Recently 'sherry' has become a legally protected name in Europe. Since consumption of sherries made in North America is limited, and none is exported to Europe in significant quantity, it is not immediately apparent whether any American companies would put up a fight over their right to use 'sherry' as a generic name in the US.

This distinction between proprietary names and generic names is well illustrated by the *Meritage story. When the varietal labeling regulation was changed from 51% to 75% in 1983, a number of CA wineries were thrown into a quandary relative to Cabernet Sauvignon and its use in blends with the other Bordeaux grape varieties (Merlot, Cabernet Franc, Malbec, and Petit Verdot for reds). Using more than 75% Cabernet Sauvignon often made the wines seem thuggish, powerful but lacking subtlety. As a practical matter, using less than 75% Cabernet Sauvignon made the wine unsaleable at a premium price because it had to be labeled with a generic name, such as claret, or a proprietary name which few consumers would recognize. Dan Berger, then wine columnist for the Los Angeles Times, came up with the idea of a coined generic name everyone could use, and initiated a contest to pick one. Meritage (rhymes with heritage) was the winner. Since then a trade organization has formed which took proprietary control over the name, for both reds and whites—regulating its use and promoting, quite successfully, its broad recognition by consumers.

Since they both serve the same purpose, sometimes proprietary names will be combined with generic names for marketing or humorous reasons: Spaghetti Red Table Wine, Adequate White Table Wine, etc.

VINTAGE DATE

This designation on a US label is optional. To use it, 95% of the wine must come from grapes grown in the year stated. The 5% allowance is to permit barrels to be topped up during ageing.

HEALTH WARNINGS

Although it is not required on export labels, the following statement on wine labels has been mandatory in the US since 1988:

Government Warning: (1) According to the Surgeon General, women should not drink alcoholic beverages during pregnancy because of the risk of birth defects. (2) Consumption of alcoholic beverages impairs your ability to drive a car or operate machinery, and may cause health problems.

The same is true of the statement 'Contains Sulfites' for wines with 10 ppm or more of SO_2. The US regulation requiring this *sulfite statement was enacted to protect a miniscule constituency of severe asthmatics who may be allergic to sulfur based compounds.

In 1999 BATF approved the use of an alternate health warning label for wine which would direct consumers either to their personal physician or to the US Dept of Agriculture's publications on dietary guidelines for information concerning the positive health effects of wine consumption (see Distribution essay, p 21), although this was hotly contended by staunchly conservative Senator Strom Thurmond.

ALCOHOL CONTENT

Federal regulations require table wines to state their alcohol content by volume on the label within 1.5% alcohol by volume of what it actually is. Consistent with this regulation, and the CA sunshine, it is also legal to use the phrase Table Wine to indicate a wine somewhere between 11 and 13.9% *alcoholic strength. A higher excise tax is levied on wines above 14% alcohol. The tax rate goes up again at 17% alcohol. Sherry-type fortified wines may have 17–20% alcohol, and their statement of alcohol level must be within 1% alcohol by volume of the actual level. Fortified wines other than sherry types must be between 18% and 20% alcohol, again with a 1% tolerance in the alcohol statement. Only sparkling wines are taxed higher in the US than fortified wines.

BOTTLER

US labels must contain the name and business location of the company that bottled the wine. As a practical matter those names might not reveal much, since companies may call themselves anything they wish merely by filing a fictitious business name statement. But the location is often informative. If the wine is bottled in Modesto, CA, the odds are very good it was made by E & J GALLO.

Several phrases prescribed for this mandatory statement are intended to reveal the bottler's role in the production of the wine, but recent court rulings have removed much of their meaning. 'Cellared by' implies the various production operations occurred at a facility not owned by the brand owner. That could mean anything from 'purchased in bulk by' to 'custom crushed under the close supervision of,' although this latter

facing: Although winter floods generate hysterical coverage by the American broadcast media and much wringing of bureaucratic hands at the US Army Corps of Engineers, their effect on vineyards is generally negligible beyond deposition of a beneficial silt layer.
overleaf above: The annual summer **International Pinot Noir Celebration** in McMinnville draws sell-out crowds from all the major producing regions of the world for its technically sophisticated, yet socially informal, sessions.
below: Netting the vineyard, seen here at **Macari Vyds**, Long Island, NY, is a time-consuming but necessary procedure to thwart greedy birds at harvest.

above: Disease-resistant, cold-hardy American **Niagara** grapes have hairy undersides to their leaves, 'slip skins,' intensely perfumed aroma, and 'foxy' flavors.

left: Many fine Napa Valley winery buildings are being reclaimed 100 years after they were first constructed. Inglenook (now **Niebaum-Coppola**) is one of several magnificent winery buildings designed by Hamden McIntyre, dean of the early Napa architects. Shown here is the staircase, and overleaf a view of the main entrance.

connotation would usually appear as 'Vinted by'. The phrase 'Produced and bottled by' requires 75% of the wine to have been made by the brand owner in their own bonded facility.

To use *estate bottled in the US the winery and the vineyard(s) must both fall within the appellation shown on the label, and the producing winery must 'own or control' all the vineyards used. 'Control' implies at least a long-term lease, or a contract with specified management practices and the right to decline grapes in any instance of non-compliance.   B.C.C.

Utah, northern tier state in the DESERT SOUTHWEST region, as well known for the strictly regulated attitudes of its large Mormon population as it is for its world-class ski resorts at Park City and Snow Bird, and for Robert Redford's Sundance Film Festival.

When the Mormons organized in Fayette, NY, wine was an integral part of their services. They brought that tradition with them to UT, and launched the wine industry there. Brigham Young sent colonies from Salt Lake City to southern UT. It is thought that John Harris brought *Mission grapes to the area between 1858 and 1860. John Naegle, a German with winemaking experience, was put in charge of plantings of these grapes. He opened Naegle Winery at Toquerville in the Virgin River Valley, a district called Dixie. Naegle's winery operated from the 1860s until state Prohibition took effect in 1910. Wine was employed by the Mormons in their Holy Sacrament, as medicine, for celebrations, and for sale to Gentiles. Dixie Mormons even paid tithes in wine. But widespread immoderate use, and the declining value of tithes paid in wine which could not be sold because of competition from CA, caused Brigham Young to ban wine outright and to replace its use in the sacrament with water in 1890. Most vines were abandoned by the advent of Prohibition.

Revival began with test plantings of Thompson Seedless by UT State Univ in Dixie in the 1960s. Commercial interests also planted Chenin Blanc in this area. Additional test plantings were made in the same area and many other parts of the contiguous four states, even as far north as Price, UT, in the 1970s by the Four Corners Regional Economic Development Commission working in concert with the Univ of AZ. Most of those plantings are now completely gone, thanks to *Pierce's disease.

Today, most wine production comes from 12–15 growers in three areas near Moab in the east-central part of the state: 5–6 acres in Castle Valley, 20 mi north of Moab; 15–20 acres in Spanish Valley, south of Moab; and 15 acres in Montezuma Canyon in the Monticello area, 60 mi south of Moab. Production is 10,000–12,000 gal annually. Soils in the area are very poor, mostly sand. There are six wineries, including one run by a religious cult called Summum which 'donates' wine to its followers in exchange for 'donations,' and La Caille, a restaurant which sells the yield of 3 adjoining acres of Seyval Blanc on its premises. A new licensee called Native Wines plans to produce *fruit wines from cultivated and wild fruit.

The region around Moab experiences similar growing conditions to the GRAND VALLEY AVA of CO, just east across the border. Temperatures can be hot during the day, regularly reaching 100°F in July and Aug. At night the cool, moist canyon winds blow off the top of the mountains, and the temperature drops 30–40°F. The last spring *frost is usually Apr 15, but the record is June 2 in this 4,200 ft high region. Overhead sprinklers offer some protection. *Hail damage is occasional and spotty, hitting one vineyard, but missing another nearby. Rainfall is a scant 7–8 in, most occurring during two-week periods in spring and fall. The latter can cause significant damage during harvest. *Chaptalization was employed for the first time in 1998, but acidity is quite adequate.

Utah Black grapes are a curiosity unique to the state. They were supplied by GENEVA in the mid-1970s, as cuttings thought to be Pinot Noir, but the vines turned out to be very winter hardy and extremely vigorous, yielding grapes with flavors resembling an American hybrid, possibly Baco Noir or a cross between Baco Noir and Pinot Noir. The native species *Vitis arizonica* is not used for commercial wine production, although it is found clinging and climbing everywhere in UT.

UT's liquor laws are restrictive. Liquor stores and wine shops are all operated by the state MONOPOLY and are scarce. There are a dozen of the former, and two of the latter for the million-plus residents of the Salt Lake City region. The state-run store in Moab attracts considerable tourist business. A winery wishing to sell wine at these retail outlets must deliver to the monopoly warehouse in Salt Lake City, which in turn distributes to the stores. Wineries may operate a tasting room, if a license to operate as a 'state packaging agency' is obtained. Wine must be sold at the winery for the same price as it is at state retail outlets. Winery tasting rooms are allowed to offer samples to visitors, but by law cannot charge for the privilege. A restaurant wishing to sell wine must purchase the products from the state stores, at full retail price. There are no volume discounts, either for consumers or for restaurants. Restaurants then resell the wine at the same price they bought it from the state store plus an allowable corkage fee. Restaurants are not allowed to solicit wine sales; the customer must actively ask to see the wine list. Restaurants are also prohibited from advertising the sale of wine and spirits (beer is allowed). Hence it is common to see signs announcing Food and Ghosts: 'Ghosts' being the name restaurant owners have invented to notify patrons they sell wine.

NOTABLE PROPERTIES

Arches, winery in Moab, 200 mi southwest of Salt Lake City, recently purchased by Colin Fryer, a businessman from Salt Lake. Winemaker is Ted Telford. Vinifera production totals 2,000–4,000 cases, of which 60% is from UT grapes, and the remainder from CO, or occasionally Elephant Butte in NM. UT/CO blends are more impressive than one might imagine. An example is Arches 1992 Syrah, made from CO grapes, a dead ringer for a good Côtes-du-Rhône, and better than any Syrah made by a CO winery. Another winner is their 1997 Desert Nectar, a LATE HARVEST Seyval Blanc with apricot and fruit cocktail aromas, sweet but not cloying, good balance and a lingering finish.   R.T.S.

VA stands for designated **Viticultural Area** in CANADA, ie approved appellations currently authorized by VQA for use in Ontario and BC. There are seven VAs at present: FRASER VALLEY, SIMILKAMEEN VALLEY, OKANAGAN VALLEY, and VANCOUVER ISLAND, which are all in BC; and NIAGARA PENINSULA, LAKE ERIE NORTH SHORE, PELEE ISLAND, which are all in Ontario. Pending VQA approval, two viticultural areas will be recognized in NS: the Annapolis Valley; and Malagash, a coastal growing region along Northumberland Strait.   L.F.B.

Valiant, dark-skinned American hybrid made in 1967 at the SD Agricultural Station for both wine and the table which has survived winter temperatures as low as –45°F.

Valle de Guadalupe, the premier fine winegrowing region in MEXICO, located 50 mi south of the US border on the Pacific Ocean side of Baja (or lower) California. The valley itself opens onto Bahia de Todos Santos at the resort town of Ensenada. Isle de Todos Santos in the middle of the bay is one of the three most prominent big wave surfing locations in the world. The Guadalupe Valley stretches for 15 mi east into the foothills of the 7,000–10,000 ft mountains which form the spine of the 1,000 mi long, 25–75 mi wide Baja California peninsula. Any more than 75 mi south of the US border, the peninsula (called simply Baja by most gringos) is arid, rugged, and sparsely populated, except for its tip at Cabo San Lucas which is a popular resort and haven for sport fishing enthusiasts intent on marlin. A single track, most of it dirt, runs the length of the peninsula. The peninsula is separated from the major land mass of Mexico by the pull-apart basin which contains the 50–100 mi wide Gulf of California. This placid warm water sea in the lee of the Baja mountains is a marine wonderland, serving as the nursery where gray whales come from AK each year to give birth.

Although the history of wine in Mexico dates from 1521, vines came to Baja at much the same time and in much the same manner that they came to Alta California, arriving with the missionaries in the latter half of

the 18th century. The first vineyards were planted at San Diego in 1769 before anyone thought about making a distinction between upper and lower California. The first vineyard in what is now Baja was planted by Spanish Jesuits in 1791 at the Mission of St Thomas Aquinas 20 mi south of present-day Ensenada. The first vines in Guadalupe Valley were planted by Dominican missionaries in 1834, but abandoned after an Indian attack in 1840. Settlement of the valley began in earnest when a pacifist Russian religious sect called Molocanes arrived in 1904 fleeing conscription into the army of the Czar. They planted grapes along with other crops.

On the western side of the Baja peninsula there are today many farming valleys running out of the central mountains toward the Pacific Ocean. Their commerce is limited by lack of water and by lack of a developed transportation system. Hence many resemble subsistence communities with a primitive road crossing the middle of the valley from north to south and a small fishing village at the western mouth of the valley on the Pacific Ocean. These communities are populated with a diverse ethnic mix. Weather patterns in these valleys are not dramatically different from those found in coastal areas anywhere south of the Tehachapi Mtns in CA (see SANTA BARBARA CO), which would include US winegrowing districts such as TEMECULA, Cucamonga, and the Ventura River watershed (see LOS ANGELES). There are more than 20,000 acres of vinifera winegrapes planted in Baja, and they supply more than 80% of the wine made in Mexico (at least that which is not then distilled into brandy). Moreover the Guadalupe Valley is north of the 32nd parallel, which puts it further from the equator than the STE GENEVIEVE plantings in TX and very similar in latitude to AVAs in AZ and NM, as well as important winegrowing districts such as the Orange River in *South Africa, the Hunter Valley and the Swan River districts in *Australia, and Aconcagua in *Chile. The Guadalupe Valley receives cooling breezes from the ocean every afternoon and often gets high level fog in the late evening. It cools off rapidly at night because

of the 300–2,300 ft drop in its elevation range. Soils are primarily granitic sand, with some loam in certain locations, but overall low fertility and a slight alkalinity. Vineyard expansion is currently limited by water resources. Annual precipitation ranges from 8–15 in depending on elevation. Some of it can arrive during the July MONSOON SEASON in the DESERT SOUTHWEST region, but those storm systems are usually east of the high mountains which form the middle of the Baja peninsula. Some rain can also arrive during Sept due to HURRICANES in the Pacific, but harvest is likely to be over by then. The harvest festival, or Fiesta de Vendimia, is held in Guadalupe Valley during Aug each year. Because agriculture is so scattered in Baja, all the vineyards need to be covered with nets in July to keep birds from pecking at the grapes.

An eastern lobe of the Guadalupe Valley, some 15 mi from Ensenada and above 2,000 ft of elevation, is called **Valle de Calafia**. A western section of the Guadalupe Valley 5 miles inland from Ensenada at 300–600 ft of elevation is called **Valle de San Antonio de las Minas**. San Antonio has the least amount of DIURNAL TEMPERATURE FLUCTUATION. It is cooler during the day, averaging 3,200 *degree days, and warmer at night. Calafia has the most temperature fluctuation and the most continental climate. Calafia averages 250 hours of temperatures below 32°F each winter, insuring vine dormancy. During the growing season it averages 3,800 degree days. Guadalupe is the overarching name likely to appear on any label, in part because the Virgin of Guadalupe is a uniquely Mexican religious symbol having to do with a legendary miracle leading to the conversion of an Indian at a location outside Mexico City in the early 1500s. It is this Indian involvement which cements the Virgin of Guadalupe in the hearts of many Mexicans. South of Ensenada at distances of 20 mi and 100 mi respectively are two coastal valleys similar to Guadalupe. The first is called **Valle de Santo Tomás**; the second **Valle de San Vicente**. Both are significant grape growing areas. In recent history they have sent their grapes to wineries in the Guadalupe Valley. The wineries were built in the Guadalupe Valley because of the proximity to Ensenada and because a road runs northeast out of Guadalupe Valley to the US border at Tecate. SANTO TOMÁS, however, completed their architecturally triumphant new winery in the valley from which they took their name in 1997.

In a major conversion from the Pedro Ximénez, Palamino, and Mission grapes which dominated Mexican wine production prior to the mid-1980s, the white wines produced in Baja today are usually Chardonnay, Sauvignon Blanc, and Chenin Blanc, the last often blended with Colombard. Too often the whites are darkly colored, bordering on brown-gold, with flabby structure and dilute flavors. Santo Tomás and MONTE XANIC wineries do better than most: Monte Xanic by acidifying their wines; Santo Tomás by sourcing grapes in the cooler San Vicente and San Antonio districts. In general red wines are more successful. The Meritage blends can be quite good, with green bean notes woven into ripe berry flavors and a full *mouthfeel. Rarely do these wines exhibit concentrated flavors, but rather the stylish length that matches nicely to food and often an expansive bouquet after 5–7 years of bottle maturation.

NOTABLE PROPERTIES
Ch Camou, elegantly designed gravity flow winery 9 mi inland from the coast at about 1,250 ft elevation. Vineyard includes a section of 50-year-old vines. Everything is drip irrigated from 45 ft deep wells. Chardonnay, Sauvignon Blanc, and Chenin Blanc are the whites; Cabernet Sauvignon, Cabernet Franc, Merlot, and Zinfandel are the reds. Harvesting is done into small lug boxes, then clusters are sorted on a triage conveyor as they enter the crusher. Whites are picked in Aug at 24°B and not acid adjusted. Chardonnay and Sauvignon Blanc are *barrel fermented, but not put through *MLF. Reds are aged in French oak. This well-financed winery has its own bottling line.

Two levels of wine are made. The Chardonnay and red Meritage blend are too ripe, flabby, and overly oaked, but the second tier wines called Flor de Guadalupe are nicely balanced and cleanly fruity. Best of the bunch is a $9 Zinfandel with 10% each of Cabs Franc and Sauvignon. It has 6 g/l of acid and comes from a DRY-FARMED vineyard 8 miles closer to the ocean than the winery, which makes 6,000 cases and exports 40% of it to Europe.

Domecq, large winery with classic visitor verandas, jumbled *amphorae sculpture in the courtyard, and cool tile floors throughout, located deep in the Valle de Calafia 15 mi inland from Ensenada at 2,000 ft of elevation. It is owned by ALLIED DOMECQ of Britain, producing 700,000 cases, but only bottling 200,000. The remainder is shipped to Mexico City for bottling. The winery owns 1,000 acres and buys grapes from 70 private growers and *ejidos*, the communally owned farms established during the Mexican Revolution. In the last half of the 1990s American winemaker Ron McClendon was busy transforming the winery from a traditional Spanish style to a more delicate and modern *New World design. The previous technique had been to extract as much as possible from the grapes using an old Spanish continuous screw press. The wines were then aged for years in large Yugoslavian oak upright casks. Wines were labeled generically, and priced based on years in cask. Most of the grapes were varieties such as Tempranillo (called Valdepeñas), Grignolino, and Portuguese Blue (Blauer Portuguieser, presumably) planted on their OWN ROOTS. McClendon's goal was to plant 250 acres of clones of *international varieties on *rootstock, and to use a new crusher and press to make fresher, less tannic wines for labeling as varietals. It is unclear whether trading rusticity for blandness will be a successful strategy. Very little wine is sold in the US. Most exports go to Europe, although they may bear *négociant labels.   B.C.C.

See also L. A. CETTO, MONTE XANIC.

Vancouver, BRITISH COLUMBIA's urban center, located at the southwestern edge of continental Canada (but not on VANCOUVER ISLAND). It is one of Canada's fastest growing cities thanks to a considerable influx of Hong Kong Chinese in the 1990s. The population of the greater metropolitan area is nearly 2 million. Exciting multi-ethnic communities provide interesting dining opportunities. Highest per capita wine consumption in Canada. This is a good wine market despite awkward distribution regulations imposed by the provincial government. Consumers can buy expensive, limited availability wines by special ordering through the provincial liquor stores. The BC Wine Institute directs the VQA program and runs twelve VQA wine stores.

Vancouver Island VA is situated off the west coast of BRITISH COLUMBIA. The west side of this 250 mi long island faces right into the teeth of oncoming Pacific Ocean storms. Hence all vineyard land and wineries are nestled 50 mi away on the east side of the island in the lee of the Vancouver Island Ranges, a ridge of mountains rising 2,500 ft.

These producers are about an hour's drive northwest of Victoria, which occupies the island's southern tip and is the capital of the province. There are about 50 acres of grapes grown around the town of Duncan, with about a half-dozen wineries, all of them started since 1990. Cooler climate and earlier ripening varieties of vinifera and hybrids are grown. Most of the soil is a mix of limestone and sand, with areas of clay, and is the result of the receding glaciation of over 10,000 years ago. Wines from this region reflect the cooler maritime climate and are lighter and crisper with a delicate (and sometimes pronounced) fruit definition.

NOTABLE PROPERTIES
Venturi Schulze Vyds was founded in 1993 by Italian-born Giordano Venturi and Australian Marilyn Shulze Venturi. Planted grapes include Pinot Noir, Pinot Gris, (Pinot) Auxerrois, Siegerrebe, Schönburger, Ortega, and Kerner. Table wine and sparkling wine are made.   R.A.I.

Ventana Vyds, premier vineyard in the ARROYO SECO AVA of MONTEREY Co better known in America for its designation on other wineries' labels than it is for its own brand name. Owner Doug Meador started during the tax break heyday of the early 1970s buying a nursery he named December-Pacific, to supply the new mist-propagated, heat-treated grapevines to vineyard syndicates which were planting all over the Salinas Valley and Paso Robles. In 1975 the tax laws changed, and all the card houses tumbled. Meador took a lease on a 275-acre vineyard with an option to buy. An expensive divorce in the mid-1980s had a deleterious effect on the fortunes and the size of the Ventana winery brand, but nothing has altered the quarter-century meteoric rise of Ventana-sourced fruit.

Top Chardonnays, Rieslings, and Gewürztraminers are made every year by a broad collection of wineries who vineyard designate their wines. Cronin and Ahlgren are two brands with 20-year vertical selections of the Chardonnay which clearly demonstrate the unusual pineapple-like aroma of the young wines, as well as their reliable 10–12-year bottle maturation potential. Rieslings are also pungent with citrus and apricot aromas no matter who makes the wine. Gewürztraminer is very perfumed and the Thomas Fogarty Winery makes a fine example. Despite these guaranteed varieties, two others are even more distinctive: Syrah and the Musqué clone of Sauvignon Blanc. Meador planted a couple of acres of Syrah in 1976 because he thought the wind in Salinas bore a resemblance to the *mistral* of the

Rhône Valley. The signature of Syrah made from Ventana Vyd grapes is black pepper spice combined with dense, jammy fruit. The wines have crisp acid, but it is the immensely concentrated fruit weight in the middle that raises them so far past the world standard, and the like-to-make-you-sneeze spiciness that makes them unique. River Run Winery makes a good one every year.

The Musqué clone of Sauvignon Blanc was a Meador discovery one day when he noticed a particular set of five vines had very luscious, tropically scented fruit, completely unlike the asparagus nose which was routine among Wente clone Sauvignon Blanc grown in the Salinas Valley. Tracing those five vines back through the genetic library plot at UC Davis, Meador found they had been called by several names including Savagnin Musqué. Professor Olmo remembered those particular cuttings having arrived in a bunch of budwood from Alsace. Meador rapidly propagated 23 acres at Ventana. These grapes effortlessly perform a trick highly regarded in Marlborough, *New Zealand, but difficult for the Kiwis to achieve without a warm vintage: a mango/guava fragrance to balance the *methoxypyrazine-driven, grassier background notes. This Ventana clone of Sauvignon Blanc is an answer waiting for CA winemakers to ask the right questions.　　　　　　　　B.C.C.

Ventura, 1974 Vineland white wine crossing of CHELOIS and Elvira whose outstanding winter hardiness makes it popular with some Canadian and a few northeastern US growers.

Verdelet, or Seibel 9110, French hybrid making delicate white wine from delicate vines which also produce for the table.

Vignoles, French hybrid making very respectable white wine in cooler Eastern wine regions. This low yielding vine was created by RAVAT from *Seibel and Pinot Noir varieties and is not the most robust, but wine quality makes up for this.

Vincent, hybrid developed in Canada.

Vincor, CANADA's largest wine company and fourth largest in North America with wineries in BC, Ontario, Quebec, and New Brunswick. Vincor is also a *négociant for several wines from France, Chile, CA, and Australia. In 1998 Vincor had 23% of the Canadian wine and refreshment beverage (coolers, ciders, etc) market. The present company had its beginnings in 1989 when John Labatt Company, owners of Ch Gai Winery, put the winery up for sale. Several employees won the bid in a leveraged buy-out and changed the name to Cartier. In 1992 Cartier merged with INNISKILLIN Winery, followed a year later by another merger with Bright's Wines. Subsequent purchases in the next two years included Okanagan Vyds in BC and London Winery in Ontario. A spin-off of their premium VQA line, Jackson-Triggs (named after Don Triggs and Allan Jackson, two of the senior managers in the buyout, now CEO and Vice President) will be a new winery and vineyard on a prime site in NIAGARA-ON-THE-LAKE.　　L.F.B.

Vin de Curé, wine produced in CANADA according to VQA regulations exclusively from fresh grapes that have been harvested after achieving a minimum of 20°B on the vine. Only Riesling and Vidal grape varieties may be used. After harvest the grapes are left to dry on frames with perforated bases in a dry place until they yield a *must of at least 32°B. No *chaptalization nor addition of *sweet reserve is allowed. The wines are similar in style to the *vin santo of Italy.
　　　　　　　　　　　　　　L.F.B.

Vineland Estates, the first winery in ON-TARIO to charge C$125 a bottle (in their restaurant) for a red wine, their 1995 Merlot, challenging the caution that Ontario can grow only white wines well. This distinction augmented their already well-established reputation as one of Ontario's foremost producers of Rieslings and Chardonnays. Herman Weis, noted German nurseryman/winemaker, had identified this NIAGARA ESCARPMENT property as a prime site for his Mosel Riesling clone 21B. By 1978 he had planted 50 acres and started a winery. Entrepreneur John Howard bought the winery from Weis in 1994 with the aim of continuing to develop its bucolic appeal as well as expand its line to include top quality reds and sparkling wines. Howard, together with his development company, now controls a total of 300 acres that include Chardonnay and Cabernet Sauvignon with smaller plantings of Pinot Meunier, Pinot Gris, Auxerrois, and Viognier. The property combines a four-story production facility, retail store, and an upscale restaurant located in the original 1840 farmhouse. Vineland's Dry Rieslings are some of the best in the world: tensely structured, with understated green apple fruit, which unfolds slowly in the aftertaste as it makes friends with one's palate.　　　　　　　　　　L.F.B.

vinifera or **Vitis vinifera,** the species of the *Vitis* genus of vines most commonly used for wine production. It includes all the European varieties Chardonnay, Cabernet Sauvignon, Merlot, and so on.

Vintage Virginia, largest of VA's many wine festivals as well as the largest in the eastern US. It features VA wines, food, crafts, and entertainment. The festival takes place annually on the first Saturday and Sunday in June, at the Great Meadows equestrian center in The Plains (Fauquier Co one hour west of WASHINGTON DC). Attendance averages 30,000 annually.
　　　　　　　　　　　　　　R.G.L.

Virginia, first of the original thirteen colonies to cultivate winegrapes, the 'Mother of Presidents' is home to many historic sites. Notable examples include: Jamestown and Williamsburg from the Colonial era; Mt Vernon and Monticello from the Revolutionary era; the Manassas and Appomattox battlefields; and Arlington Natl Cemetery from the Civil War. VA leads wine production in the MID-ATLANTIC region, with 3,225 tons of winegrapes harvested in 1998 yielding 516,175 gal, or about 206,470 cases. VA has 140 vineyards growing 1,500 acres of vines, and 53 farm wineries. Seventy-one per cent of winegrape acreage in VA is planted with vinifera varieties, with Chardonnay leading in total acreage. The rapid rise in quality of VA wines in the 1990s owes much to the work of state viticulturist Dr Tony Wolf and state enologist Dr Bruce Zoecklein through their research at VA Polytechnic Institute.

VA has six approved AVAs: MONTICELLO in the upper Piedmont in central VA; SHENANDOAH VALLEY in the west; ROCKY KNOB and NORTH FORK OF ROANOKE River in the southwest; NORTHERN NECK GEORGE WASHINGTON BIRTHPLACE in the upper Tidewater; and EASTERN SHORE on the Delmarva Peninsula. However, the most significant viticultural districts so far in VA are: central VA, especially Albemarle Co (mostly within the Monticello AVA), northern VA (Loudoun and Fauquier counties), and the Shenandoah Valley. In general wines from the upper foothills of the Blue Ridge Mtns (from Rocky Knob in southwest VA to Fauquier Co in northern VA) have performed the best. The Blue Ridge Mtns also have the advantage of drawing thousands of visitors annually who travel the Skyline Drive.

CHARLOTTESVILLE and MIDDLEBURG are the epicenters respectively of the central and northern VA wine country, and both are noted for well-heeled residents with an avid interest in horses. There are many local hunts, or horse riding clubs, in these areas and throughout the PIEDMONT in VA. Steeplechasing attracts crowds from diverse economic groups. At the Foxfield Races which run in Apr and Sept in Charlottesville, it is customary for male spectators to wear ties. There is a symbiosis of local wine and the hunt country life. VA's largest wine festivals are held in the equestrian center at Great Meadows, and one Middleburg winery bills itself as located 'in the heart of VA's hunt country.' Both Middleburg and Charlottesville are in the upper Piedmont, but their wines may be differentiated by the higher *acidity found in Middleburg, and the fuller, riper fruit aromas found in Charlottesville to the south. In Charlottesville growers need higher elevations to achieve the crispness found in Middleburg. In fact it is common for winemakers, especially with Chardonnay, to blend batches from both locations seeking balance and complexity.

NOTABLE PROPERTIES

Autumn Hill Vyds, located in Monticello AVA just over the Albemarle Co line on Rt 810 in Greene Co, although rarely open to visitors. While proprietors Ed and Avra Schwab make reliable Chardonnay, as well as Riesling, their strength is in reds. Since the 1995 vintage, the Cabernet has included higher ratios of Cabernet Franc and Merlot, resulting in richer flavors with softer tannins. These latter are also bottled as varietals, blended with small amounts of the other two grapes, and all three wines perform well in competitions. The most impressive Autumn Hill red wine to date is their Horizon Rouge, a proprietary Meritage blend including all five major red Bordeaux grapes, which won a medal in CA's ORANGE CO FAIR competition. One of the treats of the VA harvest season festivals is to visit Autumn Hill (also called Blue Ridge Winery) in early Nov, and join in a vertical Cabernet tasting, including barrel samples. Production is 2,000 cases.

Afton Mtn Vyds, aptly named for its location in the scenic Rockfish Valley in the shadow of Afton Mtn in Nelson Co, this winery has earned a reputation for the consistent quality of its refreshing dry white wines: Chardonnay, Riesling, Gewürztraminer, and a Semillon/Sauvignon Blanc blend. Also produced are Cabernet Sauvignon, Merlot, and Pinot Noir. The vineyard is 11 acres in Monticello AVA. Annual production is 3,000 cases.

Naked Mtn Vyds, winery whose barrel fermented Chardonnay, with its burgundy-like nuances, was in the 1980s (along with Piedmont's) the standard for VA Chardonnay. Owner and winemaker Bob Harper was rewarded for his consistent quality with the Governor's Cup in 1991. While the style of Naked Mtn Chardonnay has remained the same, other VA wineries have made

advances. Also produced are small amounts of Riesling, Sauvignon Blanc, Cabernet Sauvignon, and Cabernet Franc. The Chardonnay continues to place in competitions, joined by the Cabernet Sauvignon. Naked Mtn's 1997 Cabernet Franc is particularly impressive. Production is 5,000 cases. The tasting room is a Swiss-style chalet with impressive views of the northern Blue Ridge Mtns. Located near Markham, near Interstate 66.

Oakencroft Vyds was founded in 1983 near Charlottesville in Monticello AVA by Felicia Warburg Rogan and her late husband John. Mrs Rogan has contributed significantly to the VA wine industry, especially as Chair of the VA Winegrowers' Advisory Board. During the 1980s, Oakencroft wines won local medals but did not achieve high distinction. In the early 1990s however, quality took a dramatic upward turn. First, Mrs Rogan hired Shep Rouse, formerly of Montdomaine and just setting up his own winery at Rockbridge Vyds, to make her wines. Second, she acquired fruit from Redlands Vyd, which produces some of the best wines in the state. By the mid-1990s, award-winning Oakencroft wines included Cabernet Sauvignon, Merlot, and Chardonnay. The vineyard is 13 acres, located 4 mi west of Charlottesville on Garth Road. Annual production is 6,000 cases.

Oasis Vyds. Located in Hume, southeast of Front Royal, on a high plateau beneath the Blue Ridge Mtns, Oasis is one of VA's oldest and largest wineries. Oasis achieved notoriety in 1997 for its non-vintage MÉTHODE CHAMPENOISE which was awarded 92 points in Beverage Testing Institute's international competition in Chicago, putting it on a par with some top Champagnes. By 1990 Oasis was producing consistently good Chardonnay, which still performs well occasionally, and three varietal red bordeaux wines. By the mid to late 1990s however, the performance of these wines was less consistent. Riesling and proprietary white and blush table wines are also produced.

Oasis is noted for its active marketing to the upscale Hunt Country set and the professional population of Washington, DC, with features such as a cigar room at the winery, a club membership with special privileges, corporate retreats, and 'Polo wine and twilight dine' events. Oasis also features a unique event for a VA winery, a ceremonial blessing of the vines at harvest, complete with Gregorian chanters. The owner's son Tareq Salahi, a graduate of UC Davis, is winemaker. Production is 22,000 cases.

Shenandoah Vyds was the first winery established in Shenandoah Valley, near Edin-

burg in 1976. It has a reputation for crisp, dry whites with refreshing acidity. Riesling and Chardonnay are consistently fine. Shenandoah's specialty is varietally labeled Chambourcin, which has performed impressively for over two decades. Founder Emma Randel's success with Chambourcin has inspired others in the East, such as Richard Naylor in PA, to make quality red wines using this French hybrid. At Shenandoah the Founder's Reserve Chambourcin resembles a high quality Valpolicella with earthy, cherry notes and smooth tannins. Cabernet Sauvignon and Merlot are also produced. The vineyard is 40 acres, production is 8,000 cases.

Williamsburg, winery also producing the Dominion Cellars label. Williamsburg is VA's largest winery producing 50,000 cases. Located on a 300-acre property known as the Wessex Hundred, it was one of the first farms established from the Jamestown Settlement (1607). It is also near the town of Williamsburg, the state's largest tourist attraction. The winery highlights its colonial heritage, with rough-hewn floor beams, suits of armor, and candle lanterns in the tasting room. Food and drink are served in the adjacent Gabriel Archer Tavern.

As with many VA wineries, Williamsburg specializes in Chardonnay and red Bordeaux varieties. It won the VA Governor's Cup for their 1988 Chardonnay, and now offers four Chardonnay wines John Adlum, Acte Twelve, Vintage Reserve, and a single vineyard Reserve, distinguished by different degrees of barrel fermentation, *MLF, and bottle age. Williamsburg bottle ages both Chardonnay and red bordeaux styles prior to release. The Chardonnays tend to attractive mineral and earth notes, while the reds are smooth and bordeaux-like. The red bordeaux wines include a regular and reserve Cabernet Sauvignon, Merlot, and a Meritage-style Gabriel Archer Reserve. Williamsburg is conducting cooperage trials with oak from a variety of sources to identify those best suited to both the Chardonnay and red varieties. Winemaker Steve Warner reports that VA oak coopered by the French firm Tonnellerie Française offers the best results in blind tastings so far.

Wintergreen. Located a few miles south of Afton Mtn Vyds in the Rockfish Valley near Wintergreen ski resort, the winery was established in 1992 by Mike and Kathy Riddick. This is another VA winery demonstrating the quality of vineyard sites on the high Piedmont of the Blue Ridge Mtns. Wines include a regular and Black Rock Vyd Chardonnay, an off-dry Riesling, Cabernet Sauvignon, apple and raspberry wines, and proprietary blends. The Black Rock Chardonnay has subtle lime and mineral nuances, and the pure raspberry wine has naturally high acidity to balance its fresh fruitiness. Production is 3,500 cases.

See also BARBOURSVILLE, HORTON, INGLESIDE PLANTATION, JEFFERSON, LINDEN, PIEDMONT, PRINCE MICHEL, ROCKBRIDGE, WHITE HALL. R.G.L.

Wolfe, Tony, *The Mid-Atlantic Winegrape Grower's Guide* (Chapel Hill, 1995).

Gump, B., and Zoecklein, B. W., *Wine Production Analysis* (Fresno, 1990).

VQA, Vintners Quality Alliance. Wines in CANADA can be made from blends of up to 75% imported wine and still be classified as a Product of Canada. VQA was initially formed as a voluntary organization to help consumers and international trading partners identify wines that are made entirely from Canadian grapes. Today, VQA is considered ONTARIO's most significant wine-related accomplishment of the 1980s.

Growers, vintners, wine media, and provincial representatives had been meeting since the early 1980s to discuss an appellation system that would set minimum standards of production. They wanted these standards accompanied by an evaluation which would be conducted by an independent tasting panel. Varietal *typicity was to be required before granting VQA status. In June 1989 members of the WINE COUNCIL, an association of wineries first organized in 1940, voted to approve this system. In 1990 British Columbia formed a counterpart organization. Although the respective provincial organizations were maintained, in June of 1998 a national organization called VQA Canada was formed to focus on getting federal approval in law of VQA regulations similar to the legislated appellation systems in France, Italy, and other European wine producing countries. The federal system maintains consistent standards across the country with the ability to audit, and thus ensure violators are subject to sanctions and penalties. Negotiations are under way to establish provincial VQA regulations for Nova Scotia and Quebec.

The success of this program is reflected by 1998 figures in which VQA wines captured 38% of Canadian sales. In Ontario that figure was 46% in 1998. The Wine Council and LCBO are cooperating to raise that figure above 50% by the year 2000.

The term ICEWINE is an official mark of VQA Canada. The trademark means all wine labeled as Icewine in Canada, including imports and exports, must be made according to standards set by VQA.

REGULATIONS

An ability to trace the origin of a wine is the premise around which the VQA system is organized. Compared to other systems in North America, BC and Ontario's VQAs are exceptional in the stringency of their regulations. Similar to European appellation systems, grape standards and a tasting panel are part of the process to VQA approval. The approval rate varies. For instance, in 1998 only 16% of the wines submitted to VQA were refused approval. However, between Jan and May of 1999 approval was denied to 49%.

In Ontario there are two levels of appellation, each with its own set of guidelines. Wines with a Provincial Designation are made from grapes grown anywhere in the province, and from an approved list of vinifera or French hybrid grapes. Wines with the more demanding appellation of Geographic Designation are made from grapes grown in one of Ontario's three VAS only.

Provincial designation

Wines meeting the following standards may use Ontario on their label:

1. They must be made only from approved grapes, which are 66 vinifera varieties and the following French hybrids for varietal wines: Baco Noir, Chambourcin, Chancellor, Couderc Muscat, Marechal Foch, Seyval Blanc, Vidal Blanc, Villard Noir.
2. If labeled as a varietal they must contain at least 85% of the variety named and must exhibit that variety's predominant character.
3. The wine must be 100% Ontario-grown grapes.
4. All grape varieties must reach a minimum sugar level of 17.0° Brix.

Geographic designation

VQA recognizes three designated VAs in Ontario: Niagara Peninsula, Pelee Island, and Lake Erie North Shore. To employ one of these more specific appellations a wine must meet the following standards:

1. At least 85% of the grapes must come from the VA named.
2. Only vinifera can be used.
3. If labeled as a varietal they must contain at least 85% of the variety named and must exhibit that variety's predominant character.
4. The wine must be 100% Ontario-grown grapes.
5. If the vintner wishes to designate a vineyard, the site must be entirely within the VA and 100% of the grapes must come from that vineyard.

6. Wines described as Estate Bottled must be made entirely from vines owned or controlled by the winery. 'Controlled by' refers to property on which the bottling winery has the legal right to perform, and does perform, all of the acts common to viticulture under the terms of a lease or similar agreement of at least ten years' duration. The winery must control the vineyard for three years before the term 'Estate bottled' can be applied. The winery must also be located in the VA, and neither grapes nor wine may leave the winery prior to bottling.
7. Vineyard designated and estate bottled wines, as well as dessert and Icewine must meet minimum sugar levels. Those are: VIN DE CURÉ (20°B); Late Harvest (22°B); Select Late Harvest (26°B); Botrytis Affected (BA, 26°B); Special Select Late Harvest (30°B); Totally Botrytis Affected (TBA, 34°B); Icewine (35°B).

A panel from the LCBO evaluates all wines applying for the right to display a VQA medallion on their label. All wines are tasted blind. In the case of varietal wines, varietal character is an important component of the overall grade. Varietal wines are judged and scored as varietals. In the case of blended wines (proprietary), varietal character is not considered an important component of the overall grade unless the varieties are identified on the label. VQA also issues vintage reports on each VA.

PRODUCTION STANDARDS AND WINE STYLE

VQA regulations also stipulate methods for manufacturing various styles of wine such as botrytized wine, late, select late, and special select late harvest wines, nouveau styles, Blanc de Noirs, fortified wines, LIQUEUR WINES, and sparkling wines. For example, *botrytized wine must be made exclusively from fresh, ripe grapes of which a significant portion have been affected under natural conditions by the mold *Botrytis cinerea*. The grapes must be naturally harvested on the vine and achieve a minimum of 26° Brix. They must be produced as a varietal wine and must have the predominant character of wine made from botrytized grapes as determined by the VQA tasting panel. All Late Harvest wines must be produced from fresh ripe grapes of which a significant portion have been desiccated under natural conditions; *chaptalization and the addition of *sweet reserve is prohibited. Although the VQA rules set the conditions necessary to grow quality wines, they do not address such concerns as grape yields per acre or the amount of wine that may be produced from a given number of vines. Nor do the rules set out specific requirements for winemaking with a few exceptions (Icewine and Late Harvest wines in particular). If a vintner chooses to leave his Pinot Noir in barrel for two months or two years, that is his decision. If another decides to use *carbonic maceration on her Cabernet Sauvignon, or age her Riesling in oak, that is also the winemakers' choice. There are as many styles of wine as there are winemakers; however, the production of Icewine is much more highly regulated.   L.F.B.

Wagner Vyds was in the vanguard of new wineries rimming NY's FINGER LAKES following passage of the state's Farm Winery Law. With its first vintage in 1978, this family-run business also broke new ground taking wine production east of Seneca Lake, where many have followed. Wagner's 1980 Chardonnay was a landmark wine for the region, with a barrel fermented opulence that revealed new horizons for Finger Lakes wine in the richer soils and warmer mesoclimates of the area's bigger lakes. An early focus on Chardonnay, Riesling, and a few other varietals has gradually broadened into a list of 30 wines from vinifera, French hybrid, labrusca, and new varieties bred at the nearby NY Agricultural Experiment Station (GENEVA). Wagner embraces the mission of offering something for everyone from the dizzying range of Finger Lakes viniculture—and more: a microbrewery was added in 1997. All estate bottled, the wines draw upon a 250-acre vineyard growing 20 grape varieties. Production in 1998 totaled 40,000 cases. The original octagonal winery has sprouted several wings accommodating more than 800 barrels; Wagner Chardonnays, Seyval Blanc, and the dry red wines are clearly imprinted with oak. Half of Wagner's list ranges through sweetness levels culminating in Icewines. Half of production sells at the winery and its restaurant, the rest through wholesalers only within NY.   R.F.

Walla Walla Valley AVA, approved in 1984, is a sub-appellation in the larger COLUMBIA VALLEY AVA. They both extend across the border between southeast WASHINGTON and northeast OREGON. Walla Walla is the smallest AVA in WA, about 15 mi on each side. Its eastern edge abuts the Blue Mtns resulting in as much as 25 in of rain in a year, distinctly unlike the drier portions of the Columbia Basin and the Yakima Valley. Walla Walla is particularly prone to WINTER KILL when cold continental air drifts down from the Columbia Basin and settles on mostly flat vineyard land. On the valley floor are deep sedimentary sandy soils, ancient lake beds, that combine with high *degree days in the 3,000 range to produce Walla Walla Sweets, the famous mild onion.

Respect for the region is something of a conundrum in that it was pioneered by two talented winemakers who made their names using non-Walla Walla grapes: Gary Figgins at LEONETTI and his friend Rick Small at Woodward Canyon. Today Walla Walla is one of the fastest growing regions in the PACIFIC NORTHWEST, but even with increased plantings most wineries enjoy their greatest success from grapes grown outside the region. Approximately 800 acres are currently planted, mostly on hillsides, predominantly to Cabernet Sauvignon, Merlot, Syrah, and Sangiovese.

NOTABLE PROPERTIES

Oregon
Seven Hills, currently the only winery in the OR section of Walla Walla AVA. 150 acres run by Casey and Vicky McClellan who make big, richly flavored and textured Cabernet Sauvignon and Merlot. Both exhibit an intense raspberry flavor. They also dabble in Pinot Gris and Pinot Blanc from the WILLAMETTE AVA.

Washington
Canoe Ridge Vyd, begun in 1994 as a partnership between CHALONE and local investors. Winemaker John Abbott, formerly at Chalone's Acacia winery in CA, aims for balance and restrained fruit, with a slight oaky edge. The vineyard is on a prominent ridge, along the Columbia River, that rises up from the south side of HORSE HEAVEN HILLS.
Glen Fiona, winery owned by Rusty Figgins, younger brother of Gary Figgins, which produces a wonderful Syrah.
L'Ecole No. 41, winery established in 1983 by the incomparable Baker Ferguson and his winemaking wife Jean. Oppulent Semillon and full-throttled Merlot are produced today by the Ferguson's son-in-law Marty Clubb.
Pepper Bridge, vineyard owned by Norm McKibbin, growing outstanding Cabernet Sauvignon and Merlot.
Waterbrook, winery begun in 1984 by Eric and Janet Rindal. Chardonnay, especially from their own vineyard Cottonwood Creek, is consistently excellent. There is also fine Merlot and an outstanding newly released Viognier.
Woodward Canyon, winery started in 1981 by Rick Small, making consistently well-balanced Cabernet Sauvignon layered with lots of French oak. Small is also a partner in Canoe Ridge, and Chalone handles his distribution. A limited quantity of Woodward Chardonnay comes from a vineyard on sloping hillsides nearby the winery.

See also LEONETTI.   R.A.I.

warehouse wineries, catch-all phrase used to denote bonded wineries which do not own vineyards. Since they are not tied to a piece of property, they often change locations from one year to the next, frequently into or out of industrial parks. They may regress into hobbyist status, or move into landed status by acquiring vineyards and facilities in conventional agricultural districts. A primary reason they may choose to remain for extended periods in warehouse status is that their principals frequently have real jobs on the side.

A distinction should be drawn between these practitioners and the *custom crush facilities that are so popular in a places such as Napa and Sonoma. Custom crush facilities are primarily used by two types of players: (1) *négociants who buy bulk wine and then have their own proprietary blend barrel aged and bottled for them; or (2) vineyard owners who want their own grapes made into wine for a vanity label they will sell themselves. Warehouse wineries are a departure from those strictly utilitarian goals. Warehouse winemakers generally would not dream of letting someone else do the work.

Many warehouse practitioners are bit players well down the pecking order when it comes to vineyard selection. Others, however, have demonstrated their artistry most conspicuously through the years in precisely this arena of investigating overlooked vineyard resources, then creating mutually beneficial arrangements with growers who might otherwise sell their crops to bulk producers and end up seeing the vineyard's unique characteristics buried in some volume blend. The size and temperament match between warehouse winemakers and third generation owners of small plots in singular locations is just naturally symbiotic. Top examples in California include Kalin and ROSENBLUM. B.C.C.

Warren Hills AVA, one of NJ's two AVAs. The Warren Hills are in Warren Co, east of the Delaware River in north central NJ. Alba, Four Sisters, and Tamuzza wineries are located there.

Washington, state in the PACIFIC NORTHWEST region with remarkably varied terrain and a fast-growing wine industry. Vinifera grows in both the verdant maritime valleys of PUGET SOUND in western WA, as well as in the semi-arid plateaux of eastern WA. At latitudes 46°–48°N, WA more closely resembles the sunlight angle and hours of Europe's northern wine producing districts than it does its American competitor to the south, CA. WA ranks third in total wine production and second in vinifera production, shipping 3.63 million cases in 1998, way behind CA but considerably ahead of any other state. Although almost all of the vineyards in WA are located east of the CASCADE RANGE, up to a third of the wineries are situated in western WA, many of them located near CH STE MICHELLE in Woodinville, about 30 minutes' drive from SEATTLE.

At the beginning of 1998 WA had 25,000 acres of vinifera planted with 16,000 bearing. Another 4,000 acres were planted during 1998, and 5,000 planted in 1999. Projections are for 6,500 acres to be planted in 2000. There were 110 WA wineries in 1999. Since January 1999 the WA wine industry has bonded a new winery every eighteen days! Merlot is the most widely planted red variety; Chardonnay the most widely planted white. The ratio of red to white wines produced is 44 : 56. Syrah grapes are the most expensive.

In 1996 overseas exports of WA wine were 310,000 cases; in 1998 465,000 cases were exported. Much of this increase can be credited to Steve Burns, former international market manager for the CA Wine Institute, who was hired in 1996 to direct the Washington Wine Commission, which oversees wine promotion and the Washington Wine Institute, the trade's political arm. See www.washingtonwine.org.

HISTORY
Grape growing accompanied the movement of immigrant settlers into WA with plantings as early as the 1860s in Yakima, 1870s in Puget Sound, and even earlier in the Walla Walla region. The first planting occurred at Fort Vancouver by the Hudson Bay Company on the northern bank of the Columbia River across from present-day Portland. Today, Salishan Vyds continues this legacy by growing Chardonnay and Pinot Noir in southwest WA. With the introduction of irrigation at the turn of the century, vineyards expanded primarily in the Tri-Cities (Kennewick, Pasco, and Richland) area, where the SNAKE RIVER joins the Columbia, and throughout the Yakima Valley. After Prohibition new plantings were begun throughout the Columbia Valley but it was not until 1969 that they attracted any attention. In 1970 there were fewer than 500 acres of vinifera in WA and just two wineries.

CLIMATE AND TOPOGRAPHY
The CASCADE RANGE divides the state into two vastly different regions by the simple expedient of blocking rain clouds flowing from the west. Western WA, in the manner of its latitude counterparts such as the *Loire Valley or *Alsace, enjoys long sunlight hours May through Aug, but very modest temperatures. Ripening depends on detailed viticultural techniques, great site selection, favorable harvest conditions, and a good measure of luck. Western WA wines tend to be light, delicate, subtle in flavor. Chardonnay, Pinot Noir, and Riesling can be grown, but it can be a challenge to ripen many of the popular varieties. Western WA is dominated by damp air in winter and spring, usually giving way to drier, warmer air from June through Oct. In summer a high pressure system moves into place off the WA coast and winds prevail from the north instead of the west. Temperatures average in the mid-60s° F, producing 1,800–2,500 *degree days in the growing season. Annual precipitation can range from 35 to 50 in. Fortunate vineyards find climatic respite in protected pockets behind picturesque Coast Range mountains. When grapes can be harvested under ideal conditions, the wines are sublime; delicate flavors framed in light alcohols, perfectly proportioned. In less than ideal conditions they are thin and insubstantial. Recently, 1992 was an ideal vintage: moderate spring, followed by a warm, dry, and long summer, then a moderately warm fall. 1994 was downright hot and dry—some western WA vineyards even had to be irrigated. In 1996 BATF approved Puget Sound as a viticultual area, much to the delight of the determined producer/petitioners.

Eastern WA has a continental climate with extreme temperatures and much drier air. In winter, temperatures dip below 0°F when the Jet Stream moves far enough south to divert cold Alaskan air down the western side of the Rocky Mtns instead of dumping it east of the Rockies into the Plains. WINTER KILL may occur as frequently as one year in six as temperatures dip below freezing, reaching to –25°F in the freeze of 1996 when a 45% crop reduction occurred. In summer time, temperatures regularly soar above 100°F. Most grape growing occurs in the COLUMBIA VALLEY in the southeastern portion of the state. This 18,000 sq mi area has many noble winegrowing characteristics, but it lacks rain, annually averaging less than 10 in. Large irrigated vineyards watered with overhead sprinklers dot the viticultural horizon and TENSIOMETERS are frequently used to determine when and how much irrigation should be applied. Most vineyards are planted on gentle slopes. Sedimentary soils mixed with volcanic ash (Mt St Helens blew up as recently as 1980) are very productive. Wheat is grown along the edges of the valley where rainfall provides sufficient moisture. Apple orchards still dominate the landscape in much of the Columbia Valley as yields and prices have consistently outperformed those of grapes. At the end of the 1990s, however, there was a surplus of apples.

The Columbia Valley AVA, as part of the slightly larger Columbia Basin, is the largest viticultural appellation in the Pacific Northwest, a vast depression in the otherwise mountainous landscape. Within its borders are the smaller YAKIMA VALLEY and the WALLA WALLA VALLEY. Both the Columbia Valley and Walla Walla Valley appellations extend south across the border into OR. The Yakima River originates in the snow-laden Cascades, while the Snake and Columbia Rivers emanate from the immense Rocky Mountains. The Walla Walla drains out of the Blue Mtns. They all meet in the general vicinity of the Tri-Cities farming center. So the Walla Walla AVA pretty much runs east up a valley from that point while Yakima AVA runs west up a valley from that point. Columbia Valley encompasses both a huge Y along the Columbia and Snake rivers north of Tri-Cities, and a very large area south and west from that point as it follows the now mighty Columbia another 150 mi, or two-thirds of the distance to Portland, along its journey to the sea. The left fork of the Columbia Valley AVA's massive northern Y extends all the way into northern WA, past the confluence of the Okanagan River and including Grand Coulee Dam, an edifice venerated by Woodie Guthrie ('Pastures of Plenty') and centerpiece of the 20th century's most prodigious early hydro-electric project.

VITICULTURE AND WINES

Prime vineyard sites are still readily available throughout the three eastern WA AVAs and in 1999 it cost roughly $10,000 per acre to get into production, including land costs and irrigation (as compared with $10,000–20,000 for planting, trellising, and irrigation alone in CA's North Coast where the additional figure for land cost could run as high as $80,000 an acre). Most water is provided by pulling water from mountain lakes high in the Cascade Range, or by dipping into the Columbia River. Many vineyards prefer to dig their own wells, but that is costly.

Merlot, with 4,800 acres planted, shows a particular affinity for eastern WA conditions, especially in warm, dry years. Then it is concentrated and mouthfilling with blackberry and blueberry flavors. Less than stellar years can be a bit sharp, and this variety is particularly susceptible to cold winters. With 3,500 acres planted, Cabernet Sauvignon is the second most planted variety with its rich fruity nature balancing leafiness. In cooler vintages it is more obviously tannic and slightly more vegetative. Recent vintages have seesawed back and forth: 1992 was warm and dry; 1993 cool; 1994 hot; 1995 cool and wet. 1996 was the year of the devastating freeze, which hit Chardonnay and Merlot especially hard. 1997 was moderately cool while 1998 was blisteringly hot.

Of newer plantings, Syrah with 560 acres and Cabernet Franc with 820 acres seem the most promising. Syrah offers straightforward fruit flavors, juicy and rich, without the toasted qualities often associated with Rhône Syrahs. Syrah also appears to be winter hardy, even with a prolific growth pattern. Cabernet Franc has proved winter hardy in several North American regions. In eastern WA it gives delicate fruit flavors, slightly sharper than Cabernet Sauvignon. Lemberger, or *Blaufränkisch, is worthy of special mention. The original cuttings were brought from a BC nursery in 1941 to the WA State Univ research station in Prosser by Walter CLORE. Lemberger makes unique wine, possessed of *lifted blackberry aroma and a structure that can range from slightly tart to jammy. It is WA's Zinfandel.

Currently the vogue in WA is to produce red wines with higher *pH and lower *acidity. These wines are destined for short-term cellaring. There is very little evidence they will improve in flavors beyond about eight years from vintage.

WA's most exciting white wines are made from Sauvignon Blanc and Semillon. The biggest problem is overcoming consumer resistance to crisp, slightly grassy white wines. For this reason many WA wineries purchase grapes from warmer sites that highlight more melon and apple flavors. WA Semillon takes on many of the characteristics associated with Sauvignon Blanc, but also takes well to *barrel fermentation and barrel ageing. Its softer middle palate is less assertive than Sauvignon Blanc and tends to marry well with oak flavors. Because of depressed demand, most WA wineries instead make Semillon bright and fresh, highlighting the lemon-apple notes through cool fermentation in *stainless steel. Consistently these wines receive high competition marks, yet fail to achieve consumer recognition. Semillon also ages very well, developing rounder and softer fresh-fig flavors. It is not uncommon for some Semillon wines to age better than heavier red WA wines.

Chardonnay is by far the most widely planted grape in eastern WA. Quality can vary considerably by site. Again, like many Washington whites, less oak treatment is the norm. Chardonnay tends to do better in cooler vintages such as 1993 and 1995, which increase the length of flavor and reduce tropical flavors.

Riesling is WA's workhorse. It was Ch Ste Michelle's 1972 Johannisberg Riesling that put WA on the wine map when it won a *Los Angeles Times* wine tasting in 1974. It appears in sparkling wines, makes both sweet and dry table wines, is used as a blending grape, and lends itself well to late harvest wines, including icewines. Northwest consumer preference is still for slightly off-dry Rieslings that highlight fresh apple aromas and flavors. With 2,080 acres of Riesling planted, over half a million cases of Riesling are sold annually with much of it going out of state. Ironically, WA Gewürztraminer, the variety that wooed André *Tchelistcheff to consult for Ch Ste Michelle in 1967, has languished. When grown in an appropriate cool site it can deliver classic lychee aromas and flavors. Too often overcropping squanders most of its varietal distinction, although it may still deliver round *mouthfeel.

REGULATORY ENVIRONMENT

WA State Liquor Control Board (WSLCB) regulates and enforces rules adopted by the Board. It approves all labels, requires monthly price postings, and requires all wines (except for small WA wineries) to sell through licensed wholesalers. All must sell COD. WSLCB also operates state stores that offer distilled spirits, wine, and beer; competing in an industry that it regulates.

R.A.I.

Washington, DC, perhaps the most sophisticated wine market in North America, based on the average consumer's high level of wine knowledge and education. Through the 1980s, Washington attracted fine wine buyers from as far away as NC, TN, and PA because of its superior selection and prices. Intense wholesale competition, low liquor taxes, and retail stores at liberty to act as direct importers combined to make the District the center of MID-ATLANTIC wine culture. Political parties, a huge diplomatic corps, and the large upper level military population resident in the nearby suburbs, most of whom have done tours of duty in European wine producing regions such as Germany and Italy, offset the predominately Afro-American population of urban DC, which does not as a group embrace wine as its beverage of choice. In the 1990s, wholesale competition increased in neighboring regions, and some suburban consumers began buying at increasingly quality-oriented stores in MD and VA. However, DC still leads in case sales, in both volume and dollars. Sale of west coast wines is about equal with imports.

While Washington has a justly deserved reputation for the 'power lunch' wherein political deals are hatched, the evening restaurant market has developed impressively. In 1999 business was booming, especially in the Federal Triangle area, and suburbanites still come downtown for the region's best food. While many of the offerings tend toward expense account fare, the District has a Chinatown, and Ethiopian and Central American restaurants are a local specialty. Bistros are the latest restaurant trend, ranging from Pacific Rim to classic French cuisine. Restaurants are moving beyond Chardonnay, experimenting in by-the-glass selections with regional French and other less well-known wines.

The *Washington Post*, one of the nation's top two or three newspapers by virtue of its bird's-eye view on the political scene, is also one of the only five or six newspapers in the US with a staff winewriter, Ben Gilberti. The *Post* also served as launching pad for William Rice (now at the *Chicago Tribune*), who has been among America's top wine and food critics for a quarter-century.

R.G.L.

WCTU, Woman's Christian Temperance Union, founded in Cleveland, OH, in the fall of 1874, electing Annie Turner Wittenmyer as its first president. Its energies stemmed from the indiscriminate spread of alcoholic beverages throughout the country; but it also had its genesis in female emancipation. Without many legal rights in the battles involving divorce and custody, not to mention the vote or any political input into the workings of the nation (political discussions were often held in saloons where women were forbidden), women sought to express their feelings elsewhere. These two currents of political sentiment also drew momentum from the base of organizational skills and from many of the same people who had been active in the Abolitionist (anti-slavery) movement of the preceding half-century.

Vowing to 'Agitate, Educate, and Legislate' they called for total abstinence, first from alcohol but also later from drugs and tobacco. The second WCTU president Frances Willard was especially adept at fulfilling that motto. For nearly 20 years as its leader, Willard entered every social and political conversation a modern woman takes for granted. Including, of course, a strong stand on alcohol, but also such issues as women's right to vote, the eight-hour workday, federal assistance for education, divorce laws, prison reform, and others.

Today, its profile is much more low key but it is active, still agitating and still convinced that the easy availability of alcohol is a problem in world society.   P.W.F.

Wente, if not the oldest continuously operated family winery in North America, certainly the most prominent. Located in CA's LIVERMORE VALLEY, the Wente family is truly CA aristocracy and the single member of CA's top five overseas wine promoters whose history dates back prior to Prohibition. Patriarch Carl Heinrich Wente worked for Charles *Krug in Napa for three years after his arrival from Hanover, Germany, in 1880. He then acquired 300 acres in the Livermore Valley and, more importantly, sired three superstar sons. The eldest, Carl, followed his father's suggestion to attend business school. He eventually rose to become President of the worldwide Bank of America. Ernest, the next in line, studied viticulture. He gathered FIELD SELECTIONS of Chardonnay from several CA vineyards and also brought at least one from Montpellier in France. In 1936 Wente was the first CA winery to release a varietally labeled Chardonnay. This accomplishment is noteworthy, not just in hindsight because the variety has become so immensely popular, but because there were only 230 acres of Chardonnay planted in CA as late as 1960. Ernest Wente's selections of Sauvignon Blanc, sourced from Wetmore's original importation (see below), and Chardonnay budwood have led to the most widely propagated field selections of those two varieties throughout CA. 'Wente clone' is the generic phrase growers use to describe the vines

they have planted in their vineyards which became the US standard for both Sauvignon Blanc and Chardonnay.

Youngest son Herman Wente became the winemaker. In the 1940s he received a visit from the Marquis de Lur Saluces of Bordeaux who wanted 'to see how my children are doing,' a reference to vine cuttings Charles Wetmore had procured from the Marquis' Ch d'*Yquem and then planted in Livermore around 1870. No wonder. A 1937 Semillon/Sauvignon Blanc blend called Valle de Oro made by Wente had duplicated Charles Wetmore's feat by winning the Grand Prix at the Paris Exposition. The Marquis was quite impressed with Herman's range of Sauvignon Blancs, stating that it would be impossible to make a wine of that quality from Sauvignon Blanc alone in the Bordeaux climate. True enough. In Livermore, Sauvignon Blanc ripens to a cinnamon apple intensity and thicker texture (higher alcohol) than one would expect from white bordeaux without its normal Semillon component.

Wente sold sacramental wine in bulk through BEAULIEU VYDS during Prohibition, and also did a brisk trade in fresh grapes for home winemakers. That business allowed them to acquire Louis Mel's original El Mocho vineyard in the 1920s. Following the Second World War, Wente achieved national recognition when the brand was chosen by best-selling wine writer Frank *Schoonmaker for distribution under his personal Selections banner. In the 1960s the third Wente generation made a decision to remain in Livermore and resist urbanization pressures by placing their property under a ten-year perpetually renewing obligation that it be used (and taxed) as farmland. Ernest Wente's son Karl also chose to hedge his bet by purchasing 600 acres in the ARROYO SECO district of Monterey Co. *Botrytized Rieslings they made from that property at the end of the 1960s were juicy, rich, and innovative (albeit short-lived) wines. Unfortunately these failed to gain a foothold in the US mass marketplace. Wente was not then, and is not now, inclined to service small niches, no matter how much wine writers may portray those niches as a valuable artform.

The fourth generation of Wentes had decision-making roles thrust upon them in 1977 when Karl died of a heart attack at 49. His son Philip manages the vineyards plus the 2,000-acre Livermore cattle ranch. Daughter Carolyn handles marketing and winery administration as president of the company. Son Eric manages winery production. Carolyn Wente is often depicted in

the US industry as the person who took 'Brothers' out of the Wente Bros name, although she thinks her age was a bigger obstacle to overcome than her gender. She was 21 when her father died.

In 1981 the family purchased Charles Wetmore's beautiful Cresta Blanca Winery, which had stood unoccupied since 1965. In addition to its founder's seminal role in CA viticulture, Cresta Blanca had scored a couple of other wine industry firsts. Taken over by the whisky barons at Schenley during the Second World War, Cresta Blanca was the first wine brand to be nationally advertised on radio in the US. Then in 1956 Myron Nightingale (later with BERINGER) and his wife Alice produced the first ever US botrytized wine by spraying fungal spores on picked Semillon and Sauvignon Blanc bunches in the winery. The Cresta Blanca brand name was eventually sold to Guild and is now applied to a bulk facility run by CANANDAIGUA in Mendocino. The historic property with its sandstone caves has been renamed Charles Wetmore Vyd by the Wentes who have constructed a new mission style building there to house their hospitality center and restaurant. Consistent but somewhat workmanlike sparkling wines are produced in the old Wetmore facility. None of the original vines planted by Wetmore following his visit to Ch d'Yquem are still in the ground.

In 1992 the Wentes purchased the nearby Concannon winery as well. It had fallen into complete disarray. Begun in 1883 by an Irish immigrant every bit as resourceful as Carl Heinrich Wente, Concannon never quite emerged from its relationship to the Catholic Church. James Concannon had come to the west coast to sell rubber stamps. He traveled as far as MEXICO and even inveigled Dictator Porfirio Díaz to give him a franchise for Mexico City's first street cleaning system. He also got a concession from Díaz to ship millions of vine cuttings from Livermore to haciendas throughout Mexico. From the start of his vineyard operation, James Concannon's intention was to produce altar wines for his friend Joseph Alemany, Archbishop of San Francisco. This strategy stood Concannon's son in good stead during Prohibition. In fact Leon Adams, in his history of American wines, claims Joe Concannon sent a barrel of his best Muscat de Frontignan to the Pope in Rome every five years as a token of his appreciation. The most recent releases under the Concannon label have been an improvement over the flawed wines of the past, but except for the superlative Petite Sirah nothing has risen into top-flight status.

As part of their innovative effort to maintain an agriculture and winemaking base in Livermore Valley, the Wentes have lobbied hard for creation of county zoning boundaries which will require 'in fill,' or greater density, instead of mindless urban sprawl. They have succeeded in reaching an agreement with their local legislators and planning department that any future building permits for homes in the Livermore Valley will simultaneously set aside 20 acres of open space (not necessarily in the same location) or land permanently zoned for agriculture. In a complementary move the Wente's have entered into several strategic alliances which include combination golf course, vineyard, and residential developments. There is a Course at Wente Vyds designed by Greg Norman; a Ruby Hill Course designed by Jack Nicklaus; and a Poppy Ridge Course designed by Rees Jones. Residential purchasers can move into 20-acre ranchettes with both a home and a managed vineyard. Carolyn Wente says she is hopeful some of the buyers will want to establish small winery brands of their own. Land use political techniques such as these may well be the fourth generation of the Wentes' most enduring legacy to the CA wine industry.

The Wente brand wines themselves are honestly made and competitively priced. They produce 450,000 cases, half of which is sold overseas in 106 markets. Nearly half the total production is Chardonnay. Semillon and Sauvignon Blanc are offered, but since the mid-1980s both have been aimed at the soft fruit, ripe kiwi side of the spectrum. The last botrytized Semillon was made in 1983. That was also the year Philip Wente chose to make a dry Semillon the featured wine for the family's 100-year anniversary in order to acknowledge the importance of the variety to the winery's heritage. It was a last hurrah. Sales of Semillon have declined steadily from a 15,000-case highpoint in the early 1970s to 3,000 cases today. Wente sells most of that overseas. More is the pity. A museum bottle of 1983 Wente Semillon tasted in 1996 was tautly structured, balanced between forceful gravelly flavors and lean acid, its edges softened by almond and cumin notes, and exceptionally long. Carolyn and Philip Wente personally enjoy the wine, but report American retail store customers assume aged Semillon is merely old, unsold inventory. 'It is easier to be the 200th Chardonnay on the shelf than the only aged Semillon,' they say. So, having evaluated the US market, Carolyn Wente has decided to join, rather than fight it.   B.C.C.

Adams, L. D., *The Wines of America* (Boston, 1973).

Westbend Vyds. Located in the upper PIEDMONT of Forsyth Co west of Winston-Salem in NORTH CAROLINA, this winery is the state's leading quality producer, and perhaps the best in the SOUTH region. Their 42-acre vineyard grows Chardonnay (produced in regular and barrel fermented styles), Riesling, Cabernet Sauvignon, Merlot, Gamay, Sauvignon Blanc, Pinot Noir, and the hybrids Seyval, Vidal, and Chambourcin. Westbend was originally started as a vineyard enterprise by owner Jack Kroustalis. He harvested 70 tons in 1986 for sale to other wineries, then bonded his own in 1988.

Thanks to the skillful work of winemaker Steve Shepard, the Chardonnays are an elegant blend of oak and fruit elements, in a smooth, clean style, but few wineries anywhere can compete with Westbend's varietal Chambourcin with its attractive dark color, striking rose petal bouquet, and the smooth finesse of a *Rioja. It is aged sixteen months in oak. The Pinot Noir is not as impressive, which is common among wineries throughout the Piedmont. Other wines include late harvest Vidal and Muscat Canelli. Annual production is 10,000 cases.   R.G.L.

Western Connecticut Highlands AVA,

appellation in the NORTHEAST region 15–45 mi inland from the shore of Long Island Sound and 300–800 ft of elevation. Bounded approximately on the east by Hwy 8 and on the south by Hwy 84, the appellation runs almost to the NY border on the west and as far north as Litchfield. Site location is extremely important. Hopkins Vyd is on a lake. Half of their 35 acres are the vinifera varieties Chardonnay and Cabernet Franc. They do not have to MOUND their vines. DiGrazia Vyds, however, is further inland and does not have the temperature modifying benefit of a nearby body of water. They tried Chardonnay for three years, even burying the vines each winter, but still got *crown gall and virtually no crop. They plowed the vinifera under and moved on to French hybrids. Overall the AVA is modestly warmer than LONG ISLAND in the summer; colder in the winter.

See SOUTHEASTERN NEW ENGLAND.

B. C. C

West Virginia, state in the MID-ATLANTIC

region completely encompassed by the APPALACHIAN MTNS. Better known for coal, the Mountain State is the smallest wine producer in the Mid-Atlantic, with 20,000 gal in 1997. WV currently hosts twelve wineries and three approved AVAs: SHENANDOAH VALLEY in the extreme eastern Panhandle; OHIO RIVER VALLEY on the western edge of the state; and KANAWHA RIVER VALLEY in the south-central portion of the state. Grape varieties include the labruscas Delaware, Concord, and Niagara, plus Norton, French hybrids, and a few vinifera varieties. Unfortunately, the local palate sways most winemakers to finish the fresh, lively white wines from semi-dry to sweet.

West Virginia has a wide range of climate and soil conditions. Dramatic changes in elevation offer potential for good quality cool climate viticulture. The Potomac River Valley in the eastern and northern parts of the state resembles the Upper and Middle Mosel, in that both have a high sedimentary plateau dominated by shale, eroded by rivers. Potomac Highland Winery near Keyser on the North Fork of this river valley demonstrates the potential of the region to produce quality vinifera wines.

Though WV's alcoholic beverage control laws are relatively liberal for the region, with private establishments authorized to sell beer, wine, and liquor, they cannot serve or sell alcoholic beverages on Sundays before 1:00 pm. Taste preferences in a region which coined the name hillbillies for themselves are not inclined to the subtleties of dry vinifera wine, and there is a higher ratio of American hybrid and sweet fruit wines to dry vinifera or French hybrids here than in any other Mid-Atlantic state. Tourism, however, is a major component of the state's economy, and some local wineries are preparing to take advantage of that asset.

NOTABLE PROPERTIES

Fisher Ridge in Charleston was the first winery established in post-Prohibition WV. Wilson Ward makes Chardonnay. Annual production is 1,200 cases.

Potomac Highland, the state's leading winery with Riesling, Chardonnay, an impressive Pinot Noir, and a Meritage-style red blend composed of half Cabernet Sauvignon, 39% Merlot, and the remainder Cabernet Franc. Chambourcin and other French hybrids are also produced. Chardonnay, formerly made with RS, has been finished in a delicate, dry, and crisp style beginning with the fine 1997 vintage. If their Riesling were finished *dry (perhaps for 'export' to another market), the response might be surprising. Becky and Charles Whitehill are the owners. Annual production is 1,100 cases.

Vineyard Home, in Purgitsville, produces 2,000 cases annually. Wines range from Cabernet Sauvignon to Concord. Robert Pliska is the winemaker.

Schneider's in Romney is WV's largest winery at 5,500 cases. Output includes sound, if sweet, Vidal and Chardonnay. Owned by Ken Snyder. R.G.L.

White Hall Vyds. Founded by retired businessman and chemist Tony Champ and his wife Edie, this winery is one of VIRGINIA's most scenic, situated on a high plateau under the BLUE RIDGE MTNS west of Charlottesville. Few wineries in VA, or in the East, have achieved such success in so short a time. Begun in 1994, it immediately became known for impeccable quality. After sweeping the Monticello Cup awards in 1996, winning the Cup itself with a 1995 Cabernet Franc, White Hall went on to win the VA Governor's Cup the following spring for 1995 Cabernet Sauvignon. A year later, White Hall won the Governor's Cup again, this time for 1997 Gewürztraminer, the first crop from 3-year-old vines. The 1997 Chardonnay also won a Gold Medal in that Cup competition, one of only six others. The 1997 Reserve Chardonnay was the top-scoring VA Chardonnay in a national ranking of 469 wines of that variety in early 1999.

White Hall's talented young winemaker, Brad McCarthy, received no formal training in enology, but started in the business under the able direction of Shep Rouse, at Montdomaine Cellars (see HORTON). He still collaborates closely with Rouse, who has supplied much of White Hall's Vidal grapes. The White Hall white wines include a regular and reserve Chardonnay, Gewürztraminer, and Pinot Gris, and Soliterre, a CRYOEXTRACTION Vidal icewine. The reds feature the Bordeaux trio of Cabernet Sauvignon, Cabernet Franc, and Merlot, although White Hall's Cabernet Franc is packaged in a Burgundy bottle, stylistically modeled after the straight varietal *Loire prototype. Annual production is 5,000 cases. R.G.L.

Wild Horse, winery in Templeton, part of the PASO ROBLES appellation in CA's San Luis Obispo Co, although Ken Volk's excellent reputation has little to do with the 33-acre vineyard he owns at the winery site. Wild Horse was *Wine & Spirits* magazine's Winery of the Year in 1990. The year before that his Merlot won Best in America at a prestigious national competition, and his Pinot Noir took more Gold Medals than any other competitor in all that year's wine shows. But Volk firmly believes in sourcing grapes from three to six vineyards in different regions for each variety he makes in order to give himself a broad blending palette. Then he painstakingly assembles himself a winner. It would be the archetypal *New World story except for the fact that Volk is sort of a reticent personality, disinclined to call attention to himself as the creator of these works. Personality is a funny thing. Volk's father is a developer, the man who started Public Storage Inc.

Production is close to 100,000 cases a year. Vineyard sources range from VENTANA. In Monterey Co, through Talley in SLO Co to Bien Nacido, and Sierra Madre in Santa Barbara Co. Chardonnay is the biggest production item, invariably rich in the nose from *barrel fermentation, full bodied with fig-like flavors, but tapering to a long finish. Better is Volk's well-colored Pinot Noir, moderately complex in the nose with leather hints over a clean black cherry base, and not much extract, relying instead on acid for its structural rigidity. Wild Horse Merlot is not as soft and hoisin sauce-scented as it was when the grapes came exclusively from such extraordinary local vineyards as Ceres and Radike. Recent Merlot vintages have been harder edged and more cassis-like, suggesting a larger percentage of grapes from cooler coastside vineyards. B.C.C.

wild yeast, phrase used without much precision in the US to generally imply ambient *yeast arriving with the grapes from the vineyard as opposed to an introduced, commercially prepared yeast. Winemakers in *South Africa, for instance, interpret phrases such as 'wild yeast' or 'indigenous yeast' to mean a culture of Saccharomyces cerevisiae isolated out of the population of ambient yeast found in one's local vineyards. In CA those alcohol-tolerant yeasts would be considered a *pure strain* culture, albeit one with an interesting pedigree. When CA winemakers use the phrase 'wild yeast,' they mean to imply the entire ambient cocktail, in particular the non-ellipsoid shaped (ie apiculate, or apex shaped) yeasts which succumb at alcohol levels around 7%, but which produce higher concentrations of strong smelling esters. Winemakers who say they have fermented a wine with wild yeasts are rarely so doctrinaire as to claim they relied exclusively on the wild yeasts to finish the job successfully. The most common practice would be to let the wild yeasts have their way for a couple of days, then to introduce a pure strain cerevisiae culture to make sure the wine goes completely dry.

See KILLER YEASTS and Microbiology essay, p 39. B.C.C.

Willamette Valley AVA, approved in 1983, is by far the most important winegrowing region in OREGON. It is the source of most of the grapes grown there and is home to a vast majority of the wineries. At the north end of the viticultural area is PORTLAND. The Willamette Valley is a long V-shape, once an inland bay that has been gradually built up over time by lava flows, from tectonic lifting which created surrounding hills, and from eroded sedimentation. Mt St Helens, the volcano which blew a third of its mass into the sky in 1980, sits 50 mi north of Portland across the river in WA.

The Willamette Valley is surrounded by the Coast Range to the west and the Cascade Mts to the east. Much of the valley is flat, fertile farmland but surrounding hills and benchlands provide fine growing sites for cool climate grapes. The Willamette River bisects the valley as it winds through its entire length before joining the Columbia River on the northwest side of Portland. With a range of 2,052–2,255 *degree days Willamette Valley is coolest in the northern half along the western edge where marine air enters the valley through the Van Duzer Corridor, a break in the Coast Range 40 mi west of the EOLA HILLS. The northern Willamette Valley receives about 40 in of rain annually, mainly between Nov and May. Summer temperatures can get moderately hot but are quenched by cloud cover flowing in from the Pacific Ocean 30–40 mi away. Harvests are always at risk of early rains and cool temperatures. Most vintages are challenging.

Wet conditions are not always a problem in the Willamette. Nor are hot conditions always a benefit, as evidenced in the 1994 vintage which produced short-lived wines. Sometimes rain causes vineyardists to aggressively reduce crop and pull leaves, as in 1996, which can produce very pretty, albeit light-bodied wines.

A decade of Willamette Pinot Noir

Year	Sept rain (in)	Oct rain (in)	Forced ranking (10 is best)	Comment
1989	0.79	2.68	9	Great vintage
1990	n/a	n/a	8	Nice wines
1991	0.0	2.51	4	Cool; big crop; inconsistent
1992	1.26	n/a	6	Bit jammy
1993	0.10	1.40	5	Tannic
1994	0.03	4.62	7	Ripe, flattering; not aging
1995	1.46	1.63	1	Weedy
1996	7.58	5.51	2	Short term; nice fruit flavors
1997	2.34	7.21	3	May last longer; better vyd mgmt
1998	0.57	2.05	10	Early to say may be best yet

The Willamette Valley is a green, fertile, generously proportioned valley of hills. The most prominent hills are the east–west running RED HILLS OF DUNDEE and the Chehalem Mtns, within an hour's drive southwest of Portland. Further south, by 15 miles, are the Eola Hills, a north–south running set of ridges that end at the city of Salem, the state's capital. Within this northern section three distinct soil types occur. In the Red Hills, Jory soils predominate. They are of igneous origin and contain a fair amount of clay, which holds moisture longer, thus delaying harvest. Jory topsoils tend to run quite deep. Pinot Noirs grown on them are lighter in color, have more delicate fruit flavors, and often show a distinctive gamey quality. In the Eola Hills, Netalia soils predominate. These are more sand and silt, with less clay. They are also more shallow, 1.5–3 ft deep. Grapes ripen a week earlier than in the Red Hills, and Pinot Noir flavors tend more to dark stonefruits with more weight in the mid-palate. In the Chehalem Mtns and the facing Yamhill foothills, shallow topsoils are the rule, but they are of sedimentary origin and are known as Willakensie soils. Grapes ripen here two weeks ahead of the Red Hills, a week before Eola Hills. Pinot Noir flavors from this somewhat more northerly section are a bit more herbal with hints of cedar or tobacco.

Salem marks the beginning of the south Willamette Valley, not yet a separate viticultural area. Here the South Salem Hills appear for only a short distance, then the valley becomes narrower but virtually flat all the way to Eugene, where the Coast Range and CASCADE RANGE meet. Precipitation increases dramatically towards the Cascade Range foothills. Farmland gives way to dense forests. Most wineries and vineyards shelter on the lee side of the Coast Range, the west side of the Willamette Valley.

NOTABLE PROPERTIES

Adelsheim Vyd, an early player bonded in 1978 outside Newberg, a suburb of Portland. This 43-acre estate has been a consistent producer of top Pinot Noir and Pinot Gris. David Adelsheim was instrumental in putting OR on the North American wine map even before he persuaded Drouhin to make an investment.

Archery Summit, winery established in 1995 by Gary Andrus, from CA's PINE RIDGE winery. A stable of expensive vineyard designated Pinot Noirs is being produced as well as a PROPRIETARY white blend. The Pinot Noirs are big and gutsy, with a substantial whack of tannin. The entirely gravity-fed winery sits in good company, located next to DOM DROUHIN and Sokol Blosser.

Beaux Frères, located on the south side of Chehalem Mtn along Ribbon Ridge in Willakenzie soils with 25 acres bearing. There are four owners including wine critic Robert *Parker and his brother in law (*beau-frère*) Michael Etzel, who also acts as winemaker producing an unusual style of OR Pinot Noir, at once plumper and oakier than most others.

Chehalem, small winery where Harry Peterson-Nedry makes beautifully balanced wines. Pinot Gris, Chardonnay, and Pinot Noir are intensely fruity, rich, and mouth-filling.

Elk Cove Vyds, on a mountain northwest of Carlton, is owned by Joe and Pat Campbell. They are slowly turning winemaking chores over to their son, Adam. They produce structured Pinot Noir relying primarily on their 45-acre hilltop estate. Thanks to extensive crop thinning, denser plantings, and higher fermentation temperatures, their wines combine weight and angularity. Excellent Rieslings, both dry and sweet.

Ken Wright, new winery in Carlton highlighting low yield vineyards and cold SKIN SOAK prior to fermentation. Wright primarily produces vineyard designated Pinot Noirs from purchased grapes. He aims to emphasize intensity of fruit flavors with lush, seductive wines.

Montinore, winery at which Jacques Tardy, a native Burgundian, makes the wine—a lot of wine: 55,000 to 65,000 cases annually from their 300-acre vineyard. Excellent late harvest Rieslings.

Oak Knoll, reliable winery owned by the Vuylsteke family makes 30,000 cases of Pinot Noir, Pinot Gris, and Chardonnay. Also an outstanding sweet raspberry wine called Frambrosia.

Rex Hill Vyds in the Chehalem Mtns at Newberg, owned by Paul Hart and Jan Jacobsen, is one of the only early OR wineries to get off the ground with strong financial backing. That circumstance allowed them to restore a historic building, and also to offer more money to top growers for grapes, a technique which annoyed established wineries. Today winemaker Lynn Penner-Ash favors full flavored Pinot Noir, notably from their own Kings Ridge and Maresh Vyds. The winery owns or leases over 250 acres of vineyard.

Sokol-Blosser, enthusiastic winery started in 1977 by Susan Sokol and Bill Blosser, controlling 135 acres of vineyard. Their best Pinot Noir arrives under the Redland moniker, a blend of properties in Hyland and the Red Hills. They also provide a congenial venue for summer concerts.

Tyee, winery located in the South Salem Hills, the home of Barney Watson, food technologist at OR State Univ responsible for viticulture and enology trials researching clonal and site selections.

Willamette Valley Vyds, a publicly traded stock on the NASDAQ exchange located just south of Salem, and now one of OR's largest producers making 80,000 cases in 1998. The winery owns 210 acres and contracts from 60 more. Their 1998 purchase of Tualatin Vyds, a pioneer winery started in 1973 and the northernmost winery in the AVA, adds pedigree. Hiring acclaimed winemaker Joe Dobbes away from Hinman/ Sylvan Ridge added cachet. Especially noteworthy are an inexpensive and fruity Pinot Noir designated Whole Cluster and a more expensive Joe Dobbes signature model. Upcoming is a series of wines under the Griffen Creek brand made from grapes grown in the Rogue Valley. These will include Cabernet Sauvignon, Merlot, Syrah, and a Viognier which must be considered full throttle by OR standards.

Witness Tree, small winery of 6,000 cases produced from their 46-acre estate vineyard which sends nearly 10% of production to CA with good placements in restaurants there.

See DOM DROUHIN, EOLA HILLS, EYRIE, PONZI, RED HILLS OF DUNDEE.　　R.A.I.

Williams Selyem,

one of the top Pinot Noir producers in CA since 1982, in the RUSSIAN RIVER AVA of northern Sonoma Co. Begun by hobbyists Burt Williams, a pressman at the *San Francisco Chronicle*, and Ed Selyem, a part-time manager at a rural grocery store, using salvage dairy equipment in their backyard. Williams and Selyem became a CULT WINE in the mid-1980s when some of their wines were even imported into Burgundy. Throughout their tenure the two partners maintained a homespun demeanor, and the steadfast allegiance of their growers, by showing up to get grapes with a wad of cash in their pockets. As Williams loaded lug boxes of high quality, well-sorted grapes into their pick-up truck, Selyem peeled off bills for the second and third generation Italian-American farmers of these low yielding, cool climate vineyards hidden on hillsides among the redwood trees in northwestern Sonoma. The skins were *punched down by hand in open topped fermenters, and the wines aged in top quality French oak barrels. The first CA Pinot Noirs with weight and real character, they were individual, depending on the source (vineyards such as ROCHIOLI, Allan, Summa,

Z

ZAP, acronym for Zinfandel Advocates and Producers, a trade organization formed in CA for the promotion of Zinfandel. Phenomenally successful, and a model for several other trade groups focused on a single wine category or region, ZAP sponsors research such as the Heritage Collection of PRE-CERTIFICATION CLONE Zinfandel vines, it holds gala weekend events for consumer members in different Zinfandel producing regions, and at the end of each Jan it draws 5,000 paying attendees from all over the world to a new release tasting at Ft Mason in San Francisco, a somewhat ribald event that sells out months ahead of time.   B.C.C.

Ziraldo, Donald (1948–   ) of St Catharines, NIAGARA PENINSULA, the single individual who has had the most positive impact on the wine industry of CANADA. A challenger of the status quo, he was the first in 47 years after Prohibition to apply for a license to make and to sell wine. Unlike many, he has seen where the Canadian industry fits into the larger scheme of international markets. When, in 1982, he could not sell his wine to France because he was not able to prove the origins of his grapes, he returned to Canada to initiate and lead the creation of the VQA which he chaired from 1988 to 1995. As President and co-founder of INNISKILLIN, he has promoted the interests of his winery, but in equal measure he has always promoted the interests of Canadian wine generally.

He has also been able to outline the future of the Canadian wine industry in ways that inspire others. He instigated a center at Brock Univ devoted to winegrowing and winemaking in a cool climate (CCOVI). As co-chair of the fundraising campaign, he raised the C\$4 million to build it. When growers were concerned about a grape surplus, Ziraldo said, 'There is no surplus, just a lack of marketing.' He has received Canada's most distinguished citizen's award, the Order of Canada.   L.F.B.

Matching Food and Wine in North America

LARRY STONE

WITH the cultural shift in American demographics has come the interesting culinary challenge of matching wines to flavor combinations that are not traditionally enjoyed with wine in their country of origin. In succession over the last ten years has come an interest in Southwest Regional cuisine, inspired by Northern Mexican and Southwest Indian, Sonoran native culinary traditions, which among other things employed the use of very spicy and acid combinations with marinades, salsas, and unusual herbs. In the Southeast came 'Floribbean' and Pan Caribbean cuisine with the use of fruits, Yucca, and sweet sauces, a cultural descendant of African, Spanish, Creole, Criolla, and indigenous culinary currents, again with some fairly spicy seasoning. The New Orleans cuisine descended from the French colonial cuisine, in the rich old style, heavily dependent upon cream and butter, even in the newer 'New New Orleans' style cuisine led by talented Emeril Lagasse, and therefore it has been a bit more flexible with traditional wine matches. The latest ethnic cuisines to influence the general culinary tenor of American cooking has come from China, Japan, Vietnam, Thailand, Singapore, and even most recently from India. These cuisines are distinct, ranging from relatively mild Vietnamese to fragrant Indian to fiery Thai. Furthermore the range of culinary style even within the individual countries, especially within the cuisines of India and China, is so diverse that no simple panacea-like wine recommendation could hope to cover the multitude of dishes represented.

The generalizations that follow are intended to be no more than an outline, individual experimentation with special dishes is necessary. For the spicier dishes, and the heavier the use of chilis such as *de arbol*, *pekin*, *chipotle* or heaven forbid! *habanero*, more sweetness and less alcohol is required of a wine. A fiery Thai Green Curry can make most dry table wines turn soapy, but a light alcohol, Spätlese or Auslese level Rheinhessen or Rheinpfalz can tame this. The important thing to remember is that alcohol enhances the heat and bitterness of chilis, while residual sugar interferes with the sensation of hot spice and makes it less acrid, more warm and flavorful. The really hot cuisines require low alcohol wines, such as are the strength of Germany, not Alsace. The milder but fragrant spiciness of an Indian Garam Masala, for example, actually blends very well with the flowery Alsace Gewürztraminer, which is low in acid, just like the cuisine, with its use of *ghee*, coconut, and yoghurt.

Cuisines where there are sharp, acidic, and herbaceous combinations require dry, high acid wines. So for example, if one is eating a Southwestern or Mexican dish, such as chicken in a mildly spicy but acidic, tomatillo-based Veracruz Salsa Verde, the wine would be dry and medium-bodied, with a slightly herbaceous flavor, such as a typical California Sauvignon Blanc. If the salsa is made more acidic, then a New Zealand Sauvignon Blanc or a Loire Valley Sancerre would work. If there is shellfish in the dish or fruit added to the salsa, then wines like Loire Valley Chenin Blanc (Vouvray, Savennières, Coteaux du Layon) work well. A good example of this would be Vietnamese Spring Rolls with a Sweet and Sour Sauce.

There are many chefs today who practice combining different elements from different cuisines in an individualistic fashion, some of whom are mentioned in the article above. In California and Hawaii especially, where so many groups come together to live in relative peace and mutual admiration, there is a great mixing of culinary traditions. Chinese, Philippine, Thai, Japanese, French, Italian, and just plain individual style, can come together on one menu. This trend, often disparagingly called 'fusion,' is really already deep-seated, even in Europe, where French and Italian chefs add a curry here and a ginger *beurre blanc* there. It will make finding workable wine matches even more individualistic and exciting in the future.

For example Roy's Lemon Grass-Crusted Salmon with Watercress-Ginger Sauce (the sauce is a classic *beurre blanc*, served with pickled ginger as a garnish). I think a Savennières from a ripe vintage such as 1995 or 1996 would be nice with this dish, because it has a slight acidity, and a roundness rather than sweetness. It would augment the salmon flavor and the wine's quince-like flavor components would nicely match the ginger. Another example of this blending of cuisines is found in Chicago's Charlie Trotter's Seared Raw Tuna with Curried Carrot Broth, Collard Greens and Baby Carrots. This dish reflects a low acid, sweet, and fragrant touch with the broth actually containing the sweet element of apple in addition to the sweet baby carrots, but the sweetness is balanced by the bitter greens. A full-bodied, fragrant, but low acid Rhône such as a great Châteauneuf-du-Pape Blanc (e.g. Château de Rayas Blanc) or an Hermitage Blanc such as Grippat would work very well.

About the only generalization that holds for all of these new combinations, is that the hefty, tannic red wines of Europe and overly oaky New World Chardonnay are more likely to fail in combination with these experimental and non-traditional new directions in American cookery.

Classic American Foods with Wine Suggestions

BRUCE CASS

FOOD	♆ WINE
Abalone	cold climate, barrel fermented, MLF Chardonnay
Acorn squash with cinnamon	warm climate (TX, Lake Cty, eastern WA) Chardonnay
Adobo (using tamarind)	SE PA, or NC Chambourcin
Alligator	CO Chardonnay
Apple brown Betty	Okanagan Pinot Blanc Icewine
Aquacultured European flat (Belon) oysters	Amador Sauvignon Blanc (also preferred with artichokes)
Beans: Boston baked	Baja Nebbiolo
Beef: Memphis BBQ brisket	MO Norton
Beef: T-bone steak with creamed spinach and baked potato	Rutherford Bench Cabernet Sauvignon
Blackened redfish	MI or WI Chancellor
Bluefish	New Mexico Brut sparkler
Cajun crawfish etouffe with dirty rice or jambalaya	Seyval Blanc or a lighter Grenache/Mourvedre blend
Chicken: fried with buttermilk batter	woody Chardonnay
Chicken: jerk with sweet Caribbean salsa	Roussanne or Valdiguie
Chili	Petite Sirah (if chili is 3-alarm, try Baco Noir instead)
Clam chowder, cream Boston style	MI, OH, or Niagara Peninsula Chardonnay
Cole Slaw	Vidal Blanc or Chenin Blanc
Conch	warm climate Chardonnay
Corn bread with pot liquor (collard greens, okra, black-eyed peas)	WA Semillon or CA white Meritage

⚔️ FOOD	🍷 WINE
Corn on the cob	Chardonnay aged in American Oak
Dungeness Crab with sourdough	cool climate or high elevation Riesling
Elk or Caribou	Midwest Baco Noir or Howell Mtn Zinfandel
Fruit crisp (or cobbler): boysenberry, wild blueberry	Vidal Icewine or sweet Muscat
Grayling	Pinot Gris or dry Vignoles
Green chiles bisque	cold climate Sauvignon Blanc
Guacamole	CA Pinot Gris or warm climate Sauvignon Blanc
Halibut cheeks	Chenin Blanc
Ham: honey baked, bourbon basted, with jewel yams	Claret-style Zinfandel, or Okanagan Gewürztraminer
Hamburger with tomato, lettuce, onion, mayonnaise	WA Merlot or TX Cabernet Sauvignon
Hoisin sauce moo shu pork	Santa Barbara or Russian River Pinot Noir
Hot dog with relish, ketchup, and French's mustard	Sierra Foothills Barbera or Midwestern Marechal Foch
Lamb or young goat with an anchiote paste rub	Coastal region CA Cabernet Sauvignon
Lima beans	aged Livermore Semillon
Olympia (and/or aquacultured Kumomato) oyster	Finger Lakes or Northwestern Brut sparkling wine
Pacific oyster	Anderson Valley Blanc de Blanc
Paw paw (tastes like cherimoya)	MS or FL white Muscadine
Peach bisque (cold) with chive flower	Niagara Peninsula or Finger Lakes Riesling
Peanut soup (or peanut butter)	CA Sangiovese
Pecan pie	Angelica (actually best with Australian Liqueur Muscat)
Petrale sole	Dry Vidal Blanc
Pike	white Meritage or CA Arneas
Pizza with pepperoni	Russian River or Santa Barbara Syrah
Pork rib BBQ: either KC style or North Carolina style	Amador County Syrah Cabernet Franc
Possum	red Meritage
Potato: mashed with gravy, cranberry sauce, and sage stuffing	CA Gewürztraminer or MI Chambourcin
Prawns with glazed walnuts	Viognier or Okanagan Riesling
Pupusas with refried pork	Lodi Zinfandel
Quail: teriyaki grilled	OR Pinot Noir
Rattlesnake	TX Sauvignon Blanc

⚒ FOOD	♟ WINE
Salad with jicama, flowers, blood orange, star fruit, kiwi, etc	OR Pinot Gris
Salmon: wild King	Pinot Noir
Salsa and chips	Grenache
Scrod	Seyval Blanc
Sushi: California roll	Pacific Northwest Pinot Blanc
Shrimp gumbo	Baja Tempranillo or CA Sauvignon Blanc
Shrimp with cocktail sauce or Louis salad	cold climate Pinot Blanc
Soft shell crab	VA Chardonnay
Stone crab	warm climate Sauvignon Blanc
Sweet potato pie (or pumpkin pie)	Monterey Chardonnay or Orange Muscat
Tapioca with pineapple, passion fruit, or lychee	botytized Riesling or Gewürztraminer
Taro Won Ton (or poi)	Roussanne/Marsanne blend
Thai lemongrass flavored noodles	Pacific Northwest Ehrenfelser or Madelaine Angevine
Tomato with bacon, lettuce, mayonnaise (Club sandwich)	Mourvedre rosé
Turkey with mole sauce	Alexander Valley Cabernet Sauvignon
Wild rice	Central Valley or FL sherry
Yucca: fried	OH Chardonnay

US States Ranked by Vineyard Acreage

Rank	State	Acres in 1999
1	California	795,409*
2	Washington	48,000
3	New York	31,401**
4	Michigan	12,000**
5	Pennsylvania	11,073**
6	Oregon	9,000
7	Arizona	4,490 *
8	Texas	3,202
9	New Mexico	2,900
10	Arkansas	2,050
11	Ohio	1,556
12	Virginia	1,448
13	Georgia	1,199
14	Mississippi	908
15	Missouri	864
16	Florida	825
17	Idaho	686
18	New Jersey	566
19	North Carolina	528
20	Colorado	410
20	Tennessee	400

* Definitely includes significant acreage (several hundred thousand in CA) of table and raisin grapes.
** Significant acreage of Concords used for fresh juice.

Statistics compiled by P.W.F., the Chicago Wine School, from several sources including personal phone surveys. Figures are very difficult to verify, and teasing out which acres are actually employed for wine, as opposed to fresh juice or table grapes or raisins, is a virtually impossible task with usage changing every year.

US States Ranked by Number of Wineries

Rank Wineries in 1980	State		Wineries in 1999
1	California	1056	508
2	New York	136	69
3	Washington	125	22
4	Oregon	116	36
5	Pennsylvania	62	29
6	Ohio	61	44
7	Virginia	54	11
8	Missouri	40	25
9	Texas	38	11
10	Michigan	32	21
11	Colorado	26	2
12	New Mexico	25	5

Others with more than ten wineries (listed alphabetically):

Arizona
Connecticut
Georgia
Idaho
Illinois
Indiana (20)
Maryland

Statistics compiled by P.W.F., the Chicago Wine School, from BATF licensing records. As such the numbers tend to be somewhat overstated because wineries with multiple locations (including separate warehouses) are counted multiple times, and because inactive wineries often keep their license open.

Maps of North American
Wine-Growing Regions

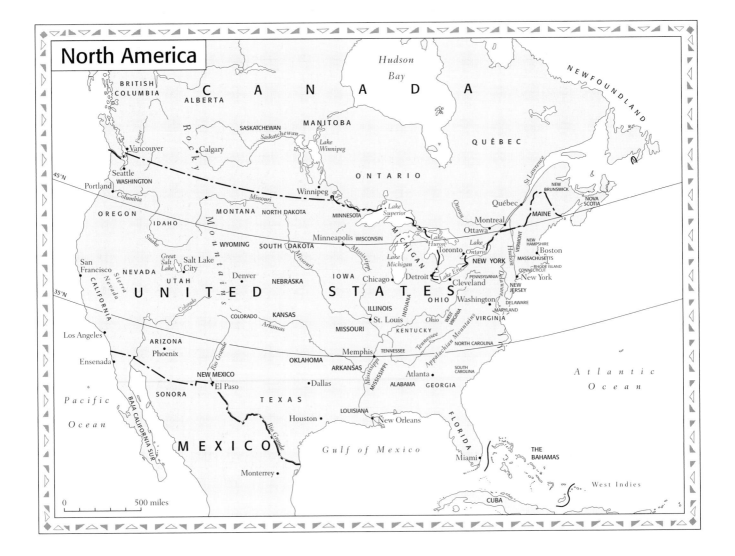

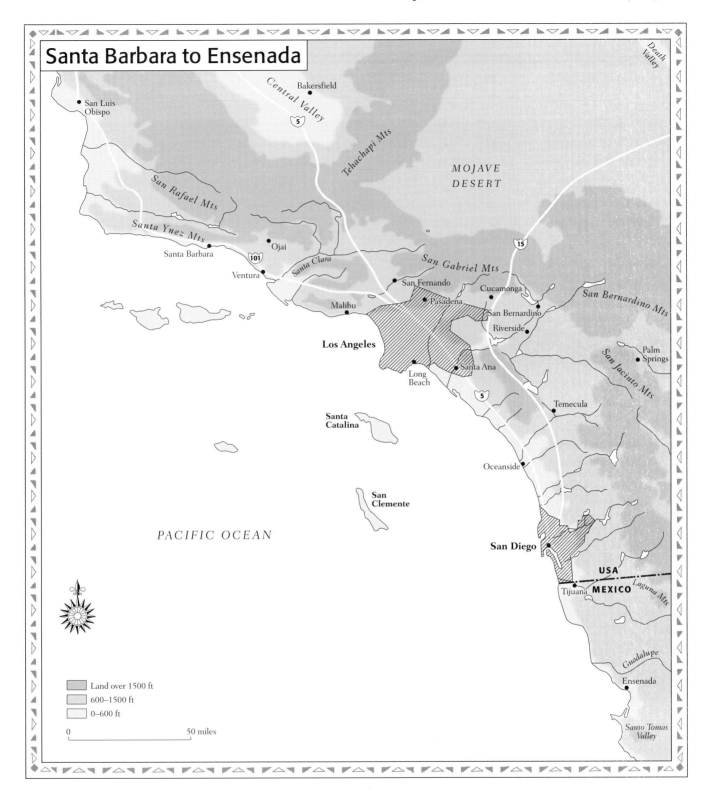

Santa Barbara to Ensenada

Land over 1500 ft
600–1500 ft
0–600 ft

0   50 miles

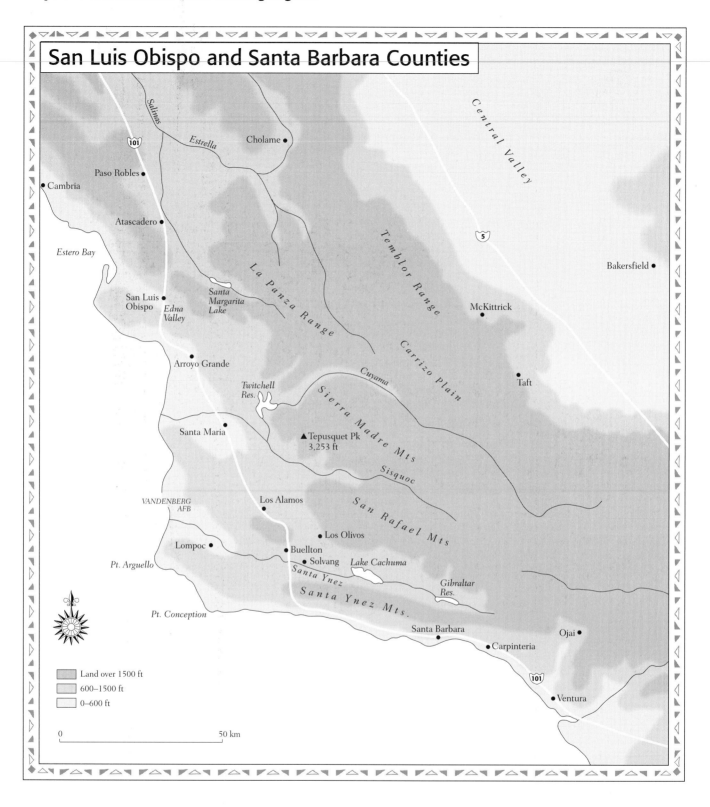

San Luis Obispo and Santa Barbara Counties

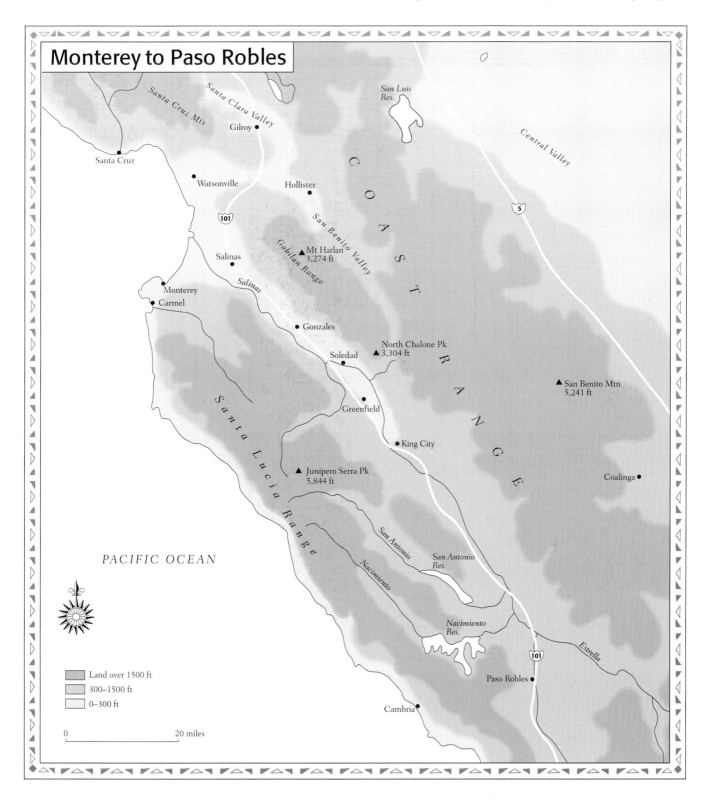

Monterey to Paso Robles

Santa Cruz Mts

Santa Clara Valley

San Luis Res.

Central Valley

Gilroy

Santa Cruz

Watsonville

Hollister

C O A S T

5

101

San Benito Valley

Salinas

Gabilan Range

▲ Mt Harlan
3,274 ft

Monterey
Carmel

Salinas

R A N G E

Gonzales

North Chalone Pk
3,304 ft ▲

Soledad

▲ San Benito Mtn
5,241 ft

S
a
n
t
a

L
u
c
i
a

R
a
n
g
e

Greenfield

King City

▲ Junipero Serra Pk
5,844 ft

Coalinga ●

PACIFIC OCEAN

San Antonio

Nacimiento

San Antonio Res.

Nacimiento Res.

Estrella

101

Paso Robles

Cambria

Land over 1500 ft

300–1500 ft

0–300 ft

0 _____ 20 miles

San Francisco Bay Area

Bodega Bay

Napa

Sonoma

Petaluma

Tomales Bay

80

101

Fairfield

The Delta

PT. REYES NATIONAL SEASHORE

680

San Pablo Bay

Vallejo

Suisun Bay

Antioch

Oakley

Pt. Reyes

Drakes Bay

San Rafael

Richmond

▲ Mt. Diablo Peak 3,895 ft

Mt. Tamalpais ▲

24

Berkeley

Bay Bridge

Golden Gate Bridge

San Francisco

Oakland

Livermore

580

San Francisco Bay

680

San Mateo

PACIFIC OCEAN

Palo Alto

▲ Mt Hamilton 4,261 ft

Santa Clara Valley

San Jose

Santa Cruz Mts

Eagle Rock 2,488 ft ▲

17

Morgan Hill

101

Hecker Pass

Gilroy

Land over 1500 ft

300–1500 ft

0–300 ft

Santa Cruz

Monterey Bay

0   20 miles

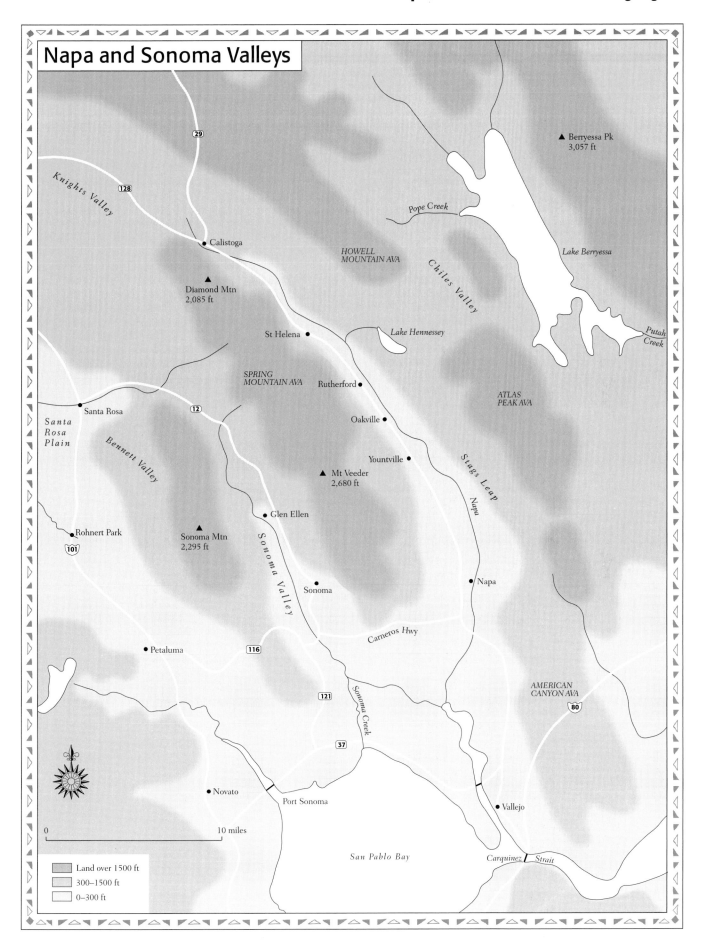

Napa and Sonoma Valleys

29

128

Knights Valley

▲ Berryessa Pk
3,057 ft

Pope Creek

• Calistoga

*HOWELL
MOUNTAIN AVA*

Chiles Valley

Lake Berryessa

▲ Diamond Mtn
2,085 ft

Lake Hennessey

*Putah
Creek*

St Helena •

*SPRING
MOUNTAIN AVA*

Rutherford •

*ATLAS
PEAK AVA*

• Santa Rosa

12

Oakville •

*Santa
Rosa
Plain*

Bennett Valley

Yountville •

▲ Mt Veeder
2,680 ft

Stags Leap

Napa

• Rohnert Park

• Glen Ellen

101

▲ Sonoma Mtn
2,295 ft

Sonoma Valley

Sonoma •

• Napa

Carneros Hwy

• Petaluma

116

*AMERICAN
CANYON AVA*

121

Sonoma Creek

80

37

• Novato

Port Sonoma

• Vallejo

0   10 miles

San Pablo Bay

Carquinez Strait

Land over 1500 ft

300–1500 ft

0–300 ft

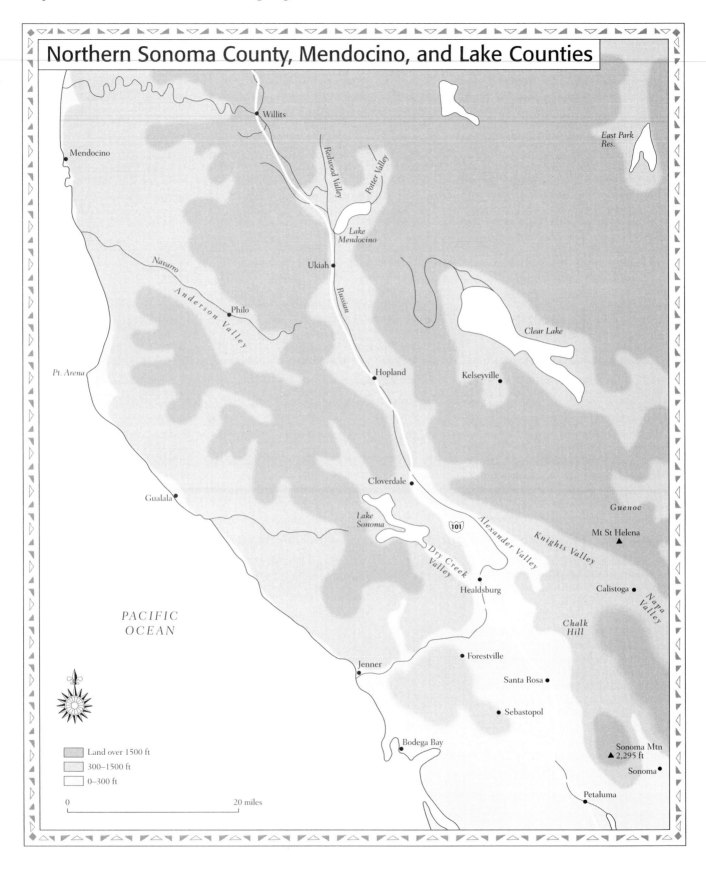

Northern Sonoma County, Mendocino, and Lake Counties

Willits

Mendocino

East Park Res.

Redwood Valley

Potter Valley

Lake Mendocino

Navarro

Ukiah

Russian

Anderson Valley

Philo

Clear Lake

Pt. Arena

Hopland

Kelseyville

Cloverdale

Gualala

Guenoc

Lake Sonoma

101

Alexander Valley

Knights Valley

Mt St Helena ▲

Dry Creek Valley

Calistoga ●

Napa Valley

Healdsburg

Chalk Hill

PACIFIC OCEAN

● Forestville

Jenner

Santa Rosa ●

● Sebastopol

Sonoma Mtn ▲ 2,295 ft

Bodega Bay

Sonoma ●

Petaluma

Land over 1500 ft
300–1500 ft
0–300 ft

0   20 miles

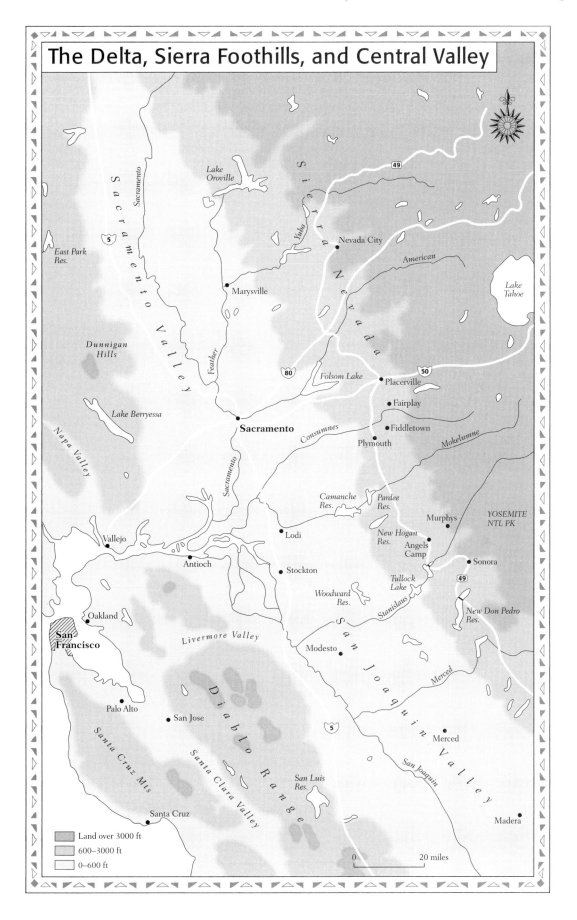

The Delta, Sierra Foothills, and Central Valley

Sacramento

Lake Oroville

Sierra Nevada

49

Yuba

Nevada City

American

East Park Res.

5

Sacramento

Marysville

Lake Tahoe

Dunnigan Hills

Feather

80

Folsom Lake

Placerville

50

Fairplay

Lake Berryessa

Sacramento

Sacramento

Consumnes

Fiddletown

Plymouth

Mokelumne

Napa Valley

Camanche Res.

Pardee Res.

Murphys

YOSEMITE NTL PK

Vallejo

Lodi

New Hogan Res.

Angels Camp

Sonora

Antioch

Stockton

Tullock Lake

49

Woodward Res.

New Don Pedro Res.

Oakland

Stanislaus

San Joaquin Valley

San Francisco

Livermore Valley

Modesto

Merced

Diablo Range

Palo Alto

San Jose

5

Merced

Santa Cruz Mts

Santa Clara Valley

San Luis Res.

San Joaquin

Santa Cruz

Madera

Land over 3000 ft

600–3000 ft

0–600 ft

0   20 miles

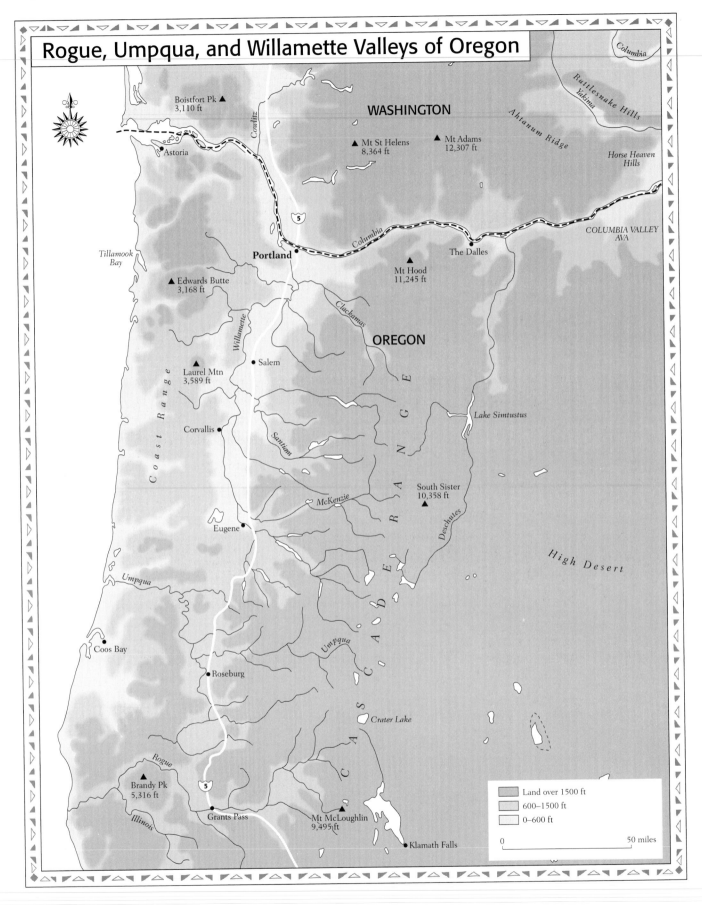

Rogue, Umpqua, and Willamette Valleys of Oregon

Columbia

Rattlesnake Hills
Yakima

Boistfort Pk ▲
3,110 ft

WASHINGTON

Astoria

Cowlitz

▲ Mt St Helens
8,364 ft

▲ Mt Adams
12,307 ft

Ahtanum Ridge

Horse Heaven
Hills

Columbia

The Dalles

COLUMBIA VALLEY
AVA

Tillamook
Bay

Portland

▲ Edwards Butte
3,168 ft

▲ Mt Hood
11,245 ft

Willamette

Clackamas

OREGON

Laurel Mtn
3,589 ft
▲

Salem

Coast Range

Santiam

Corvallis

Lake Simtustus

McKenzie

South Sister
10,358 ft
▲

Deschutes

Eugene

High Desert

Umpqua

Coos Bay

Umpqua

Roseburg

C A S C A D E   R A N G E

Crater Lake

Rogue

Brandy Pk
5,316 ft
▲

Illinois

Grants Pass

Mt McLoughlin
9,495 ft

	Land over 1500 ft
	600–1500 ft
	0–600 ft

0   50 miles

Klamath Falls

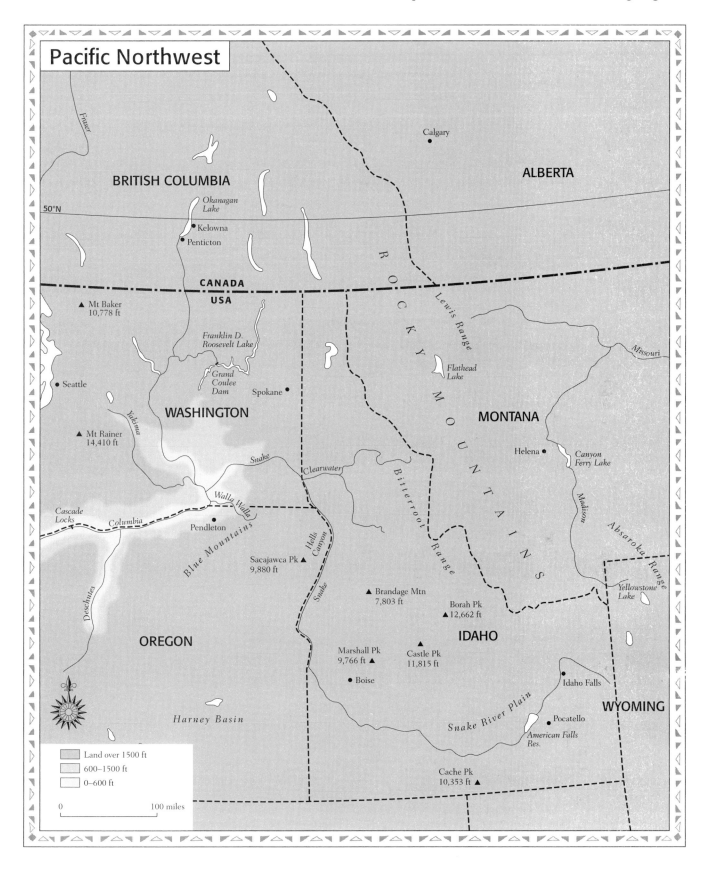

Pacific Northwest

BRITISH COLUMBIA

ALBERTA

50°N

Calgary

Fraser

Okanagan
Lake

• Kelowna

• Penticton

CANADA
USA

▲ Mt Baker
10,778 ft

Franklin D.
Roosevelt Lake

ROCKY

Lewis Range

Missouri

• Seattle

Grand
Coulee
Dam

Spokane •

Flathead
Lake

WASHINGTON

Yakima

▲ Mt Rainer
14,410 ft

Snake

Clearwater

MOUNTAINS

MONTANA

Helena •

Canyon
Ferry Lake

Cascade
Locks

Columbia

Walla Walla

Bitterroot Range

Madison

Absaroka Range

Pendleton •

Blue Mountains

Sacajawca Pk ▲
9,880 ft

Hells Canyon

Snake

▲ Brandage Mtn
7,803 ft

Borah Pk
▲12,662 ft

Yellowstone
Lake

OREGON

Marshall Pk
9,766 ft ▲

Castle Pk ▲
11,815 ft

IDAHO

WYOMING

• Boise

Idaho Falls •

Snake River Plain

• Pocatello

Harney Basin

American Falls
Res.

	Land over 1500 ft
	600–1500 ft
	0–600 ft

Cache Pk
10,353 ft ▲

0   100 miles

279

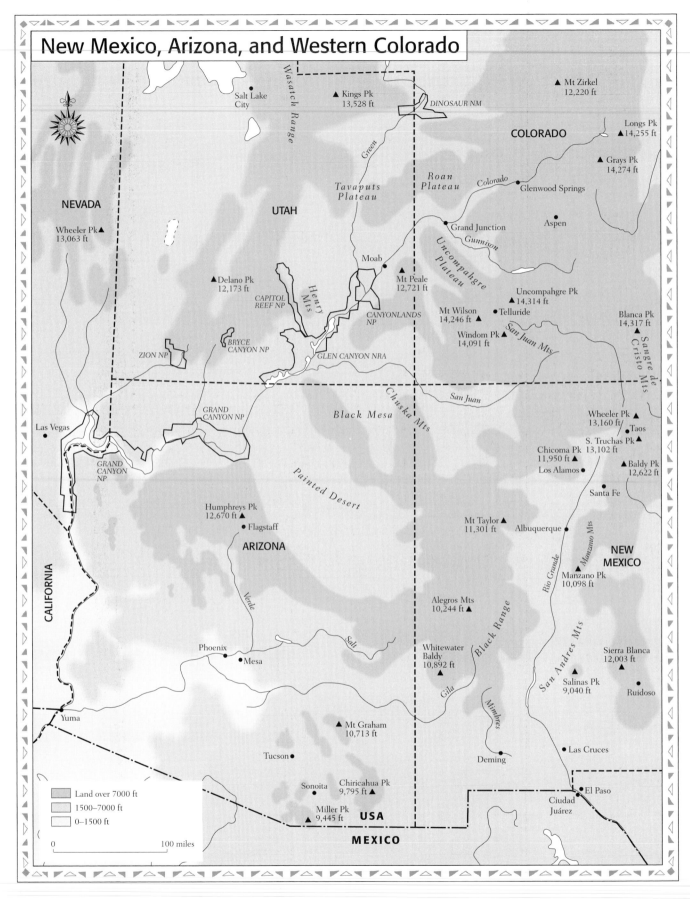

New Mexico, Arizona, and Western Colorado

▲ Mt Zirkel
12,220 ft

Salt Lake
City

▲ Kings Pk
13,528 ft

DINOSAUR NM

COLORADO

Longs Pk
▲ 14,255 ft

Wasatch Range

Green

*Roan
Plateau*

Colorado Glenwood Springs

▲ Grays Pk
14,274 ft

NEVADA

UTAH

*Tavaputs
Plateau*

Grand Junction

Gunnison

Aspen

Wheeler Pk▲
13,063 ft

▲ Delano Pk
12,173 ft

*CAPITOL
REEF NP*

*Henry
Mts*

Moab

▲ Mt Peale
12,721 ft

*Uncompahgre
Plateau*

Uncompahgre Pk
▲ 14,314 ft

Telluride

Blanca Pk
14,317 ft

Mt Wilson
14,246 ft ▲

San Juan Mts

*Sangre de
Cristo Mts*

*CANYONLANDS
NP*

Windom Pk ▲
14,091 ft

*BRYCE
CANYON NP*

ZION NP

GLEN CANYON NRA

San Juan

Wheeler Pk ▲
13,160 ft

Chuska Mts

Black Mesa

Taos

*GRAND
CANYON NP*

S. Truchas Pk ▲
Chicoma Pk 13,102 ft
11,950 ft ▲

▲ Baldy Pk
12,622 ft

Los Alamos

Las Vegas

*GRAND
CANYON
NP*

Painted Desert

Santa Fe

Humphreys Pk
12,670 ft ▲

Mt Taylor ▲
11,301 ft

Albuquerque

Manzano Mts

Flagstaff

NEW
MEXICO

ARIZONA

Rio Grande

Manzano Pk ▲
10,098 ft

Verde

Alegros Mts
10,244 ft ▲

Black Range

Sierra Blanca
12,003 ft
▲

Salt

Whitewater
Baldy
10,892 ft

San Andres Mts

Salinas Pk
9,040 ft

Ruidoso

Phoenix

Mesa

Gila

Mimbres

Yuma

▲ Mt Graham
10,713 ft

CALIFORNIA

Las Cruces

Tucson

Deming

Sonoita Chiricahua Pk
9,795 ft ▲

El Paso

Miller Pk
▲ 9,445 ft

USA

Ciudad
Juárez

MEXICO

	Land over 7000 ft
	1500–7000 ft
	0–1500 ft

0   100 miles

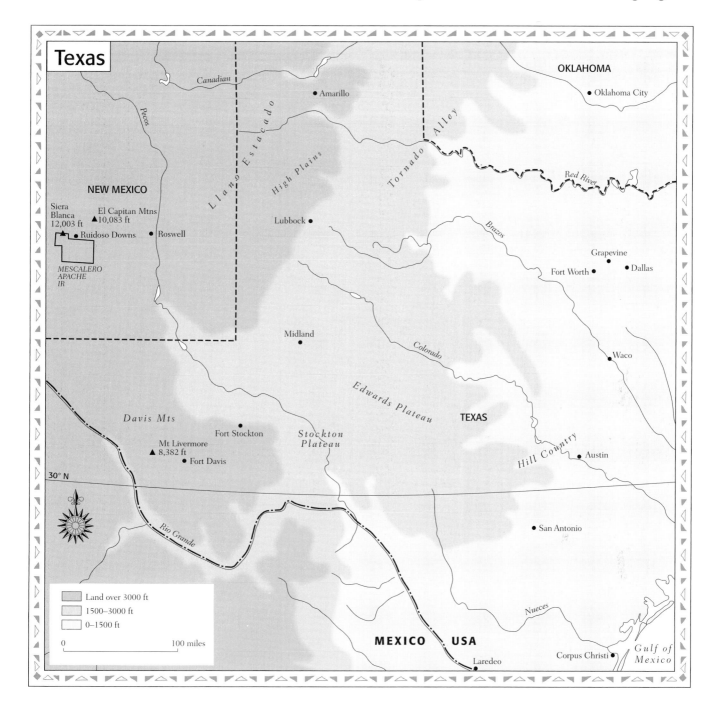

Texas

OKLAHOMA

Canadian

● Amarillo

● Oklahoma City

Pecos

Llano Estacado

High Plains

Tornado Alley

Red River

NEW MEXICO

Siera
Blanca
12,003 ft
▲

El Capitan Mtns
▲10,083 ft

Lubbock ●

Brazos

▲ ● Ruidoso Downs   ● Roswell

Grapevine
●
Fort Worth ●   ● Dallas

MESCALERO
APACHE
IR

Midland
●

Colorado

Waco
●

Davis Mts

Edwards Plateau

TEXAS

Fort Stockton
●

Stockton
Plateau

Mt Livermore
▲ 8,382 ft   ● Fort Davis

Hill Country

● Austin

30° N

Rio Grande

● San Antonio

Land over 3000 ft

1500–3000 ft

0–1500 ft

Nueces

0   100 miles

MEXICO   USA

Laredeo
●

Corpus Christi ●

Gulf of
Mexico

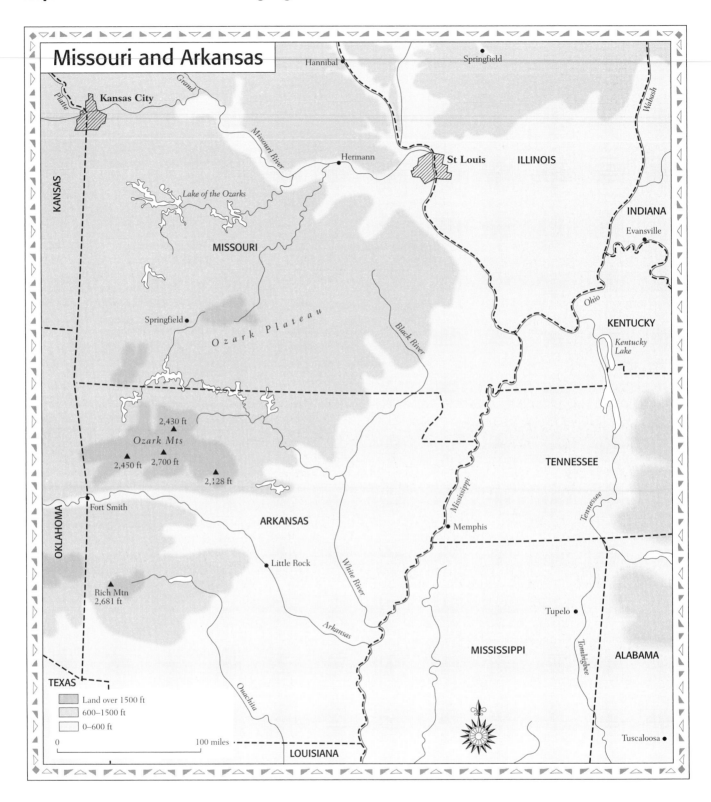

Missouri and Arkansas

Hannibal

Springfield

Kansas City

Grand

Platte

KANSAS

Missouri River

Hermann

St Louis

ILLINOIS

Lake of the Ozarks

MISSOURI

Wabash

INDIANA

Evansville

Springfield

O z a r k   P l a t e a u

Black River

Ohio

KENTUCKY

Kentucky Lake

2,430 ft ▲

Ozark Mts

2,450 ft ▲   ▲ 2,700 ft

▲ 2,128 ft

TENNESSEE

OKLAHOMA

Fort Smith

ARKANSAS

Mississippi

Tennessee

Memphis

Little Rock

White River

▲ Rich Mtn 2,681 ft

Arkansas

Tupelo

TEXAS

Land over 1500 ft

600–1500 ft

0–600 ft

0   100 miles

Ouachita

MISSISSIPPI

Tombigbee

ALABAMA

Tuscaloosa

LOUISIANA

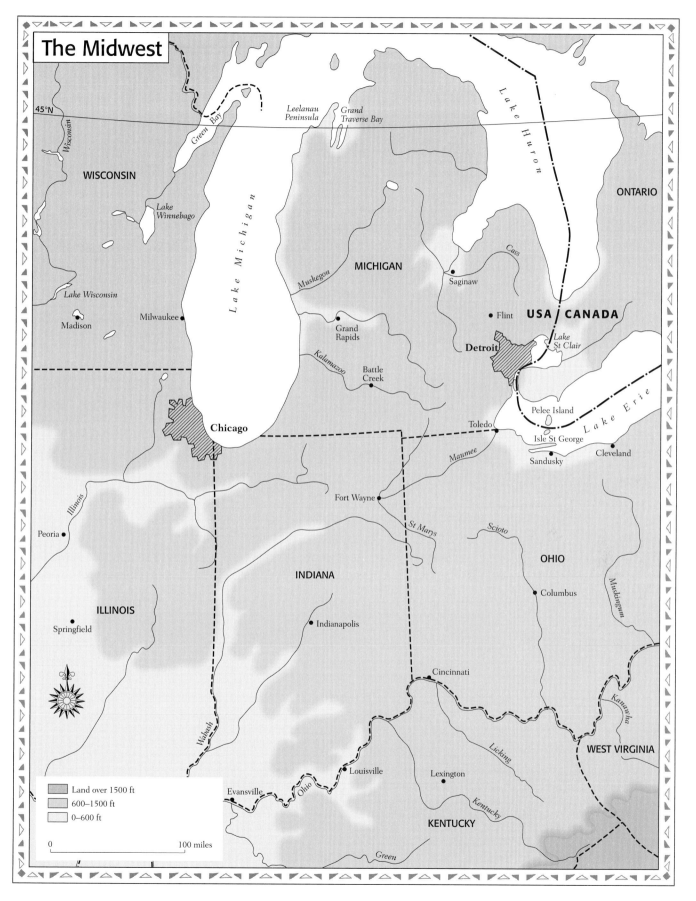

The Midwest

45°N

Wisconsin

WISCONSIN

Green Bay

Leelanau Peninsula

Grand Traverse Bay

Lake Huron

ONTARIO

Lake Winnebago

Lake Wisconsin

Madison

Milwaukee

Lake Michigan

Muskegon

MICHIGAN

Cass

Saginaw

Flint

USA / CANADA

Grand Rapids

Detroit

Lake St Clair

Kalamazoo

Battle Creek

Pelee Island

Lake Erie

Chicago

Toledo

Isle St George

Sandusky

Cleveland

Illinois

Maumee

Fort Wayne

St Marys

Scioto

OHIO

Peoria

INDIANA

Columbus

Muskingum

ILLINOIS

Indianapolis

Springfield

Cincinnati

Kanawha

Wabash

Licking

WEST VIRGINIA

Evansville

Ohio

Louisville

Lexington

Kentucky

KENTUCKY

Green

Land over 1500 ft

600–1500 ft

0–600 ft

0   100 miles

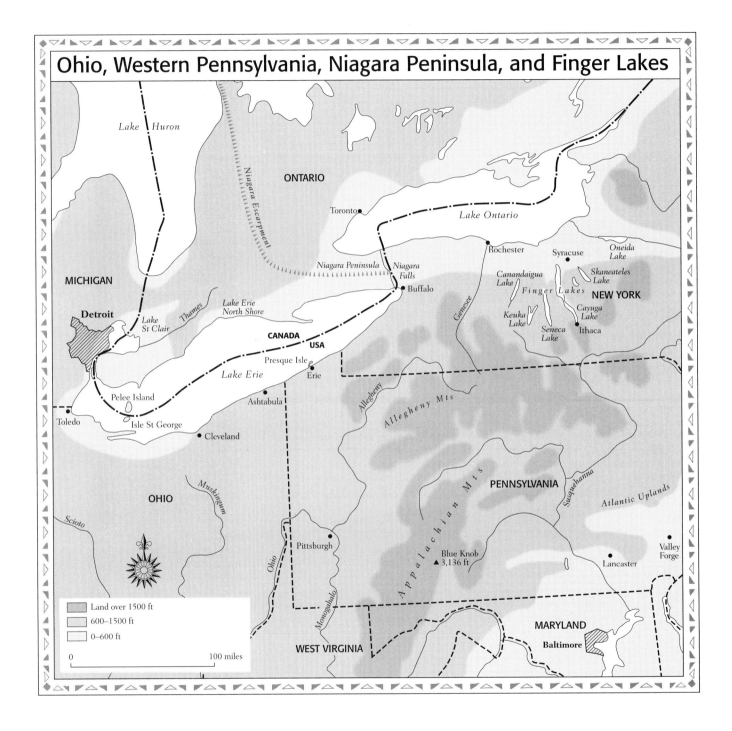

Ohio, Western Pennsylvania, Niagara Peninsula, and Finger Lakes

Lake Huron

ONTARIO

Niagara Escarpment

Toronto

Lake Ontario

Rochester

Syracuse

Oneida Lake

Niagara Peninsula

Niagara Falls

Canandaigua Lake

Skaneateles Lake

MICHIGAN

Buffalo

Finger Lakes

NEW YORK

Thames

Lake Erie North Shore

Genesee

Keuka Lake

Cayuga Lake

Detroit

Lake St Clair

CANADA

USA

Seneca Lake

Ithaca

Presque Isle

Pelee Island

Erie

Toledo

Isle St George

Ashtabula

Lake Erie

Allegheny

Allegheny Mts

Cleveland

Muskingum

OHIO

Ohio

Scioto

Pittsburgh

Appalachian Mts

PENNSYLVANIA

Susquehanna

Atlantic Uplands

Blue Knob
▲ 3,136 ft

Lancaster

Valley Forge

Monogahalo

MARYLAND

Baltimore

WEST VIRGINIA

Land over 1500 ft

600–1500 ft

0–600 ft

0   100 miles

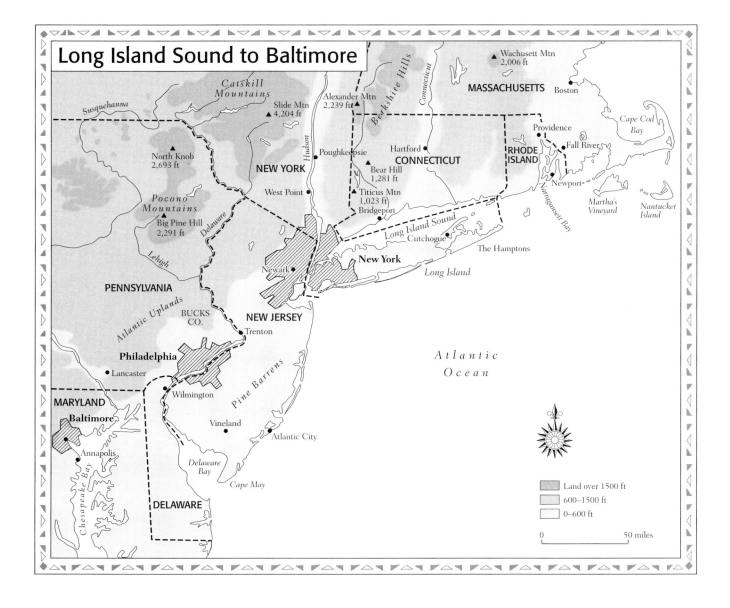

Long Island Sound to Baltimore

Susquehanna

Catskill Mountains

Slide Mtn
▲ 4,204 ft

Berkshire Hills

▲ Wachusett Mtn
2,006 ft

MASSACHUSETTS Boston

Alexander Mtn
2,239 ft ▲

Connecticut

North Knob
▲ 2,693 ft

Poughkeepsie

Hartford ●

CONNECTICUT

Providence ●

Cape Cod Bay

NEW YORK

Bear Hill
▲ 1,281 ft

**RHODE
ISLAND**

Fall River ●

*Pocono
Mountains*

West Point ●

Hudson

▲ Titicus Mtn
1,023 ft

Newport ●

*Martha's
Vineyard*

*Nantucket
Island*

Big Pine Hill
▲ 2,291 ft

Delaware

Bridgeport

Cutchogue ●

Narragansett Bay

Lehigh

Newark ●

New York

Long Island Sound

The Hamptons

Long Island

PENNSYLVANIA

Atlantic Uplands

BUCKS
CO.

NEW JERSEY

*A t l a n t i c
O c e a n*

Philadelphia

Trenton ●

● Lancaster

Pine Barrens

MARYLAND

Wilmington ●

Baltimore

Vineland ●

● Atlantic City

Annapolis ●

*Delaware
Bay*

DELAWARE

Cape May

Chesapeake Bay

	Land over 1500 ft
	600–1500 ft
	0–600 ft

0   50 miles

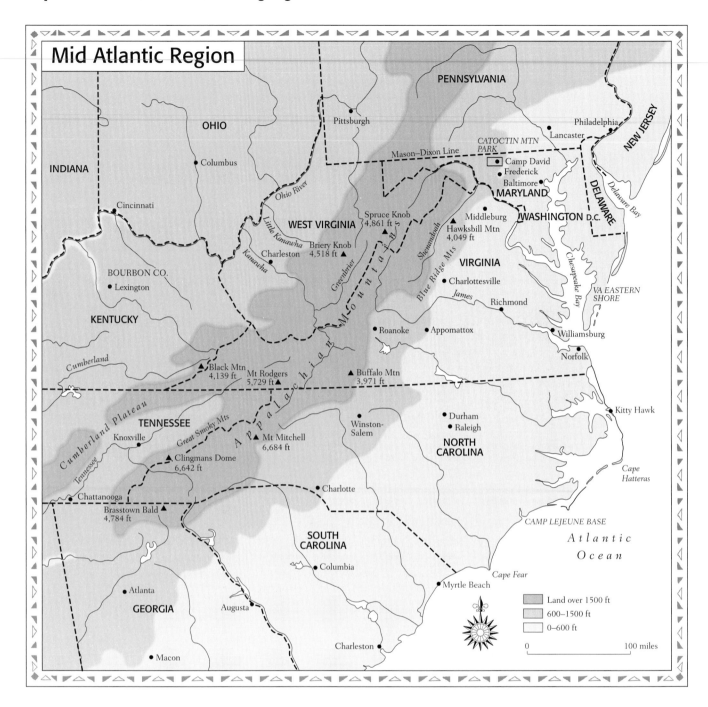

Mid Atlantic Region

PENNSYLVANIA

OHIO

Pittsburgh

Philadelphia

Lancaster

CATOCTIN MTN PARK

Mason–Dixon Line

Camp David

Frederick

Baltimore

INDIANA

Columbus

MARYLAND

WASHINGTON D.C.

DELAWARE

Delaware Bay

Cincinnati

Ohio River

Little Kanawha

WEST VIRGINIA

Spruce Knob 4,861 ft

Middleburg

Hawksbill Mtn 4,049 ft

Chesapeake Bay

Charleston

Kanawha

Briery Knob 4,518 ft

Shenandoah

VIRGINIA

VA EASTERN SHORE

BOURBON CO.

Greenbrier

Blue Ridge Mts

Charlottesville

Lexington

James

Richmond

KENTUCKY

Williamsburg

Cumberland

Roanoke

Appomattox

Norfolk

Black Mtn 4,139 ft

Mt Rodgers 5,729 ft

Buffalo Mtn 3,971 ft

Kitty Hawk

Appalachian

Cumberland Plateau

TENNESSEE

Great Smoky Mts

Winston-Salem

Durham

Raleigh

Knoxville

Mt Mitchell 6,684 ft

Tennessee

Clingmans Dome 6,642 ft

NORTH CAROLINA

Mountains

Chattanooga

Charlotte

Cape Hatteras

Brasstown Bald 4,784 ft

CAMP LEJEUNE BASE

SOUTH CAROLINA

Atlantic Ocean

Columbia

Atlanta

Cape Fear

GEORGIA

Augusta

Myrtle Beach

Land over 1500 ft

600–1500 ft

0–600 ft

Charleston

0   100 miles

Macon

Owl Creek Vyd (Cobden, IL) *see* Illinois
Ozark Highlands AVA (MO) 188
Ozark Mountain AVA (AR/MO/OK) 66, 188 *see also* Arkansas

Pacheco Pass AVA (CA) 212 *see also* Santa Clara Valley
Pacheco Ranch Winery (Ignacio, CA) 74 *see also* Bay Area
Pacific Star (Ft. Bragg, CA) *see* Mendocino
Page Mill Winery (Los Altos Hills, CA) 214 *see also* Santa Cruz Mtns AVA
Pahlmeyer Winery (Oakville, CA) 68, 117 *see also* Atlas Peak
Pahrump Valley Vyds (Pahrump, NV) *see* Nevada
Paicines AVA (CA) 209 *see also* San Benito Co
Palagyi, Raymond L. (licensee, Conneaut, OH) *see* Ohio
Palmer Vyds (Riverhead, NY) 189
Palomares Canyon 153
Pandosy, Father 183
Panoz, Donald 105
Panther Creek Cellars (McMinnville, OR) *see* Willamette Valley AVA
Paoletti, John P. (licensee, Calistoga, CA) *see* Calistoga
Paradigm Winery (Oakville, CA) 70, 182 *see also* Oakville
Paradise Ridge Winery (Santa Rosa, CA) *see* Sonoma Co
Paradise Vintners (Paradise, CA) *see* Sierra Foothills AVA
Paragon Vyds 118, 210
Paraiso Springs Vyds (Soledad, CA) *see* Monterey
Paramount Distillers 126, 142, 183
Parducci, John 149
Paris International Exposition 153, 200, 212, 251
Park City Cellars (Park City, UT) *see* Utah
Parker, Fess (Los Olivos, CA) 123
Parker, Gabriel and Barbara (licensees, Grapevine, TX) *see* Texas
Parker, Robert M., Jr 14, 34, 70, 133, 158, 187, 198, 254
Paroschy, John 104, 186
Parras 163
Parsons Family Winery (York, ME) *see* Northeast
Paschina, Luca 73
Pasek Cellars (Mt Vernon, WA) *see* Washington
Paso Robles AVA (CA) 190
Paso Robles Winery (Paso Robles, CA) *see* Paso Robles
Pastori Winery (Cloverdale, CA) *see* Alexander Valley
Paterini Winery (Ellsworth, PA) *see* Pennsylvania
Patrick M. Paul Vyds (Walla Walla, WA) *see* Walla Walla Valley AVA
Patton, Dennis 190
Patz & Hall Wine Co (Rutherford, CA) 191
Paul Hobbs Winery (Kenwood, CA) *see* Sonoma Co
Paul Thomas Cellars (Sunnyside, WA) *see* Yakima Valley AVA
Pauli Ranch (Potter Valley, CA) *see* Mendocino
Paumanok Vyds (Aquebogue, NY) 191
Pavan, Angelo 99
Pawlisch, James T. (licensee, La Valle, WI) *see* Wisconsin
Payette, Tom 195
Peace Valley Winery (Chalfont, PA) *see* Pennsylvania
Peaceful Bend Vyd (Steelville, MO) *see* Missouri
Peachy Canyon Winery (Paso Robles, CA) 191 *see also* Paso Robles
Peconic Bay Vyds (Cutchogue, NY) *see* Long Island
Pedrizzetti Winery (Morgan Hill, CA) *see* Hecker Pass
Pedroncelli Winery (Geyserville, CA) *see* Alexander Valley
Peirano Estate Vyds (Graton, CA) *see* Lodi
Peju Province (Rutherford, CA) *see* Rutherford AVA
Pellegrini Family Vyds (Kenwood, CA) *see* Sonoma Co
Peller, Joseph 94
Peller, Estates and Andras 66
Pelligrini Vyds (Cutchogue, NY) 192
Pend D'Oreille Winery (Sandpoint, ID) 141 *see also* Idaho
Penman Springs Vyd (Paso Robles, CA) *see* Paso Robles
Penn Oaks Winery (Deep Creek, MD) *see* Maryland

Penn Shore Vyds (North East, PA) *see* Lake Erie AVA
Pennsylvania Wine Company 164
Pepi, Robert 146
Pepperwood Springs Vyd (Philo, CA) 65 *see also* Anderson Valley
Perdido Vyds (Perdido, AL) 61 *see also* Alabama
Perrin family 230
Perrone, Osea 200
Perry Creek Vyds (Somerset, CA) 122 *see also* Fair Play
Perry Vyds (Calistoga, CA) *see* Calistoga
Pesenti Winery (Templeton, CA) *see* Paso Robles
Peter Michael Winery (Calistoga, CA) 147 *see also* Knights Valley
Petersen, Dick 68, 171, 207
Peterson, Joel 204
Peterson, Ron 194
Peterson, Tom 62
Peterson & Sons Winery (Kalamazoo, MI) *see* Michigan
Peterson Barrett, Heidi 105, 111, 138, 176, 182, 207
Peterson Winery (Healdsburg, CA) *see* Sonoma Co
Peterson-Nedry, Harry 254
Pezzi-King (Healdsburg, CA) 116 *see also* Dry Creek Valley
Pheasant Ridge (Lubbock, TX) *see* Texas High Plains AVA
Philip Togni Vyd (St Helena, CA) *see* Spring Mtn AVA
Phillips, Jean 176
Phillips Farms Vyds (Lodi, CA) *see* Lodi
Phoenix Winery (Napa, CA) *see* Napa Valley
Pickberry Vyd 223
Piedmont Vyd (Middleburg, VA) 193
Piedra Creek Winery (San Luis Obispo, CA) *see* Edna Valley
Piestengel 142
Pietra Santa Winery (Kenwood, CA) *see* Sonoma Valley AVA
Pikes Peak Vyds (Colorado Springs, CO) *see* Colorado
Pillar Bluff Vyds (Lampasas, TX) *see* Texas
Pillar Rock Vyds (St Helena, CA) *see* Napa Valley
Pillsbury Inc 4, 62, 75
Pina Cellars (Rutherford, CA) *see* Rutherford AVA
Pindar Vyds (Peconic, NY) 155 *see also* Long Island
Pine Ridge Winery (Napa, CA) 194
Piney Woods Country Wines (Orange, TX) *see* Texas
Pinnacles Vyd 120
Pintler Cellars 108, 140
Piper Heidsieck, Sonoma 104, 143
Pipestone Vyds (Paso Robles, CA) *see* Paso Robles
Placerville 119, 122
Plane's Cayuga Vyd (Ovid, NY) *see* Finger Lakes
Plateau Vyds (Murrieta, CA) *see* Temecula
Ployez Winery (Lowerlake, CA) *see* Lake Co
Plum Creek Cellars (Palisade, CO) 107 *see also* Colorado
Plump Jack Winery (Oakville, CA) *see* Oakville
Plymouth Colony Winery (Plymouth, MA) *see* Southeastern NE AVA
Poalillo Vyds (Paso Robles, CA) *see* Paso Robles
Point Reyes Vyds (Point Reyes Station, CA) *see* Bay Area
Pommery 65, 104
Pompei Winery (Cleveland, OH) *see* Ohio
Pon, Ben 76
Ponderosa Vyd (Ponderosa, NM) 178 *see also* New Mexico
Ponderosa Vyds (Lebanon, OR) *see* Oregon
Pontin Del Roza Winery (Prosser, WA) *see* Yakima Valley AVA
Ponzi Vyds (Beaverton, OR) 194
Pool, Dwayne 184
Pope Valley Winery (Pope Valley, CA) *see* Napa Valley
Poplar Ridge Vyds (Valois, NY) *see* Finger Lakes
Portage Wine Company (Suffield, OH) *see* Ohio
Porter Creek Vyds (Healdsburg, CA) *see* Russian River AVA
Portet, Bernard 227
Portteus Vyds (Zillah, WA) *see* Yakima Valley AVA
Post Winery (Altus, AR) 67 *see also* Arkansas
Poteet Country Winery (Poteet, TX) *see* Texas

Potomac Highland (Keyser, WV) 252 *see also* West Virginia
Potter Valley AVA (CA) 128, 160 *see also* Mendocino
Pozzan Winery (Rutherford, CA) *see* Rutherford AVA
Prager Winery & Port Works (St Helena, CA) *see* St Helena AVA
Preate Winery (Old Forge, PA) *see* Pennsylvania
Prejean Winery (Penn Yan, NY) *see* Finger Lakes
Presidio, San Francisco 74
Presque Isle Wine Cellars (North East, PA) *see* Lake Erie AVA
Preston Family Winery (Pasco, WA) *see* Columbia Valley AVA
Preston Winery (Healdsburg, CA) 195
Prial, Frank 89
Price, David and Suzanne (licensees, Camino, CA) *see* El Dorado
Pride Mountain Vyds (Santa Rosa, CA) *see* Spring Mtn AVA
Pritchard, Keith E. (licensee, Canal Winchester, OH) *see* Ohio
private clubs 235
'Produced and bottled by' (on a label) 241
Prohibition 3
Prospero Winery (Pleasantville, NY) *see* Hudson River
Puchta, Adam (licensee, Hermann, MO) *see* Hermann
Puget Sound AVA (WA) 196
Pugliese Vyds (Cutchogue, NY) *see* Long Island
pulque 162
punch-down 36

Quady Winery (Madera, CA) 197
Quaker Ridge Winery (Washington, PA) *see* Pennsylvania
Querétaro 163
Quilceda Creek Vintners (Snohomish, WA) 198
Quilter, Thomas and Mary (licensees, Waldo, OH) *see* Ohio
Quinn, Katie 63
Quivira Vyds (Healdsburg, CA) *see* Dry Creek Valley
Quixote Winery (Napa, CA) *see* Napa Valley
Qupe Wine Cellars (Santa Maria, CA) 198

R. H. Phillips (Esparto, CA) 200
Rabbit Hill Winery (Fiddletown, CA) *see* Amador Co
Rabbit Ridge Vyds (Healdsburg, CA) *see* Russian River AVA
Rack & Return 36
Radanovich Winery, Inc. (Mariposa, CA) *see* Sierra Foothills AVA
Rafanelli Winery (Healdsburg, CA) 116 *see also* Dry Creek Valley
Rainey Valley Winery (Glenoma, WA) *see* Washington
Rainsong Vyds (Cheshire, OR) *see* Oregon
Raleigh, Sir Walter 224
Ramey, Dave 103, 158, 191
Rancho De Philo (Alta Loma, CA) *see* Los Angeles
Rancho De Solis Winery (Gilroy, CA) *see* Hecker Pass
Rancho Sisquoc Winery (Santa Maria, CA) *see* Santa Maria
Randel, Emma 245
Rapazzini Winery (Gilroy, CA) *see* Santa Clara Valley AVA
Rapidan River brand 195
Raptor Ridge Winery (Hillsboro, OR) *see* Willamette Valley AVA
Rasmussen, Kirk Edward (licensee, Macomb, MI) *see* Michigan
Rattlesnake Hills 108, 257
Rausse, Gabriele 73
Ravenhurst Champagne Cellars (Mount Victory, OH) *see* Ohio
Ravenswood Winery (Sonoma, CA) 199
Ray, Martin 79, 172
Raymond Vyd & Cellar (St Helena, CA) 205 *see also* Rutherford AVA
Reagan, administration and Nancy 4, 19
Rebec Vyds (Amherst, VA) *see* Virginia
Rechsteiner, David E. (licensee, Johnstown, OH) *see* Ohio
Recht, Jacques 111, 141

Index

PICTURE ACKNOWLEDGEMENTS

Between pages 48–9

1 Picking Icewine grapes: Cephas Picture Library / Kevin Argue, 2 Harvesting Cabernet Sauvignon grapes at Trefethen Vyds, Napa Valley, CA: Cephas Picture Library / Mick Rock, 3 Biltmore Estate, NC: Corbis / Richard A. Cooke, 4 Vineyard and mountains, CO: Kirk Irwin—I & I Images.

Between pages 112–13

5 Montage of labels arranged by Nick Clarke, 6 Morning fog, St Helena, Napa Valley: Cephas Picture Library / Kevin Judd, 7 Monticello Vyd, VA: Corbis / Buddy Mays, 8 Greta Ranch Vyds, Okanagan Valley, BC, Canada: Cephas Picture Library / Steve Elphick, 9 Sunset over lower Mississippi River: Tony Stone Images / Nathan Benn.

Between pages 176–7

10 Franzia Winery, Central Valley, CA: Cephas Picture Library / Mick Rock, 11 Clos Pegase Winery, Napa Valley, CA: Janet Price, 12 Groth Winery, Napa Valley, CA: Cephas Picture Library / Bruce Fleming, 13 Tensiometer in use, Mt Veeder, CA: Cephas Picture Library / R & K Muschenetz, 14 Donald Ziraldo: Sara Matthews, 15 Helen Turley at the Bryant Family Vyds, Napa Valley, CA: Cephas Picture Library / R & K Muschenetz.

Between pages 240–1

16 Flooding at St Helena, Napa Valley, CA: Cephas Picture Library / Bruce Fleming, 17 McMinnville International Pinot Noir Festival, OR: Doreen L. Wynja, 18 Netting at Macari Vyds, Long Island, NY: Sara Matthews, 20 Niagara grapes (*vitis labrusca*): Cephas Picture Library / Fred R. Palmer, 19 Grand staircase of Niebaum-Coppola Winery, Napa Valley, CA: Courtesy of Niebaum-Coppola Estate Winery / Gerald French, 20 Niebaum-Coppola Winery, Napa Valley, CA: Cephas Picture Library / Bruce Fleming.